MOBILE COMPUTING

MOBILE COMPUTING

For

(All Indian Universities, Engineering and Technical Colleges and Institutions, IIT's and IIT Organizations)

Rishabh Anand

Khanna Book Publishing Co. (P) Ltd.

4C/4344, Ansari Road, Daryaganj, New Delhi-110002

Phone : 011-23244447-48 E-mail : contact@khannabooks.com

Website : www.khannabooks.com

MOBILE COMPUTING
Rishabh Anand

ISBN : 978-93-81068-62-5

First Edition 2012

Published by:
Khanna Book Publishing Co. (P) Ltd.
4C/4344, Ansari Road, Daryaganj, New Delhi-110 002
Phone: 011-23244448 Telefax: 011-23244447
E-mail: contact@khannabooks.com
Website: www.khannabooks.com

Regd. Off: 1694-95, 1st Floor, Nai Sarak, Delhi-110006 (India)
Phone: 011-23283211 Telefax: 011-23256658

Cover Design & Layout by
Akriti Print & Graphics, Delhi

Printed in India by
S.P.S. Printers & Binders, Delhi

Dedicated to
My Mother whose love and affection made
me capable of writing this book
and
Shri Guru Maharaj Ji of Shri Anandpur

Preface

Mobile computing gains in last years an increasing importance. It penetrates into new areas of everyday life. With increasing computing power that is available in recently developed mobile devices the mobile computing approach is used in new areas (where its use would not be possible few years ago). Due to specific properties of mobile devices the traditional approaches to the traditional schemes for communication between users and the devices are not applicable. Another important issue that is linked with new applications in the field of mobile computing is derived from the fact that portable information appliances are pervading the everyday life and ambient intelligence is starting to surround us. Adapting multimedia applications and services to these delivery environments and enabling ensembles of multimedia appliances to organize themselves spontaneously and ad hoc will be major technical issues that have to be solved in near future.

Although mobile computing is still in its infancy, some basic concepts have been identified and several seminal experimental systems developed. Mobile Computing contains chapters that describe these concepts and systems, and the book describes applications that are currently being deployed and tested. Mobile Computing is a valuable reference book that may also be used as a text for a course on the subject.

The importance of Mobile Computing is well known in various engineering fields. The book is structured to cover the key aspects of the subject Mobile Computing.

The book uses plain, lucid language to explain fundamentals of this subject. The book provides logical method of explaining various complicated concepts and stepwise methods to explain the important topics. Each chapter is well supported with necessary illustrations, practical examples and solved problems. All care has been taken to make students comfortable in understanding the basic concepts of the subject.

The book not only covers the entire scope of the subject but explains the philosophy of the subject. This makes the understanding of this subject but explains the philosophy of the subject. This makes the understanding of this subject more clear and makes it more interesting. The book will be very useful not only to the students but also to the subject teachers.

The author hopes that the book will fulfill the pressing need of interested readers and welcome any suggestions towards the improvement of the book.

Rishabh Anand

Acknowledgement

We all marvel at the beautiful rose. The rose, with all its beauty and grandeur. But seldom we pause and thank the kind of gardener who patiently manured and watered it. The book I have written is the fruit of such unseen hands.

I wish to express my profound thanks to the people around me who helped to make this book a reality.

I am especially grateful to my teachers and my colleagues specially Mrs. Aparna Mahajan, Mr. Sanjeev Kumar, Mrs. Rashmi Mahajan, Wg.cdr. P. Patnayak, GpCapt. H.S. Dua, Wg.cdr. Onkar Singh, Mrs. Dimple Saproo, Mrs. Naresh Kumari, Mrs. Chitra Kaul, Director M.M Jha, Mrs. Savita Khazanchi, Mrs. Meenakshi and other faculty members who influenced my academic grown during my study.

There was, in and always will be the love of my students whom I taught, for what is written in this book has been the fruit of experience that I taught them. Finally, thanks to my parents and to rest of my family for their patience and support during the long hours of writing this book and above all there is the one Almighty whose humble children we are. It is his blessings we cherish and pray for. It is the blessing I wish for you.

I deeply express my heartful thanks to the publishers Khanna Book Publishing Co., for publishing this book in such a beautiful get-up and well in time.

Rishabh Anand

✍ *Message to My Students*

As you have signed up for this course and probably your teacher has adopted this book! You had no say about the choice, although you can form and express your opinion on the book after reading it. What I really meant is that although this is an easy book to study from (in my opinion), it is no-nonsense book. It does not have cartoons or nice-looking photographs to amuse you. From here on it is all business and hard work.

This book has many examples. Some of these are simple, for the purpose of illustrations of new ideas and subject matter. Some examples are made quite elaborate, in order to develop desired technical skill and confidence. Furthermore, the objective of this book is to present the complex subject in a clear and thorough manner.

I hope that you will enjoy this book, and it will be remain as major text book in your college career. My advice to you is not sell it back at the end of semester. If you do, not only will you be violating the "buy low and sell high" axiom of finance but definitely be missing it during your higher semester or project assignments.

When you finish the journey through this book, having variety of experiences, ideas and thoughts. You are welcome to express your opinion at **rishabh.anand009@yahoo.com.**

Rishabh Anand

Contents

Unit 1

Wireless Communication Fundamentals

1.1 INTRODUCTION

Mobile communication refers to the conversation established between two users at two different places with their hand held equipment. Initially the focus of mobile communication was towards voice but later it also dealt with data. Today cellular phones provide many services. That include electronic mail, internet access, short message service, electronic address book, games, calculator. Further research is in process to attract people towards commercial product.

The size of the cellular phone is such that subscribers can handle it easily wherever they roam. The frequency range for mobile transmission included 825 to 845 MHz range as its comfortable range. The information and technology field is greatly revolutionized due to the arrival of cellular phones.

The first generation digital cellular wireless network was the advanced mobile phone system (AMPS). It provided 19.2 kbps data rate.

The second generation wireless systems are the popular global system for mobile communications (GSM), personal communication service (PCS) and it provided 9.6 kbps data rate to deliver the data, with dedicated channels.

1.2 EVOLUTION OF MOBILE COMMUNICATION

The wireless communication has developed worldwide from the year 1897 by means of radio and the development of the technology is due to revolution in the fields like

(*i*) RF circuit fabrication

(*ii*) Large scale circuit integration

(*iii*) Digital circuit design

(*iv*) Miniaturization technologies.

The impact of development of mobile communication is personal communication services. The cellular concepts emerged appreciably and slowly developed by Bell Laboratories in the period between 1960 and 1970. An exponential growth of wireless communication was observed. While comparing wireless technologies with other communications the penetration of wireless application is more in our day-to-day life. The cellular as well as personal communication services have revolutionized the communication field.

The drastic growth of mobile communication is compared here with some of other technologies in a graph.

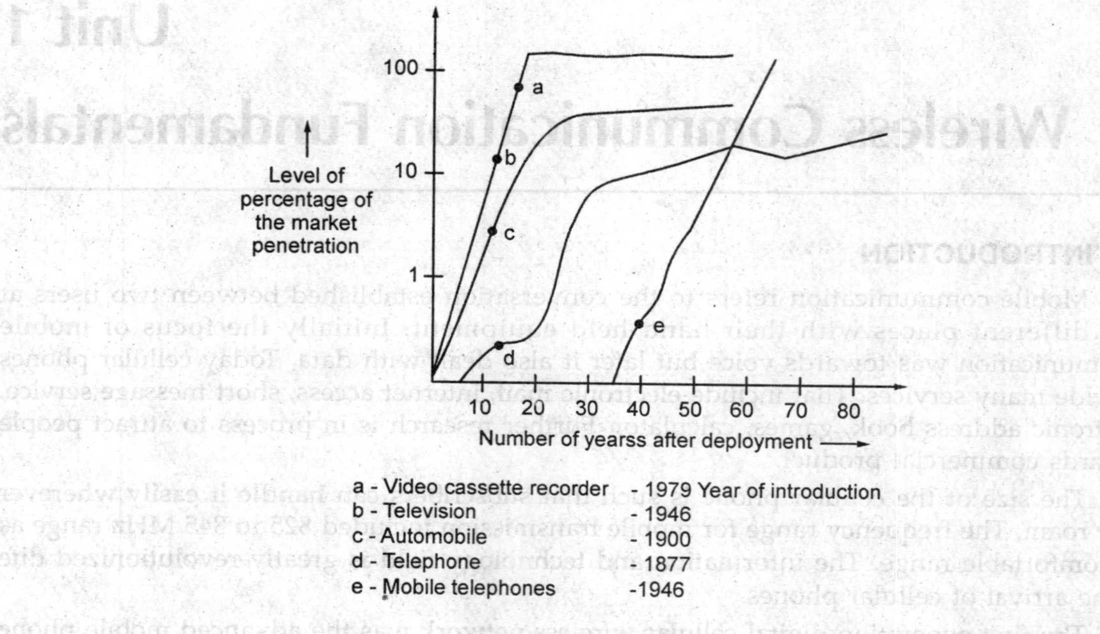

Fig. 1.1

The cellular mobile communication technology emerged slowly and developed worldwide. At the same time it has penetrated into the market for long time with high demand than other technologies. It has an appreciable growth rate as seen in the graph.

In the year 1934 the police radio systems used the Amplitude Modulation (AM) systems for transmission purposes. In early cellular the major problem faced was vehicular ignition noise. It is also interesting that in 1960's the majority of mobile users were not linked through PSTN and they were not capable to dial the telephone numbers directly. In the year 1995 the number of mobile users in US was 37% of the total population. The growth of cellular mobile users was approximately from 25000 to 25 million and this took roughly one decade. (From 1984 to 1993).

The number of consumers in wireless communications increases every year worldwide.

In early days the FM push-to-talk telephone systems were popular. In the period of 1940 this system used frequency of 120 kHz, such that only one person can talk at a time. It was known as half duplex mode. But the FCC increased the number of channels in each market and at the same time it does not need an extra spectrum allocation. It was possible with new technologies enabling reduction in bandwidth from 120 kHz to 60 kHz. Later automatic channel trunking was also possible and it was named as Improved Mobile Telephone Service (IMTS). With this IMTS full duplex mode was brought in. In the year 1968 AT and T Bell Laboratories recommended the concepts of the cellular mobile communication to the respective FCC and in the year 1983 FCC assigned 666 duplex channels for the US mobile systems named as Advanced Mobile Phone System (AMPS). It is also worthnothing that FCC insisted to have 'duopoly' in each city. That is in each city/market only two service providers were allowed to have a healthy competition in the market. An additional 166 channels of 10 MHz frequency were permitted in US cellular system to meet the demand scenario.

US Cellular radio service :

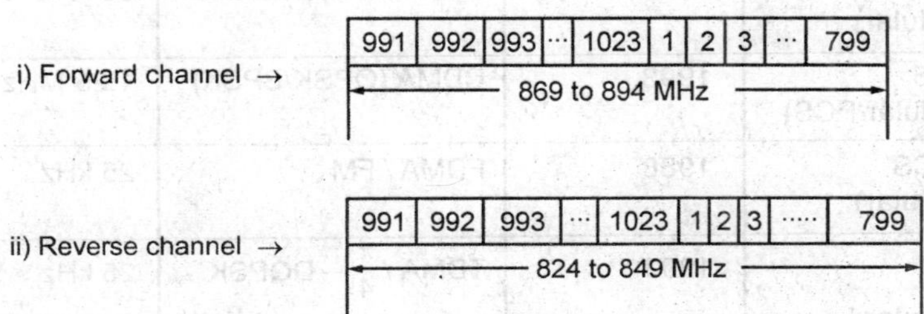

Some of the main problems the cellular mobile system faced are

(*i*) Interference

(*ii*) Less encryption techniques

(*iii*) Spectrum inefficiency.

In the year 1991 the US Digital Cellular (USDC) system was implemented and this USDC Standard or Electronic Industry Association Interim Standard IS-54 enabled the main advantage of replacing few single user analog channels with that of the digital channels.

Comparing AMPS with USDC system the digital USDC provided more capacity to the cellular mobile world. It was due to the reasons, the USDC applied the techniques mentioned below.

(*i*) $\frac{\pi}{4}$ differential quadrature phase shift keying.

(*ii*) Speech coding.

(*iii*) Time division multiple access.

Later a better cellular mobile system using Code Division Multiple Access (CDMA) was developed by the Qualcomm, Inc which was then standardized by the respective Telecommunications Industry Association (TIA) and the system was named as Interim Standard (IS-95).

The IS-95 allowed many number of mobile users by Direct Sequence Spread Spectrum (DSSS) technique. The CDMA cellular phone systems were independent of interference problems and provided better call quality than the first generation (1G) AMPS cellular system.

Some of the mobile standards of North America, Japan and Europe are listed below.

	Mobile standard	Year of introduction	Multiple access / Modulation	Bandwidth of channel
1. North America	(*a*) AMPS (Cellular)	1983	FDMA / FM	30 kHz
	(*b*) USDC (Cellular)	1991	TDMA / $\frac{\pi}{4}$ DQPSK	30 kHz
	(*c*) CDPD (Cellular)	1993	(FH/Packet) / GMSK	30 kHz
	(*d*) IS-95 (Cellular/PCS)	1993	CDMA (QPSK/BPSK)	1.25 MHz
2. Japan	(*a*) JTACS (Cellular)	1988	FDMA / FM	25 kHz
	(*b*) PDC (Cellular)	1993	TDMA / $\frac{\pi}{4}$ – DQPSK	25 kHz
	(*c*) NTT (Cellular)	1979	FDMA/FM	25 kHz
	(*d*) PHS (Cordless)	1993	TDMA / $\frac{\pi}{4}$ – DQPSK	300 kHz
3. Europe	(*a*) ETACS (Cellular)	1985	FDMA / FM	25 kHz
	(*b*) GSM (Celluar/PCS)	1990	TDMA / GMSK	200 kHz
	(*c*) CT2 (Cordless)	1989	FDMA / GFSK	100 kHz
	(*d*) DECT (Cordless)	1993	TDMA / GFSK	1.728 MHz

AMPS - Anlog Mobile Phone System.

USDC - US Digital Cellular.

CDPD - Cellular Digital Packet Data.

IS-95 - Intaerim Standard-95.

JTACS - Japanese Total Access Cellular Systems.

PDC - Pacific Digital Cellular.

NTT - Nippon Telephone and Telegraph Company.

PHS - Personal Handy Phone System.

ETACS - European Total Access Cellular System.

GSM - Global System for Mobile.

CT2 - Cordless Telephone. (CT2)

DECT - Digital European Cordless Telephone.

In the examples of cellular, cordless and PCS systems each one of them has unique advantages and facilities with respect to mobile communication technology. Thus the transition from analog mobile phones to digital mobile phones was made along a number of years and today digital cellular telephony is very popular worldwide due to its several technical advantages, including cellular coverage capability.

Examples of the cellular radio communication.

1. Cellular telephone system.
2. Cordless Telephone (CT) system.
3. Paging system.

These examples are given below.

Example 1 : Cellular telephone system

The cellular telephone system mainly helps to connect a Public Switched Telephone Network (PSTN) and any distant/near user provided the user is available within the corresponding radio range. (A basic cellular system is given below.) The mobile switching center or Mobile Telephone Switching Office (MTSO) connects the mobile units (called parties) to the PSTN. Every cell of the particular geographical area has its own base station with a transceiver, an antenna, and also a control circuitry.

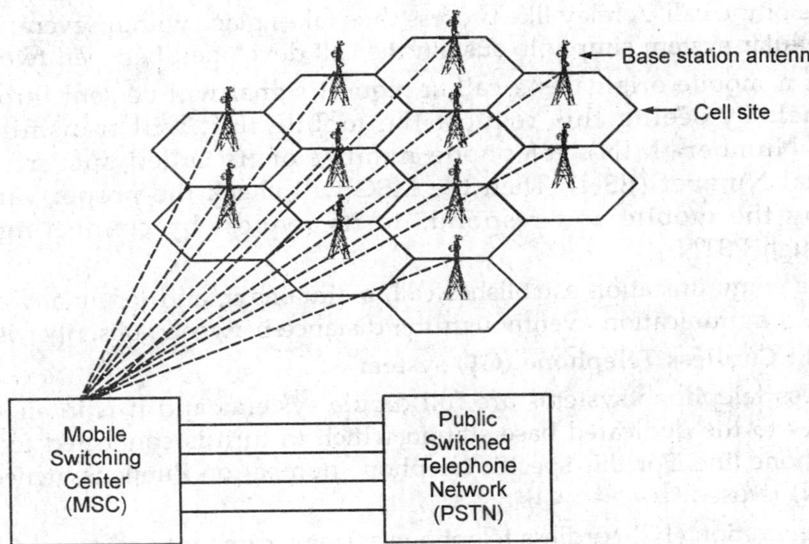

Fig. 1.2 Cellular system

The base stations are capable of handling many full duplex cellular communications. The mobile switching center can handle atleast 5000 telephonic conversation at a time and 1,00,000 cellular users/subscribers in a network. The cellular communication is made possible between mobile units and the base stations with the help of Common Air Interface (CAI) which specifies four channels.

They are :

1. Forward Control Channels (FCC)
2. Reverse Control Channels (RCC)
3. Forward Voice Channels (FVC) and
4. Reverse Voice Channels (RVC).

The control channels mentioned here are also termed as setup channels. They will have calls that are in progress but they usually send and receive data messages carrying call initiation and requests for services.

The Forward Control Channels (FCC) are also termed as "BEACONS" since they continuously broadcast the traffic requests for the mobile units within the cellular system. As soon as the cell phone is switched on it scans the control channels searching for the strongest signal of a base station. When the call progresses the mobile switching center adjusts the power transmitted (P_T) of the mobile unit and alters the channel of the mobile unit and also the base station so as to maintain the call quality eventhough the mobile unit is non-stationary.

The call in progress continues irrespective of the frequency changes from one base to another base station. Such a call continued process without termination is called as 'Hand off technique. As the mobile moves and the signal strength reduces when it is away from its base station of cell, the next base station of the neighbouring cell where the mobile enters in will take charge of the call. A relay like process thus takes place within several base stations of the entire cellular system simply to sustain the call developed between two subscribers.

Whenever a mobile originates a call, a request signal will be sent through reverse control channel. By seeing this request the mobile unit will transmit its Mobile Identification Number (MIN), telephone number of its called subscriber, and the Electronic Serial Number (ESN). Then the MSC will check the proper validity of the signals sent by the mobile and responds to its request by connecting the called subscriber through PSTN.

The mobile communication establishes call, maintains it, and terminates as the call is over. It enables communication eventhough the distance between subscriber is large.

Example 2 : Cordless Telephone (CT) system

The cordless telephone systems are full dipole systems and it is intended to link a portable handset to the dedicated base station which in turn is connected to a particular dedicated telephone line. For this specific telephone number on Public Switched Telephone Network (PSTN) is used.

The first generation (1G) cordless telephone systems came into existence in 1980's. But the distance the system covered was only few meters.

Later the second generation (2G) cordless systems the distance was not a problem and the subscribers used cordless systems in mobile environment also. The system was good only if the subscriber availability was within the coverage of base station.

Fig. 1.3 Cordless Telephone (CT) system

The cordless system also work together with paging system such that the roaming subscriber can first be paged and he or she can respond to it with the help of cordless telephone. In the simple cordless system shown above it illustrates that the cordless handset is linked to PSTN through the base station (fixed port). The cordless handset has a wireless link with its dedicated base station. The cordless systems are divided into two namely Analog CT and Digital CT.

In the early days these cordless systems were analog (Analog CT). They provided analog voice transmissions and enabled mobility within a limited distances. But they had many demerits such as

(*i*) Poor call qualities

(*ii*) Interference

These problems urged the need for digital cordless (Digital CT) systems. They provided better voice quality similar to wired telephone system.

Example for digital cordless system is

CT2 / Common Air Interface (CAI)

Some of the main criteria of CT2 system are

(*i*) Voice signal is digitized through 32 kb/sec Adaptive Differential Pulse Code Modulation (ADPCM) technique.

(*ii*) Bit stream compression facility.

(*iii*) Final bit stream transmission at a rate of 72 kb/sec through Gaussian Frequency Shift Keying (GFSK).

(*iv*) Immune to errors.

(*v*) Supports data transmissions effectively upto 32 kb/sec.

(*vi*) Traffic can be separated with the Time Division Duplex (TDD) access technique.

Note : This CT2 standard does not provide for the mobility status and the later version CT2 + standard was used for this purpose.

Example 3 : Paging systems

The paging systems are communication systems and they can transmit brief messages to subscribers. The message sent may be an alphanumeric message, numeric message or even a voice data. Paging systems also include news headlines, faxes and stock quotations. It may be sent to a particular paging subscriber through the paging system access number with a modem or a telephone keypad. Such a message is called as page.

In a technique called 'simulcasting' the wide paging systems sends a page from each base station simultaneously.

The important performance metrics used in decision-making process under hand off situations (mobility management) are listed below.

1. Probability of call blocking.
2. Probability of call dropping.
3. Probability of call completion.
4. Hand-off delay.
5. Rate of hand-off.
6. Probability of an incomplete hand-off.
7. Probability of hand-off blocking.
8. Interruption time duration.
9. Hand-off probability.

Strategies used to calculate the instant of hand-off are :

1. Relative signal strength method.
2. Relative signal strength with hysteris method.
3. Relative signal strength with threshold method.
4. Prediction techniques.

In a wide area paging system a paging control center is available that connects the PSTN to different paging terminals.

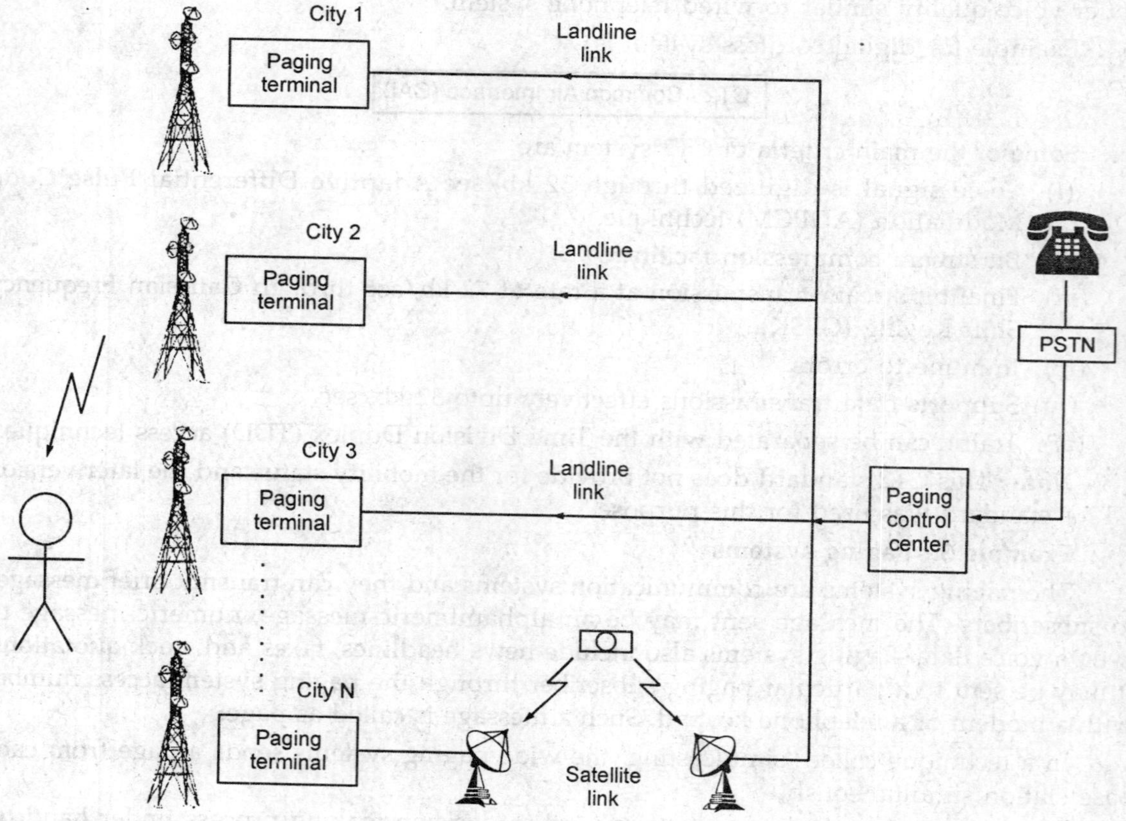

Fig. 1.4 Wide area paging system

Thus paging systems enable communication with subscribers irrespective of their roaming state. But the system requires large transmitter powers in the order of kilowatts and uses only low data rates for providing proper coverage.

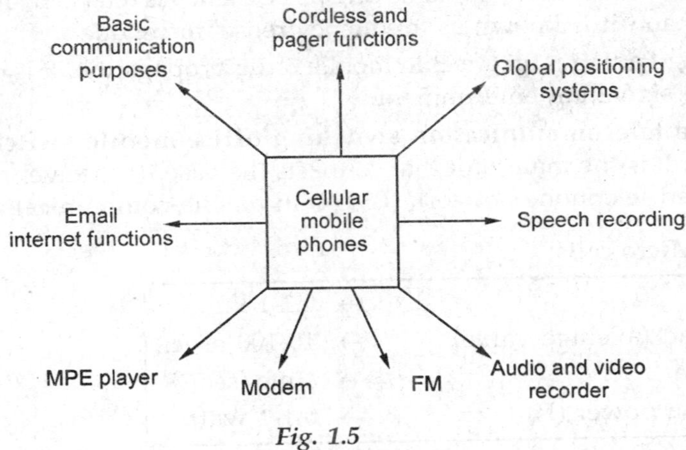

Fig. 1.5

There are several functionalities possible with cellular mobile phones as shown above which includes the pager functions too. It is helpful in sending short messages which are highly used by subscribers. The short message or page is sent to a subscriber wherever he is, and it is the main advantage of these system in spite of low data rates and large transmitter power requirements.

1.3 CELLULAR MOBILE COMMUNICATION

Important Terminologies

1. **Cell :** It is smallest geographical area considered for cellular mobile communication radio coverage and the shape of a cell is hexagon.
2. **Base station (BTS) :** Base station provides functionalities between mobile unit and mobile switching centre (MSC). BTS is located in each cell.
3. **Cell splitting :** In high cellular traffic regions, a larger cell is divided into smaller cells to have complete radio coverage.
4. **Hand-off :** When mobile unit moves from one cell to another call, the call in progress will be handed over from one base transceiver to the base transceiver of the new cell where the mobile unit enters so that the call in progress is not disturbed and continues smoothly. This process is called as "Hand-off".
5. **Cell sectoring :** A cell can be divided in to many sectors for example 3 sectors to 6 sectors in each hexagonal cell. Also the directional antenna should focus on each sector.
6. **Umbrella cell pattern :** A single large cell (Macro cell) consists of many small; (micro cell) cells and there will be interaction between micro and macro cells.
7. **Control channel :** They are used for necessary exchange of information related to setting up and establishing cell base stations and the mobile units.

8. **Traffic channels :** They are used for carrying data or voice connections between different users.
9. **Frequency reuse :** It is a concept followed in cellular communication for efficient spectrum utilization. The same carrier frequency is reused by many cells in a cellular cluster and it is known as 'frequency reuse' technique.
10. **Fading :** Fading is an effect in mobile radio propagation. It is common in mutlipath mobile signalling environment.
11. **Mobile telecommunication switching office/mobile switching centre (MTSO/MSC) :** It is the main unit that connects the base transceiver station and the public switched telephone network (PSTN) in mobile communication.

Parameters for Micro cells

Cell radius	→ 0.1-1 km.
Delay spread (average value)	→ 10-100 nsec.
Max bit rate	→ 1 mb/sec.
Transmission power (P_T)	→ 0.1-1 watt.

Parameter for Macro Cells

Cell radius	→ 1 - 20 km.
Delay spread (average value)	→ 0.1- 10 μsec.
Max bit rate	→ 0.3 mb/sec.
Transmission power (P_T)	→ 1 - 10 watt.

12. **Page :** It is a brief message that is broadcast over an entire service area, generally in a simulcast type by many base stations at a time.
13. **Forward Channel :** It is a radio channel used for transmission of information from base station to the mobile unit.
14. **Reverse Channel :** It is a radio channel used for transmission of information from mobile unit to the base station.
15. **Simplex Systems :** These are the communication systems that provide only one way communication.
16. **Subscriber :** A mobile phone user who pays subscription charges for using a cellular mobile communication system.
17. **Mobile Station :** Mobile station is mainly intended for use while in movement at any location. It can be hand-held personal units that is portable or installed in moving vehicles.
18. **Full Duplex Systems :** The transmission and reception is typically on two different channels (FDD) even though new cordless systems are using TDD scheme. It is a communication system that allows two way communication simultaneously.
19. **Half Duplex Systems :** The communication systems that allow two way communication by using same radio channel for both transmission and reception. The user can transmit or receive at any time.

20. **Transceiver :** It is a device used for both transmitting and receiving radio signals.
21. **Roamer :** It is a mobile station that operates in a service area other that the subscribed service area.
22. **PSTN :** It is the public switched telephone network to which the mobile telephone switching center (MTSO) is connected.

1.4 MOBILE COMPUTING ENVIRONMENT

It is the computation made over physical mobility. Mobile computing system permits the user to perform a task from a distant place from the device. The user of a mobile computing environment will be able to access data, information, or other logical objects from any device in any network while on move. The mobile computing is also known by different names according to its role in that context. Few examples are listed below.

1. Virtual home environment

It is denoted as "VHE". It is possible under VHE to operate a device like heater in a person's home though he is away from his place. He has a virtually available feeling at his home.

2. Nomadic computing

The entire mobile computing environment is nomadic in nature and it moves with the roaming user. It is possible for both remote and local services.

3. Wearable computer

The wearable computers are used like wearable accessories like shoes, clothes etc. by human beings. A person can wear it provided these computers have extra attributes than conventional mobile computers. The wearable computers are those which can be adorned by a person like an accessory hat, shoe etc.

4. Anywhere, Anytime Information

This is the generic definition of ubiquity, where the information is available anywhere, all the time.

1.5 MOBILE COMPUTING-STRUCTURE VIEW

The three tier structure depicted is used mainly for mobile environment. They are presentation tier, data tier and application tier.

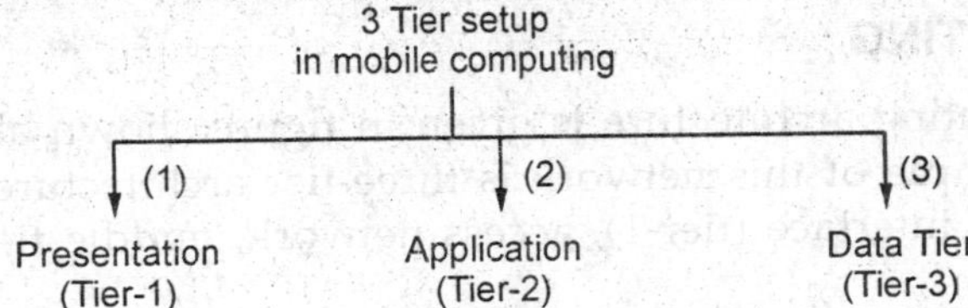

The presentation layer is concerned about user interaction. Its applications run on the client devices. This layer also includes web browsers, and the customized client programs.

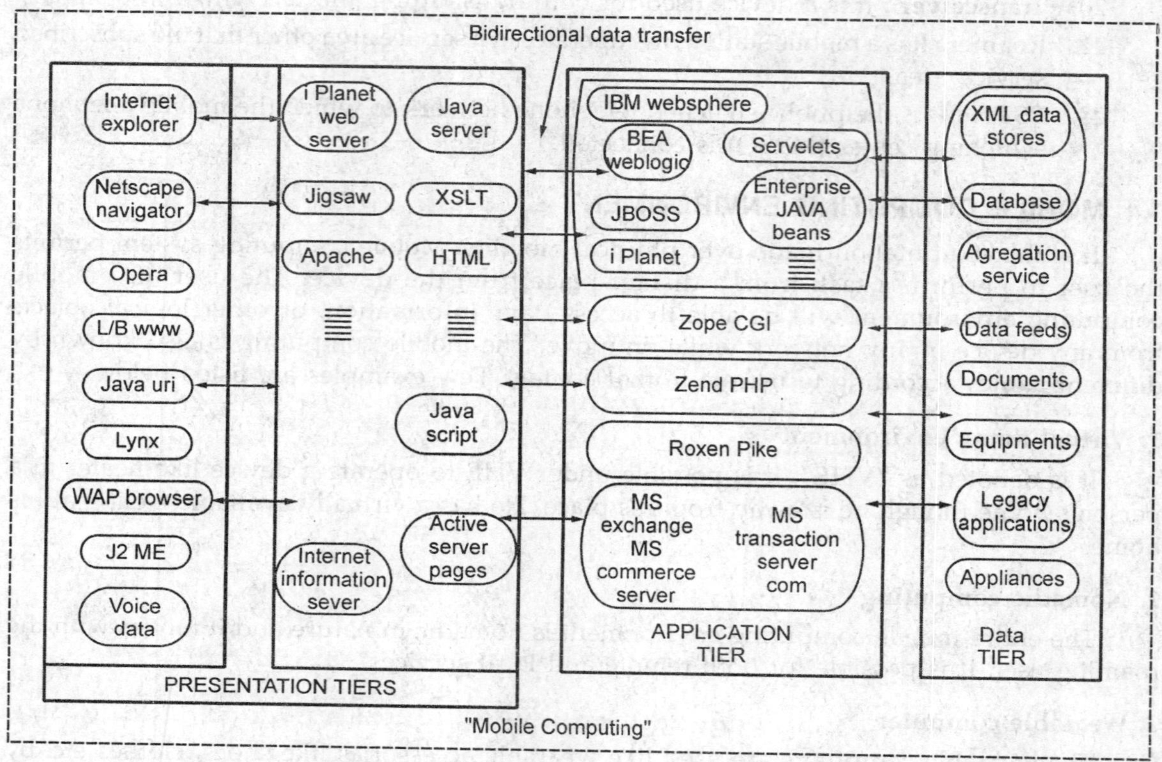

Fig. 1.6 Architecture of mobile computing

The application tier is known as middle tier which is like an "engine" to the automobile. It plays a vital role in wireless LAN applications. It performs the processing of user input, obtaining information and then making decisions. This layer includes technology like Java, ".NET" services, cold fusion web logic, iplanet, 'Z end' etc. It is database independent.

The middleware also covers a wide range of software systems, mobile application support etc. The two independent open objects can be connected through this middleware as a software gateway.

There are many classifications available under middleware.

1.6 MOBILE COMPUTING

The mobile computing architecture is given in figure shown above. They are simple and efficient. One example of this network is three-tier architecture as in the diagram. It mainly consists of user interface (tier-1), access network, middle tier (tier-2) are data tier (tier-3).

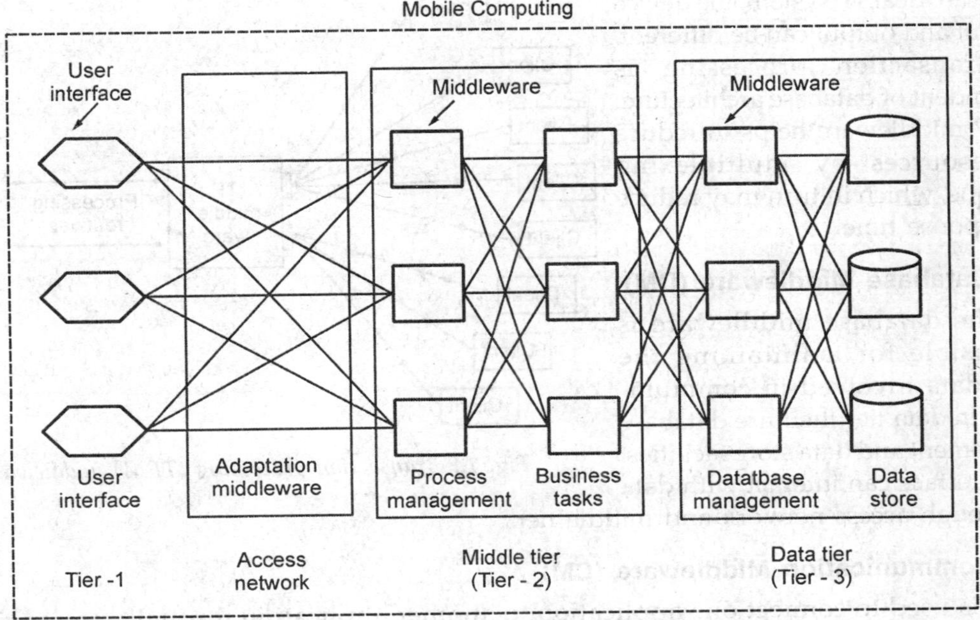

Fig. 1.7 An example for mobile computing - "Three tier architecture"

The first layer is the user interface or a presentation tier.

(*a*) Message-oriented middleware are (MOM).
(*b*) Transaction processing middleware (TPM).
(*c*) Communication middleware (CM).
(*d*) Database middleware (DM).
(*e*) Distributed object and components (DOC).
(*f*) Transcoding middleware (TM).

1.6.1 Message-Oriented Middleware (MOM)

The message oriented middleware is generally asynchronous, peer to peer which works in a subscribe method. One or many objects may subscribe to a particular event. When an event occurs it will be subscribed or published by asynchronous loosely coupled object. The MOM monitors the occurrence of events. The Request/Response scheme is more flexible with MOM method. Hence the message oriented middle is more appropriate for event driven applications. An example for MOM under Java is known as Java Message Service (JMS).

1.6.2 Transaction Processing Middleware (TPM)

It is suited for developing transaction based distributed applications.

The number of client requests are properly mapped to different application tasks through application service routines.

In an ideal TP system, the device for input and output can be different. The transaction processing is independent of database architecture. The TP middleware helps to reduce the resources by multiplexing technique, which in turn may reduce the response time.

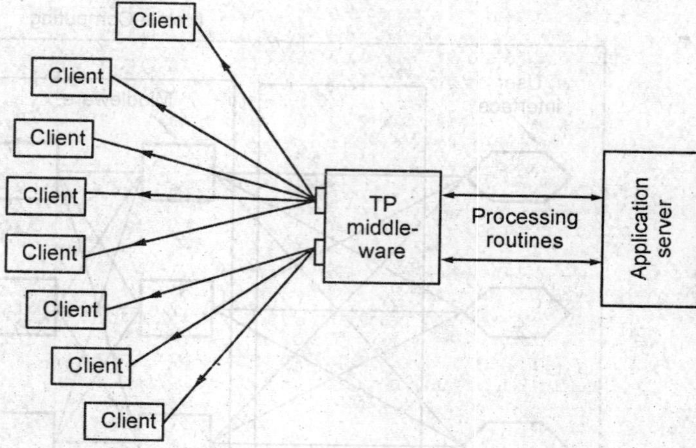

Fig. 1.8 Transaction processing (TPM) middleware

1.6.3 Database Middleware (DM)

The database middleware is responsible for maintaining the entire data involved in communication. In data tier their are database management and data store facilities. User interface can interact with data tier through access network and middle tier.

1.6.4 Communication Middleware (CM)

It is used to connect one application to another application through communication middleware. In telecommunication field there are numerous elements in the core and the user interface is via the telnet. The communication between nodes are finally established.

1.6.5 Distributed Object and Components (DOC)

The Common Object Request Broker Architecture termed as CORBA is on of the best example for distributed objects and components. Many network programming tasks like framing, error handling etc. are simplified using CORBA. Many number of clients can be handled with high reliability and hit rates.

1.6.6 Transcoding Middleware (TM)

To attend the request or need of the user/client, the transcoding middleware is used to transform one format of data to another format. Actually content adaptation is done by transcoding to meet the requirement of each device.

The application tier or the so called middleware has to play role in mobile computing architecture. The reliability of the entire system is enhanced by the performance of middleware.

1.7 FUNCTIONS OF MOBILE COMPUTING

A computing environment is said to be mobile if it supports, few of the characteristics mentioned below.

1. User Mobility

Though the user roams from one place to another he should be able to use the same service. This service may be a remote network or home network.

2. Bearer Mobility

In this case the user may move from one bearer to another bearer but use the same service.

3. Agent Mobility

The user-agent or the applications should be able to move from one node to another. Examples could be aglets, crawler software, or even a malicious worm or virus software that moves from one node to another.

4. Host Mobility

In host mobility the user device can be either a server or a client. If it is a host mobility the mobility of that IP should be given more care. But if it is server or host mobility, some complexities will change.

5. Service Mobility

Though the user changes from one service to another service it should remain enabled and if a user is sending a mail and he refers some information in his PC stored file for adding in his mail he should be allowed to do so.

Frequency allocation

Table 1.1 Frequency allocation for communication

Band	Downlink Band (MHz)	Uplink Band (MHz)
1. UHF-military	≅ 250 to 270	≅ 290 to 310
2. C Band commercial	3700 to 4200	5925 to 6425
3. X-military	7250 to 7750	7900 to 8400
4. Ku Band commercial	11,700 to 12,200	14,000 to 14,500
5. Ka Band commercial	17,700 to 21,200	27,500 to 30,000
6. Ka Band military	20,200 to 21,200	43,500 to 45,500

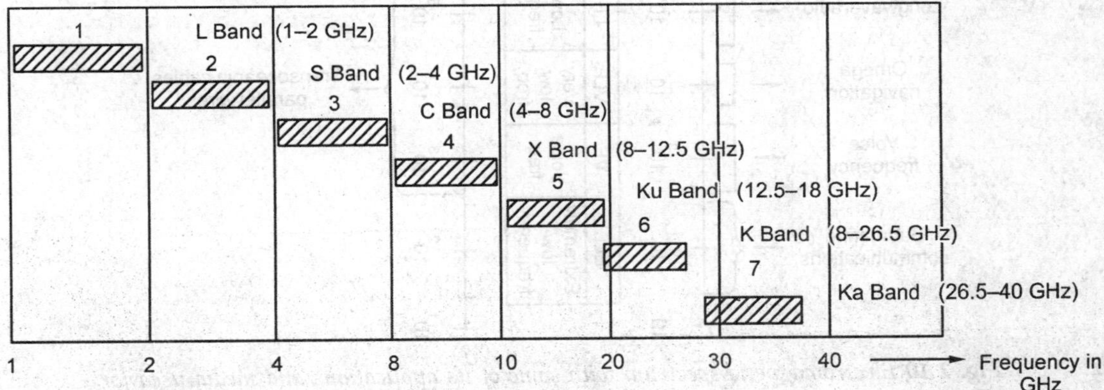

Fig. 1.9 Arrangement of frequency spectrum used for various communication services

From the Fig. 1.9 it is clear that the various frequency bands are used for different communication services.

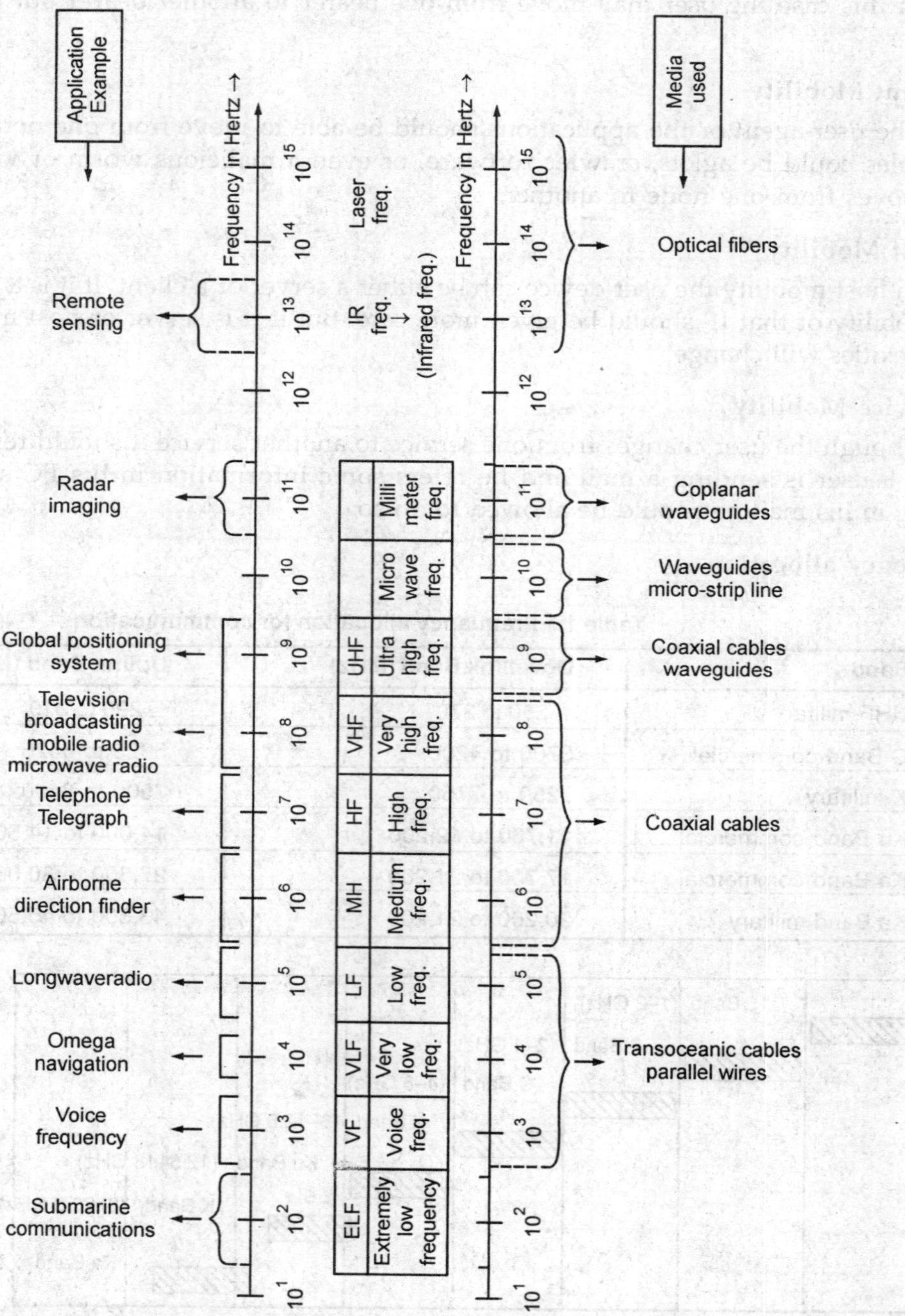

Fig. 1.10 Electromagnetic spectrum with some of its applications and media used for different frequencies of transmission

Example :

Table 1.2 Few Frequency ranges used in communication

Band		Example of services provided
L	-	Mobile satellite service (MSS)
S	-	MSS, space research
G	-	Fixed satellite service (FSS)
X	-	FSS military application
Ku	-	FSS, broadcast satellite service (BSS)
K	-	FSS, BSS
Ka	-	Local multichannel distribution services (LMDS)

Frequency range	Term used
RF frequency	Less than 1 GHz
Microwave frequency	1 GHz to 40 GHz
Millimeter wave frequency	More than 40 GHz

Table 1.3 Frequency range and bands

Frequency range	Band
1 to 2 GHz	L band
2 to 4 GHz	S
4 to 8 GHz	C
8 to 12 GHz	X
12 to 18 GHz	Ku

1.8 SIGNALS

A signal can be defined in many ways. Some definitions are as follows

"A function when it becomes realizable is said to be a signal".

"A signal can be defined as a function of variables that convey information". When a function depends on one (single) variable it is, called as one-dimensional. If a signal depends on two or more number of variables it is called as multi-dimensional.

E.g. Two-dimensional signal-video signal

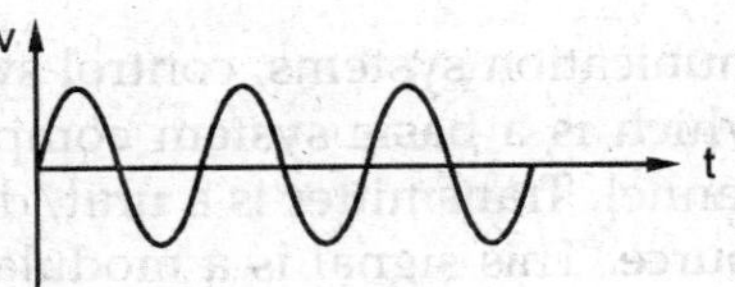

a) Input sinusoidal signal

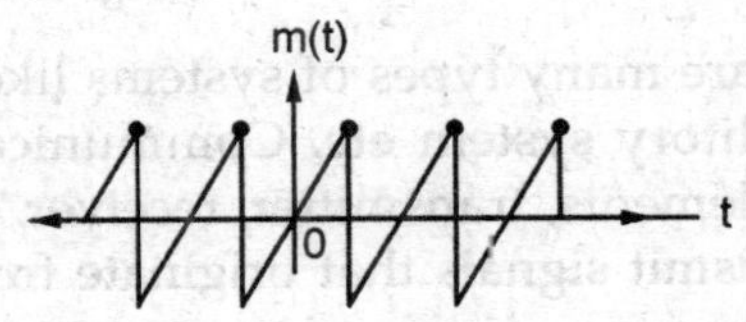

b) Continuous time signal (periodic signal)

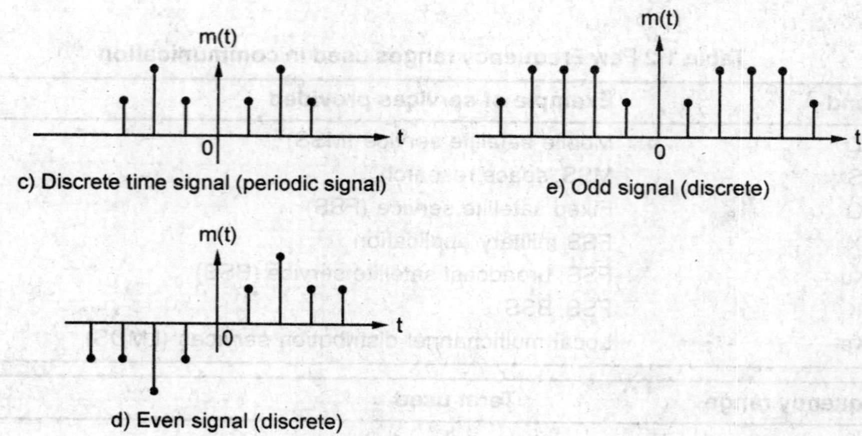

Fig. 1.11 Examples of "signals"

1.9 SYSTEM

A system can be defined as an "entity" that can manipulate the signal entering through it to perform a function by which yielding an output new signal.

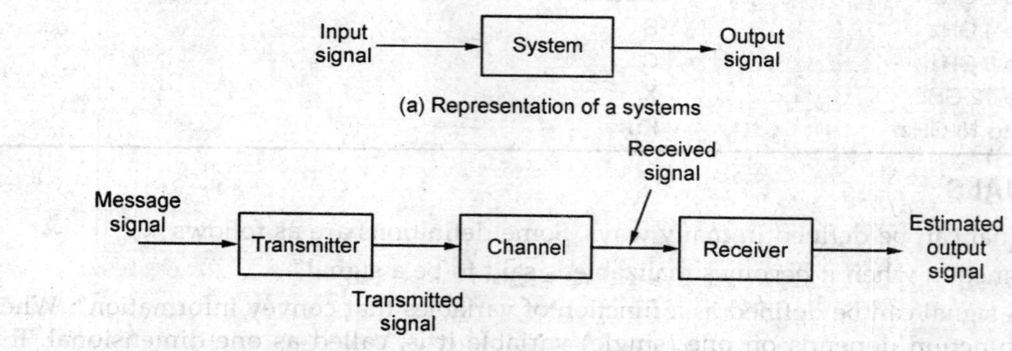

Fig. 1.12 System example

There are many types of systems like communication systems, control systems remote sensing auditory system etc. Communication which is a basic system comprises of three important elements, transmitter, receiver, and channel. Transmitter is a unit/device that can send or transmit signals that originate from a source. This signal is a modulated signal.

A receiver is an unit/receiver that received the signal that was manipulated and transmitted by a system. This signal will be demodulated, at the destination end.

A channel is a path or medium that allows signals to travel through it.

Noise is an unwanted form of energy that may be added up with the signal when it is travelling through the channel.

Note : There are two types of communication available.

They are 1. Broadcasting

2. Point-to-point communication

In first type, a single large transmitter transmits signal/information and multiple receivers receives it.

In the second method, point to point communication, single transmitter transmits signal/information to a single receiver. This one-to-one correspondence is the concept used in point-to-point communication.

1.10 TYPES OR CLASSIFICATION OF SIGNALS

For classification of signals (one-dimensional) their different features are considered here. One dimensional signals are single valued functions of the time period. The term single valued refers to a single value of the function for every instant of time period.

The main classification of signals based on their different features are given below.

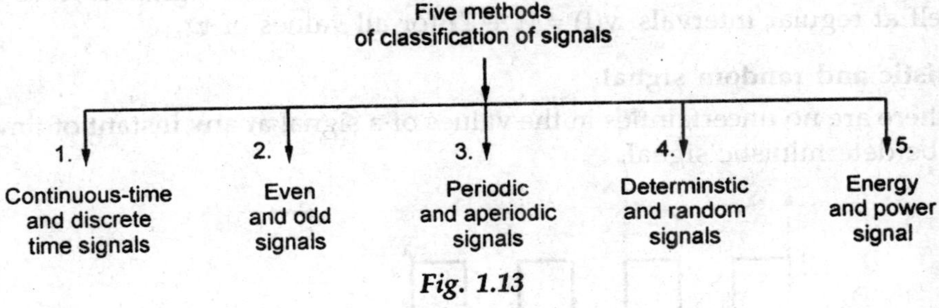

Fig. 1.13

1. Continuous time signal :

- A signal y(t) is said to be a continuous time signal if the signal is defined for all the values of time 't'. They are produced naturally when one energy (say light) or waveform is converted into another waveform (like electrical signal).
- **Discrete time signal :** A signal y(t) is said to be a discrete time signal if the signal is defined only at discrete (finite) time instants. Usually in discrete signal the variable that has finite values only and they will be equally/uniformly spaced.

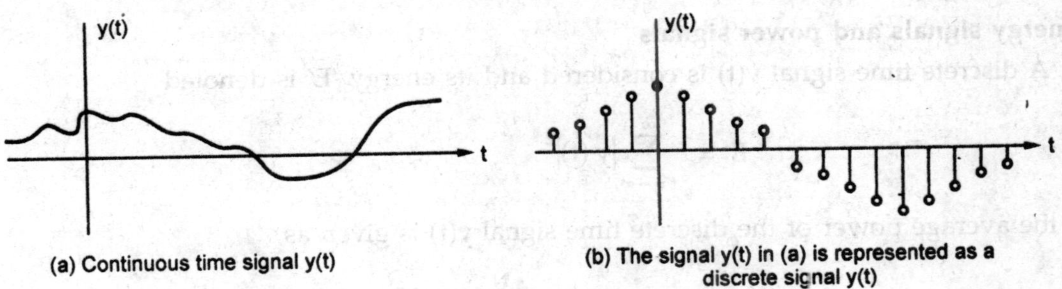

(a) Continuous time signal y(t)

(b) The signal y(t) in (a) is represented as a discrete signal y(t)

Fig. 1.14

The discrete time signal having finite values that are uniformly spaced as shown in Fig. 1.14 (b).

2. Even and odd signals :

- A continuous time signal y(t) is called an even signal only if it satisfies a condition

$$y(-t) = y(t) \text{ for all values of 't'.}$$

- A signal y(t) is called an odd signal only if satisfies the condition.

$$y(-t) = -y(t) \text{ for all values of 't'}$$

$$\text{eg : } y(t) = \cos \omega t \rightarrow \text{even signal}$$

and

$$y(t) = A \sin \omega t \rightarrow \text{odd signal}$$

3. Periodic signals and A-periodic signals

- A signal y(t) is called as periodic signal if it satisfies a condition y(t) = y (t + T) for all values of 't' and T is a constant. Periodic signal will repeat its self at regular time intervals.
- A signal y(t) is called as A-periodic or Non-Periodical signal. It does not repeat itself at regular intervals. y(t) ≠ (t + T) for all values of t.

4. Deterministic and random signal

- If there are no uncertainties in the values of a signal at any instant of time it is said to be deterministic signal.

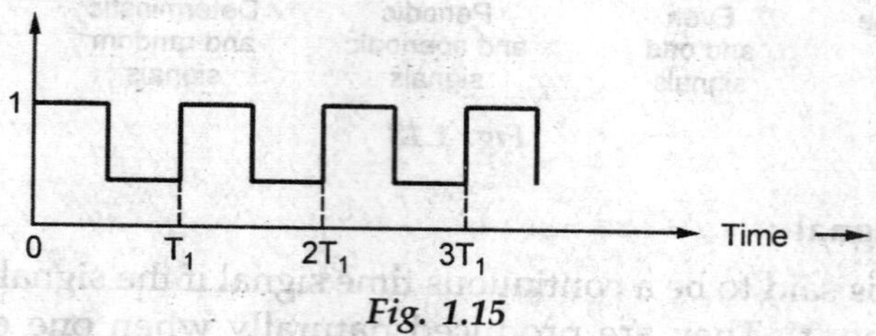

Fig. 1.15

E.g. Deterministic signal—A square wave of definite values

- If there are uncertainties in the values of a signal before its actual occurrence such a signal is said to be random signal.

E.g. Noise signal that generates in an amplifier.

5. Energy signals and power signals

A discrete time signal y(t) is considered and its energy 'E' is denoted as

$$E = \sum_{t=-\infty}^{\infty} |y(t)|^2$$

and the average power of the discrete time signal y(t) is given as

$$P = \lim_{N \to \infty} \frac{1}{2N+1} \sum_{t=-N}^{N} |y(t)|^2$$

where N is fundamental period

Note : For a continuous time signal the total energy can be given as

$$E = \int_{-\infty}^{\infty} y^2(t)\,dt$$

and the total power of the continuous time signal can be given as;

$$P = \frac{1}{T}\int_{-T/2}^{T/2} y^2(t)\,dt$$

where T is fundamental time period.

1.10.1 Basic operations on a signal

There are two basic categories of operations that can be performed on signals when they are passed through systems.

The operations are performed on

1. Dependent variables
2. Independent variables.

The operations that can be performed on dependent variable are

(*i*) Addition
(*ii*) Multiplication
(*iii*) Integration
(*iv*) Differentiation
(*v*) Scaling

(*i*) Addition

Consider two continuous time signals $m_1(t)$ and $m_2(t)$. The output resultant signal n(t) is obtained by addition of these two signals and it is given as

$$n(t) = m_1(t) + m_2(t) \;......$$

An example of addition is mixing of two signals like audio and video signals in an audio mixer device.

(*ii*) Multiplication

Consider two continuous time signals $m_1(t)$, and $m_2(t)$. The output signal n(t) is obtained by multiplying these two signals, and it is,

$$n(t) = m_1(t) \times m_2(t) \;......$$

Example

An AM radio signal which comprises of an audio signal mi(t) along with a d.c. component and a carrier signal $m_2(t)$.

***(iii)* Integration**

Consider a continuous time signal m(t). The output signal n(t) is obtained by integrating this signal m(t) with respect to the time period 't'.

$$n(t) = \int_{-\infty}^{t} m(\tau)\, d\tau \ldots.$$

Where 't' is known as integration variable.

Example

The operation of a capacitor is just integrating the current that is flowing through the capacitor 'C'.

***(iv)* Differentiation**

Consider a continuous time signal m(t). The output signal n(t) is the derivative of the input signal m(t) with respect to time 't' and it is given as,

$$n(t) = \frac{d}{dt} m(t) \ldots.$$

Example

An inductor's operation is just finding the derivative value of the current flowing through the inductor 'L'

***(v)* Scaling (Amplitude scaling)**

Consider a continuous time signal m(t). The output signal n(t) is obtained by just applying an amplitude scaling to the input signal m(t) and it is given as,

$$n(t) = C\, m(t) \ldots.$$

Where 'C' is a scaling factor.

Example

The electronic passive component resistor 'R' performs an amplitude scaling function.

The operations that can be performed on an independent variable are

(i) Reflection

(ii) Time scaling

***(i)* Reflection**

Consider a continuous time signal m(t). The output signal n(t) is obtained by replacing the value of time period from (+ t) to (– t) and it is given as,

$$n(t) = m(-t) \ldots.$$

Hence the signal n(t) is a reflected signal/version/mirror image of the input signal m(t).

Example

The even signals [i.e. m(t) = m(– t)] are examples of this operation.

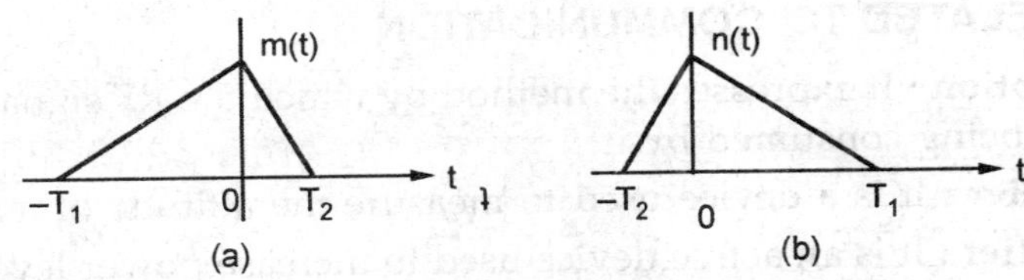

Fig. 1.16 The signal n(t) in (b) is a reflected/mirror image of the input signal m(t) in (a) where [t = – t]

(ii) Time scaling

Consider a continuous time signal m(t). The output signal n(t) is obtained by multiplying the variable 't' by a scaling factor 'a' and it is given as,

$$n(t) = n(at) \; ....$$

Where 't' is an independent variable and 'a' is a scaling factor.

The above mentioned operations (reflection and time scaling) are mainly applied on independent variable.

1.11 ANTENNAS - AN OVERVIEW

An antenna is a device that can radiate or receive electromagnetic signal. Antenna can be an active or passive device. The passive antenna is a hunk of a metal which is configured in a special way. In case of an active antenna it has power supply connectivity at some point. Antenna can carry RF signal and power signal. The shape and size of antenna may be a largest dish (receives satellite signals) or a miniature size dish for different kind of applications. The functionality of an antenna mainly depends on two things. The frequency of its design and the direction of the signal.

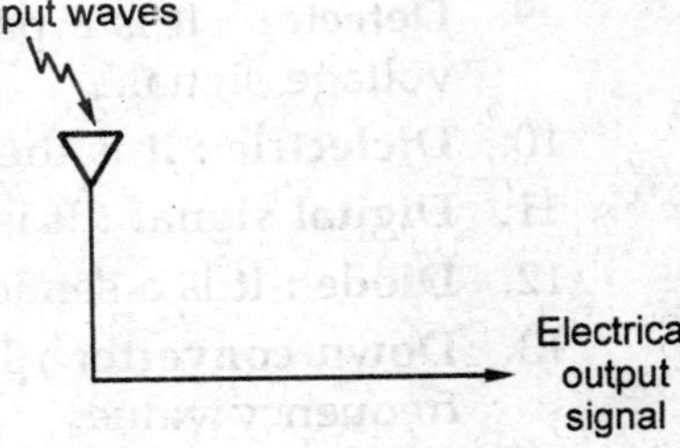

Fig. 1.17 Antenna

1.11.1 VSWR

The expansion for the term VSWR is voltage standing wave ratio. It expresses the amount of leakage of RF signal, which is useful in the measurement of 'match'. The amount of leakage of signal is inversely proportional to the match. For better matching the leakage should be minimum.

VSWR is expressed as A : 1 where 'A' represents the amount of leakage. If the value of A is high then leakage will be more. For 1 : 1 relation it expresses perfect match without leaking which is practically impossible.

1.11.2 Polarization

The RF signal travels (radiated) in open air and it (sinewaves) has its own orientation called as polarization. The polarization of the signal may be vertical or horizontal. But when the RF signals vary continuously from horizontal to vertical polarization as it travels and it is called as circular polarization.

1.12 TERMS RELATED TO COMMUNICATION

1. **Absorption :** It expresses the method by which the RF signal penetrates a material and is being consumed by it.
2. **Altimeter :** It is a device used to measure the altitude of a signal from ground.
3. **Amplifier :** It is an active device used to increase power level of a signal. The gain value gets increased as the signal is amplified.
4. **Amplitude modulation :** The process of super imposing the high frequency signal (carrier signal) on a modulating signal is called as modulation.

   If the amplitude of the carrier is varied in accordance with that of the modulating signal it is called as amplitude modulation.
5. **Analog signal :** An electrical signal that varies over a time period and has positive and negative cycles is called as analog signal.
6. **Antenna :** It is a RF component used to radiate electromagnetic signal. Antennas can be active or passive.
7. **Attenuator :** It is a RF component used to reduce the value of the signal and is measured in decibels. Attenuator can be fixed or variable.
8. **Bandwidth :** It is a measure that expresses the range of frequency.
9. **Detector :** It is a passive RF component that can convert RF power signal into a voltage signal.
10. **Dielectric :** It is the material that does not conduct electricity.
11. **Digital signal :** It is an electrical signal that varies over a time period.
12. **Diode :** It is a semiconductor device and acts as a switch.
13. **Down converter :** It is used in receiver and also called as mixer. It reduces the frequency value.
14. **Directional coupler :** It is a coupler that will work in only one direction.
15. **Earth station :** The ground segment with all required facilities for transmitting and receiving radio frequencies with satellites is called as earth station. It can also monitor and control the communication process.
16. **Impedance matching :** The process of converting the output impedance value of a RF device (which is not 50 ohms) and enables it to be connected to any other component with proper matching.
17. **Multipath :** If a signal takes more than one path to reach the intended receiver it is said to undergo multipath effect.
18. **Noise :** It is an unwanted form of energy.
19. **Transceiver:** A combination of transmitter and receiver is known as transceiver.
20. **Attenuation :** It is an important criteria that has to be considered with antennas. Whenever the output signal is lesser than the input signal it is called as "loss". Any signal passing through a device that is exhibiting loss has to experience "attenuation". If it is so the signal is said to be attenuated.

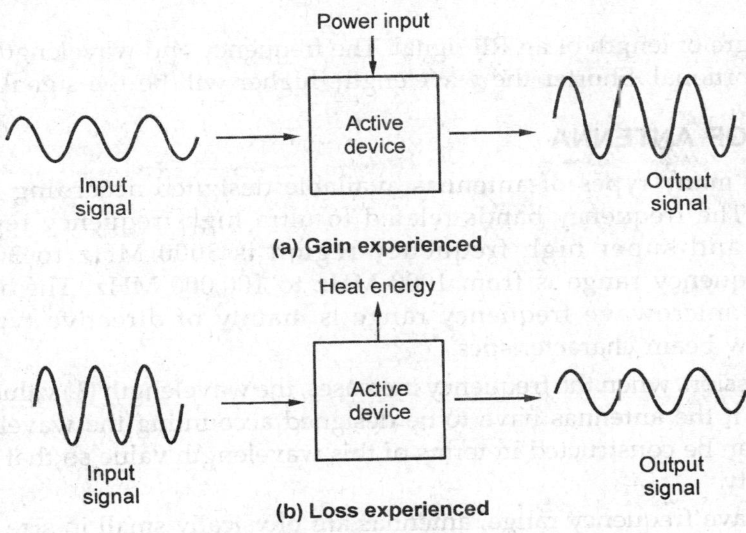

Fig. 1.18 A signal experiencing gain and loss criteria

1.13 SKIN EFFECT, ABSORPTION AND REFLECTION

1. Skin effect

Whenever the RF signal is around a conductor say metal it hangs there on the surface of the conductor. If a detector is placed inside the conductor then it is very difficult to detect the presence of RF signal and such an effect is called as skin effect.

2. Absorption

The RF signal generally tries to escape the boundaries of conductor and freely travels in open air. But when the passive device that exhibits insertion loss influence the signal, then the signal is said to experience 'absorption' since the device has absorbed the Rf signal.

3. Reflection

The RF signal is absorbed by a device with insertion loss. On the other hand the signal is transmitted in another direction. It is called as 'reflection'. Hence RF signal gets either absorbed or reflected or partially absorbed depending on the media through which it travels.

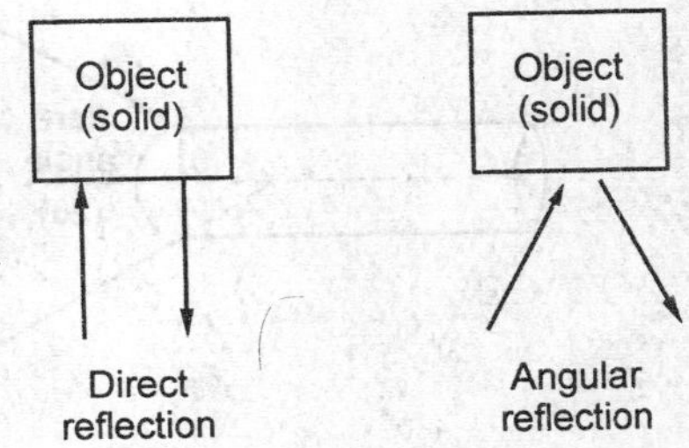

Fig. 1.19 Direct and angular reflection concepts

4. Transistor

A semiconductor device that is used in amplifiers to increase gain.

5. Uplink

The signals transmitted from ground station to satellite is known as uplink (In gigahertz range).

6. Wavelength

It is measure of length of an RF signal. The frequency and wavelength of the signal are inversely proportional. Shorter the wavelength, higher will be the signal frequency.

1.14 TYPES OF ANTENNA

There are many types of antennas available designed according to the frequency requirements. The frequency bands related to ultra high frequency region is 300 MHz to 3000 MHz and super high frequency region is 3000 MHz to 30,000 MHz. The microwave frequency range is from 1000 MHz to 100,000 MHz. The antennas that are used for these microwave frequency range is mainly of directive type that has high gain and narrow beam characteristics.

In transmission, when the frequency increases, the wavelength (λ) value will get reduced and to balance it the antennas have to be designed accounting the wavelength parameter. The antennas can be constructed in terms of this wavelength value so that they can provide better directivity.

In microwave frequency range, antennas are physically small in size and they use the metallic reflectors to provide required directivity. Usually they are curved surfaces in shape. There are many types of antennas used in microwave frequency range like,

(*i*) Horn antenna
(*ii*) Parabolic reflector
(*iii*) Lens antenna

1.14.1 Horn Antenna

A horn antenna is also called as open waveguide. When this waveguide is opened at one end and excited at another end it act as a radiator. It can radiate in a efficient way when compared to a two wire transmission line. Generally one end (mouth) of the wave guide is kept open and hence the waveguide assume the shape of electro-magnetic horn and it is just like a transmission line.

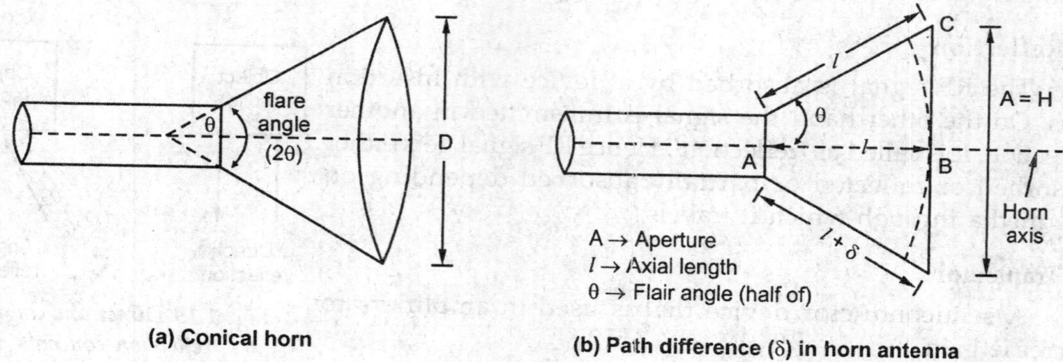

(a) Conical horn **(b) Path difference (δ) in horn antenna**

Fig. 1.20 Horn antenna

When flairing is done in both directions/both the walls of waveguide (F and H) of rectangular waveguide, a pyramidal horn can be obtained and flaring the walls of the circular waveguide will result in a conical horn.

From the triangle ABC in Fig. 1.20 (b), the angle 'θ' is given as, 9 = $\cos^{-1}$

$$\theta = \cos^{-1}\left(\frac{l}{l+\delta}\right)$$

Where 'δ' is the permissible variable phase angle.

and $$(l+\delta)^2 = l^2 + \left(\frac{H}{2}\right)^2 \ldots$$

$$= \left(l^2 + \frac{H^2}{4}\right) \ldots$$

When the 'δ' value is very small if can be neglected,

Hence $$2\,l\,\delta = \frac{H^2}{4}$$

$$l = \frac{H^2}{8\delta}$$

The 'l' and 'θ' expressions are the important design equations for a horn antenna.

The horn antennas are mainly used in microwave frequency ranges for moderate power gain case.

Note: If high power gain is required then parabolic reflectors are more suitable than horn antennas.

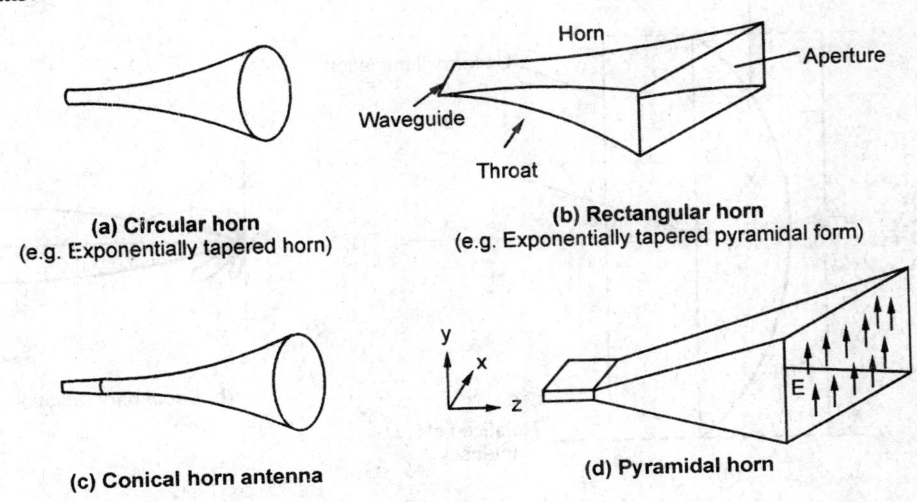

Fig. 1.21 Circular and rectangular horn antennas

Some examples of circular and rectangular horns are shown above. A rectangular horn which has flare at both sides is called as a pyramidal horn. The Fermat's principle, known as "principle of equality of path length" is suitable in design of horn antenna. Other types of horn antenna are septum horn, ridge horn, corrugated horn and aperture matched horn antenna.

1.14.2 Parabolic Reflector

The surface produced by a parabola's revolution about its axis is known as "paraboloid". A practical parabolic reflector is curved, three dimensional surface. The surface produced is also called as a 'Microwave dish'.

From these diagrams it is evident that the mouth of a parabolic reflector is circular.

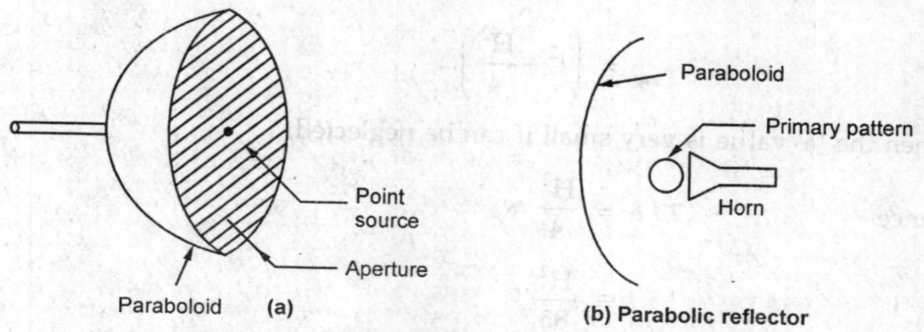

Fig. 1.22 Parabolic reflector

When an antenna applies parabolic reflector the radiation pattern will have sharp major lobe along with smaller minor lobes. The axis of the major beam will be in same direction as that of the parabolic reflector.

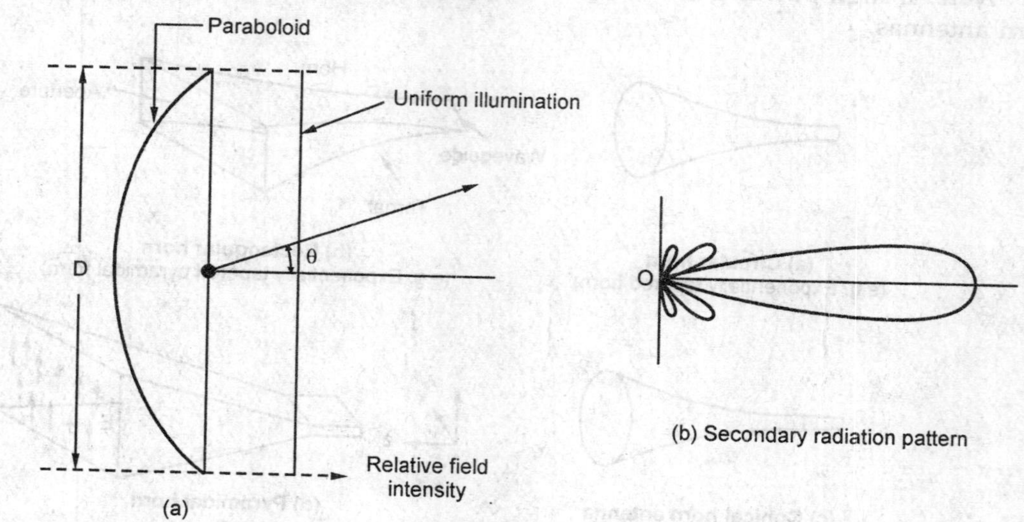

Fig. 1.23 Large paraboloid with radiation pattern (having uniformly illuminated aperture area)

When the primary antenna or feed is isotropic in nature there is a chance that paraboloid will generate a beam of radiation and if the circular aperture is very large then beam width between the first null for a circular aperture is denoted as BWFN and it is given as

$$\text{BWFN} = \frac{140\lambda}{D_\lambda}\text{deg}$$

where $D \rightarrow$ Diameter of the antenna aperture in m and $D_\lambda \rightarrow$ diameter of aperture, λ.
$\lambda \rightarrow$ wavelength in free space.

Then the beamwidth in between the nulls (first) of a rectangular aperture is,

$$\text{BWFN} = \frac{115\lambda}{l_\lambda}\text{deg}$$

Where $l_\lambda \rightarrow$ length of the antenna aperture λ, of a large uniformly illuminated antenna aperture.

The directivity is, $D = 4\pi\left(\frac{\text{Area}}{\lambda^2}\right)$

For a circular aperture case,

$$D = 4\pi\left(\frac{\pi D^2}{4\lambda^2}\right)$$

For circular aperture = $D = 9.8\left(\frac{D}{\lambda}\right)^2 = (9.8\,D_\lambda^2)$

Where $D_\lambda \rightarrow$ diameter of an aperture in λ,

Note 1 : Power gain 'G_p' of circular aperture is,

Considering a $\lambda/2$ dipole antenna

$$G_p = (6\,D_\lambda^2)$$

An antenna using parabolic reflector is used in several communication applications. It has large coverage capability and accuracy.

Note 2 : The power gain G_p with respect to halfwave dipole for a circular aperture paraboloid is $G_p = \left(\frac{4\pi A_c}{\lambda^2}\right)$ where $A_c \rightarrow$ capture area.

1.14.3 Lens Antenna

The frequency band used in a lens antenna begins at 1000 MHz and upto 3000 MHz its operation is effective. The lens antenna acts like an optical lens. The types of lens antenna are of two types, (*i*) Dielectric lens or H plane metal plate lens antenna (*ii*) E-plane metal plate lens. The lens antennas becomes heavy at lower frequencies.

(*i*) They are the delay lenses where travelling wavefronts are retarded/suppressed by the lens media used.

(*ii*) They are the fast lenses where travelling wavefronts are accelerated by lens media.

There are two types of dielectric lens antenna.

(*a*) Metallic dielectric type.

(*b*) Non metallic dielectric type.

The delay lens antennas are considered as end-fire antenna with monofilar axial mode helical and polyrod antennas. The director structured yagi uda antenna of multiple elements is another basic type of antenna and the delay lens antennas of these structures are mainly elementary lens type.

The different forms of lens antennas are shown below.

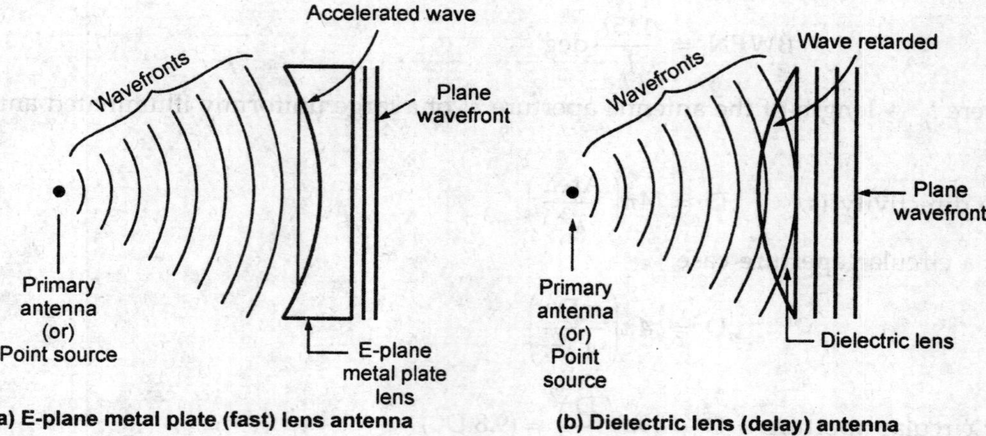

Fig. 1.24 Lens antenna

The three forms of rudimentary lens antennas has better performance like parabolic reflector antenna.

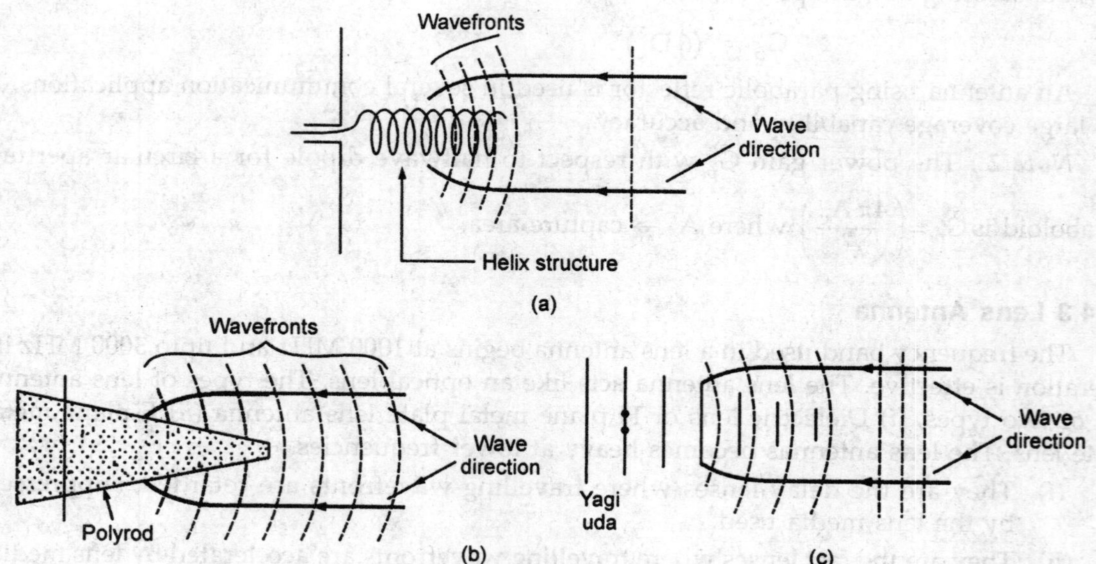

Fig. 1.25 Three forms of the rudimentary lens antenna

The monoflair axial-mode helical antenna design is simple. The parameters that have to be considered in its design are,

(*i*) Gain of the antenna
(*ii*) Beamwidth
(*iii*) Impedance
(*iv*) Axial ratio

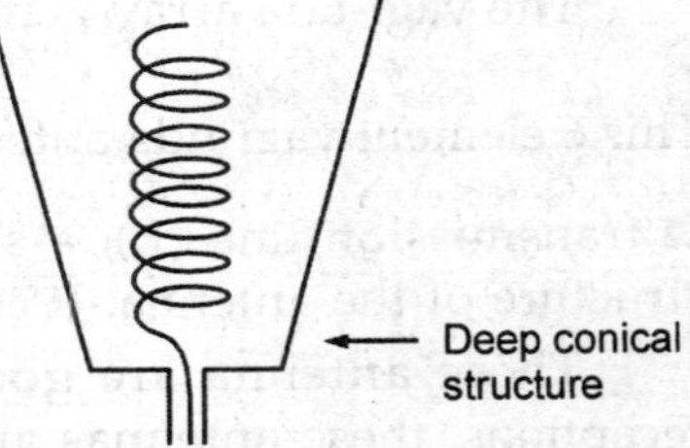

Fig. 1.26 Deep conical helical structure

Depending upon the number of turns in helical structure, the spacing between the turns and the frequency used the parameters axial ratio and impedance will change. The other two parameters gain and beamwidth values are interdependent. They are inversely proportional to each other. All the above four parameters will determine the bandwidth (BW). The side lobes can be reduced by having a deep conical helical structure.

The entire bandwidth will be utilized if all the parameters are accurate. It is worth noting that the helix circumference about '1 λ' value corresponds to the center frequency of the bandwidth.

1.14.4 Polyrod Antenna

In polyrod antenna, the electromagnetic waves are guided by dielectric rod. An amount of power would escape and radiate through the walls of the guide and this characteristics is used in polyrod antenna. The dielectric rod used here is made up of the material polystyrene.

The dielectric rod is fed by a waveguide which is energized by the coaxial transmission line. The polyrod antennas act like an end fire antenna. These antennas may also use dielectric sleeve of square cross section or circular cross section if the interior portion of the dielectric sleeve is fully air filled. The polyrod antennas are suitable for many applications.

1.14.5 Yagi-Uda Antenna

The yagi-uda antenna is constructed with an array of many director elements and a driven element. A feedline is the main element of the structure. There is an equal spacings allowed between any two directors. The full construction is completed by having a reflector at one end of yagi-uda antenna, and a narrow bandwidth is used for its functionality. If the reflector is lengthened, the narrow bandwidth can be broadened upto the value of 1.5 λ. The director elements also has to be shortened.

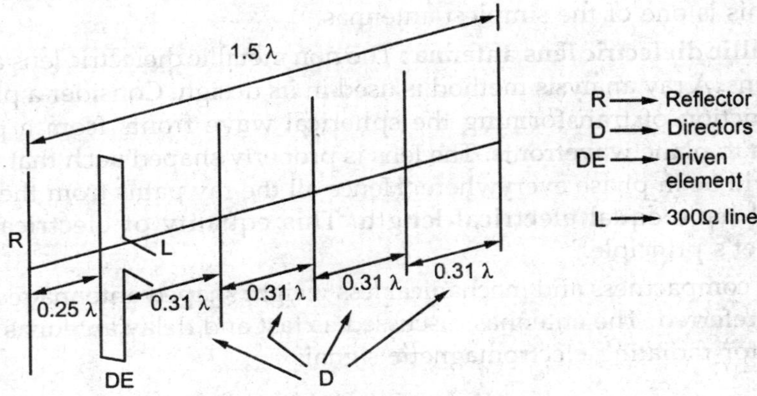

Fig. 1.27 6-element yagi-uda element

The yagi-uda array is mainly used for television signal reception as home application.

This 6 element yagi-uda antenna has a folded $\frac{\lambda}{2}$ dipole as driven element and it is fed by 300 Ω transmission line (L), a single reflector and four director elements and shown in the structure of the antenna. It can provide up to 12 dB maximum gain.

These antenna are good at ultrahigh frequency ranges. For domestic television receptions, these antennas are used conventionally.

1.14.6 Artificial Dielectric Lens Antennas

The metallic or artificial dielectric antennas have advantage of lesser weight. When compared to its design of wavelength the size of metal particles used should be small. Also the space between the metal particles should be less than the wavelength to suppress any diffraction effects.

The particles used would be metal spheres, rods or strips. A plano-convex lens consisting of metal spheres is used here where the spheres are kept in a Lattice structure. An oscillating current is made to flow on these spheres by radiating electromagnetic signal from a primary or a point source antenna.

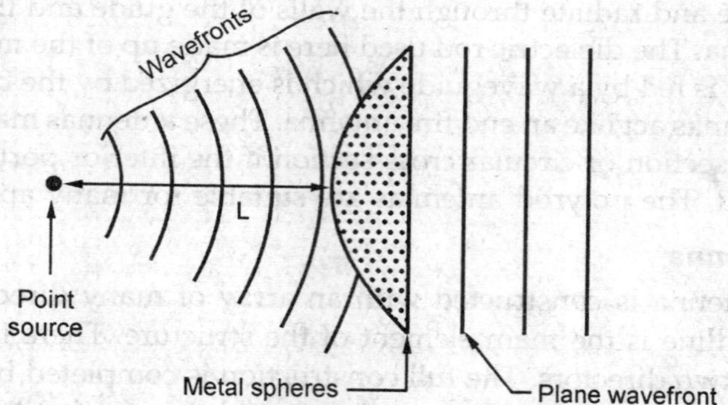

Fig. 1.28 Metallic (or) an artificial lens antenna

Metal discs or strip shaped particles are better than these spheres since they possess less weight. This is one of the simplest antennas.

Non metallic dielectric lens antenna : The non metallic dielectric lens antenna is similar to an optical lens. A ray analysis method is used in its design. Consider a plano-convex lens. It does the function of transforming the spherical wave fronts from a primary or point source antenna to plane wavefronts. The lens is properly shaped such that the field over the plane waves will be in phase everywhere. Hence all the ray paths from the source to that of the plane will have equal electrical length. This equality of electrical path length is called as Fermet's principle.

For better compactness and mechanical less weight shaped antenna requirements, these antennas are preferred. The antennas discussed as fast and delay antennas are thus suitable lens antennas for radiating electromagnetic signals.

1.14.7 Smart Antennas

The smart antennas or adaptive antenna arrays (consists of array of antenna elements) can increase the performance level of wireless communication networks. Smart antenna or antenna arrays have many advantages.

(*i*) Wider radio coverage through range extension.

(*ii*) Increased capacity.

(*iii*) Mitigates fading in multipath environments,

(*iv*) Maximum data rates are possible.

These smart antennas find usages in wireless communication, direction finding in emergency applications, vehicular traffic monitoring etc. With adaptive antennas/smart antennas the Intersymbol (ISI) interference generated due to delayed multipath components and also the fading effect are reduced. These smart antennas offer many advantages over sector and omni directional antennas. As the number of subscribers increase they support continued mobile communication with reducing ISI and other fading effects. The system capacity interference reductions are important criterion associated with cellular communication and smart antennas are suitable to produce optimum results on each of these parameters.

1.15 CAPACITY

The capacity is a parameter related to spectral efficiency of the system and the traffic offered by each user. The spectral efficiency S_E is calculated in channels/km^2 /MHz and it is given by

$$S_E = \frac{B_t / B_{ch}}{B_t \cdot N_c \cdot A_c} = \frac{1}{B_t \cdot N_c \cdot A_c}$$

Where $B_t \rightarrow$ Total bandwidth of the system available for voice channels.

$B_{ch} \rightarrow$ Bandwidth per voice channels.

$N_c \rightarrow$ Number of cells per cluster.

$A_c \rightarrow$ Cell area in km^2

The system capacity is expressed in channels/km^2 and it is given by,

$$C = (S_E)(B_t)$$

$$= \frac{B_t}{B_{ch} \cdot N_c \cdot A_c}$$

$$C = \frac{N_{ch}}{N_c \cdot A_c} \qquad \left[\because N_{ch} = \frac{B_t}{B_{ch}}\right]$$

The system capacity 'C' can be increased in many ways like increased by the bandwidth allotted to the system, reducing bandwidth of channel, reducing the number of cells in a particular cluster, applying cell splitting technique to reduce cellular area etc. The main factor "Number of users" affects the system capacity 'C' value.

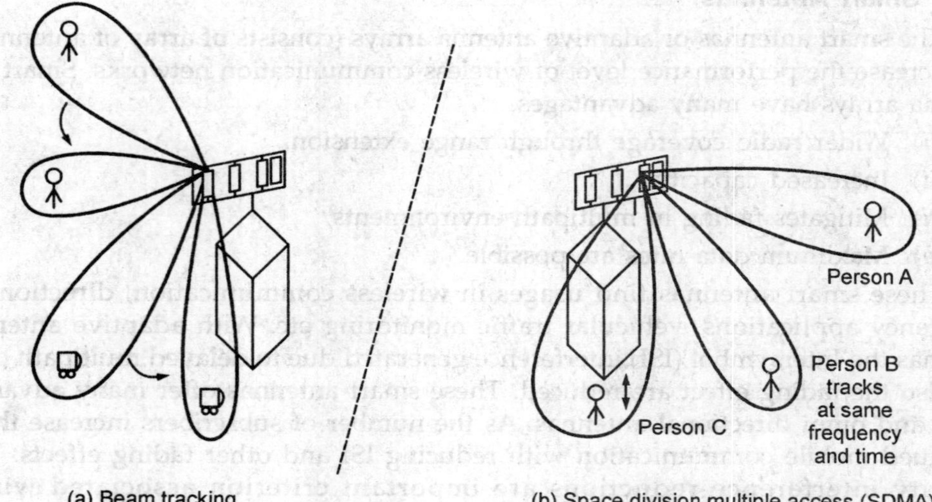

Fig. 1.29 Smart antennas-techniques

The smart antennas with their radiation patterns help adaptively to maximize communication quality. Smart antennas along with space division multiple access (SDMA) technique, enhances beam tracking in mobile communication. It ensures greater efficiency and increase frequency reuse in cellular environment. With smart antennas the system capacity can also be increased by two strategies namely "interference reduction" on the downlink and "interference rejection" on uplink. The directional beams are steered towards the mobile units to reduce interference levels. In turn it helps to reduce the probability of co-channel interference when compared to a system which is using omnidirectional base station (BS) antennas. Interference reduction can be achieved by using an antenna array with steered or a set of switched beams. But for small amount of time period the co-channel interference will be strong whenever the mobile unit is available within the main beam of adjacent co-channel base station.

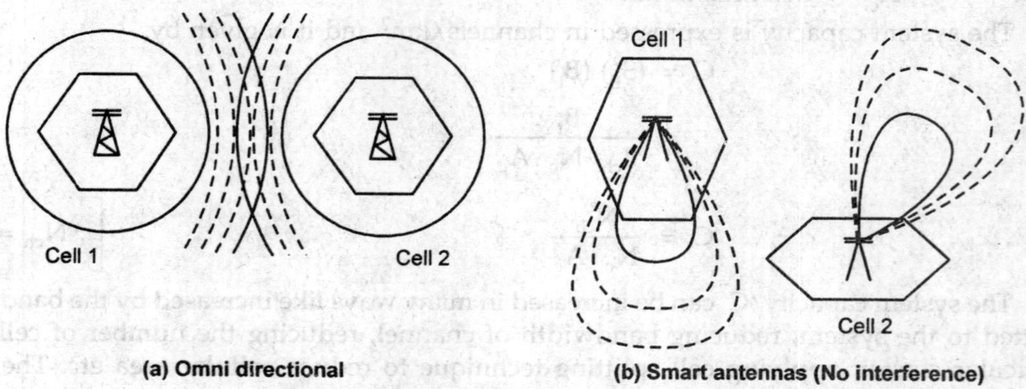

Fig. 1.30 Interference reduction with smart antennas

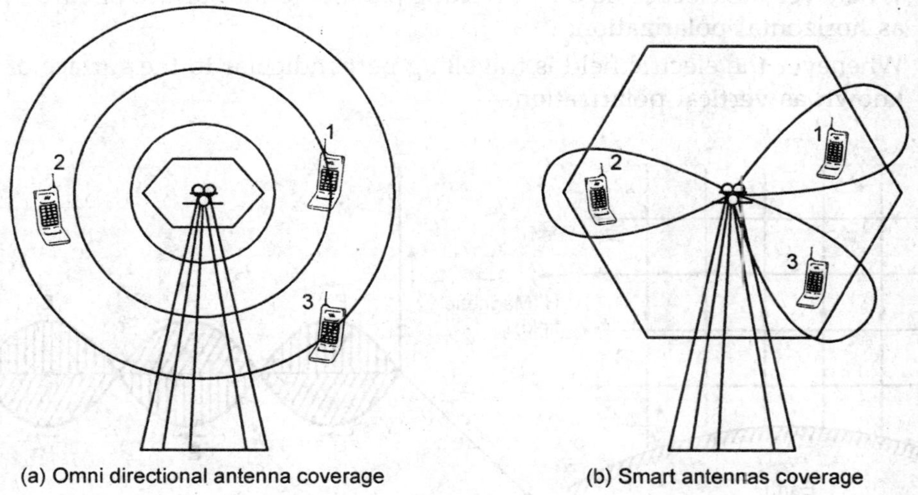

Fig. 1.31 Better coverage with smart antenna system

Smart antennas combine multiple antenna elements as an array of antennas and the radiation pattern and antenna beamwidth is such that increases radio coverage very efficiently.

In mobile environment beam tracking is more accurate in smart antennas compared to omni directional antennas. Hence for better coverage, reduced interference, reduced fading under multipath effects smart antennas are highly appropriate.

1.16 SIGNAL PROPAGATION

1.16.1 Propagation of Electromagnetic Waves

The electromagnetic waves travel in straight line with the speed of light. They possess electric field and magnetic field which are at right angles to each other and also to the direction of wave propagation. The radio waves are also a form of electromagnetic radiation. Some important properties of the radio waves are, intensity, direction of travel, plane of propagation and frequency. The polarization of an electromagnetic wave is just the orientation of electric field vector with respect to the earth's surface.

Polarization are of two types

Linear Polarization

When the polarization remains as constant then such a type is called as linear polarization.

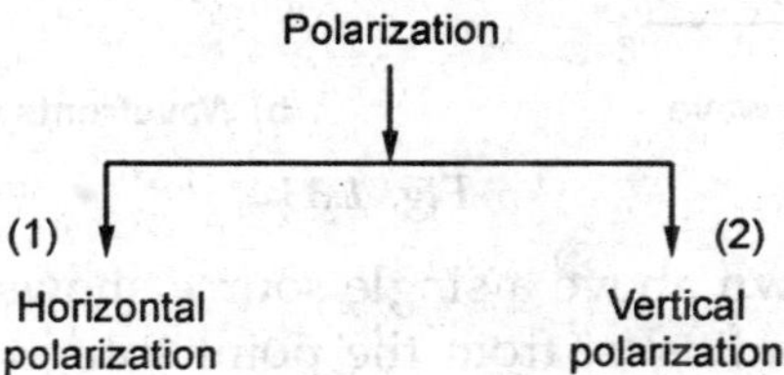

1. Whenever the electric field is travelling parallel to the surface of earth, it is known as horizontal polarization.
2. Whenever the electric field is travelling perpendicular to the surface of earth, it is known as vertical polarization.

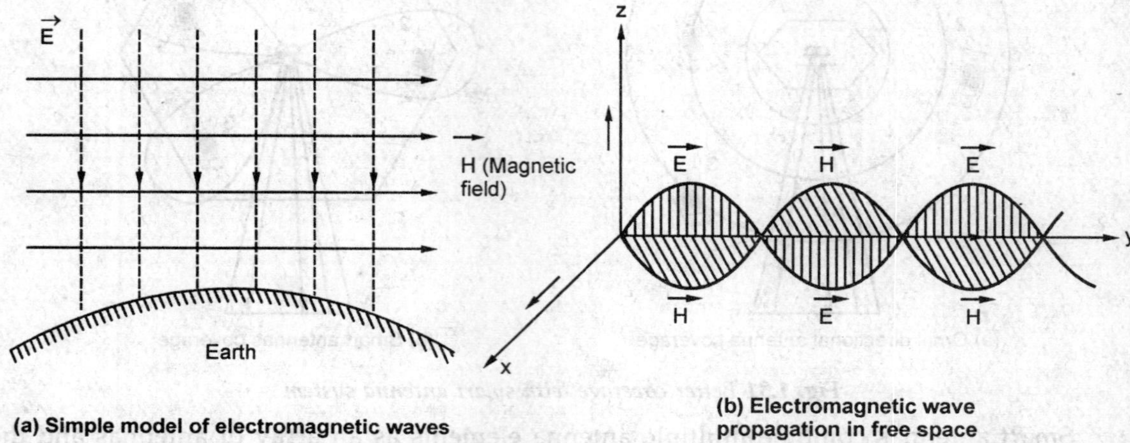

Fig. 1.32 Propagation of Electromagnetic waves H → Magnetic lines; E → Electric field

The electromagnetic waves (E.M) or signals are defined in many ways. One of the definition is "they are simple oscillations which propagates with the velocity of the light energy (3×10^8 m/s)". The E.M wave consists of electric and magnetic fields that are moving forces in their nature. The wave propagation, direction of movement of electric field, and magnetic filed are normal to each other. These lines of force and E.M wave propagation in free space are given in Fig. 1.32 (a) and (b).

Wavefront

The plane waves are simpler in its propagation as in Fig. 1.33 (a) whereas wavefronts travel in a complex way. Consider a point source, which is a single location and the rays emerge from it travels in all directions as in Fig. 1.33 (b).

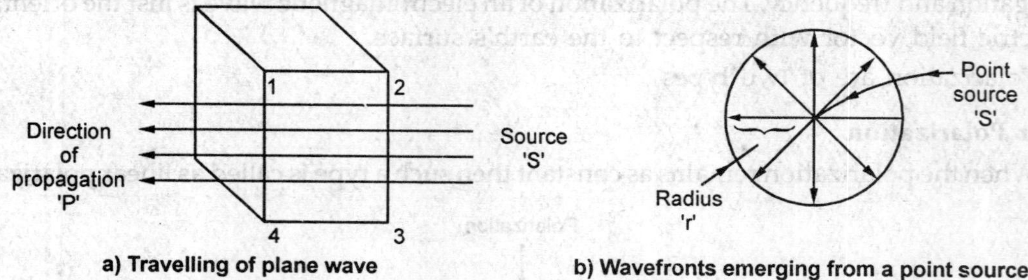

Fig. 1.33

In 'point source' as shown above a single source shows the rays that emerges from it constitutes wavefront. The radius 'r' from the point source to the boundary is equal at a time instant. The wavefronts are almost parallel, in free space conditions. In case the point source is at a distance then it will lead to formation of plane wavefront.

1.16.2 Electromagnetic Radiation

As said earlier the radio waves are made up of magnetic and electric fields (H&E). The magnetic fields are continuous in nature. The strength of the magnetic field produced around a conductor, is represented as 'H' and, it is given as,

$$H = \frac{1}{2\pi d}$$

Where $d \rightarrow$ Distance in meter.

$H \rightarrow$ Magnetic field (ampere turns per meter).

The electric fields are produced by the voltage potential's difference between the two conductors. It is represented as 'E' and,

$$E = \frac{q}{4\pi \varepsilon d^2}$$

Where $q \rightarrow$ Charge between the two conductors in coulombs.

$E \rightarrow$ Electric field strength in volts per meter,

$e \rightarrow$ Permittivity in farads per meter.

$d \rightarrow$ Distance between the two conductors in meters.

Note : Free space permittivity = 8.85×10^{-12} F/m.

or

The permittivity of the air.

1.16.3 Attenuation

1.16.3.1 Wave Attenuation and Absorption

When the signal passes through vacuum space there will be no loss of signal, as the waves propagates. But there is a reduction in the level of power density and this is called as attenuation. There is another type of loss known as 'absorption loss' which is due to particles available in earth's atmosphere, which is not vacuum.

The reduction in power density in correspondence to the distance is equal to the power loss parameter which is generally called as 'wave attenuation'. It is denoted by 'W_a'.

$$W_a = 10 \log\left(\frac{P_1}{P_2}\right)$$

Where (P_1/P_2) represents the power density ratio.

The concept of absorption is also attractive. Since the earth's atmosphere is not a vacuum and it consists of molecules and atoms of different substances like liquids, gases etc and some of them have the property of absorbing electromagnetic signal when it is radiated into space. At this time the wave energy may be transferred from the waves to that of the gases or molecules, of atmosphere. The waves may also transfer energy with free electrons (valence electrons) and ions. In case the ions do not make collisions with the gas molecules energy will be again given back to electromagnetic waves. Hence there will be no absorption of energy taking place. On the other hand if the ions collide with the gas molecular (say) then ions may release the energy and in turn will not provide the energy to the electromagnetic waves. This will surely result in 'absorption concept'.

It can be said that greater the particle's energy the probability of collision is higher and resulting in more absorption.

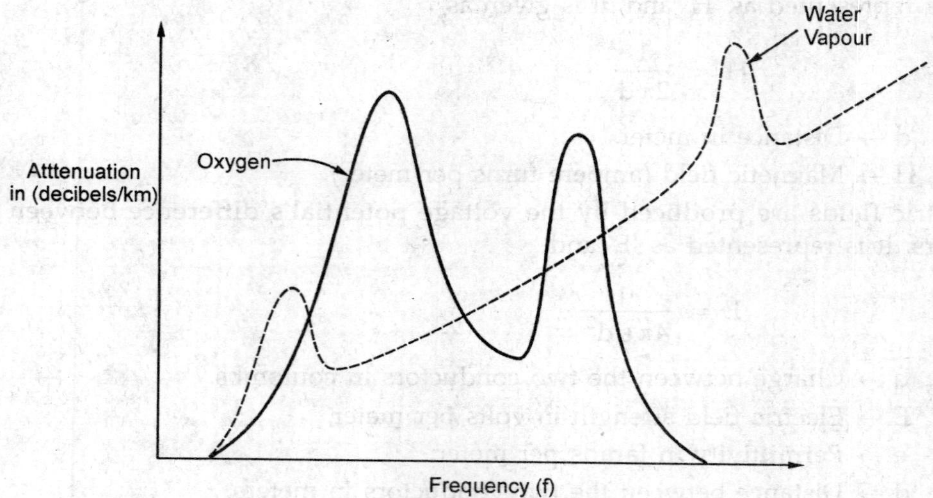

Fig. 1.34 Absorption of electromagnetic waves in atmosphere considering water vapor and oxygen

As the frequency increases the probability of attenuation increases very fast in case of water vapor, and in case of oxygen the level of attenuation is tolerable where initially it rises and then decreases suddenly though the frequency increases.

It is essential to study the various aspects that influence the cellular signals transmission to estimate the accuracy of reception on the other side. Generally the radio channel finds it difficult with wireless systems than wired systems due to the reasons like frequency of operation, terrain contour, velocity of the mobile terminal and other factors.

In the lower frequency range (≃ less than 500 MHz) in the signal spectrum the loss of signal strength is much smaller (at the initial few meters). Other than frequency ranges, atmospheric gases may absorb signals above 60 GHz transmitted which in turn accelerates attenuation as a function of the distance.

In cellular transmission, the radio signal propagation is more different for indoor and outdoor areas.

In urban area the man made noise is the main cause for the increase in interference level. The signal strength falls as the square of the distance. In urban areas the line of sight (LOS) between transmitter and receiver is highly obstructed due to tall buildings and terrain contour. At the mobile frequency range (≃ 800) the wavelength of the signal is very small and simply it can be treated as rays. The propagation mechanisms may be different for indoor and outdoor units. The propagation mechanisms for indoor area are

1. Reflection and transmission
2. Diffraction
3. Scattering

And for outdoor area the fading of signals is more due to signal scattering. The multipath scattering is due to tall buildings, natural obstacles and other factors. The line of sight link between base station antenna and that of the mobile unit is hardly possible.

1.16.4 Important Properties of Radio Waves

The radio waves possess important properties similar to optical properties. The wave propagation can be altered by optical effects such as reflection, refraction, interference and diffraction. These terminologies are similar in operation to some other terms.

Example

- Refraction of wave can be considered as bending.
- Reflection can be considered as bouncing.
- Interference can be treated as colliding.
- Diffraction can be considered as scattering.

Since light waves are nothing but high frequency electromagnetic waves, it is considered that science of optics can help the propagation of radio waves.

The refraction, reflection, interference and diffraction are the main properties in optical communication. Since the radio waves while travelling (propagating) undergoes these kinds of properties, optical science also suits radio wave propagation.

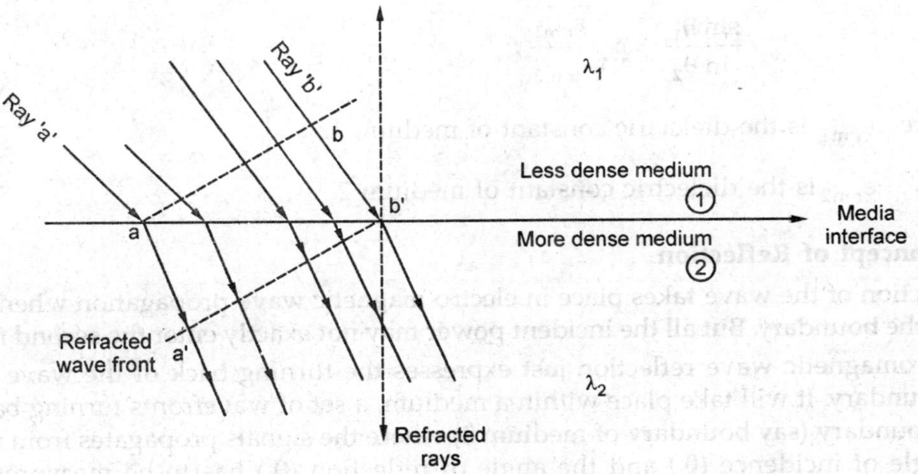

Fig. 1.35 Refracted ways between two media

It this case the wavefront at a particular plane boundary which is between two media with various densities. For example medium 1 is less dense than the mědium 2. From the diagram the ray a enters the denser medium first than ray b, and ray b enters denser medium after a time delay. The refracted wavefront a' b'.

A bunch of refracted rays emerge when they enter a medium (say 2) which is denser than the medium 1.

The index of refraction or refractive index is very important in the sense that the amount of bending or refraction at the point of interface of two materials of different density depends on this refractive index.

$$\text{Refractive index} = r = \frac{C}{V}$$

Where r is the refractive index.

C is the speed of light (3×10^8 m / sec).

V is the speed of light in a particular given material (m/sec).

Note : Refractive index (r) is unit less parameter. From the discussion of refractive index, Snell's law can be represented with refractive index and angles (degrees) involved in the wave propagation. The Snell's law states that $n_1 \sin \theta_1$ is equal to $n_2 \sin \theta_2$.

$$n_1 \sin \theta_1 = n_2 \sin \theta_2$$

$$\frac{\sin \theta_1}{\sin \theta_2} = \frac{n_2}{n_1}$$

Where $n_1 \rightarrow$ Refractive index of material 1 (say M_1).

$n_2 \rightarrow$ Refractive index of material 2 (say M_2).

$\theta_1 \rightarrow$ Angle of incidence in degree.

$\theta_2 \rightarrow$ Angle of refraction in degree.

$$\frac{\sin \theta_1}{\sin \theta_2} = \sqrt{\frac{\varepsilon_{r\,m1}}{\varepsilon_{r\,m2}}}$$

Where $\varepsilon_{r\,m1}$ is the dielectric constant of medium 1.

$\varepsilon_{r\,m2}$ is the dielectric constant of medium 2.

1.16.4.1 Concept of Reflection

Reflection of the wave takes place in electro magnetic wave propagation whenever the wave hits the boundary. But all the incident power may not exactly enter the second material.

Electromagnetic wave reflection just expresses the turning back of the wave when it hits the boundary. It will take place within a medium, a set of wavefronts turning back after hitting a boundary (say boundary of medium 2) where the signals propagates from medium 1. The angle of incidence (θ_i) and the angle of reflection (θ_r) has to be measured as the wavefronts are reflected.

The waves are reflected as it hits the boundary and in this case it is considered as semi-rough surface. Here the signal reflected as it touches the semirough surface. If it is scattered in random direction it is said to be diffuse reflection and when reflection emerges due to a smooth surface it is said to be specular (mirror like) reflections. If the cosine of angle of incidence of the wave is greater than the value $\frac{\lambda}{8\,D}$, it is termed as 'Rayleigh Criterion'.

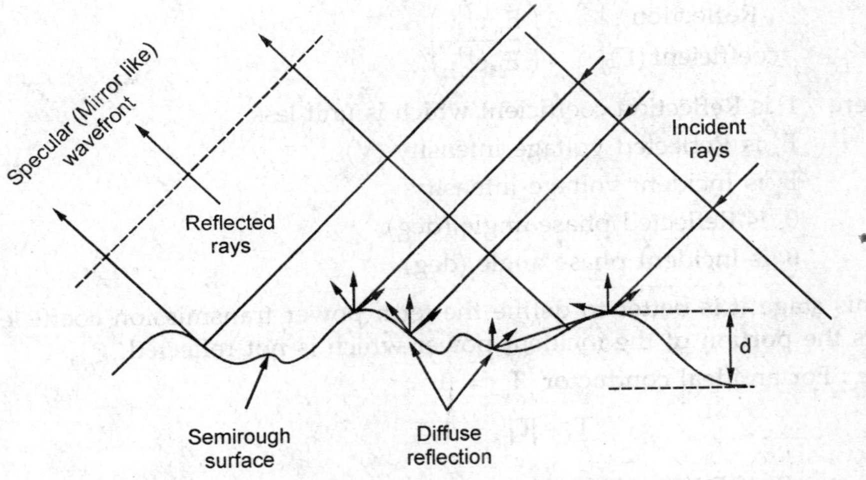

Fig. 1.36 Reflection concept with semirough surface

In Rayleigh criterion $\frac{\lambda}{8\,D}$,

D $\rightarrow$ Depth of the surface irregularity

and λ $\rightarrow$ Wavelength of the incident wave.

This criterion holds good as long as,

$$\cos\theta_1 > \frac{\lambda}{8\,D}$$

Also the surface or boundary is assumed as smooth surface to meet this condition mentioned above.

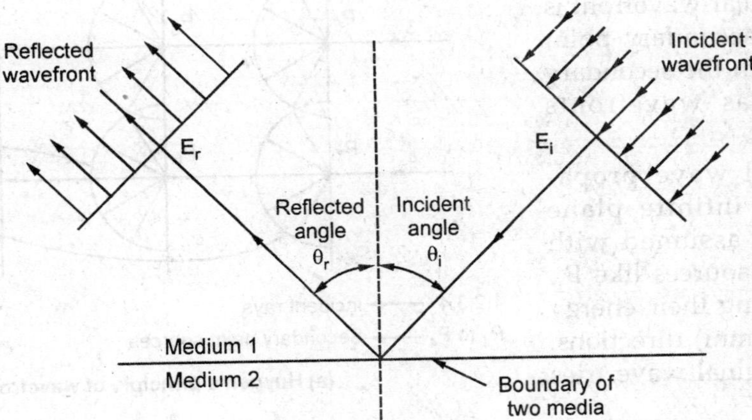

Fig. 1.37 Electromagnetic reflection

In reflection of the wave, the incident angle θ_i is equal to the reflected angle θ_r. The reflection coefficient Γ represents the ratio of reflected voltage intensity to the incident voltage intensity.

For an ideal case say for a perfect conductor reflection coefficient is unity ($\Gamma = 1$).

$$\left.\begin{array}{r}\text{Reflection}\\ \text{coefficient }(\Gamma)\end{array}\right\} = \left(\frac{E_r\, e^{j\theta_r}}{E_i\, e^{j\theta_i}}\right)$$

Where Γ is Reflection coefficient which is unit less.

E_r is Reflected voltage intensity (V).

E_i is Incident voltage intensity.

θ_r is Reflected phase angle (deg).

θ_i is Incident phase angle (deg).

In this stage it is better to define the term power transmission coefficient say (T_c). It represents the portion of the incident power which is not reflected.

Note : For an ideal conductor $T_c = 0$

and $T_c + |\Gamma| = 1$

1.16.4.2 Concept of Diffraction

Diffraction is nothing but redistribution of energy within a particular wavefront as it approaches closer to the edge of an object (opaque object). Diffraction is the concept that expresses the characteristics of wave when it passes around corners of an object or an obstacle. An important principle known as "Huygens principle" is that each and every point on a particular wavefront is considered as a secondary point source from which the secondary waves termed as wavefronts radiates outward.

The normal wave propagation with an infinite plane consideration is assumed with many secondary sources like P_1, P_2, P_3 etc. radiating their energy outward in all (omni) directions. But the main original wave tries

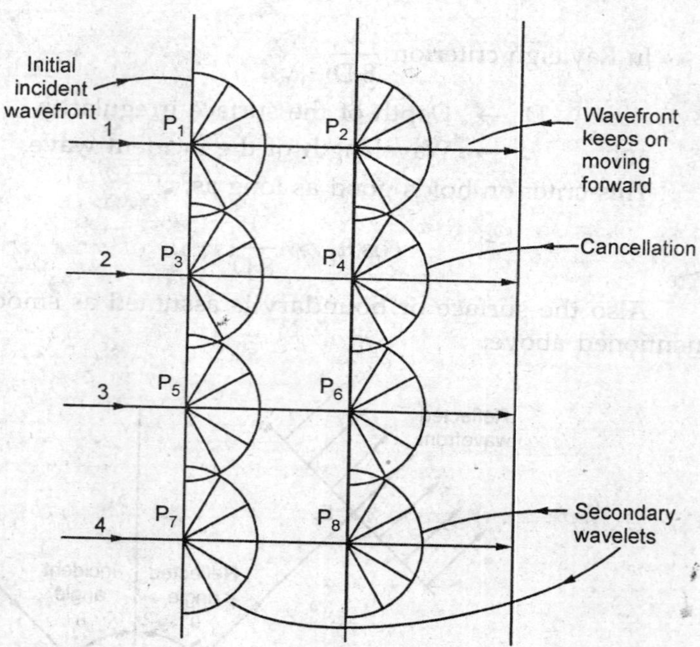

(a) Huygen's principle of wavefront

to maintain its same path in the forward direction even though many secondary wavelets get cancelled midway.

It is shown with one example.

The wavefronts propagates, spreads out and then scatters. This scattering effect of wavefronts is known as 'diffraction effect'.

Note : If the secondary wave sightly sneaks around the obstacle's corner, it is said to be 'shadow zone' of the wave propagation.

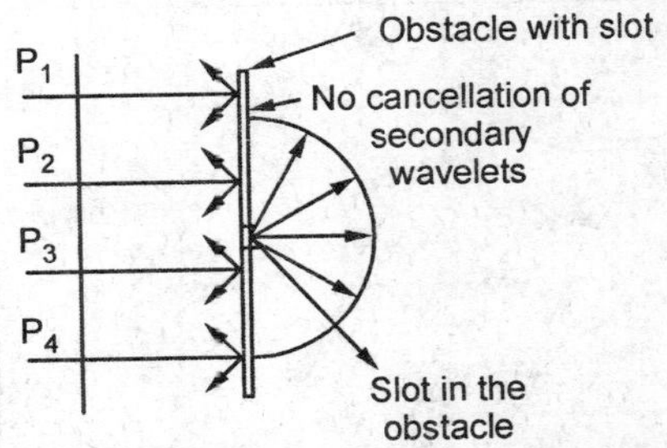

(b) Finite wavefront passing through a slot

Fig. 1.38 Electromagnetic wave diffraction

1.16.4.3 Interference

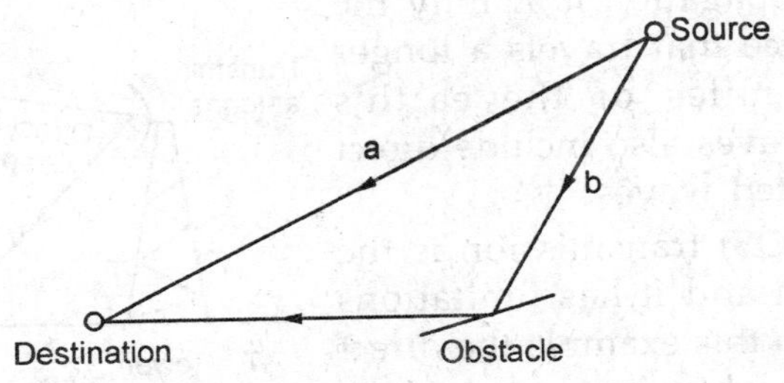

Fig. 1.39 Interference of two waves a and b

Interference represents the interfering act or nature which might take place in wave propagation. When two or more electromagnetic waves meet at the same point then there occurs linear superposition of waves and interference principle is subject to it. The linear superposition principle states that the net voltage intensity at a particular same point in space is equal to the sum of the intensities of the individual waves (where waves are assumed as vectors).

In the addition of two voltage vectors, the total voltage is just not the summation of magnitudes but also the addition of phases.

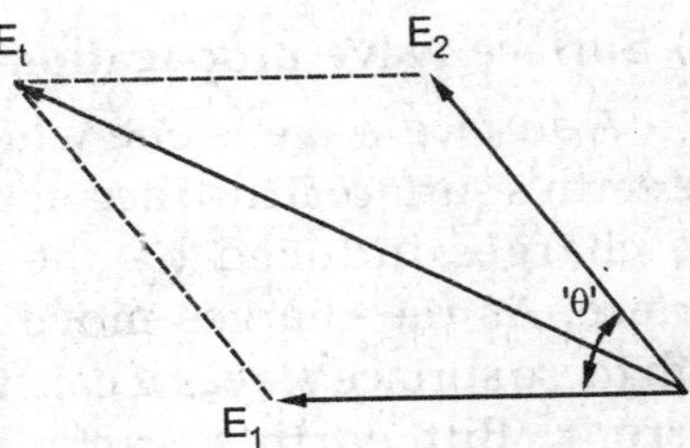

Fig. 1.40 Sum of two voltage vectors

1.17 TYPES OF PROPAGATION

When electromagnetic waves travel within the earths atmosphere it is known as terrestrial waves and the corresponding communication between different points is terrestrial radio communication.

In terrestrial radio communication which is with respect to earth's atmosphere it mainly has three oceans of wave propagation.

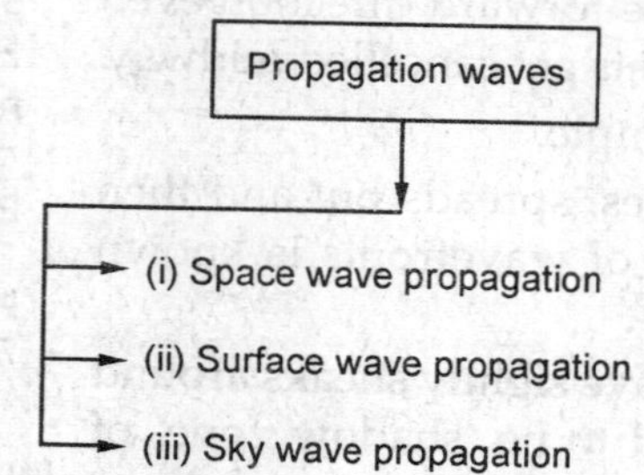

Each type of wave propagation is discussed in detail in this chapter.

(*i*) Space wave propagation

The space wave propagation is mainly the energy radiated into space that travels a longer distance in terms of miles of the earth's atmosphere. The space waves also include direct waves and ground reflected waves.

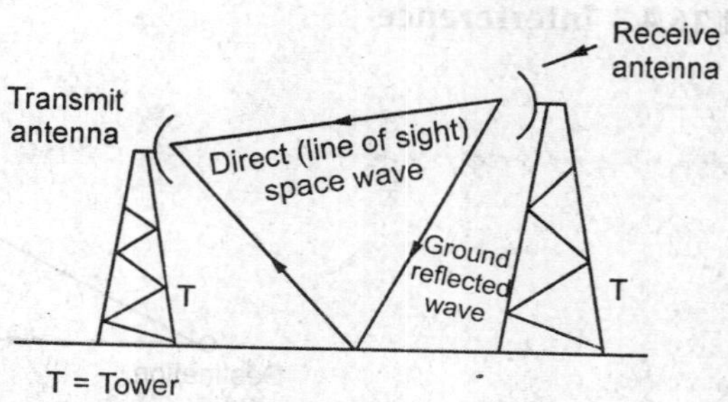

Fig. 1.41 Space-wave propagation concept

The line of sight (LOS) transmission is the direct wave transmission and it has limitations with earth's curvatures. In this example the direct wave in space travels straight where some wave hits the earth's surface and subjected to reflection. The ground reflected wave travels towards receiving antenna and as the waves propagates and reaches the receiver the signals received undergoes further analysis.

(*ii*) Surface wave propagation

A surface wave is one which is guided by the earth's surface. As this wave travels near the earth's surface it also accompanies the charges induced by the earth surface. As the charges move along with these surface waves it constitutes current. But earth's surface has resistivity too so that the charges are dissipated in several directions. Hence surface waves resemble a transmission line in this aspect.

The main application of these waves are in ship related communication, including navigation. The frequency range involved with these surface wave propagation is 15 kHz. The earth mainly has gradient density that is the density decreases as the distance from earth's surface increases ; as in the diagram shown above.

(a) Surface wave movement

(b) An example of surface wave propagation

Fig. 1.42 Surface propagation

It is worth noting that frequency selection is very important such that excessive wavefront tilt should be avoided so that wavefront may not die as the wave propagates over the earth's surface.

(*iii*) Sky wave propagation

Whenever the electromagnetic waves are directed above the horizon level then it is termed as sky waves. Generally a large angle will be provided as the skywaves propagates keeping earth as reference. When skywaves radiate into sky usually they are neither reflected nor refracted to the earth due to ionosphere. Because of this characteristics skywaves are also termed as ionosphere propagation. The three layers D, E and F layers of ionosphere influences sky wave propagation.

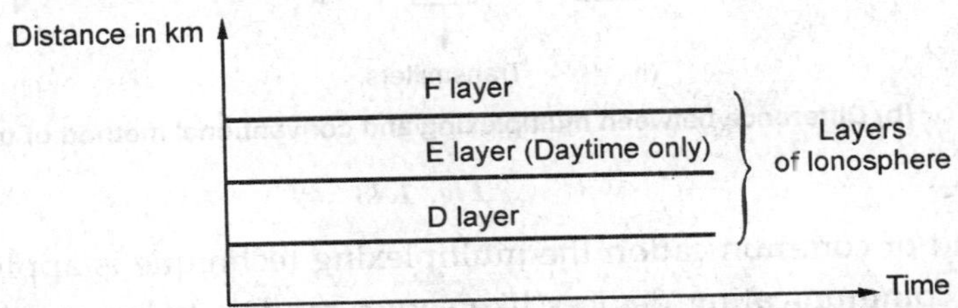

The ionosphere is highly dense during maximum sunlight and ionosphere occupies the region of space roughly 50 to 400 kilometers above the earth's surface. In skywave propagation the electromagnetic waves bend towards the regions of low electron density in ionosphere and propagates according to the density of ionosphere which depends on availability of sunlight.

1.18 MULTIPLEXING

Multiplexing is a technique used to accommodate more channels at a time so that each can have its own data/information which travel from transmitter to receiver. It is a concept of "many to one", and hence many channels are combined into a multiplexer (MUX) and sent as a single stream of data towards receiver. If a multiplexer (MUX) is used as transmitter it must be balanced with a demultiplexer circuit (DEMUX) at the receiver to receive the single stream of data and split them again into original set of channels which was the input to MUX unit.

Today the data traffic is highly voluminous and so the high capacity of data stream can be managed only by sharing the link (transmission link) between two devices.

The scheme of multiplexing is represented as block diagrams.

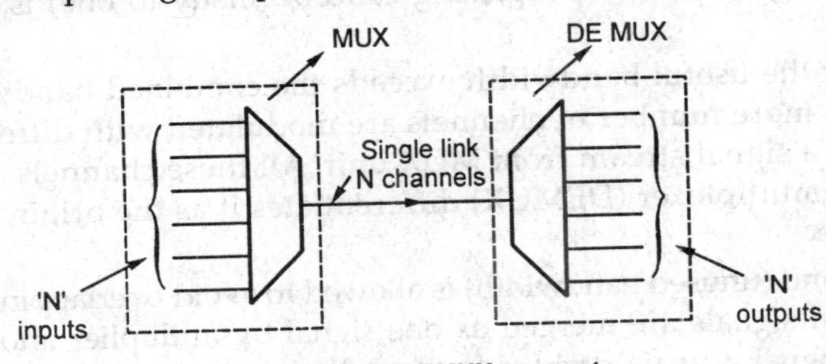

(a) MUX and DEMUX concept

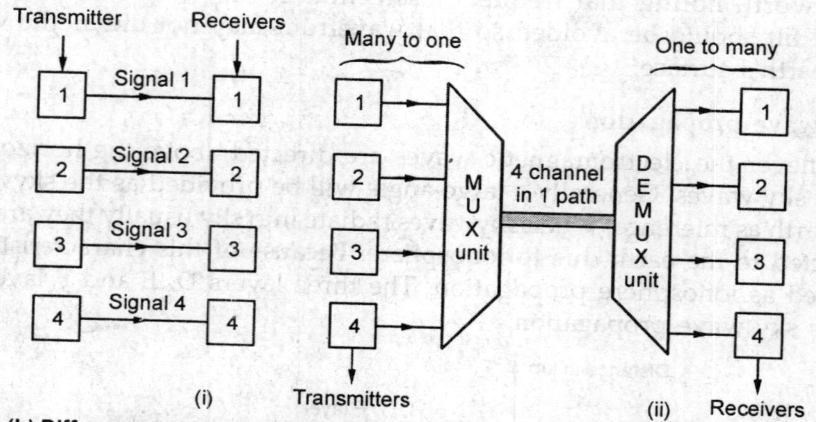

(b) Difference between multiplexing and conventional method of transmission

Fig. 1.43

In the field of communication the multiplexing technique is applied widely.

The data communicating devices like server models today requires higher data rates and hence this technique is used to a greater extent.

1.18.1 Types of Multiplexing

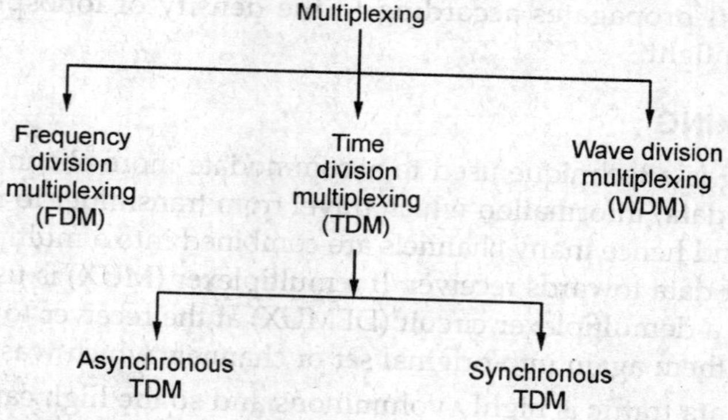

Frequency division multiplexing

The frequency division multiplexing concept (many to one) is shown in the diagram below.

Whenever the useful bandwidth exceeds the combined bandwidth of the signals to be transmitted, more number of channels are modulated with different carrier frequency and are sent as a signal stream from MUX unit. All these channels are transmitted as one channel and demultiplexer (DEMUX) differentiates it as the original individual channels at receiver side.

A guard band (unused bandwidth) is allowed to avoid overlapping of different channels. Four transmitted signals are merged as one signal by multiplier and sent as one complete signal and the signal is again divided by demultiplexer to get back four original signals.

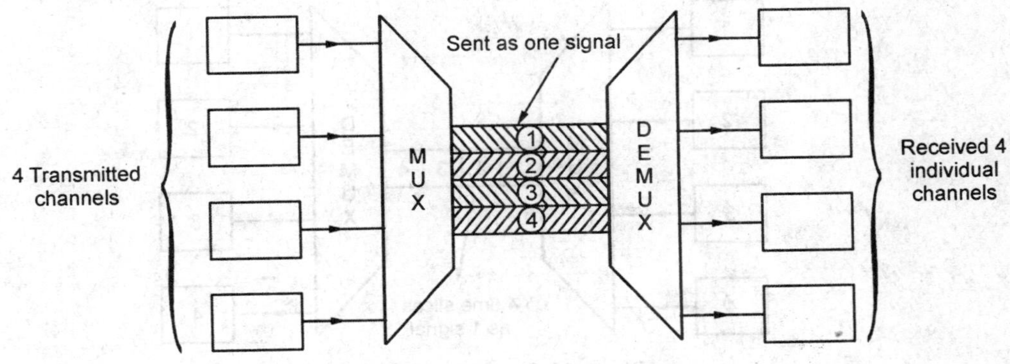

Fig. 1.44 Overview of FDM

In this FDM method it is like four different small links merged together as one main link by MUX and again split as 4 small links (channels) by DEMUX unit.

In FDM the channels are slices of frequencies f_1, f_2, f_3 etc. whereas in TDM method the channels are the slices of time. The third technique wave division multiplexing (WDM) is a scheme where it opts the same FDM scheme but with respect to light signals. The WDM unit combines the different light signals as one main ray that can travel through a fiber optic cable, which is shown below. Multiple light sources are combined to produce a single light beam. Each signal may have different wavelength (X).

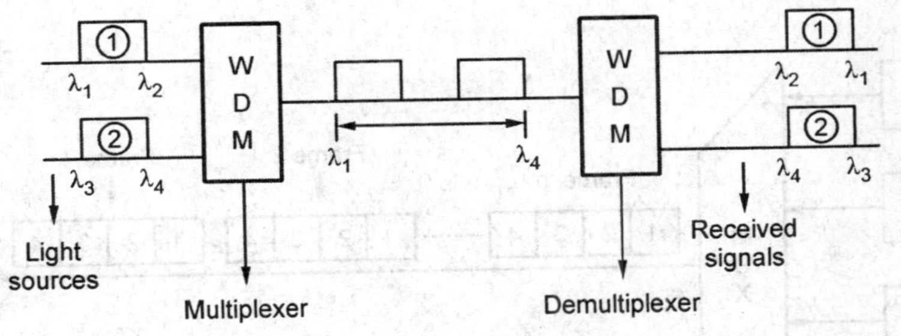

Fig. 1.45 Wave division multiplexing (WDM)

The demultiplexer at receiver gets the single light beam and splits it into original individual light sources for example 1 and 2 with λ_1 and λ_4 wavelengths.

Time division multiplexing (TDM)

In TDM multiple transmission can occupy an individual link by subdividing the link and also interleaving its portions.

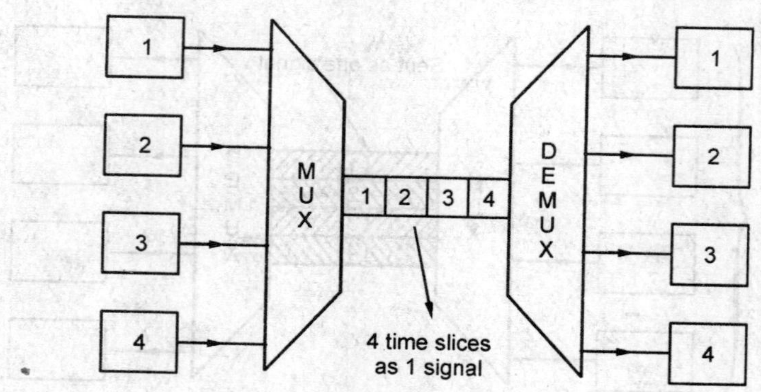

Fig. 1.46 Overview of TDM

TDM's overview is shown above. Also the portions of these four signals occupy the link sequentially during its journey towards demux.

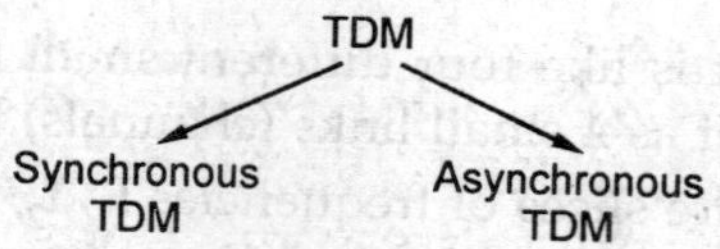

Synchronous TDM scheme

The multiple input signals sent to MUX and each frame has sequential slots for each signals.

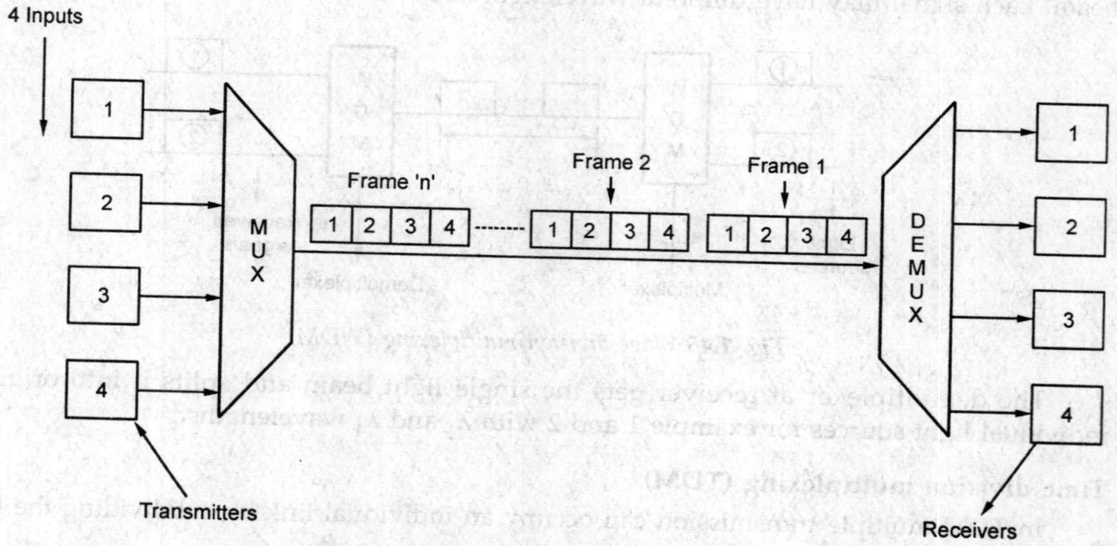

Fig. 1.47 Concept of multiplexer and demultiplexer units

If there are 4 inputs available to MUX under synchronous TDM then each frame is allocated with at least 4 slots within it. The data is sent at same data rate. Hence number of input lines are equal to the number of time slots in each frame.

'Bit stuffing' is permitted in TDM, where MUX unit adds extra bits to source stream to enhance speed of the devices.

Asynchronous TDM

It is a kind of statistical time division multiplexing (TDM). This asynchronous method is mainly a flexible method or said to be "not fixed".

Here the number of time slots in frame need not be equal to the number of input signals. The timeslots are three in frame for four number of input signals. The total speed of input can also be greater than that of the path. In general asynchronous TDM can handle more number of device than synchronous TDM.

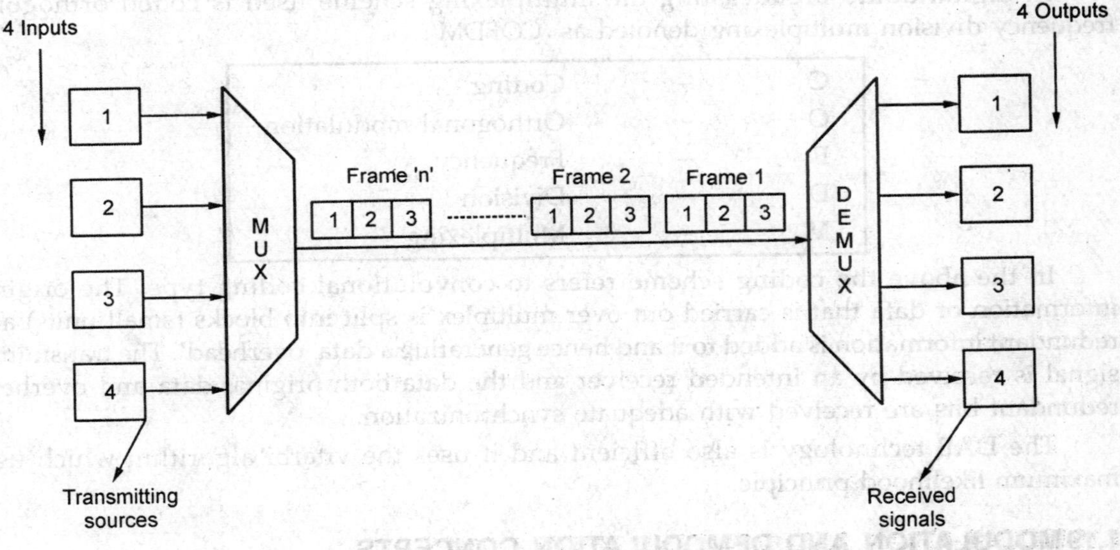

Fig. 1.48 Asynchronous TDM scheme

In synchronous TDM since time slots are fixed and preassigned if a particular connecting device does not transmit the communication path is wasted and this risk is eliminated in asynchronous TDM scheme is lightly flexible and not fixed.

The time slots are not preassigned. Variable length time slots are allowed here.

All the multiplexing schemes are matched with demultiplexing unit at the receiver and it also called as "inverse multiplexing". The FDM, TDM and WDM techniques are intended to do 'many to one' signal transmission and their corresponding demux units does the 'one to many' conversion to get back the original input signals or channels.

Frequency division multiplexing (FDM)

It is the process where more information channel bandwidths are shifted in frequency with others available in turn to form a wider bandwidth containing information (data). The shifting or translating scheme is used mainly with bandwidths such that it avoids mutual interference.

Orthogonal concept in DAB

Whenever the phase relationship of two sinusoidal signals (RF signals) is 90°, then the relationship between them is said to be orthogonal. They are also said to be in quadrature with each other. The subcarrier frequency spacing is in reciprocal of the symbol time period. In DAB modulation scheme the subcarriers that are successive have quadrature relationship with each other.

1.18.2 Scheme of Multiplexing

Coded Orthogonal Frequency Division Multiplexing (COFDM)

In digital audio broadcasting the multiplexing scheme used is coded orthogonal frequency division multiplexing denoted as 'COFDM'.

C	–	Coding
O	–	Orthogonal modulation
F	–	Frequency
D	–	Division
M	–	Multiplexing

In the above the coding scheme refers to convolutional coding type. The original information or data that is carried out over multiplex is split into blocks (small units) and redundant information is added to it and hence generating a data 'overhead'. The transmitted signal is received by an intended receiver and the data both original data and overhead redundant bits are received with adequate synchronization.

The DAB technology is also efficient and it uses the viterbi algorithm which uses maximum likelihood principle.

1.19 MODULATION AND DEMODULATION CONCEPTS

Modulation is the process of superimposing the high frequency carrier signal on the information bearing signal or the message signal.

On other hand demodulation is the process of detecting the information signal from the modulated signal and it is termed as demodulation.

1.19.1 Need for Modulation

It is important in view of practical antenna length.

The wavelength of the signal should be nearly (approx) equal to the length of the antenna. If the wavelength is expressed with the notation 'λ' then, it is equal to the ratio of velocity and frequency and its is expressed in meters.

$$\text{Wavelength} = \lambda = \frac{\text{Velocity}}{\text{Frequency}} \text{ meters}$$

When the signal is modulated and transmitted the height of antenna need not be a higher range like 15000 meters (say).

In order to transmit a signal of frequency of 20 kHz, then an antenna height of 15,000 meters is required.

$$\text{Wavelenth} = \frac{3 \times 10^8}{20 \times 10^3}$$

$$= 15{,}000 \text{ meters}$$

It is really impossible to construct such a tall antenna and therefore modulation is a must to have an antenna of reasonable heights.

Secondly the efficiency of radiation is very poor in the audio range. It is very difficult to transmit audio signals directly into space.

Thirdly the operating range is also an important criteria that necessitates modulation. When the frequency of the signal is high the energy contained within it high such that operating range will be more effective to transmit audio signals.

1.19.2 Types of Modulation

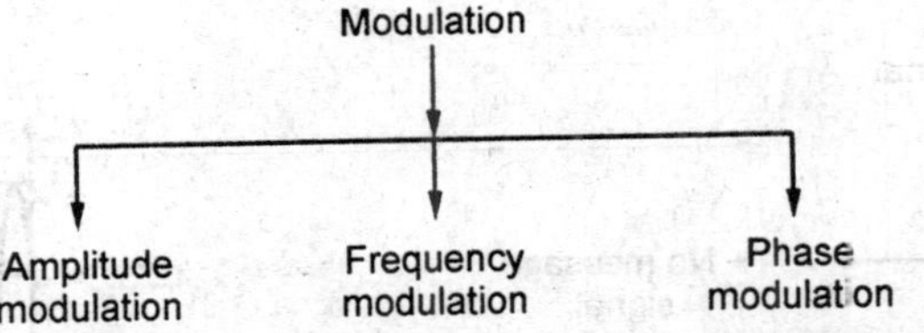

The above are the three types of modulation where the characteristic of the carrier wave is changed in accordance with that of the information signal.

The important terminologies related to modulation are:

1. Modulation factor
2. Gain
3. Maximum voltage → V_{max}
4. Minimum voltage → V_{min}
5. Side band frequency
6. Noise reception
7. Quality of audio
8. Carrier power
9. Side band power
10. High frequency

1.19.2.1 Amplitude Modulation

In amplitude modulation the amplitude of the carrier is varied in accordance with the message signal.

The frequency component of the signal is kept constant and the amplitude alone is varied.

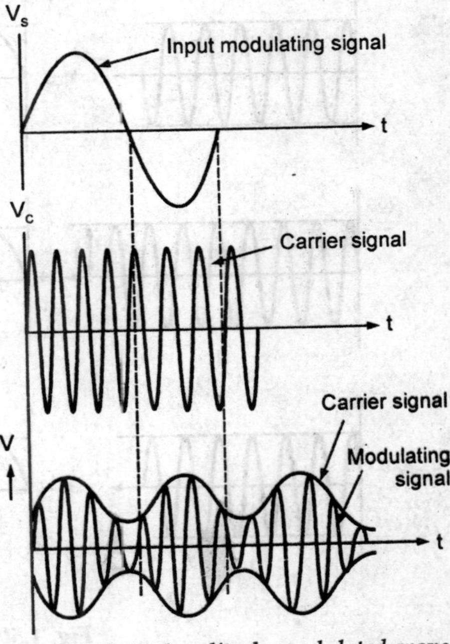

Fig. 1.49 Amplitude modulated wave

In the diagram shown above the carrier signal's amplitude varies in relation with that of the message signal. The level upto which the modulation is changed is also important.

The range value upto which it changes is termed as modulation factor and denoted as m

$$\left.\begin{array}{r}\text{Modulation}\\ \text{factor (m)}\end{array}\right\} = \frac{\text{Change of amplitude of the carrier signal}}{\text{Unmodulated carrier signal}}$$

Comparisons of signal amplitude changes with that of the carrier signals amplitude.

(*a*) In diagram 'a' when there is no message signal that is the amplitude of message signal is zero the carrier signal is not at all modulated. The output signal amplitude is exactly same as that of the carrier signal.

(*b*) In the second case whenever the amplitude of the message signal is one half of the carrier signal amplitude, the amplitude of the carrier signal changes between 0.5a and 1.5a. The modulation factor will be 50%.

Change in carrier amplitude = 1.5a – a.
= 0.5a

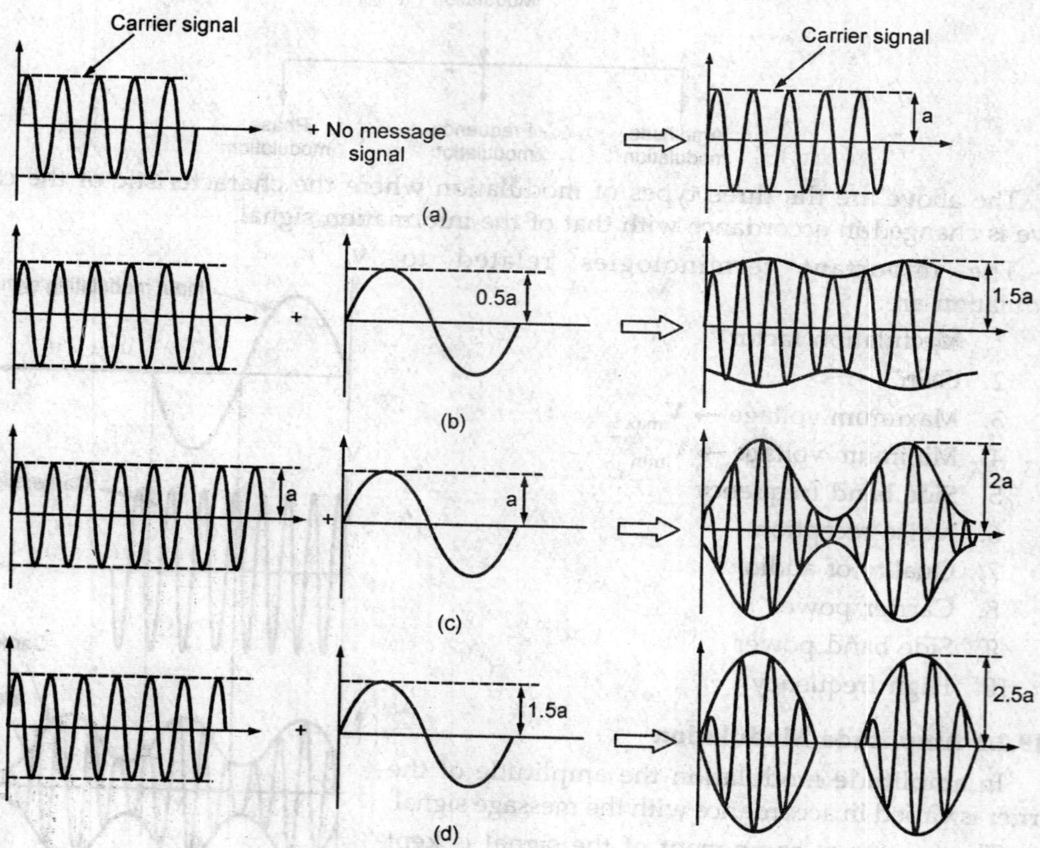

Fig. 1.50 Inferences from the four cases a to d

$$\text{Modulation factor (m)} = \frac{0.5a}{a}$$

$$a = 0.5$$

$$\therefore \quad m = 50\ \%$$

(*c*) In the third case the amplitude of the message is equal to the amplitude of the carrier signal. It varies between two values zero and 2a.

The amplitude change of carrier signal = 2a – a = a

$$\text{Modulation factor} = \quad m = \frac{\text{Change of carrier amplitude}}{\text{Amplitude of unchanged normal carrier}}$$

$$m = \frac{a}{a} = 1$$

$$m = 100\%$$

In this case the carrier is said to be 100% modulated or modulated to the maximum acceptable level where noise is within control.

(*d*) In the fourth case, when the amplitude of the message signal is one and half times that of the message signal then the maximum value of the carrier wave is equal to 2.5a.

$$\text{Change of carrier wave} = 2.5a - a$$

$$\text{Modulation factor} \quad (m) = \frac{1.5a}{a}$$

$$= 1.5 = 150\ \%$$

Thus in four different cases it is clear that according to the amplitude level of the information signal there is a change in the modulated output signal amplitude and in turn the value of the modulation factor 'm'.

Derivation of modulation factor (m)

In the graph shown below let us consider the amplitude of normal carrier signal as V_c and the amplitude of the input signal is V_s.

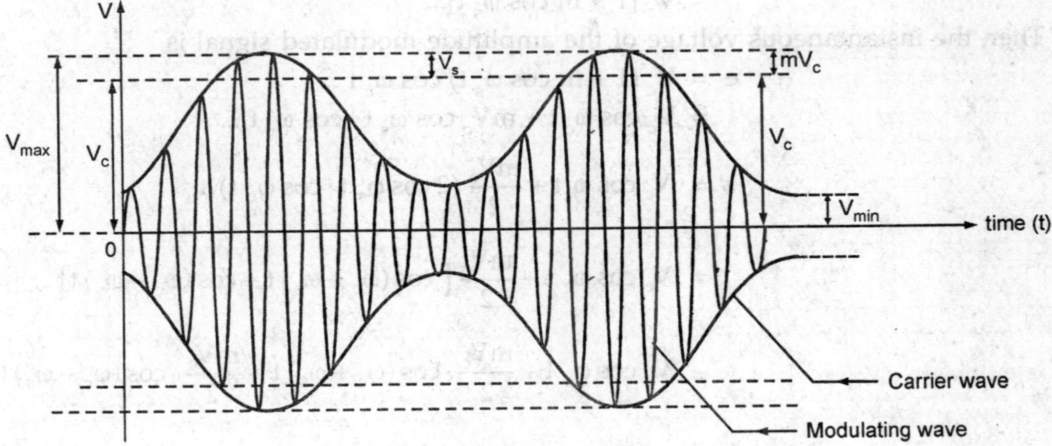

Fig. 1.51 Amplitude modulation signal

$$\therefore \quad V_s = \frac{V_{max} - V_{min}}{2} \quad ...(1)$$

where $V_s = m\,V_c$ ...(2)

Substitute equation (1) in equation (2) then,

$$\frac{V_{max} - V_{min}}{2} = m\left(\frac{V_{max} + V_{min}}{2}\right)$$

$$= m \text{ (after simplifying both sides in equation (3))}$$

This 'm' termed as modulation factor is very much significant since it expresses the strength and also the quality of the signal transmitted.

Derivation : Amplitude modulation

The carrier signal is expressed as,' e_c'

$$e_c = V_c \cos \omega_c\, t \quad ...(4)$$

In equation (4), 'e_c' is instantaneous voltage (amplitude) of the carrier signal, and 'V_c' is the amplitude of carrier.

$$\omega_c = 2\pi f_c \quad ...(5)$$

where 'ω_c' is the angular velocity at carrier frequency 'f_c'. If the signal amplitude is 'mE_c' (i.e. the maximum signal change is mE_c) then,

$$V_s = mV_c \cos \omega_s\, t \quad ...(6)$$

In equation (6), V_s is the instantaneous voltage (amplitude) of the signal and mV_c is the amplitude of the signal.

$$\omega_s = 2\pi f_s \quad ...(7)$$

where ω_s expresses the angular velocity of the signal at signal frequency say 'f_s'.

The amplitude of the modulated signal will depend on the changes in amplitude of the carrier signal in accordance with the amplitude of the modulating signal.

$$= V_c + mV_c \cos \omega_s\, t...$$

$$= V_c\,[1 + m \cos \omega_s\, t]...$$

Then the instantaneous voltage of the amplitude modulated signal is,

$$e = V_c\,(1 + m \cos \omega_s\, t) \cos \omega_c\, t \,...$$

$$= V_c \cos \omega_c\, t + mV_c \cos \omega_s\, t \cdot \cos \omega_c\, t \,...$$

$$= V_c \cos \omega_c t + \frac{mV_c}{2}(2 \cos \omega_s\, t \cdot \cos \omega_c\, t) \,...$$

$$= V_c \cos \omega_c\, t + \frac{mV_c}{2}\left[\cos(\omega_c + \omega_s)\, t + \cos(\omega_c - \omega_s)\, t\right]...$$

$$= V_c \cos \omega_c\, t + \frac{mV_c}{2} \cdot \cos(\omega_c + \omega_s)\, t + \frac{mV_c}{2} \cdot \cos(\omega_c - \omega_s)\, t$$

From the above equation the three main points are

(*a*) The amplitude modulated (AM) wave contains three frequencies namely f_c, $(f_c - f_s)$, and $(f_c + f_s)$.

(*b*) The AM wave consists of three waves say sinusoidal waves.

- The wave with amplitude 'V_c' and corresponding frequency 'f_c'.
- The second wave with amplitude of $\frac{mV_c}{2}$ with frequency component $f_c + f_s$.
- The third wave with amplitude $\frac{mV_c}{2}$ with frequency component $f_c - f_s$.

(*c*) The difference of carrier and signal frequencies $(f_c - f_s)$ represents the lower sideband. The sum of carrier and signal frequencies $(f_c + f_s)$ represents the upper sideband.

The AM wave thus consists of three signal components namely carrier components and the lower and upper sidebands respectively.

AM wave-sidebands representation

The sideband frequencies in amplitude modulation is represented in the following graph. If the carrier frequency is 'f_c' the two side band frequencies are $(f_c - f_s)$ and $(f_c - f_s)$.

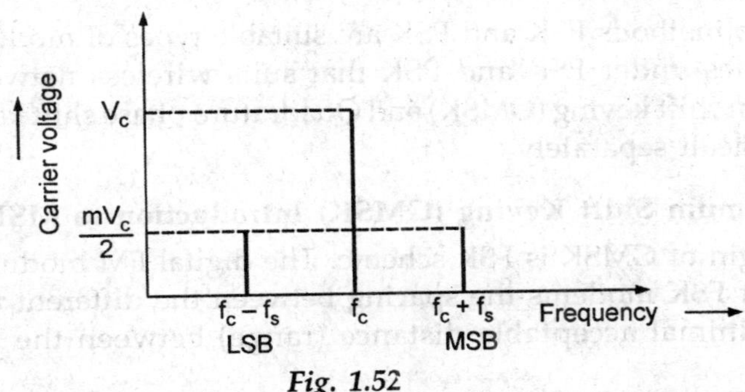

Fig. 1.52

The carrier frequency 'f_c' is centered and the two side frequencies are generally close to it. It is possible to transmit three signals namely f_c, $f_c - f_s$ and $f_c + f_s$ simultaneously.

In the reception side in amplitude demodulation a tuned receiver can be used in the circuit to receive the reactive frequencies f_c, or lower side band$(f_c - f_s)$ or the upper sideband $(f_c + f_s)$ respectively.

1.19.3 Digital Modulation Schemes

Digital signal transmission schemes used for wireless applications are discussed in detail in this chapter. There are many modulation methods available for digitized transmissions.

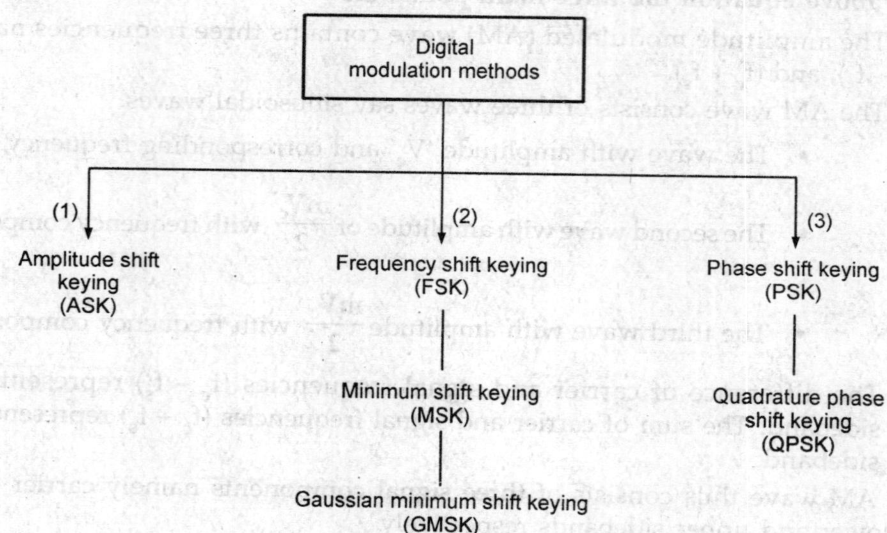

In the three main keying methods ASK, FSK, PSK the ASK is not suitable for cellular transmission. The reason is that in ASK the digital '1' is represented by the presence of signal and digital '0' is represented by the absence of the signal and its is not suitable for cellular communication.

The other two methods FSK and PSK are suitable types of modulations where specific modulation schemes under FSK and PSK that suits wireless network transmissions are Gaussiaix minimum shift keying (GMSK) and Quadrature phase shift keying (QPSK) methods. Each of them are dealt separately.

(*i*) Gaussian Minimum Shift Keying (GMSK) Introduction to MSK

The basic origin of GMSK is FSK scheme. The digital FM modulation is called as FSK where in design of FSK modems the spacing between the different tones (1's and 0's) are important. The minimal acceptable distance (range) between the tones in the signal is $\frac{1}{2}$T (0.5 T), where T represents the symbol duration, when a FSK modulation has minimum acceptable range between tones as 0.5 T then that FSK modulation is termed as minimum shift keying scheme (MSK). It is a kind of continuous phase-frequency shift keying (CPFSK) method. Hence MSK is also said to be a type of continuous phase FSK, strictly with a modulation index value as 0.5.

MSK Transmission and Reception

In MSK transmission (modulation), the carrier signal is multiplied with cos (πt / 2T) and will generate two phase-coherent signals for example $\left(f_c - \frac{1}{4T}\right)$ and $\left(f_c + \frac{1}{4T}\right)$. These are FSK signals and they should be separated for which narrow bandpass filters are used.

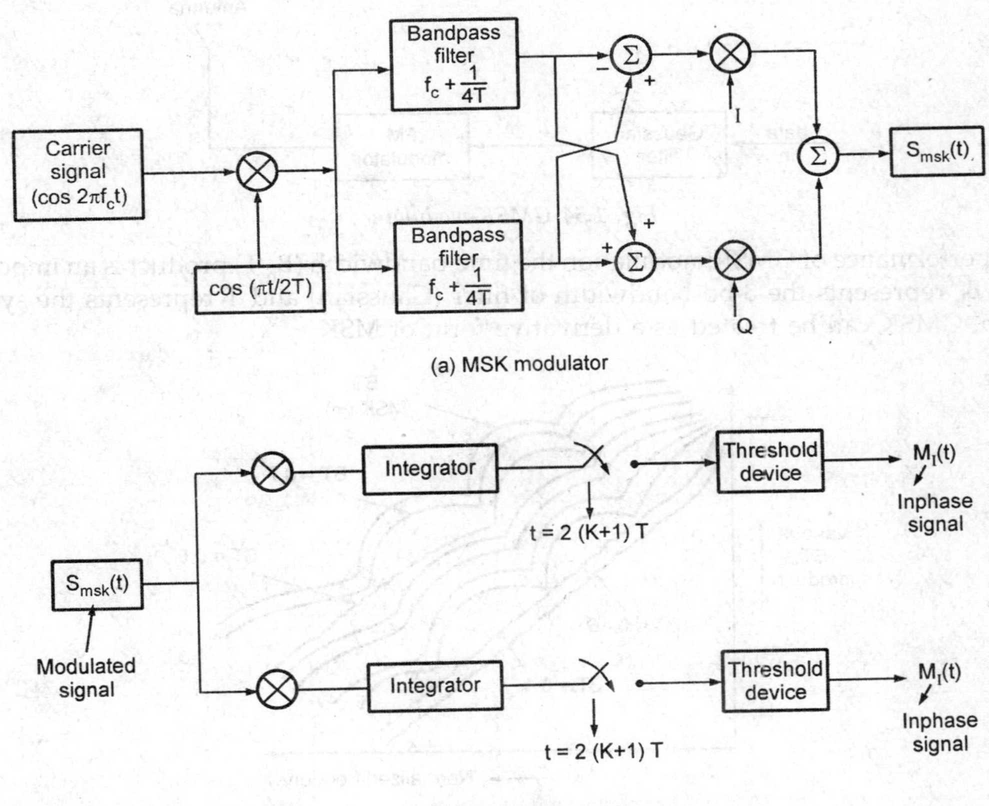

Fig. 1.53 MSK modulator and demodulator

Consider the in-phase and quadrature carrier signals be $x_1(t)$ and $x_2(t)$. These carrier signals are multiplied with the odd and even data bit streams as $m_1(t)$ and $m_Q(t)$. The output will a MSK modulated signal $S_{MSK}(t)$, at the end of a modulator block. At the MSK demodulator the $S_{MSK}(t)$ signal is multiplied with corresponding quadrature and in-phase carrier signals $x_1(t)$ and $x_2(t)$. The output signals of the two multiplier units are then integrated for a particular bit period for example two bit periods and passed decision devices. By checking the signal level the threshold device finally decides whether the signal is a digital '1' or digital '0'. The output data will $m_1(t)$ the in-phase signal and $m_Q(t)$ the quadrature signal, and they can be combined to get the demodulated signal or message.

From minimum shift keying technique the popular GMSK signal can be obtained.

Gaussian Minimum Shift Keying (GMSK)

In generating GMSK signals gaussian filters are used with MSK signals.

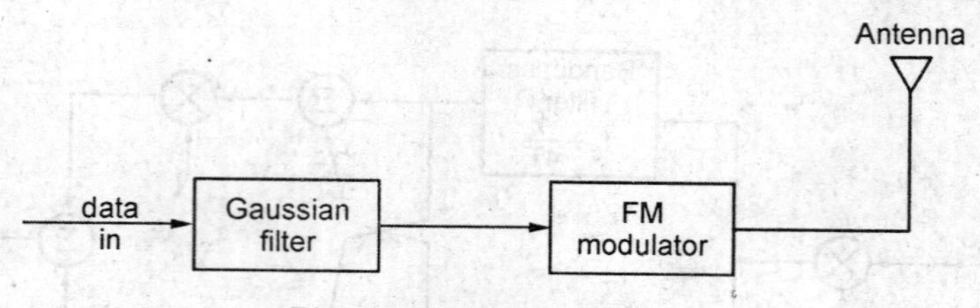

Fig. 1.54 GMSK-modulator

In performance of GMSK modulation the time-bandwidth (B_b T) product is an important criteria. B_b represents the 3-bd bandwidth of filter (Gaussian) and T represents the symbol duration. GMSK can be treated as a derivative form of MSK.

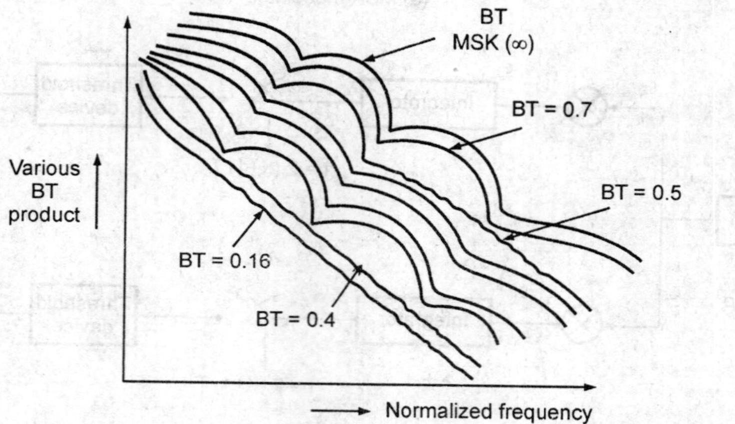

Fig. 1.55 GMSK-power spectral density

The GMSK signal can be detected coherently or non-coherently like MSK and FSK signals. GMSK is very popular mainly for its spectral and power efficiency. GMSK can be defined from the base band symbol duration 'T' and bandwidth 'B'. Hence it is convenient to define GMSK by 'BT' product values. The RF power spectrum of this GMSK signal/ message for several values of BT product is plotted in Fig. 1.55. When the BT values becomes equal to infinity (∞) the power spectrum of MSK resembles equivalent to GMSK.

To generate GMSK signal a message bit stream (say NRZ-non return to zero data) is passed though a gaussian filter with a determined response. For example a GMSK filter with an impulse response given as

$$h_g(t) = \left[\frac{\sqrt{\pi}}{\alpha} \exp \frac{-\pi^2}{\alpha^2} \cdot t^2\right]$$

Where α is roll off factor of filter related to Bandwidth 'B', t is time period

[$t = kT_b$; $T_b \rightarrow$ bit period] and $k \rightarrow$ an integer.

The GMSK signals can also be detected using the coherent detectors or non coherent detectors. It is simpler to recover GMSK signal by sampling the output signal of the FM demodulator unit.

(ii) Quadrature Phase Shift Keying Technique (QPSK)

The QPSK scheme has bandwidth efficiently twice as that of the binary phase shift keying (BPSK) scheme. The phase angle values of carrier signal in QPSK takes one of four different values. They are 0, π/2, π and 3π/2 and each value mentioned corresponds to a pair of message/information bits.

The QPSK signal is given as, S_{QPSK} (t) that is

$$S_{QPSK}(t) = \sqrt{\frac{2E_s}{T_s}} \cos\left(2\pi f_c t + (i-1)\frac{\pi}{2}\right), \ldots$$

$0 \leq t \leq T_s$; 1 = 1, 2, 3, 4

Where T_s is symbol duration (time period) and T_s = twice the bit period.

f_c is carrier frequency.

E_s is signal amplitude level.

Each symbol in QPSK will correspond to two bits, and hence E_s is equal to $2E_b$.

Therefore the distance/range between the two neighbouring (adjacent) points is keying constellation is equal to $2\sqrt{E_b}$ value.

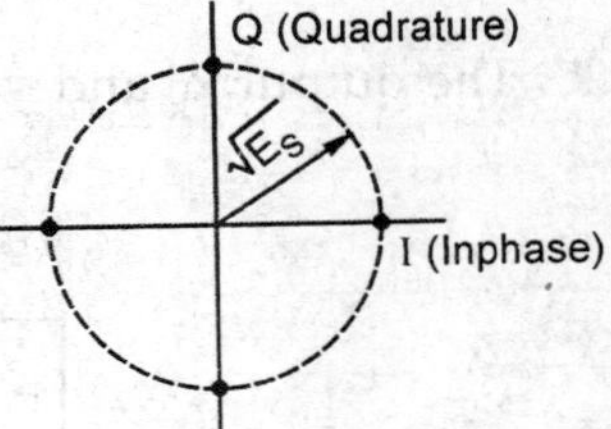

Fig. 1.56 QPSK constellation with carrier signal phase values as 0, $\frac{\pi}{2}$, π and $\frac{3\pi}{2}$

For QPSK signal transmission two carrier signals with phase angle differences like $\phi_1(t)$ and $\phi_2(t)$ are necessary. At first the input signal (unipolar bit stream) has to be converted to a bipolar non return to zero (NRZ) data sequence using a unipolar to bipolar converter device. This data bit stream with bit rate 'R_b' is denoted as m(t) and it is divided/split into two data bit streams as $m_1(t)$ and $m_Q(t)$ and known as in phase bit stream and quadrature bit stream or even bit stream and odd bit stream. These two bit (binary) stream are modulated individually with two carrier signals like $\phi_1(t)$ and $\phi_2(t)$ that are in quadrature fashion. Then the summation of two different modulated signals is made to generate a QPSK output signal of the modulator.

The power spectrum of QPSK output signal is properly confined within the band allocated will be done by filtering the modulator output, the QPSK signal.

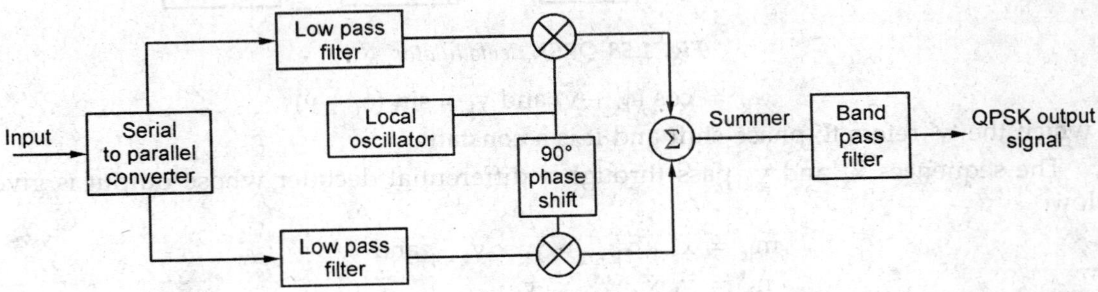

Fig. 1.57 QPSK modulator

The output of QPSK modulator is a smooth signal after removing any spurious signals mixed with the bit stream.

In QPSK demodulator generally a band pass filter is utilized at the front end to filter the received signal. There are several types of QPSK detection schemes. They are baseband differential detection, FM discriminator detection and IF differential detection. We discuss baseband differential detection method in detail.

The baseband differential detector is shown in the block diagram above. The input signal $\frac{\pi}{4}$ QPSK is demodulated using two oscillator signals that operate in same frequency but not in the same phase. If $\phi_k = \tan^{-1}\left(\frac{Q_k}{I_k}\right)$ is the phase of the carrier due to the data bit 'k'. The output x_k and y_k are expressed as,

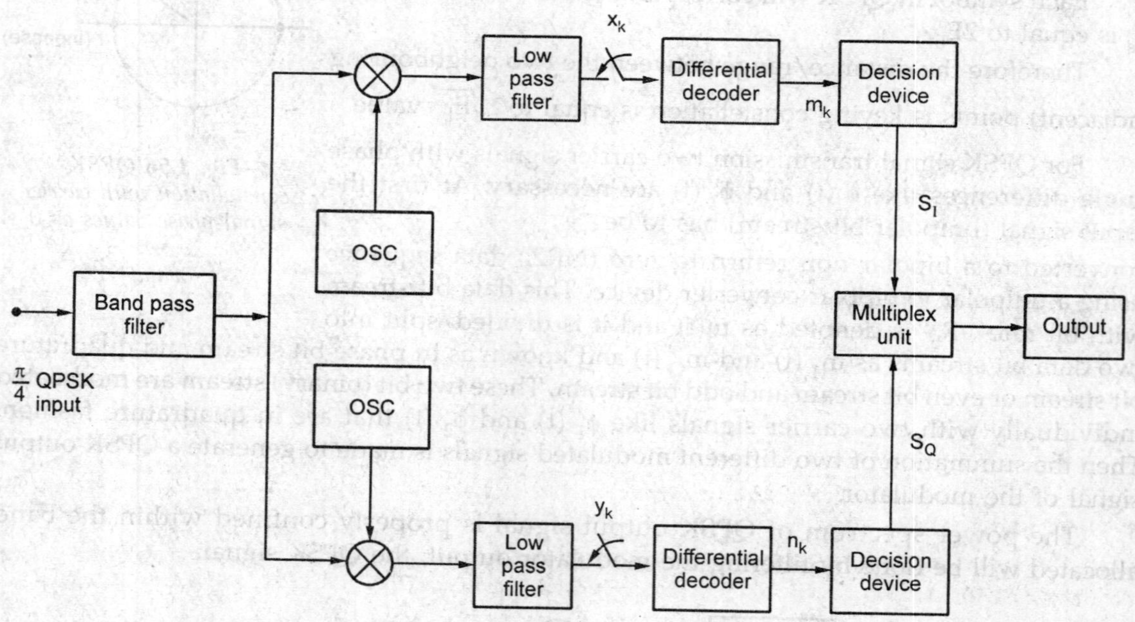

Fig. 1.58 QPSK demodulator

$$x_k = \cos(\phi_k - \nu) \text{ and } y_k = \sin(\phi_k - \nu)$$

in which the 'ν' refers to phase shift and it is a constant.

The sequences x_k and y_k pass through a differential decoder whose output is given below.

$$m_k = x_k \times x_{k-1} + y_k \times y_{k-1} \text{ and}$$
$$n_k = y_k\, x_{k-1} - x_k\, y_{k-1}$$

Then the output of the decoder is expressed as

$$m_k = \cos(\phi_k - \nu)\cos(\phi_{k-1} - \nu) + \sin(\phi_k - \nu)\sin(\phi_{k-1} - \nu)$$
$$m_k = \cos(\phi_k - \phi_{k-1})$$
$$n_k = \sin(\phi_k - \nu)\cos(\phi_{k-1} - \nu) + \cos(\phi_k - \nu)\sin(\phi_{k-1} - \nu)$$
$$n_k = \sin(\phi_k - \phi_{k-1})$$

The output m_k and n_k of the differential decoder is applied to the decision device and then to the multiplex unit. The two signal at the input of multiplex are known as inphase and quadrature phase signals S_1 and S_Q.

$$S_1 = 0 \text{ if } m_k < 0 \text{ and}$$
$$S_Q = 0 \text{ if } n_k < 0$$

The S_I and S_I are the demodulated bits of the output of baseband differential QPSK detector.

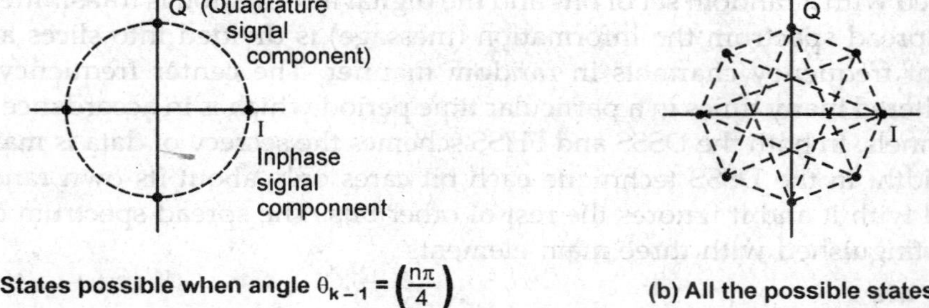

Fig. 1.59 QPSK signal constellation diagram

In Fig. 1.59 the constellations diagram for different phase angle θ_k is plotted in 1.59(*a*) and constellation for all possible states for angles (θ_k) is given in Fig. 1.59 (*b*). Generally in $\pi/4$ QPSK modulation the signalling points of the signal that is modulated are always selected from two different QPSK constellations that are shifted by an angle $\pi/4$, with each other. In the Fig. 1.59 (*b*), the constellations of QPSK signal for all possible states also represents a combined constellations of $\theta_{k-1} = n\,\pi/4$ and $q_{k-1} = n\frac{\pi}{2}$ constellation. From these diagrams it is clear that for every symbol there will a phase transmission so that timing recovery and synchronization between transmission and reception will be accurate. In all the constellation the link available between any two points represents a phase transition.

1.20 SPREAD SPECTRUM

This technique is used to increase the bandwidth of digital communication system. The input signal is fed into the channel encoder where a set of digital signals are generated from pseudonoise generator and added in modulator. These set of bits are called as pseudonoise signal. The signal is sent through channel. At the demodulator side the same pseudonoise code which was spread at transmitter is despread and the original data or information is extracted as output of channel decoder. The spreading code is also called as pseudocode or spreading sequence.

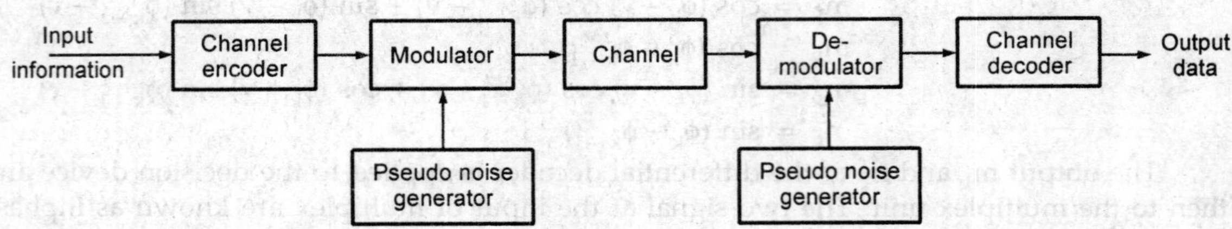

Fig. 1.60 Model of spread spectrum technique

The signal is spread over a larger bandwidth and it enables very high degree of security for signal transmission and reception. The direct sequence spread spectrum (DSSS) and frequency hopping spread spectrum (FHSS) are the two types of spread spectrum techniques used under spread spectrum. In direct sequence spread spectrum each bit to be transmitted is multiplied with a random set of bits and the digital information is transmitted. In frequency hopping spread spectrum the information (message) is divided into slices and transmitted at different frequency channels in random manner. The center frequency of the carrier signal is altered many times in a particular time period which is in accordance with a random set of channels. In both the DSSS and FHSS schemes the secrecy of data is maintained at cost of bandwidth. In the DSSS technique each bit cares only about its own random set of bits multiplied with it and it ignores the rest of other bits. The spread spectrum communication can be distinguished with three main elements.

They are :

1. It requires larger bandwidth.
2. This bandwidth is spread with respect to code and not the data.
3. The receiver should synchronize properly to recover data. Hence it is possible for many users to access the same frequency (f) band simultaneously.

1.20.1 Advantages of Spread Spectrum (SS)

1. it reduces different kinds of noises.
2. It provides immunity from multipath distortion, and jamming problems.
3. This technique can be highly applied in cellular applications along with code division multiple access (CDMA) method of multiplexing.
4. The spread spectrum technique is used for hiding encrypting data signals.

All these three methods will be dealt in detail in this chapter. Earlier to it, it is better to understand the method of generation of spreading sequences (PN sequences), PN properties.

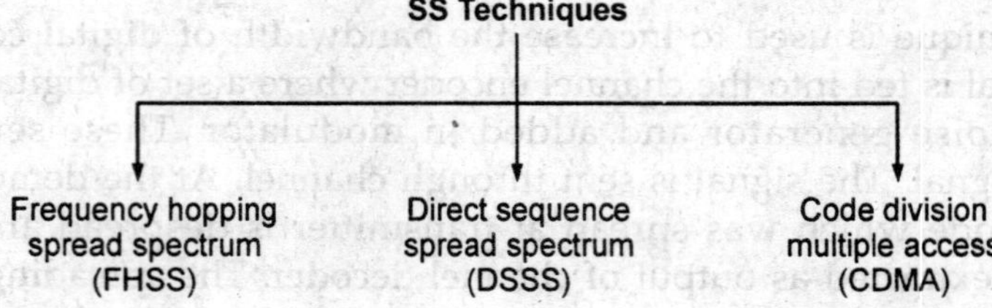

Spread Spectrum Sequence-Generation

The pseudonoise signal is generated by pseudonoise code generator. This signal is actually a sequence of digits. The spreading technique involves XOR operation of input signal with the spreading sequence (sequence of digits). At the receiver side the spreading is removed by the same spreading code multiplication with necessary synchronization and the original signal is retrieved. The data rate and bandwidth saving is high.

The degree of redundancy is also good.

The pseudonoise is denoted as PN sequence. It should be same at transmitter and at receiver side. In the PN sequence is produced by PN generator and it will repeat itself in random nature.

The PN sequence is popular because of two important points. They are,

1. Unpredictability.
2. Randomness.

The randomness of the sequence is weighted by correlation properly and uniform distribution. The correlation properly is concerned with similarity of number of terms in sequences at various time shifts, and at the most difference is allowed. The uniform distribution of numbers is that the distribution of numbers in a sequence is uniform.

The **advantages** are many in this spread spectrum technique.

1. The vital reason for using this technique is highest security.
2. Then the problem of jamming is avoided.
3. In military application spread spectrum technique was mainly used to maintain high degree of security.
4. The message is transmitted at different frequencies from the transmitter and hence except the intended receiver a third party cannot receive the message or data.
5. Today not only in military applications but the commercial field also attracted towards spread spectrum techniques.
6. There are many advantages like hiding of information from the intruders.
7. Since wider bandwidth is used to spread information it makes the jamming and interference more difficult.
8. High degree of assurance for faithful reproduction of data.
9. Even though bandwidth is wasted in spread spectrum technique it is used in defence area where security of data is highlighted.

1.20.2 Demerits of Spread Spectrum

1. The main drawback of this technique is that bandwidth wastage.
2. This technique is not economical.

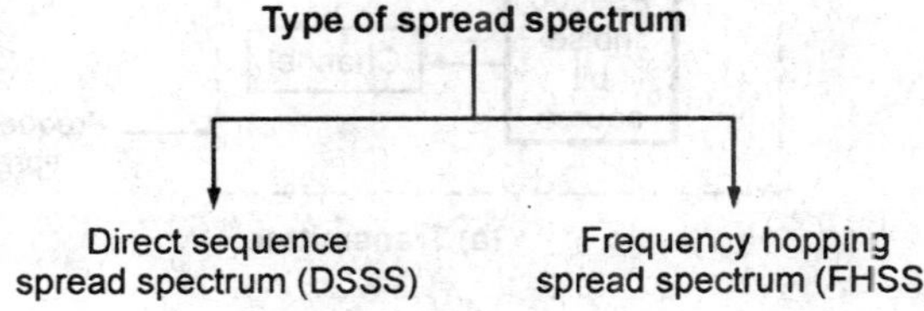

DSSS	FHSS
• Each bit of the information is multiplied with a sequence or stream of bits.	• Signal is transmitted over a random series of radio frequencies.
• The spreading code spreads this signal across a wider band width in direct proportion to number of bits used.	• Receiver has to hop between various frequencies to synchoronize with message of transmitter.

For transmitting the signal under "Frequency Hopping" technique the message is sent over a series of random frequencies. At the receiver side hopping between two frequencies in synchronization with transmitter and finally picking up of message is done. An example of frequency hopping spread spectrum (FHSS) is shown in Fig. 1.61.

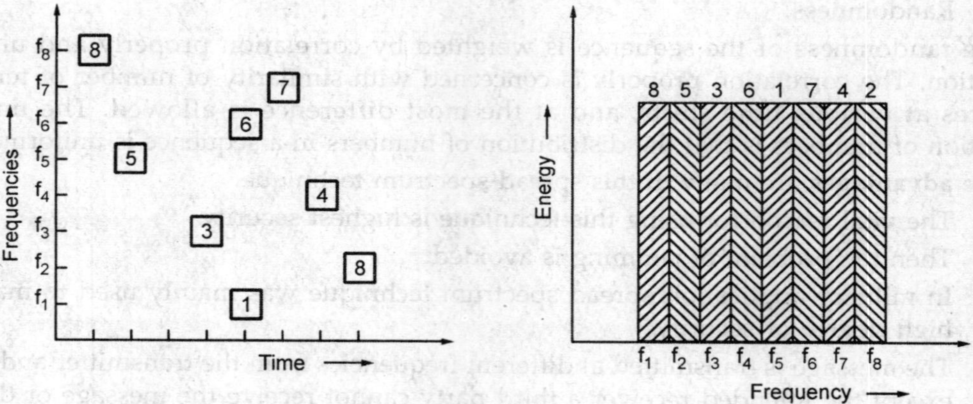

Fig. 1.61

Many channels are allocated for the FH signal. There are 2^i carrier frequencies which forms 2^j channels. The spacing between two carrier frequencies and hence the width of each channel corresponds to bandwidth of the input signal applied. The transmitter operates in one channel at a time for a fixed time period. Both the transmitter and receiver use the same code to tune into a sequence of channels in proper synchronization.

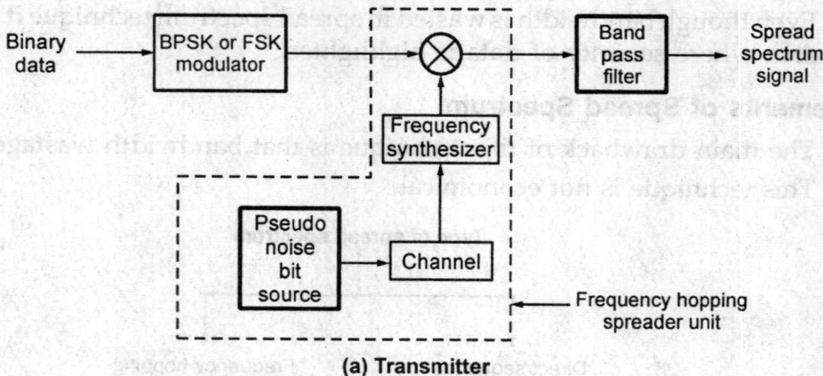

(a) Transmitter

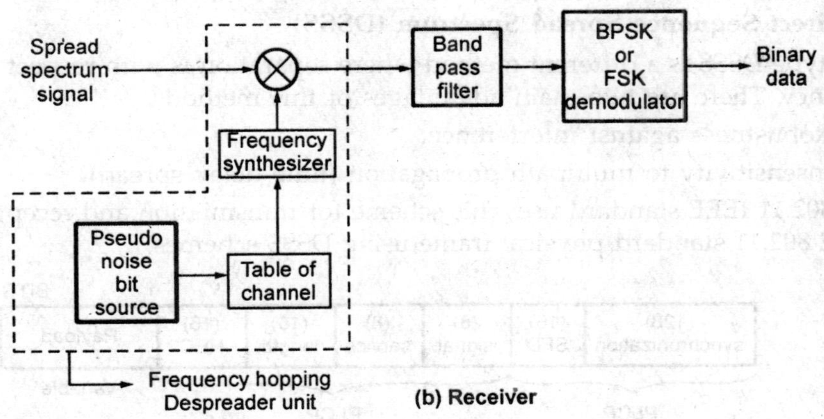

Fig. 1.62 Frequency hopping spread spectrum (FHSS) system

The frequency hopping spread spectrum method use the principle of calculating product of 2 signals. The binary information are fed into a modulator or transmitter using some digital to analog encoding scheme such as frequency shift or binary phase shift keying techniques. A table of frequencies is maintained to which the pseudonoise code or PN sequence or pseudonoise number source serves as an index. This helps to form the spreading code sequence. Each and every 'j' bit of this PN sequence source specifies one of the "2^j" carrier frequencies. At the successive time interval a carrier frequency (f_c) will be selected.

We can define the frequency shift keying (FSK) input to the frequency hopping spread spectrum system as

$$S_d(t) = A\cos(2\pi(f_0 + 0.5(b_k + 1)\Delta f)t)$$
$$\text{for } kT < t < (k+1)T$$

Where A → Amplitude of signal

f_0 → Base frequency

b_k → Value of the given k^{th} bit of data (i.e. 0 or 1)

T → Bit duration; Data rate = 1/T.

Δf → Frequency separation (or) deviation

The output of frequency synthesizer has both sum and difference frequencies. The band pass filter (BPF) is used for intended passing of sum frequencies and blocks the difference frequencies. The output of the frequency hopping spread spectrum synthesizer is,

$$S(t) = \frac{1}{2}A\cos\left(2\pi\left(f_0 + \frac{1}{2}(b_k + 1)\Delta f + f_k\right)t\right)$$

The intended receiver receives the signal and multiplies it with the replica of the spreading code used at the transmitter side. As said at the transmitter side, the bandpass filter (BPF) at the receiver pass only the sum frequencies and blocks the other difference frequencies.

1.20.2.1 Direct Sequence Spread Spectrum (DSSS)

This type DSSS is a different method where separation is with respect to code and not the frequency. There are two main advantages of this method.

1. Robustness against interference.
2. Insensitivity to multipath propagation (time delay spread).

The 802.11 IEEE standard uses this scheme for transmission and reception. The format of an IEEE 802.11 standard physical frame using DSSS schemes.

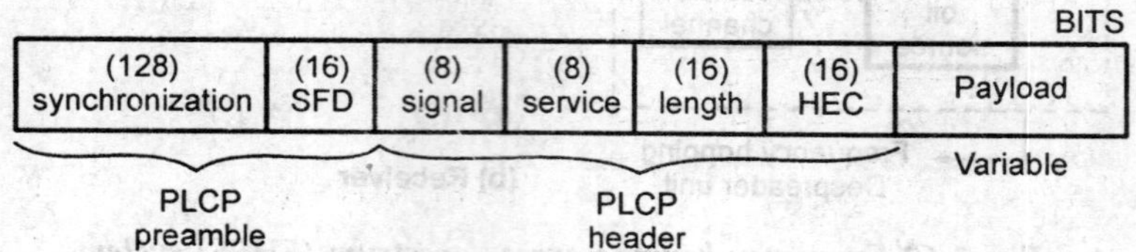

Fig. 1.63 Format of IEEE 802.11 standard physical frame using direct sequence spread spectrum

The format of DSSS shows that is has seven fields in total. Also it basically has two parts first is the PLCP (that is preamble and header) and second is payload part (MAC data). The payload part uses 1 to 2 Mbits/s for transmission and the first part PLCP uses 1 Mbits/s for the same. The seven fields of the direct sequence spread spectrum format has their own distinct functions. They are listed below.

1. Synchronization

The 128 bits of this field are used for synchronization, gain setting, frequency offset compensation and energy detection. The synchronization field consists of scrambled 1 bits.

2. Start frame delimiter (SFD)

If consists of 16 bits in this field which is used for synchronization at the beginning of a frame.

3. Signal

There are two values defined for this third field which has eight bits and this field indicates the data rate of the payload.

4. Service

This service field of 8 bits is mainly reserved for future use and it indicates a complaint frame.

5. Length

In this field 16 bits are used for length indication of the payload.

6. Header error check (HEC)

It has 16 bits and the signal. Service and length fields are protected by this checksum using a polynomial.

1.20.2.2 Format of Frequency Hopping Spread Spectrum (FHSS)

The main advantage of frequency hopping spread spectrum is that it allows for the coexistence of multiple network in a particular same area by separating different networks using various hopping sequence. This standard defines 79 hopping channels for North America and 23 for Japan. The hopping pattern selection is achieved by using a pseudorandom hopping pattern.

These are some of the examples of hopping sequences used in different countries. When dealing with modulation shift keying techniques FHSS PHY is compatible with gaussian frequency shift keying technique (GFSK). For example for a 1 Mbits/s a two level GFSK is used and for a 2 Mbits/s a four level GFSK is used. In frequency hopping spread spectrum the frame consists of two basic parts the PLPC part (that is preamble and header) and the payload as second part. The format consists of six fields. Each field has its own specific function. They are listed below.

1. Synchronization

It is the first part of PLCP preamble and it has 80 bits, usually with bit pattern as 010101... This field is concerned with synchronization of the receivers.

2. Start frame delimiter

It consists of 16 bits which indicates the start of the frame and hence helps synchronization of frames. This is the second part of PLCP preamble.

3. PLCP-PDU length word (PLW)

The first field of PLCP leader indicates the length of the payload in bytes which includes 32 bit CRC at the tail end of the payload. The PLW can range from 0 to 4,095. This field consists of 12 bits.

4. PLCP signalling field (PSF)

It consists of 4 bits. It is used to indicate data rate of the payload.

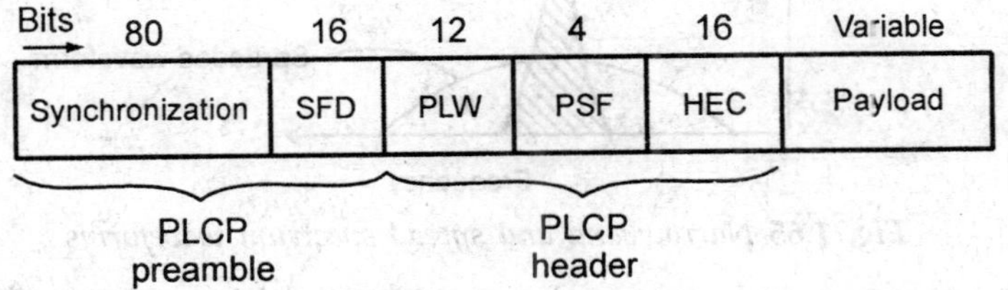

Fig. 1.64 Format of 802.11 standard physical layer used with frequency hopping spread spectrum

5. Header error check (HEC)

The PLCP header is safeguarded by a 16 bit checksum, with generator polynomial as g (x) = ($x^{16} + x^{12} + x^5 + 1$). The HEC field thus consists of 16 bits.

1.20.3 Special Features of Spread Spectrum Systems

1. Reduced interference problems in communication.
2. Secured transmission and reception.
3. For signal hiding low density power spectra is used.
4. High resolution ranging is achieved.
5. Code division multiplexing for CDMA applications.
6. Cost of implementation is less.
7. Anti jamming capability.
8. Integrated components (IC) are available for related designing process.
9. As the number of RF channels increases [number of simultaneous users increases]. The degradation of system performance is acceptable.
10. Increased capacity.
11. Efficient spectrum utility.
12. Direct spread spectrum sequence (DSSS) is very much useful in defence area where high degree of security is required.
13. Frequency hopping spread spectrum (FHSS) is useful in many application areas like cellular mobile communication and spectrum bandwidth is completely used.

1.20.4 Spread Spectrum-graphical analysis

In communication system the information is modulated and transmitted. The transmission power is spread over the entire band. It is shown in the graph below.

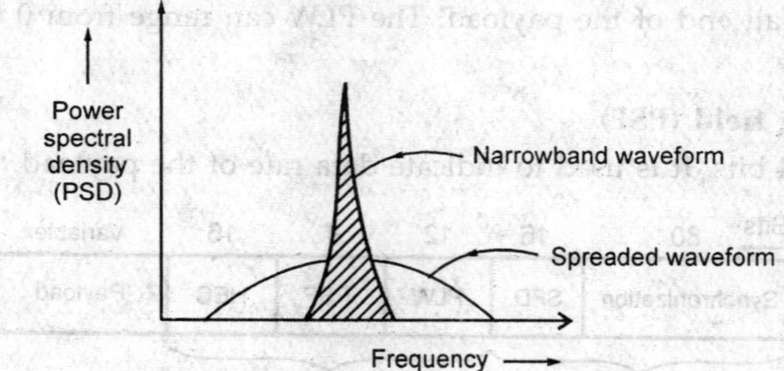

Fig. 1.65 Narrowband and spread spectrum waveforms

This spread spectrum techniques, due to the stretching of signal, occupies a larger bandwidth. On one side wastage of bandwidth may not be appreciable but in terms of defence, and military application security is more important than bandwidth economy criteria and this technique is well suited in defence area.

1.21 MEDIUM ACCESS CONTROL (MAC)

The medium access control (MAC) algorithms perform several mechanisms for regulating user access to a physical medium. It provides traffic regulations in data communications. From the open system interconnect (OSI) model the MAC belong to the layer 2 called as data link control layer (DLC). The layer 2 has two subdivisions namely logical link control (LLC) and MAC layer. In multiplexing schemes used for wireless data transmissions MAC layer provides regulations for the data traffic.

With MAC layer access to physical medium is done using time division multiplexing (TDM), code division multiplexing (CDM), space division multiplexing (SDM), or frequency division multiplexing (FDM) schemes.

The MAC layer establishes, maintains and also release the channels for next higher layers by methods of activating and deactivating the channels used. The logical channels can be multiplexed on to the physical channels by the MAC layer. Thus MAC performs important function for cellular wireless networks.

Motivation for a Specialized MAC

For the wireless domain their are many medium access control (MAC) algorithms are used. The MAC comprises mechanisms that can regulate user access to required medium using a multiple access scheme either TDM, FDM, CDM or SDM. The MAC resembles traffic regulations in the highway/multiplexing. MAC belongs to the layer 2, (OSI) the data link control layer (DLC). This layer 2 is subdivided into logical link control (LLC), and MAC.

DLC → MAC / LLC

Fig. 1.66

MAC with CDM assign specific codes to allow the separation of various users in a code space. The MAC schemes can be elaborated from wired networks say, for example, the carrier sense multiple access with collision detection (CSMA/CD).

A sender can sense the medium weather it is free or not. The sender will wait if the medium is busy. In case sender detects a collision signal in its sending process then it will send a jamming signal.

In case of wireless network the strength of signal will get reduced in proportion to the square of the distance. In wireless environment there is a chance of several obstacles.

Hidden and Exposed Terminal

Consider a sender 1 use a carrier sense and detects an idle medium. As the sending procedure starts assume there occurs collision, due to sender 2. Such a situation dealt in hidden and exposed terminal.

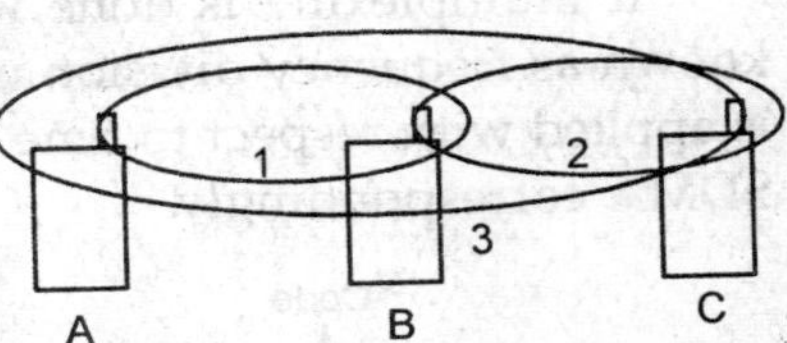

Fig. 1.67 Hidden and exposed terminal

In the example shown below the terminal A starts to send towards B. The terminal C wants to send information to B and it senses the medium. If the medium appears to be free (carrier sense fails), C starts sending and it leads to collision at junction of B.

The terminal A cannot realize this collision taken place and it continues with its own transmission.

In other case consider B sends to A and C wants to send data to other mobile that is not in interference ranges of A and C. Now the C senses carrier and finds that the carrier is busy. The terminal C postpones the transmission

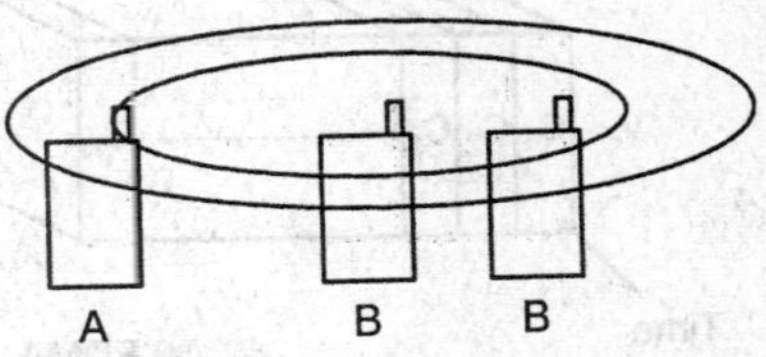

Fig. 1.68 Near and far terminals

until it detects the medium as idle. If there is a collision at B it does not affect A since it is very weak and it propagates to A.

In this case the terminal C is exposed to terminal B.

In near and far terminal case, assume the terminals A and B are sending with same amount of transmission power. The signal strength reduces in proportion to square of the distance involved. For example, B's signal would drown out A's signal and hence terminal C cannot receive the A's signal. If C acts as bare station and coordinating medium accessing job. Then terminal B would drown out terminal A on the physical layer.

The wireless network using CDM has the problem of near/far effect. The signals arrives at the receiver with approximately uniform strength.

On the other hand if a person is closer to one but talks to a third person standing away from him will speak loudly to the third person to overcome the speech of the person close to him. The method of using codes (CDM) helps in reducing interference in wireless environment.

Also an accurate power control is required to receive all the senders with same strength at the receiver end.

1.21.1 Multiple Access Schemes-FDMA, TDMA, CDMA and SDMA

Introduction

With the multiplexing technique several users can share a particular medium with minimum interference. The efficiency of medium utility is high using this technique. For wireless environment there are several multiple access techniques available.

Multiplexing can be applied in four possible dimensions. They are namely

(*i*) Frequency Division Multiple Access (FDMA)
(*ii*) Time Division Multiple Access (TDMA)
(*iii*) Code Division Multiple Access (CDMA)
(*iv*) Space Division Multiple Access (SDMA)

If multiplexing is done with respect to assigning frequencies for each channels it is known as frequency division multiplexing technique (FDMA). Similar to it if this technique is applied with respect to time or code or space then they are limited as TDMA, CDMA and SDMA correspondingly.

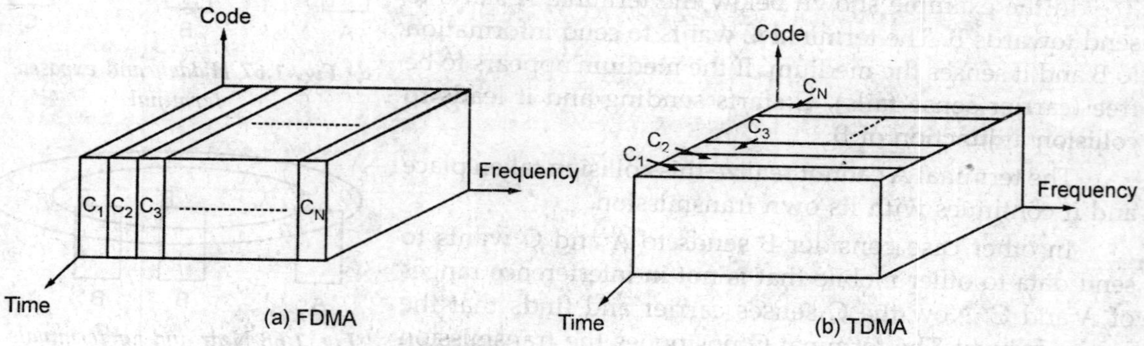

(a) FDMA (b) TDMA

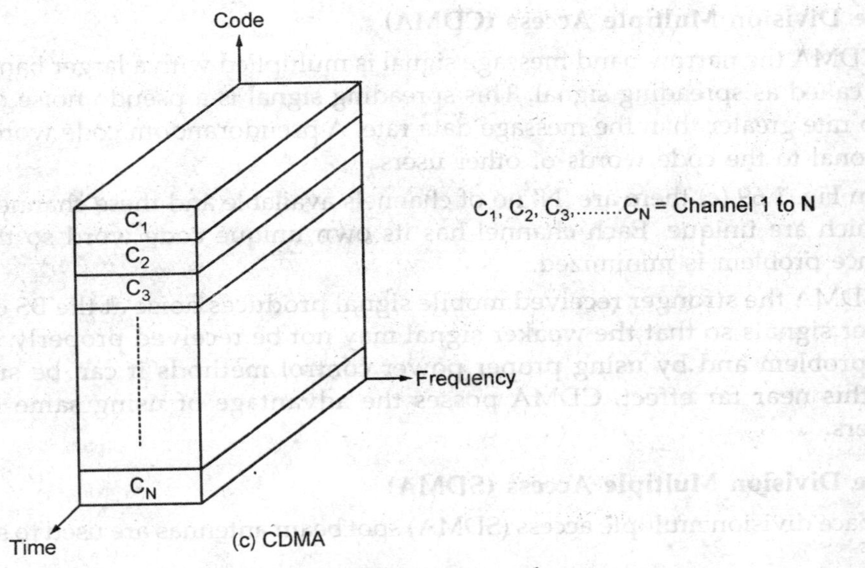

Fig. 1.69 Multiple access schemes

(*i*) Frequency Division Multiple Access (FDMA)

In FDMA individual channels (c_1, c_2,... c_N) are assigned to individual subscriber/user as in Fig. 1.69 (a). A unique frequency band or a channel is allocated to each subscriber, and assignment of channels is done on demand basis. If there is a request for service a channels will be assigned to that user.

(*ii*) Time Division Multiple Access (TDMA)

In TDMA systems the entire radio spectrum is split into time slots (slices) and each slot is allocated to individual user. The method used by TDMA system is also known as "buffer-and-burst" method. With TDMA only digital message/data and its modulation are used where as FDMA engages analog FM systems. The transmission of signals from several users is interlaced together into a frame structure which is then repeated continuously. A frame basically consists of the following.

1. Information message 2. Tail bits and 3. Pre-amble

In the TDMA/TDD technique, in a frame information half of the time slots are used only for forward link where as other half of time slots are used for reverse link channels. TDMA is popular because a single carrier frequency is divided as many time slices and they are used by a large number of subscribers by providing one time slice to one user.

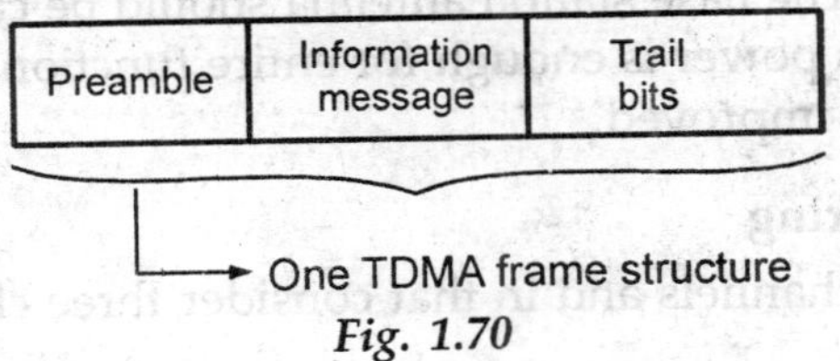

Fig. 1.70

(*iii*) Code Division Multiple Access (CDMA)

In CDMA the narrow band message signal is multiplied with a larger bandwidth signal which is called as spreading signal. This spreading signal is a pseudo noise code sequence with chip rate greater than the message data rate. A pseudorandom code word of each user is orthogonal to the code words of other users.

As in Fig. 1.69 (c) there are 'N' no of channels available and these channels are allotted codes which are unique. Each channel has its own unique code word so that in CDMA interference problem is minimized.

In CDMA the stronger received mobile signal produces noise at the BS demodulators for weaker signals so that the weaker signal may not be received properly. It is called as near-far problem and by using proper power control methods it can be suppressed. In spite of this near far effect, CDMA posses the advantage of using same frequency by many users.

(*iv*) Space Division Multiple Access (SDMA)

In space division multiplè access (SDMA) spot beam antennas are used to serve multiple users.

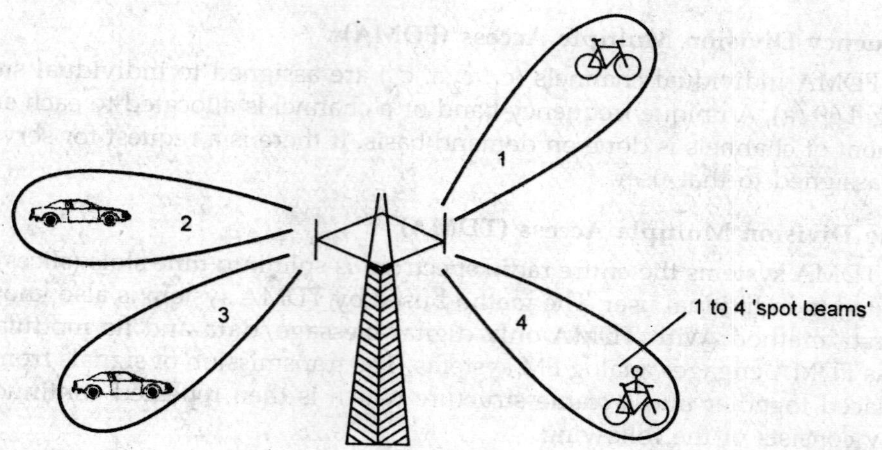

***Fig. 1.71** SDMA spatially filtered antenna at base station serves multiple subscribers*

The covered regions (with many users) will be served by a single frequency like TDMA/ CDMA or various frequencies like FDMA. Sectorized antennas and adaptive antennas can be used for SDMA technique. Using the same channel, all the users in the systems can establish communication. The base station antenna should be capable of spatially filter each user accurately so that less power is enough for entire functionality and the reverse link for every user will be greatly improved.

Space Division Multiplexing

Assume there are n_i channels and in that consider three channels n_1, n_2 and n_3.

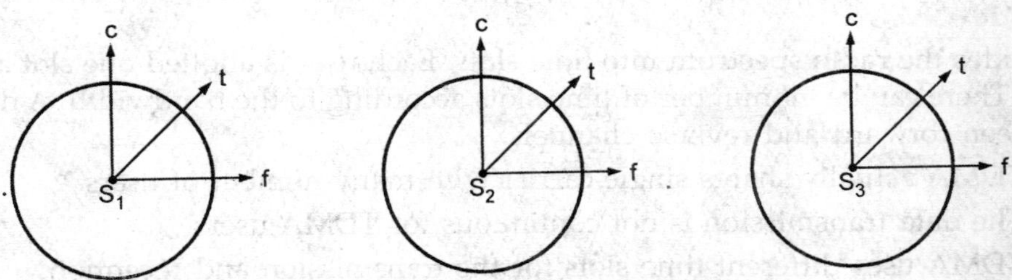

Fig. 1.72 Space division multiplexing

For these channels n_1, n_2 and n_3 three spaces S_1, S_2 and S_3 are allotted as shown here. In SDM multiplexing the interference will be very low but the space required to serve all the channels is high. If the number of channels are more total space used by this techniques will also be more.

All the access schemes can also be grouped as narrow band technique and wideband technique according to the method of bandwidth allocation.

1.21.2 Wideband system - Advantages

The transmission bandwidth of a single channel is larger than coherence bandwidth of the channel with wideband systems. Multipath fading does not affect wideband systems. The CDMA and TDMA system uses either time division duplexing TDD or frequency division duplexing FDD techniques.

1.21.3 Features of Three Multiple Access (FDMA, TDMA and CDMA) Techniques

1. FDMA

- The FDMA scheme can carry only one telephone circuit at same time.
- If a FDMA channels is not used at particular time, then it will be idle and any other user cannot use it.
- The base station and the mobile station transmit at a time without any break after the assignment of voice channel.
- The FDMA channel bandwidths are narrow.
- The FDMA cell site system cost are higher when compared to that of the TDMA system.
- This technique needs proper RF (radio frequency) filtering to reduce adjacent channel interference (ACI).
- The FDMA systems are less complex than TDMA schemes.
- Duplexers are used by FDMA mobile schemes.
- Synchronization and framing bits are required for FDMA systems since continuous transmission is taking place.

Note : In FDMA system use, same antenna at base station is shared by all channels and the power amplifiers are basically nonlinear. These affect the signal and "signal spreading" takes place in frequency domain which in turn generates intermodulation (IM) frequency. It is very important to reduce IM while dealing with FDMA schemes.

2. TDMA

It divides the radio spectrum into time slots. Each user is allotted one slot and only he can use it. There can be 'n' number of time slots according to the bandwidth. A delay can be used between forward and reverse channels.

- TDMA actually shares single carrier with many number of users.
- The data transmission is not continuous for TDMA users.
- TDMA uses different time slots for the transmission and reception.
- The transmission rates are very high in TDMA schemes and hence adaptive techniques are used.
- High synchronization is required in TDMA systems due to their burst transmission.
- Preamble is important in TDMA which bears synchronization and address information.
- Thetbandwidth is allotted to different users on demand basis.

3. CDMA

- The code division multiple access schemes provide individual code for each users. Multipath fading is reduced in CDMA.
- CDMA has to meet self-jamming problem.
- Near-far effect is a disadvantage in CDMA technique.
- Since each user is provided with a separate code, CDMA assures interference free communication.
- It uses frequency hopping (FHSS) or Direct Sequence Spread Spectrum (DSSS) methods for spread spectrum mechanisms.
- CDMA guarantees high degree of security than other schemes.
- The channel datarates are very high.

1.21.4 Comparison of SDMA, TDMA, FDMA and CDMA Techniques

Sr. No.	Approach	TDMA	FDMA	CDMA	SDMA
1.	Principle	Message sending time into disjoint time-slots, fixed pattern/demand driven.	Message is in different segments of frequency as disjoint subbands.	Spreads the spectrum using orthogonal codes.	Segment space into sectors/cells.
2.	Terminals	All the terminals are active for short time periods on same frequency.	Every terminal has its own frequency, which is uninterrupted.	All the terminals are active at same moment which is uninterrupted.	Only one terminal is active in one sector/one cell.

3.	Signal Separation	Synchronization is done in time domain.	Filtering in frequency domain is done.	Code plus special receivers arrangement.	Directed antennas/cell structure.
4.	Advantage	– Full digital in nature. – Flexible – Easy to establish.	– Robust – Easy establishment – Simple	– Flexible. – Soft handover – Less planning is enough.	– Simple. – Increases the capacity.
5.	Disadvantages	– Requires a guard space – Synchronization is difficult.	– Not flexible – Resources are limited.	– Receivers are complex in nature. – Needs more complicated power control for senders.	
6.	Application	Used in mobile networks.	Combined with TDMA/SDMA for hopping and reuse mechanisms.	– Integrated with TDMA/FDMA for application. – This is a complex scheme.	It is used only in combination with TDMA, FDMA (or) CDMA scheme for applications.
7.	Scheme	Time slices are used	Frequency slices are used.	Individual codes for each user.	Segments the space in each sector.

1.22 CELLULAR WIRELESS NETWORKS

The world, of communication has tremendously developed by the growth of the cellular wireless networks. The cellular or mobile telephones are novel equivalent of wireless telegraphs which provides a two way communication. The development of cellular wireless networks were divided into generations namely first generation (1G), second generation (2G), 3G, 4G and so on. In 1G technology analog techniques were found. Later digital technologies slowly emerged and caught up the entire wireless communication era in its hands. Many wireless devices are being introduced in wireless communication. First, importance was given to voice data, and then it was focused on 'data' including internet applications. The advanced mobile phone system (AMPS) was popular in early days and this network offered data services using the network known as 'cellular digital packet data' (CDPD), that provides a data rate of 19.2 kB/sec.

Later, in second generation wireless network systems, the global system for mobile communication (GSM) took all the importance in wireless applications. Also personal communication services (PCS) namely IS-136, IS-95 emerged at the same time.

Other technologies, wireless application protocol (WAP), wireless local area network (WLAN) and general packet radio service (GPRS) were developed which again lifted the cellular technological development to greater heights.

As the generation standards 1G, 2G, 3G etc. were developed one by one the cellular wireless networks provided large number of user friendly features in mobile phones.

These latest techniques like WAP, WLAN, GPRS, GSM topics are covered in detail in this book.

Now some basic ideas about wireless communication including its operation, frequency reuse technique, diversity techniques for mobile signal reception, adjacent channel interference are discussed under this chapter.

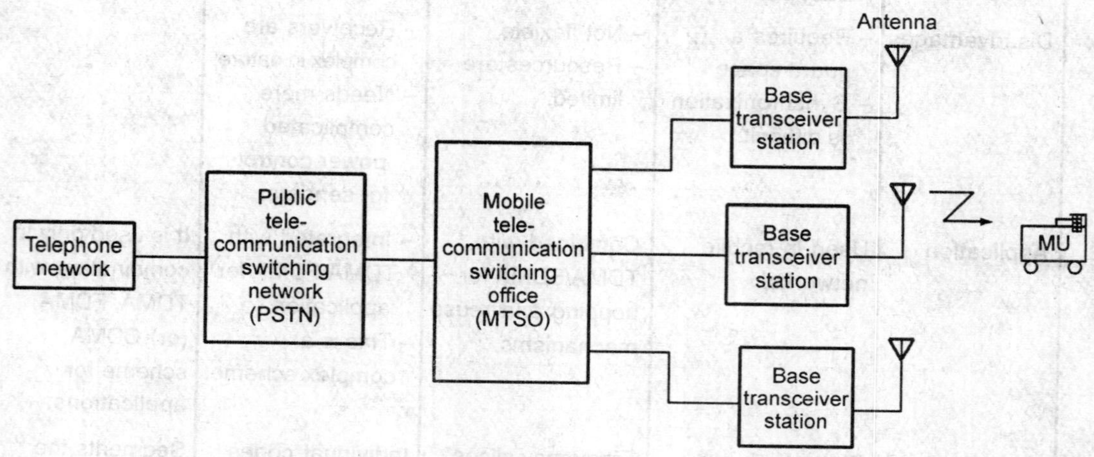

Fig. 1.73 Overview of cellular system (MU-mobile unit)

1.22.1 Operation of Cellular System

The principle elements of a cellular system are

- Mobile Unit Initializing
- Paging
- Mobile Originated Call

The base station is located approximately in the centre of each cell. It also includes antenna, transceivers (transmitter and receiver) and controller for communicating with the different channels in that call. In a random manner any subscriber may communicate with the base station. The base station should be efficiently equipped with a transceiver system to respond to the signal from subscriber. The cellular system should properly place and answer the calls. The channels are of two types termed as control channels and traffic channels which are very important between the base station and subscriber for sustaining communication.

The control channels are used to interchange (exchange) information to set up and to maintain calls. The mobile unit will establish contact with nearest base station.

The traffic carry are intended to carry voice or data between different users. If a mobile user signals to its nearest base station the important sequence of operations carried out are discussed in detail in the following topic.

Sequence of Operations :

1. Mobile unit initialization.
2. Mobile originated call (Request for connection).
3. Paging.
4. Call acceptance.
5. Ongoing call.
6. Hand-off procedure.

1. Mobile unit initialization

The mobile unit when it wants to establish a call, and as soon as it is turned on it selects the strongest set up channel available and finds the frequency band with the base station within which the mobile unit can operate. Actually it monitors the strongest available signal. The user can be identified and can be registered with the help of handshaking signals. During the 'on' time of mobile unit (turned on status) the scanning procedure is repeated in regular time intervals to account for the motion of the mobile unit.

2. Mobile originated call (Request for connection)

Whenever the mobile unit wants to originate a call, it initially checks for an idle set up channel availability with the forward channel. Then it sends the number of the called party on the pre selected set up channel available at that time. The base station (BS) transmits the request of mobile unit to the MTSO. This is followed by paging function.

3. Paging

As the request is received by the MTSO from the base station it tries to complete the connection to called party (called mobile unit). According to the mobile number the MTSO sends a paging message/information to a set of base station on the assigned set up channel. This function is followed by call acceptance.

4. Call acceptance

The mobile number on set up channel is recognized by called mobile unit and it responds to base station (BS). The MTSO then sets up a circuit between the called and calling base station respectively.

5. Ongoing call

When the call is established and maintained exchange of voice/data signals takes place between mobile units with base station and the switching office (MTSO).

6. Hand-off

The traffic channel should change as the mobile unit moves (roams) from one cell to another cell region. The call should not be disturbed or terminated but maintained properly by this hand off technique. The call is handed over next base station where the mobile unit is available at that moment. Hence the call is not interrupted though the subscriber is roaming. The related functions of these important function of cellular system are summarized below.

(*a*) Call drop
(*b*) Call blocking
(*c*) Call termination
(*d*) Call from/to fixed and mobile subscriber (including remote distant area)

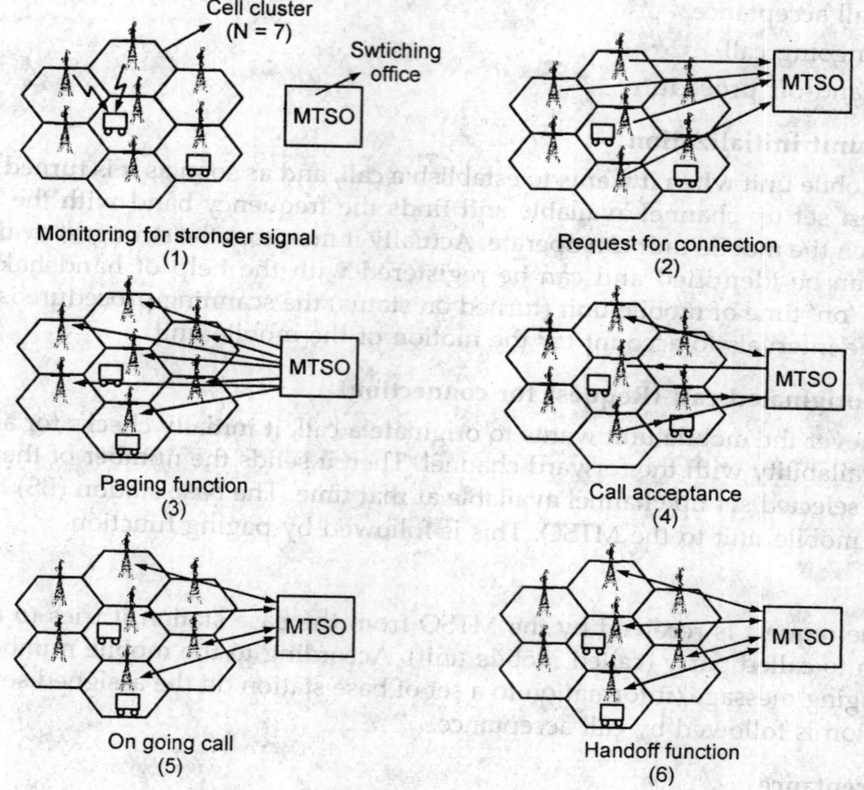

Fig. 1.74 Operations in a cellular mobile system

1 to 6 → "Stages in establishing a call".

The line of sight (LOS) at sea level (for single antenna) is denoted as 'D' and

$$D = \sqrt{2h}$$

where h → Height of the antenna above sea level in feet

D → Distance to the radio horizon in miles.

At sea level the distance between two antennas is the summation of radio horizon for transmit antenna (D_t) and radio horizon for receive antenna (D_r) in terms of miles.

$$D = D_t + D_r$$

Note : The maximum distance between a transmitter and receiver antenna over an average terrain is denoted as D_{max}.

where D_{max} → Distance in kilometers between transmitter and receiver.

$h_t \rightarrow$ Height of transmitting antenna above the sea level in meters.

$h_r \rightarrow$ Height of receiving antenna above the sea level in meters.

Sequence of steps (functions) involved when two mobile users are in communication, through MTSO/MSC.

1. Mobile unit initialization (originating).
2. Paging.
3. Call accepting.
4. Call ongoing.
5. Hand-off.

Also the other functions that may be introduced in progress of call are,

1. Call blocking.
2. Call drop.
3. Call termination.

1.23 PAGING SYSTEMS

They are communication systems that send brief messages to a subscriber. The message may be an alphanumeric message, numeric message or a voice data. Today paging systems may include news headlines, faxes and stock quotations and it may be sent to a particular paging subscriber through the corresponding paging system access number with a telephone keypad or a modern. The message issued is called as a page. The page message is broadcast over a radio carrier through the geographical service area using the base stations. Under simulcast technique the wide area paging systems transmits a page from each base station simultaneously. It is also shown in the operation of establishing a call from a mobile unit and base station (BS).

Performance metrics used in decision-making under handoff situations are listed below.

1. Probability of call blocking.
2. Probability of call dropping.
3. Probability of call completion.
4. Hand-off delay.
5. Rate of hand-off (Number of hand-offs per unit time)
6. Probability of an incomplete hand-off.
7. Probability of hand-off blocking.
8. Interruption time duration.
9. Hand-off probability.

List of strategies used to calculate the instant of the hand-off are

1. Relative signal strength method.
2. Relative signal strength with hysteresis method.
3. Relative signal strength with threshold method.
4. Relative signal strength with combined (hysteresis and threshold) method and
5. Prediction techniques.

Increased functionality and applications of cellular mobile phone.

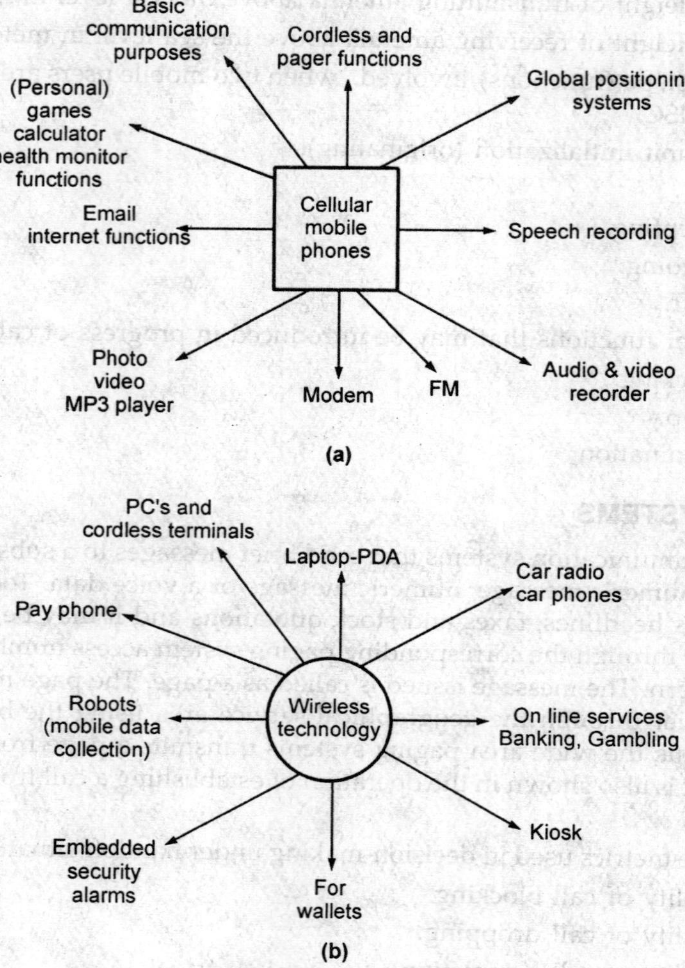

Fig. 1.75 Cellular mobile phone

1.24 ADJACENT CHANNEL INTERFERENCE (ACI)

Adjacent channel interference is denoted as ACI. It is an example or non-cochannel interference. The interference that results due to adjacent signal frequency is termed as adjacent channel interference. It may result due to an imperfect receiver unit. When nearby frequencies adds up with actual signal frequency then adjacent channel interference takes place. Due to this leaking of adjacent signal frequencies into actual signals frequencies wireless communication degrades in its performance. ACI can be reduced by proper filtering and also channel allocations.

Another cause for ACI is 'frequency reuse'. Since the separation between adjacent channels is very less interference of adjacent channel frequency is more. Hence channel separations are a must to reduce ACI value.

1.24.1 Methods of reducing ACI

By proper channel assignments and filtering, ACI problem can be reduced since each channel is assigned a small bandwidth of the channels available. Care can be ensured in channel assignments so that adjacent channel interference can be reduced to the maximum. It is a trade off between adjacent channel interference reduction and frequency reuse factor When frequency reuse is high there are more chances for interferences due to neighboring channels and due to less frequency separation concept. For example, if the closeness in a mobile is 30 times as close to the base station as another mobile, it is important to measure signal to interference ratio (S/I).

Signal to interference ratio = $\frac{S}{I} = (30)^{-a}$, for a path loss exponent value a = 6. Also power control should be properly done by the base station to reduce interference at the subscriber's mobile unit.

1.24.2 Frequency reuse concept

A smallest geographic area is termed as cell. Each cell has a base station and base station antennas are designed mainly to enhance coverage. The process of allocating channel groups and selecting for all the cellular base station within the particular system is called as frequency planning or frequency reuse. As in the diagram below the corresponding cells (with same numbers) use the same set (group) of channels and it is the main aim of frequency reuse concept where the bandwidth is saved.

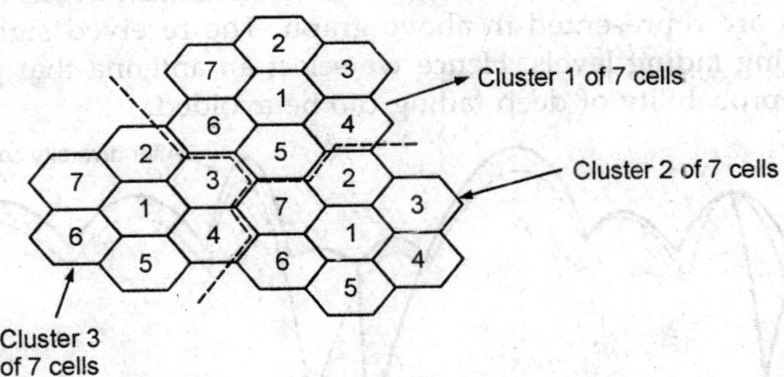

Fig. 1.76 Frequency reuse concept

The cells with same numbers uses the same set of frequencies.

Frequency reuse concept can also be explained with an example.

The frequency division multiplexing (FDM) which applies the principle of dividing the bandwidth of frequencies into slices allocating to many channels. In satellite communication 24 channels can be accommodated into the 500 MHz by this frequency reuse concept. Each frequency allocation is done by two carriers with orthogonal polarization. A 4 MHz guard band is allowed in 40 MHz (approx) channel bandwidth. Then subtracting the guardband from a channel bandwidth, 36 MHz bandwidth is allowed for a channel. This technique is used in many applications.

They are 1. 600 channels of 40 Kbps each (for each channel).
2. Single 50 Mbps data stream.
3. 1200 voice-frequency voice channels arrangement.
4. In digital video signals.

1.25 DIVERSITY TECHNIQUES

The diversity is a good technique applied in mobile communication receiver circuits where there is multipath environments. The diversity techniques uses the nature of the propagation path characteristics for improving the sensitivity of receivers. If will improve the wireless links, at less costs. It does not require prior training because a training sequence is not needed by a transmitter like an equalizer. Diversity technique finds a way of analyzing signal paths for multipath cellular environment.

The diversity decisions made at the receiver end and they are not known to the transmitter.

1.25.1 Diversity Concept

The simple concept of diversity is that even if a radio signal path experiences a deep face, there will be another independent signal path available for analysis.

Consider the above diagram. A received signal is observed with many variations. Assume two antennae with a specific separation between them are located on a terminal. They experience different fading levels as the mobile terminal moves. An example of received signal variations are represented in above graph. The received signal levels differ with their corresponding fading levels. Hence we select an antenna that possess higher signal level so that the probability of deep fading can be avoided.

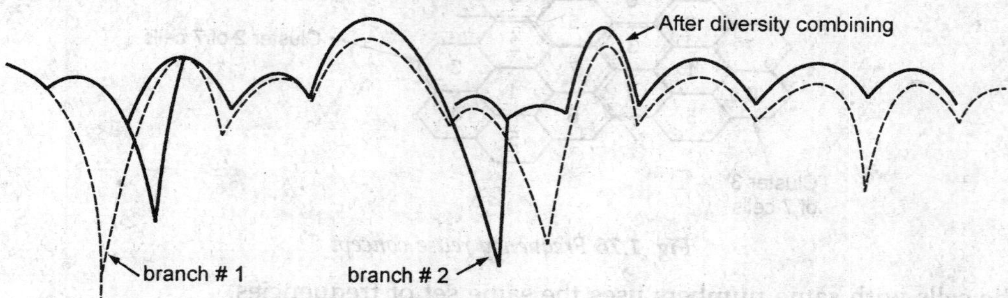

Fig. 1.77 Received signal level variations at various diversity branches

In this diagram signal level of the antenna #1 suffers fading whereas signal level of antenna #2 fades in seldom cases. Note that branch #1 is deeply faded where as branch #2 is not highly faded.

1.25.2 Types of Fading

There are two types of fading small-scale and large-scale fading

(*a*) Small-scale fading

The small-scale fading are mainly characterised by rapid amplitude fluctuations and deep fades of less wavelengths (λ). The small-scale fading is due to signal fades caused by multiple path and reflections with respect to mobile movement.

(b) Large-scale fading

The large-scale fading is generated by shadowing effects which is due to changes in both the nature of surroundings and the terrain profile involved. The large scale fading is log-normally spreaded with particular standard deviation value of approximately 10 decibels in the urban area.

1.25.3 Kinds of Diversity

The two basic kinds of diversity are termed as

(*i*) Microscopic diversity and (*ii*) Macroscopic diversity.

(*i*) Microscopic diversity

To counteract small-signal fading that is to avoid deep fading in the signal received under small distances can be minimized by this technique. It can prevent small signal fades in case of less antenna separations, if two antennas are used.

By choosing the signal of higher strength most of the time, the receiver can reduce the fading effects. In the graph shown below. The small signal fades rapidly where as large signal fades gradually with respect to an indoor environment.

(*ii*) Macroscopic diversity

In large signal fading, the signal strength reduces that is because of shadowing problems. By choosing a base station that is not shadowed when compared to other

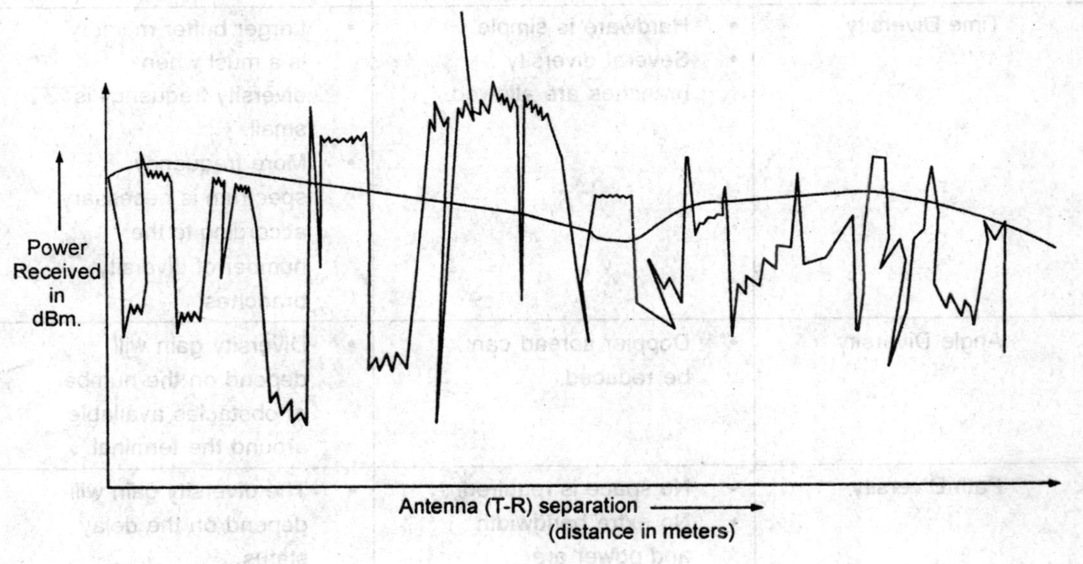

Fig. 1.78

base stations, the mobile unit can acquire a better signal to noise ratio (SNR) in its forward path. Such a type of counteracting to large scale fading effects or the method of diversity used to reduce large scale signal fades is termed as macroscopic diversity technique. This is highly useful at the base station receiver end.

Table 1.4 some of the advantages and disadvantages of different diversity schemes.

Table 1.4

Sr. No.	Diversity scheme	Advantages	Disadvantages
1.	Polarization Diversity	• No space and extra bandwidth is required.	• 3 dB extra power is a must • Two branch diversity schemes is only possible.
2.	Space Diversity	• Several diversity branches are allowed. • It is also applicable to macroscopic diversity. • No extra bandwidth or power is required.	• Large hardware size is required. • Larger antenna spacing is a must for the microscopic diversity at the base station.
3.	Frequency Diversity	• Several diversity branches are allowed.	• Relevant power level of frequency spectrum are important.
4.	Time Diversity	• Hardware is simple. • Several diversity branches are allowed.	• Larger buffer memory is a must when diversity frequency is small. • More frequency spectrum is necessary according to the number of diversity branches.
5.	Angle Diversity	• Doppler spread can be reduced.	• Diversity gain will depend on the number of obstacles available around the terminal.
6.	Path Diversity	• No space is required. • No extra bandwidth and power are required.	• The diversity gain will depend on the delay status.

1.25.4 Important Diversity Techniques

The important diversity techniques are discussed in the following ways

Types of Diversity Techniques :

1. Space diversity technique.
   - (i) Selection diversity
   - (ii) Feedback diversity
   - (iii) Maximal ratio combining method
   - (iv) Equal gain combining.
2. Polarization diversity technique.
3. Time diversity technique.
4. Frequency diversity technique.
5. Directional diversity technique.
6. Path diversity technique.
7. Macroscopic diversity technique.
8. Transmitter diversity technique.

Each diversity technique is unique in its functionality but aims towards a common goal of reducing the fading effects in multipath receiver circuit.

1.25.5 Space Diversity Technique

The space diversity scheme is also called as 'antenna diversity scheme'. In conventional methods of wireless communication, the availability of direct path between transmitter and receiver is not assured. Hence the occurrence of Rayleigh fading will be present.

But the antenna space diversity can achieve independent fading changes by applying spatially separated antennas.

In the space diversity scheme the receiver configuration is quite simple. Several number of diversity branches are selectable. For producing diversity reception at each and every cell site, multiple base station receiving antennas are used effectively. It is important to note that main scattering takes place in ground which is in the vicinity of the mobile unit, and hence to attain decorrelation the antennas at base station have to be placed with necessary separation distances. This separation distance can be in order of tens of wavelength (λ) value with respect to base station. Generally the space diversity technique can be used at base station or mobile or at both ends.

Also in case the antenna spacing is greater than $\frac{x}{2}$ then it is sufficient to obtain low fading correlation between the diversity branches, and antenna spacing of 50 λ to 100 λ is a must at the base station end.

A general schematic of space diversity is shown below. There are 'n' branches with separate gain values namely G_1 G_2 ... G_n and a set of demodulators to generate required output.

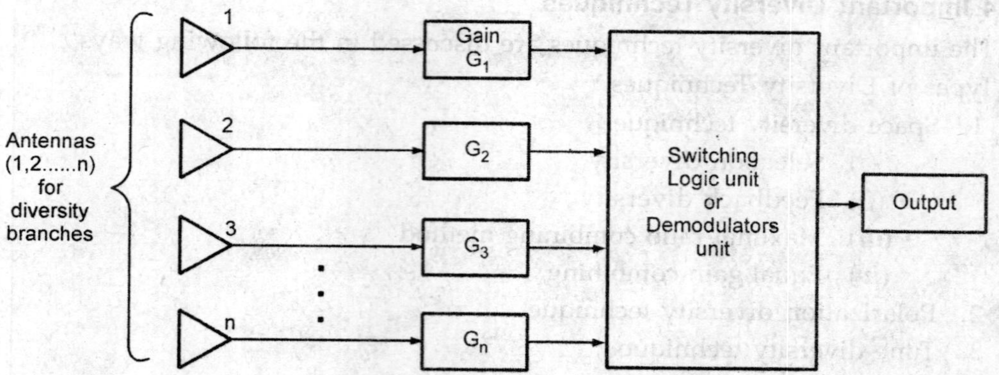

Fig. 1.79 Simple block diagram of Space diversity technique

1.25.6 Space Diversity Combining Schemes

(i) Selective diversity

In selective diversity combining, the branches having the strongest received signal will be selected. In selective diversity method 'n' number of demodulators are used and their gains can be adjusted to give mean signal to noise ratio (SNR) for every diversity branch. Then the antenna signals will be sampled. Finally the best signal that possess good signal strength will be sent to a demodulator. It is also seen that practical diversity system has to be designed carefully such that reciprocal of the mobile signal fading rate is longer than the internal time constant values of selection diversity circuitry.

(ii) Feedback Diversity

The feedback diversity technique is also known as scanning diversity. In this method the 'n' signals are scanned in a proper sequence and monitored to pick a signal in the sequence which is above the preset threshold value say 'α'.

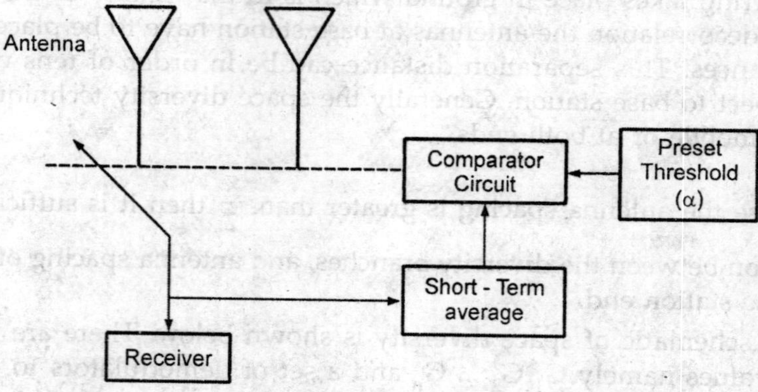

Fig. 1.80 Feedback diversity technique

Then scanning process will be initiated for the received signals. But the demerit of this method is that the fading level reduction is less than the other diversity techniques. In this method for the received signals (m) the best signal of better strength is measured by comparing every signal with a preset threshold value 'a' as shown in the diagram.

One of the merit of feedback diversity is its easier implementation than other methods.

(iii) Maximal ratio combining technique

The concept of this method is all the branch signals [N] are combined coherently with necessary weighting coefficients for every diversity branch signal, so that the reduction of fading will be better leading to overall improvement of system performance.

A block diagram for this method is shown below. Unlike selection diversity, the signal are cophased before addition process and for this individual receiver and phasing circuits is a must for all the antenna elements.

In the output, signal of maximal ratio combiner will be such that the sum of individual signal to noise ratio (SNR) values will be equal to the SNR of output signal measured.

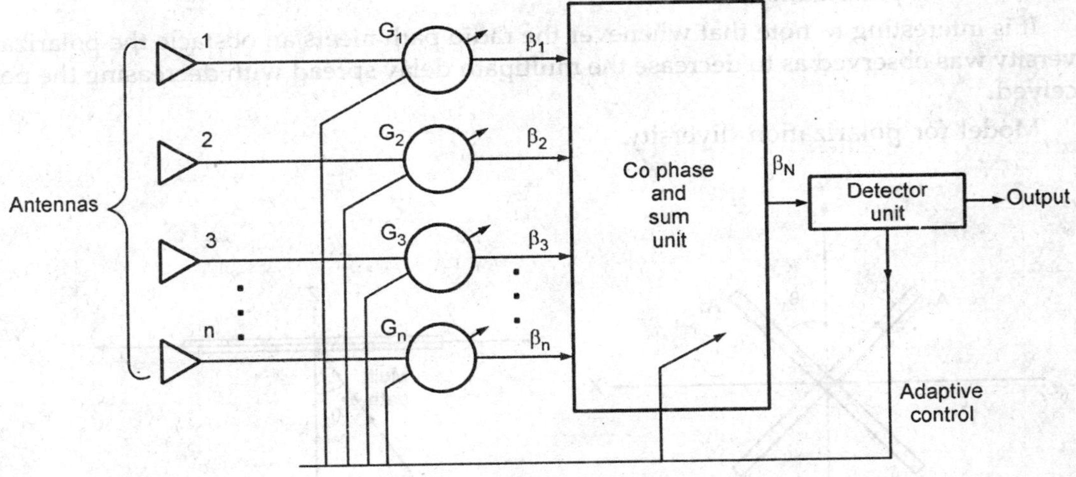

Fig. 1.81 Maximal ratio combiner technique

Advantages :

1. Maximal ratio combiner generates an acceptable SNR value.
2. Accuracy is high.
3. Produces best reduction of fading.

(iv) Equal gain combiner technique

In the equal gain combining, all the diversity branches are coherently added with a same weighting factor. On the other hand this scheme also cophases all the diversity branches and finally adds them up. As the signals are cophased from all branches they provide an equal gain factor. When compared to maximal ratio combining, the configuration of this method is simple. By applying equal gain combining it is convenient for the receiver to get back the signals.

One of the demerits of this method is that it degrades the SNR value by 0.5 dB at the output of combiner if two branches are involved. If ten branches are involved in the reception, then the SNR degradation would be roughly upto 1 dB value.

1.25.7 Polarization Diversity

In polarization diversity both horizontal and vertical polarization are involved. In case if a signal is transmitted by a pair of polarized antennas and they are received by another pair of antennas, then two uncorrelated fading signals will be received because different fading variations are experienced by horizontal and vertical polarizations and due to different reflection coefficient values of the tall building walls.

The measured vertical and horizontal polarization signal paths between base station and mobile is found to be uncorrelated. Also the decorrelation in vertical and horizontal polarization for signals is due to multiple reflections in the radio channel between base stations and mobile antennas. There will he an amount of dependence of received polarization on transmitted polarization.

It is interesting to note that whenever the radio path meets an obstacle the polarization diversity was observed as to decrease the multipath delay spread with decreasing the power received.

Model for polarization diversity.

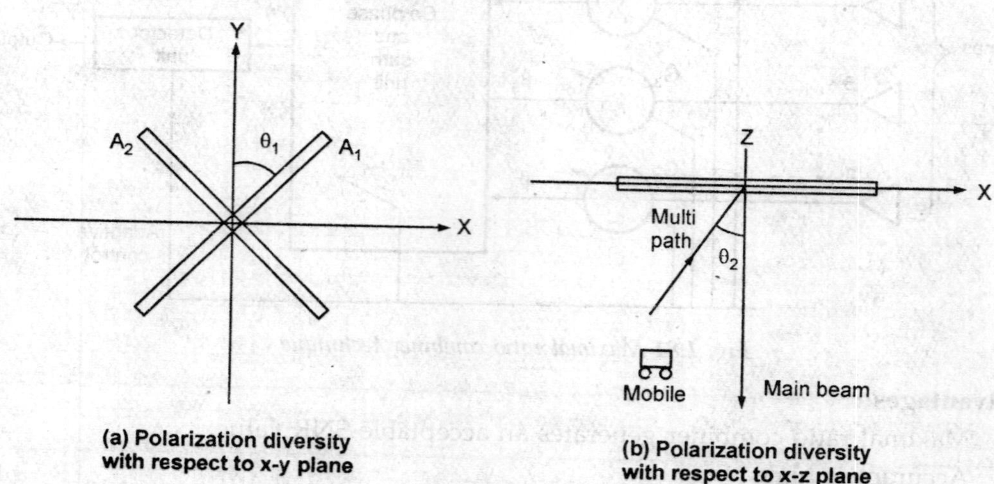

Fig. 1.82 Model for the base station polarization diversity

Consider that the signal is being transmitted with horizontal or vertical polarization from a mobile unit. This signal is received by polarization diversity antenna say with two diversity branches.

Assume that the polarization diversity antenna consists of two antenna elements say A_1 and A_2 making an angle of $\pm \theta_1$ with that of the y axis. Then a mobile station is located in a particular direction that makes an offset angle θ_2 from the direction of mean beam of the diversity antenna.

The two signals a and b that arrive at base station are

$$a = r_1 \cos(\omega t + \phi_1)$$
$$b = r_2 \cos(\omega t + \phi_2)$$

in which a and b are levels of the received signals when $\theta_2 = 0$; Assume that r_1 and r_2 possess independent Rayleigh distributions and the phase angles ϕ_1 and ϕ_2 have independent uniform distribution values.

The correlation coefficient of the signals received at A_1 and A_2 can be determined by three factors.

They are,

1. Polarization angle.
2. Cross polarization discrimination.
3. Offset angle from that of the main beam direction of diversity antenna setup.

By these factors the value of correlation coefficient can be determined.

Note : As the offset angle '82' grows higher the correlation coefficient also becomes higher value.

Thus polarization diversity is one of the best technique in diversity reception and it can be applied for mobile unit and the base station.

1.25.8 Time Diversity

In time diversity method, the information is transmitted repeatedly at specific time spacings that which would exceed the coherence time of the mobile channel, and this will lead to repetition of signals for several times; irrespective of fading conditions.

Thus when an identical information is sent for different time slots, it is possible to obtain diversity branch signals.

The time diversity technique is well suited for spread spectrum CDMA system, in which RAKE receiver is used for reception.

1.25.9 Frequency Diversity

In this method of frequency diversity, the information is transmitted on many carrier frequencies. The idea behind this is that if the frequencies are separated by more than that of the coherence bandwidth of the mobile channel would be uncorrelated with each other and it will not experience same fading status. Also under channels, uncorrelated situations, the occurrence of fading will be multiple of the individual fading probability (occurrences).

The frequency diversity scheme is applied in microwave fields whenever line of sight (LOS) links is used. That is in LOS links they may carry many channels in the frequency division multiplex mode (FDM). There are chances of deep fades in frequency diversity due to tropospheric propagations and the resulting refractions of the signal.

The fading variation independence factor between the separated frequency components is a main effect with respect to land mobile communication and it is known as frequency diversity effect. Thus the frequency diversity is a popular diversity reception technique.

1.25.10 Directional Diversity

The received signals would arrive from different incident angles due to any one of the propagation mechanisms namely reflection diffraction or scattered signals around the mobile terminal. By using selective directive antennas the independent faded signals (since all the paths arising from various angles are mutually independent of each other) can be received. This -type of diversity is suitable to apply in mobile terminal end where limited directions of signals at base station is linked.

1.25.11 Path Diversity

In path diversity method, the signals are coherently combined. That is both the direct and delayed signal components are combined together. Thus the diversity branches are generated only after signal reception, and this method is also called as Implicit diversity. As an example an adaptive equalizer and RAKE diversity are also categorized as path diversity schemes.

Advantages of path diversity schemes are :

(*i*) No extra power is required

(*ii*) No extra antennas are required and

(*iii*) No extra frequency spectrum is required.

Demerit of path diversity scheme :

This diversity method is very sensitive to Rayleigh fading conditions, and hence the propagation path conditions has to be given more attention.

1.26 RAKE RECEIVER

In general the CDMA receivers can combine all the delayed versions of the transmitted signal and provides better signal to noise ratio at destination side. By using a specific correlation receiver unit the 'RAKE' receiver collects all the delayed versions/ shifted versions of the original signal. Each and every correlator unit is capable of searching a particular range of time delays and it is termed as "Search window". The RAKE receiver given below is also known as "diversity receiver" designed particularly for CDMA technique. Here diversity of the signals are achieved by using the uncorrelated multipath components with one another whenever the relative propagation delay values are greater than the chip time period. Hence the 'RAKE Receiver' mainly makes use of the multiple correlations for signal reception in mobile communication. In this particular example 'N' number of correlators are used for detecting the multipath components. For obtaining an accurate estimate of the transmitted signal as a whole rather than a single component the multiple components are weighted after the 'n' correlators units. Based on the output signal values the detection and the bit decisions are done. A weighting state (network) provides a linear combination of the outputs from correlator for the bit detection purpose. It should be noted that if bit decisions are done with respect to a single correlation then probability of bit error rate is higher.

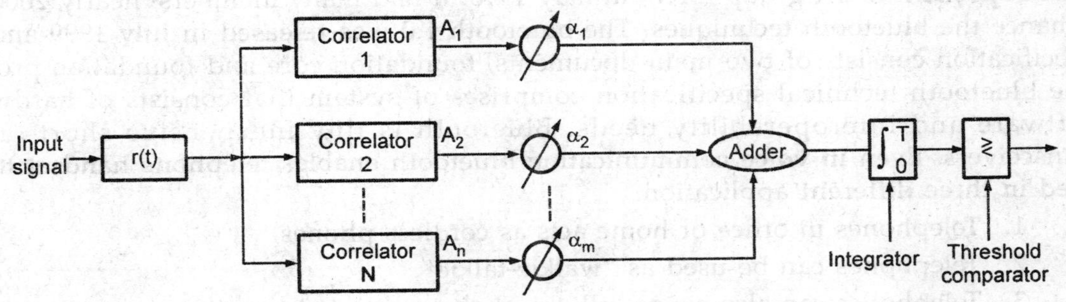

Fig. 1.83 'RAKE' receiver

Assume that the outputs of the 'N' number of correlators are $A_1, A_2 \ldots A_n$ which are weighted by $\alpha_1, \alpha_2, \alpha_3, \ldots \alpha_n$ values. If the SNR/power is smaller for a particular correlator then its weighting factor will also be a smaller value. The general overall signal can be represented as A' and it is given as.

$$A' = \sum_{n=1}^{N} \alpha_n \cdot A_n$$

where $\alpha_n \rightarrow$ Weighting coefficients

For having a better performance to produce efficient signal reception, selection of weighting coefficients which is based on output values (actual output) of correlator is an important criteria in the 'RAKE' receivers.

Difference between wireless and fixed telephone networks

The transfer of data (information) in a public switched telephone network (PSTN) takes place in four ways.

1. The trunk lines comprised of optical fibers.
2. Microwave links.
3. Satellite links.
4. Copper cables.

But the wireless networks are established such that whenever the subscriber moves from one place to another the network setup is rearranged, so that coverage region holds good. The wireless networks are flexible to change where as fixed networks are very difficult to change. But the main constrain with wireless networks are the bandwidth. The channels bandwidth for fixed networks can be increased for high traffic but cellular bandwidth provided to wireless networks cannot be changed.

The global telecommunications company, Ericsson mobile communications, which is based in Sweden first initiated its interest in bluetooth technology in 1994. The aim to develop this technology is to enable communication between mobile unit and other devices like personal computer. PC cards, headsets and many other devices. Later other companies also started to work in this area and joined together and to form a group called special interest group (SIG), in may 1998. It had many members, nearly 2000, to enhance the bluetooth techniques. The bluetooth 1.0 was released in July 1999 and its specification consists of two main documents, foundation core and foundation profile. The bluetooth technical specification comprises of system that consists of hardware software and interoperability needs. Bluetooth is tiny inexpensive short-range transceivers. Even in voice communication bluetooth enables telephone handset to be used in three different application.

1. Telephones in office or home acts as cordless phones.
2. Telephones can be used as "walkie-talkie".
3. Telephones can also act as cellular phone connected to cellular structures with corresponding cellular charges.

Hence bluetooth enhances the uses of voice channels. Video transmission is also supported by bluetooth techniques.

The bluetooth modules of different applications does not cause harm to public or private sectors and they do not interfere in any other networks.

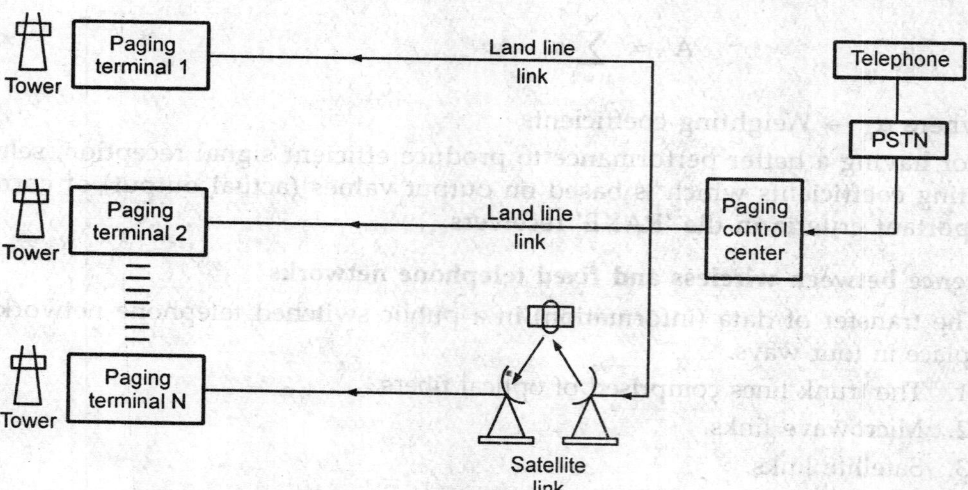

Fig. 1.84 Wide area paging system-an example

As in the example given, above the satellite uplink and downlink facilitates the performance efficiency to grow higher for a paging system. Time delays are avoided and the data rates are high in wide area paging systems.

REVIEW QUESTIONS

1. What is known as mobile communication ?
2. Define a cell.
3. What is known as cell splitting ?
4. What is MTSO ?
5. Write a short note on hand-off.
6. What is the difference between full duplex and half duplex systems ?
7. What is known as virtual home environment ?
8. List any three functions of mobile computing.
9. Define 'signal'.
10. Draw the diagram of basic communication system.
11. Differentiate the discrete and continuous time signal.
12. Mention few operations that can be performed on a signal.
13. What is an antenna ?
14. What is known as amplitude modulation ?
15. What is known as attenuation ?
16. What are types of antenna ?
17. What is known as smart antenna ?
18. Define propagation and polarization.
19. Write a short note on wavefront.
20. What is known as wave attenuation ?
21. List some of the properties of radio waves.
22. Define reflection.
23. Define diffraction.
24. What are the three types of propagation of electromagnetic waves ?
25. What is known as multiplexing ?
26. Write short note on TDM.
27. What is a 'COFDM' ?
28. What is the need for modulation ?
29. Draw the AM signal.
30. "When modulation index (m) changes the amplitude modulated output signal will also definitely change." Show few cases to justify this with different values of 'm'.
31. What is known as minimum shift keying and Gaussian minimum shift keying method ?
32. Explain QPSK modulation.
33. What is the advantage of spread spectrum ?
34. What are the two types of spread spectrum ?
35. Explain frequency hopping spread spectrum.
36. Draw the format of 802.11 standard.
37. Explain medium access control.
38. Differentiate and compare TDMA, FDMA and CDMA techniques.
39. Explain cellular wireless networks, with its operation.

40. Explain paging systems.
41. Explain adjacent channel interference.
42. What is known as diversity technique ? Explain in detail.
43. List any two advantages of diversity technique.
44. How adjacent channel interference can be reduced ?
45. Differentiate a signal and system.
46. Explain polarization concept.
47. Define VSWR.
48. Give one example for an even signal.
49. Explain lens antenna in detail.
50. Explain 'RAKE receiver' in detail.

❑❑❑

Unit 2

Telecommunication

2.1 COMMUNICATION AND TELECOMMUNICATION

The term "communication" refers to the process of conveying information or message from one place to another place. For establishing a communication the necessary components are transmitter, receiver and a channel. The channel is also called as transmitting medium or a path through which information is sent.

But "Telecommunication" is a term that refers to long distance communication where the receiver will be at a distant end (far) from the transmitter. It is more effective if electromagnetic waves are radiated into space to have a distant (tele) communication.

The telephone system involves a large distance between the calling and called party. The telephone communication is a best example for telecommunication. Conventionally a pair of wires (for forward and reverse) are being used for telephone systems and public switched telephone network (PSTN) is the centralized system through which call progress and termination takes place.

The telephone system's operation is dealt in this chapter.

Some terms related to telecommunication system :

(*i*) POTS

The simplest telephone service known as plain old telephone service allows users accessing the public telephone network with a pair of wires called as local loop.

(*ii*) Telephone

It is derived from a Greek word 'tele' which has the meaning 'from a far' and the word 'phone' has the meaning 'sound', 'audio' or 'voiced sound'.

Telephone is an instrument used to produce sound (speech) by means of the electricity and enables conversation over a large distance between two users/subscribers.

(*iii*) PTN

Public telephone network system has a data modem or telephone used in the telephone circuit. The PTN is capable of interconnecting many subscribers through switches and hence it is also called as Public Switched Telephone Network (PSTN).

(iv) Base band transmission

It is related to transmission of raw electrical signal.

(v) Wire pair

A pair of wires used for telecommunication between any two subscribers by a copper conductor.

(vi) Attenuation

It is "Dissipation of signal strength" as the signal travels through the transmission medium. It is usually expressed in decibels (dB). Attenuation or loss is represented as $L = 10 \log \frac{P_1}{P_2}$; where P_1 is power of the signal when it enters the wire and P_2 is the power signal at a distant end.

Attenuator symbol

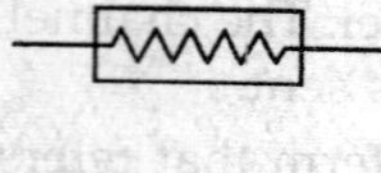

Amplifier symbol

(vii) Cross talk

Cross talk is common in the telephone cable, and it is a kind of an unwanted signal induced in pair of wires from nearby wire pairs. This problem of cross talk can be solved by using twisted wire pairs.

(viii) Delay distortion

Delay distortion is a parameter that varies with the length of the line. It is caused by capacitance between one wire and the other wire of a pair.

(ix) Bandwidth of twisted pair wire

Generally PSTN subscriber access provides 2 MHz over a length of mile. Common impedance of the cable will be 75 and 50 ohms.

(x) Limitations of telecommunication

Voice transmission will slowly become inaudible for < 30 km. Distance is a limiting parameter in telecommunication system's performance.

(xi) Transmission media

It is the channel or path used for transmitting and receiving signal between the transmitter and receiver.

e.g.
- Wired pair
- Coaxial cable
- Fiber optic cable
- Radio wave transmission in "Atmosphere" (air) as media.

(*xii*) Frequency response of coaxial cable

The frequency response at 100 kHz loss will be $\approx 1\,\text{dB}$ and at 10 MHz loss $\approx 12\,\text{dB}$.

(*xiii*) Uses of optical fiber cable includes

- Wideband terrestrial links
- Cable television
- As data network backbones

(*xiv*) Types of signalling (examples)

- Supervisory signalling,
- Addressing signalling

(*xv*) AT&T

It is the "American Telephone and Telegraph Company" which runs AT&T's research and development and AT&T's manufacturing wing etc. But AT&T does not control Bell Operating Groups (BOG).

(*xvi*) ITU

It is an international standardization known as "International Telecommunications Union".

The three important organizations under ITU are International frequency registration board, consultative committee on International Radio and the consultative committee on International telegraphy and telephony.

The main functionalities of the International Telecommunication Union (ITU) are split into four wings. They are shown in the Fig. 2.1.

A list that comprises of the common transmission data rates (speed) and their corresponding applications are summarized here along with the different transmission media used by the applications or devices involved in them. Refer Fig. 2.2 for more information about various transmission speeds.

2.1.1 Functions of a Telephone Set

1. It identifies the subscriber whenever there is an incoming call with an alert audible signal.
2. Verifies with telephone network when the receiver is lifted off hook by providing (sending) a signal to the telephone network.
3. Conversion of sound signal (audio signal) to electrical signal at transmitter and vice-versa in receiver side.
4. It sends destination telephone numbers mechanically or electrically to the central office through the local loop setup.
5. Regulates the level of amplitude of speech signal to maintain smooth speech levels of two subscribers when call is in progress.

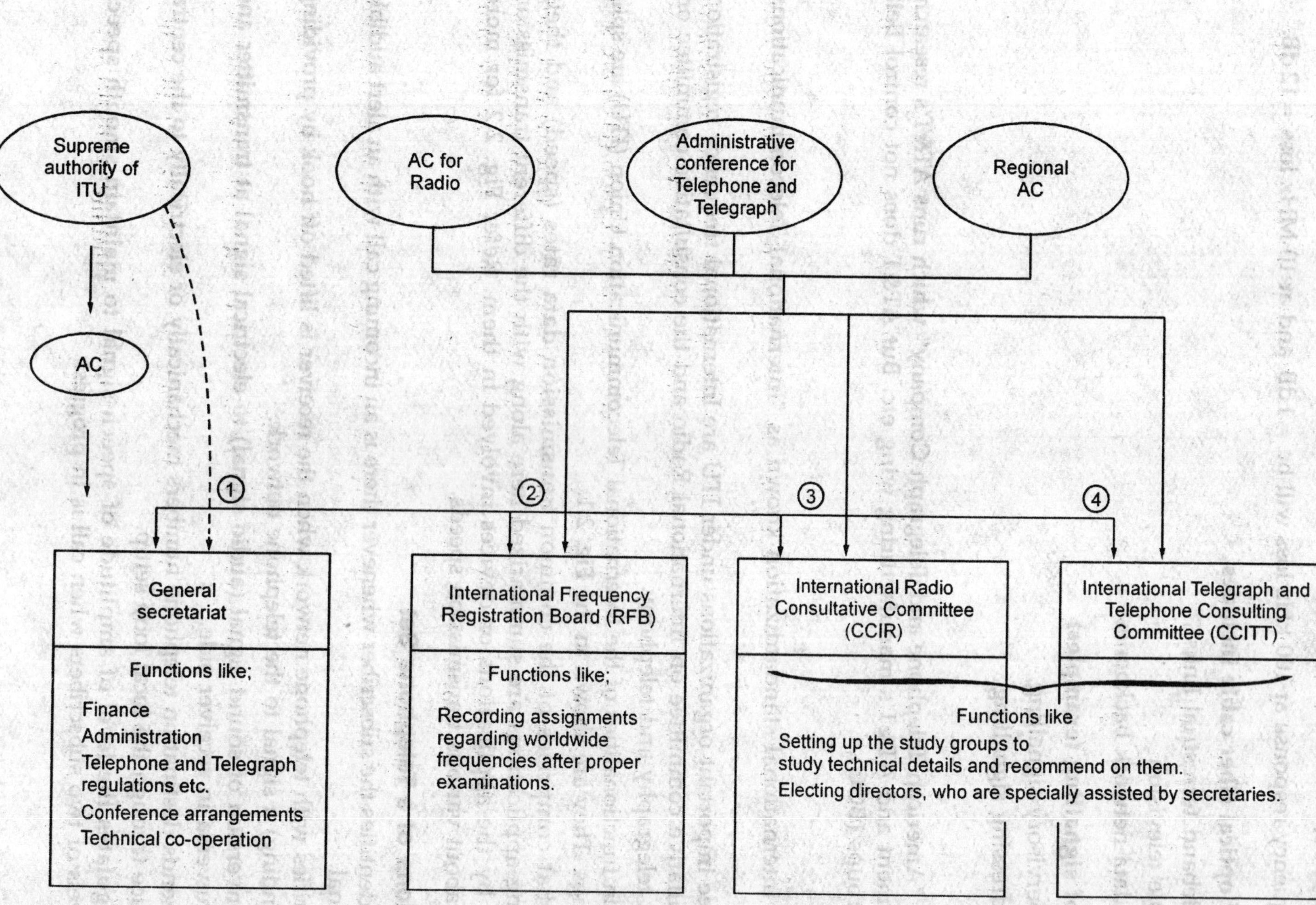

Fig. 2.1 International Telecommunications Union (ITU)—Organization and function (AC - Administrative Conference)

6. When a subscriber wants to make an outgoing call, the telephone office is alerted and 'handset lifted off hook' state verified.
7. Enables speakers to hear his own speech by taking back a small amount of speech signal and feedback to speaker so that amplitude of speech will be in a tolerable level.
8. Provides a closed circuit (busy state) and an open circuit (idle state) whenever telephone is in on/off states.
9. Enables on and off hooks, ringing, busy, dial pulses, dial tone and touch tone signals by the call progress.

2.1.2 Public Telephone Network - an Overview

For establishing telecommunication technology in early days there was many telephone companies which were independent and known as 'Public Telephone Network (PTN)'. It forms a longest form of computer network. The telephonic signals forms a pair of wires that connects two telephones with each other. Many transmission system are interconnected to form a "tandem connections" to establish a call when two parties need to communicate.

The telephone system as a whole has to facilitate three main phases.

1. Call establishment
2. Monitoring the call
3. Call termination

For providing such a bidirectional type of communication the functions involved are switching function, signalling function and transmission functions. The functionality of the above is given below.

- Switching function : It identifies and makes connection with subscribers to a particular transmission path.
- Signalling function : It supplies and also interprets the control signals and supervisory signals that are necessary to complete an operation. The public telephone network (PTN) mainly accommodates two different types of subscribers namely "private" and "public". The private line circuits are designed as specific or dedicated circuits. The private telephone companies also lease equipment and form networks and develop intended database required for them within the public telephone network. Therefore PTN can also be called as service provider. The subscribers under this PTN setup are connected through switching techniques and therefore called as Public Switched Telephone Network (PSTN).

Under cellular communication also PSTN plays a vital role. The signalling from base transceiver reaches the mobile switching center MSC (or MTSO) which is then connected to the PSTN respectively.

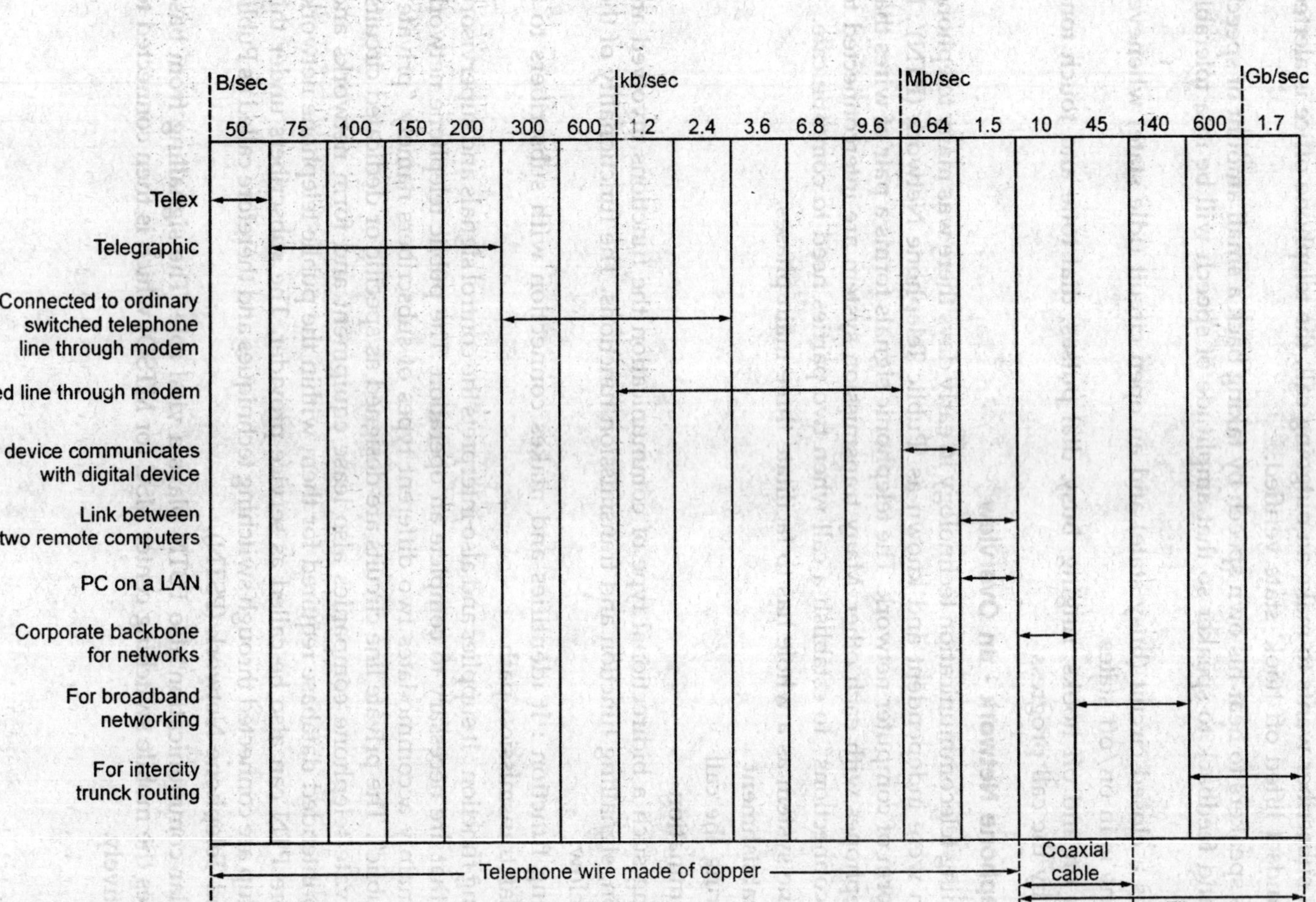

Fig. 2.2 Various transmission speeds and corresponding application areas

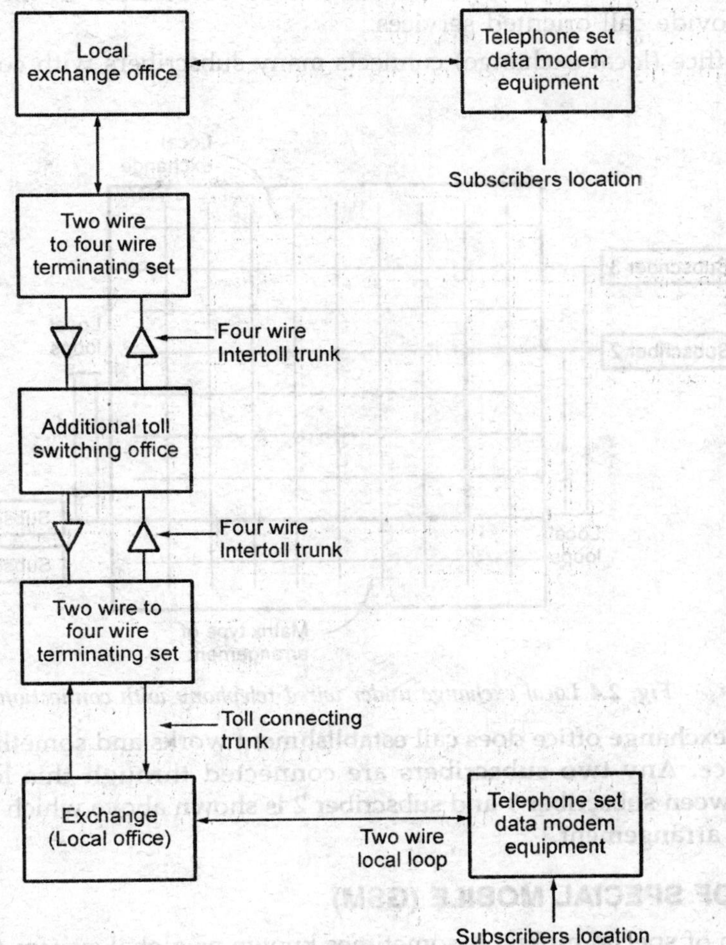

Fig. 2.3 A "Wired telephonic connection"

Whenever the subscribers are linked (connected) to a particular toll office through the toll connecting trunks, the information/message is handled with a two wire basis. A pair of wires take care of call transmission and reception functions.

The functions like, (*a*) Switching (*b*) Routing are also undertaken.

The message is connected to inter toll trunk lines through the two wire to four wire termination set. It is possible to have many toll switching offices and it depends on call origination and destination stations.

The telephone exchangers are placed with proper planning such that it can cover a large dwelling area of the subscribers. The call between two subscribers may require one or many exchanges to have a established call, but on the otherhand a call may originate and terminate within a exchange. This type of call is known as "Intraoffice" or "Intraswitch call".

The wired telecommunication hence enabled connection in the entire subscribers network to provide call oriented services.

A local office (local exchange) connects many subscribers with connections available centrally.

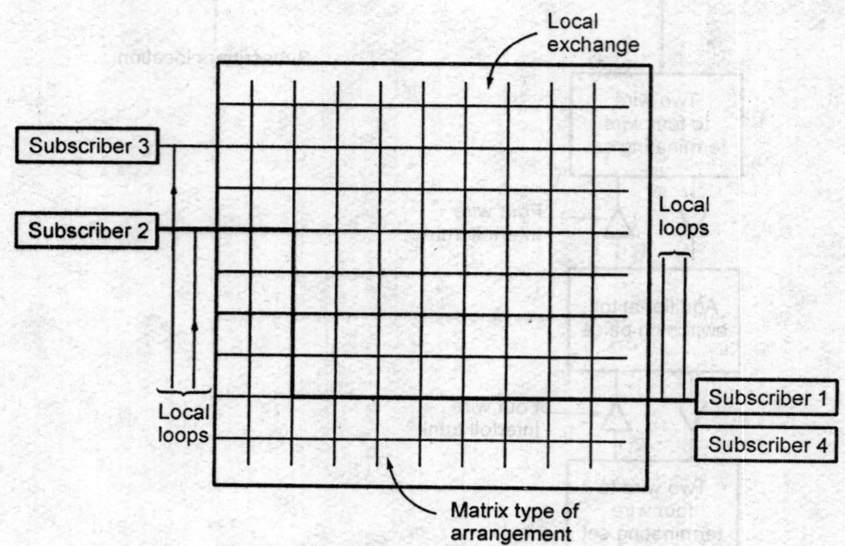

Fig. 2.4 Local exchange under wired telephony with connection

The local exchange office does call establishment works and sometimes it is also called as central office. Any two subscribers are connected through this local exchanges. A connection between subscriber 1 and subscriber 2 is shown above which resembles a simple matrix type of arrangement.

2.2 GROUP OF SPECIAL MOBILE (GSM)

The group of special mobile is sometimes known as global system for mobile and it is a second generation cellular mobile standard. Actually in 1980's many mobile systems with closer carrier frequencies under analog mobile phone systems faced many interferences and other problems, in European countries. A better approach which is a second generation digital system is the global system for mobile with acronym 'GSM'. In the age before GSM European countries used various cellular mobile standards which were not much efficient. GSM was initially functioning in 900 MHz band of frequency. The group of special mobile committee was a functioning group of CEPT. In the year of 1992 GSM modified its name to "Global system for mobile communications". The standards setting for GSM was under European Technical Standards Institute (ETSI).

In European countries GSM was first marketed in the year 1991. After two years other countries also evinced interest in this digital standard used for cellular communications technology.

The main aim of GSM was to provide 'roaming facility' for subscribers and to follow ISDN guidelines. It provides voice services that are compatible with ISDN standards.

GSM lies under second generation systems, that replaced first generation analog systems. Considering satellite uplink and downlinks, GSM was deployed using 890-915 MHz for uplinks and 935 to 960 MHz for downlink transmissions. GSM system used in United States in the band of 1900 MHz was called as personal communications services (PCS). There are many GSM solutions known as GSM 900, GSM 1800 etc.

GSM phone - functional block diagram

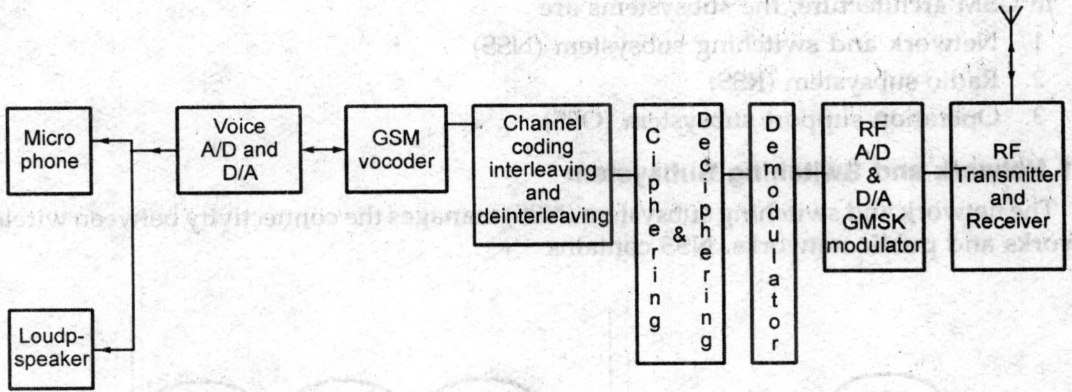

Fig. 2.5 GSM phone-functional block diagram

The global system for mobile (group of special mobile) GSM phone functional block diagram is shown above. The transceiver antenna system receives or transmits RF signal. The analog to digital conversion and digital to analog conversions are done in opposite directions depending upon transmission or reception. Microphone and loudspeakers are used in similar two directional ends.

The channel coding is done with, interleaving technique. Modulation and demodulation are done for transmission and reception. Equalization technique is also applied. Modulation scheme adopted is Gaussian minimum shift keying digital modulation. The antenna is of MIMO (Multiple Input and Multiple Output) nature. User authentication is possible with GSM phones.

Depending upon the services provided by this standard there are six important category/examples.

1. Transactional service – Shopping – Booking	2. Travelling related services – Roaming – Weather	3. Personal service – Health monitoring – Budgeting
4. Mobile office – E-mail – Modem – Fax	5. Fun – Gambling – Online games	6. Security services – Emergency calls – Alarm provisions

There are three subtopics which are important under GSM.

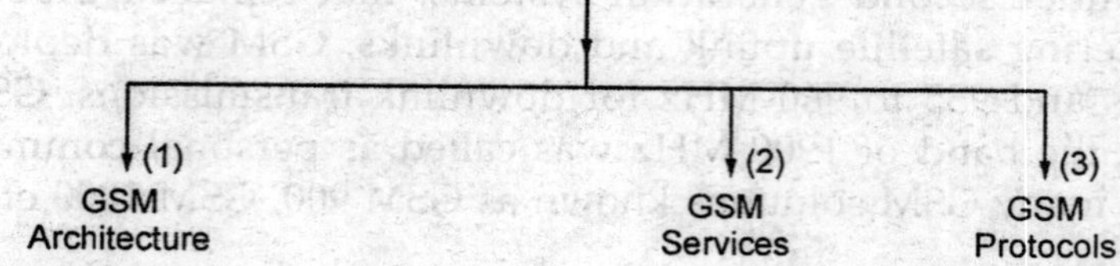

1. GSM Architecture

In GSM architecture, the subsystems are

1. Network and switching subsystem (NSS)
2. Radio subsystem (RSS)
3. Operation support subsystem (OSS)

2.2.1 Network and Switching Subsystem

The network and switching subsystem (NSS) manages the connectivity between wireless networks and public networks. NSS contains

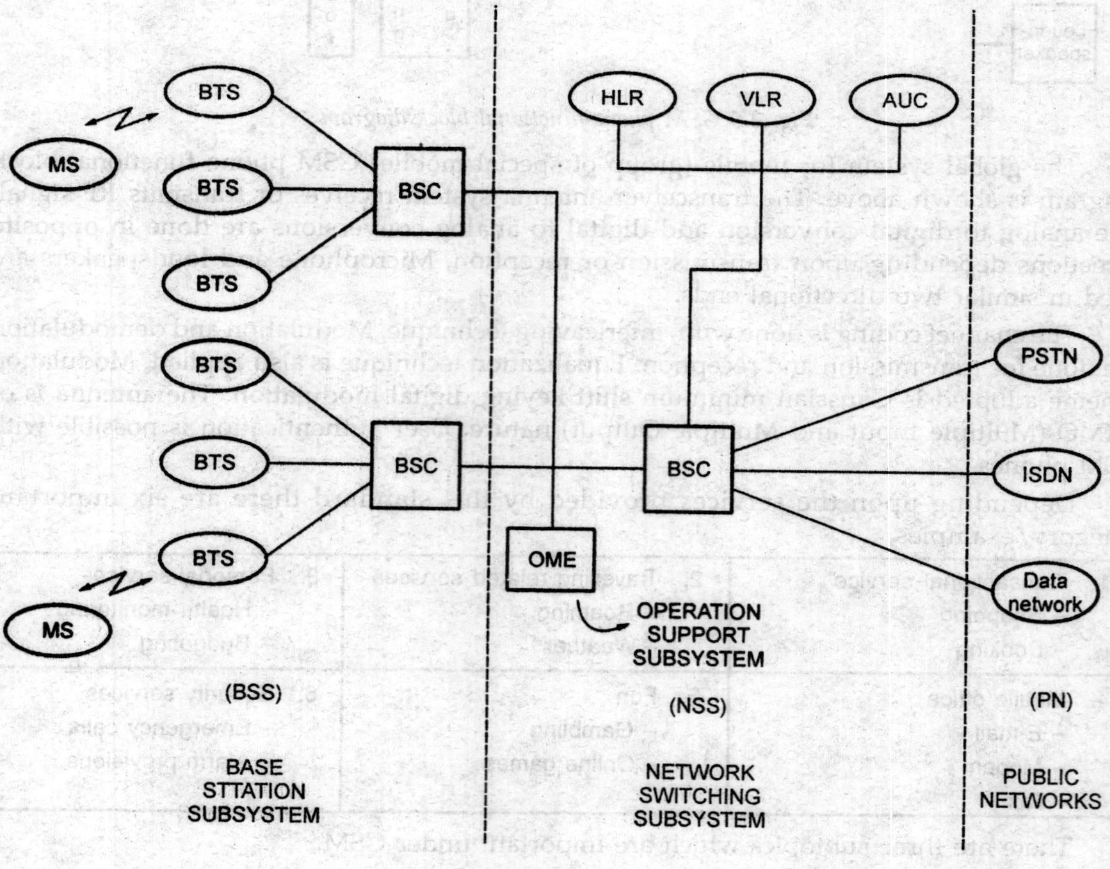

Fig. 2.6 GSM system architecture

(*i*) Mobile Services Switching Centre (MSC)
(*ii*) Home Location Register (HLR)
(*iii*) Visitor Location Register (VLR)

(*i*) Mobile Services Switching Centre (MSC)

The mobile switching centres acts as highly reliable ISDN switches. It establishes connections between BSC's and all other MSC's. A single MSC can manage many BSC's of a particular region. A typical gateway MSC is termed as GMSC and it has additional fixed networks like PSTN and ISDN.

(*ii*) Home Location Register (HLR)

The home location register is very important database used in GSM standard in the sense it consists of all user related information.

It consists of mobile subscriber ISDN number, the related services and authentication key facilities. The information regarding users (subscribers) are linked to it. HLR also involves itself with charging and accounting details of subscribers.

(*iii*) Visitor Location Register (VLR)

VLR is responsible for any visitors or new users entering the network. Whenever a new mobile subscriber (MS) enters the local area (LA) then visitor location register VLR has to take immediate action so that it copies all related information about that new user.

2.2.2 Radio Subsystem (RSS)

In GSM architecture the radio subsystem 'RSS' consists of two main parts.

(*i*) Mobile stations (*ii*) Base station subsystem

In a GSM network, it has many base station subsystems (BSS's) where each one is controlled by a base station controller called 'BSC'. It is equipped to perform all functions which are important to maintain an individual mobile station. The BSS unit also consists of many base transceiver stations BTS's.

The base station controller can manage many BTS's. It can reserve many radio frequencies, handling over functions from one base transceiver station to another base transceiver station. It can also perform paging operation of MS. The multiplexing of many radio channels onto a fixed network is possible.

The subscriber identity module termed as 'SIM' with all user related information are available with mobile station (MS). The International mobile equipment identity (IMEI) is used for identifying a mobile station in the network.

All authentication functions and specific user functions (e.g. charging) are possible only with SIM card.

Few important things contained in a SIM card are

1. Identifiers
2. Card type
3. Serial number
4. List of subscribed services

5. Personal Identity Number (PIN)
6. Authentication key (K)
7. PIN unblocking key (PUK)
8. International Mobile Subscriber Identity (IMSI)
9. Compatible with locking of SIM in case of wrong PIN (for a three time trial).

2.2.3 Operation Subsystem (OSS)

All functions related to networking operations and maintenance are done by operation subsystem. Using the SS7 signalling the OSS can access other entities also.

It consists of

(*i*) Operation and maintenance centre
(*ii*) Authentication centre (AuC)
(*iii*) Equipment identity register (EIR)

Operation and Maintenance Centre (OMC)

The functions managed by the operation and maintenance systems are

1. Traffic monitoring
2. Subscriber and security management including billing
3. Status of network entities in a report form.

OMC is subjected to the concept of TMN Telecommunication Management Network, which is standardized by ITU-T. OMC monitors and maintains each MS, BSC, BS and MSC within entire GSM system.

It is also responsible for integrity and performance of each subscriber equipment within the system.

Authentication Centre (AuC)

The user identification, protection of all user information are taken care of by authentication centre. It can also be kept safe as a part of home location register (HLR).

Equipment Identity Register (EIR)

EIR is responsible for all devices identification used in a network. It also maintains a list of stolen devices and malfunctioning devices.

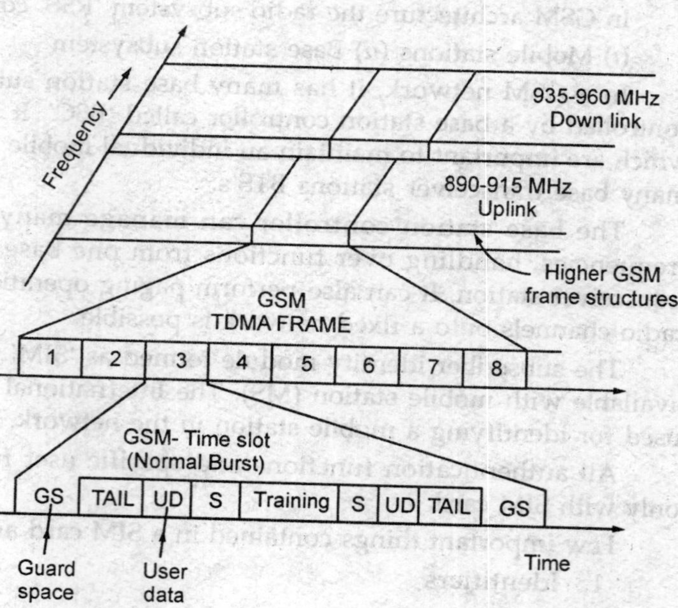

Fig. 2.7 GSM (i) TDMA frame (ii) Slots (iii) Bursts

Significance of Radio Subsystem

The frequency band used for uplink or (forward link) was 890-915 MHz and for downlink (Reverse link) was 935-960 MHz. The original frequency band for GSM was 25 MHz. The forward and reverse frequency bands are generally split into channels each with 200 kHz wide and they are known as Absolute Radio Frequency Channel Numbers (ARFCN's). It denotes forward and reverse channel pair and it is separated in the frequency of 45 MHz. TDMA concept can be used for time sharing to cover all subscribers.

Data can be transmitted as portions known as burst. It (time slot) will contain user and signalling information. The middle of the time slot of the GSM frame has the training sequence (TS) which is used to adapt the needed parameters of the receiver, and to select the strongest signal in multipath propagation environment.

2.2.4 Channels

GSM has different types of logical channels and they are separated as traffic channels and control channels.

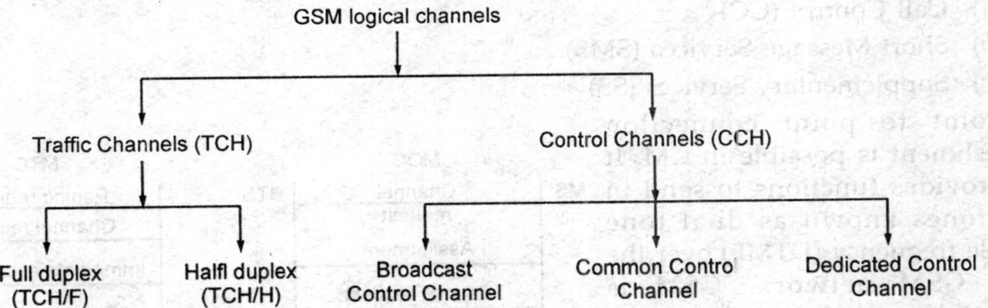

GSM uses traffic channels to transmit user data which can be voice, fax etc. This traffic channel may be full duplex or half duplex. For full duplex the data rate is 22.8 kb/sec and it is only 11.4 kb/sec in case of half duplex channels. For GSM standard a data rate of 13 kb/sec is good. If full duplex channel scheme is used 13 kb/sec is used for actual data transmission rate while the remaining is used for error correction purposes.

The control channels in GSM are responsible for mobility management.

2.2.4.1 Broadcast Control Channel

It is denoted as BCCH. It is used for signal information by Base Transceiver Station (BTS) to all MS, in a cell. There are few important channels known as frequency correction channel (FCCH), synchronization channel (SCH). The FCCH is used for frequency correction information by BTS. SCH is helpful to transmit information about time synchronization. Basically FCCH and SCH are subchannels of BCCH.

The Common Control Channel (CCCH) is related to information transferring with respect to connection setup between BS and MS, (exchanged whenever required). Whenever a call has to be setup the MS seeks help of Random access channel (EACH) for sending data to base transceiver station. All channels described so far are uridirectional. The dedicated control channels are bidirectional.

The dedicated control channels (DCCH) maintain a low data rate using stand alone dedicated control channel (SDCCH) till the MS establishes TCH with the BTS. Signalling to MS regarding usage of TCH or SDCCH for connection setups BTS makes use of access grant channel (AGCH), under common control channels. In DCCH there are SACCH and FACCH. The TCH and SDCCH has slow associated dedicated control channel (SACCH) and this channel is used for exchanging system information like signal power level and channel quality.

The channels (FACCH) are used for exchanging large amount of data in less period of time. Out of the three layers in GSM architecture the network layer plays a vital role in the sense it contains radio resource management (RR), mobility management (MM) and call management (CM).

The functions like call set, call maintenance and releasing radio channels are taken care by RR. Then registration, identification, authentication updating location, providing temporary mobile subscriber identity (TMSI replaces IMSI) are done by mobility management (MM). Finally the call management (CM) consists of three entities known as

(*a*) Call Control (CC)

(*b*) Short Message Services (SMS)

(*c*) Supplementary Services (SS)

Point to point connection establishment is possible in CM. It also provides functions to send in band tones known as dual tone multiple frequency (DTMF) over the entire GSM network. GSM is compatible with four 16 kbit/sec channels into a single channel of 64 kbit/sec and hence pulse code modulation (PCM) can be applied for GSM. For signalling operations between BSC and MSC signalling system No. 7 (SS7) is used.

The advantage of using this GSM standard is its world wide localization of users facility. The particular phone number allotted is same and unique world wide and is quite a complex free design Roaming of subscribers between two providers in one country or in different countries is possible even with different providers.

To find or locate a MS the main features required are listed below :

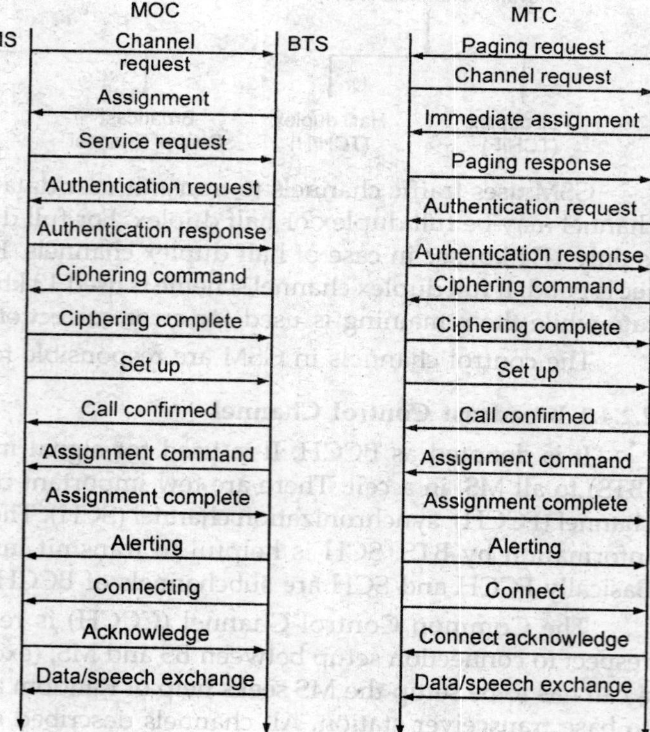

Fig. 2.8 Flow of message in MOC and MTC

(i) International Mobile Subscriber Identity (IMSI)
(ii) Mobile Station International ISDN Number (MSISDN)
(iii) Temporary Mobile Subscriber Identity (TMSI)
(iv) Mobile Station Roaming Number (MSRN)

Two opposite terms mobile terminated call (MTC) and mobile originated call (MOC) work very accurately in this network. MTC works in a situation where the calling station is outside the GSM network. MOC suits it to an environment when a call is purely initiated i.e. when MS transmits a request signal for a new connection in the GSM network.

The flow of messages for MTC and MOC under GSM are unique in nature.

In GSM network the movement of mobile station is around 250 km/hr. As the cell size is small (few km's) the faster will be the coverage done by MS.

When the mobile station moves out of the coverage range of base transceiver station (BTS) handover is a must or when traffic is very high in a cell the handover is very important.

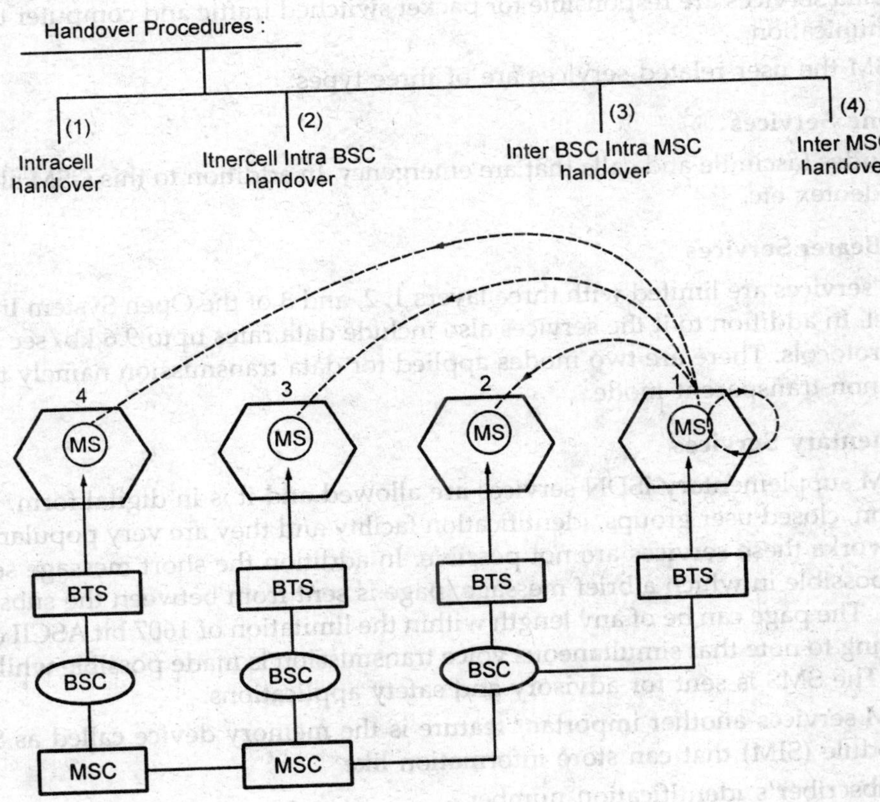

Fig. 2.9 Handover procedures

1. In Intracell handover the base station may decide to change carrier frequency while narrow band interference is high which disturbs transmission.

2. In second case though the mobile station enters another cell it is still in the proper control of BSC of cell. In this case the BSC will change handover at the new carrier frequency of that new cell.
3. In case 3, GSM has to provide some handover functions between the cells those are controlled by different BSC's. This is because the BSC's can control only limited number of cells in a network. Then the handovers has to be controlled overall by the MSC.
4. In fourth case in Inter MSC handover, the handovers may be required between different MSC's.

2.2.4.2 GSM Services

The GSM Services can be classified as

- Tele services or
- Data services The tele services are responsible for' mobile or base originated traffic.

The Data services are responsible for packet switched traffic and computer to computer data communication.

In GSM the user related services are of three types.

1. Telephone Services

It includes fascimile and calls that are emergency. In addition to this GSM also includes Teletex, Videotex etc.

2. Data or Bearer Services

These services are limited with three layers 1, 2, and 3 of the Open System Interconnect (OSI) model. In addition to it the services also include data rates upto 9.6 kb/sec and packet switched protocols. There are two modes applied for data transmission namely transparent mode and non-transparent mode.

3. Supplementary Services

In GSM supplementary ISDN services are allowed and it is in digital form. It includes call diversion, closed user groups, identification facility and they are very popular. In analog mobile networks these services are not possible. In addition the short message services are also made possible in which a brief message/page is sent from between the subscriber and base station. The page can be of any length within the limitation of 1607 bit ASCII characters. It is interesting to note that simultaneous voice transmission is made possible while a SMS is being sent. The SMS is sent for advisory and safety applications.

In GSM services another important feature is the memory device called as Subscriber Identity Module (SIM) that can store information like

(*i*) Subscriber's identification number,
(*ii*) User specific information,
(*iii*) Privacy keys, and
(*iv*) Network where the user is entitled.

This SIM is activated with a personal ID number (four digit number) and gets services from GSM phones. Only if the SIM card (or smart card) is inserted the phone will be activated or the GSM phone will be in non-operational state.

Next to SMS, SIM services in GSM an on-the-air privacy is provided in the standard that guarantees high degree of privacy by encryption at transmitter end.

2.2.4.3 Call Operation in GSM

In GSM there are two types of logical channels known as traffic channels (TCH's) and control channels (CCH's). These traffic and control channels are intended for different functions for having a call operation. Let us consider a call originating in a GSM phone. At first the broadcast channel (BCH) checks whether the subscriber unit is synchronized with the base station near by. The subscriber has to be locked on to the cellular system and it can be understood by the frequency correction, synchronization and broadcast channel messages. For making a call the user of a GSM mobile dials the numbers and sends the same by pressing the send button. Then the mobile transmits the random access channel (RACH) data and the base station responds to it with a message. The FCCH is a data burst that occupies 'TS O' of the GSM frame.

The subscriber unit monitors this 'TS O' may get its Absolute Radio Frequency Channel Number (ARFCN) and TS (time slot). Then it tunes to the ARFCN (new) and TS. These ARFCN and TS are stand alone dedicated control channels (SDCCH) and once if the user unit is tuned to it the user unit waits for the SACCH frame that tells about the timing advance and transmitter power commands. Then the BTS sends relevant value over SACCH for the mobile for further processing. Only then the user is able to send burst type messages, required for the speech traffic.

The PSTN connects the user who has dialled to the MSC and the MSC switches the correct path to the respective serving BTS. Through the base station the mobile is commanded using SDC channel for retuning to new value of ARFCN and a TS (time slot). Now the speech traffic is possible and the call is in progress.

The process is somewhat similar when it is initiated at the PSTN end. A PCH is broadcast at first. The mobile unit once receives the page information it acknowledges the same with a random access message. The mobile station is locked to the same ARFCN said previously.

The base station assigns new physical channel to the mobile unit for having connection to SDCCH and SACCH.

The subscriber/user establishes the timing advance and the authentication on the SDCCH. Then the base station gives a new physical channel assignment for the mobile over the SDCCH. The TCH assignment is thus made. The call from the mobile phone or from the PSTN is originated and with the help of different channels in GSM the call operation is developed in the cellular system.

2.2.5 Security in GSM

The degree of security in GSM is higher with respect confidentiality information in subscriber identity module (SIM) and authentication centre (AuC). Any unauthorized trial will be disabled and a PIN is maintained in this aspect.

1. Confidentiality

To maintain confidentiality encryption and decryption techniques are used. The information about user (subscriber) is encrypted. Only an authorized person can decrypt it.

2. Encryption

All information that are user related are encrypted. This ensures more privacy from the point of subscribers. If authentication process is over the base transceiver station and mobile station can work with proper encryption by using cipher key say 'K_c'. The subscriber identity module (SIM), MS and the network calculate the same key 'K_c' which is based on a particular random value and the key itself is not transmitted. The cipher key 'K_c' is not generated using an individual key 'K_i', but generated using some random value with a particular algorithm intended for this purpose. The base transceiver station (BTS) and the mobile station (MS) can encrypt at one end and decrypt at the other end. For example cipher key of 64 bits, is used.

3. Authentication

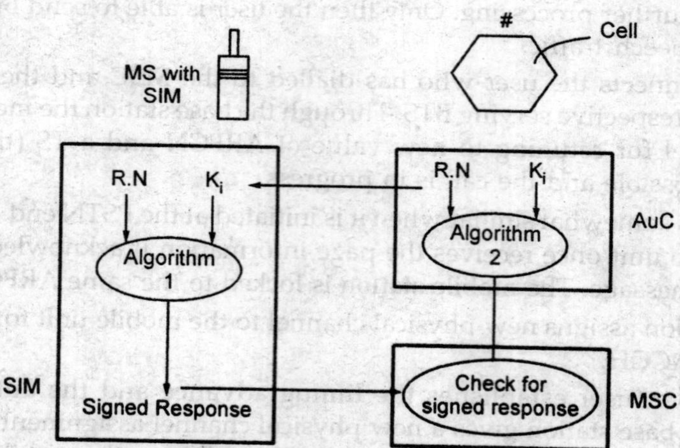

Fig. 2.10 Subscriber (user) authentication

Users can opt for any type of service that a GSM network can offer. The authentication is based on the SIM card that stores user related information. A random number (R.N) and authentication key (K_i) along with the specific algorithm is used for developing user authentication.

The access control generates a random number (R.N) and the SIM provides a signed response where authentication centre (AuC) does the basic generation of random values random number R.N, signed response and secret key 'K_c'. Ultimately this is sent to home location register (HLR). The visitor location register VLR sends random number R.N to the SIM where the subscriber and network does the same type of functions. When both match, the VLR will accept the subscriber (new) or simply it will reject it and hence higher user authentication is made possible in GSM networks.

Comparison of IS136, IS95 and GSM standards [2G standards].

Table 2.1 Comparison of second generation mobile telephone systems

Parameter	IS136	IS95	GSM
Year 1991	1993	1990	
Type of access	TDMA	CDMA	TDMA
Spacing between forward and reverse channels	45 MHz	45 MHz	45 MHz
Bandwidth of channel	30 kHz	1250 kHz	200 kHz
Maximum power of mobile unit	3 W	0.2 W	20 W
Number of users per channels	3	35	8
Base station transmission band	869 MHz to 894 MHz	869 MHz to 894 MHz	935 to 960 MHz
Carrier signal bit rate	48.9 kbps	9.6 kbps	270.8 kbps
Bit rate of speech code	8 kbps	8/4/2/1 kbps	13 kbps
Frame size	40 msec	20 msec	4.6 ms

2.2.6 GSM Codecs (Encoder and Decoder)

2.2.6.1 GSM Encoder

The GSM codec block diagram is shown in Fig. 1.15.

There are four processing units available in the GSM encoder. They are

(*i*) Pre-Processing (PP).

(*ii*) Short-Term Prediction (STP).

(*iii*) Long-Term Prediction (LTP).

(*iv*) Regular Pulse Excitation (RPE).

At first the sequence of speech signal is pre-emphasized and they are ordered into many segments each with 20 msec duration. Then they are hamming windowed. This process is followed by second process of STP. In short-term prediction filtering the Logarithmic Area Ratios (LAR) of the corresponding reflection co-efficients x_n (k) are found. But the LAR parameters have different dynamic range values and probability distribution function. Also same number of bits for transmission are not used for all of them.

The LAR parameters can be decoded by LPC inverse filter for reducing error l_n.

In third processing phase namely LTP analysis calculation of pitch period t_n and gain value g_n are found so as to minimize LTP residual r_n.

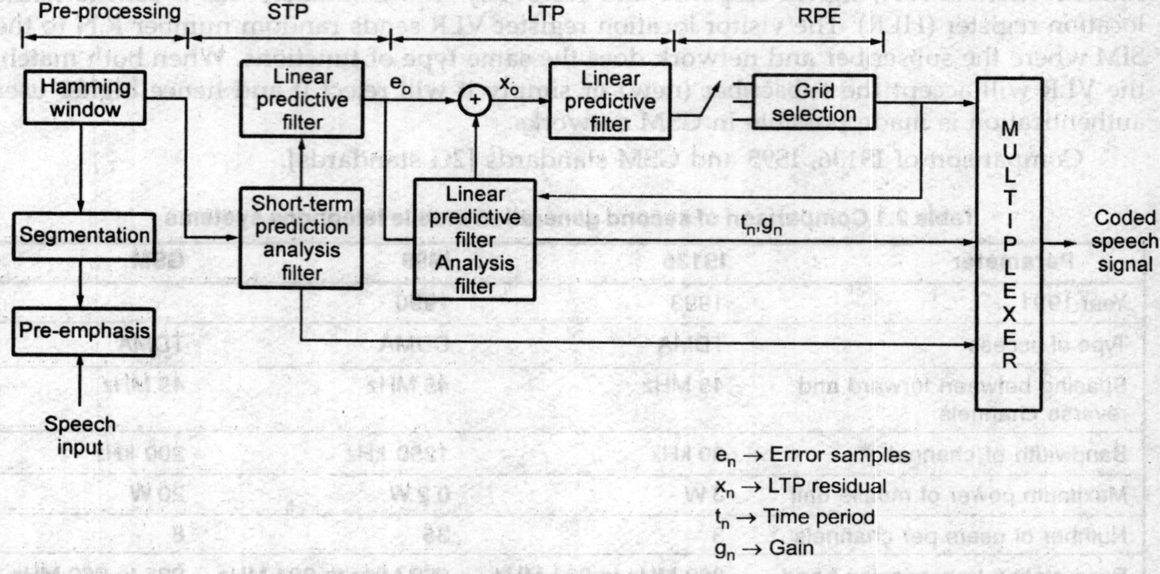

Fig. 2.11 Block diagram of GSM coder

In speech coding era the GSM codec is very popular. The original speech coder that is used in European digital cellular standards was Regular Pulse Excited Long-Term Prediction (RPE-LTP) codec unit. When compared to all other speech codecs RPE-LTP was found to be a better codec after conducting many tests. This codec provides a bit rate of 13 kB/sec. The advantages of using the RELP codec and multi-pulse excited long term prediction (MPE-LTP) codec were combined in the RPE-LTP codec. The RELP was French proposed and the MPE-LTP was proposed by Germany.

2.2.6.2 Comparison of RELP and MPE-LTP Codecs

RELP codec	MPE-LTP codec
Provides good quality speech.	Produces excellent speech quality.
Liable to noise generation.	Has high complexity and not completely affected by bit error in the channel.

Also by adding a long term prediction loop with the RELP codec the main features of MPE-LTP codec can be incorporated into RELP and at the same time the bit rate can be reduced from 14.7 kB/sec to 13.0 kB/sec without quality degradation.

A simple block diagram of a GSM coder and decoder are discussed below.

To reduce the value of x_n, it is important to find pitch extraction which is done by LTP just by calculating the delay (d) value. It may maximize the cross-correlation available between present short-term predicted error sample l_n and a sample previous to it say e_{n-d}.

Hence the gain g_n and extracted pitch value t_n in LTP analysis are transmitted and then encoded at a data rate of 3.6 kB/sec. Finally the LTP residual 'x_n' is weighted and then decomposed into three excitation sequences and their energies are carefully analyzed to find the one with highest energy level and represented as LTP residual 'x_n'. Then pulses in excitation sequence are given a sequence of treatments mentioned below.

(*i*) Normalized to maximum amplitude.

(*ii*) Quantized.

After quantization they are transmitted at a data rate of 9.6 kB/sec.

2.2.6.3 GSM Decoder

In the GSM speech decoder block diagram there are four main operations performed which are reverse to that of GSM speech encoder sequence of operations.

The excitation signal is received by the decoder unit. The four operations done in GSM decoder are given below.

(*i*) RPE decoding

(*ii*) LTP synthesis filtering

(*iii*) STP synthesis filtering

(*iv*) Post-processing

The excitation parameters are decoded in the RPE decoder and then sent to LTP synthesis filter where the long-term signal is synthesized by using the gain and extracted pitch values g_n, x_n. These RPE decoder and LTP synthesis are first and second processing steps. In the third processing step of STP synthesis phase the reflection coefficients x_n are used to generate the original speech signal which was the input of GSM encoder unit.

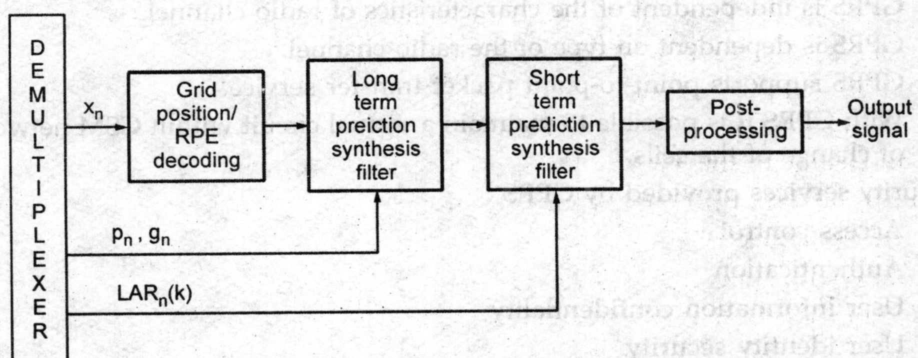

Fig. 2.12 Block diagram of GSM decoder

2.2.6.4 Bit-ordering Scheme

In the GSM coder output, every 260 bits are properly ordered with respect to their importance into different groups of 50, 132 and 78 bits each. Each of these groups of bits are named as below.

Bits in the first group (50-bits) → "Ia bits"

Bits in the second group (132-bits) → "Ib bits"

Bits in last group (78-bits) → "II bits"

Note : In these above categories mentioned the first group (50-bits group) of bits contribute more important speech information and hence Cyclic Redundancy Check (CRC) bits are appended with them for protection. The two groups Ia and Ib bits are convolutionally encoded for the Forward Error Correction (EEC) scheme.

The last group (II bits) of bits are of less important and generally they are not provided with error correction (or) detection.

2.3 GENERAL PACKET RADIO SERVICE (GPRS).

The General packet radio service (GPRS) provides efficient packet mode of data transfer. GPRS is popular because it provides a cost effective packet services supporting Internet applications.

GPRS allows other services like,

- Unicast
- Multicast and
- Broadcast

The important concepts of GPRS are :

(*i*) The GSM system is capable of allocation time slots [from one to eight] in a time division multiplexing access frame for the GPRS radio channels.

(*ii*) Demand based time slot allocation.

(*iii*) Depending on a coding technique it is possible to have data rate up to 150 kbps with GPRS.

(*iv*) The maximum data rate is not limited by GPRS.

(*v*) GPRS is independent of the characteristics of radio channel.

(*vi*) GPRS is dependent on type of the radio channel.

(*vii*) GPRS supports point-to-point packet transfer service.

(*viii*) With GPRS it is possible to maintain a virtual circuit within GSM network in case of change of the cells.

Security services provided by GPRS :

1. Access control
2. Authentication
3. User information confidentiality
4. User identity security

Reliability classes possible in GPRS (as per ETSI) :

Reliability Class	Service Data Unit (SOU)	SOU Probability Probability	Duplicate SDU
1	10^{-2}	10^{-2}	10^{-5}
2	10^{-4}	10^{-6}	10^{-5}
3	10^{-9}	10^{-9}	10^{-9}

GPRS provides many services without restricting data rates of transmission. The service precedence namely high, low, normal, reliability class, throughput and delay are determined by Q_OS profile. The delay in GPRS is mainly due to transmission delay and channel access delay in the network and GPRS does not append additional delay. Many security services like user authentication, access control, user information confidentiality, user identity confidentiality are enabled with GPRS. There are also two important network elements available that plays a vital role in performance of GPRS.

They are GPRS support nodes called as GSN. There are many interfaces available for flexibility and system efficiency. The gateway GPRS support node acts between GPRS network and external packet data networks (PDN). The CGSN is connected to other external networks like X.25 standard.

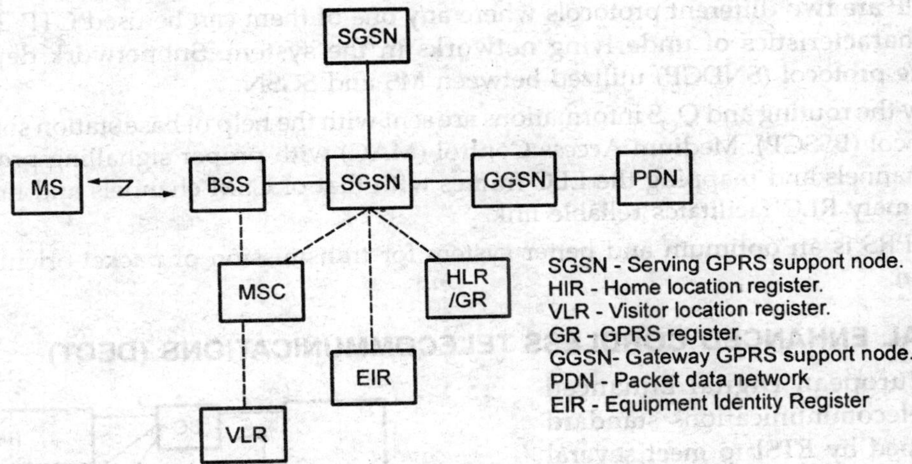

Fig. 2.13 'GPRS'-General packet radio service architecture

The General Packet Radio Service (GPRS) facilitates packet mode transfer for specific applications. This scheme involves a fully packet oriented data transmission.

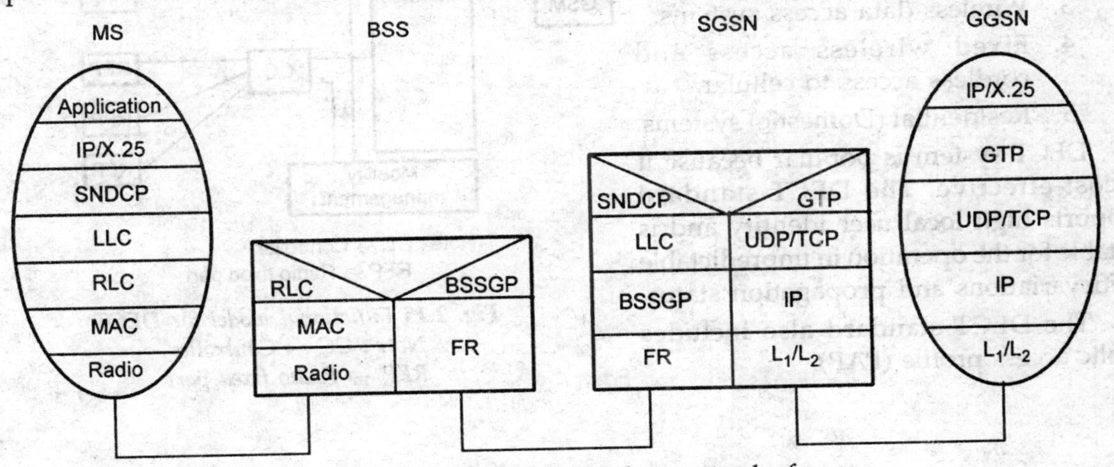

Fig. 2.14 GPRS - Transmission plane protocol-reference

For GPRS the GSM scheme allots between one and eight time slots within a TDMA frame structure. Demand assignment of time slots is possible and hence flexibility is high with GPRS. Fixed and preassigning of TDMA time slots is not a must. Point to point packet transfer service is allowed in GPRS which enables maintaining circuits in GSM network. A data rate of 150 kb/sec is generally met. The GPRS concept is not dependent on channel characteristics.

The data packets are transmitted from the PDN through the SGSN and GGSN which is directed to MS finally via BSS. The proper procedures of mobility management are also met. For data encryption purpose, a temporal identifier Temporal Logical Link Identity (TLLI) and a Ciphering Key Sequence Number (CKSN) are used. In GPRS transmission plane protocol structure, using the GPRS tunnelling protocol (GTP) all data transfer are done within GPRS (between GSN's). The reliable protocol TCP or non-reliable protocol namely UDP are two different protocols where any one of them can be used GTP. To adopt different characteristics of underlying networks in the system. Subnetwork dependent convergence protocol (SNDCP) utilized between MS and SGSN.

Mainly the routing and Q_OS informations are sent with the help of base station subsystem GPRS protocol (BSSGP). Medium Access Control (MAC) with proper signalling procedures for radio channels and mapping the LLC frames with that of GSM channels and radio link protocol namely RLC facilitates reliable link.

The GPRS is an optimum and better system for transmission of packet-oriented data transmission.

2.4 DIGITAL ENHANCED CORDLESS TELECOMMUNICATIONS (DECT)

This European Digital Enhanced Cordless Telecommunications standard was developed by ETSI to meet several applications. Some of them are,

1. Small business systems.
2. Large business systems.
3. Wireless data access systems.
4. Fixed wireless access and cordless access to cellular.
5. Residential (Domestic) systems.

DECT system is popular because it is cost-effective. The DECT standard supports high local user identity and is suitable for the operation in unpredictable trafficvariations and propagation status.

The DECT standard also includes public access profile (PAP).

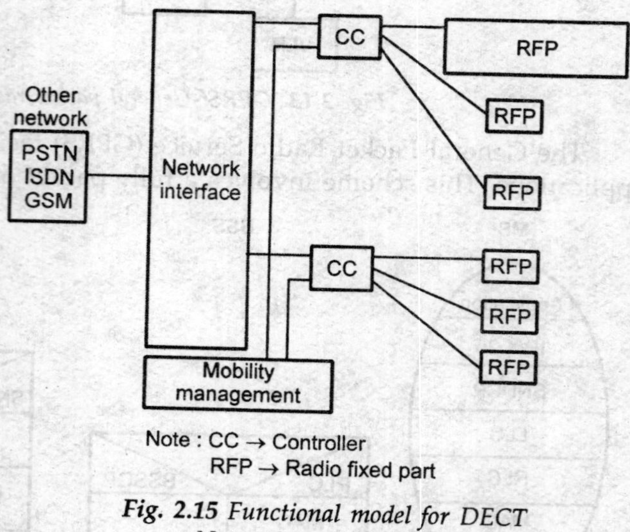

Fig. 2.15 Functional model for DECT
Note : CC → Controller
RFP → Radio fixed part

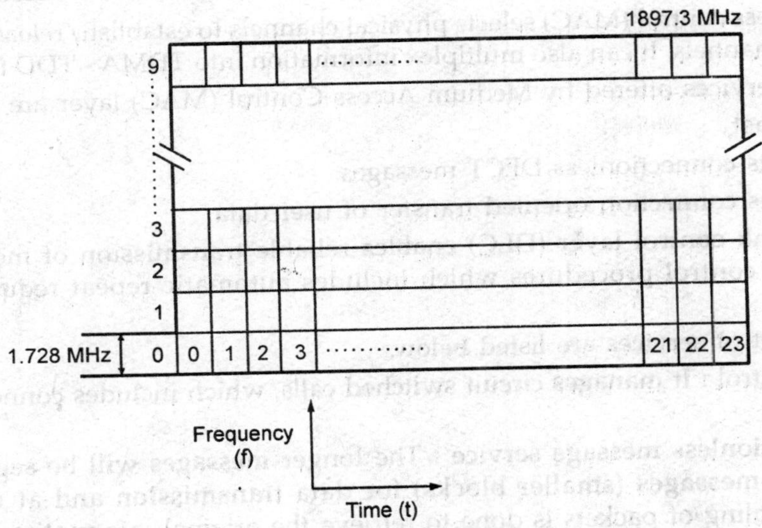

Fig. 2.16 Radio channel structure of DECT

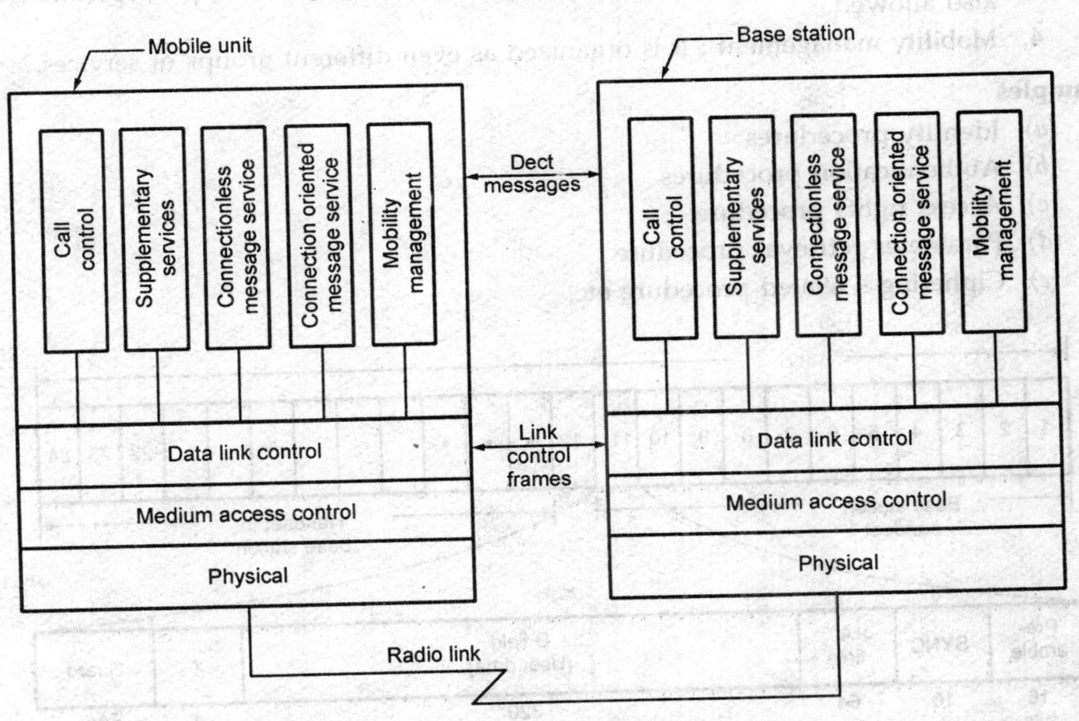

Fig. 2.17 DECT protocol architecture

The protocol architecture which supports DECT operations is shown above. The modulation method used is Gaussian filtered FSK with a frequency deviation of 288 kHz. It resembles Gaussian minimum shift keying (GMSK) technique. The data rate is 1.15 Mbps.

The medium access control (MAC) selects physical channels to establish/release connections on the selected channels. It can also multiplex information into TDMA - TDD frames format.

The three services offered by Medium Access Control (MAC) layer are :

1. Broadcast
2. Supports connectionless DECT messages.
3. Supports connection oriented transfer of user data.

The Data link control layer (DLC) enables reliable transmission of messages using proper data link control procedures which includes automatic repeat request and error detection.

The other set of services are listed below.

1. Call control : It manages circuit switched calls, which includes connection setup/ release.
2. Connectionless message service : The longer messages will be segmented into smaller messages (smaller blocks) for data transmission and at receiver side reassembling of packets is done to retrieve the original information.
3. Supplementary services : Services independent of calls that support operations are also allowed.
4. Mobility management : It is organized as even different groups of services.

Examples

(*a*) Identity procedures
(*b*) Authentication procedures
(*c*) Access rights procedure
(*d*) Parameter retrieval procedure
(*e*) Ciphering - related procedure etc.

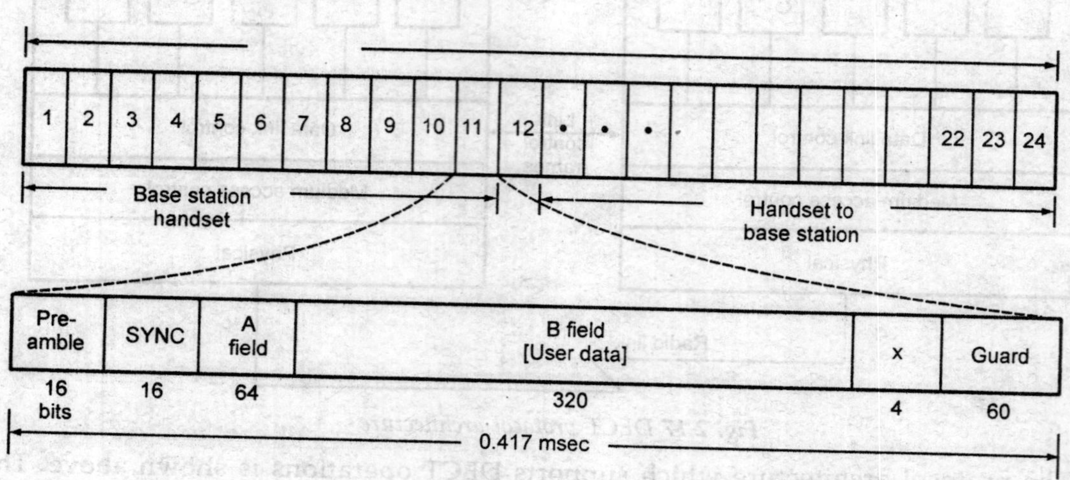

Fig. 2.18 Frame and time slot formats in DECT format

The Time Division Multiplexing (TDMA/TDD) frame format is shown above. Each (single) frame occupies 10 msec consisting of 24 TDMA time slots. For example 12 time slots may define 12 logical channels, in forward direction. (Transmission from base station to handset) where rest of the 12 time slots for reverse direction (Transmission from handset to base station).

A carrier (single carrier) supports 12 full duplex. That is 12 time slots for forward direction which is followed by 12 time slots in the reverse direction.

A single time slot consists of six fields.

1. Preamble (16 bits)
2. Synchronization (Sync = 16 bits)
3. A field (64 bits)
4. B field (320 bits)
5. Guard (G = 60 bits)
6. X field (4 bits)

The 'A' field is used for network control and the 'B' field contains user data. The 'X' field has four parity checking bits that enables base stations and terminals to monitor the quality of transmission.

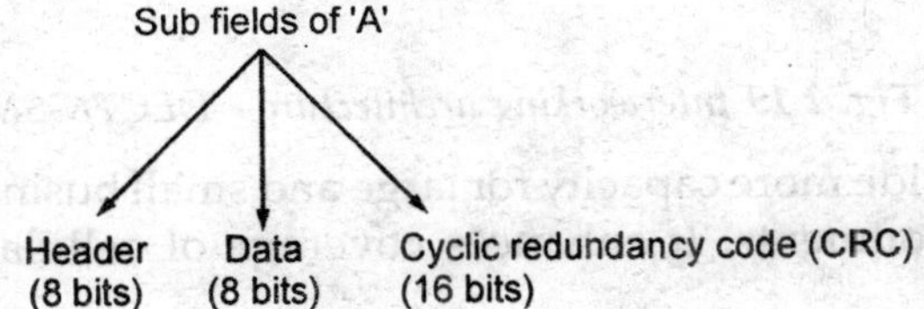

Some of the DECT specifications are listed below :

Parameter	DECT
Frequency Band	1.88 GHz to 1.9 GHz
Access scheme	TDD/TDMA/TDMA schemes
Bandwidth	20 MHz
Number of carriers	10
Handoff	Possible
Speech rate	32 kbps
Speech coding method	ADPCM
Modulation (keying technique)	GFSK (Gaussian FSK)
Mean output power level	10 mW
Maximum cell radius	30 m to 100 m
Transmission data rate	1.152 Mbps

2.4.1 DECT/GSM Interworking Network

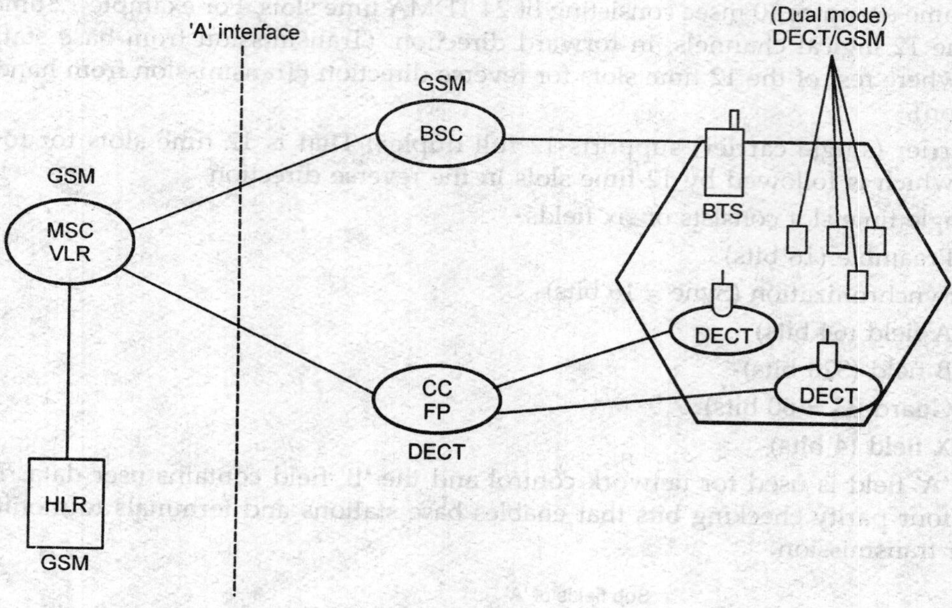

Fig. 2.19 Interworking architecture - DECT/GSM

DECT can also provide more capacity for large and small business (PPX and key systems) and public access environments. It enhances coverage of cellular mobile. It requires few specifications like,

1. Protocol descriptions and access mapping
2. Service description and provision
3. Implementation of GSM - supplementary services
4. Interconnection of DECT fixed part (portion) and GSM - MSC through interface 'A' as in diagram. The mobility is limited to coverage area.

2.5 IMT-2000 AND UMTS

Introduction

For development of mobile technologies the International Telecommunication Union (ITU), invited proposals for Radio Transmission Technologies (RTT) for International Mobile Telecommunications IMT-2000 system. The IMT-2000 is a worldwide expanded communication system and it provided a path for terminal and user mobility technologies. It also included various environments such as vehicles, indoor use, satellites and also pedestrians etc. The novel IMT-2000 system utilized the frequency bands 1885-2025 and 2110-2200 MHz ranges.

Later the European proposal for this IMT-2000 which is prepared by ETS is termed as Universal Mobile Telecommunications Systems (UMTS). An intended proposal for radio interface RTT is namely UMTS terrestrial radio access (UTRA). This scheme was formulated roughly around 1998.

An enhancement of GSM towards UMTS is nothing but enhanced data rates for the GSM evolution .

2.5.1 UMTS - an Overview

The European proposal for IMT-2000 is called as Universal Mobile Telecommunication System (UMTS). It. made a big revolution in the third generation era. The group of special mobile (GSM) enhancement towards UMTS is often known as "EDGE" technology which stands for enhanced data rates are upto 384 kbits/sec using 200 kHz wide carrier with same frequencies as that of GSM. The basic structure of UMTS comprises of user equipment, radio network subsystem and core network. UMTS supports FDD and TDD modes. The FDD mode for UTRA uses the wideband CDMA (W-CDMA) with direct sequence spread spectrum (DSSS) scheme. Hence the up and downlinks under FDD uses different frequencies. The uplink carrier is around 1920 to 1980 MHz.

GSM also fits itself into ETSI and termed as global multimedia mobility (GMM). UMTS provides different services such as :

1. Real time services
2. Bearer services
3. Non real time services
4. Circuit and packet switched methods of transmissions.

2.5.2 UMTS - Architecture

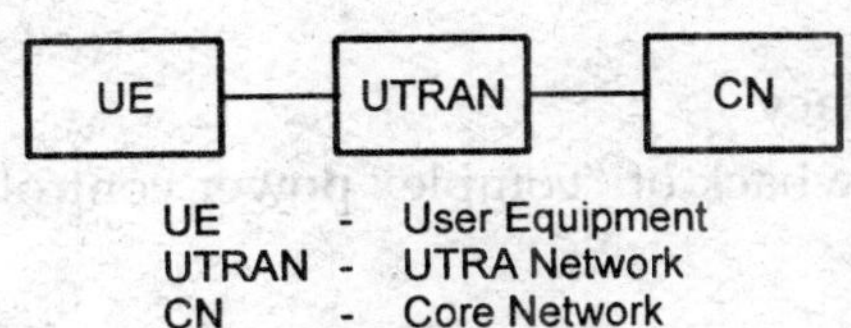

Fig. 2.20 UMTS - architecture

The UTRA network called as 'UTRAN' enables cell level mobilities and it has many radio network subsystems (RNS). The main functions of RNS is listed below.

1. Call handover control
2. Channel ciphering and deciphering
3. Radio resource management

In the architecture of UMTS, the user equipment (UE) is connected to core network 'CN' via UTRAN block.

Functions like

1. Gateways to other (external) networks
2. Inter system handover are handled by core network.

There are two-types of modes compatible with UTRA system

(*a*) UTRA FDD mode

(*b*) UTRA TDD mode.

The wideband CDMA namely W-CDMA is used for UTRA FDD and up and downlinks use separate frequencies. FDD mode can provide 250 channels (approx), for handling user traffic; (e.g. voice channel facility). Direct sequence spread spectrum (DS) coding is compatible and data rate of 2 Mbits/sec can be achieved here. Many logical and physical channels can be assigned. User data (from layer two and higher layer) is sent over uplink dedicated physical data channel (uplink DPDCH) and in UTRA, the FDD mode makes use of wideband CDMA (W-CDMA) along with direct sequence spreading (DSS). The mobile uplink frequency range is from 1920 MHz to 1980 MHz and the downlink frequency used by base station is from 2110 MHz to 2170 MHz. It is possible to accommodate 250 channels approximately with this specified frequency spectrum range. Like GSM, in UTRA technology there are logical and physical channels available for the users. In uplink the uplink dedicated physical data channel (uplink DPDCH) is used to transport user data/information. The uplink dedicated physical control channel (uplink DPCCH) is used in transport layer to control data (like data used for controlling power).

The control data from mobile station is carried by physical random access channel (PRACH) for random access purposes.

In downlink case the user data/information and control data from layer one are carried by downlink dedicated physical channel (DPCH downlink). The chip rate may be 4.096 Mchip/sec and it may be extended for different applications in future upto 16.384 Mchip/sec.

The modulation scheme used is QPSK. CDMA technique which is compatible with UTRA has many features like,

(*i*) Localization of mobile stations.

(*ii*) Soft handovers.

(*iii*) High degree of accuracy.

CDMA scheme has a drawback of "complex power control" during a "call progress".

2.5.3 UTRA - TDD mode

The time division duplexing mode of the UTRA technology makes use of wideband TDMA/CDMA for the medium access and the up/down links uses the same frequency. The data rate is 2 Mbit/sec for about 120 channels (approx) in case of the user traffic. The direct sequence (DSS) type of spreading code is applied and the modulation scheme used is QPSK. In TDD the power controlling can be slower than the FDD because the number of power controlling cycles in one second are less. It is worth noting that the frame structures of FDD and TDD are same and hence both the schemes can coexist in necessary conditions.

2.6 SATELLITE COMMUNICATION - BASICS

Definition - Satellite

The satellite is also called as a space craft or a secondary body that revolves around the earth or primary body. It follows the Keplers laws which governs the two different bodies (primary and secondary) which interact in space through gravitation.

There are many types of satellites operating with different frequencies. For example communication satellites are launched for communication related applications (say mobile satellites for mobile communications).

According to the different frequency bands the satellite services will vary.

The two related tabulations can be shown for general and different frequency band assignments with respect to the applications.

2.6.1 Important terminologies in Satellite Communication

Satellite

Satellite is an artificial body (or secondary body) revolves around the earth which is a primary body.

Uplink

It is a link where transmission of signals from the earth to the satellite take place.

Downlink

It is a link where transmission of signals from satellite to earth take place.

Transponder

It is available in satellite and is used to convert the uplink signal received to the downlink signal form.

Orbit

It is a path taken by the satellite while rotating around the earth.

Equatorial orbit

It is an orbit taken just above the earth's equator.

Earth station

It is the ground station where the transceiver antenna and other equipment are available for the satellite.

Types of orbits

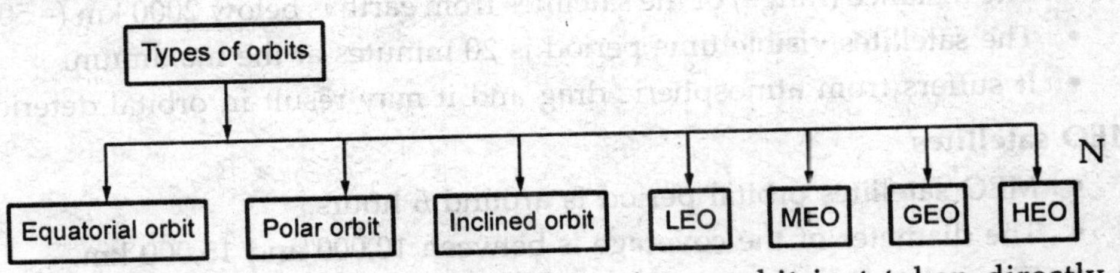

- An equatorial orbit as mentioned above is an orbit just taken directly above the earth's equator line.
- A polar orbit is an orbit that passes through both the poles of the earth.
- All the orbits that do not pass through the earth's poles are said to be "inclined orbits".
- Low earth orbit (LEO) : The low earth orbit is closer to earth and the range is below 2000 km only. Iridium satellites are also known as big LEO satellites.

- Medium earth orbit (MEO) : It is an orbit with range from earth is approximately from 5000 km to 12,000 km. MEO satellites lies in this orbit and also MEO stays between LEO and GEO.
- Geostationary orbit (GEO) : It is an orbit where the range is above 10,000 km from the earth. The satellite in this orbit rotates with the same velocity as that the earth's speed of rotation around sun. Since both the speeds of revolution are nearly equal this GEO satellites are assumed to be in stationary position from the earth. GEO satellites are well suited for communication purposes and they are also called as "communication satellites".

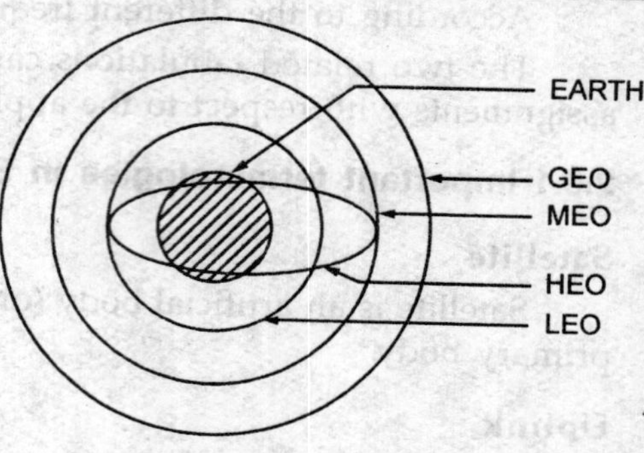

Fig. 2.21 Important satellite orbits

- Highly elliptical orbit (HEO) : HEO lies between MEO and LEO or MEO and GEO. It can provide coverage beyond the 76 degrees, and higher propagation delay. HEO is used for high attitude regions for satellite communication.

Note :

(*i*) Iridium system is an example for big LEO satellite system.

(*ii*) 'ORBCOMM' satellites are example for little LEO satellite system. 'ORBCOMM' represents an orbital communication system.

2.6.2 Characteristics of MEO and LEO Satellites

1. LEO satellites

- The orbital period lies between 1.5 to 2 hours.
- The diameter of the satellite coverage is approximately 8000 km.
- The propagation delay is lesser than 20 msec time period.
- The distance (range) of the satellites from earth is below 2000 km (– 500 to 1500km).
- The satellites visible time period is 20 minutes at the maximum.
- It suffers from atmospheric drag and it may result in orbital deterioration.

2. MEO satellites

- MEO satellites orbital period is around 6 hours.
- The diameter of the coverage is between 10,000 and 15,000 km.
- The signal propagation delay is lesser than 50 msec.
- The satellites visibility remains for few hours when viewed from earth. MEO satellites need more number of handoff s than the LEO satellites.

Merits of LEO satellites

LEO satellites provide

- Low propagation delay.
- Better coverage.
- Lower path loss.

- Frequency spectrum is used efficiently.
- Position determination.
- Less complexity than other system.
- Operation range below 2000 km (approx).

Merits of MEO satellites

MEO satellites provide

- Global coverage.
- Operation range below 12000 km (approx).
- Medium propagation delay.
- Robust in nature.
- Minimum path loss.

Demerits of LEO satellites

- It requires long period of deployment.
- Defective satellites have to be replaced regularly.
- Routing mechanisms are complex.
- Range is a constraint.
- Large numbers of satellites are required for its function.

2.6.3 Characteristics of different satellite configuration

Sr. No.	Characteristics	Satellite type		
		GEO	MEO	LEO
1.	Satellite visibility	24 hours	2-4 hours	10-20 minutes
2.	Altitude range	36,000 km	10,000 to 20,000 km	500-2000 km
3.	Round-trip delay	500 msec	40-80 msec	5-10 msec.
4.	Satellite life time	20-30 years	10-15 years	4-8 years
5.	Constellation cost of satellite	Low	Medium	High

2.6.4 Main services provided by satellite

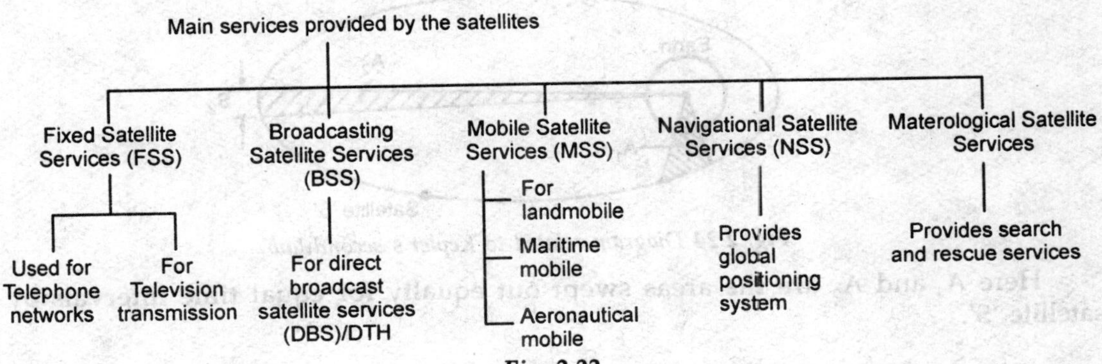

Fig. 2.22

2.6.5 Fundamental laws governing the satellite

The satellites are governed by Kepler's laws of planetary motion. There are three laws.

(*i*) Kepler's first law

It states that the path followed by a satellite around primary will be an ellipse.

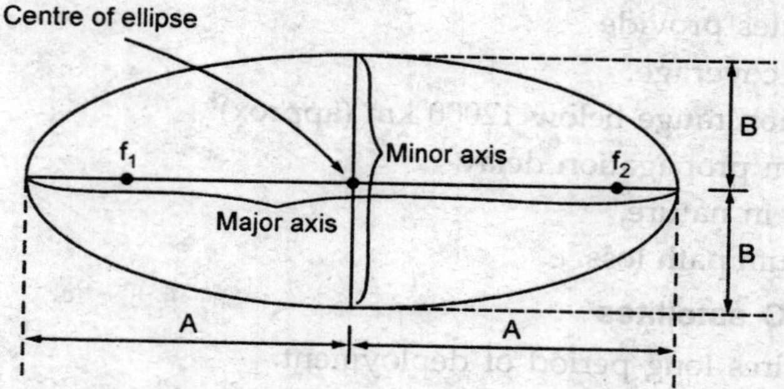

Fig. 2.23 Ellipse related to Kepler's first law

In this diagram f_1 and f_2 are the two focal points. 'A' denotes semimajor axis and 'B' denotes semiminor axis.

The value of eccentricity (e) is given as,

$$e = \frac{\sqrt{A^2 - B^2}}{A}$$

The eccentricity (e) and the semimajor axis (A) are two of the satellites orbital parameters.

Conditions :

1. Whenever eccentricity lies between 0 and 1, $0 < e < 1$ the orbit is said to be elliptical.
2. Whenever eccentricity is equal to 0 ($e = 0$), the orbit is said to be circular.

(*ii*) Kepler's Second Law

It states that for equal time intervals a satellite will sweep out equal areas in its orbital plane focussed at the barycenter.

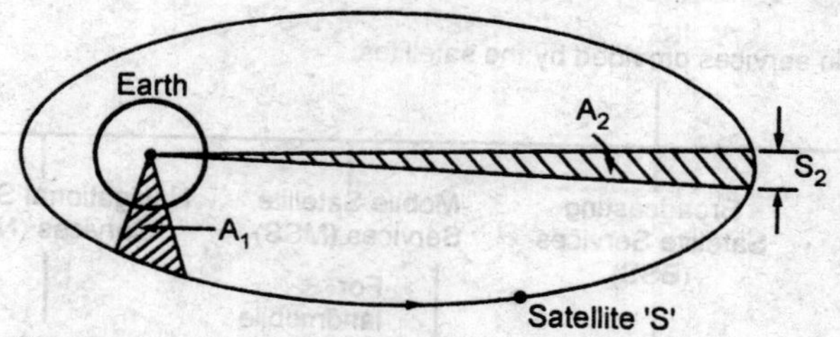

Fig. 2.24 Diagram related to Kepler's second law

Here A_1 and A_2 are the areas swept out equally for equal time intervals by the satellite 'S'.

(iii) Kepler's Third Law

The Kepler's third law states that the square of the periodic time of orbit is proportional to the cube of the mean distance between the two bodies. This mean distance is equal to the semimajor axis 'A'. It can be represented as

$$\text{Mean distance} = A^3 = \frac{\mu}{n^2}$$

where 'μ' is the earth's geocentric gravitational constant and 'n' is the mean motion.

Note : The orbital period 'P' is given as $P = \frac{2\pi}{n}$, where 'n' is mean motion in radians per second.

Hence from Kepler's third law it is clear that there exists a fixed relation between the size and time period.

The important orbital elements (Keplerian element set) are listed below :

1. Semimajor axis (A)
2. Eccentricity (e)
3. Mean anomaly (M_O)
4. Argument of perigee (ω)
5. Inclination (i)
6. Right ascension of assending node (Ω)

Out of the six Keplerian element set the semimajor axis and eccentricity gives the shape of the ellipse. Mean anomaly (M_O) represents position of satellite in the orbit at a particular time period (epoch). The rotation of orbits perigee is given by argument of perigee (ω).

The earths equatorial bulge and flattening at the poles known as oblateness is important in the sense that it makes variations in the values of ω and Ω.

- **Apogee and perigee heights**

The farthest and closest heights of the satellite position from earth is known as apogee and perigee denoted as 'h_a' and 'h_p' respectively.

The line that joins the perigee and apogee points through the earth's center is called as line of apsides.

- **Ascending node**

It is the point where the orbit crosses the equatorial plane that goes from south to north.

- **Descending node**

It is the point where the orbit crosses the equatorial plane that goes from north to south.

- **Line of nodes**

It is the line joining the ascending node and descending nodes through the earth's center.

- **Inclination**

It is the angle between orbital plane and earth's equatorial plane.

The orbital perturbations are mainly due to oblateness of earth. The perturbations are classified as

1. Effects of a non-spherical earth
2. Atmospheric drag.

Hence when dealing with satellite communications it is a must to consider these two perturbing effects.

- **Foot Print**

It is the coverage area of any satellite launched in a particular orbit. Wider the foot print higher will be the coverage area which has to be focussed by the satellite with respect to the earth.

- **Satellite foot print**

A particular region covered by the satellite is the shaded portion on the earth shown above and is known as satellite's foot print.

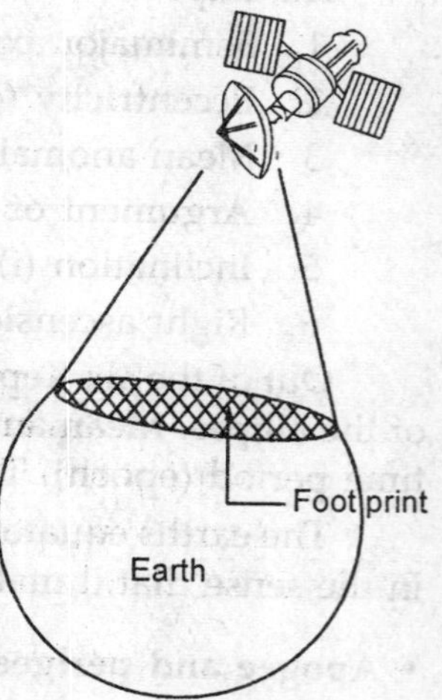

Fig. 2.25 Foot print of a satellite

If the foot print is a larger geographical area then radio coverage area will be equivalently high.

If the foot print is a smaller geographical area then radio coverage by the satellite will be low.

For efficient satellite networking better (high) coverage (foot print) is a very important criterion.

The satellite channel allocation applies frequency division scheme. In GEO systems larger bandwidth of 500 MHz is used. This frequency spectrum is subdivided into many channels namely 40 MHz each. The channel allocation scheme has three different methods namely,

(*i*) Frequency division multiple access (FDMA)
(*ii*) Code division multiple access (CDMA) and
(*iii*) Time division multiple access (TDMA).

In the three schemes frequency division multiple access is mainly used for satellite communication. The two forms of FDMA scheme are,

1. Fixed assignment multiple access (FAMA) and
2. Demand assignment multiple access (DAMA).

When using the FDMA, for allocating satellite channels some criteria are taken into consideration and it is usually divided into three main parameters. They are,

(*i*) Cross talk (*ii*) Intermodulation noise and (*iii*) Thermal noise

2.7 SATELLITE NETWORK CONFIGURATION

Satellite is also known as secondary body that circulates the primary body earth in a particular orbit. The earth station monitors the satellite communication and sends signal to the satellite. This is called as uplink. In similar way the amplified or analyzed signals are retransmitted from satellite to the earth and it is known as downlink. The uplink and downlink powers are expressed in terms of decibels.

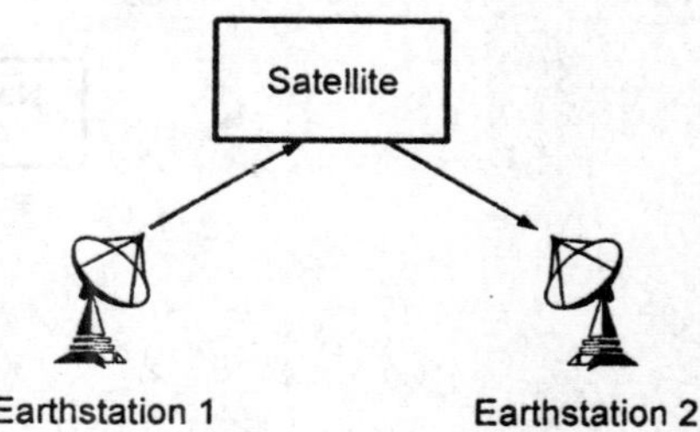

Fig. 2.26 Satellite-point to point link

The orbit is the path through which the satellite circulates the earth.

The antenna used must be bidirectional in nature used both for transmitting and receiving purposes.

Satellite Networks

Satellite networks are developed with reliable equipment which serve many applications including cellular networks.

Example (*i*) VSAT

One of the example for satellite network is termed as VSAT.

'VSAT' is Very Small Aperture Terminal.

The frequency band used for VSAT is 'Ku' band of K band.

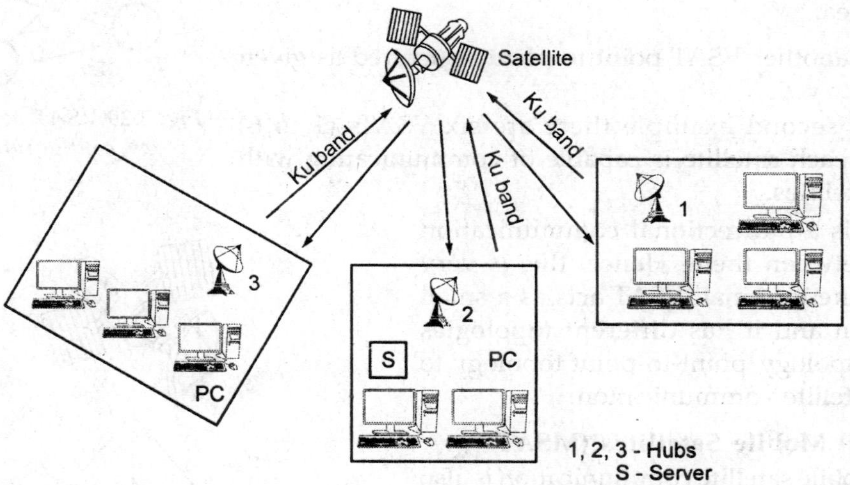

Fig. 2.27 VSAT-satellite network

The VSAT acts as small earth station. Two types of topologies namely mesh and point to point VSAT arrangement in satellite communication is shown below.

(a) VSAT - mesh topology

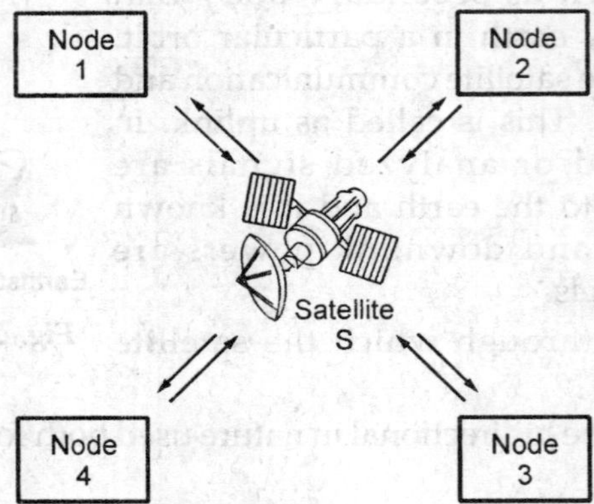

Fig. 2.28 VSAT configuration with mesh topology

There is a bidirectional communication between the VSAT node and the satellite(s). Here four VSAT terminals are considered and a full duplex communication is possible. They communicate with the common satellite to transmit and receive signals.

VSAT is an efficient satellite network and many VSAT terminals can be used in a particular zone to improve satellite coverage area.

(b) There is another VSAT point to point structured as given below.

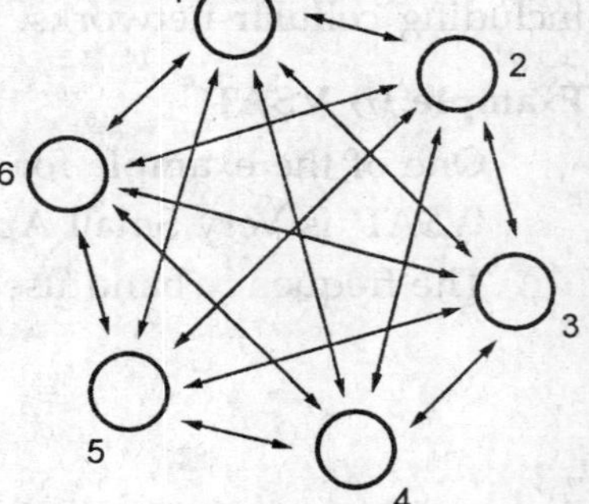

Fig. 2.29 VSAT point to point configuration

In this second example there are six VSATs (1 to 6) shown and each satellite is capable of communicating with all other satellites.

There is a bidirectional communication available between them. Hence, this is very small aperture terminal. VSAT acts as a small earth station and it has different topologies like mesh topology, point-to-point topology to establish satellite communication.

Example (*ii*) Mobile Satellites (MSAT)

The mobile satellite communication is also called as "Ultra small aperture terminal" in satellite networks. For 'direct communication' purposes MSAT's are used. A mobile satellite (MSAT) is capable of tracking a mobile unit, telephone exchange and operation center for establishing a satellite network for the mobile communication as a leading application.

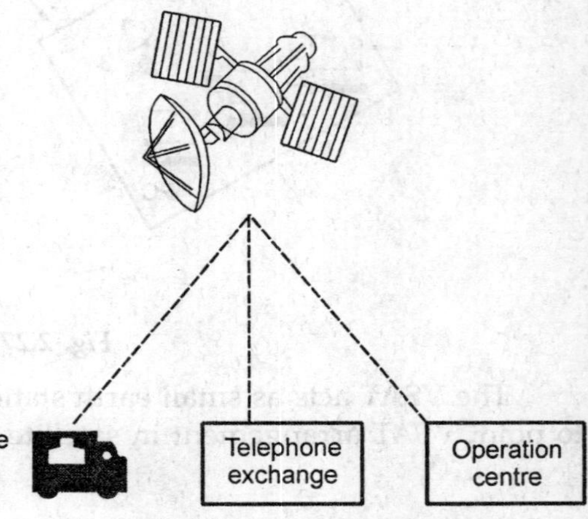

Fig. 2.30 MSAT-Network structure

Table : 2.2 (*a*) Common range for all satellite services

Sr. No.	Frequency range in GHz (gigahertz)	Frequency band designations
1	0.1 - 0.3	Very high frequency (VHP)
2	0.3 - 1.0	Ultra high frequency (UHF)
3	1.0 - 2.0	L
4	2.0 - 4.0	S
5	4.0 - 8.0	C
6	8.0 - 12.0	X
7	12.0 - 18.0	Ku
8	18.0 - 27.0	K
9	27.0 - 40.0	Ka
10	40.0 - 75	V
11	75- 110	W
12	110 - 300	mm (millimetre)
13	300 - 3000	µn (micrometre)

Table 2.2 (*b*) ITU frequency bands designation

Sr. No.	Band Number	Symbols used	Frequency range
1	4	VLF (very low frequency)	3 - 30 kHz
2	5	LF (Low frequency)	30 - 300 kHz
3	6	MF (Medium frequency)	300 - 3000 kHz
4	7	HF (High frequency)	3 - 30 MHz
5	8	VHF (Very high frequency)	30 - 300 MHz
6	9	UHF (Ultra high frequency)	300 - 3000 MHz
7	10	SHF (Super high frequency)	3 - 30 GHz
8	11	EHF (Extremely high frequency)	30 - 300 GHz

2.8 ALLOCATION OF FREQUENCY FOR MOBILE SATELLITE SERVICES

Example

- The region I includes Europe, Africa, Mongolia and USSR.
- The region II including North and South America and Greenland.
- The region III includes Asia, Australia and the South west Pacific.

$\simeq$ 805 to 890 MHz - Region II and III

$\simeq$ 1545 to 1559 - For downlink transmission.

$\simeq$ 1446 to 1660 - For uplink transmission.

2.9 IRIDIUM SYSTEM : (BIG LEO SYSTEM)

The Iridium system enables constellation of more number of satellites in close paths to the earth. The Iridium system provided the first proposal for services from space to handheld phone sets. The constellation consists of six polar orbital planes which are 60° apart with eleven satellites in each. The main advantage of this scheme so far discussed enables 100% global coverage including the poles. Though the satellites are in motion with respect to earth it enables more coverage. The important characteristics of the Iridium system are tabulated below :

	Characteristic of Iridium System	Value in approx
1	Geometry	Polar orbits
2	Orbit altitude	900 km
3	Satellites per orbit	11
4	Number of orbits	6
5	Satellite lifetime	Upto 6 years
6	Access technique	Time division multiple access

Each satellite in this technology has 48 spot beams generated by phased array antenna setup.

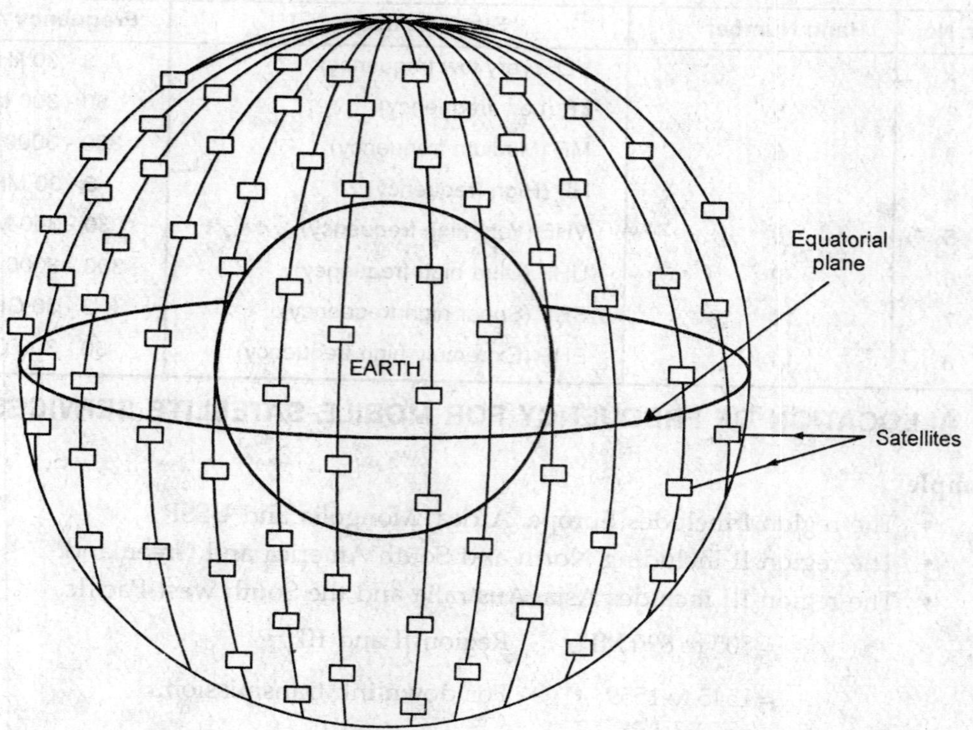

Fig. 2.31 Iridium network orbital constellation

In this figure of Iridium network the orbital constellation is shown where 66 satellites in 11 polar orbital planes are possible at the maximum.

Actually this technique adopts the NON-GEO orbits and has to give up synchronization of satellite revolution to earth rotation, for the cost of the satellite being closer to that of the earth. There are many advantages of this LEO approach of Iridium setup which includes,

- Minimum propagation delay.
- Enables interactive voice services.
- Reduction in path loss.
- Compatible with mobile services.
- Good for real time applications.

The Iridium system is specially designed for 66 satellites in 11 different polar orbits.

2.9 A ORBCOMM (LITTLE LEO SYSTEM)

The Orbital Communications Corporation (Orbcomm) is a low earth orbiting (LEO) satellite system. It provides two way data communication services and position determination. It consists of four main orbital planes each enclosing eight satellites which are spaced from each other by 45° ± 5°.

Each main plane is at 45° and at an altitude of 775 km. The main orbital planes are circular. Two sublimental orbits composing two satellites are at an inclination of 70°. These two orbits provide enhanced polar coverage. Gateway Earth Stations (GES), Network Control Center (NCC) and Satellite Control Center (SCC) form the ground segment which provides access to the public switched telephone network and mobile systems. When compared to the geo stationary satellites, these Orbcomm satellites are smaller in size. The Orbcomm system provides subscribers with the position determination service using dopier positioning.

The advantages of Orbcomm satellite is that the range is small when compared to geo stationary satellite. Hence free space loss is less and propagation delay is also reduced. Orbcomm systems provide more than 60,000 messages per hour. Though the Orbcomm is US based, it has agreements with companies in Canada, Russia, South Africa etc.

Note :

1. The distance between satellite antenna and the earth station antenna is denoted as 'D' and given as

$$\frac{P_T}{P_R} = \frac{(4\pi D)^2}{\lambda^2} \quad ...(1)$$

$$\frac{P_T}{P_R} = \frac{(4\pi f D)^2}{c^2} = D^2 = \left[\left(\frac{P_T}{P_R}\right) \cdot \frac{c^2}{(4\pi f)^2}\right] \quad ...(2)$$

where P_T → Signal power at the transmitting antenna.

P_R → Signal power at the receiving antenna.

l → Wavelength of the carrier.

c → Speed of light energy, i.e. 3×10^8 m/sec.

and D → Distance between the antennas.

Also, the free space loss L (dB) is

$$L\ (dB) = 10 \log \frac{P_T}{P_R} \quad ...(3)$$

$$= 20 \log \left(\frac{4\pi D}{\lambda}\right) \quad ...(4)$$

$$= -20 \log (l) + 20 \log (D) + 21.98 \text{ dB} \quad ...(5)$$

where λ and D are expressed in same units say meters.

2. For the geostationary orbit satellites (GEO)

This free space loss is (at equator),

$$L\ (dB) = -20 \log (\lambda) + 20 \log \underbrace{(35.863 \times 10^6)}_{D} + 21.98 \text{ dB}$$

$$L\ (dB) = [-20 \log (\lambda) + 173.06]$$

2.10 IMPORTANCE OF THE MULTIPLE ACCESS TECHNIQUES

The radio spectrum is shared by the mobile users simultaneously. The sharing may be based on frequency, time, and code. The wireless telephony applies duplexing technique where talking and listening is enabled at a time. For example frequency division duplexing (FDD) offers two bands of frequencies for every user.

The simplex channel consists of a forward and a reverse channels and hence each duplex channel consists of one simplex channel.

These forward and reverse channels are separated with a frequency band in the entire system. On the other hand time division duplexing known as TDD make use of time instead of frequency to have the same forward and reverse channels.

Both FDD and TDD schemes have advantages and disadvantages. The multiple access schemes with any one of these techniques are used for wirelesss communications.

2.10.1 Different Multiple Access Schemes (Techniques)

The important multiple access schemes used are

1. Time division multiple access (TDMA)
2. Code division multiple access (CDMA)
3. Frequency division multiple access (FDMA)

Concepts of FDMA, TDMA and CDMA - multiple access techniques

Frequency division multiple access (FDMA)

In wireless environment, individual users are allotted individual channels. The channels or frequency band is unique for each user/subscriber. The entire allowed radio spectrum is divided into many slices of frequency bands and each band or channel is allocated to each user. The allocation of radio channel can also be done on demand basis.

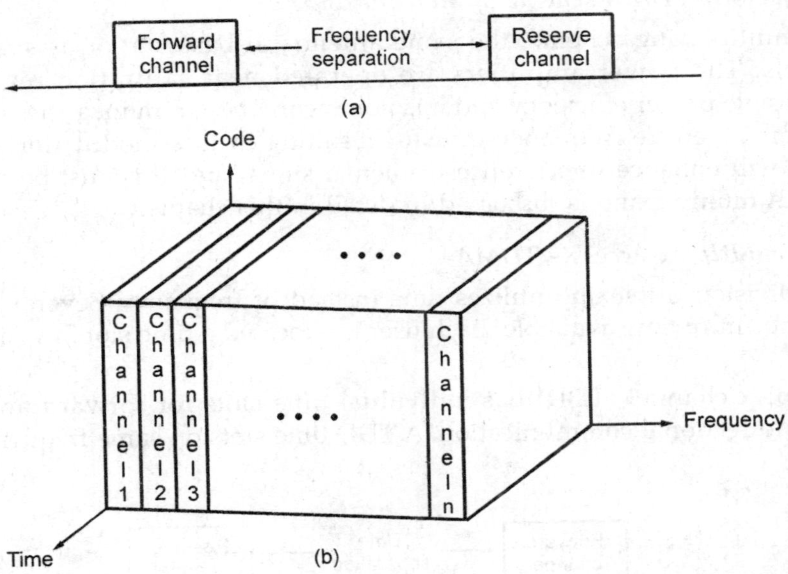

Fig. 2.32 *(a) Two simplex channels allocation in FDD (b) FDMA scheme*

In conventional telephonic systems, bidirectional communication is possible simultaneously and it is essential for cellular communication also. Such a simultaneous talk and listen facility is known as duplexing. Under frequency division multiplexing, duplexing is done using frequency and hence it is termed as frequency division duplexing (FDD).

In FDD, the duplex channel contains dual simplex channels namely forward and reverse channel as in Fig. 2.33 (*a*). The forward frequency band provides radio traffic from base station (BTS) to the mobile unit where as the reverse frequency radio band provides radio traffic from mobile unit to the base station. A duplexer device is kept in mobile unit and base station for enabling simultaneous conversation.

Note : The separation in frequency between the forward and reverse channel is constant in the entire system for all the channels.

In Fig. 2.33 (*b*) the principle of FDMA multiplexing scheme is shown where the entire bandwidth is divided in frequency slices and assigned to every user.

Some features of FDMA scheme

- FDMA requires proper filtering at receiver side to avoid adjacent channel interference (ACI).
- In FDMA scheme, if a channel is not in use it will be idle and it will not be used by some other user. Hence, there is a chance of resource wastage.
- FDMA channel can handle one phone circuit at a time.
- Complexity is less.
- Narrow bandwidth.
- If voice channel are assigned in FDMA, the mobile unit and base station start transmitting simultaneously.

Non-linear effects in FDMA scheme of multiplexing

In this multiplexing scheme, the same antenna at base station is shared by several radio channels. The power amplifiers are operated near saturation region for getting maximum possible power efficiency and it is nonlinear. These nonlinearities cause spreading of signals over the entire frequency domain resulting in intermodulation (IM) frequency generation. It will enhance interferences in actual signal and IM must be minimized. The types of FDMA multiplexing is discussed in detail in this chapter.

Time division multiplex access - TDMA

In time division duplexing utilizes time instead of frequency. Several users share the time slots of the entire time available. Each user is allocated a time slot in which it can access the channel.

Each duplex channel (TDD) has individual time slots for forward and reverse time slots to have bidirectional communication. A TDD time slots on same frequency is shown in Fig. 2.33 (a).

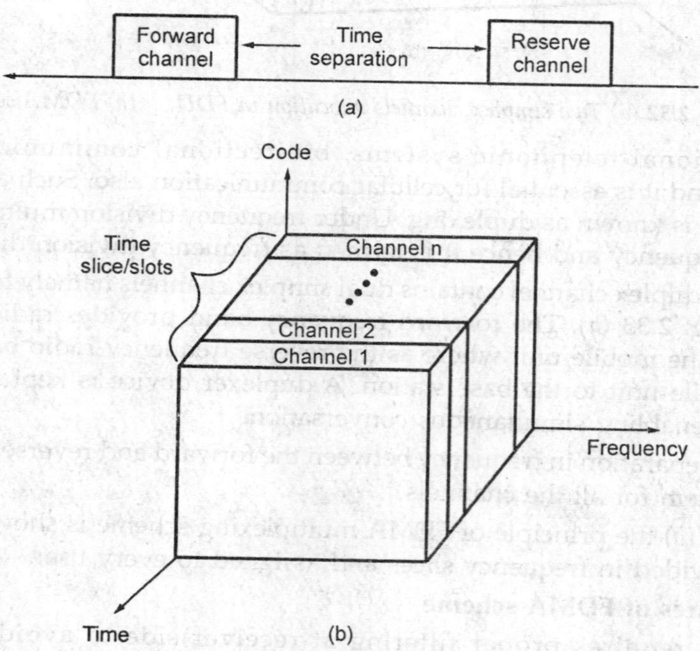

Fig. 2.33 (a) Simplex time slots allocation in TDD (b) TDMA scheme

This TDD mode enables every transceiver (transmitter and receiver) to operate as a transmitter or receiver. The TDD mode is generally used in cordless phones.

The principle of TDMA multiplexing scheme is shown in Fig. 2.33 (*b*). In TDMA system the entire radio spectrum is divided into time slots where a single user is allowed to use the radio channel in a time slot. In TDMA digital data transmission and digital modulation are allowed.

Many users can access their channel in their respective time slots. The transmission from several users are interlaced into a single frame as shown in Fig. 2.34.

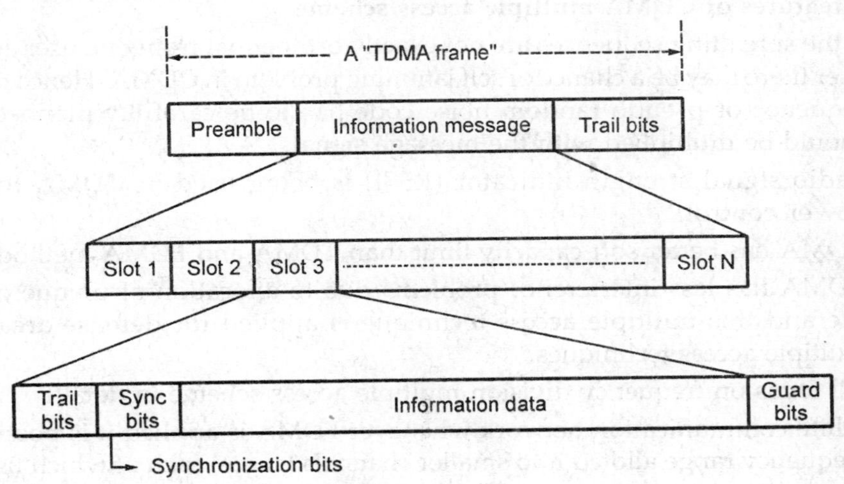

Fig. 2.34 TDMA frame format

In this format the preamble field contains the synchronization and address informations. The guard bits are used to allow synchronization of the different receivers between various frames and time slots. It is assumed that there are 'N' number of time slots for 'N' number of users so that each user can access the channel in their allowed time slot.

Some features of TDMA

- Each user in TDMA multiple access scheme shares same carrier frequency but with non overlapping time slots.

Code division multiple access (CDMA) :

In CDMA technique many users share the same carrier frequency (f_c). The narrowband message signal is also multiplexed with a spreading signal of larger bandwidth. This spreading signal is actually a pseudo noise code sequence and it has higher chip rate that the data rate of the message signal

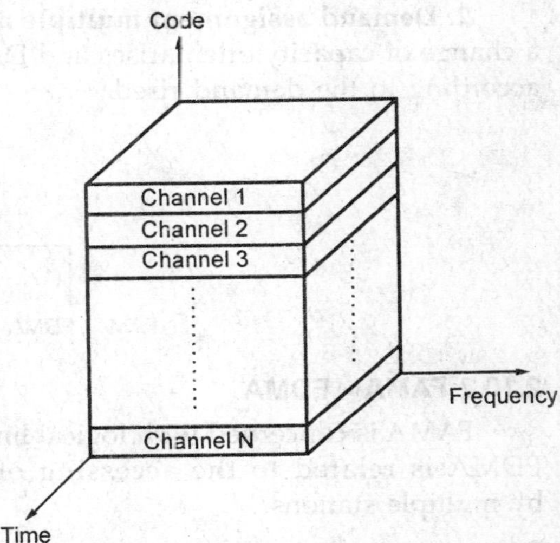

Fig. 2.35 Code division multiple access

Since same channel is shared by several users, there may be a problem of near far effect. In CDMA, the main advantage when compared to other multiple access schemes is reduced level of interference. Since each user/subscriber is allocated an individual pseudo random codeword that is orthogonal to all other codewords of remaining users at the receiving end the receiver selectively tunes to receive the intended signal of the user. Proper power control measures are done in CDMA to avoid near far problems.

Some features of CDMA multiple access scheme

- If the spreading sequences are not exactly orthogonal from one user and to another user there may be a chance of self jamming problem in CDMA. Hence this spreading sequence or pseudo random noise code has to be carefully planned and then it should be multiplied with the message signal.
- Radio signal strength indicator (RSSI) is being used in CDMA to have better power control.
- CDMA has better soft capacity limit than TDMA and FDMA methods.
- CDMA has less interference problems due to allocation of unique codes to each use and this multiple access technique is applied for defense areas than other multiple access techniques.

We will focus on frequency division multiple access scheme in detail.

In satellite communication network whenever FDMA is applied it is possible to divide the entire frequency range alloted into smaller channels (slices) each of which uses frequency modulation.

Access of frequency division multiplexing is quite good with satellite networks which in turn helps mobile communication. The limiting factors of FDMA are thermal noise, cross talk and intermodulation noise.

Types

There are two types of FDMA allowed.

1. Fixed assignment multiple access : It is denoted as "FAMA".

In the FAMA scheme the satellite channels are assigned in a predetermined fashion and distributed such that random changes in capacity changes are not allowed.

2. Demand assignment multiple access (DAMA) : In case of multiple stations there is a change of capacity often arises and DAMA scheme is flexible and channel may be alloted according to the demand rised.

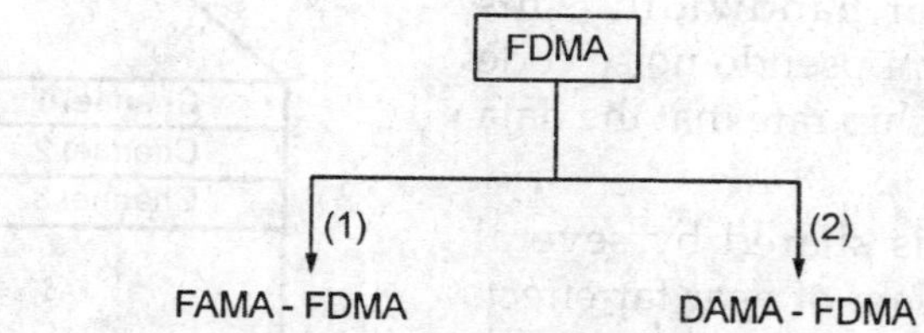

2.10.2 FAMA - FDMA

FAMA is concerned with logical links between the stations which are preassigned. The FDMA is related to the accessing of satellite links using different frequency band by multiple stations.

When the satellite receives the smaller channels that is from the 36 MHz (say) band of frequency it simply translates it to required range of frequency in gigahertz ranges and then retransmits the signal.

This FAMA-FDMA is preassigned and not flexible with needs of traffic changes.

2.10.3 DAMA - FDMA

This DAMA-FDMA scheme is a better method than the previous FAMA-FDMA method particularly in C band. It is better to neglect groupings in channel assignments and just dividing the entire bandwidth for example 36 MHz band of frequency into individual channels, and this technique is also known as single channel per carrier SCPC scheme. It is flexible with C band. The SCPC is also good with remote regions.

But SCPC finds complexity with fixed channel assignment. The efficiency can be increased with DAMA method, where for establishing a full duplex links between any two earth stations is possible because dynamic allocation of satellite channels is allowed. An example of such DAMA-SCPC scheme is discussed below where a pool of links available with centralized facility.

For example : SPADE System

'SPADE' is an acronym used for single channel per carrier pulse code modulated multiple access demand assignment equipment. Here the earth stations are connected permanently through the technique called common signalling channel (CSC). Because the demand assignment of channel as per requirement of traffic common signalling channel 'CSC' is very much required.

For example assume there are six earth stations 1, 2, 3, 4, 5 and 6. Each earth segment (1 to 6) has ability to generate any one carrier frequency out of the band alloted using the frequency synthesizers. If one station say '6' is initiated from another earth station say '3' then the station '3' will select the frequency pair in random manner and this selected frequency pair from the available list will be intimated to the earth station '6' through the central pool CSC. The same signalled information has to be then acknowledged by the station '6'. Then the entire circuit will be established and all other earth segments (stations) will be instructed to remove this frequency opted from their list.

The total round trip time for call initiation to signal acknowledgment by station '6' is around 600 ms.

Note : During the round trip time gap in case if the opted frequency is alloted to some other station (say 2) then the station 3 will immediately select some other pair of frequency from the list and same procedure will be repeated with the monitoring of CSC.

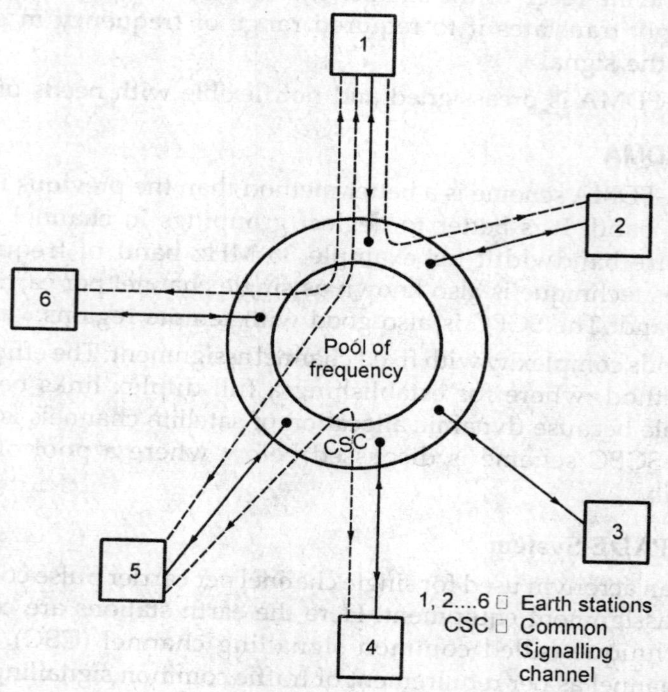

Fig. 2.36 Spade system

2.11 BROADCAST SYSTEMS

e.g. Direct to Home (DTH)

The Direct to Home (DTH) systems were designed and developed for transmitting entertainment television for home receiving with proper receivers. The main factors influencing this type of satellite service is

- Acceptability of the cost.
- Scrambling and conditional access.
- Uplink system design.
- Acquisition facilities.
- Proper programme mixing (quality, language option, degree of interactivity).
- Incompatibility with other Direct to Home (DTH) schemes.

The DTH is a simplest application of satellite service, where multiple receivers receive their own downlinks. The downlink frequencies are,

- 2100 to 2128 MHz (S band BSS)
- 3.4 to 4.2 GHz (C band FSS)
- 10.7 to 12.2 GHz (Ku band FSS)

- 12.2 to 12.9 GHz (Ku band BSS)

The DTH receivers are designed for a particular downlink frequency. The equivalent isotropic radiated power (EIRP) has an impact on DTH dish antenna diameter. Doubling of the EIRP value will allow the reduction of dish antenna diameter by a factor of 1.414. Thus squeezing of diameter of dish antenna will definitely increase the EIRP value. Therefore if a DTH system has highest EIRP value then it can have smallest sized receiving dish antenna. Then the DTH selects circular polarization or linear polarization for its downlink.

The scrambling is a technique that can be used in DTH to provide authentication of the programming that unauthorized receiver cannot receive the message.

In this DTH reception which digitized and it is an arrangement to meet uplink compression and downlink decompression systems. The direct to home system is also called as DIRECT TV. The signal in uplink is compressed and encrypted. Reed Solomon encoder (RS coding) is used and assures for error free signals which is then modulated and transmitted. The received signal is demodulated, decoded and then decrypted to get back the original signal. The encryption and decryption is done for security purposes. The signal is decompressed and again converted to analog form available for home TV reception.

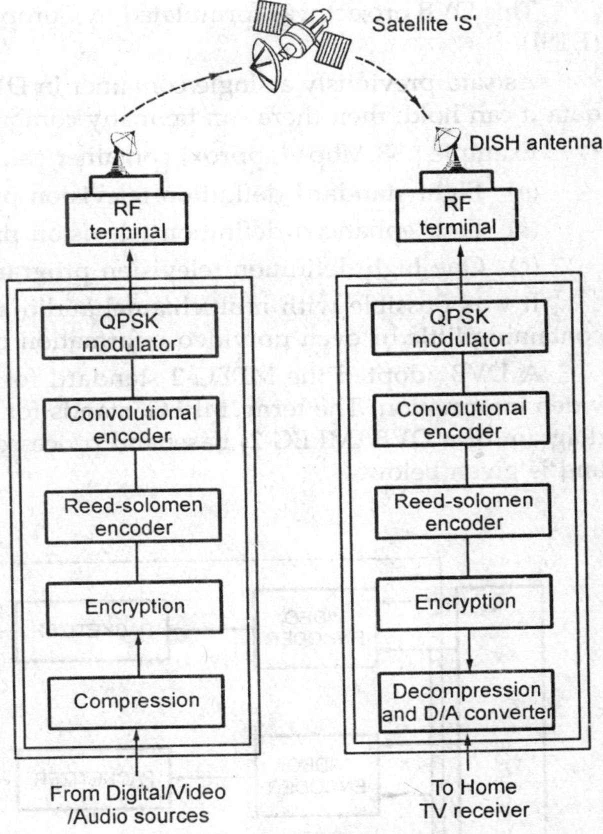

Fig. 2.37 Digital direct to home DTH transmission system

2.12 DIGITAL VIDEO BROADCASTING (DVB)

The digital video broadcasting standard DVB is a term used to inter digital television and data broadcasting services. Many standards work on these kind of services. They were also developed by the project on digital video broadcasting simply called as "DVB project".

The "DVB" is a better mechanism which can be applied for data broadcasting. Like reservoir or container DVB keeps different form of data in a single entity (in a container). For example a container delivers sound or data, compressed image to the receiver. It has the advantage of sending audio information synchronized with its corresponding video data in general and sometimes even if audio and its video information does not reach the receiver simultaneously. The asynchronous type of reception does not degrade the picture information say in case of conventional television programmes.

This DVB project was formulated by European Telecommunications Standards Institute (ETSI).

As said previously a single container in DVB system say for example is of 38 Mbps of data it can hold, then there can be many combinations of data.

Example : 38 Mbps (approx) container can hold,

(*a*) Eight standard definition television programmes (SDTV)

(*b*) Four enhanced definition television programmes (EDTV) or

(*c*) One high definition television programme (HDTV).

It was possible with multichannel audio and other data services. A multimedia data containing little or even no video information can be transmitted.

A DVB adopted the MPEG-2 standard for its source coding techniques of audio and video information. The term 'MPEG' stands for "Motion picture experts group". The block diagram of a DVB (MPEG-2) baseband processor is capable of completing many functions and is given below.

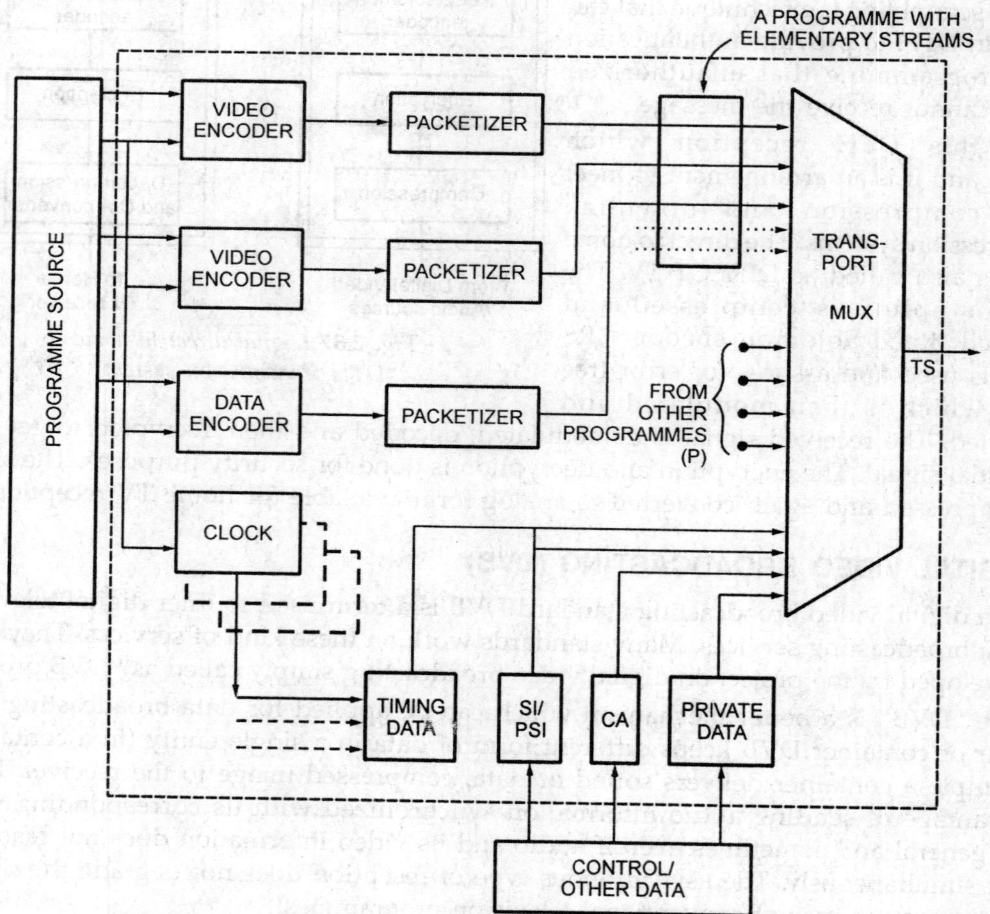

Fig. 2.38 Digital video broadcasting (MPEG-2) baseband processor

A basic service type under DVB is a radio programme that comprises of single audio elementary stream. A conventional television broadcast consists of three elementary streams :

1. Stream 1 → Coded video
2. Stream 2 → Coded stereo audio
3. Stream 3 → Teletext

The data is then fragmented as packets and the different elementary streams of a programme are multiplexed with the respective packetized elementary streams (P) of other programmes if any to form a transport stream (TS) finally. If synchronized properly the decoder can interpret the time stamps and then determines relevant time to decode and submit the associated information to the end user.

In a MPEG technology the sequence of time limited transmissions is referred as a "programme", and the service is equivalent to channel assignment for that application.

2.12.1 Satellite DVB System

A basic model of satellite transmission channel which is digital in nature comprises of five important elements or modules.

1. Baseband processing unit (BPU)
2. Satellite channel adaptation (SCA)
3. Transmission channel (C)
4. SCA at receiver side
5. BPU at receiver side

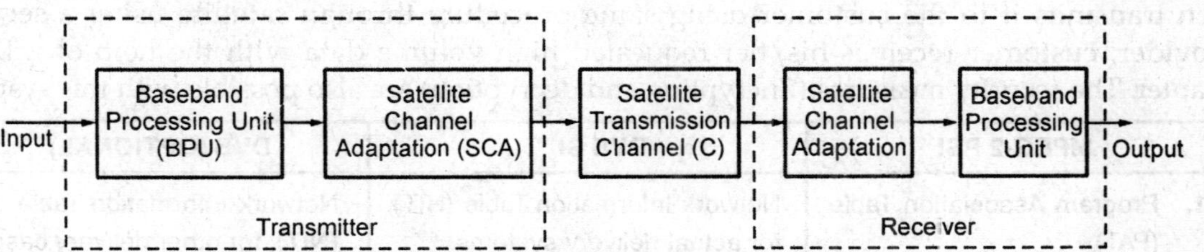

Fig. 2.39 Model of "DVB satellite system"

The service content may be a mixture of video, audio and data. The Transport Stream (TS) includes Programme Specific Information (PSI), Conditional Access (CA), Service Information (SI) and also private data.

Service Description Table

This table lists the parameters and names for each individual service within a moving pictures experts group (MPEG) for the set top boxes.

Event Information Table

It provides the status information regarding the current transmission and additional information for set top boxes.

Time and Date Table

This table contains latest information (with updation) for the set top boxes.

Hence the service information is contained in the data stream. It specifies the contents of the container.

DVB system can also be used for two other functions.

1. High Bandwidth Applications 2. Asymmetrical Internet Access

DVB system is flexible in satisfying customer requests.

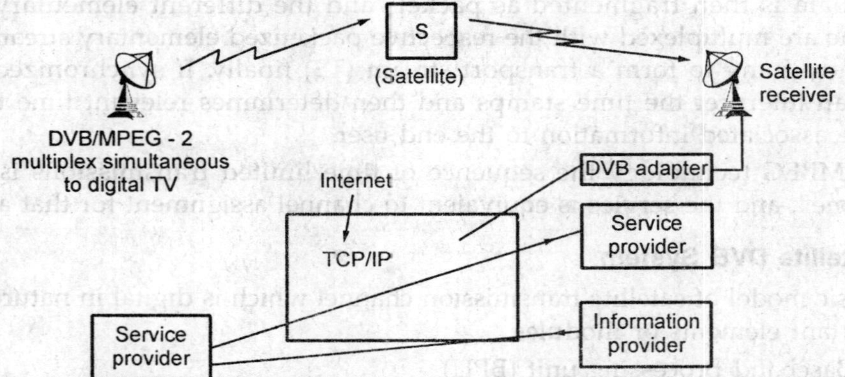

Fig. 2.40 High bandwidth internet related applications in DVB system

In case a customer needs to download a high volume information, then the information/ message provider sends this information to satellite provider through a particular service provider. The satellite then multiplexes data stream with other digital television channels and then transmits it to the customer using same procedure through satellite using a service provider; customer receives his/her requested high volume data with the help of a DVB adapter. The security measures (Encryption and decryption) are also possible with this system.

MPEG-2 PSI	DVB SI	DVB (OPTIONAL)
1. Program Association Table (PAT)	Network Information Table (NIT) for actual delivery systems.	Network Information Table (NIT), for other delivery cases.
2. Conditional Access Table (CAT)		Bouquet association table (BAT)
3. Program Map Table (PMT)	Service Description Table (SDT), for actual transporting systems.	Service Description Table (SDT), for other type of transport systems.
4. Transport Stream Description Table (TSDT)	Event Information Table (EIT)	Event information table for actual TS. Event Information table for other TS (transport streams).
5.	Time and Date Table (TDT)	Running Status Table (RST)
6.		Time Offset Table (TOT)
7.		Stuffing Table (ST)

Fig. 2.41 "DVB"-service information

The programme specific information (MPEG-2) data consists of three types of table.

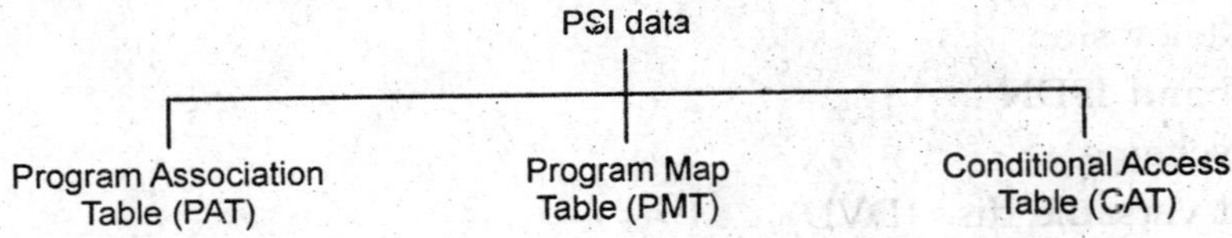

These three tables provide information for the multiplex unit in which they are actually contained and they do not provide data about other transport streams irrespective of the network where they are.

2.12.2 Program Association Table (PAT)

It always has PID value as zero to make its access flexible. PAT supplies full possible services (programmes) available in the transport stream which can be identified by their program number. The programme number zero usually points to the network information table denoted as NIT. At any time the list of available services can be verified with the help of PAT.

2.12.3 Program Map Table (PMT)

Each and every program or service in the transport stream (TS) has an associated program map table (PMT). It identifies elementary streams which comprises the program, and also descriptive information relating to the programme, like data on audio and video encoding parameters conditional access information etc. It indicates programme clock reference "(PCR), for that particular programme. In general the elementary streams of a programme and PCR's are identified in the programme map table (PMT) by the transport packet PID values respectively. But one PMT can describe many programmes and it is not restricted with one programme alone.

2.12.4 Conditional Access Table (CAT)

The conditional access table (CAT) should provide any elementary stream if available in the transport stream that are scrambled and should list the entitled management messages denoted as 'EMM' streams.

The output of the transport MUX unit will be a single data stream which is ready for transmission and further storages. It may be variable or fixed data rate and it may also contain different data rate streams. Error free transmission is not much guaranteed within multiplier units DVB systems.

Hence the main goal of DVB system to have digital television broadcasting with satellite transmissions, cable television and also terrestrial transmission are made possible.

The main advantage of DVB system is its container flexibility since it works well with different types of information. The server related information is available within data stream which is used to specify the content of container (C).

In DVB architecture the main point is an integrated receiver - decoder (IRD) termed as 'set top box' and it can be connected to a high resolution monitor.

Some functional technologies possible with DVB system are

1. Cable television
2. Broadband ISDN
3. ADSI scheme
4. Digital versatile disc (DVD)
5. Digital video tape recorder (DVTR)

The various levels of quality available quoted earlier are

(a) Standard definition TV (SDTV)
(b) Enhanced definition TV (EDTV)
(c) High definition TV (HDTV)

With these technologies DVB can provide upto 1920 × 1080 pixels picture accuracy.

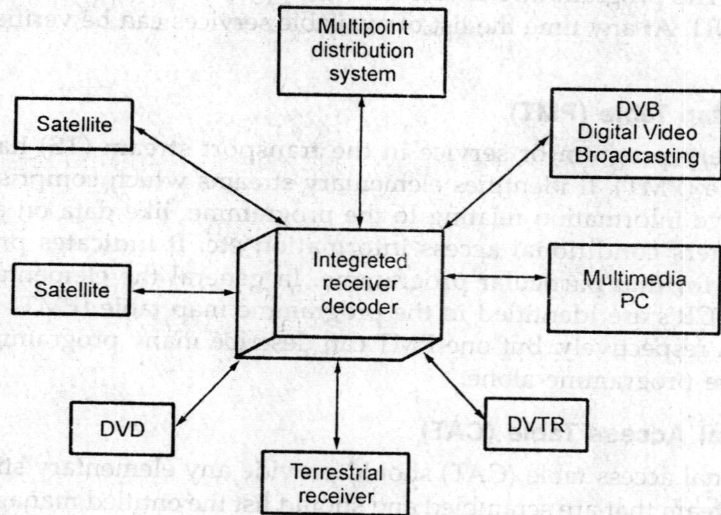

Fig. 2.42 'Digital' video broadcasting system applications

Contents of a container in DVB system :

(a) Network information table (NIT)
(b) Service description table (SDT)
(c) Event information table (EIT)
(d) Time and data table (TDT).

Network Information Table

It lists the services of a particular provider and contains additional information for the set top boxes.

Along with service relatea tables in DVB system the list of all possible services table are important since each one of them has unique functionality.

DVB - service information data has nine various tables :

(*a*) Service description table (SDT)
(*b*) Bouquet association table (BAT)
(*c*) Event information table (EIT)
(*d*) Running status table (RST)
(*e*) Time and date table (TDT)
(*f*) Time offset table (TOT)
(*g*) Stuffing table (ST)
(*h*) Selection information table (SIT)
(*i*) Discontinuity information table (DIT)

(*a*) Service description table (SDT)

The SDT also provides data/information like name of the service provider and name of the service. The service description table consists of data describing services which are contained within a transport stream, where the services provides information like name of service provider and name of the service. This in turn can be used by the receiver.

(*b*) Bouquet association table (BAT)

It provides information regarding the service "bouquets". It is basically of services meant as a single entity.

Information obtained from BAT :

(*i*) Name of the service and
(*ii*) List of services for each and every bouquet.

(*c*) Event information table (EIT)

The event information table provides data or information in proper chronological (time to time updated) order related to the events contained within every service or programme. Information like event name, duration and start time are denoted by EIT.

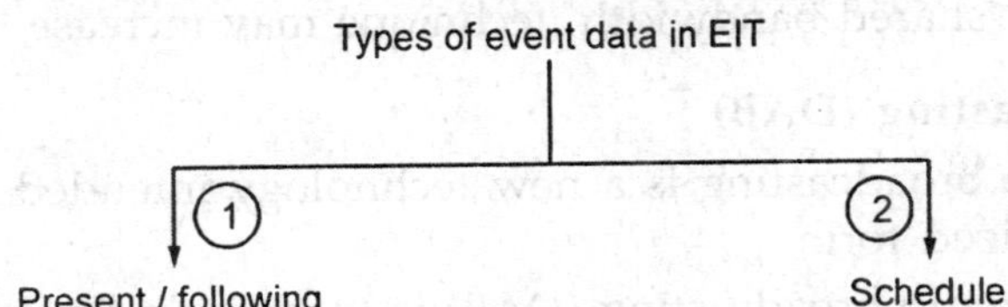

The first type (1) refers to current event which is on process and next will be the event "following" of a particular service. The second type (2) consists of a events list which may take place at some time period. This table (EIT) is usually optional.

(*d*) Running status table (RST)

It allows updated timing status with more accuracy of many events. Any scheduling changes hence will be reflected by 'RST'.

A 'DIT' is usually inserted at some transition points wherever the service information is discontinuous in nature. The two tables SIT and DIT are not used with partial transport streams that is used for broadcast services.

(e) Time and date table (TDT)

It is also used to express time information, which is generally present time. Information regarding summer or winter time is not transmitted in TDT.

(f) Time offset table (TOT)

This table conveys information or data regarding summer or winter time periods. It is also user friendly in its operation, when the user seeks information about summer or winter time with local time offset for different countries TOT will provide the data and DVB system is more attractive.

(g) Stuffing table (ST)

This table is used mainly to invalidate the presently existing tables at the delivery status of a system.

(h) Selection information table and discontinuity information table (SIT and DIT)

If SIT is available in bit stream it shows that it is a "partial" transport stream which comes from an interface that is digital.

Advantages of DVB system

(i) Typical data rates (speed) for each user are 6-38 Mbits per second for downlink through satellites where the other link will be of 33 kbits per second with a proper modem arrangement.

(ii) Transmission of this type of information is done along with television programmes using the free spaces in the data stream. Therefore it avoids usage of extra lines for customer care tracks.

Disadvantages of DVB system

(i) This technology allows 'shared satellite links' for many users where complexity is high.

(ii) Also the 'shared bandwidth' technique may increase the interference level.

Digital audio broadcasting (DAB)

The digital audio broadcasting is a new technology intended for broadcasting audio programming in digitized form.

Goals of digital audio broadcasting (DAB) is to provide the following,

(a) Higher fidelity
(b) Mobile services
(c) New services
(d) Greater noise immunity.

There are many systems (types) used for digital broadcasting but they are based on analog technology with few specific digital feature like LCD frequency displays and synthesized tuning.

The example for LCD frequency displays are digital tuners which refers to analog AM or FM receivers where the tuned frequencies are displayed as digits.

Terrestrial digital audio broadcast

DAB system was developed as a Research project for the European Union (Eureka project number EU147) and was standardized by European Telecommunications standards Institute to deliver high quality digital radio services. DAB systems can also use single frequency networks (SEN) such that all senders transmitting same radio programme can use the same frequency. DAB makes use of VHF and UHF frequency bands. DAB is mainly based on orthogonal frequency division multiplexing for transmitting digital data over a radio channel. The DAB technology make use of MP2 audiocoding technique which is created as a part of project "Eureka 147" standard. The system also includes the following main features.

1. Modulation and error correction coding schemes.
2. Selection of an audo codec system.

'DAB' system also has the advantage that the stations do not have to be retuned in accordance with mobile status. Area to area change takes place according to movement (say travelling in an automobile) retiming is not required. This DAB system can also carry "radio text" which is termed here as "Dynamic label segment" or DLS from the station giving the real time information such as "traffic updates" or "song titles." There is also provision available that this could also be extended to full screen static pictures. The united kingdom was the first and foremost country to receive a wide range of radio station through DAB. The "Eureka 147" DAB scheme makes use of wide bandwidth broadcast technology and typically a spectra was allocated for it in band III and L band. The scheme allowed "operation from anywhere" above 30 MHz.

2.13 SPECIAL FEATURES OF DIGITAL AUDIO BROADCASTING (DAB)

(*a*) Perception of a service threshold.
(*b*) Effective elimination of multipath interference.

Perception of a service threshold

DAB technology can be efficient when viewed from receiver side with factors like

1. Radio propagation
2. Local geography
3. Influence of tall buildings and metallic reflective structures like warehouses, bridges etc.

Whenever the received signal becomes marginal, with most of the consumer receivers, and since there is no 'threshold' warning the audio output signal for the entire multiplex gets muted until the strength of the signal is recovered. This may also be misunderstood that the receiver unit is faulty.

Elimination of multipath interference

The digital audio broadcast (DAB) was mainly developed for eliminating multipath interference or fading problem.

It is possible to eliminate multipath fading whenever a strong signal is available. DAB is well suited in following applications.

(*a*) For moving automobiles for which the FM multipath fading is a complex problem.

(*b*) Whenever multipath fading is more serious (say when integral antennas used for domestic environments).

2.13.1 Comparison between DAB and FM

DAB	FM
1. It is a digital radio system.	It is analog radio system.
2. It offers more radio stations.	It offers less radio stations compared to DAB.
3. Not much spectrum efficient.	Better spectrum efficient than DAB.

There is also a chance of integration of frequency spectra components of one modulated subcarrier to zero at the respective corresponding components from adjacent subcarrier signals. This ultimately generates two merits of DAB scheme.

1. Elimination of many bandpass inters hardware setup for extracting subcarrier at the receiver is possible.
2. After modulation the subcarrier spectrum occupies the proper bandwidth with tolerable overlapping of signals.

2.13.2 Modulation

The differential quadrature phase shift keying (DQPSK) method of modulation is used in DAB system. It is incoherent in nature. The principle of DQPSK differs from QPSK method, in the sense that the modulated carrier phase for the present symbol (current symbol) depends on its phase relative to that of its previous one. The modulation scheme incorporates a form of coding say Gray coding in only one symbol change when moving from symbol state to next adjacent symbol. DAB technology is compatible with differential quadrature phase shift keying method of modulation.

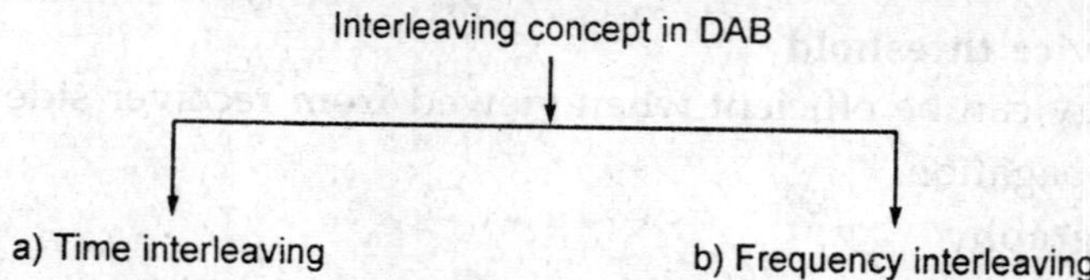

(*a*) Time interleaving in DAB

The data buffering is made possible in DAB type of transmission. It enables the data symbols to be transmitted over radio frequency path in a different time period order than they were generated the audio signal source say in studio. These data symbols at the receiver side are again reassembled and then returned to original time period order before the conversions back to analog type of signals that is to feed the receivers part to audio output. This process is also called as time interleaving. But there is a chance of multipath interference to degrade the data available and hence the choice of time interleaving to make proper averages in a mobile status is very important to nullify or to reduce bursts over a time period.

But the data buffering may insert a delay (d) between the receiver and the source (say studio). In case the delay is not much bothered in view point of applications it can be permitted. But for real time signal dealings the delay may result the broadcast with inaccurate results.

(*b*) Frequency Interleaving

In direct audio broadcast the subcarrier centre frequencies. The multipath and other selective fading affects the radio frequency (RF) multiplex bandwidth at any one particular time period and now the frequency interleaving scheme averages 'bursts' of the errors which is the result of the process.

The DAB technique is compatible with both time interleaving and frequency interleaving concepts.

Single Frequency Networks (SFN)

The greater advantage of DAB scheme over FM is the single frequency networks termed as SFN. In this case synchronization of transmitter and receiver is important. These networks allow building up of substantial service areas with effective utilization of frequency. When service areas of different transmitters overlap, any of their signals will be slightly delayed, hence leading to the same old problem of 'Multipath Interference'. 'Networks development design' is therefore a main criteria to consider to reduce interferences. It is also better to provide filtering with a filter circuit in the receiver side to retrieve a virgin desired data which is maximum possible way to suppress interferences.

REVIEW QUESTIONS

1. Define the term telecommunication.
2. What is known as attenuation?
3. Define ITU and POTS.
4. What are the three main phases of PTN?
5. What is the function of a telephone?
6. List any two transmission media.
7. Write a short note on PTN.
8. Explain a wired, telephone system.
9. What is known as handover procedure in GSM?
10. What is known as a vocoder?
11. What is known as GSM?
12. Define operation subsystem (OSS) in GSM.
13. What are the functions of network and switching subsystem?
14. Write a short note on radio subsystem.
15. List some of the teleservices of GSM.
16. Explain the architecture of GSM with all its subsystems.
17. What is known as mobile originated call?
18. List few types of handover methods in GSM.

19. Write a short note on security issues in GSM.
20. What is the function of 'serving GPRS support node' in GPRS?
21. Draw the GPRS architecture.
22. Write a short note on GPRS.
23. What are the advantages of DECT system?
24. Explain system architecture of DECT system.
25. What is the use of global network in DECT?
26. Write a short note on UMTS.
27. What are the advantages of IMT-2000 cellular system?
28. Draw the simplified architecture of UMTS.
29. What are TDD and FDD modes in UMTS?
30. Give two examples for satellite network.
31. Explain the transmission plane protocol reference under GPRS.
32. Explain the logical channels and security issues in a GSM.
33. List any five DECT specifications.
34. Explain UMTS architecture in detail.
35. What is known as IMT-2000 standard?
36. Write a short note on UTRA-TDD mode.
37. Define the term 'satellite'.
38. Define satellite uplink and downlink.
39. What are the advantages of a MEO satellite?
40. Define Kepler's first law.
41. What are the services provided by satellite?
42. What is known as a satellite footprint?
43. What are the two forms of FDMA multiplexing scheme?
44. Explain VSAT and MSAT satellite networks.
45. Write a short note on big LEO system.
46. Explain FDMA in detail.
47. Explain TDMA and CDMA multiple access techniques in detail.
48. Explain DTH and DVB systems.
49. Explain the network information table and functional technologies of DVB system.
50. Explain the digital audio broadcasting (DAB) systems.

□□□

Unit 3
Mobile Network Layer

3.1 MOBILE INTERNET PROTOCOL (MOBILE IP)—OVERVIEW

Whenever the user is connected to an application(s) across the Internet it is said to be in mobile status. The routers actually uses the IP address in IP datagram to do the routing function. The network portion of an IP address helps routers to send datagram from source computer to network where the target computer is attached (connected) with. Mobile IP can also deal with dynamic IP addresses.

Terminologies related to mobile IP :

- **Home address :** The IP address on the network is known as home address.
- **Home network :** A mobile node is designated to a network which is called as home network.
- **Foreign agent :** The router on the foreign network is called as foreign agent.
- **Foreign network :** Whenever the mobile node moves the attachment point to another network then it is called as foreign network.
- **Home agent :** The mobile node that communicates with the router of its home network is called as a "home agent".
- **Care of address :** It is the address that is used to identify the location of foreign agent.

Mobile IP is most often found in wireless WAN environments where users need to carry their mobile devices across multiple LANs with different IP addresses. It may also be used in 3G networks to provide transparency when internet users migrate between cellular towers.

3.1.1 Mobile IP

The 'MOBILE IP' is similar to the handoff or roaming situation in cellular mobile network. The handoff technique helps the user to continue conversation inspite of his mobility. Likewise the user who is connected through Internet and his point of attachment changes dynamically. But all the connections established are maintained without any disturbances though his underlying network properties change.

Mobile IP is an Internet Engineering Task Force (IETF) standard communications protocol that is designed to allow mobile device users to move from one network to another while maintaining their permanent IP address.

Basically the IP address changes from one network to another network. It holds good if the user is static in his particular network. The 'MOBILE IP' enhances the efficiency of network and friendly with the users.

Mobile IP provides an efficient, scalable mechanism for node mobility with Internet using Mobile IP, nodes may change their point of attachment to the Internet without changing their IP addresses. This allows them to maintain transport and longer layer connections while moving. Node mobility is realized without the need to propagate host specific routes throughout the Internet routing fabric.

Goals and assumptions and requirements of Mobile IP

Assume an user is moving from his home network to which his computer is configured at. As soon as he leaves his home network he may not receive any packet and he has to reconnect the computer (wired or wireless). If routing mechanisms are considered carefully the above problem can be solved easily. The goal of Mobile IP is to enable packet transmission efficiently without any packet loss.

Consider a host computer sends an IP packet with the header containing destination address along with other fields.

The destination address determines the receiver of the data packet and relating physical subnet.

For example, the destination address will be 129.13.43.99. It shows that the receiver has to be connected to the physical subnet with network prefix as 129.13.43. At this moment the routers in internet look at the destination address of the packets incoming and it forwards them with respect to the look-up tables. For the sake of simplicity the prefixes alone are stored on which further optimizations shall be applied.

If the receiver is reachable within the physical subnet it will get the packets. Once it moves outside the subnet then it will receive the packets or packets cannot reach it. Thus a host requires the "Topologically Correct Address". Thus to achieve the goals of Mobile IP the entire system should be designed properly.

3.1.2 Quick Solution

Moving to a location that is completely a new IP address is assigned. It is difficult to find a mobile host on internet platform that has changed the address.

The IP address with regard to present location is dynamically adapted (Dynamic DNS). But if the mobile is moving frequently this approach also may not be useful. The domain name system (DNS) uses caching for improving scalability. It does not present consistent views of name and address.

Routes are built for extremely fast forwarding, but not for fast updates of routing tables. Routers are the 'brains' of the internet, holding the whole net together.

A better approach is to design proper routing. The changes in routing will not be allowed by service providers or the system administrators. Only to compromise with mobile status it may be allowed but at the cost of poor stability of the system.

The ultimate goal towards mobile IP is to provide correct topological address and to enable packet transactions in spite of moving hosts from their home networks.

Some of the requirements of mobile IP includes

(*i*) Compatibility

(*ii*) Transparency

(*iii*) Scalability

(*iv*) Efficiency and

(*v*) Security

Summary of goal of mobile IP

* To support end-system mobility the entire system should have.

1. Efficiency
2. Maintaining scalability
3. Compatibility with the existing Internet protocols and other related applications.

3.2 ENTITIES AND TERMINOLOGIES

(*i*) Mobile Node (MN)

A mobile node (MN) is a router or an end-system that is capable of changing its point of connection to the internet with the help of mobile IP. Mobile need not be smaller devices. For example a router onboard of an aircraft is a mobile node.

(*ii*) Home Network

A home network is nothing but a subnet to which a mobile node belongs to (with corresponding IP address). Within the home network there is no need of mobile IP.

(*iii*) Correspondent Node (CN)

For a mobile node atleast one partner is required. The correspondent node (CN) acts as partner for MN and CN can be mobile or a fixed node.

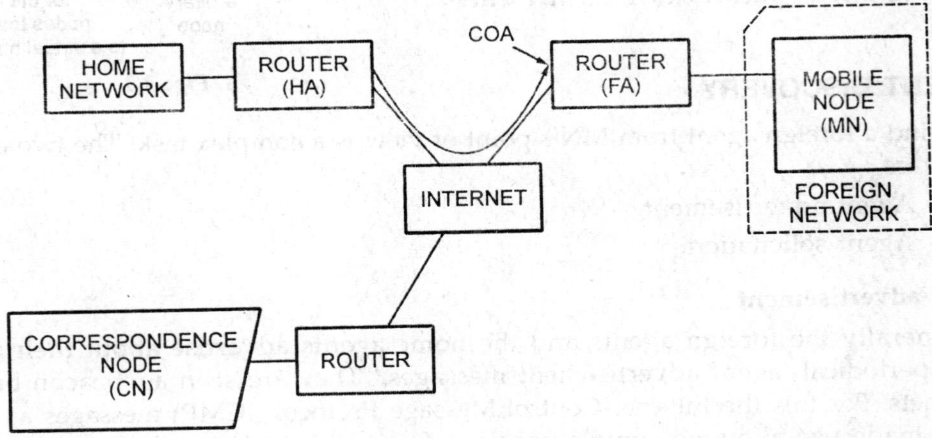

Fig. 3.1 Mobile IP network

(iv) Foreign Network (FN)

The foreign network is a current subnet to which the mobile node visits. It is completely different from home network.

(v) Foreign Agent (FA)

The FA provides many services to the mobile node during its visit to that the foreign network. This FA can act as default router for the mobile node.

(vi) Care-of Address (COA)

The current location of MN is defined by care-of address (with respect to IP). The packets sent to that of the MN are delivered to COA and they are not delivered directly to the MN's IP address. The address at which the packets finally exit is known as tunnel. The COA express the tunnel endpoint.

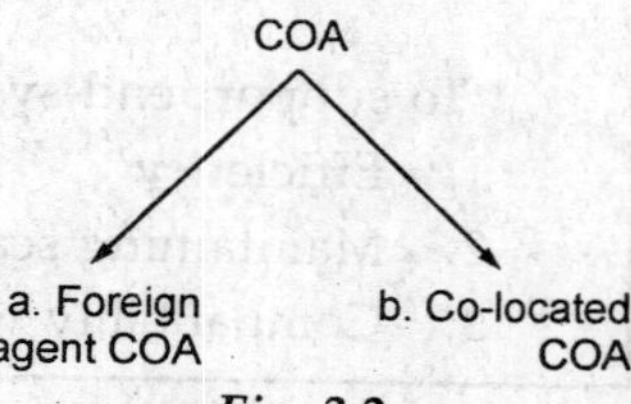

Fig. 3.2

(a) Foreign agent COA

The COA may be an IP address of foreign agent (FA). It can be located at FA.

(b) Co-located COA

The COA will be co-located if the mobile node (MN) has acquired an extra IP address that acts as COA. This address may be topologically correct. Here the tunnel end point will be at the MN.

Note : The co-located addresses can be acquired using the services like dynamic host configuration protocol (DHCP).

(vii) Home Agent (HA)

It is located in home network and it provides several services for the MN. Only at HA the tunnel for packets towards MN will start.

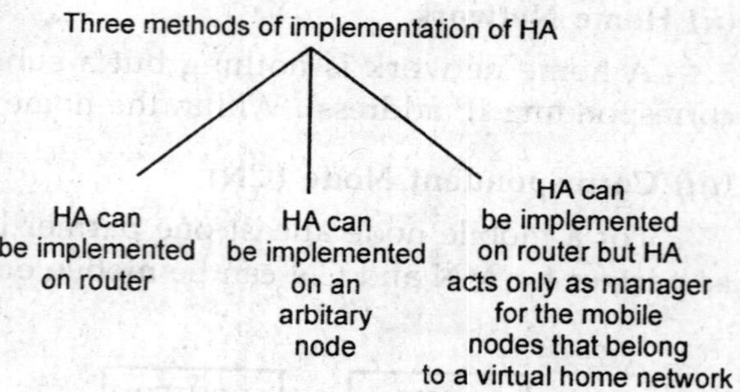

Fig. 3.3

3.3 AGENT DISCOVERY

To find a foreign agent from MN's point of view is a complex task. The two discovery methods are :

1. Agent advertisement
2. Agent solicitation.

1. Agent advertisement

Generally the foreign agents and the home agents advertise about their presence through periodical 'agent advertisement messages.' They are seen as 'beacon broadcast' into subnets. For this the Internet Control Message Protocol (ICMP) messages as per RFC 1256 are made use allowing some extensions for mobility status. An example of agent advertisement according to RFC 1256 is with some extension is shown in diagram.

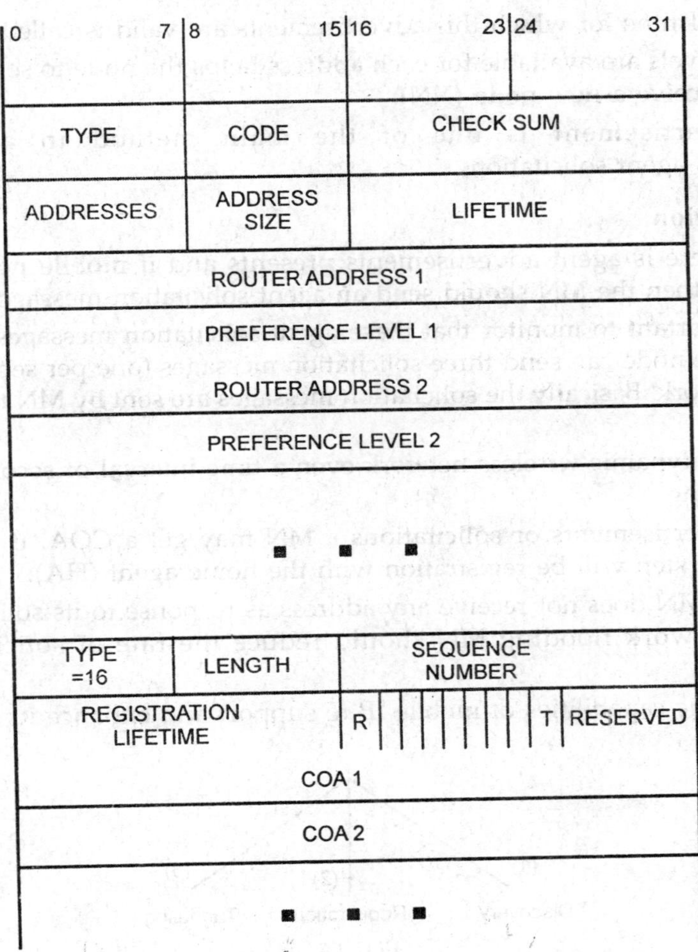

Fig. 3.4 Agent advertisement packet

The upper part of it represents ICMP packet where as the lower part is the mobility extension. Some of the fields are not shown here. Some of the fields namely type, code, lifetime, addresses, preference levels, lengths etc. are shown respectively.

The mobile nodes (MN) has to be reached with correct link layer's address. The 'Time to live' (TTL) field of the packet will be set to 1, for all the advertisements so as to avoid the forwarding process.

The respective fields in the ICMP are usually defined as given below. In the Fig. 3.4. The type is set to a value 9, next the code is set to 0, when the agent routes the traffic from the non-mobile nodes.

The foreign agents are required to send their packets form the mobile nodes and the number of addresses are available in addresses.

The length of time for which this advertisements are valid is called as 'Lifetime'.

Preference levels are available for each address helps the node to select the router that is interested to receive a new node (NN).

Agent advertisement is one of the main method in agent discovery. The second one is agent solicitation.

2. Agent Solicitation

In case if there is agent advertisements presents and if mobile node (MN) did not receive any COA then the MN should send an agent solicitation messąge.

But it is important to monitor that these agent solicitation messages do not flood the network. A mobile node can send three solicitation messages (one per second) as soon as it enters a new network. Basically the solicitation messages are sent by MN to search a foreign agent (FA).

For a highly dynamic wireless network even a time interval of second between these messages is too long.

By these advertisements or solicitations a MN may get a COA. If MN is in foreign network then next step will be registration with the home agent (HA).

Note : If the MN does not receive any address as response to its solicitation messages then to avoid network flooding MN should reduce the rate of solicitation messages exponentially.

The three basic capabilities of mobile IP to support and enhance its operations are as follows :

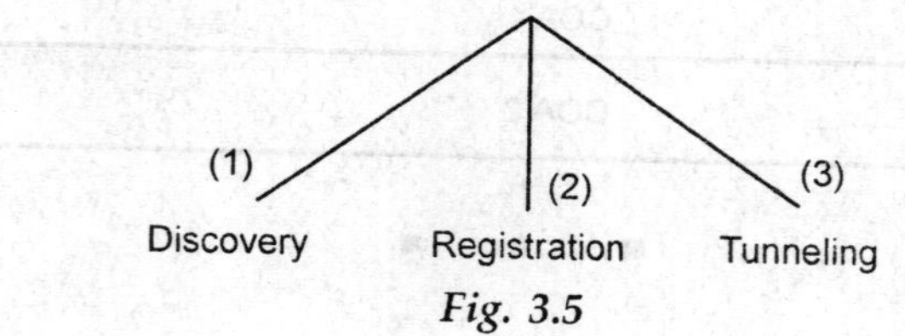

Fig. 3.5

1. Discovery

Mobile node makes use of discovery procedure for identifying the home agents and also the foreign agents.

2. Registration

Mobile node makes use of registration (authenticated) procedure to intimate the care-of-address to a home agents.

3. Tunneling

It is used for forwarding the IP diagram from home address to a care-of-address.

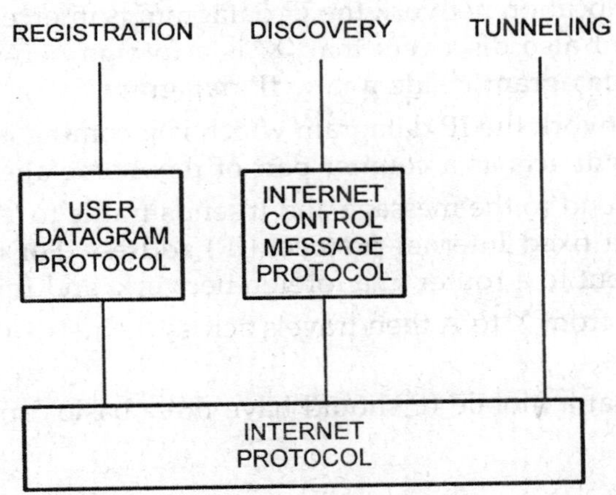

Fig. 3.6 Mobile IP—protocol support concept

Mobile IP

Mobile Internet protocol is denoted as mobile IP. A schematic diagram of it is shown below. The connectivity in the network is represented as link.

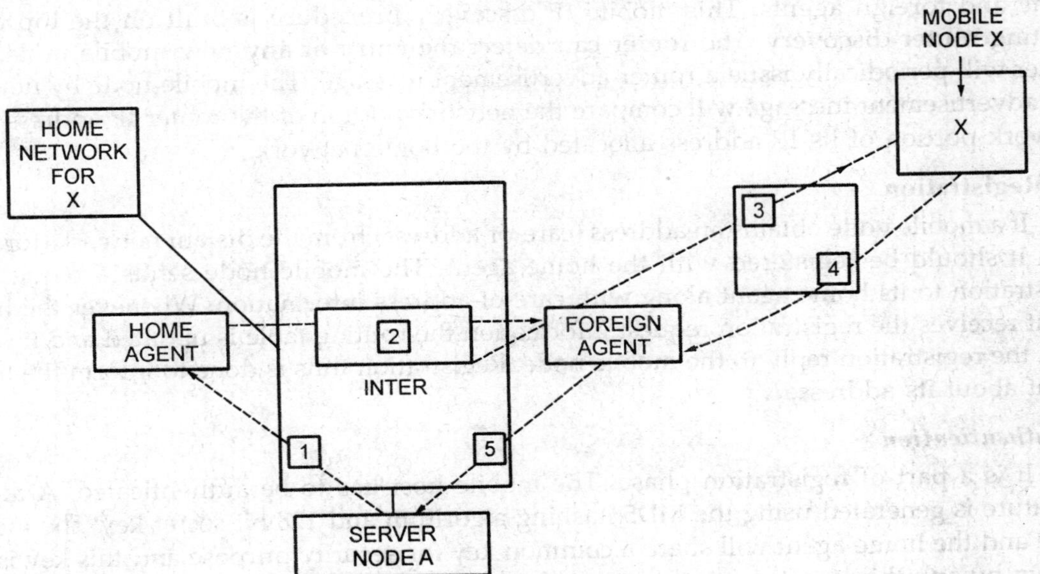

Fig. 3.7 Mobile IP schematic diagram architecture

Case study

The server 'A' (say) wants to send an IP datagram to a node X. The home address of X is known to A. The server A does not know whether X is in its home network or not. A sends packet to X with home address of X as its destination Internet protocol address in the IP header. The IP datagram then routed to X's home network area.

At the X's home location network the IP datagram is intercepted by the available home agent. The home agent also discovers that 'X' is a foreign network. Then the home agent encapsulates the full datagram inside a new IP datagram.

At the distant network the IP datagram which is incoming is intercepted by the foreign agent. The foreign agent acts as a counter part of this home agent in the foreign network.

X intends to respond to the message and it sends traffic to 'A'. In this, example A is not mobile. Hence A has a fixed Internet protocol (IP) address. For routing X's IP datagram to A, each datagram is sent to a router in a foreign network, and this router is a foreign agent.

The IP datagram from X to A then travels across the network using A's address (IP) as its destination address.

It is important that a mobile IP should have three basic capabilities.

(*i*) Discovery

(*ii*) Registration

(*iii*) Tunneling

Each of the above are discussed in detail below.

(*i*) Discovery

Each mobile node uses a particular discovery procedure to identify the respective home and foreign agents. This mobile IP discovery procedure is built on the top of an existing router discovery. The router can detect the entry of any new mobile node. The router will periodically issue a router advertisement message. The mobile node by noticing this advertisement message will compare the network portion of the router IP address with network portion of its IP address allocated by the home network.

(*ii*) Registration

If a mobile node obtains an address (care-of-address) from the distant network (foreign) then it should be registered with the home agent. The mobile node sends a request for registration to its home agent along with care-of-address information. Whenever the home agent receives the registration request information the routing table is updated and it sends back the registration reply to the mobile node. Registration thus is done to inform the home agent about its address.

• ***Authentication***

It is a part of registration phase. The mobile host has to be authenticated. A digital signature is generated using the MD5 hashing algorithm and 128 bit secret key. The mobile node and the home agent will share a common key for security purpose and this key is not known by any third party or intruders. A triplet (home address, registration life time and care-of-address) is maintained at the home agent at the end of registration. This is known as binding the mobile node.

The registration process has four important steps.

1. The mobile node sends a registration request to foreign agent for forwarding its service from the foreign agent.
2. This request from mobile node is relayed to home agent of mobile node by the foreign node.

3. The home agent rejects or accepts it and reply is sent.
4. Finally the foreign agent relays the reply message to the corresponding mobile node which actually requested it.

(*iii*) Tunneling

In the tunneling operation of mobile - IP, IP - within - IP encapsulation (embedding) mechanism is applied. For this a new IP header called as runnel header is added by home agent. Therefore the home agents address is the tunnel source IP address itself.

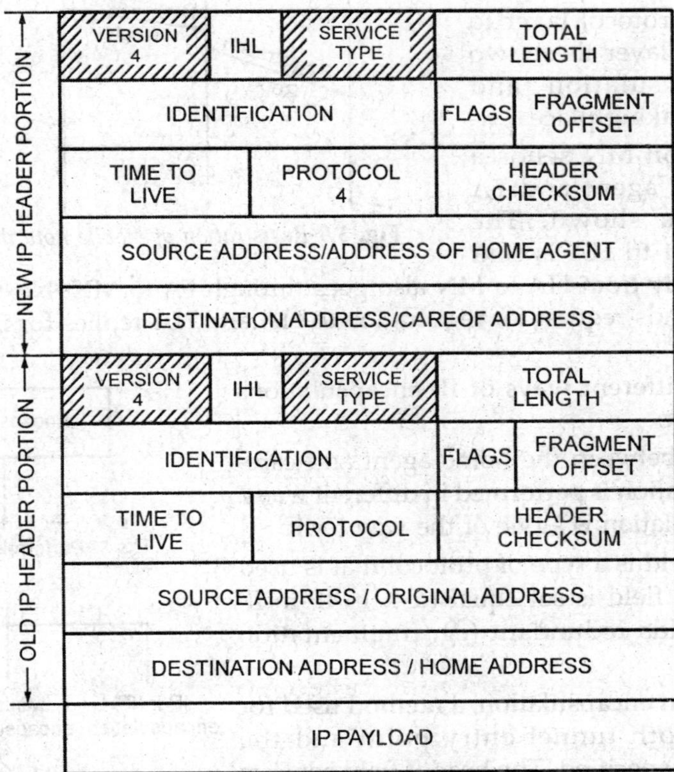

Fig. 3.8 IP encapsulation in mobile IP

Note : Shaded fields in the IP encapsulation represents the fields that are carried directly from inner IP header to that of the outer IP header portion.

3.4 TUNNELING AND ENCAPSULATION

Tunnel

It establishes a virtual pipe for the packets available between a tunnel entry and endpoint. The packets that enters the tunnel will forwarded and they will leave it with no change. Thus tunneling is sending a packet via a tunnel and it is achieved by 'Encapsulation'.

Encapsulation

It refers to a mechanism of arranging a packet header and data. Putting them together in the data part of the new packet. On the otherhand taking or eliminating data part of another packet is called as decapsulation.

Note : Whenever a packet is sent from higher protocol layer to the lower protocol layer these two operations encapsulation and decapsulation are taking place.

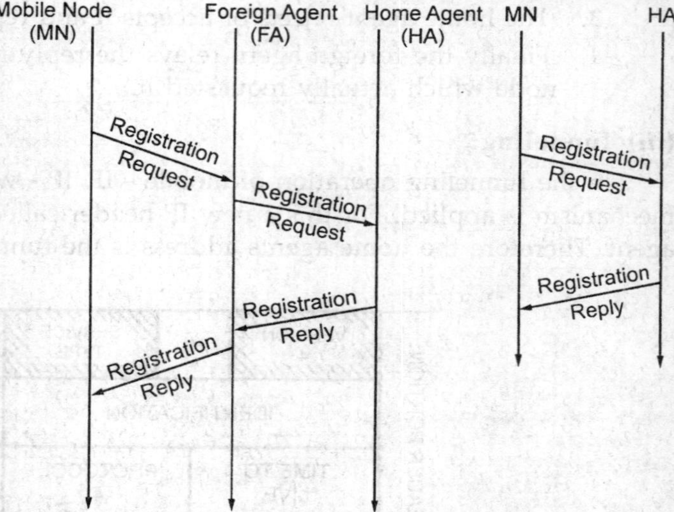

Fig. 3.9 *Registration of mobile note through HA or FA.*

For registration MN sends a request to foreign agent and FA replies to MN as shown. The registration request to HA is sent through FA and reply from HA to MN also goes through FA to MN. Next is without the FA intervention MN sends request for registration to HA and HA replies for it directly as shown in Fig. 3.10.

Some of the different ways of IP encapsulations are discussed below.

For tunneling between the home agent and care-of-address encapsulation is performed in different ways. An IP-in-IP encapsulation is a one of the way for it.

Encapsulation

Performing ways

IP-in-IP encapsulation | Minimal encapsulation | Generic routing encapsulation

Fig. 3.10

The IP-in-IP field is a type of protocol that is used in IP payload. The. field is set equal to 4. In IP-in-IP there are many fields redundant (eg. fragmentation field).

Next is minimal encapsulation, a method used for mobile IP. Here both tunnel entry point and the endpoint are clearly specified. The header field consists of the value 55 under minimal encapsulation protocol. The address of MN is needed here. A bit 'S' is maintained as a field content. The original sender address of the CN is included.

The IP-in-IP encapsulation and minimal encapsulation methods works only for the IP and the third method is generic routing encapsulation (GRE), it permits encapsulation of the packets of a protocol suite into payload part of packet of some other protocol suite. Simple procedure of it is shown below. The original data, header and GRE header forms the new data. The header of second protocol suite will be put in the front end.

The minimal value of header is only 4 bytes for GRE. The C bit field is set, if the checksum field consists of a valid IP checksum of the header and the payload data. The R bit is set that shows if the routing and offset fields 'tire present with valid information. Similarly the C bit mentioned earlier also expresses if the checksum field is present with valid information.

IP encapsulation formats

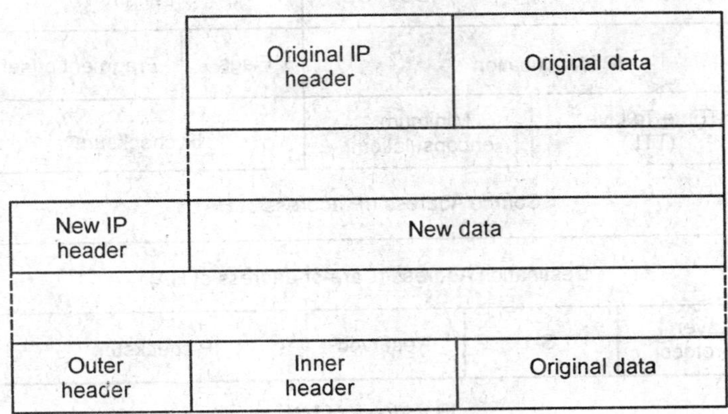

Fig. 3.11 IP encapsulation format

Version	IHL	DS (TOS)	Length	
IP identification			Flags	Fragment offset
TIME TO LIVE (TTL)	IP-in-IP		IP checksum	
SOURCE ADDRESS (IP address of HA)				
DESTINATION ADDRESS (Care-of-address of COA)				
Version	IHL	DS(TOS)	Length	
IP identification			Flags	Fragment offset
TIME TO LIVE (TTL)	Layer & protocol		IP checksum	
IP address of CN				
IP address of MN				
TCP/UDP/ ......PAYLOAD				

IHL → Internet Header length

TOS → Type of service

Fig. 3.12 IP-in-IP encapsulation

Version	IHL	DS (TOS)	Length	
IP identification			Flags	Fragment offset
Time To Live (TTL)	Minimum encapsulation		IP checksum	
Source Address (IP address of HA)				
Destination Address (Care-of-address of HA)				
Layer 4 protocol	S	Reserved	IP checksum	
IP address of MN				
Original sender IP address when s is set				
TCP/UDP/ .... PAY LOAD				

* S → If bit S is set, it means that original sender address is include

* TTL → Should be high so that packet will reach the end point

Fig. 3.13 Minimal encapsulation

		Original header	Original data
Outer header	GRE header	Original header	Original data
New Data	New Data		

Fig. 3.14 Generic routing encapsulation (GRE)

The routing field has variable length and it consists for the source routing.

Checksum field is valid ⇒ If C is set
Offset field is valid ⇒ If R is set

A key field is offered in GRE for authentication purpose. The offset in bytes is represented by offset particularly for the first source routing entry value. The routing field has variable length.

There is a field in GRE called as recursion control field that differentiates GRE from other encapsulation methods.

Recursion field in GRE represents a counter to show number of recursive encapsulations that are allowed.

The reserved field has to be ignored or zero on reception. For GRE the version field is zero.

3.5 OPTIMIZATION

In mobile IP protocol all the data packets to the mobile node should go through home agent. Because of this there will be unwanted overheads between HA and CN in network so that latency will increase.

Thus it is important to optimize the routes in network. For this the CN has to be informed about current location of the MN. An optimized mobile IP protocol requires four additional messages. They are tabulated below.

Sr. No.	Message required	Description
1.	Binding request	If a node wants know about mobile node (MN) it sends a request to home agent (HA).
2.	Binding ACK	On request the node will return this message after getting binding update message.
3.	Binding update	This is a message sent by HA to CN mentioning correct location of MN.
4.	Binding warning	The message is sent by a node if it decapsulates a data packet for MN, and it is not present FA for the MN. The message contains target address and MN's home address. In turn a binding update message will be sent to the node by HA.

These are the four messages that a mobile IP should contain if it has to optimized.

3.6 DYNAMIC HOST CONFIGURATION PROTOCOL (DHCP)

DHCP was developed from protocol called as Bootstrap protocol (BOOTP). This standard was released in 1985. It supports static information for clients that includes IP addresses. To manage dynamic configuration information and dynamic IP addresses IETF standardized an extension to 'BOOTP' known as dynamic host configuration protocol (DHCP).

3.6.1 Application of DHCP

1. DHCP helps to drag the management of IP addresses from distributed client servers to centrally managed servers.
2. In the sites with more TCP/IP clients, DHCP yields support to manage large number of clients effectively.
3. DHCP is useful in sites with fewer TCP/IP addresses than the number of clients.
4. In sites that needs frequent movement from host to host with different locations DHCP is used.

5. DHCP is used in sites where laptop computers have to move among different networks within a particular site.
6. It is used for diskless clients.

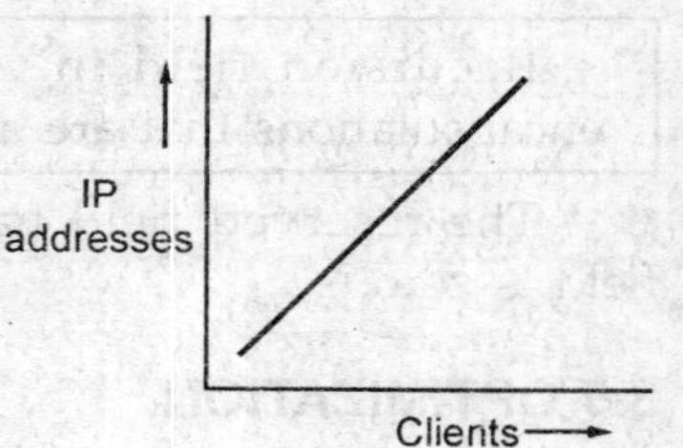

Fig. 3.15 Client Vs number of IP addresses

As the number of clients grows up the need for IP addresses is more. There is a chance of scarcity of IP addresses availability. This scarcity can be minimized with the help of DHCP. There are two ways possible.

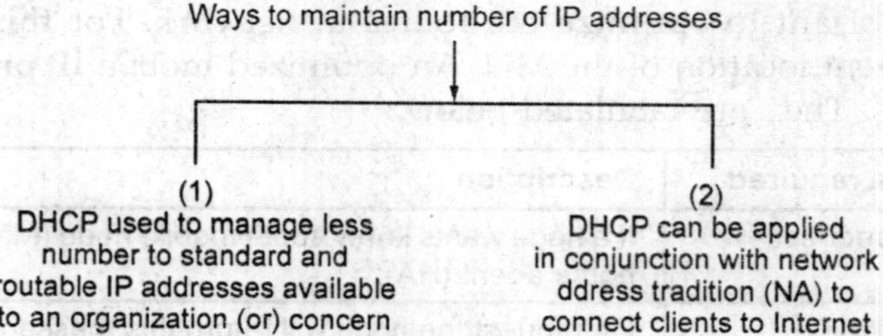

Fig. 3.16

By using these methods accessible IP addresses are made easy to some extent in networking.

The dynamic host configuration protocol was developed from Bootstrap protocol (BOOTP). The BOOTP is client server protocol which was designed to furnish four information. The problems associated with BOOTP are given below.

Problems with BOOTP

When a node (computer) is attached to TCP/IP Internet (connection established) should be aware of these above said four information.

1. Its subnet mask
2. Internet protocol (IP) address.
3. Internet protocol (IP) address of a router.
4. Internet protocol (IP) address of a name server.

Actually this Bootstrap protocol (BOOTP) is not a dynamic configuration protocol. Whenever a client requests IP address the server machine with BOOTP searches a table which matches physical address of client with Internet protocol (IP) address. This link between client and IP address is predetermined.

BOOTP cannot address a few problems like

1. If a host moves from a physical network to another network.
2. If a host seeks a temporary Internet protocol (IP) address.

There are critical situation where BOOTP cannot decide what to do next.

3.6.2 Significance of Dynamic Host Configuration Protocol

But Dynamic host configuration protocol DHCP provides dynamic configuration. It is an extension to the BOOTP and compatible with it. If a host is running BOOTP client it can also request a configuration (example : static configuration) from a DHCP server node. The advantages of DHCP are :

1. Whenever a host moves from one network to another network or to connect or disconnect with a network.
2. DHCP also provides temporary IP address for a particular predetermined time period.

3.6.3 Components of Dynamic Host Configuration Protocol

The dynamic host configuration protocol (DHCP) is built on a client-server model. It has designated server hosts allocating the network addresses and delivering configuration parameters to the dynamically configured hosts. The term 'client' refers to host that request initialization parameters and the term 'server' refers to a host that can provide initialization parameters through dynamic host configuration protocol. The DHCP mainly provides configuration parameters to the Internet hosts. It consists of two components.

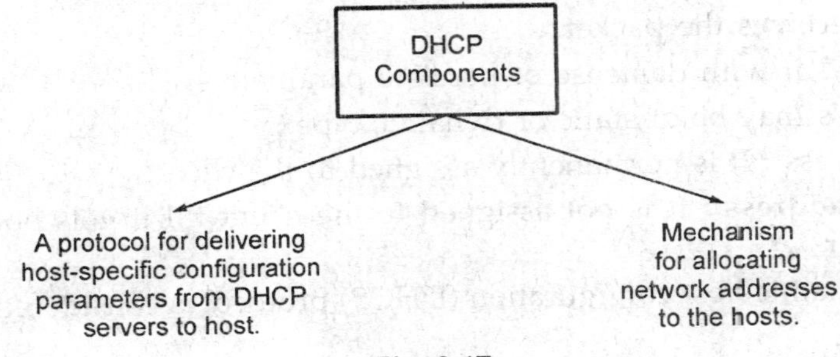

Fig. 3.17

The DHCP supports three important mechanisms for the IP address allocation.

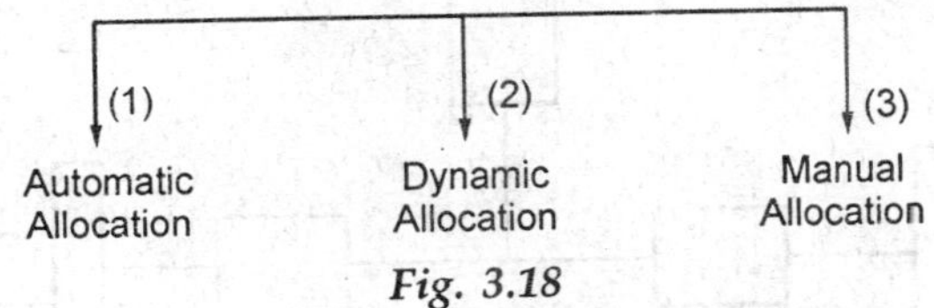

Fig. 3.18

1. Automatic allocation is also possible. Wherein the DHCP assigns permanent IP address to a particular client.
2. With the dynamic allocation DHCP assigns IP address to a client for, a particular period of time.
3. In the manual allocation a client's IP address is assigned by network administrator, where the DHCP is used to inform the address assigned to the client.

Note : Whenever permanent IP address pool is not required and if temporary IP addresses are enough for a set of clients in this case it is better to have dynamic allocation mechanism.

Only in dynamic allocation method automatic reuse of an address is done.

Importance of DHCP

DHCP is a widely used protocol for configuring hosts like PC's, printers and workstations. The DHCP servers allocates mainly IP addresses from a pool of IP addresses to a set of clients with the help of network administrator as discussed so far. Hence dynamic host configuration protocol which was created by Internet Engineering Task Force (IETF) streamlines the efficiency of the network connectivity that is used by mobile IP protocols.

The DHCP protocol is used by three different agents as we know server, client and relay agent. This DHCP server is actually a central server configured on a site's network that can provide DHCP services. The client (software program) interacts with DHCP server.

The client/server relationship is perfectly used by DHCP for allocating IP addresses and keeping track of their usage. Whenever a user boots a particular client system and that system broadcasts a request for DHCP server for issuing an IP address.

The DHCP can also pass additional information for a booting system.

Sequence :

1. Client issues request for booting.
2. Server receives the packet.
3. Compares it with database of possible parameters.

The IP address may be of static or dynamic type.

Static IP address : It is permanently assigned to the client.

Dynamic IF address : It is not assigned to the client till it gets booted and address given by the server.

Hence the dynamic host configuration (DHCP) protocol is considered as "a protocol of choice".

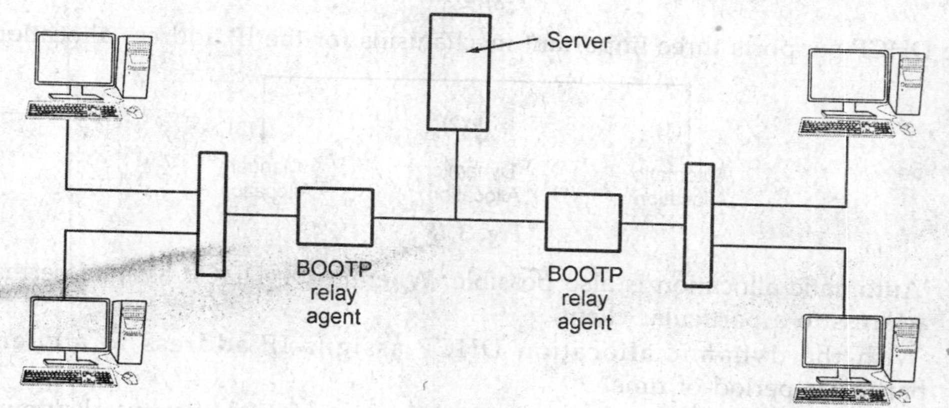

Fig. 3.19 DHCP—Client/server environment

Note : The DHCP responds to a particular period of time (server responds with IP address) which is also known as "lease" for which period the client makes use of the address assigned to it.

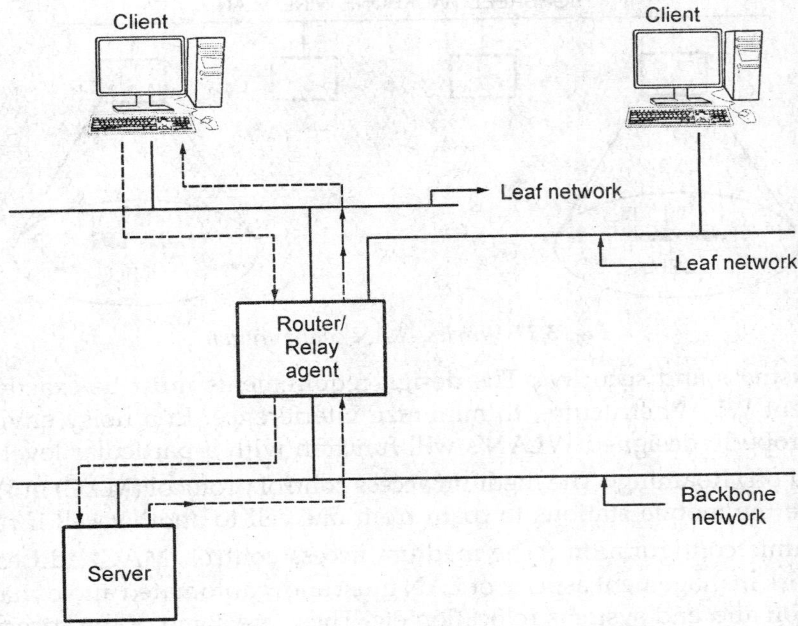

Fig. 3.20 DHCP—Client/server Interaction sample

With this client/server interaction setup DHCP enables computers on a network to configure themselves.

DHCP makes it possible for users of wireless devices to move within an organization that is with various networks, (from home to work) for this the DHCP client and server work together to handle the roaming status and to assign IP address on new networks efficiently.

The wireless LAN should meet some basic requirements. It should have high capacity, full connectivity, to cover short distances etc.

Advantages of WLAN

1. Number of nodes : WLAN must support many nodes across many (multiple cells).
2. Service area : The coverage of WLAN should have a diameter from 100 m to 300 m.
3. Power consumption : The battery life should be long and reliable for all wireless users.
4. Throughput : To maximize capacity the medium access control protocol (MAC) should make use of WLAN to the maximum.
5. Co-located Network Operation : Whenever interference between different WLAN's is possible then WLAN will start to interact, in the possible areas.
6. License free operation : The users (customers) should operate WLAN products without securing license for frequency range that is used by LAN.

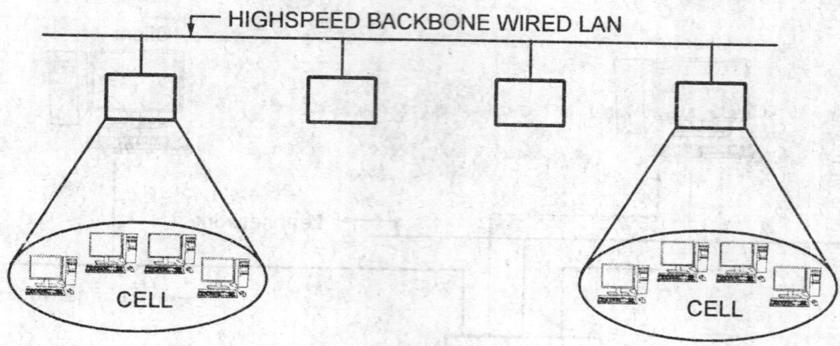

Fig. 3.21 Wireless LAN configuration

7. Robustness and security : The design requirements must be exactly done for an efficient WLAN structure, to minimize interference. In a noisy environment also the properly designed WLAN's will function with a particular level of security.
8. Hand off/Roaming : The medium access control protocol (MAC) in WLAN should enable the mobile stations to roam from one cell to another cell if required.
9. Dynamic configuration : The medium access control (MAC) addressing and the network management aspects of LAN must allow automated and dynamic addition, deletion and end systems relocation etc. These are some of the specific aspects for an efficient WLAN set up where dynamic configuration is very important.

3.7 ROUTING

The importance of routing is essentially the distributing ability with the shortest path that is possible. Each node in the network prefers a shortest neighbour to it. The process of forwarding continues till the packet reaches the destination. The objective of routing concept is to reach the destination with an optimal path. The routing should also satisfy the needs of an ad hoc network. The router should be capable of performing few important functions.

1. Router should provide a link between the networks.
2. It should provide routing and delivery of data between processes on the end systems attached to various networks.
3. Routing should be such that it is able to do all functions without modification of architecture of networks and subnetworks.

Router should also be able to make differences among networks like addressing schemes, interfacing methods and maximum possible packet sizes.

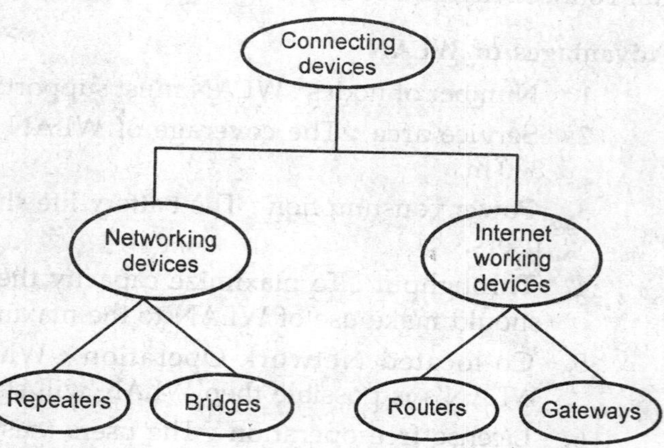

Fig. 3.23 Connecting Devices in a network

When two or more devices are connected for sharing the data/resources it forms a network. The network so formed can be a local area network (LAN). Depending upon the coverage distance the network is also classified as local area network (LAN), metropolitan area network (MAN) and wide area networks (WAN). When entirely separate networks change information (data) between them it is known as internetwork or simply Internet. Now it is important to connect or link many local area networks (LAN's) into an Internet requires more (additional) internetworking devices called as routers and gateways. Hence the Internet is nothing but interconnection of networks.

The important devices associated with Internet as

1. Repeaters
2. Bridges
3. Routers
4. Gateways

The repeaters mentioned here acts on the physical layer. The bridges make use of addressing protocols and influences flow control of a LAN setup, and are active in data link layer (DLL). The routers provides between two similar (but separate) local area networks (LAN's). Router is highly active in network layer of OSI model.

The last one called as gateways facilitates translation services between the incompatible LAN's and active in all the layers. The bridge device in a network has many types.

1. Simple bridge 2. Multiport bridge 3. Transparent bridge

Whenever the bridges used to connect different LAN's many aspects are given consideration. Some of them are listed below :

(*a*) Frame format
(*b*) Data rate
(*c*) Payload size
(*d*) Address bit order

The bridges and repeaters in a network are mainly hardware devices that are capable of doing special tasks.

But the devices called routers are different from these types. They consists of software that makes them to find which of the available paths is appropriate for a particular type of transmission at that time. They can function at three main layers. They are

1. Physical layer
2. Datalink layer
3. Network layer of OSI standard model

Router can relay the packets among different networks (i.e. interconnected networks). Routers acts like stations on a network. Router switches the packet from a network to other network which wants to receive it Routers thus directs the packets to the router of destination side in the proper path. It has addresses, and links to which it continues the job and two or more networks at a particular instant of time period. (Refer Fig. 4.16 on next page.)

There are four networks connected through routers denoted as 'R' here. These routers are responsible to direct the packets of data in right direction towards destination. If the received packet's address of node to which it has to be sent is foreigner to that particular router then router is capable of determining the correct relay point in the network to which this received packet should be actually sent such that it reaches its destination in that network successfully. The concepts considered in routing are

1. Least cost routing
2. Adaptive routing
3. Non adaptive routing

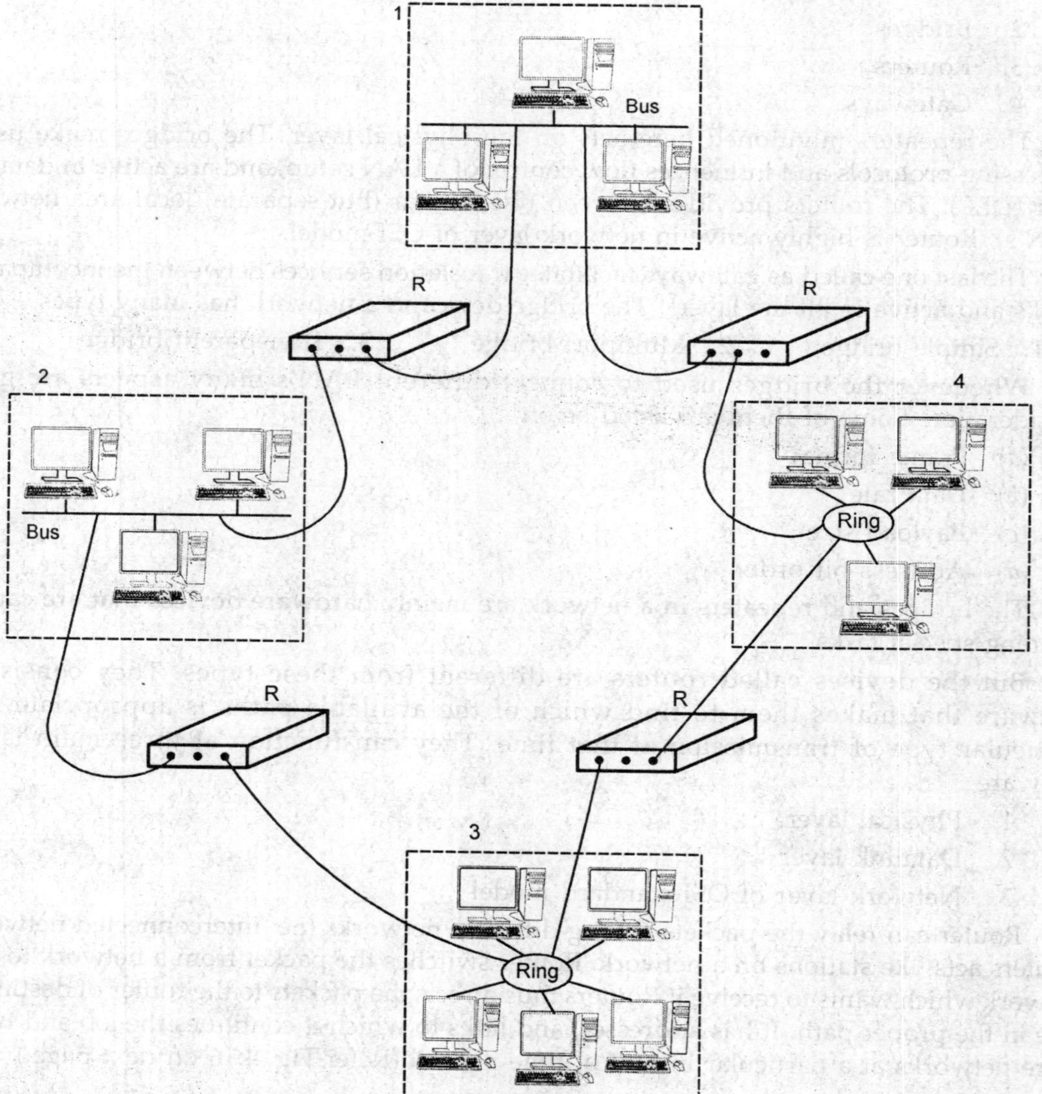

Fig. 3.23 Routers (R) in an Internet with four networks (1, 2, 3, 4)

3.7.1 Routing Types

1. Least Cost Routing

This routing is based on efficiency of the system. The shortest path also denotes the cheapest path possible. The number of hops required for the packets to reach the destination also counts. The less number of hops is economical and expresses an efficient routing.

If the pathway requires least number of relays it is termed as hop-count routing. In this scheme every link is treated to be equal length. The decision of best short route is made by finding the summation of all lengths of all the links used by the path.

2. Adaptive Routing

In this routing method depending upon the changes in topology and nature of the given network every router will select a new route (way) for every packet.

If a router decides a pathway, it passes the packet (data) to next router on the same path and then does not worry about it. The new router may follow the same path for transmission or selects a different path also.

The life time determination of the packet is also an important factor. The hand off mechanism from one router to another router enables lesser logic and control factors which must be present in the frame. The acceleration of the packet is also enhanced. Each packet added with a packet field called "packet life time" or "time to live" (TTL) which is considered before a packet is lost or destroyed.

3. Non Adaptive Routing

In this scheme the routing decisions are made according to changes of network topologies. Thus routing method may be adopted according to expected efficiency.

3.7.2 Destination Sequenced Distance Vector Routing (DSDV)

The destination sequenced distance vector routing (DSDV) is a table driven algorithm based on Bellman Ford routing mechanism. It is highly useful for mobile networks. There are two types of mobile networks namely,

1. Infrastructured network
2. Ad hoc network

In the first type it has the fixed and wired gateways and in the second type it consists of infrastructureless mobile network. It has no fixed routers. All the nodes are flexible with dynamic connections in the network in a arbitrary manner. The applications of ad hoc network are meetings where quick information sharing is a must and emergency search and rescue operation cases etc. The ad hoc network of early days had few drawbacks like the following.

1. High power consumption
2. Low bandwidth
3. High error rates

The routing information must be properly advertised by broadcasting or multicasting the packets that are transmitted periodically.

Decision has to be made based on the data and delaying of advertising the routes are allowed. The idea of delaying is to avoid many number of rebroadcasts in the network due to instability.

The two types of protocols are table driven routing protocol and source initiated (demand-driven type) routing protocol.

The table driven routing protocol tries to maintain consistent and up-to-date routing related information from each node to every other node in the network.

The DSDV protocol under this category requires every mobile station to advertise to every current neighbour. The entries of the list may dynamically change and it makes way for requirement of frequent advertisements to take place. Hence every node can have knowledge about every other mobile computer.

The DSDV protocol enables shortest number of hops for a route to a destination. The mobile computers frequently link with base stations that allows them to exchange information with other computers connected in the wired networks.

In an ad hoc network movement of host (mobile host) is supported by this protocol. For example the mobile host (MH_1, MH_2, MH_3 ...) can move in an ad hoc network.

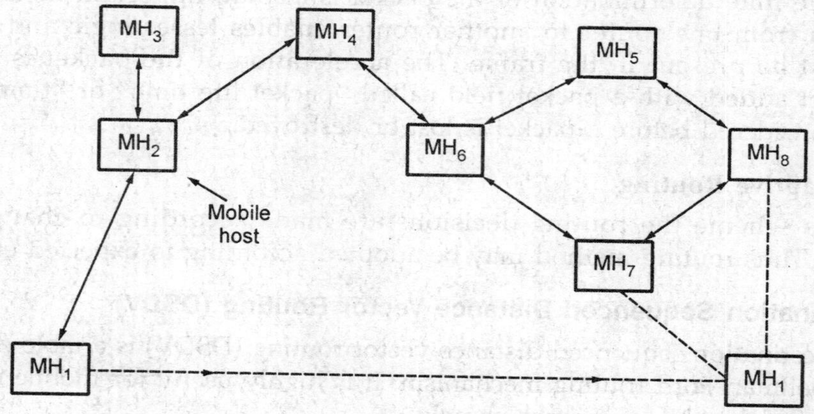

Fig. 3.24 Movement enabled in an ad hoc network

The movement of each mobile host (MH_i) is possible and each one has its sequence number. A table is maintained and updated as the hopping takes place. Advertisements of routing information in the network is made whenever required. The DSDV routing protocol well suits the movement of mobile hosts.

The fluctuations of routing has to be avoided. The updation of routes are done as per few important criteria.

1. Routes are preferred if sequence numbers are same and still the metric is lower.
2. Routes are preferred (most of the time) if the sequence numbers are newer.

To avoid damping fluctuations setting time has to be properly used. The setting has three fields keyed with first field.

1. Destination address field
2. Last settling time field
3. Average settling time field.

Advantages of DSDV protocol

1. The Dynamic sequenced distance vector (DSDV) routing protocol guarantees loop free paths to every destination.
2. Effective protocol under table driven category for movement of mobile hosts.
3. It maintains stability.
4. Compatible with Ad hoc networks.
5. It is good for the system in steady state condition.
6. DSDV protocol models mobile computers as routers that co-operates to forward packets according to the needs of the network.
7. It can be utilized at either network layer (layer 3) or below the network layer (above the MAC layer), with few additional information along with the routing informations.
8. DSDV uses settling time and sequence number and hence enables the routing table free from damped fluctuations.

3.7.3 Dynamic Source Routing (DSR)

The dynamic source routing (DSR) protocol is an on-demand protocol which is designed for multihopping wireless ad hoc networks. It provides two functions.

1. Route Discovery
2. Route Maintenance

Route Discovery : It is performed whenever a node wants to send a packet of data to a particular destination for which it does not have a route.

Route Maintenance : It identifies a link failure on an active route or path. Once route failure is found then it is informed in such a way that it is maintained. Both the route discovery and route maintenance are available on an on-demand situation. Information cannot be exchanged in a periodical way.

A main difficulty in operation with dynamic source routing (DSR) is handling congestion. While dealing with DSR protocol it is important to consider mobile status of devices. The impact they have created is high. Since ad hoc devices consists of mobile devices, stability of routes in the network often change. Due to changes in delivery, the packets become instable, as the mobile network enter and exit freely.

It is better to select lesser number of hops on a particular route. Distance matters a lot, and as the range of transmission increases the quality of wireless radio channel starts decreases providing less reliable transmission. This in turn increases more packet losses and necessitates retransmission thus reducing system efficiency.

Node mobility impacts on routes available. It is also complex to monitor congestion levels in the network. Final throughput will be less due to this level of mobility of nodes. If it is high stability of routes will decrease and throughput will naturally decrease. These may be known to the initiator because of the collapse of the routes created by high mobility in the network.

Hence protocols including dynamic source routed protocol (DSR) dealing with mobile ad hoc networks has to take into account so many criterion for improving the entire system's performance.

3.7.4 Alternative Metrics

The network routing protocols can be adaptive or non-adaptive. For a dynamic network and node mobility to have an improved performance adaptive ad hoc network routing protocols suit very well. The mobile ad hoc network known as 'MANET' protocols are flexible with network dynamics. 'MANET' protocols are better than other existing protocols.

The "Network dynamics" includes changing the network topology, shared medium contention, data congestion, varying traffic distributions, varying traffic patterns etc. Any node movement will create changes in network topologies, due to link additions and link breakages. The new changes like link additions needs network protocol responses to have reliable and accurate network services.

The route changes if any, will alter the traffic distribution in the network and in turn varies congestion that is experienced by each node in the network. A mobility metric must properly express and indicate the performance of network protocol and it should be protocol independent.

A mobility metric should capture any network changes that take place and indicate the resulting performance of a MANET protocol.

Hence the metric should provide feedback and allow proper adaptation of a single protocol.

There are few requirements for mobility metric to enable adaptive ad hoc network 'MANET' protocols.

(*a*) A good indicator of protocol performance.

(*b*) Feasible to compute with respect to node resources.

(*c*) Independent of any specific protocol.

(*d*) Computable in a distributed environment without knowledge of global network.

(*e*) Computable in real network implementations.

(*a*) A good indicator of protocol performance

(*i*) Data packet delivery ratio.

(*ii*) End-to-end delay.

(*iii*) Protocol overhead.

The performance of protocol must be properly predicted by the mobility metric.

If there is a small change in an end-to-end delay in the network it should be reflected in the mobility metric's value changes. Whenever the node in the network receives a feedback from mobility metric then it can adjust the delay parameter to be within the boundaries allowed.

(*b*) Computable in a distributed environment without global network knowledge

If a metric needs information from some other node of other network and adds that information also then the demand on the network will grow.

(*c*) Feasible to compute with respect to node resources

A node in a network may have resource constraints like limited battery power, limited processing ability, less memory. A mobility metric should be feasible enough to compute by each node in that network inspite of all the above resource constraints.

(d) Independent of specific protocols

A general mobility metric should be used by any adaptive protocol and it must not stick on to a specific protocol's presence. Whenever there is independence of a protocol then that mobility metric suits many networks layers also.

(e) Computable in real network implementations

The mobility metric should be present for a real network nodes in real network implementing conditions. It should be done just with simulation results and relevant parameters. Many aspects of link duration are considered.

(i) Link duration as an indicator of protocol performance.

(ii) Link duration meeting network requirements.

e.g. Indication of protocol performance feasible to compute with respect to node resources available.

(iii) Usage of link duration for adaption in networks.

Therefore link duration mobility metric helps to enable MANETs. The mobility metric is flexible and good in performance with adaptive ad hoc networks to indicate the performance of protocols used in network establishments.

3.7.5 Possible Metric Alternatives

Introduction

In any network number of hops used for data transfer is treated as routing metric. But bandwidth is another factor to be considered for routing metric.

In addition to these factors the least interference routing (LIR) is also important that will account interferences taking place in network.

A simple example for possible interference in ad-hoc network topology is shown below.

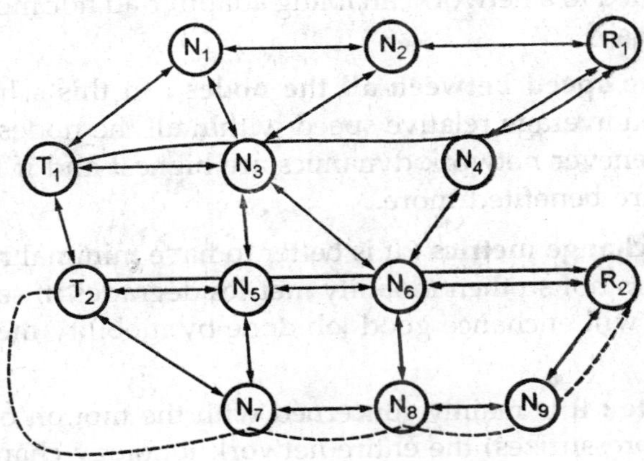

T_1, T_2 ... → Transmitter/Sender

N_1, N_2 ... → Nodes

R_1, R_2 ... → Receiver

Fig. 3.26 Least interference routing an example

Sender T_1 wants to send information to R_1. Similarly T_2 wants to, send, information to R_2. In the diagram the T_1 takes three paths using three hops.

The three different possible paths are

(*i*) T_1, N_3, N_4, R_1

(*ii*) T_i, N_3, N_2, R_1

(*iii*) T_1, N_1, N_2, R_1

Taking any one path the transmitter T sends packets to the receiver R.

Also at each node possible interference can be calculated. The amount of interference depends on number of neighbours that could overhear the transmission.

Thus analysis of routing behaviour at a node has to consider these main parameters to obtain accurate results.

1. Mobility model parameters.
2. Information unique to a protocol.
3. Average relative speed between all the nodes.
4. Minimum route change metrics.
5. Link change rate.

1. Mobility model parameters : The parameters includes pause time or node speed. With mobility model input parameters like mobility metric make links for adaptability of the protocols to an artificial input which may not be available in real network implementation.

2. Information unique to a protocol : Protocols have feedback mechanism. For example the dynamic source routing protocol can adapt to route requests time outs based on the end-to-end delay of the route requests.

Hence a custom feedback metric mechanism for each protocol will be more flexible scheme that can be applied to a network. Enabling adaptive ad hoc mobile network (MANET) protocols suites this case.

3. Average relative speed between all the nodes : In this scheme mobility metric is allowed that is based on average relative speed within all the nodes. Hence a stable link is somewhat possible whenever network dynamics are highest and if feedback mechanism is used network nodes, are benefited more.

4. Minimal route change metrics : It is better to have minimal route changes in ad hoc networks scenario. If it is not so then mobility metrics degrades in some of its performance. Minimal multihopping will enchance good job done by mobility metric to enable adaptive networks.

5. Link change rate : It is mainly concerned with the motion of nodes relative to one another which forces (pressurizes) the entire network topology changes or change in node interconnections. Link change rate is not related to node mobility. Hence the link change rate that will influence changes in network topology is treated as main criteria in mobile ad hoc networks (MANETs).

3.7.6 Link Duration-Overview

Link duration predictive value can be taken as mobility metric. The stability of links is a very important parameter. If the links are longer stability will be high and if the links are shorter (in terms of time period) then stability will reduce. An average link duration metric is then considered. Hence it combine the link change rate and the weight values.

REVIEW QUESTIONS

1. Define 'mobile IP'.
2. List any three important features of mobile IP.
3. What is known as home address?
4. Write short notes on Link and tunnel.
5. Write short note on Internet protocol.
6. Explain architecture of mobile IP.
7. Write a note on Tunnelling.
8. What is known as DHCP.
9. What are the applications of DHCP?
10. How DHCP helps to maintain proper number of IP addresses.
11. What are the advantages of DHCP?
12. What is a 'BOOTP'?
13. What are the constraints in using 'BOOTP'?
14. Write a short note on 'Routing'?
15. List/our devices which are connected with internet.
16. What is the function of a 'Router'?
17. Define 'gateway'?
18. Explain : (*a*) Gateways (*b*) Bridges and (*c*) Repeaters.
19. What are types of a bridge device?
20. Explain the different aspects that can influence LAN's which are connected with bridges.
21. What are : (*a*) Least cost routing (*b*) Adaptive routing (*c*) Non adaptive routing? Explain.
22. What is 'DSDV'? Explain in detail.
23. What are the three mechanisms applied for IP address allocation?
24. Explain dynamic source routing in detail.
25. Write a short note on DSDV and DSR.
26. What is known as alternative metrics?
27. What are the possible metric alternatives?
28. Write a short note on : (*a*) Minimum route change metrics and (*b*) Link change rate.
29. Define 'link duration'.
30. Explain 'Mobile IP' in detail.
31. Explain the goat, entities and IP packet delivery in mobile IP.
32. Explain :
    (*i*) Tunneling concept and
    (*ii*) IP packet delivery

32. Explain DHCP and IP encapsulation.
34. Explain agent advertisement and discovery in mobile IP.
35. Explain :
    (*i*) Registration
    (*ii*) Optimization concepts
36. What is the use of binding cache in mobile IP?
37. What are the limitations of minimal-encapsulation in Mobile IP?
38. Explain the header-fields of IP-in, IP, minimal generic routing encapsulation.

❑❑❑

Unit 4

Transport and Application Layers

4.1 INTRODUCTION

- **Network**

A network can be defined in many ways. One of its definition is "A network is a set of connected devices that can communicate with each other". Examples of such devices are computers and printers.

- **Internet**

The Internet is nothing but a group of networks that communicate with each other. Internet is a combination of many networks connected together.

Internet has several applications like electronic mail, web browsing etc. which are the part of today's life style. The Internet is an organized and structured system. It is used by industries, educational institutions, libraries etc. in many countries.

- **Traditional TCP**

Brief history of TCP/IP :

In the year of 1973 the importance of protocols which support end to end data packet delivery came into the data communication. The Transmission Control Protocol (TCP) is an end to end protocol that assures faithful data packet delivery. TCP has many important concepts like,

(*i*) Datagram

(*ii*) Encapsulation and

(*iii*) Gateway functionalities.

TCP was divided into two subdivisions.

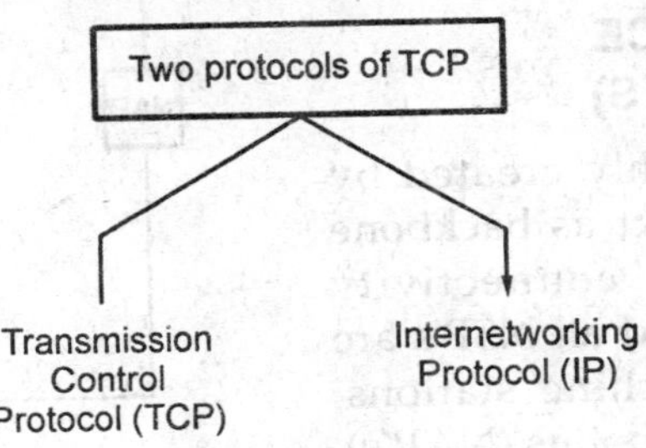

Fig. 4.1

Responsibilities of TCP and IP in broadway.

Protocol	Responsibility
IP	Responsible for datagram routing.
TCP	Responsible for functions such as. 1. Error detection 2. Segmentation 3. Reassembly

The combination or Internet working of these two protocols was named as TCP/IP protocol suite.

Also connection between networks were possible with three important networks in the year 1977, namely packet radio, packet satellite and Advanced Research Projects Agency Network (ARPANET).

Internet Environment

A basic Internet environment with few levels for establishing connectivity throughout the world is done with the help of large service providers like,

(*a*) International Service Provider (ISP)

(*b*) National Service Provider (NSP)

(*c*) Regional Internet Service Provider (RISP) and

(*d*) Local Internet Service Provider (LISP)

Internet is not just a hierarchical structure. Many number of local area networks (LANs) and wide area networks (WAN's) are connected via connection and switching devices. Some of the international service providers (ISP) are listed below :

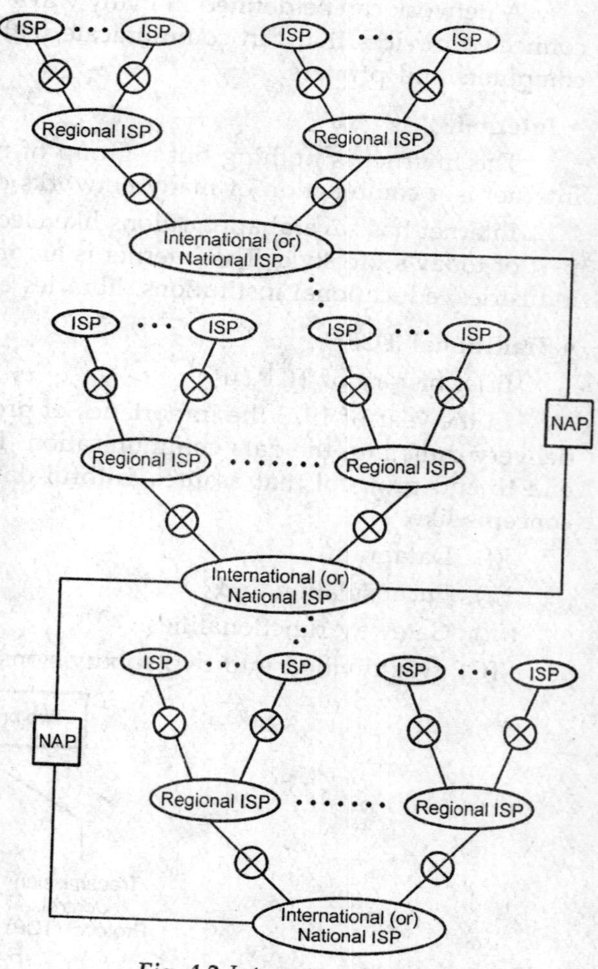

Fig. 4.2 Internet environment

4.2 NATIONAL SERVICE PROVIDERS (NSP'S)

The NSP's are mainly created by large companies. They act as backbone network and provides connectivity between the end users and all NSP's are connected through switching stations, known as network access points (NAP's).

Some of the NSP's can also be connected through private switching offices/stations known as "Peering stations".

The regional ISP's (RISP) are the Internet service providers and they are basically small ISP's which can connect few NSP's. They provide lesser data rate when compared to ISP's.

The last component in the Internet environment is the local Internet service providers (LISP's). They enable direct services to the end users. The LISP can be linked to RISP or even to ISP's directly. The structure of the Internet is given in above diagram. These service providers and together they facilitate world wide connectivity.

The TCP/IP are the two important protocols. Before discussing TCP/IP in detail the term "protocol" has to be made clear.

Protocols

'Protocol' is a set of rules which governs data communication. A protocol provides information about,

(*i*) What is being communicated

(*ii*) When it was communicated

(*iii*) In what way it is communicated.

The major components of a protocol are known as :

(*a*) Syntax

(*b*) Semantics and

(*c*) Timing

(*a*) **Syntax :** It represents the format of the data/information and the order in which the data is available.

(*b*) **Semantics :** It represents the exact meaning of every section of bits.

(*c*) **Timing :** The timing parameter generally provides two information. They are

(*i*) When the data has to be sent

(*ii*) How fast the data has to be sent.

It determines the speed of the data transfer usually in megabits per second. To begin with, the Open System Interconnect system (OSI) should be clearly understood.

In the year 1947, the International Standards Organization (ISO) which is a multinational structured body was dedicated to the world wide agreement on accurate international standards.

An International Standards Organization that covers all the requirements/aspects of the network data communication is called as "Open System Interconnection" popularly termed as OSI model.

The OSI model has seven layered architecture. To remember a OSI model the following mnemonic sentence shall be used.

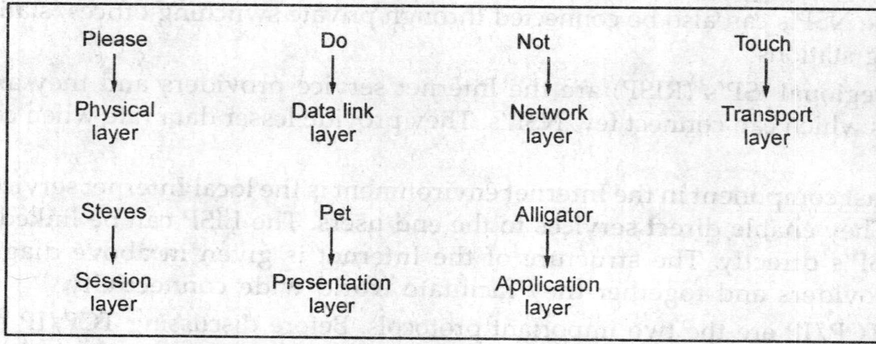

The OSI model and the TCP/IP protocol suite are discussed in detail in the following chapters.

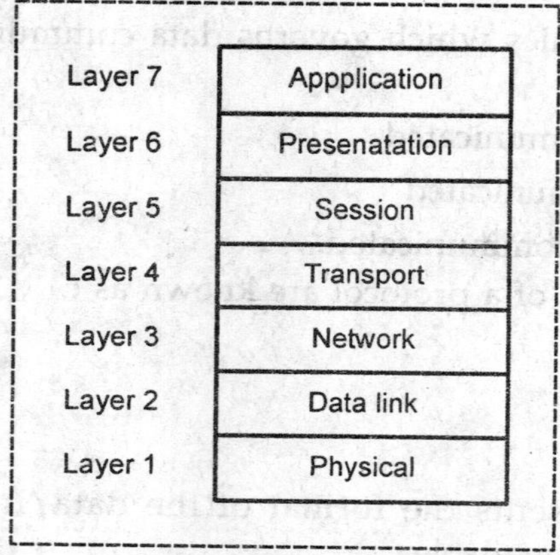

Fig. 4.3 Seven layers of OSI model

4.2.1 Functions of layers of OSI model :

1. Physical layer : It is related to transmission of unstructured stream of bits over the physical medium. It deals with the mechanical, electrical, functional and the procedure aspects to access the physical medium.

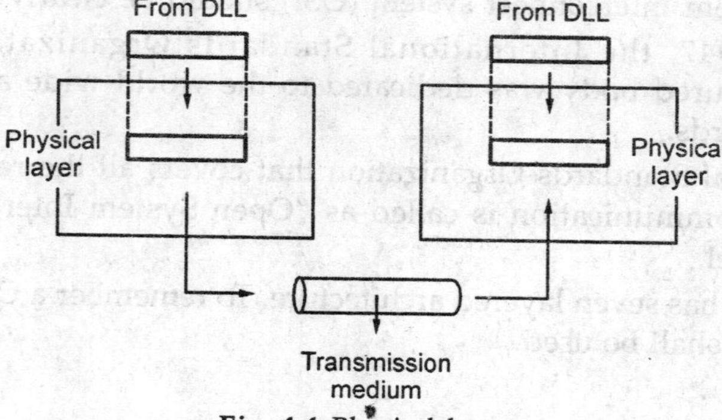

Fig. 4.4 Physical layer

Parameters related to physical layer

- ***Representation of individual bits***

This layer consists of a stream of bits. (Bits are of 1's and 0's). The bits are encoded into signals, and the physical layer mainly defines the encoding type.

- ***Characteristics of interfaces and media***

Physical layer defines the nature or characteristics of the interface acting between transmission medium and devices.

- ***Data rate***

It denotes the transmission rate, defined by physical layer. The physical layer defines the duration of each bit. This transmission data rate expresses the number of bits sent each second.

- ***Bit synchronization***

At bit level the sender and receiver should be synchronized.

Line configuration :

The devices must be properly connected to the medium which is done by physical layer. For example in multipoint configuration the link is shared between many devices.

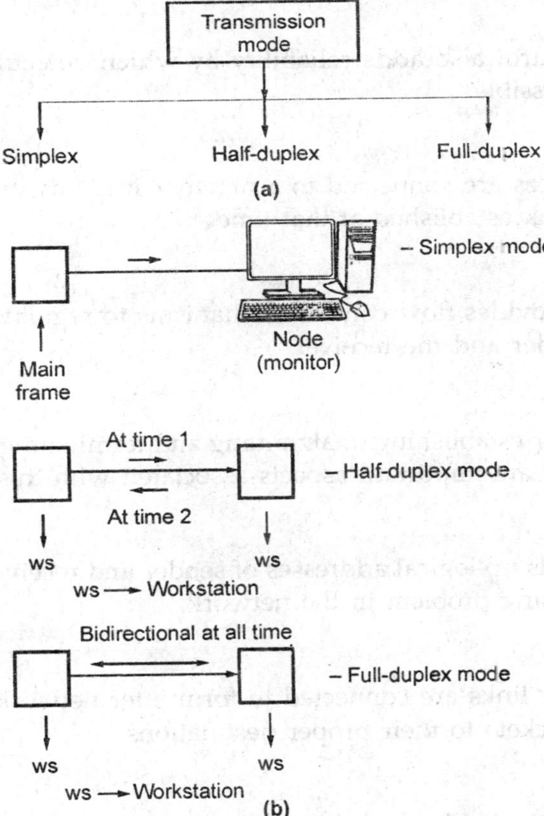

Fig. 4.5 (a) Transmission modes used in physical link (b) Concept of different modes

2. Data link layer/Data link control layer (DLC)

It takes care for reliable transfer of information across the physical link. It divides the entire length of data into blocks (frames) and sends them with proper synchronization, flow control and error control.

This layer is responsible for node-to-node delivery without error.

Function of Data-link layer

Framing function

The DLC divides the bit stream into manageable units called as frames. This fragmentation of entire message received from physical layer into small data units (frames) is the main responsibility of data link layer.

Physical addressing

After framing the physical address is used in order to distribute it to different systems in a network by the data link layer.

A header information is added to each frame which bears both source and destination address.

Error control

The data link control also adds reliability by which detecting and retransmitting of lost frames is made possible.

Access control

When many devices are connected to a network it is possible to know which device has control over the link established at that time.

Flow control

Data link layer provides flow control mechanisms to regulate a balanced (same) data flow rate between sender and the receiver.

3. Network layer

It is responsible for establishing, maintaining and terminating connections. The logical addressing and routing are important aspects associated with this layer.

Logical addressing

Network layer adds up logical addresses of sender and receiver to header information. This eliminates addressing problem in the network.

Routing function

When networks or links are connected to form inter network then routing should be proper to direct the packets to their proper destinations.

4. Transport layer

It is responsible for reliable and transparent data transfer between end points. Also it provides end to end data recovery and flow control. This layer takes care of data transfer from source to destination and vice-versa. It establishes connection between two end ports.

Features :

1. Service-point addressing : The transport layer header includes address known as service-point address which is also called as port address.
2. Connection control : The layer can be connectionless or connection oriented. In case of connection oriented type transport, all the data is sent and connection is terminated.
3. Segmentation and reassembly : The entire message is divided into small units called as segments and transmitted which are then reassembled as original message at the receiver side.

5. Session layer

It establishes control structure for communication between the applications. It also manages and terminates connections between all co-operating applications.

Synchronization : Session layer permits a process to add check point to data stream for synchronization purpose.

Dialog control : The session layer is also called as network dialog controller. It permits two systems entering the dialog. The communication between two processes is made possible, for both duplex and full duplex types.

The session layer does three things between two systems :

1. Establishes Interaction
2. Maintains Interaction
3. Synchronizes Interaction

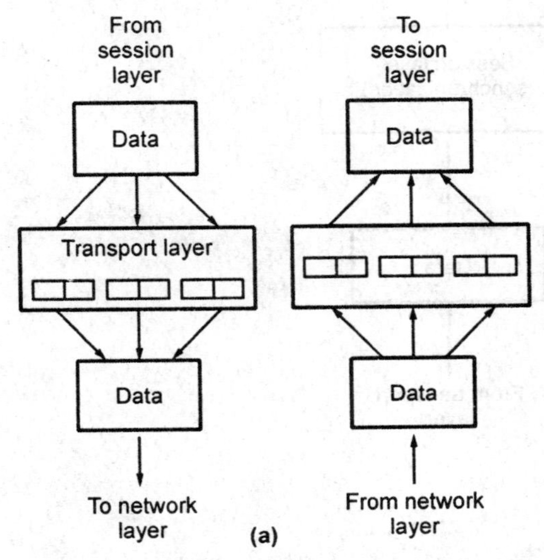

Fig. 4.6 (a) Concept of transport layer

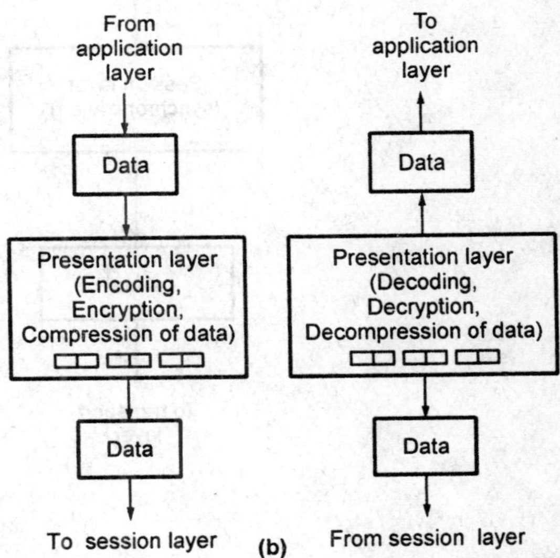

Fig. 4.6 (b) Concept of presentation layer

- ***Translation***

The information content of processes in systems may be in the form of numbers, characters, strings etc. Before transmitting the bit stream information should be changed.

- ***Encryption and Compression***

Encryption is mainly intended for privacy. Sender and receiver alone can recognize the data and any intruder cannot capture the message.

If encryption is done in transmitter and then decryption should be done at receiver side to balance and retrieve the data. The same type of transform as encryption is done at receiver.

Another function is the 'compression'. It reduces the total number of bits that has to be transmitted. It is very distinct and highly important in multimedia transmissions which includes text, video and audio signals.

6. Presentation layer

It provides full independence to the application processes from data (information) in data representation. It is related with syntax and semantics of the data between the two systems.

The presentation layer is interlinked with session layer and application layer.

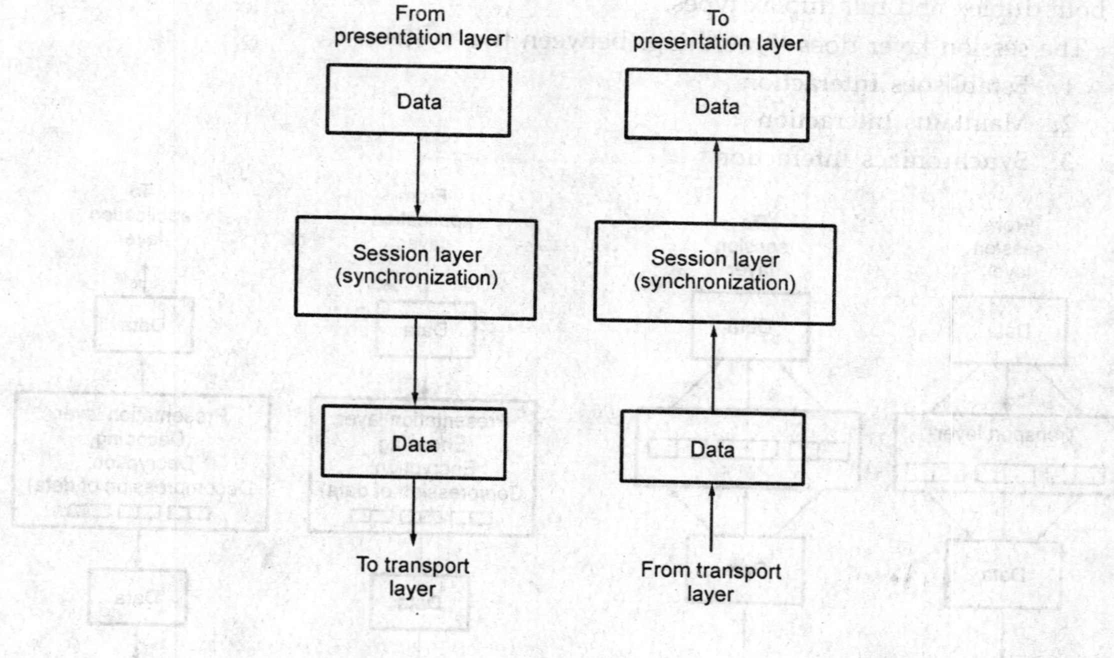

7. Application layer

It provides distributed information services, and allows access to OSI model for users.

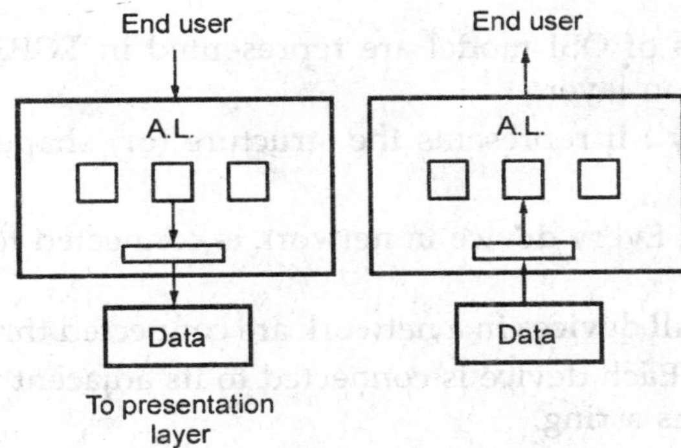

Fig. 4.7 Concept of Application layer

This layer provides support and user interfaces for the services like remote file transfer and transfer, electronic mail (e-mail) etc. Many types of distributed information services can be supported by this layer.

Example : File Transfer Access Management (FTAM)

In this application it allows and enables the user to access files in remote computer.

4.2.2 Transmission Mode

The direction of transmission between two devices may be simplex, half-duplex or full-duplex. In a simplex mode only one device can transmit data whereas the other can only receive data and it is called as one-way communication. But in a half-duplex mode two devices can transmit and receive (send and receive) but not at same time period. Finally in a full-duplex mode (simply duplex) the devices can send and receive at same time.

- **Physical Topology**

The topology represents the way how devices are physically connected to form a network as a whole. There are many distinct topologies. For example mesh topology, star topology, ring topology and bus topology. Each type are unique from the other.

- **Network Virtual Terminal**

It is a software version of physical terminal that allows the user for logging on to the remote host. A software emulation of the terminal is also created at remote host. The users terminal can interact with it and enables communication.

Note : The TCP/IP (Transmission control protocol/Internet working protocol) exactly does not match with OSI model discussed so far. But it resembles it in many ways. The TCP/IP suits has five main layers.

1. Physical link
2. Data link

3. Network link
4. Transport link
5. Application link

The three top layers of OSI model are represented in TCP/IP suite with a single layer known as application layer.

- **Network topology :** It represents the structure (or) shape of the network.

Examples :

1. Mesh topology : Every device in network is connected to every other device in it.
2. Star topology : All devices in a network are connected through a central devices.
3. Ring topology : Each device is connected to its adjacent (next) device in such a way that it forms a ring.
4. Bus topology : All devices in a network have a common link (or) devices are connected to a common link.

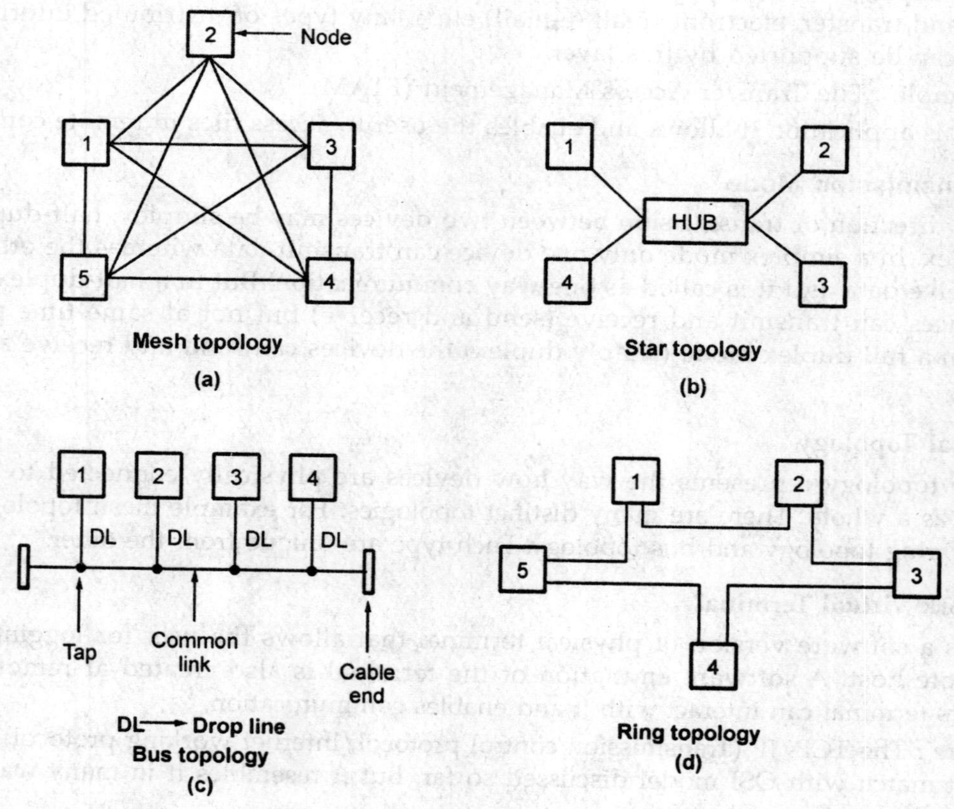

Fig. 4.8 Different topologies

4.2.3 Interaction between seven layer structures in OSI model

The OSI reference model with internal seven layers interaction is given below.

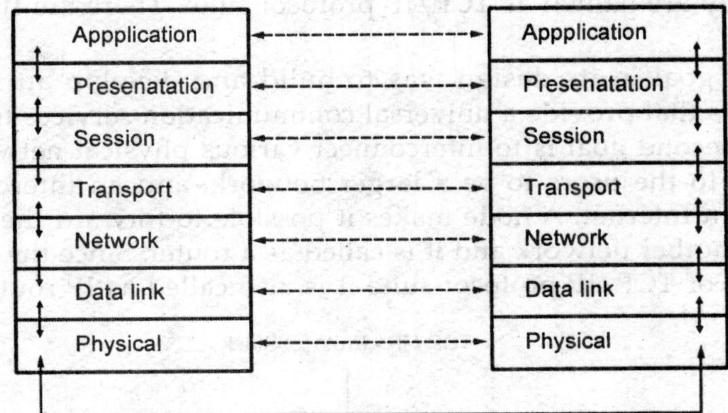

Fig. 4.9 OSI-reference model

In these seven layers each and every layer provides a particular set of functions to the layers above it and also to the next layer below it. The functions of each layer is listed in the tabulation below.

Summary of functionalities in OSI model

Layer	Function
Application layer	Network applications such as terminal emulation and also file transfer.
Presentation layer	Formatting of data and encryption function.
Session layer	Establishment and maintenance of the sessions.
Transport layer	Provision of reliable and unreliable end to end delivery.
Network layer	Packets delivery and routing.
Data link layer	Framing of units of information and error checking.
Physical layer	Transmission of bits on the physical hardware unit.

4.3 TRANSMISSION CONTROL PROTOCOL (TCP)

To support mobility the transmission control protocol (TCP) is applied for several applications.

Most of the applications rely on transport layer like TCP or UDP is user datagram protocol. There are two main functions of transport layer in internet namely checksumming and multiplexing/demultiplexing of data. TCP needs some special environments so as to be applied for mobile applications. UDP is connectionless and it does not guarantee reliable data delivery. But TCP offers connections between any two applications and it guarantees reliable data delivery.

4.4 GOALS OF TCP

The transmission control protocol and Internet protocol (IP) are the two important protocols and they are named as TCP/IP protocol suite. There are two important goals of TCP/IP.

(*i*) The first goal in its design was to build and develop an interconnection of different networks that provide a universal communication services that is internetwork or Internet. The second goal is to interconnect various physical networks to form what actually appears to the users to be a larger network, and an interconnection of such networks forms an Internet. A node makes it possible to forward the data packets from one network to another network and it is called as a router. Since the routing function is a part of IP layer of TCP/IP protocol suite it is also called as IP router.

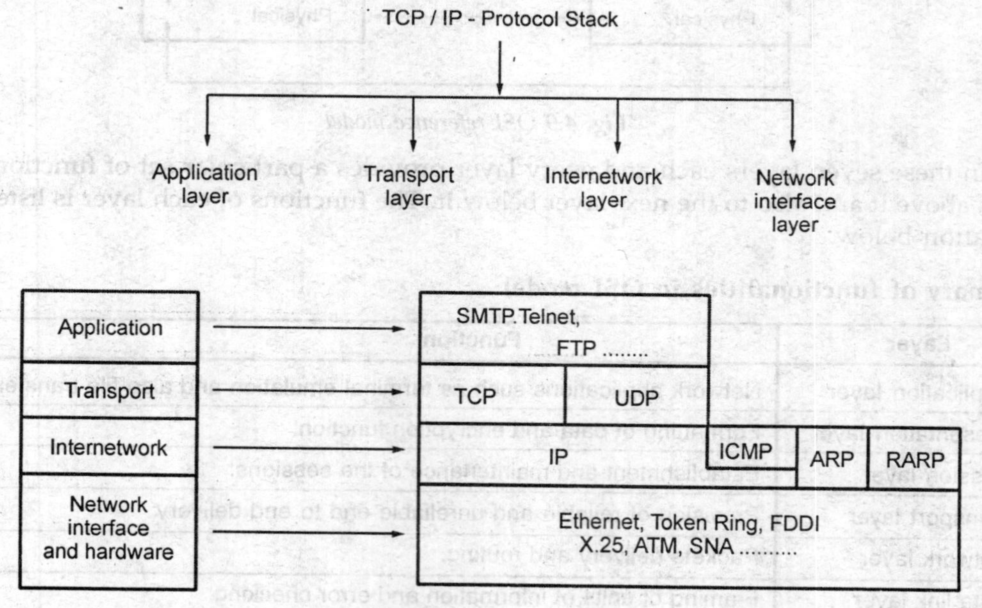

Fig. 4.10 TCP/IP-Architectural model

Each of the above four layers have different application functions like SMTP, Telnet etc. There are few important characteristics for the application protocols. They are :

(*i*) TELNET

(*ii*) FTP (File transfer protocol)

(*iii*) SMTP (Simple mail transfer protocol) etc.

For transport mechanism they use either TCP or UDP.

TCP is a peer-to-peer, connection oriented protocol, and there is no master-slave relation available.

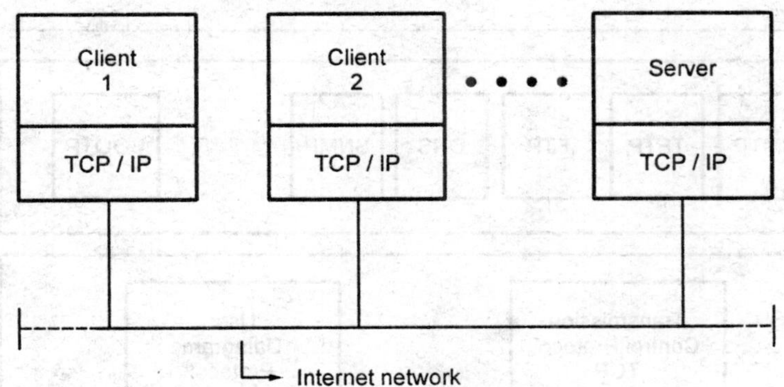

Fig. 4.11 Client server model—in TCP/IP

Here server is an application available for the Internet users, and the client is a requester of that service. A client part is invoked to make a request by the user for his application and it inturn provides the service, using the TCP/IP as transport vehicle. 'Request' and 'Reply' signals are interchanged. A server is capable of attending several requests (multiple clients) simultaneously.

4.4.1 Advantages of TCP/IP over OSI model

(*i*) The cost involved in designing TCP/IP protocol suite is comparatively less,

(*ii*) With TCP/IP suite as a basic foundation it is easy to build Internet systems.

(*iii*) The department of defense (DOD) uses TCP/IP protocol suite for all the software purchases and its operational needs were supported only by TCP/IP protocols.

4.5 TCP/IP PROTOCOL ARCHITECTURE—FIVE LAYERED STRUCTURE

The TCP/IP protocol suite is characterized by five layers and the different layers are

1. Application layer
2. Transport layer
3. Physical layer
4. Internet layer
5. Network access layer

Each layer is intended to do specific functions.

The architecture of TCP/IP is different from seven layer open system interconnect (OSI) model.

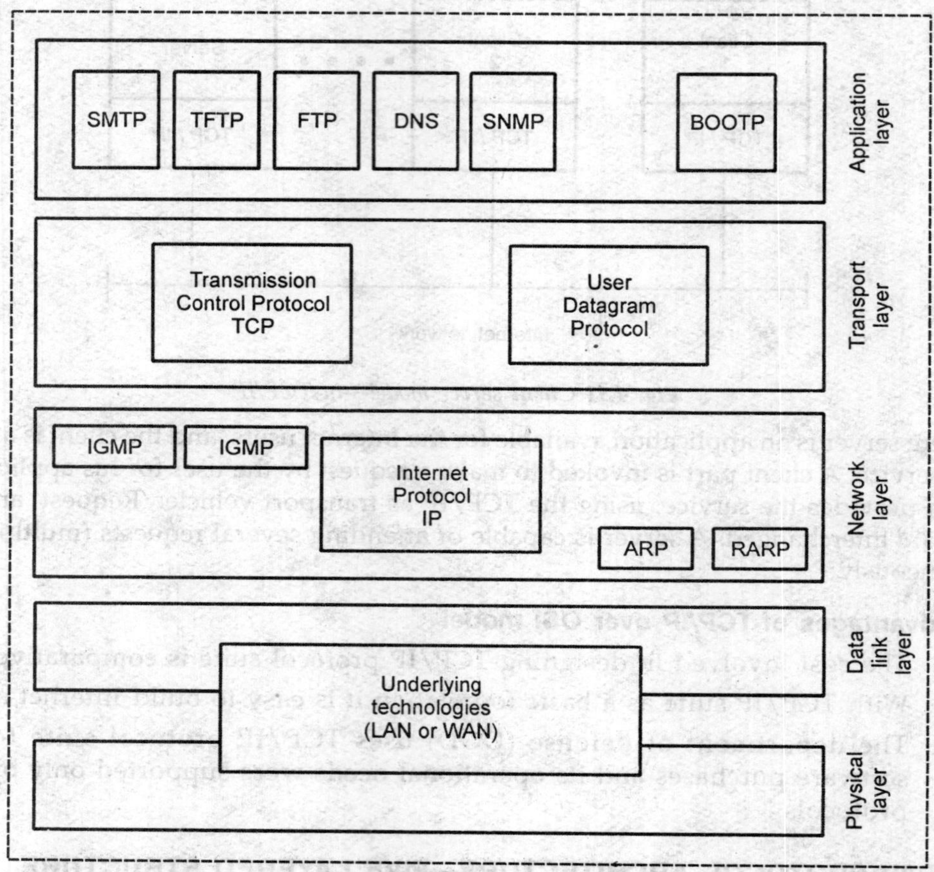

Fig. 4.12 TCP/IP Protocol suite—A five layered structure

TFTP : Trivial file transfer protocol
SMTP : Simple mail transfer protocol
FTP : File transfer protocol
ARP : Address resolution protocol
RARP : Reverse address resolution protocol
SNMP : Simple network management protocol
DNS : Domain name system
IGMP : Internet group management protocol
ICMP : Internet control message protocol
BOOTP : Bootstrap protocol

4.5.1 Layers of TCP/IP

1. **Application layer :** This layer provides communication between the applications, processes on separate hosts environment.
2. **Transport layer :** It provides data-transfer services and it is reliable to have end to end client service. The details of the underlying networks are hidden from application layer by this transport layer. Sometimes this layer is also referred as host-to-host layer.
3. **Internet layer :** It is mainly related to data routing and ensures packet delivery at the destination host. The networks linked in between may be connected through router devices.
4. **Network access layer :** It is related to logical interfacing between a subnetwork and an end system available.
5. **Physical layer :** It represents the characteristics of the transmission media, encoding schemes and also the rate of signalling.

4.6 TCP/IP—OPERATION

Any 'communication' developed for data transmission may contain many networks and they are called as 'subnetworks'. Connecting the computer with the subnetwork is done by token ring. The blocks of data is then transferred from one host to another host by implementing Internet protocols (IP) in the end systems. Each entity in the network should have an unique address. Within each host, every process has its own address and it allows the transport protocol (TCP) to deliver data/information to each relevant process.

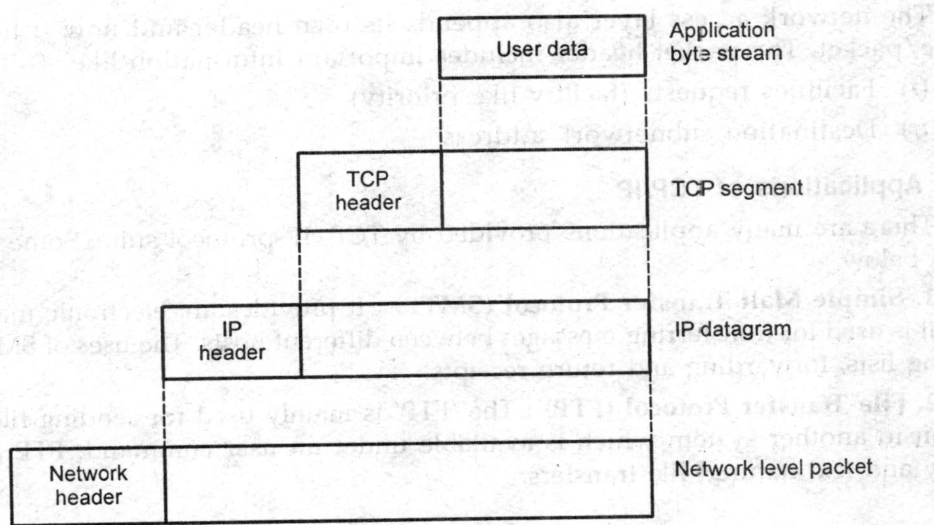

Fig. 4.13 Protocol data units—in TCP/IP protocol architecture

To control all the operations the user data and control data should be sent to the appropriate host. In this "sending of data" process usually a block of data is passed to TCP, and TCP will receive all the data first and then the entire block will be broken by TCP into smaller pieces for simplified processing. A control information known as TCP header' is appended along with each piece of data. Hence a 'TCP segment' is formed.

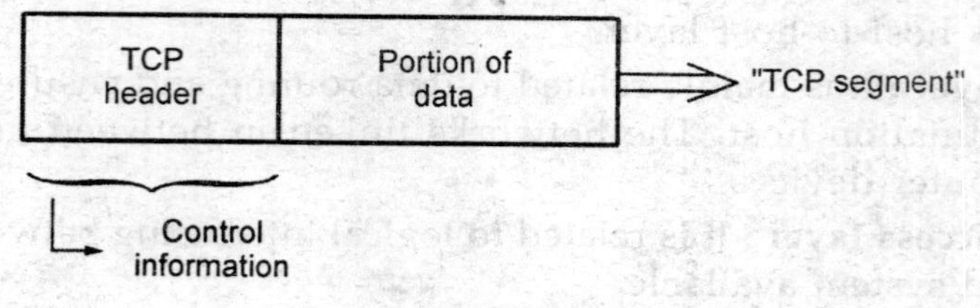

Fig. 4.14

Many items can be included within the TCP header like,

(*i*) Destination port

(*ii*) Checksum

(*iii*) Sequence number

When the TCP segments are handed over to Internet Protocol (IP) with necessary instructions, where to send those segments, the IP will append a IP header with relevant control information and the segment is now known as IP datagram.

These IP datagrams will be finally sent to network access layer and it is ready for transmission process towards first subnetwork in the network in the path to destination host.

The network access layer also appends its own header and now it has formed a frame/packet. The packet header includes important information like

(*i*) Facilities requests (facility like priority)

(*ii*) Destination subnetwork address

4.6.1 Applications of TCP/IP

There are many applications provided by TCP/IP protocol suite. Some of them are listed below.

1. Simple Mail Transfer Protocol (SMTP) : It provides an 'electronic mail' function. Also it is used for transferring messages between different hosts. The uses of SMTP includes mailing lists, forwarding and return receipts.

2. File Transfer Protocol (FTP) : The 'FTP' is mainly used for sending files from one system to another system which is available under an user command. FTP allows both binary and text natured file transfers.

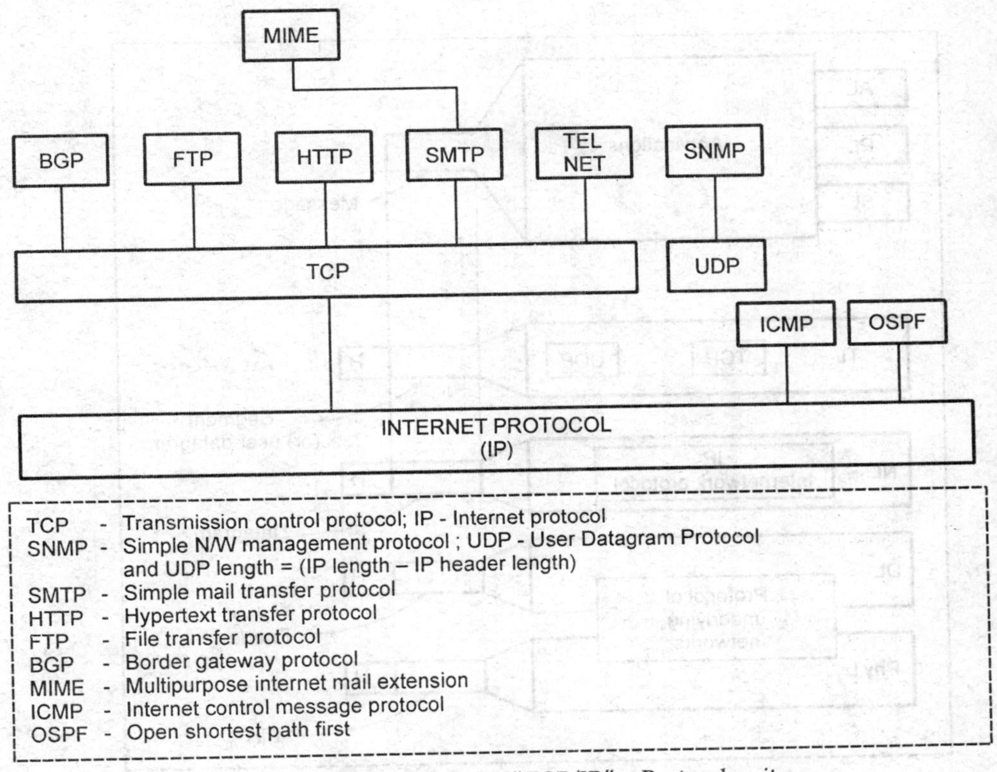

Fig. 4.15 Protocols in "TCP/IP"—Protocol suite

3. TELNET : It enables remote log-on facility, by which user operates (log-on) as if he is connected to the system directly. There are two TELNET modules available. They are "User TELNET" and "Server TELNET". With a TCP connectivity the terminal data traffic takes place between these 'User TELNET' and 'Server TELNET'.

4.7 TCP/IP and OSI Model—A Comparison

The TCP/IP protocol suite was developed prior to OSI model. TCP/IP as discussed earlier has five layers. Out of that the transport layer plays a vital role. At the layer the TCP/IP suite defines two different protocols.

1. TCP (Transmission Control Protocol)
2. UDP (User Datagram Protocol)

The data units are encapsulated at different layers of TCP/IP suite. Each data unit constitutes 'message'. The transmission control protocol or user datagram protocol creates a data unit (information unit) which is also called as user datagram or segment. The data unit created by IP layer is termed as datagram. But its (datagram) movement is monitored by the TCP/IP protocol suite.

The TCP/IP protocol suite supports Internet work protocol denoted as IP, at the network layer. The IP is also said to be a transmission mechanism and is used by TCP/IP protocols. The advantage of IP is that it guarantees error-free communication.

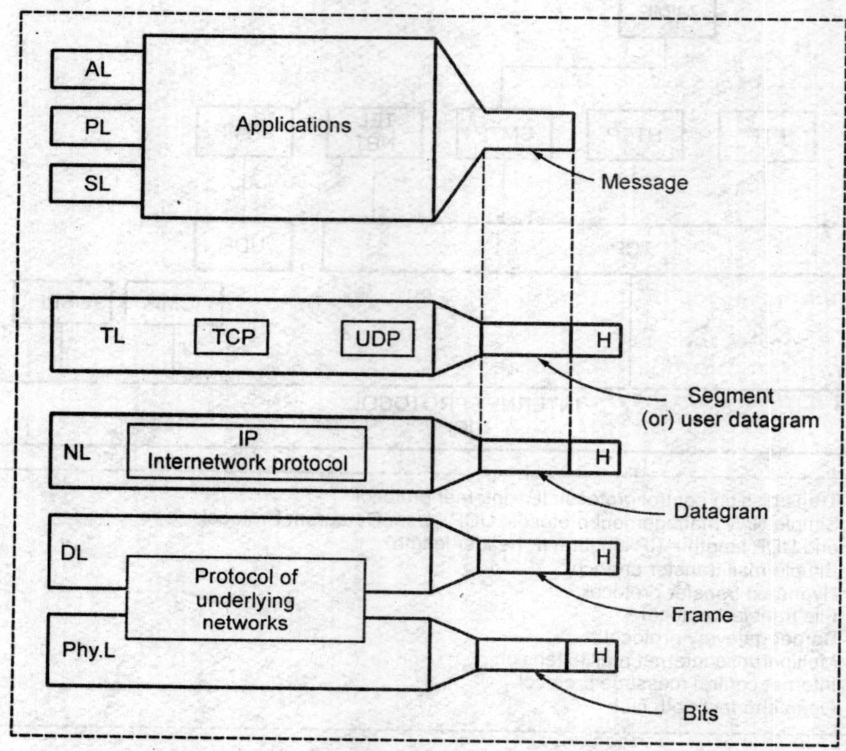

Fig. 4.16 TCP/IP and OSI model

Note : Layers denoted in Fig. 4.7 :

AL	:	Application layer
PL	:	Presentation layer
SL	:	Session layer
TL	:	Transport layer
NL	:	Network layer
DL	:	Data link layer
Phy.L	:	Physical layer

Datagram

The packets are defined as datagrams in an IP layer.

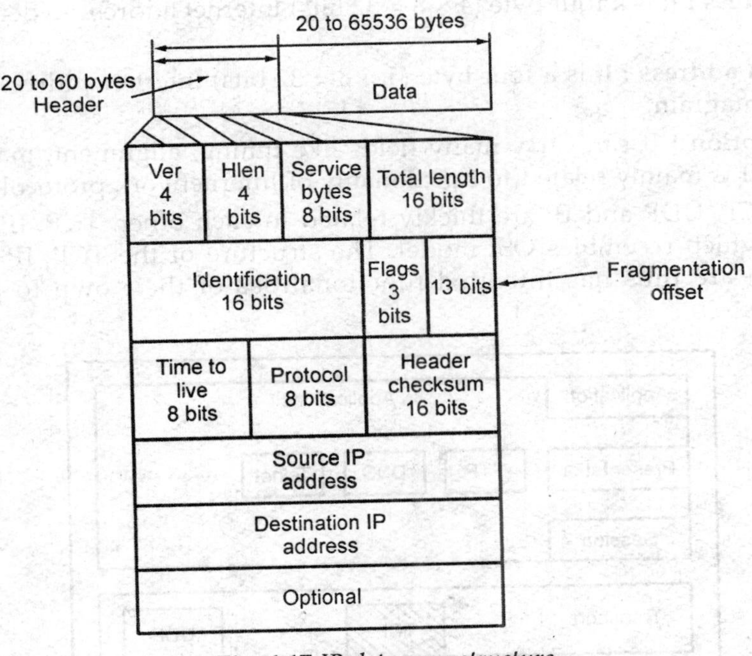

Fig. 4.17 IP datagram structure

Datagram is a packet of variable length which can go upto 65,536 bytes. It has two parts (fields)

1. Header (20 to 60 bytes)
2. Data

Version (Ver) : The IP version number is defined in this field

e.g. 1. IPV4 for version 4
 2. IPV6 for version 6

Header length (Hlen) : It defines the header length as multiples of four bytes.

Service type : It has bits that defines the priority of the datagram itself.

Total length : This field is allotted 16 bits to define the length of IP datagram.

Identification : It is mainly used to identify fragmentation that belongs to different networks 16 bits are allotted for this job.

Flags : It deals with fragmentation of the data.

Fragmentation offset : It is a pointer that points to the offset of the data in the original datagram.

Time to live : This field is used to define the total number of hops that a datagram has to travel before discarding operation.

Protocol : This field has 8 bits. It defines which upper layer protocol data is encapsulated at that time say for example TCP or UDP or ICMP etc.

Header checksum : It has 16 bit field to check the integrity of the packets.

Source address : It is a four byte (4 × 8 = 32 bits) Internet address to define the original source.

Destination address : It is a four byte (4 × 8 = 32 bits) Internet address to identify the destination of datagram.

Optional/option : It can carry many fields like timing, alignment, management and control routing. It is mainly related to functionality of Internetwork protocol (IP) datagram.

Thus the TCP, UDP and IP are thickly related to each other. TCP/IP protocol suite has five layers which resembles OSI model. The structure of the TCP/IP suite and also the IP datagram are thus has intended functionalities of their own to provide many services for users.

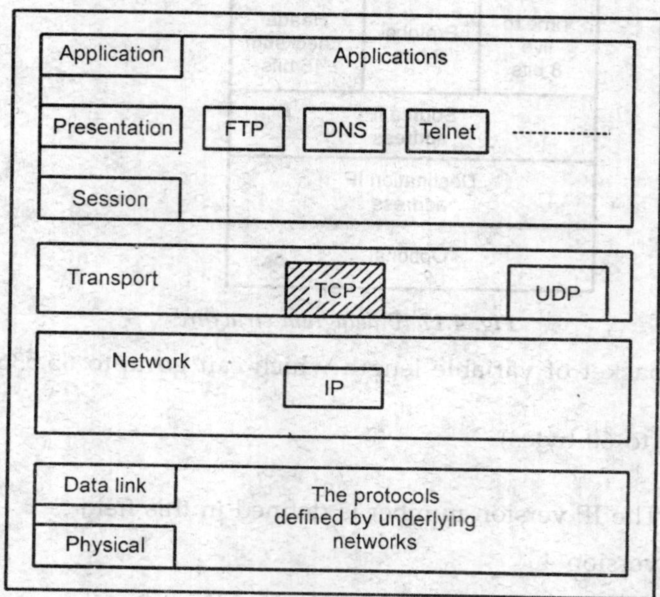

Fig. 4.18 OSI model and TCP/IP suite

Note : OSI model → It has seven layers

TCP/IP suite → It has five layers where the application layer consists of session, presentation and application layer.

Though TCP/IP suite was prior to OSI model it has few resembleness with OSI model respectively.

Improvements of TCP/IP

TCP is popularly called as connection-oriented and reliable transport protocol.

A transport layer protocol generally has many duties. The main duty of TCP/IP is to improve data transmission so as to have process-to-process communication. Data flow control is achieved using sliding window protocol. It also provide necessary connection mechanism for application programs.

Important functionality

- The data stream is chopped into the form of transportable units by the transport layer.
- The transport layer also checks whether all the segmented units are properly received in correct order at the receiver.
- If the entire data stream is completely transmitted then transport layer will close the connectivity.
- The host-to-host and process-to-process are the two ways of communication.
- The Internet protocol (IP) is linked to the communication at system level which is called as host-to-host communication.
- The messages corresponding to an application program is delivered by TCP.

Port addresses

For establishing communication between a remote computer and a local computer the following parameters are important.

- Local client program
- Local host
- Remote host
- Remote server program

To identify the local computer (host) and the remote computer two identification marks are used namely.

- IP address
- Port number which are integers from 0 to 65,535.

Consider a client and server program located at different points. The client program uses a temporary (ephemeral) port number and the server program uses permanent (well-known) port number. These port numbers are used for authorized identification.

Some permanent port used by the TCP are tabulated below.

Protocol	Port	Description
TELNET	23	Terminal network
Users	11	Active users
SMTP	25	Simple mail transfer protocol
RPC	111	Remote procedure call
DNS	53	Domain name server

Improved TCP services

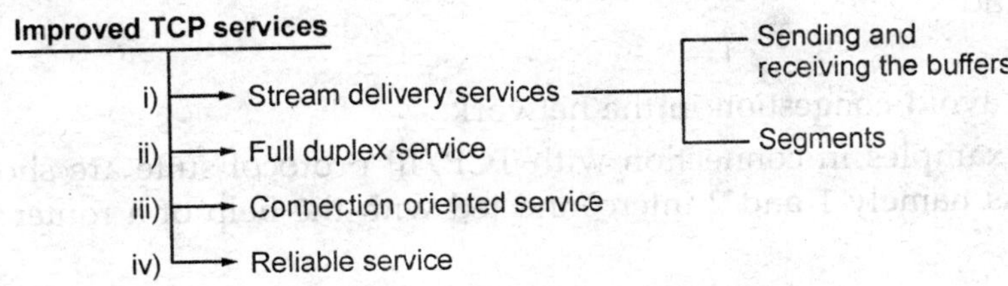

Fig. 4.19

(i) Stream delivery service : TCP is also known as stream oriented protocol. An application program/process transmits a group of bytes to user datagram protocol (UDP) for delivery purposes. There may be several groups of data sent to UDP but the UDP considers only one group of data at a time.

TCP monitors the sending process and receiving process for an ordered sequence of bytes transmission and reception of the exact replica of the data stream. The data bytes are assumed to travel in a tube like structure.

Under sending and receiving processes TCP requires buffers for data storage. For each direction there is sending and receiving buffers available. For implementation of these buffers a circular array of 1 byte positions are considered. The buffer at the receiver end has to receive the corresponding data streams. If any bytes are empty it has to be filled by the data from the network.

Before transmitting data few points have to be noted such as : For TCP, the IP acts as a service provider and it has to send data/message in the form of ordered bytes. TCP has to get the data bytes and it groups them into packet form known as segments. A header information is appended along with this segment. The transmitter and receiver should be transparent with all the processes they adopt and they should be synchronous with each other for better reception of data streams. It is worth noting that the segments at transport layer need not be same and of fixed size.

(ii) Full duplex service : The data flow which is possible at a time in both directions and it is known as full duplex service. Hence each TCP will have both transmitting and receiving buffer and the data segments are transmitted in both directions.

(iii) Connection oriented service : TCP itself is a connection oriented protocol. When two processes (A and B) at different sites want to communicate a sequence as follows takes place.

- TCP of A informs the TCP of B and gets approval status from TCP of B.
- TCP of A and TCP of B exchanges data streams in both directions.
- If all data are sent and buffer is in empty condition the TCP's of A and B processes will destroy their buffers.

Such a kind of sending and receiving of data is highly improved with TCP/IP.

(iv) Reliable service : TCP is a well known reliable transport protocol. The safe and accurate reception of data is arrived with help of this TCP protocol suite.

Also for smooth operation TCP uses four timers namely

(a) Retransmission timer

(b) Persistence timer

(c) Keep alive timer and

(d) Time-waited timer

TCP also takes care to avoid congestion in the network.

Some of the Internet examples in connection with TCP/IP protocol suite are shown here. Consider two networks namely 1 and 2 interconnected with the help of a router.

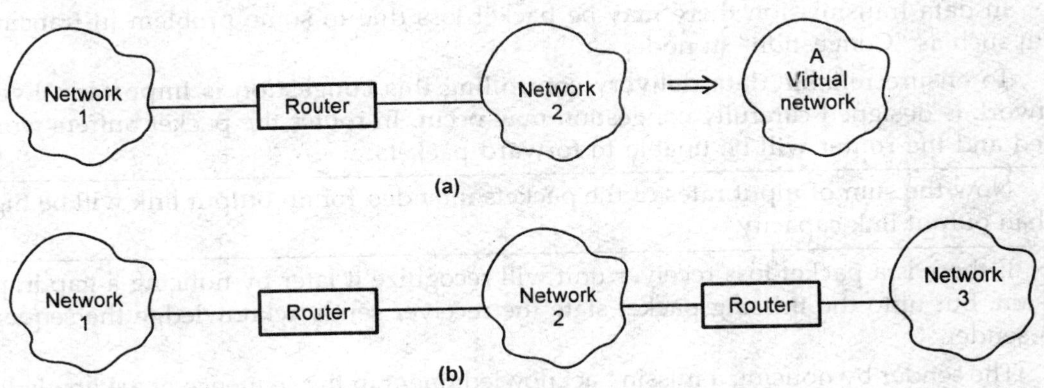

Fig. 4.20 Internet examples (a) Two networks interconnected
(b) Multiple networks interconnected

The two interconnected set of networks in Fig. 4.20(*a*) is seen as one logical network and a router enables communication between two networks. More than one router may be used in case of multiple networks interconnected. The router has few fundamental properties :

(*i*) From the network point of view a router is a normal host.

(*ii*) From user point of view the routers are invisible and they form one large internetwork.

The Internet protocol (IP) address comprises of two parts and the IP address = <network number><host number>. This network number is unique throughout the Internet and the host number is assigned by the organization that controls the network identified by the network number.

4.8 TRADITIONAL TCP

In mobile environment TCP applies several mechanisms to improve efficiency. The topics to be discussed in traditional TCP are

(*i*) Congestion control

(*ii*) Fast retransmit/Fast recovery

(*iii*) Slow start

(*iv*) Implications on mobility.

Each of these topics are dealt here in detail.

(*i*) Congestion control

The TCP is basically designed for fixed type of networks with fixed end systems. For data transmission takes place using

- Network adapters
- Fiber optics
- Copper wires
- Special hardware for routers.

In data transmission there may be packet loss due to some problem in transmission path such as "Congestion" in node.

To ensure reliable data delivery controlling this congestion is important. Even if a network is designed carefully congestion may occur. In router the packet buffers would be filled and the router will be unable to forward packets.

Now the sum of input rates of the packets intended for an output link will be higher than output link capacity.

If there is a packet loss receiver unit will recognize it later by noticing a gap in packet stream. But upto the missing packet state the receiver sends acknowledge the sequence to the sender.

The sender by noticing a missing acknowledgment in the sequence of acknowledgment recognizes a packet loss occurrence, due to congestion in path.

To avoid congestion now TCP reduces the rate of packet transmission drastically so that accumulation of packets gets slow down.

Note : In heavy load TCP guarantees sharing of bandwidth. Also by using reliable hardware like special routers, network adapters and software the congestion in transmission path can be controlled.

(*ii*) Fast retransmit/Fast recovery

Two important features will lead to reduce congestion threshold. They are :

1. Fast retransmit
2. Fast recovery.

If the sender receives acknowledgments continuously for same packet then sender assumes that the receiver has received packets upto acknowledged packet in the sequence. The gap in packet stream may be due to an error in transmission path or due to a severe congestion.

Once packet loss is noticed by sender it retransmits the missing packets before the allotted time expires. Such a behaviour is called as 'fast retransmit'.

If acknowledgments are received continuously it shows that there is no congestion and the sender would continue the same current congestion window. The sender always performs a 'fast recovery' from packet loss strategy. By this mechanism efficiency of TCP is improved.

(*iii*) Slow start

If there is missing acknowledgment due to a packet loss TCP reacts fast. It may not come out of congestion quickly. But its behavior exhibits slow start after the congestion detection. The sender calculates a congestion window and its start size is one segment.

After arrival of an acknowledgment sender increases the window by one. Then after arrival of two acknowledgments, sender increases congestion window by two. It continues and if another two acknowledgments are received the congestion window is again increases by two and now it will be equal to 4. Such a mechanism is called as exponential growth of congestion window in slow start technique.

Every time an acknowledgment coming back will take one round trip time (RTT)

So far we noticed that congestion window was doubled every time. But the steps might be very large and hence doubling is not good. The exponential growth of congestion window stops at the congestion threshold.

Note : As the congestion window reaches the congestion threshold level then after that if an acknowledgment is received then the window will be increased only by (linearly) and doubling the size is avoided.

(*iv*) Implications on mobility

The mobility itself may induce packet loss. Always soft handover may not be possible from one system to another.

Fundamental design problem in TCP is if there is packet loss the cause for it cannot be distinguished easily. Sometime error control mechanism is misused for congestion control. But end result will be packet loss for both cases.

When using the mobile IP there may be some packet available in transit to the old agent (foreign agent) where as the mobile node is moving to a new foreign agent. So that there may be packet loss. Thus packet loss may also be induced by mobility from one node to another.

4.9 INDIRECT TCP

The traditional TCP had the problem of poor performance with wireless links. Also the TCP available within a fixed network cannot be altered. Due to these reasons the 'Indirect TCP' (I-TCP) emerged slowly. The I-TCP emerged slowly. The I-TCP segments the TCP connection into two parts namely,

1. Fixed part
2. Wireless part.

In the below diagram the mobile host is connected through a wireless link and an access point (AP) to the wired internet. The correspondent host resides here. The foreign agent can control the mobility of mobile host. Also it can handover the existing connection to next foreign agent whenever the mobile moves on.

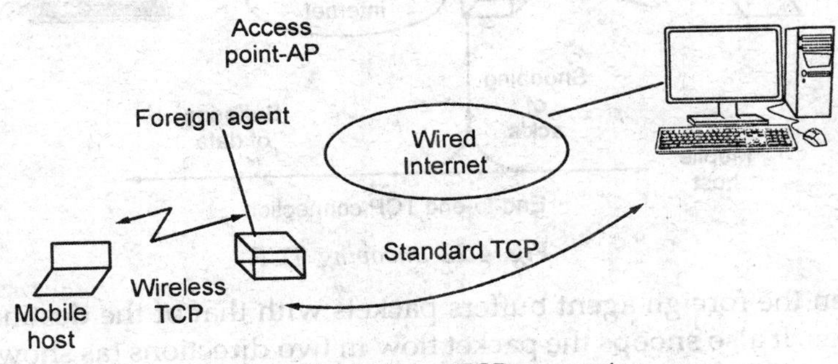

Fig. 4.21 Indirect TCP segments

If handover takes place I-TCP needs several actions to happen. The I-TCP has many advantages and they are listed below :

- The I-TCP does not need any changes in TCP protocol when used by hosts in fixed network. All optimizations for TCP works between correspondent host and foreign agent.
- Because of the strict partitioning into two connections in I-TCP the transmission errors if any would not propagate into fixed network.
- In I-TCP new mechanisms can be introduced between foreign agent and mobile host. It allows different tests to be applied.
- It is also possible to apply different transport layer protocol between mobile host and foreign agent. Compressed headers can also used in I-TCP.

But with the technique of segmentation in I-TCP there are also same demerits. Some of the demerits are listed below :

- The correspondent node is not aware of portioning done. A crashing access node may crash applications that runs on correspondent node and assumes a reliable end-to-end delivery.
- Increased handover latency creates problem.
- The foreign agent involved should be a trusted entity or otherwise their will be security problems.

4.10 SNOOPING TCP

Main drawback in I-TCP is the segmentation of single TCP connection into two connections. Because of this original end-to-end TCP semantic will be lost. But here the function of enhancement is buffering data closer to mobile host so as to perform local retransmission when there is a packet loss. A correct place for TCP enhancement is the foreign agent (in mobile IP terms) as shown below.

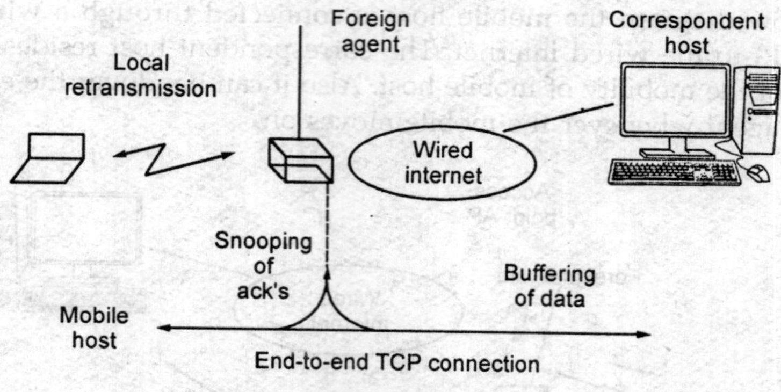

Fig. 4.22 Snooping TCP

As it is seen the foreign agent buffers packets with that of the destination mobile host. In addition to this, it also snoops the packet flow in two directions (as shown) and recognizes acknowledgments. By buffering packets to a foreign node there is a chance of local retransmission in case of packet losses in wireless link. Till receiving acknowledgments from mobile host the foreign agent continues buffering process. If it does not receive acknowledgment then either packet or acknowledgment could be lost.

As an alternate it could receive a duplicate ACK but it also reflects that a packet has been lost. Now a faster retransmission is made by foreign agent and time cuts will also be shorter. The foreign agent can filter any duplicate ACK's so that unwanted retransmissions are avoided.

Unnecessary traffic on wireless link can be avoided since the foreign agent is capable of discards duplicates of packets that was already transmitted and acknowledged.

With snooping TCP there are many advantages. Some of them are summarized below :

(*i*) The end-to-end semantic of TCP is not changed.

(*ii*) As soon as a mobile host reaches a new foreign agent a handover of state is not required.

(*iii*) The correspondent host involved need not be changed.

(*iv*) It does not account whether the next foreign agent had applied enhancement or not.

4.10.1 Demerits of Snooping TCP

(*i*) It does not differentiate the behavior of wireless links as in the case of I-TCP.

(*ii*) Usage of negative acknowledges results in more number of mechanisms.

(*iii*) Only if the encryption used above transport layer this snooping TCP can work or otherwise it will not work.

4.11 MOBILE TCP

It is important to address the problem of occurrence of lengthy and frequent disconnections.

The mobile-TCP (M-TCP) has same goals as I-TCP and snooping TCP; to avoid the sender window from disconnection or shrinking if bit errors cause but not the congestion causes current problem.

- This Mobile-TCP aims to improve system throughout.
- M-TCP lower delay time.
- M-TCP maintains end-to-end semantics of TCC.

M-TCP is used in situations arising due to frequent or lengthy disconnections. The M-TCP also segments TCP connection into two as I-TCP. But an unmodified TCP is used on standard host-supervisory host (SH) connection.

The M-TCP achieves low bit error rate, in case of wireless links.

The supervisory host (SH) supervises all the packets transmitted to mobile host (MH) and ACK's sent by MH's. In case ACK not received from MH then SH decides that the MH is disconnected. Now it sets the sender's window size as '0' and sender is now said to be in persistent mode.

The sender's state remain constant whatever be the time for which the receiver is disconnected. This is persistent mode.

An adapted TCP is used by wireless link and it is capable of recovering from packet losses. It does not use slow start. The M-TCP also needs a bandwidth manager to provide fair sharing over wireless links.

4.11.1 Merits of M-TCP

- Maintains end-to-end TCP semantics.
- It can avoid unwanted retransmissions in case of MH disconnections.
- Lost packets will be retransmitted automatically.

4.12 FAST RETRANSMIT/FAST RECOVERY

As the mobile host (MH) registers at new foreign agent with the help of mobile IP it will send duplicate acknowledgments to the corresponding hosts. The idea is to transmit three duplicate Ack's. By this the corresponding host is forced to enter into fast retransmit mode. That is the correspondent host will continue to transmit with same rate (i.e. previous rate it used when mobile host moved to another foreign agent).

On the other hand the MH will go into slow start as it had moved to new foreign agent and it will also make MH to enter into fast retransmit.

4.12.1 Merits

- Simple design approach
- Minor changes in mobile host's software is only required.

4.13 TRANSMISSION/TIME-OUT FREEZING

If connection problems exists MAC layer has noticed even before the connection was actually interrupted with respect to TCP. MAC layer does not decide that the disconnection is due to congestion. But the MAY layer informs TCP layer regarding upcoming loss of connections.

Thus as a result TCP stop transmission and it freezes the present state of the congestion window. Once the MAY layer knows about interruption at earlier stage it informs it to correspondent and mobile host.

On the other hand if connectivity is detected by MAC layer it informs TCP to resume its operation again which was stopped earlier.

4.13.1 Merits

- Resumes TCP connection in spite of longer interruptions.
- It is independent of ACK's and usage of sequence numbers.

4.13.2 Selective Retransmission

One of the important advantage of extension of TCP is the usage of 'selective retransmission'. The TCP-ACK's are cumulative, and they acknowledge the receipt of packets upto a particular packet. Now the sender retransmits all packets from the last packet onwards.

This is 'go-back-n retransmission' method. The bandwidth is wasted due to sending many packets once again.

An alternate to this is selective retransmission. The TCP requests indirectly for selective retransmission. The receiver is capable of acknowledging single packets and the sender can determine in particular about which packet is to be retransmitted.

4.13.3 Merits

- Sender will retransmit only the packet that was lost.
- Bandwidth is saved.

4.14 TRANSACTION-ORIENTED TCP

Consider an application is running on mobile host (MH). The MH sends short requests from time to the server. If the application that is running reliable packet transfer it would use TCP. Due to this several packets are required over the wireless links. The sequence of steps are given below.

- At first TCP use a three-way handshake for establishing connection.
- For transmission of request and closing connections through three-way handshake atleast 4 (1 + 3) additional packets are needed.

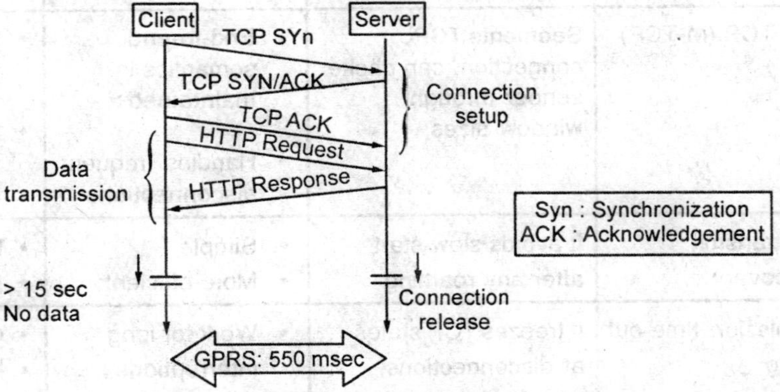

Fig. 4.23 TCP connection setup overhead

- If there is a heavy traffic for a long time this requirement is minimum or otherwise it will be of waste to have more packets to handle less packet transmission.

In this example an overhead scenario is shown. The web services depend on HTTP and it need reliable transport system. TCP is used for this purpose in Internet.

The TCP connection has to established before a HTTP request is sent. Assume GPRS is used as wire area transport system.

There is an one-way delay equal to 550 msec. To set up a TCP connection it may take more than one second.

The transaction-oriented TCP (T-TCP) emerged in this regard to provide more efficiency T-TCP can combine the packets for both connection establishment and release with that of the user data packets. By this approach the additional number of packets can be reduced. If there is seven additional packets required this T-TCP can reduce it upto two packets.

Merit

- Reduction in overhead.

Demerits

- Needs changes in mobile host and correspondent hosts.
- Has security problems.

Summary of the classical enhancements to the TCP are tabulated below regarding mobility scenario.

Sr. No.	TCP approach	Mechanism involved	Merits	Demerits
1.	Indirect TCP (I-TCP)	It segments TCP connection into two	• Simple • Isolation of wireless link is possible	• Loss of the TCP semantics. • Security problem.
2.	Snooping TCP (S-TCP)	Snooping of data and ACK's	• Transparency • MAC integration • Security problem	• Inadequate isolation of the wireless links
3.	Mobile TCP (M-TCP)	Segments TCP connection, can choke sender through window sizes	• End-to-end semantics is maintained • Handles frequent disconnections	• Poor isolation of wireless link. • Security problem.
4.	Fast retransmit fast recovery	It avoids slow-start after any roaming	• Simple • More efficient	• Not transparent • Mixed layers
5.	Transmission time-out freezing	It freezes TCP states at disconnections, later it resumes after reconnection.	• Work for long interruptions	• Changes in TCP • MAC dependent
6.	Selective retransmission	Lost data only retransmitted.	• Highly efficient	• Complex • Need more buffer spaces
7.	Transaction-oriented TCP (T-TCP)	Combine connection setup/release	• Efficient for few applications	• Not transparent • Security problems

4.15 TCP OVER 2.5G/3G WIRELESS NETWORKS

Transmission control protocol (TCP) is optimized for recent days wireless scenario, to meet the requirements of GSM/GPRS, UMTS etc. Some of the characteristics like data rate, latency, jitter and packet loss has to be considered when addressing various applications for 2.5G and 3G networks. They are discussed below.

***(i)* Data rates**

The future 2.5G and 3G wireless networks will have initial data rates around 64 kbits per second for uplink (From mobile unit to base station) and 115 to 384 kbits per second for downlink (From base station to mobile unit). The data rates are asymmetric because the data transactions will be more in downloading due to many users than uploading. Uploading *is* restricted by the battery resource. An asymmetry of 3 to 6 times in data rates is followed for cellular communications.

***(ii)* Latency**

In wireless networks many algorithms like forward error correction (FEC), inter leaving summing etc are used. The round trip time is improved by FEC from milliseconds to seconds.

***(iii)* Jitter**

The wireless systems suffers from delay spikes. Latency time increases due to loss of radio coverage, blocking or handover problems. The larger delay variations are also said to be delay spikes.

***(iv)* Packet loss**

Packet losses may occur due to handover procedures. Due to link-level retransmissions the rate of loss has reduced appreciably. The higher layers recovery at link layer appears as jitter.

Note : To adapt TCP to wireless environments some of the configuration parameters are very important.

They are listed below :

- Larger windows based on bandwidth. Larger maximum transfer unit to have faster TCP (MTU).
  Limited transmit (useful when small data is sent)
- Selective acknowledgment (SACK)
- Explicit congestion notification (ECN).
- Time stamp
- No header compressions.

These configuration parameters are deployed in Japan and they would be in other regions also.

4.16 CONGESTION STRATEGIES IN TCP/IP

The two congestion strategies are

1. Slow start and additive increase
2. Multiplicative decrease.

1. Slow start and additive increase

Slow start : At initial state TCP sets congestion window size to maximum possible segment's size. The increase in window size is continued till a threshold (i.e. half the level of window size allowable) level is reached. It is known as slow start and it is not an efficient method since it misleads the processes which are not at all slow.

Additive increase : The exponential growth of window size has to be reduced as the threshold level is attained. The additive increase strategy continues till the window size reaches the window size of receiver so as to avoid congestion.

2. Multiplicative decrease

At the time of congestion in a network the probability of 'segment lost' will be higher than 'segment getting corrupted'. Hence when a time out occurs the threshold level has to be reduced to half the value of previous congestion window size and a new start should take place. Size of threshold has to be reduced for each and every 'time-outs'. Hence the threshold size reduces exponentially which is called as "multiplicative decrease". This procedure is a better method to avoid congestion in a network. This cycle of systematic steps slow start, additive increase and multiplicative decrease can be repeated for any required number of time.

Note :

- The Internet protocol is also called as connectionless protocol and uses datagram approach.
- IP provides more reliability.
- IP should be paired with TCP for an efficient functionality of datagram (IP packet) delivery at the intended receiver.
- This IP is a best transmission mechanism that is used perfectly by the TCP/IP protocol suite.

4.17 WIRELESS APPLICATION PROTOCOL (WAP)

The wireless world of web development is tremendous as it changed the field of communication more brighter. The wireless application protocol forum popularly known as WAP forum was actually founded in the year 1997. The main objectives of this WAP forum was,

(*i*) To bring diverse Internet contents like web pages, push services etc.

(*ii*) To provide other data services like stock quotes to mobile terminals (PDA's) and digital cellular phone units.

(*iii*) To provide better protocol suite to support world wide wireless communication, the Internet applications.

(*iv*) To support wireless networks like CDPD, GSM, UMTS etc.

Many solutions were derived by the "WAP Forum" to meet these requirements they are :

(*a*) Scalable : The protocols and other services should be able to be in scale with the customer needs.

(*b*) Interoperable : It allows the terminals and softwares from several vendors to communicate with many networks of different providers. Hence internetworks communication is made possible.

(*c*) Efficient : To provide proper quality of service suitable to the requirements of wireless and the mobile networks.

(*d*) Reliable : To provide predictable and consistent platforms for deployment of services.

(e) Secure : It should have provisions to secure data and to preserve data integrity and devices.

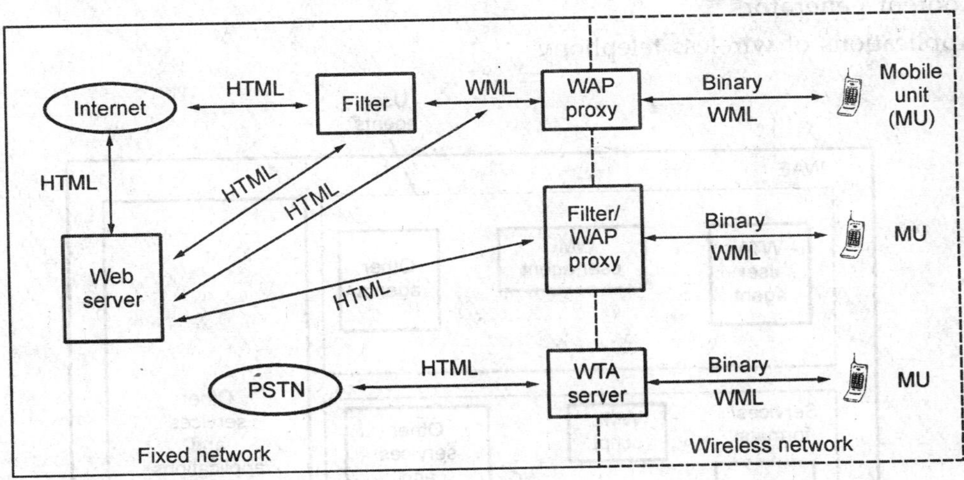

Fig. 4.24 Integration of various WAP components— an example

WTA → Wireless telephony application

HTML → Hypertext markup language

WML → Wireless markup language

In the Fig. 4.24 it is evident that various scenarios are possible for integrating many WAP components into the existing fixed and wireless networks. It is shown as a part of the full figure. The other part of the figure is the fixed network which comprises of networks such as public switched telephone network (PSTN) and traditional Internet.

The protocols used and the services of the networks existing cannot be changed. The wireless networks provides WAP enabled wireless, mobile devices. There are special type of filters used to translate hypertext markup language (HTML) into wireless markup language (WML). The same function can also be done by gateways available between fixed and wireless network. Gateways can acts as proxies for accessing web. Finally the wireless telephony application (WTA) translates the signalling of telephone networks into the WML events which can be displayed at handled devices. Through the wireless application environment (WAE) the wireless clients of various services, telephony and web are integrated.

The WAE forms the top layer in the layered architecture of wireless application protocol (WAP). In this chapter the WAP is discussed in detail.

4.17.1 Wireless Application Environment (WAE)

In wireless network environment for the data is transmission the wireless handsets size, weight and portability are important bottlenecks and has to be addressed with at most care. These influences the user interface less powerful CPU with less memory capacity.

The wireless application environment finds solutions for meeting the requirements in transmission of wireless data.

The important elements of WAE model are

1. WAE - User agents
2. Content generators
3. Applications of wireless telephony

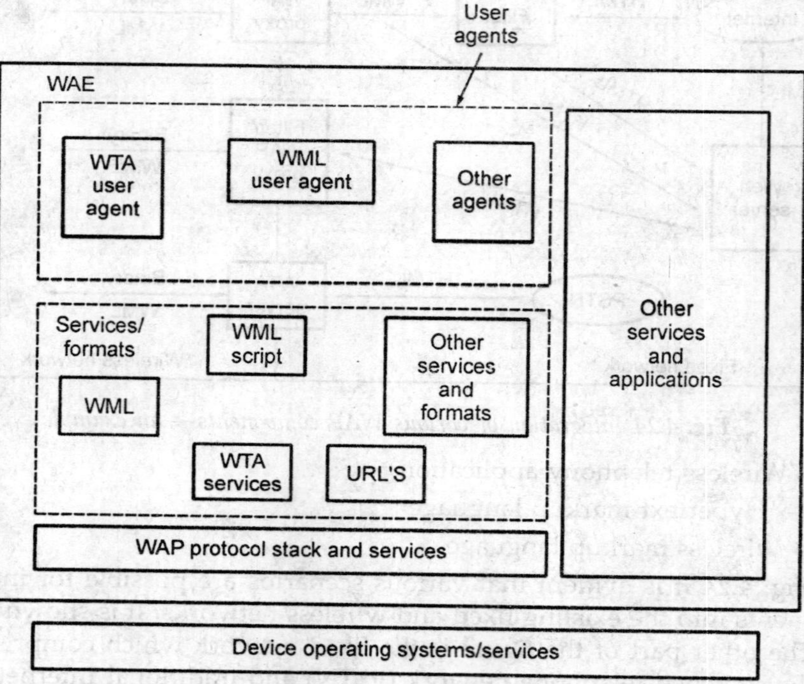

Fig. 4.25 Wireless applications environment-client components

WAE - User agents

It is a software that provides functionality like display content to end user and executes in user's wireless component (device).

Content generators

These are services/applications on server (origin server) that produces standard content formats in response to the requests from user agents side.

Content encoding

It allows WAE user agent to navigate the web content.

Wireless Telephony Application (WTA)

With WTA related applications developers use micro browser to initiate telephone calls and to give response to events, that is from telephone network.

The services are provided by wireless session protocol as mentioned below :

1. The content push facility from server to client.
2. It establishes reliable sessions from server to client and releases it in proper order.
3. Exchanging content between server and client with compact encoding.
4. A common level of protocol functionality with usage of capability negotiations.

WAP is actually a collection of service primitives which defines WSP and users of WSP in wireless application protocol (WAP).

A wireless session protocol (WSP) acting as client makes requests to WSP acting as server (i.e. a web server). This request in accompanied with four parameters. They are listed below.

1. Server address
2. Client address
3. Request capability
4. Client headers

Stacks arrangement with WAP

The wireless application protocol tries to make use of many technologies from Internet. A simple protocol stack may not require new protocols. For this purpose based on the simple stack many complex stacks can be developed by simply appending security with a most reliable transaction service. This reliable service is compatible with applications regarding distributed computing like CORBA.

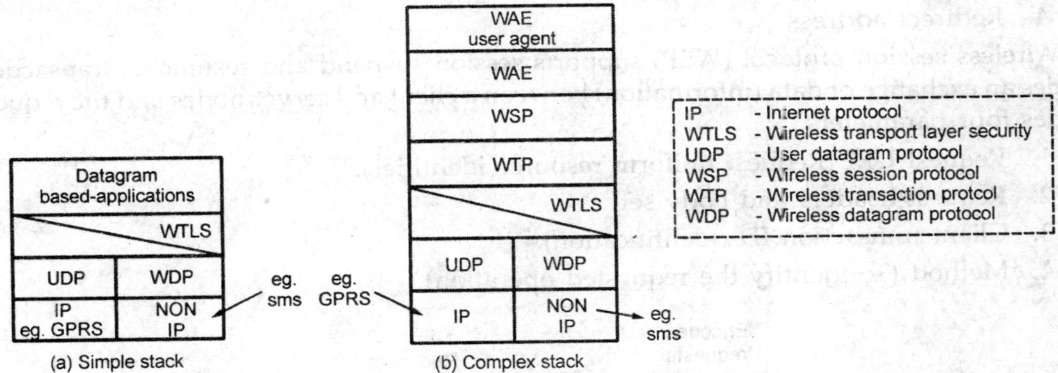

Fig. 4.26 Protocol stacks arrangement in WAP - an example

For a complex WAP applications like WML a full stack arrangement of protocols may be required (Fig. 4.26(*b*)). Hence WAP is flexible to integrate many technologies from that of the Internet to complete an application.

Table 4.1 M-Wireless Session Protocol (WSP) capabilities

Sr. No.	Name	Type	Class	Description
1.	Size of client SOU	Positive integer	n	The size cf largest transaction service data sent to client during the session (s).
2.	Aliases	List of addresses	i	It indicates which alternative addresses used by peer to access the session service.

3.	Header code pages	Set of code page names	n	A set of extension header code pages are supported by client and server.
4.	Maximum outstanding request method	Positive integer	n	Many method invocations can be active at same time during session (s).
5.	Protocol options	Facilities and features	n	It may include confirmed push, session resume and acknowledge headers
6.	Size of server SOU	Positive integer	n	The size of largest transaction SOU which may be transmitted to server during session (s).

- n : Negotiable
- i : Informational

In WAP the "S-Disconnect" primitive is mainly used for session termination, and the request primitive for termination includes many parameters like;

1. Redirect security
2. Reason code
3. Error headers and the error set
4. Redirect address

Wireless session protocol (WSP) supports session suspend and resume. A transaction includes an exchange of data (information) between a client and server nodes and the request includes four parameters.

1. Request URI (Request uniform resource identifier).
2. Request headers and body set.
3. Client transaction ID (identification).
4. Method (To identify the requested operation).

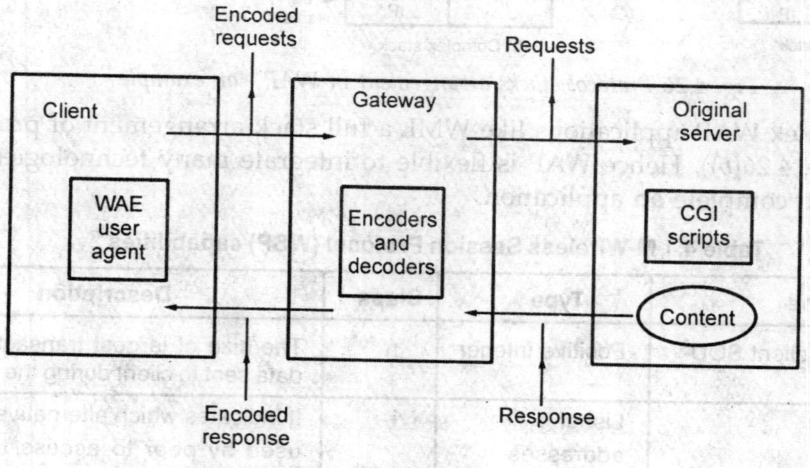

Fig. 4.27 Programming model of WAP

Architectural Goals

The goals of WAP Forum architecture is listed below.

(*a*) Enable the personalisation and customisation of the device, the content delivered to it, and the presentation of the content.

(*b*) Provide secure access to local handset functionality.

(*c*) It facilitates network-operator and third party service provisioning.

(*d*) Defines a layered, scalable and extensible architecture.

(*e*) Provide support for secure and private application and communication in a manner that is consistent and interoperable.

(*f*) Provides a web centric application model for wireless data services that utilises the telephony, mobility and other functions of wireless devices and networks and enables maximum flexibility and ability for vendors to enhance the user experience.

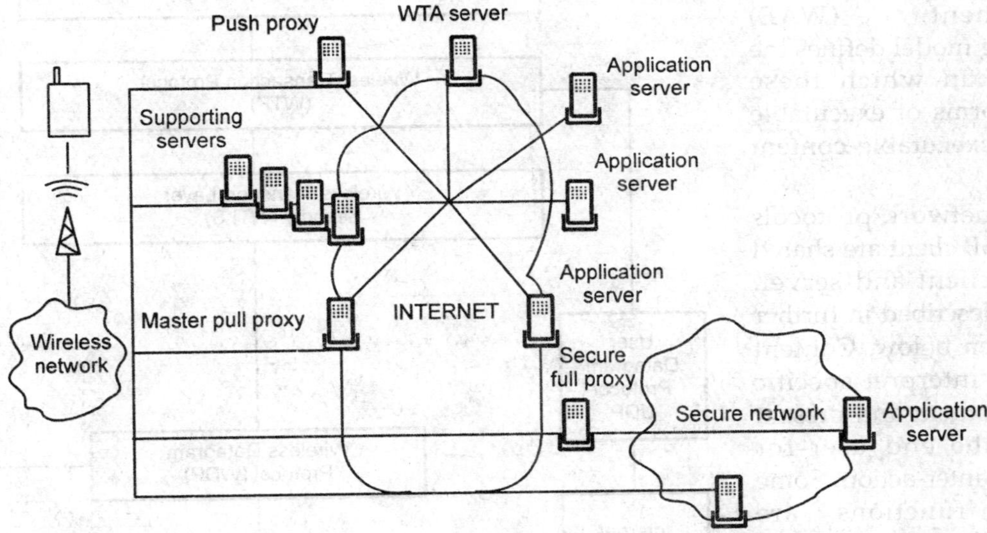

Fig. 4.28 An example of a WAP-network

The WAP clients communicate with application servers through a number of different proxies or directly. WAP clients supports the proxy selection mechanism that can allow them to utilise approximate proxy for a given service or to connect to that service directly. The proxies can be utilized to augment a request. They translate between WAP protocols and worldwide web (www) protocols (TCP, HTTP) so as to allow the WAP client to submit request to the origin server.

The proxies may be located in many places including wireless carriers or independent service providers in order to facilitate feature enhancements coupled to the wireless networks or to optimise communication between device and

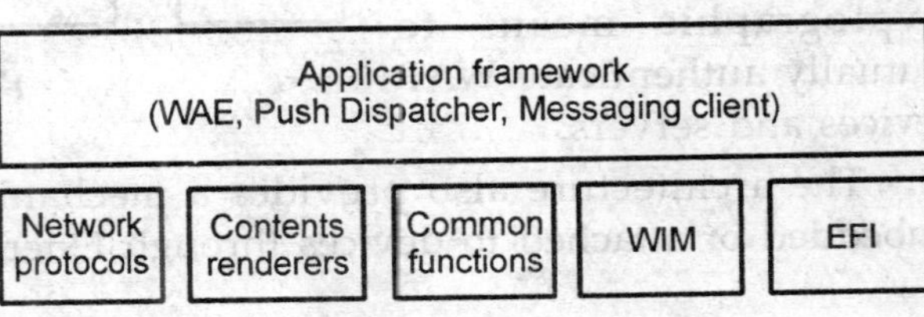

Fig. 4.29 WAP-client architecture

application server. The supporting servers provide support functions required by devices, proxies and the application servers. These functions includes user, agent profiles, provisioning etc.

WAP Client Architecture

The application frame-work provides the device execution environ-ment for WAP appli-cations. WAP applications are comprised of markup, script, style sheets and multimedia content all of which are rendered on the device. The WAP Application Environment (WAE) processing model defines the structure in which these various forms of executable and non-executable content interact.

The network protocols on the WAP client are shared between client and server. They are described in further detail given below. Content Tenderers interpret specific forms of content and present them to the end user for perusal or inter-action. Some common functions are defined to be utilised by the application framework, including persistence and data synchronisation.

The Wireless Identity Module (WIM) contains the identity of the device and the cryptographic means to mutually authenticate WAP devices and servers.

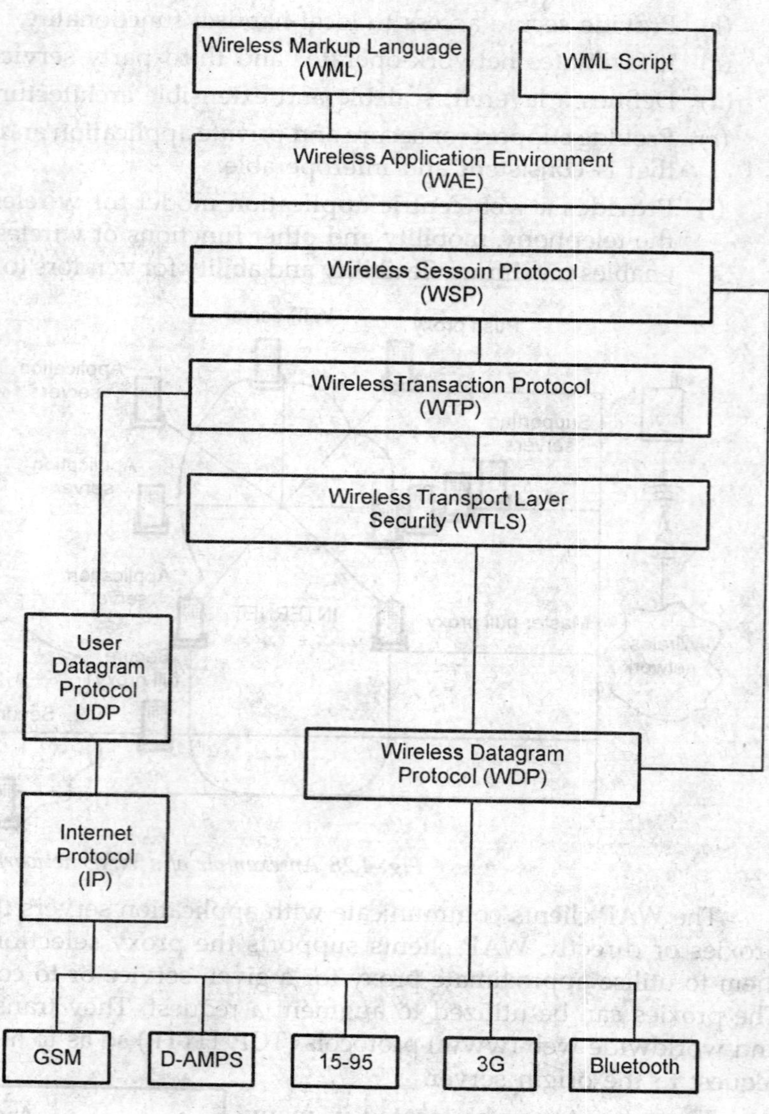

Fig. 4.30 Protocol stack of WAP

The architecture also provides a mechanism to access external-functions that are embedded or attached to devices through External Functionality Interface (EFI).

Components of WAP Architecture in detail

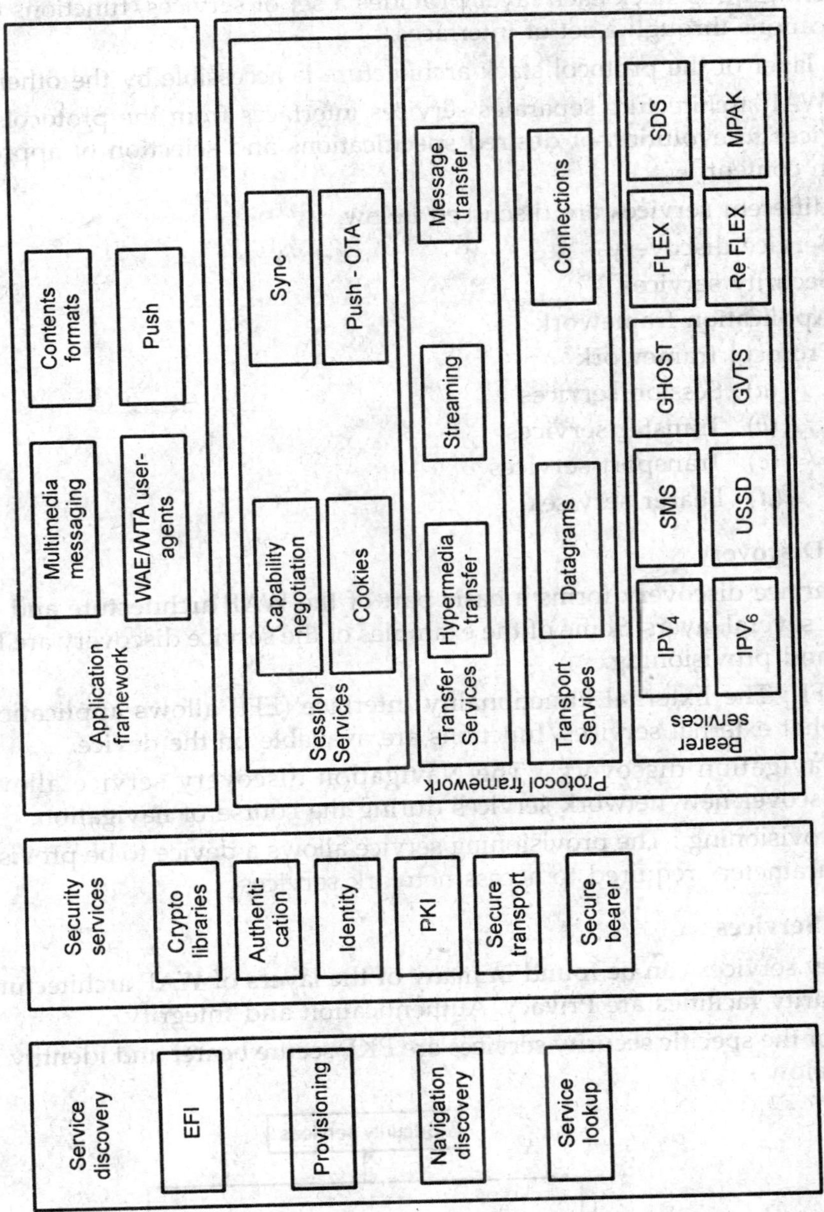

Fig. 4.31 WAP stack architecture

The protocol stack architecture is in a general and detailed fashion in above two diagrams.

The WAP architecture provides a scalable and extensible application development environment for mobile communication components. A layered architecture design of protocol stack for WAP as given in above figure helps to achieve such an application oriented environment. In this stack each layer provides a set of services/functions to other services and applications through a set of interfaces.

Each layer of the protocol stack architecture is accessible by the other layers.

The WAP architecture separates services interfaces from the protocols which provide those services to evolution of desired specifications and selection of appropriate protocol for a given content.

The different services are discussed below.

1. Service discovery
2. Security services
3. Application framework
4. Protocol framework
   (*a*) Session services
   (*b*) Transfer services
   (*c*) Transport services
   (*d*) Bearer services

1. Service Discovery

The service discovery forms a basic part of the WAP architecture and its services can be found at several layers. Some of the examples of the service discovery are EFI, Navigation discovery and provisioning.

(*a*) EFI : The External Functionality Interface (EFI) allows applications to discover what external services/functions are available on the device.

(*b*) Navigation discovery : The Navigation discovery service allows a device to discover new network services during the course of navigation.

(*c*) Provisioning : The provisioning service allows a device to be provisioned with the parameters required to access network services.

2. Security Services

Security services can be found in many of the layers of WAP architecture. Some of the general security facilities are Privacy, Authentication and Integrity.

Some of the specific security services are PKI, secure bearer and identity. These services are listed below.

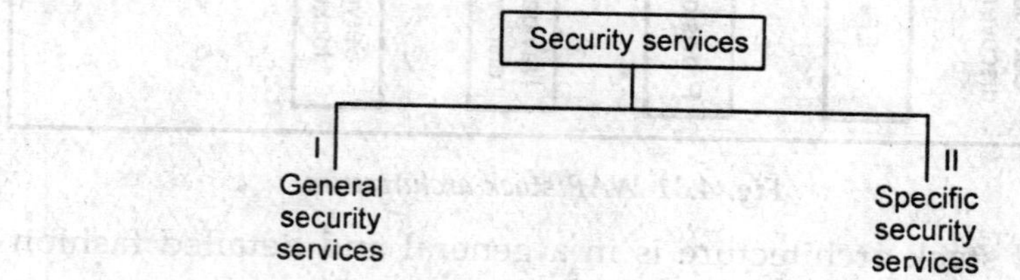

[I] (*i*) Privacy

It facilitates to ensure that communication is private and cannot *be* known by any third person.

(*ii*) Authentication

It facilitates to establish the authenticity of parties to the communication.

(*iii*) Integrity

If facilitates to ensure that communication is unchanged and uncorrupted.

[II] (*i*) Identity

The WIM provides the functions that can store process information needed for user identification and authentication.

(*ii*) PKI

The set of security services that enable the use and management of public-key cryptography.

(*iii*) Secure bearer

Some bearer networks provide bearer level security.

3. Application Framework

It provides a general purpose application environment. The main objective of the application framework is to develop an interoperable environment that will allow the service providers and operators to build applications and services that can reach wide variety of wireless platforms.

Some of the application framework are,

(*i*) **Push :** The push service provides a general mechanism for the network to initiate the transmission of data to applications resident on the WAP devices.

(*ii*) **WAE/WTA User Agent :** WAE is a micro browser environment allowing for the markup, scripting, telephony services etc. and programming interfaces, all optimised for use in the hand-held mobile units.

(*iii*) **Multimedia Messaging (MMS) :** It provides for the transfer and processing of multimedia messages such as electronic mail and instant messages to that of the WAP devices.

4. Protocol Framework

(*a*) Session services

These session services provides for the establishment of shared state between network elements. Some of the session services are given below.

(*i*) **Push-OTA :** The Push-OTA (Over The Air) session service provides for network - initiated transactions to be delivered to wireless devices that are able to receive data.

(*ii*) **Sync :** The sync service provides for the synchronization of replicated data.

(*iii*) **Cookies :** The cookies service allows applications to establish state on the client or the proxy which survives multiple hypermedia transfer transactions.

(b) Transfer services

These services provide for the structured transfer of information between the network elements. Some of the transfer services are given below.

(i) **Streaming :** They provide a means for transferring isochronous data like audio and video information.

(ii) **Message transfer :** They provide the means for transfer asynchronous multimedia messages such as electronic mail or any instant messages. The MMS Encapsulation is a protocol used to transfer messages between WAP devices and MMS services.

(iii) **Hypermedia transfer :** The hypermedia transfer service provides for the transfer of self-describing hypermedia resources.

(c) Transport services

These services offer a set of consistent services to other upper layer protocols and links/maps those services to the bearer services available.

Some of the transport services are given below.

(i) **Datagrams :** The datagram service provides data transport in which self-contained, independent entities of data carries required information to be routed from source to destination node independent of earlier exchanges between the nodes.

(ii) **Connections :** The connection service provides data transport service in which communication will take place in three phases namely connection establishment, two-way reliable data transfer and connection release.

(d) Bearer networks

The bearer services includes short message packet data and circuit-switched data. The bearers offer differing level of quality of service with respect to error rate, delays and throughput. The transport service layer provides interface between bearer services and remaining WAP protocol stack.

Thus the different network services of WAP protocol stack enables efficient wireless communication.

Network Architecture

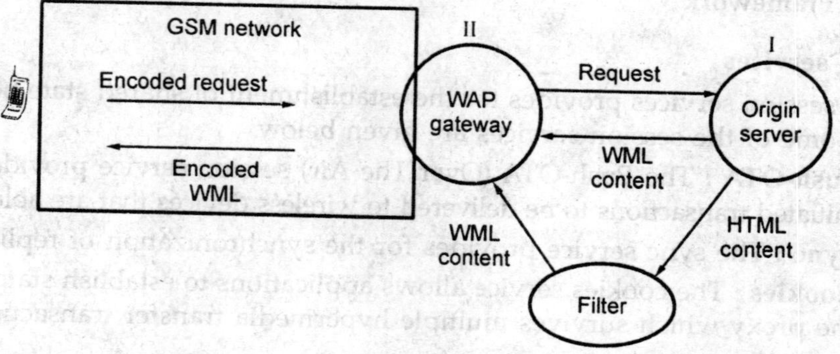

Fig. 4.32 Wireless application protocol (WAP)-network configuration

The wireless application protocol (WAP) network architecture is shown above. The server at origin (say) at position I is connected with handheld mobile unit. i.e. the mobile unit communicates with the server through the mobile network. The server is a standard HTTP or a web server. The contents received by the WAP handset are encoded in a binary format that is in wireless markup language (WML).

This facilitates proper delivery in band limited mobile network. The function of WAP gateway located between Internet and mobile network (II) receives the request (WAP request) from mobile handset and decodes it from binary format into text form and then forwards it to the origin server. This server provides only HTML (Hypertext markup language) contents and hence the HTTP responses of origin server is first sent to HTML filter (III). It translates HTML text into a WML format. The wireless application protocol (WAP) verifies the contents, and encodes into WML byte code format which is finally sent to WAP handset.

The WAP mainly provides end to end security as communication is directly possible with WAP protocols. The WML mentioned above is an XML language (wireless XML) which describes the WAP content of WAP handsets.

The WML documents are aggregated into set of cards where each of them represents a unit of interaction between user agent and user. These cards are also grouped into "deck" which is a basic WML unit. The WAP defines a user interface standard model for mobile handheld devices.

The WAE discussed previously mainly defines WAP application layer that provides proper environment for mobile users on wireless platforms. WAE supports user agent profile (UAP), which enhances its capability to the application servers and other network entities and hence contents based on the mobile handsets capabilities can also be generated accurately.

4.17.2 Wireless Application Protocol (WAP 2.0)—Advantages

This WAP 2.0 protocol focuses on the schemes combining wireless applications with the Internet. The WAP 2.0 provides support for the protocols like IP, TCP and HTTP. It is also flexible with air interface technologies and then corresponding bearers. For example GPRS and 3G cellular standards are interoperable with it. Then delivery of data to mobile phones, personal digital assistants (PDA) is also possible.

These devices also have the better hardware factors like battery life, ROM, limited RAM etc. The WAP provides many features and it is attractive since it is user friendly by providing several user interface (UI) designs.

WAP 2.0 reduces processing power and efficiently uses network resources to increase performance.

4.17.3 WAP 2.0

The wireless application protocol (WAP) forum released its first specification termed as WAP 1.0 in the year 1998. Then WAP forum viewed interoperability with many additional features. The WAP 2.0 is next generation standard which was released later and intended to a set of work under wireless with Internet operations. It has backward compatability with the previous WAP technologies.

The main architectural components of WAP 2.0 is listed below.

1. Protocol stack support
2. WAP application environment
3. Addition services and capabilities
4. Networks and network bearers
5. TCP/IP as transport protocol
6. Processors
7. Mobile friendly technology

All these seven components are discussed in detail with an example in this chapter.

1. Protocol stack, support

In WAP 1.0 version the WAP stack was introduced and WAP 2.0 appends high support and services on the stack based on Internet stack that includes support for TCP, HTTP etc. The version WAP 2.0 provides connectivity model on a broader range of networks and other wireless bearers.

2. WAP application environment

It is generally viewed as the WAP browser and the WAP 2.0 application environment has evolved to develop standards for the Internet markup language.

3. Additional services and capabilities

The WAP specifications have had items that were neither part of 'WAP Browser' nor the 'WAP Stack' but helped to enrich the environment defined in the WAP specification list. It is worth noting that with WAP 2.0 there is a considerable increase in the number of features present to operators, developers and end users. The WAP protocols are largely based on Internet technologies.

WAP was developed to use the Internet technologies for wireless networks and other devices.

4. Network and network bearers

Networks in the world over are switching on to high speed bearer such as General Packet Radio Service (GPRS) and High Speed Circuit Switched Data (HSCSD). For the introduction of third generation (3G) mobiles with higher bandwidth such as W-CDMA. This enables new type of content such as streaming media, video etc. over the higher capable network bearers.

5. TCP/IP as transport protocol

Today several wirelss network technologies provide IP packet support as primary data transport protocol. A mobile profile of TCP wireless links are used in the Performance Implications of Link Characteristics (PILC) working group thus enabling interoperability over the internet with common TCP.

6. Processors

Hardware manufacturers today are keen on introducing smaller devices which are more efficient, consuming less power and much faster in their performance. Due to VLSI technology more sophistication is achieved. Therefore new wireless devices provide enhanced services and have a variety of capabilities.

7. Mobile friendly technologies

Today catering to the needs of the mobile user has become very important. The WAP forum has therefore worked with standards like Internet Engineering Task Force (IETF) to address the issues generated by the wireless usage of the web. This has resulted in more user friendly mobile technologies.

For example, the basic profile for Extensible Hypertext Markup Language (XHTML) is incorporated with the core elements of the XHTML language in order to provide a bigger framework for enhancement and expansion.

The Components of WAP 2.0

The main components of WAP 2.0 are like "Application support", "Protocol support" and others.

The wireless application environment (WAE) provides interaction between web/WAP applications and the wireless devices containing WAP microbrowser.

The markup language XHTML mobile profile (XHTMLMP) is supported by the version WAP 2.0. Then it is possible to have services for wireless devices with languages compatible to them. The WAE also provides WBMP images, V Calender, V Card etc. WAP 2.0 supports an application centric approach by defining the XHTML-MP and few other technologies including several elements.

WAP Programming model

This model is aligned with that of the web programming model. The WAP extends the web architecture by adding the telephony support with the WTA that enables a push model and the server available there can send the content to the client.

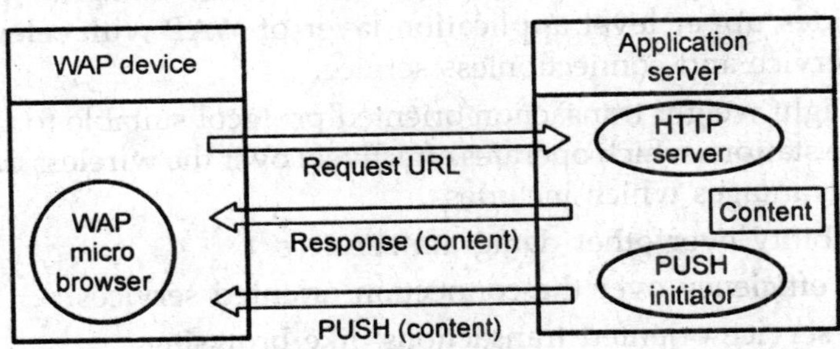

Fig. 4.33 WAP—"Programming model"

The WAP 2.0 version does not require a WAP proxy because the communication link between the origin server and the client can be conducted using the HTTP/1.1 But a WAP proxy is important for providing 'PUSH' functionality.

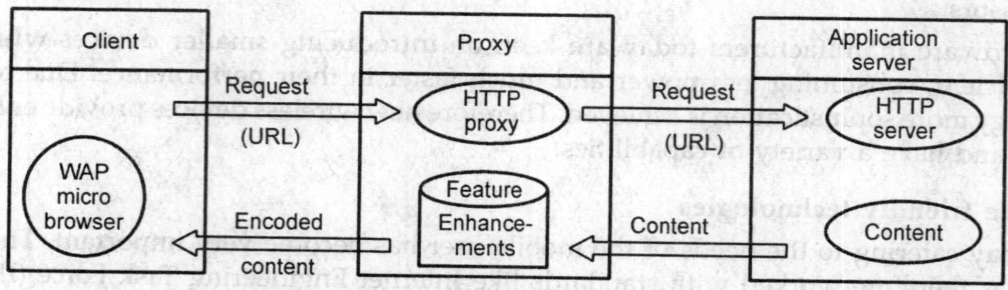

Fig. 4.34 WAP—'Optional proxy model'

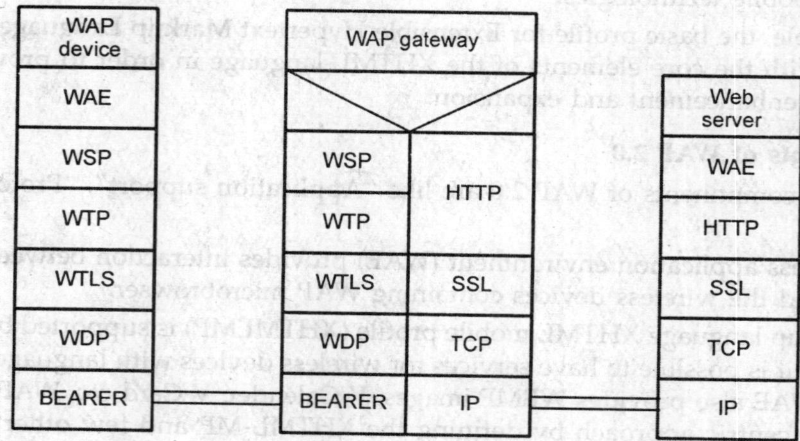

Fig. 4.35 WAP—1.x 'Gateway'

When an IP connectivity is available to that of the mobile device it is then supported by WAP 2.0.

The protocol layers are wireless session protocol (WSP), wireless transaction protocol (WTP), wireless transport layer security (WTLS) and wireless datagram protocol (WDP). In this the WSP provides upper level application layer of WAP with relevant interfaces for connection mode service and connectionless service.

The WTP is a light weight transaction oriented protocol suitable for implementation in 'thin' clients/mobile stations which operates effectively over the wireless datagram networks. WTP has several advantages which includes,

- High reliability over other datagram services.
- Improved efficiency over the connection oriented services.
- Supports 'service oriented transactions' like browsing.

The wireless transport layer security (WTLS) is designed to provide privacy, authentication and data integrity between different communicating applications. It also provides upper level layer of WAP with secure transport service interface for managing secured conditions. The WDP is a general datagram service providing consistent service to upper layer protocol for transparent communication with underlying bearer services.

It provides common interface to upper layers to function independently. The protocol layers for the networks supporting Internet protocol are

(*i*) Wireless profiled HTTP

(*ii*) Transport layer security

(*iii*) Wireless profiled TCP.

WAP 2.0 also supports several enhanced services, like WAP push, User agent profile (UA prof), Wireless telephony application (WTA), External functionality interface (EFT), Persistent storage interface. Data synchronization, Multimedia messaging service (MMS), Provisioning and Pictogram services.

Uses of WAP 2.0 additional services

WAP Push : Using a push proxy this service allows content to be transmitted or pushed to the devices by the server based applications through a 'Tush Proxy'. The push functionality is relevant to the real time applications that can send notifications to their users like messaging, stock price and traffic updated alerts.

User Agent Profile (UA Prof)

It provides a mechanism for elaborating capabilities of clients and preferences of users to a particular application server. It is possible to recognize the importance of the user's privacy, personal information that is submitted in requests may also be controlled by user. Thus UA prof supports client-server transaction model by transmitting client and the user information to the servers with the request.

The wireless telephony application (WTA) provides tools that provide for a range of advanced telephony services, supporting data functionality. The call handling services like making calls, answering calls, redirecting calls, placing calls on hold are combined with other data services.

The external functionality interface (EFI) mainly specifies interfacing between WAE and other entities with related applications.

The persistent storage interface (PSI) specifies a standard set of services coupled with well defined interface for accessing, organizing, storing and retrieving data on wireless device.

WAP 2.0 version supports data synchronization of data transfer.

The **multimedia** messaging service (MMS) provides the basic framework to implement messaging solutions. That is delivery of varied types of contents as messaging.

Also **provisioning service** provides a standard approach for providing WAR clients with information needed to operate on wireless network environments. A common set of tools are used by the network manager under this type of service.

Finally the 'pictogram' is a service that permits the usage of images (tiny) in a consistent manner and such type of tiny images can also be used to convey and permit communication in smaller space overcoming conventional limitations that were previously available as an obstacle.

WAP 2.0 is thus an enhanced specification which builded from the previous versions. It adopts in the latest standards and protocols so as to cater to increased bandwidth, dataspeed, small devices with enhanced processing power. WAP 2.0 allows increased access to the Internet, while being compatible to the previous versions of WAP.

REVIEW QUESTIONS

1. Define network.
2. Define Internet.
3. Mention any one important aspect of IP and TCP protocols.
4. What is known as NAP?
5. Define protocol.
6. What are the main information provided by the protocol?
7. Define syntax, semantics and timing.
8. What is known as National service provider?
9. What are the seven layers of OSI model?
10. What is the function of physical layer?
11. What are the types of transmission mode?
12. Define 'data link layer'.
13. List the functions of the network layer.
14. What is known as fragmentation?
15. What is the significance of transport layer and session layer?
16. Explain the concept involved in the presentation layer.
17. What is the importance of application layer 1 .
18. Explain network topology.
19. Write short note on :
    (*a*) Mesh topology
    (*b*) Star topology
    (c) Ring topology and
    (*d*) Bus topology.
20. Explain OSI reference model in details with functionalities of all the seven layers.
21. Explain the goals of TCP/IP.
22. What are the advantages of TCP/IP over OSI model?
23. List few application protocols.
24. Explain the TCP/IP operation in detail.
25. What are the layers of TCP/IP?
26. What are the applications of TCP/IP
27. List the protocols available in TCP/IP.
28. Explain the IP datagram structure in detail.
29. Define 'Fragmentation Offset' and 'Flags' in Internet protocol.
30. Write stort note on
    (*a*) Header length (*b*)Identification.
31. Explain stream delivery service in TCP/IP.
32. Explain the improved services of TCP/IP.
33. Write short notes on :
    (*a*) Full duplex service(*b*)Connection oriented service
34. What is known as congestion strategy ?

35. Define WAP.
36. Define WAE.
37. What are the elements of WAE ?
38. Write short note on 'Wireless Telephony Application'.
39. Explain WAP and WAE in detail.
40. Explain 'Wireless Session Protocol' in detail.
41. Explain the protocol stack of WAP.
42. Write short note on WAP 2.0 version.
43. Explain the programming model of WAP.
44. What are the advantages of WAP 2.0 version?
45. Write short note on 'Pictogram'.
46. Define :
   (*i*) Multimedia messaging service,
   (*ii*) Persistent storage interface.
47. Explain the advantages of TCP/IP.
48. What are the advantages of
   (*i*) Wireless application protocol and
   (*ii*) Wireless session protocol.
49. What is the use of 'ver' and 'Hlen' fields in IP ?
50. Explain the following :
   (*a*) TCP segment
   (*b*) Applications of TCP/IP
   (*c*) TCP/IP protocol suit
   (*d*) Client-server model in TCP/IP.
51. Explain transmission/time-out freezing and traditional TCP.
52. Explain (*i*) Indirect TCP and (*ii*) Snooping TCP.
53. Explain selective transmission and transaction oriented TCP.
54. Write a short note on congestion control.
55. What is fast retransmit/fast recovery?
56. Why mobility results in packet loss?
57. Why access point maintains buffers in direct TCP?
58. How handover takes place in indirect TCP/IP?

❑❑❑

Unit 5

Database Issues

5.1 HOARDING TECHNIQUES

In mobile computing environment to increase the use of entire system it is very important to enable continued working inspite of either connectivity or no connectivity available. The tasks on process should not be disturbed. If there is disconnected status then to handle the problem of allowing disconnected operations on the shared data is dealt by the Coda file system. It is possible to have a disconnected operation/computing with atleast some information rather than no information. Thus more data availability is required than its consistency. In a distributed mobile computing system there should a balanced trade off between data availability and data consistency.

In UNIX-like environments the Coda file system supports disconnected operations on the shared files. To enhance data availability caching at clients is mainly used with server replications.

There should also be a balance between speed cache validation after any disconnection and accuracy of invalidation. It is achieved by many versions of time stamps. The clients hoard the files when they are in connection with data server.

The 'HOARDING' is nothing but a cache maintenance scheme used for facilitating any disconnected operations. Some of the main points to note under hoarding are,

(*a*) What are the data files need to be hoard?

(*b*) How and when we can perform hoarding scheme?

(*c*) How to deal the cache misses?

(*d*) How to reconcile the data item's cached version with the server's version?

There should be high priority allowed to decide about 'what to hoard'? An user-assigned priorities can also be entertained. In regular time intervals a 'HOARD WALK' has to performed to check or monitor that no uncached object be in high priority then cached objects. The hoarding walk ensures whether the cache is in the equilibrium state. That is the user expectations regarding information availability in disconnected state from network is met by hoarding walk.

Types

Simple types of hoarding are :

- Manual hoarding technique
- Automatic hoarding technique

In manual hoarding a mobile user should decide the data sets that he wants to take before entering into mobile, and manually copy and with proper synchronization in reverse direction upon the return, and decide where to store the new set of files and directories.

All these tasks are time consuming and more complex, if a mobile user has number mobile devices (more than one). In case if the data comes from various heterogeneous type of sources (say different systems) the procedures in manual hoarding is again complicated.

But in automatic hoarding these problems are solved. In case an user want to enter into mobile he first connects to the 'mobility account' by using any mobile device. Now an incremental hoarding process gets started and contents mobile device are updated. The hoarding process will be active as long as the user is being connected. Thus all database management activities involving copying and synchronization are done automatically in this technique.

5.1.1 Three-tier Architecture

A three tier architecture that supports automatic hoarding of data from multiple, heterogenous type of source is shown below.

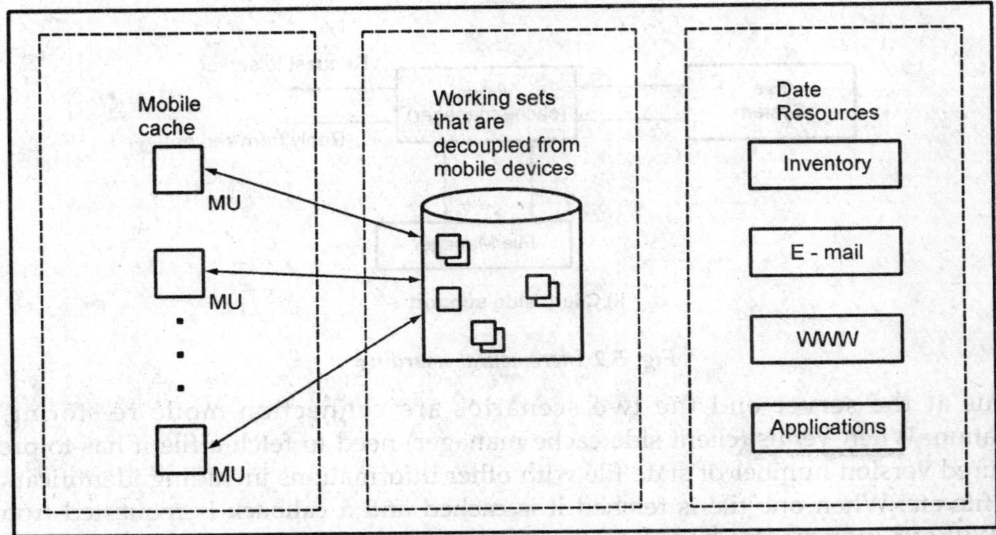

Fig. 5.1 Three-tier hierarchy for data management in mobile environment

The three tiers are :

(*a*) Data resources (e.g. email servers, web servers etc.)

(*b*) Working set (decoupled from mobile devices)

(*c*) Mobile caches (has copies of user's working set)

The mobile nodes can be separated from data source by introducing a middleware shielding them from changes effected on any one side. Middleware is data warehouse and it acts as mobility-aware store. As the user is connected it can accumulate his working set. If he roams it will update the changes taken place. Proper synchronization is also maintained. The three-tier system uses hoarding technique in data management.

5.1.2 Incremental Hoarding

Hoarding is necessary in preparation for an anticipated disconnections. The hoarding is based on Coda file system and it is using the Revision Control System (RCS). The implementation has two parts namely server side and client side. In server side connection mode restoring a user can directly open a code file, modify it and save it. Then reintegration will take place only in disconnection mode when the write propagation is disabled. Assume Venus as client side cache manager.

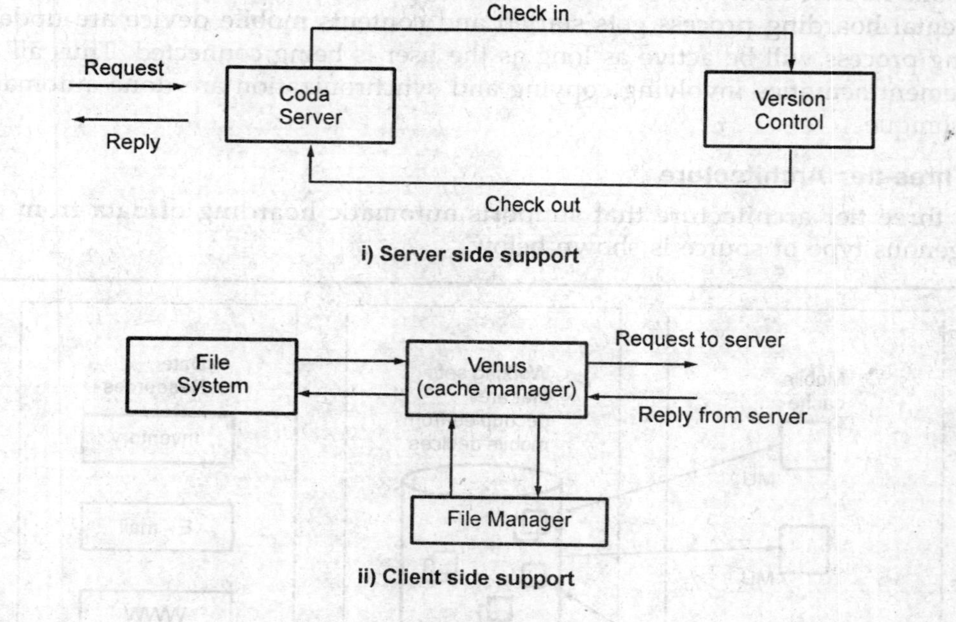

Fig. 5.2 Incremental hoarding

Thus at the server end the two scenarios are connection-mode re-storing and reintegration. When Venus (client side cache manager) need to fetch a file it has to provide the required version number of state file with other informations including identification of fetched file etc. When one file is fetched it is cached and a callback is requested from the server. Without incremental hoarding the Venus will simply discard the cached file. To implement incremental hoarding on file system a state file manager is first implemented.

Whenever one cached file is callback broken (by server) then Venus will discard the stale state file from cache library. Now the stale file manager will take charge of the situation.

Though the cached file was deleted by Venus it is stored by stale file manager.

In actual code file system Venus will fetch the whole file and hence version number is not a compulsory. But if the version number provided is 'O' it shows that Venus has no state version of file current used and hence server will retrieve the up-to-date version of the file. In case version provided by Venus is greater than 'O' then a difference between provided version and the up-to-date version will be by with the help of Revision Control System (RCS). This difference will be transferred to the Venus using a File Transfer Protocol (FTP).

Note : The information set by system server is about up-to-date file and not the difference file. For mobile data management the different hoarding techniques are being used. The hoarding and synchronization are independent of mobile device.

Flexible synchronization is obtained through programmable and proper conditional consistency specification of mobile data items. The hoarding and data consistency maintenance from heterogenous types of data sources is done by using data warehouse as middle layer in the structure.

5.2 CACHING OF DATA

Introduction

A "cache" is nothing but small, fast memory used for holding data that is often used.

The process of caching relevant data at hosts is an important tool that helps to improve the distributed system performance. The performance improvement includes improvement in query response time and data throughput.

An effective caching scheme includes,

(i) What to cache. It deals with "when to cache" and for "how long to cache".

(ii) When and how invalidate cached date items. It includes level of granularity also

(iii) Data consistency that is provided to the user

(iv) Cost involved in the process.

Also efficient caching schemes for the mobile environments should account the factors like :

- Data accessing pattern.
- Communication/access costs.
- Mobility pattern of client.
- Location dependence of data items and
- Connectivity characteristics etc.

In computing applications environment a computer system consists of many cache memories. A cache memory is small and fast to handle data. Data caching is an important application in computing environment. Data caching is important for improving the data availability since they are characterized by the narrow bandwidth wireless links. The cache maintenance protocols has to be energy efficient and it should be robust inspite of disconnections. It has to be adaptive for varying quality of service that is provided by wireless network.

The two different cache consistency requirements are : (*i*) Strong cache consistency (*ii*) Weak cache consistency.

The first one specifies that the cache data should be updated always. To achieve this two approaches used are,

(*a*) Polling

(*b*) Invalidating data.

In the second method it allows data inconsistency to some level of acceptance. One method to attain weak cache consistency is to apply TTL based consistency strategies.

There are three conventional strategies used for cache consistency maintenance :

1. Polling every time
2. FTL-based approach
3. Invalidation based approach.

In first two methods the client will initiate consistency verification. That is the data consistency is checked and used by the client.

5.2.1 Cache Invalidation

In invalidation-based strategies server will initiate cache consistency. It is classified into stateful and stateless approaches.

In the stateless approach the cache contents of clients are not maintained and the server is not aware of it.

On the other hand in stateful approach server will keep track of cache contents of the clients. The stateful approach can be categorized in two types and they are,

(*i*) Synchronous approach.

(*ii*) Asynchronous approach

Next the cache maintenance is done for push-based information.

Push-based information dissemination

The push-based information schemes are used for information access where the clients will initiate data transfers. The push-based architectures are developed in which data is pushed from server to the client. Thus the frequently accessed information (hot data) is being periodically broadcast by server using the broadcast channel is used. This push-based architectures are used for cache management scheme.

In conventional methods of cache management caches are used for storing the data that is often used, whereas in push-based environments the cost of receiving data should also be accounted.

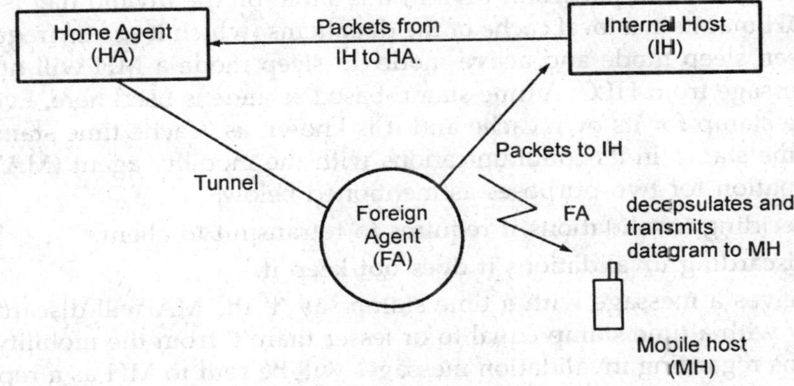

Fig. 5.3 Delivering message to MH

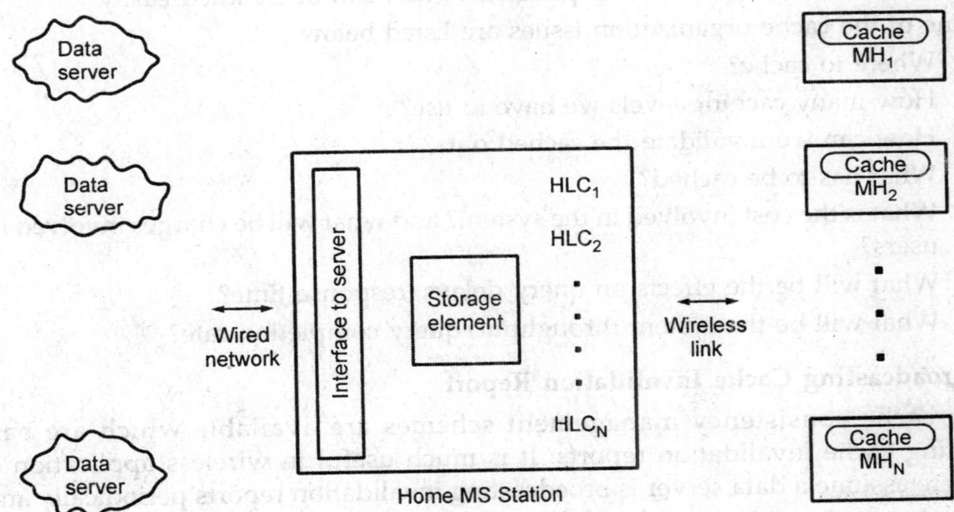

Fig. 5.4 Caching architecture

The method of message delivery to mobile host in mobile IP is shown above. The packets are routed to home agent from Internet host through home address. The care-of-address of the mobile host is the tunnel's end-point. From the foreign agent data packets are routed to IH as shown. The FA is also capable of decapsulating datagram to mobile host (MH).

In the system architecture a local home location cache (HLC) is maintained by mobile host (MH). In case a MH is in roaming status the HLC of it will be duplicated at MSS. For each MH a HLC is being maintained by MSS and ready at any time. If there is any invalidation reports they will be sent asynchronously and then buffered at MSS until an acknowledgment

(ACK) is received from that particular MH. In this situation the invalid flag is set to 'TRUE' status. Every MH maintain a local cache of the data items (which it access frequently). A MH alternate between sleep mode and active mode. In sleep mode a MH will not receive any invalidation message from HLC. A time-stamp-based scheme is used here. Every client will maintain a time stamp for its own cache and it is known as 'Cache time stamp.' The client includes this time stamp in its communications with the mobility agent (MA) and the MA uses this information for two purposes as mentioned below,

1. For deciding invalidations if requires to retransmit to client.
2. For discarding invalidations it does not keep it.

If MA receives a message with a time stamp say 't' the MA will discard invalidation messages if any with a time stamp equal to or lesser than 't' from the mobility host's PILC. The informations regarding invalidation messages will be sent to MH as a report. Later the MH will wake up after a sleep mode and it transmits probe message to HLC with the cache time stamp. As a response to this probe message the HLC will send an invalidation report. Thus by this lengthy procedures the mobile host will find which data item (s) was changed when it was disconnected. The sleep patterns of MH can be handled easily.

Some of the cache organization issues are listed below :

- Where to cache?
- How many caching levels we have to use?
- How can we invalidate the cached data?
- What has to be cached?
- What is the cost involved in the system? and what will be charges involved towards users?
- What will be the effects on query delays/response time?
- What will be the system throughput/query completion rate?

5.2.1.1 Broadcasting Cache Invalidation Report

The cache consistency management schemes are available which are based on transmitting cache invalidation reports. It is much useful in wireless application era. As shown here assume a data server is broadcasting invalidation reports periodically and these invalidation reports contains all invalidations in one window.

A cache invalidation will consist of two parameters say ide, tsmp in it.

eg. : (ide, tsmp) ; where ide is the identifier of data item and tsmp is the time stamp that shows the modification time period.

$t - w \leq tsmp < t$; where

$w \rightarrow$ is the window of time units in cache invalidation,

$t \rightarrow$ is the time of sending invalidation reports.

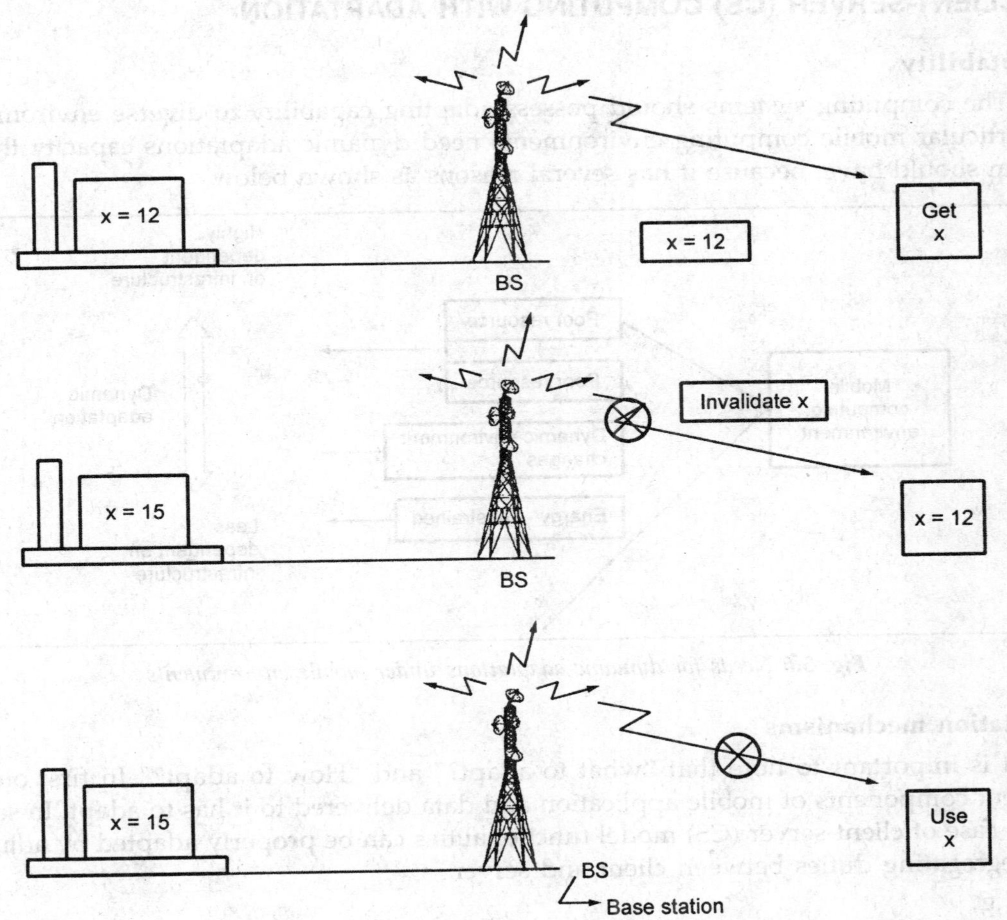

Fig. 5.5 Problem with the callback invalidation technique

As an invalidation report is received at the mobile, mobile starts to perform the operations to validate the cache.

Note : The window size (w) will decide the time allowed for a client to sleep in disconnected mode.

All clients in wireless computing experiences a delay for accessing a cached entry and it continues until a new invalidation report arrives. On receiving a report (R), mobile client will validate the cached entry. Thus broadcasting invalidation reports is an useful task that is continuously monitored and once there is a broadcast a sequence operations takes place as response to it and mobile client tries to validate the cached data effectively.

Note : The invalidation report scheme has the characteristics and it is given below.

(*i*) The entire cache will be invalid in case the client is in disconnected state for a time period more than broadcast period.

(*ii*) The scheme assume a stateless server and it does not addresses the mobility issues directly.

5.3 CLIENT-SERVER (CS) COMPUTING WITH ADAPTATION

Adaptability

The computing systems should possess adapting capability to diverse environments. In particular mobile computing environments need dynamic adaptations capacity that the system should have, because it has several reasons as shown below.

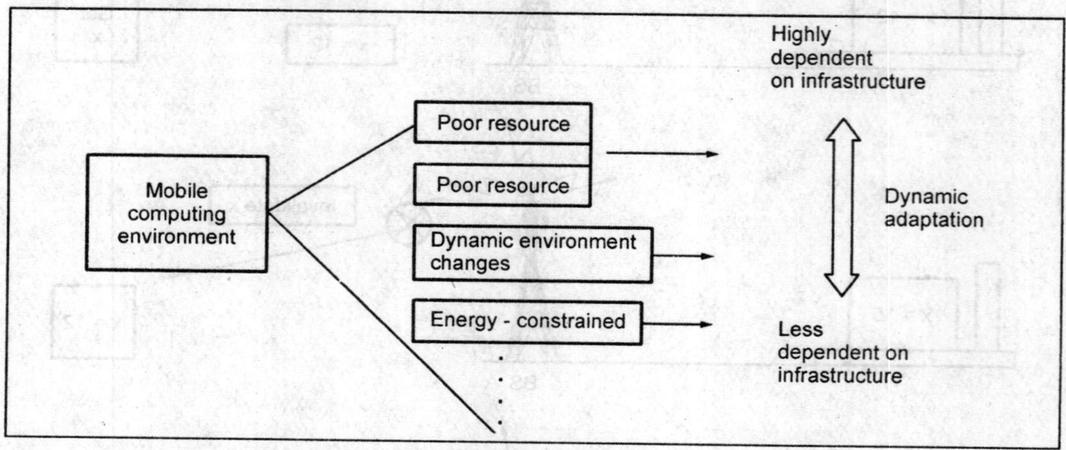

Fig. 5.6 Needs for dynamic adaptations under mobile environments

Adaptation mechanisms

It is important to note that "what to adapt?" and "How to adapt?" In first one the different components of mobile application and data delivered to it has to adapt. In second one in case of client-server (CS) model functionalities can be properly adapted by adjusting and segregating duties between client and server.

E.g.

- At the time of disconnections.
- At the time of strong connectivity.

For distributed computing CS paradigm is highly used. In a conventional CS model at the time of design their roles are well defined, for example their own run times etc.

A client or system (middleware) could dynamically select the server as to request the service. But this server may maintain the client's the information to which it serves. It is not compulsory. The state information be maintained as soft or hard state. The soft state needs no explicit actions but hard state information once installed need explicit deletions. The soft state information is used in different protocols like Resource Reservation Protocol (RSVP).

In case of file servers (data servers) the CS model is used and it has many characteristics like,

- Performance enhancement is attained by caching and prefetching techniques.
- End-to-end authentication and encryption techniques used and provides high security.

Advantages of CS model (Implemented by Coda file system) are :

1. The client-server (CS) model simply decomposes a larger distributed system into smaller nucleus system operations that are more dynamic periphery of the clients.
2. CS model provides more scalability, availability and performance.

Impacts of mobility on CS model

To perform expensive computations the CS model allows a resource-poor mobile client for requesting a resource-rich server system. In case if a client send a request to a server then it goes to sleep to save energy. Later it wakes up and obtain the needed result / response from the server.

But the boundary available between the clients and server should have dynamic adjustments, so that an efficient performance with higher adaptability can be achieved.

Such a client-server model is called as " EXTENDED CS MODEL".

Note : The clients with less functionalities are called as thin clients. It is also available is mobile computing environment under CS model.

5.4 POWER-AWARE AND CONTEXT-AWARE COMPUTING

Power-aware mobile computing

The wireless networks are classified into two types namely (*i*) Infrastructure networks (*ii*) Ad hoc networks.

In first type it is "infrastructure based" and in second type it is "independent of infrastructure." The end nodes communicate with each other in multihop fashion. In these networks the routing methods will consume more battery power. It is important that power saving is one of the main criteria.

The power-aware routing metrics has to be considered seriously. The main metrics applied to evaluate ad hoc routing protocols are nothing but shortest hop, local stability and shortest delay.

The two types of traffic considered under power aware analysis are unicast and broadcast. The unicast traffic is that the traffic in which the packets are send towards single receiver, whereas the broadcast traffic is intended for several network nodes.

The unicast traffic is accounted with respect to power consumption. There are five different routing metrics defined.

(*i*) Energy consumed by one packet.

(*ii*) Time for network partition.

(*iii*) Variance in power levels across mobiles.

(*iv*) Cost for one packet

(*v*) Maximum mobile cost.

To conserve energy it is important to minimize all metrics except the time parameter since it has to be maximized. Also shortest-hop routing protocol is not much suitable. A simple comparison of shortest-hop routing. Shortest-cost routing and power-aware routing showed that power-aware routing had no extra delay. For this comparison the metrics considered were delay, average maximum node cost and average cost for single packet. The routing algorithm should be efficient such that congested paths has to be avoided.

If routing parameters are adjusted carefully an energy efficient routing may be attained.

Local information-based algorithm

Many of the routing protocols shall be considered as global algorithms incorporate that can global topology and related information. They also use global positioning system (GPS) receiver set up for providing location oriented information to network nodes that allows the nodes to use least transmission for reception purpose. The networks may be of any type mobile, static or quasi static in nature. The ultimate goal of power-aware metric is that to reduce the total power required for routing a message from source (S) to destination (D).

Cost-aware metric

In case of cost-aware metrics the main goal cost-aware algorithms is to extend network node's worst-case lifetime.

If power-aware and cost-aware algorithms are combined and applied to manage routing metrics then message will be routed from S to D efficiently with reduced power and cost. Thus the ultimate goal of "power cost" algorithms is to reduce the total power required and to avoid the network nodes with shortest battery lifetime problem. At the same time the system design has to be cost effective.

The algorithms used are loop free in their characteristic.

In localized algorithms every node has to be capable to make forwarding decisions, depending on its own location. Thus each node is expected to be aware of geographic locations of all its neighbouring nodes in the network. It should be aware of the time of establishment also. The routing table provides location informations of the destination node involved and accurate datas regarding the location of other nodes.

Note : If the information of activity of all nodes and their positions are known clearly then for obtaining power-saving the Dijkstra's single source, a shortest weighted path method can be used. It will lead to optimal power-saving and reduced cost.

5.4.1 Power-aware Algorithm

In case of localized power-saving routing algorithm every node A select its neighbour (one of its neighbour) B and let D is the neighbour node of A, then

$$P\ (A, B) = u(r) + v(s)$$ where u(r) is the

power needed to transmit from A to B and v(s) is the power needed for transmission from B to D.

The algorithm will proceed until the destination is reached. The value of P(A, B) can still be minimized and,

$$P\ (A, B) = u(r) + t\ v(s)$$

where 't' is known as network parameter. Generally for analysis purposes 't' will be set as unity.

5.4.2 Power-cost Routing Algorithm

The two main factors power and cost can be merged in a single routing algorithm. It is based on sum or product of two metrics. In sum of the two, the power cost can be mentioned as,

$$P(B, A) = \alpha\, u(r) + \beta\, f(A)$$

Where f(A) is sum of cost involved and α and β are suitable selected values. In next case of product of the two, the power cost of transmitting one message from A to B (neighbouring node) is expressed as,

$$\text{Power cost} \quad (A, B) = f(A)\, u(r).$$

In above two cases 'r' is considered as distance between nodes A and B in the network.

As said previously, the power cost algorithm can find an optimal power cost by using Dijkstra's single-source, shortest weighted path algorithm.

Analysis

In power cost routing algorithm let B be the neighbour node of node A such that it minimizes power cost (Pc) as,

Pc (A, B) - Power-cost (A, B) + v(s) f(A) in which s is zero for D when D is a neighbouring node of A. This Pc algorithm is known as 'power cost 0' ; Pc (A, B) = f(A) u(r).

The power-cost (Pc), will refer to power cost (A, B) = f(s) u(r) + u(r)' f(A). Now packet is delivered to B and not to D.

The algorithm continues till the destination node is reached. Thus a localized optimum power and cost metrics has to be achieved by selecting proper routing metric method and hence lifetime of each node in the network is long with efficient cost and battery power saving metrics.

(*ii*) Context-aware computing

Definition

The English word 'context' originates in Latin verb termed as "contexere" and it means "to weave together." This is a general meaning for the word context. But a computer friendly definition for the word context has several definitions and it is categorized under two classes such as :

(*i*) Enumeration-based

(*ii*) Role-based.

In first one the context is expressed in the terms of several categorizations and in second one it is expressed interms of its role in the context-aware computing environment. This a step taken in the direction of the application-aware adaptation is called as context-aware computing. The applications adapts to the changes in availability of computing and the communication resources. It also includes the contextual informations like,

- Time
- Where the system is residing currently.
- Action performed by user.
- Intension of performing the action etc.

Thus context-aware (context-sensitive) application needs contexual information which has to be collected from different sources. The design and complete development of context-aware applications are related to the issues like,

1. How it is possible to provide context-aware informations to application.
2. How it is possible to develop the applications to react for changing environment of context informations.

Next let us consider the main categories mentioned earlier enumeration-based and role-based types.

(*a*) Enumeration-based category

One of the definition in the terms of different categories is to express 'context' is just from the Schilit's definition for it. It includes,

- Computing context (includes network connectivity, bandwidth etc.)
- User context (Includes profiles, location etc.)
- Physical context (Includes traffic conditions, temperature etc.)
- Temporal context (Includes time, day, week, month and year etc.)
- Context history (Includes recording of mobile computing, user informations etc.)

Also there are various context types that can be used by an application like :

Who	-	Social context
What	-	Functional context
Where	-	Location context
When	-	Temporal context
Why	-	Motivating context

In addition to these contexts user's emotional informations are called as 'emotional context' and informations related to environment (temperature etc.) are called as 'environmental context.'

Note : The informations related to sophisticated functions likes low-level context information, artificial intelligence technique etc. are classified under high-level context information.

(*b*) Role-based category

It is important to understand that how context-information can be used by the mobile applications. It also said as "The set of environmental states that can determine either an application's behavior or where an event occurs."

Here there are two types of contexts possible

- Active Context.
- Passive context.

Active context is used by an application for adapting its behavior. Passive context is provided for the user just to understand the situation. This context is not critical to adapt like active context.

Various types of Context-aware Computing

The term context-aware is also said to be mobile applications because,

- The contexts of users fluctuates very often as the user roams.
- The requirement for context-awareness is high in mobile computing environment.

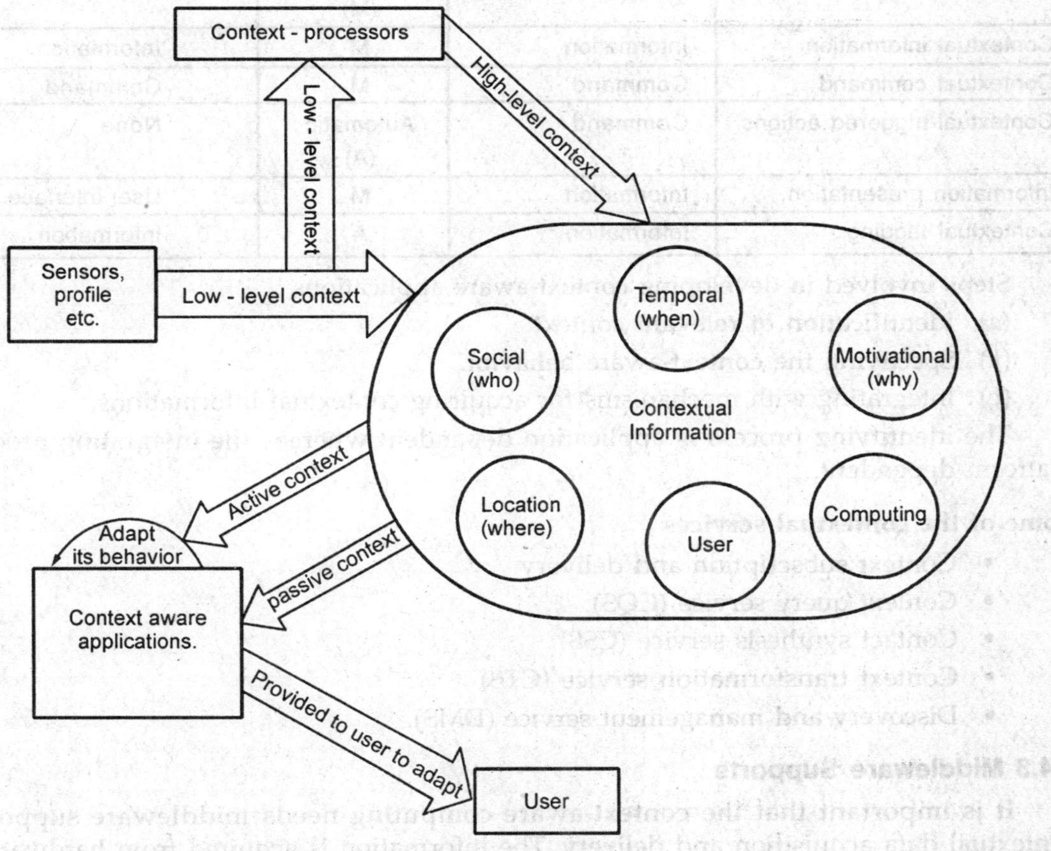

Fig. 5.7 Types of contexts

The context-aware applications has to be proactive in getting contextual informations. Proactive in the sense that it is automatically initiated by system itself or by the application. Otherwise is has to be reactive that is reacting in response to the user request.

A context-aware application can do various tasks and provide either context information (or) non-context information to the user and may be proactive (or) reactive in nature.

Capabilities for context awareness

1. Contextual sensing
2. Contextual adaptation
3. Contextual resource discovery
4. Contextual augmentation.

Some of the types of context-aware applications.

Application type	Function/Service	Initiation	Adaptation
Contextual selection	Information	Manual (M)	Informations
Contextual information	Information	M	Information
Contextual command	Command	M	Command
Contextual-triggered actions	Command	Automatic (A)	None
Information presentation	Information	M	User interface
Contextual tagging.	Information	A	Information

Steps involved in developing context-aware applications :

(*a*) Identification of relevant context.

(*b*) Specifying the context-aware bahavior.

(*c*) Integrating with mechanisms for acquiring contextual informations.

The identifying process is application dependent whereas the integrating process is platform dependent.

Some of the contextual services

- Context subscription and delivery
- Context query service (CQS)
- Contact synthesis service (CSS)
- Context transformation service (CTS)
- Discovery and management service (DMS).

5.4.3 Middleware Supports

It is important that the context-aware computing needs middleware support for contextual data acquisition and delivery. The information is acquired from hardware and software sensors, recorded inputs, and other application environments. Also same type of context data could be derived from different sources.

In case of mobile environment context awareness should be very high so as to adapt to frequent changes as the user is in mobile status. A middleware is a software that could support as a medium between other softwares and enables interoperability between the heterogenous components. The context-aware computing uses middleware for its functionalities.

5.5 TRANSACTIONAL MODEL

A transaction is a set of interdependent and related steps that forms a logical unit of a work.

The entire set of all steps may either succeed or fail as it runs. A simple database transaction consists of two updates namely update 1 and update 2.

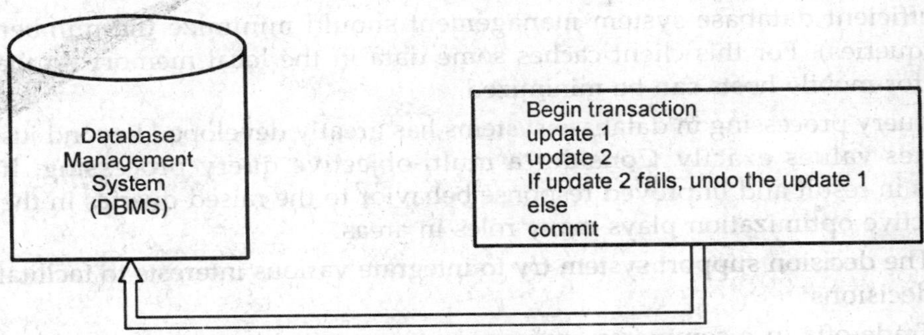

Fig. 5.8 A simple database transaction system

Consider there is a transaction taking place. The transaction will block the database which it is modifying and makes it unavailable for other transactions that try to modify it.

The process of isolating data from any outside interference is one of the main advantage of transaction.

As shown above once the transaction operations gets complete, it ends with commit operation. This commit operation will then release the transaction lock, such that making the database available to other transactions.

5.5.1 Roil-back Process

Consider a transaction which has started and modification of a database is on process. Now if an error had occurred then all the transaction may get fail and rather than leaving the database with partial results the transaction will release the database with older values that was available before transaction had started. Such a going back to initial state is known as "roll-back" process.

5.5.2 Two-phase Commit Transaction

The two-phase commit is a type of database transaction that is adapted for distributed usages across the multiple databases. It uses a transaction monitor for coordinating concurrent update procedure.

Each and every transaction should maintain consistency in database and in two phase commit transaction facilities beyond individual databases are available.

An example to this is "funds transfer". In database issues thus transaction is one of the main function that ensures better system performance.

5.6 QUERY PROCESSING

Query

A query for example represents uplink request sent by the client for data to the data server. By noticing the query the server responds to it by sending the requested data and it is known as downlink.

An efficient database system management should minimize the number of uplink requests (queries). For this client caches some data in the local memory so that the total overhead for mobile hosts can be minimized.

The query processing in database systems has greatly developed beyond just matching of attributes values exactly. Consider a multi-objective query processing. It produces correctness in result and improved response behavior to the raised queries in the system. A multi-objective optimization plays many roles in areas.

- **The decision support system try to integrate various interests to facilitate strategic decisions.**
- Trade-offs in e-commerce environment-
  e.g. between the price and quality to product etc.
- Personal user preferences requesting for a web services for executing a complex task.

Example

Multi-objective retrieval :

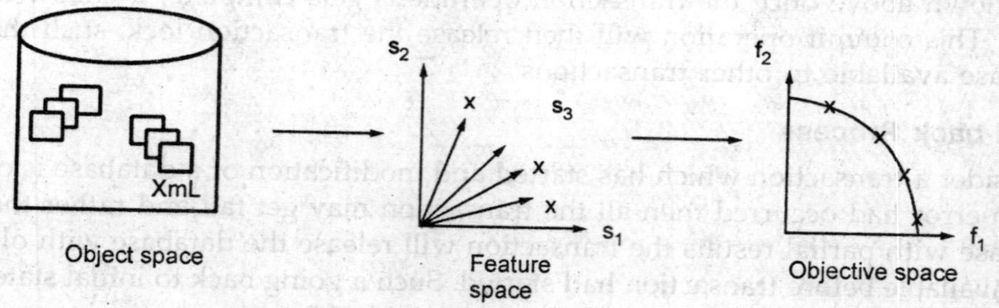

Fig. 5.9 Multi-objective retrieval

Consider a database consists of 'N' number of objects (o) and $o = \{o_1, o_2, ... o_N\}$, and there are 'P' characteristics S_k (o), ($l \leq k \leq p$) to describe the available objects (e.g. aggregation of attribute values) and 'm' monotonic functions say f_i ($l \leq i \leq m$) aggregating subset with the help of objective functions. The main objective of process is to find best database objects considering all 'm' scoring functions mentioned above. For simplicity we assume that all the characteristics S_k are the scoring functions for evaluation some characteristics of the database objects assigning normalized scores and for example a numeral domain for retrieval is used.

Let the characteristics of database objects be table, XML documents, images etc. They are evaluated in a feature space and the scores are aggregated by user specific objective functions as shown above. For a better optimization each database object 'O' a 'm' dimensional vector containing the aggregated scores (f_1, (S_1, (0), ... S_p(0)),...., f_m (S_i(0),.... ,S_p(0))) for every objective (f_i). The process has to be continued until best vectors are being selected.

For, utility-based retrieval models 'top k retrieval' algorithm is used, where global aggregation of objective scores can be processed.

Then the skyline queries in database management known as Pareto optimality is popular to handle query.

In case of personalization in database retrieval and considering user preferences three operators namely score aggregation, pareto accumulation and lexicographic optimization are used. The user preferences are build into queries and arbitrary combinations are being allowed. An efficient query processing is an important task that helps to save time and bandwidth and it is always suggested to reduce number of uplink requests/queries sent to the server.

5.6.1 Recovery

In database issues recovery is also a main task to address. Recovery means to the coming back to needed state from a failure.

A successful completion of a given job will be objective in overall data management. But in execution there may be partial or total failure may take place. Recovery from it should take only a minimal time. During recovery phase it has to be monitored by overall system manager that failure should not take place. In the recovery phase each file has to be checked for any error. If so action has to take place to eliminate errors. The recovery procedure ensures a stable error less data zone availability. Thus the recovery process enhances the performance efficiency of database management in the entire system. It will also lead to stable storage implementations effectively.

5.7 QUALITY OF SERVICE (QOS)

The mobile computing applications must not maintain low QoS when it has abundant resources. The goals should include saving energy. There should be trade-off between increasing delay in packet delivery and overhead of paths reconstruction such that better QoS will be achieved. The network topology may change in mobile environment say if sensor nodes stop functioning due to lack of power or any fault. There should be additional sensors to deploy according to dynamic need and it should be well planned at designing time so that suitable QoS level can be maintained in system.

This QoS concept is important for distributed multimedia systems. The QoS requirements should be supported by networks involved, protocols and the operating system (OS). The QoS specifications are primarily used for reserving necessary resources and to schedule tasks. There are three scenarios available for reduced QoS in case of multimedia database system. They are,

- Reduced video quality
- Reduced reliability constraints
- Relaxed synchronization requirements.

In the mobile computing, database management should give more attention in maintaining appropriate QoS and it should monitor that the network, protocols etc. Qos.

REVIEW QUESTIONS

1. What is known as hoarding technique?
2. Define data caching method.
3. What is known as power-aware computing?
4. What is known as context-aware computing?,
5. What is use of power-cost computing mechanism?
6. What is the use of transactional model?
7. Write short note on query processing.
8. Define recovery.
9. Define quality of service.
10. Write short note on cache invalidation.
11. Explain (*i*) Hoarding and (*ii*) Caching mechanisms.
12. Explain power-aware and context-aware computing.
13. Write short notes on
    (*a*) Query processing.
    (*b*) Recovery.
    (*c*) Quality of service.
14. Explain transactional models in detail.
15. Explain client server computing with adaptation in detail.
16. Explain caching invalidation mechanisms in detail.
17. Write short notes on (*i*) Recovery and (*ii*) Hoarding techniques.
18. Explain power-aware computing in detail.
19. Give the advantages of power-aware and cost-aware computing mechanisms.
20. Explain transactional models and quality of service in detail.
21. What are the hoarding techniques? Explain in detail.
22. What is query processing explain in detail.
23. What is context aware? Explain in detail about context aware computing?
24. What are the problems involved in client mobility?
25. Discuss the various transactions models in detail.

□□□

Unit 6
Data Dissemination

Communication asymmetry

The distributed data management meets several challenges due to various characteristics of the wireless networks. There are two types available in mobile wireless networks. They are

(*i*) Architecture-based mobile wireless networks
(*ii*) Architecture less mobile wireless networks.

In most cases when compared to wired links the wireless links have low bandwidth. The wireless links are subject to disconnections frequently and it would lead to weakly connected links. Hence the mobile clients are often disconnected from their respective data servers.

These disconnections of mobile clients from their data servers may be two types, voluntary or involuntary.

But an user would always need connection transparency with the server so as to complete the intended application.

Thus data management for mobile wireless networks is really a challenging task. The challenges of data management system includes the points like,

(*i*) How to ensure data availability inspite of disconnections.

(*ii*) How to manage weekly connected mobile wireless links between clients and server.

(*iii*) How to support constant resource availability to complete the applications.

Resource availability refers to battery power at the mobile node. The problems of limited power at mobile node has to be addressed carefully.

Next important criteria is minimized use of resource consumption (bandwidth and energy).

Asymmetric communication links

Some of the wireless links has the characteristics of presence of the asymmetric communication links.

Consider an architecture-based wireless network, the capacity of downstream communication link is higher than the capacity of uplink communication link.

To get an upstream channel a MN has to compete with several other nodes in its accessing process.

> Downstream → Base station to mobile nodes
> Upstream → Mobile to base station.

But for accessing an uplink channel after competing with several other nodes the MN needs more battery power. This is because the MN has to keep its battery powered up from the time it has initiated request to the response it receives from data server.

Hence the asymmetric nature of wireless communication link is another challenge for data management in wireless links to ensure low resource consumption and data access latency.

Finally the mobile wireless computing environments has another characteristics to address is location and time-dependent nature. To maintain a location-dependent and time-dependent informations some efficient techniques such as cache invalidation and prefetching has to be used in mobile wireless networks.

In mobile computing one of the main task is accessing information from remote servers. Remote data can be accessed just by sending a query to remote server. By seeing this query the server sends the data requested. Such a data access mode is called as 'PULL MODE' or on-demand mode.

> In pull mode the mobile node must send a query to the server and for this wireless access it can use uplink channel.

But this complete procedure needs more battery power. Also bandwidth requirement is high.

There is also another method of data access known as PUSH MODE. That is data can be delivered to mobile node by pushing data to it.

Data broadcasting is done periodically by the data server using the broadcast channel. Indexing information related to the time of data availability. The pushing information is also known as publishing mode of the data dissemination.

> In push or publishing mode to deliver data it is pushed or published to the mobile node.

Some of the advantages of pushing mode of data dissemination are listed below :

- The data items requested frequently is called as 'hot data items'. It advantage of this method is it avoids on-demand data transfers for same data.
- Because of it the push mode is highly scalable.
- This mode also avoids energy consuming uplink transmissions to the data server.

In mobile computing environment a cell's wireless bandwidth is divided into three logical channels. They are :

1. Uplink request channel.
2. On-demand downlink channel.
3. Broadcast downlink channel.

But for implementations the wireless bandwidth is partitioned into two physical channels namely on-demand and broadcast channels.

Cache maintenance for the push mode information dissemination

A cache is a smaller and fast memory used for holding frequently used data items.

The data caching is important in mobile computing environment because these environments has only narrow bandwidths. Data caching is for improving data availabilities and to access latencies in the system so that improves overall performance.

For wireless networks the pull-based mode is not suitable. The push mode is optimum for cache management. The algorithms suitable for pushed-based information system considers the cost of cache miss. For architecture based wireless networks the pull-based techniques are not suitable.

An important metric to analyze cache management algorithms is the hit ratio. In mobile computing environment the hit ratio is not the only metric for evaluating compute cache management algorithms. The cache miss cost depends on data timing and data size.

6.1 DATA MANAGEMENT ISSUES IN MOBILE ENVIRONMENT

The mobile computing environment is observed as a distributed computing. The complete database may be distributed among wired components as in mobile switching stations. This is one approach. But in next approach the entire database is being distributed in wired and wireless components of the computer systems. Some of the parameters that influence and complicate database management are,

(*i*) Design of database.

(*ii*) Replication of data.

(*i*) Design of database

The mobility of clients (hosts-MH) and disconnection between hosts and servers is very difficult to predict. In addition to this the dynamic nature of constantly changing location has to be updated carefully and it also adds more complexity to system design.

(*ii*) Replication of data

In mobile computing scenario the data is partially replicated in different places and the availability of these duplicates is updated periodically. There is also consistency management and version control available.

In this chapter we will focus on caching of data and different mechanisms like push-based and pull-based methods. Caching the relevant data at mobile hosts is an important tool to improve performance of distributed system. While designing an efficient caching system the points like when to cache, how long to cache, when to invalidate cached items at what granularity level and at what cost data it is provided to the host etc. Also some of the factors lias to be considered for a cache system in mobile computing environment. It includes,

Data access pattern Update rate Access costs Mobility pattern of host Bandwidth Disconnection pattern Location dependency of information

In design approaches if all these parameters are attended carefully an efficient cache management can be developed for mobile scenario.

In this chapter we will focus on the topic data scheduling. One of the popular data scheduling methodology in which data broadcasting is planned effectively is push-based data scheduling. In this method the server broadcasts data proactively to its clients according to the broadcast program that is developed by data scheduling algorithm. The order and frequency with which data items are being broadcast by the broadcast program. It's different types are given below.

Push-based data scheduling 1. Flat broadcast 2. Probabilistic-based broadcast 3. Broadcast disks 4. Optimal push scheduling

6.2 TWO INFORMATION DELIVERY METHODS IN WIRELESS SCENARIO

Data broadcast and point-to-point are the two fundamental data delivery methods for the wireless data application environments.

A logical is established between the client and server. As in the case of wired links in point-to-point access queries will be sent to server and the results will be returned by server to the clients. But in broadcast access data is simultaneously transmitted to the users who are residing in broadcast area. The client is given liberty and to decide whether to select the data or not to select.

There is also a special broadcast system known as ON-DEMAND BROADCAST, the client will submit the queries to the server.

When comparing broadcast and point-to-point data access methods, the broadcast method is a more attractive method for many reasons. Because the broadcast system can attend multiple users and servers to their requests.

A wireless communication system employs a broadcast component for delivering information. This approach is also economical to afford.

Some demerits or challenges the broadcast and point-to-point schemes has are power conservation and bandwidth consumption.

In case of wireless data system the access efficiency and power conservation are the two issues to address. Access efficiency reflects the fastness in serving a request whereas the power conservation parameter is related how to minimize power consumption.

Then the two performance matrices for broadcast system are access time t_1 and tune in time t_2.

It is also important that access time should not be wasted by broadcasting irrelevant data items. Because it will reduce efficiency of a broadcast system.

In broadcast system three important mechanisms/models are available.

Broadcast Mechanisms (BM)/Models (BM)
1. Push-Based BM
2. On-demand or Pull-based BM
3. Hybrid BM

6.3 CLASSIFICATION OF DATA DELIVERY MECHANISMS

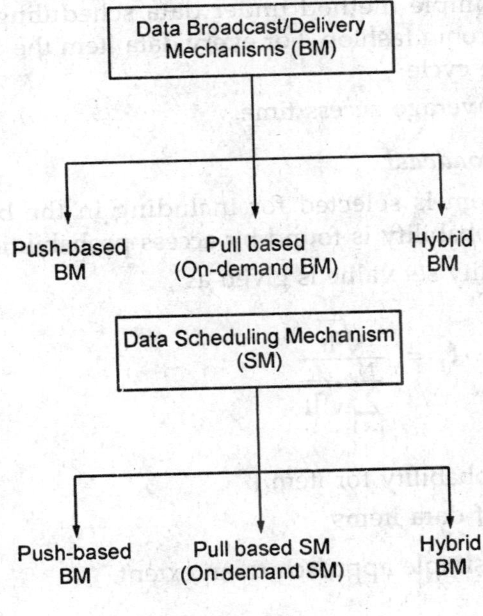

Fig. 6.1

In push-based BM server uses a periodic or a periodic broadcast program and disseminates information. In on-demand BM the server disseminates information with respect to requests that are submitted by the clients.

In last approach hybrid BM, both the push-based and pull-based data delivery mechanisms can be combined and applied.

Similar to data delivery mechanisms there are also three data scheduling mechanisms namely, push-based scheduling mechanism (SM), pull-based (SM) and hybrid (SM), corresponding to the three data delivery (broadcast) mechanisms.

Different data scheduling methods for three broadcast (delivery) mechanisms are discussed in detail in this chapter.

(*a*) Push-Based Mechanisms

In the push-based data broadcast/delivery technique the server will broadcast data proactively to all the clients according the program (for broadcast) that is generated by data scheduling program. The frequency and order of data flow are mainly determined by broadcast program. There are four types of push-based data scheduling algorithms are available. They are listed below :

(*i*) Flat broadcast.

(*ii*) Probabilistic-based broadcast.

(*iii*) Broadcast disks.

(*iv*) Optimal push scheduling.

(i) Flat broadcast

Flat broadcast is a simple method under data scheduling. Here the data items are being broadcast in round robin fashion. For every data item the access time is uniform. It is half the broadcasting time cycle.

Demerit : Has poor average access time.

(ii) Probabilistic-based broadcast

In this method an item is selected for including in the broadcast program with a probability P_i in which probability is found by access probabilities of the data items.

An optimum probability set value is given as

$$f_1 = \frac{\sqrt{q_i}}{\sum_{j=1}^{N} \sqrt{q_1}}$$

where $q_1 \rightarrow$ Access probability for item j

$N \rightarrow$ Number of data items

This method is also a simple approach to an extent.

Demerit :

(*i*) This method has a large access time for one data item,

(*ii*) Performance not good.

(*iii*) Broadcast disks

The hierarchical dissemination architecture is also called as broadcast disk in which the data items are being assigned to logical disks such that data items of same access probabilities are combined as one group on a same disk.

According to broadcast frequencies allocated to different disks the data items are selected from each disk. This is possible by just dividing each disk into equal sized, smaller units known as chunks. Then from each disk broadcasting the chunks at particular time is done and cyclic sequential system is adopted.

> Minor cycle :
>
> It is defined as a subcycle containing one chunk from one disk and so on. Such that data in minor cycle will be repeated only once.

Some of the steps in broadcast disks generation algorithm.

{

Calculate : Items are ordered in decreasing probabilities.

Allocate : Allocate items from different disks with same range of access probability.

Select : Select proper broadcast frequency.

Split : Splitting every disk into smaller sized chunks.

}

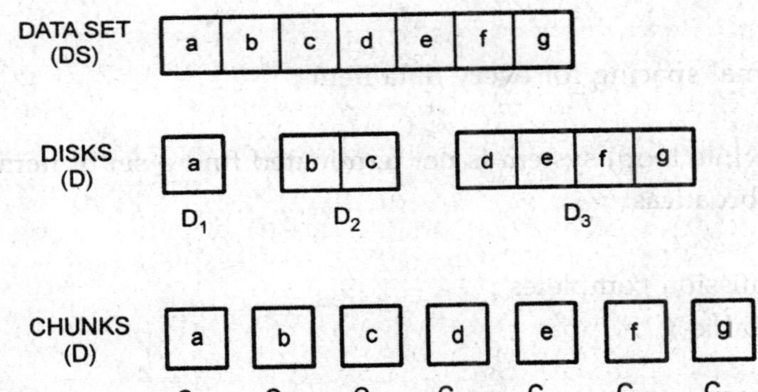

Fig. 6.2

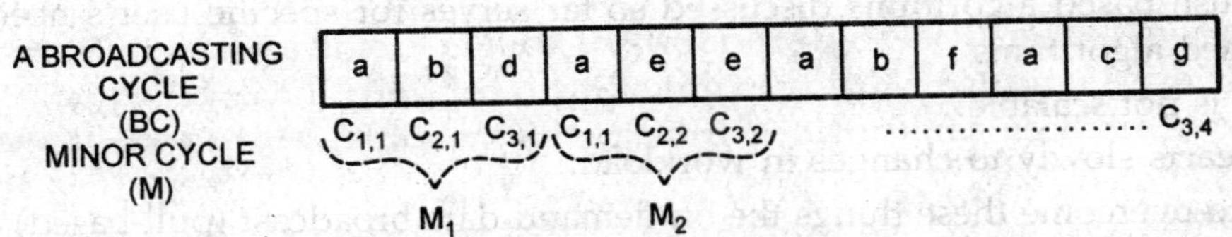

Fig. 6.3 7-data item, 3-disk broadcast program example

In the above example shown there are seven data item available. They are divided into three groups of same accessing probability (P_i) and they are assigned to separate disks in the broadcast.

The three disks ($D_1 - D_3$) are interleaved in one broadcast cycle. In the resultant broadcast cycle it contains four minor cycles ($M_1 - M_4$).

In this method the data items of high popularity will be broadcast frequently if the number of disks, spinning speed, size and the assigned items to different disks.

***(iv)* Optimal push scheduling mechanism**

In optimal push scheduling it is stated that minimum expected latency of accessing is being achieved when two criteria are met. They are :

- If time instances of the data items are spaced equally on the broadcast channel.
- The spacing s_x of consecutive instances of item x is proportional to square root of length l_x and it is inversely proportional to the square root of the access probability q_x.

$$\boxed{s_x \propto \sqrt{l_x / q_x}}$$

Note : But the two conditions are not attained at some time.

For providing better results an algorithm known as Heuristic algorithm is efficient and it maintains two variables say A_x and B_x for every item x.

Example algorithm :

{

Calculate optimal spacing for every data item ;

Initiate time 't' ;

When (using while loop) system is net terminated find a set of item 's' ;

Select item to broadcast ;

Process .... ;

Wait till transmission completes ;

Increate time value ;

}

This algorithm performs closer to the analytical lower bounds.

6.4 ON-DEMAND DATA SCHEDULING (PULL-BASED MECHANISMS)

The push based algorithms discussed so far serves for specific user's needs. Demerit of push-based algorithms :

- It is not scalable.
- Reacts slowly to changes in workload.

Thus to overcome these things the on-demand data broadcast (pull-based) are applied for data dissemination. If supports broadcast and services through the broadcast and lower-bandwidth uplink channels.

The uplink channel can be either a wired or a wireless channel.

By monitoring the broadcasts channels the clients can retrieve their required item say Y.

6.4.1 On-demand Scheduling Techniques (ODS)

They are mainly meant for fixed-sized data items, variable sized data items and the energy efficient scheduling techniques. Their is also possibility of applying hybrid scheduling techniques.

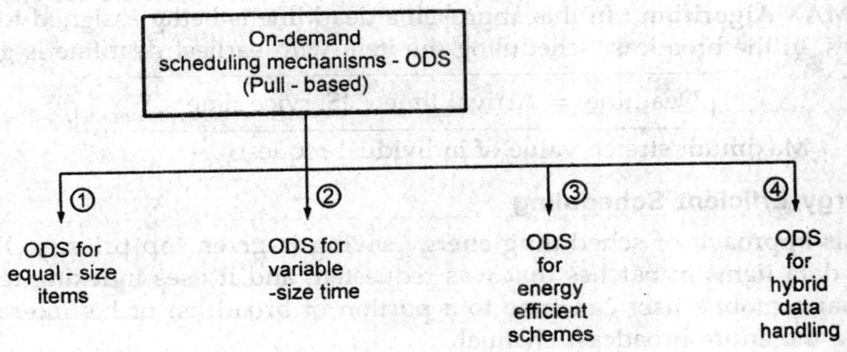

Fig. 6.4

6.4.2 ODS for Equal-size Items

When equal-size data items are considered the average access time performance is used as main objective. There are three scheduling algorithms proposed and they are called as,

(*i*) First-Come-First-Served (FCFS) : The data items are being broadcasts on their requests.

(*ii*) Most Requests First (MRF) : In this approach the data item that has largest number of pending requests is sent first. In arbitrary manner the ties are broken.

(*iii*) MRF Low (MRFL) : It *is* same as that of the MRF. It breaks the ties in favour of item with low probability.

(*iv*) Longest Wait First (LWF) : In this approach the data item with large total waiting time period.

6.4.3 ODS for Variable Size Items

To evaluate the performance of this mechanism a performance metric called as 'stretch' is used. It is the ratio of access time of request to the service time to attend it. When comparing to the access time the stretch is considered as a more reasonable performance metric for the items of different sizes of the data item requested. The algorithms used are considered as preemptive.

(*i*) Shortest Remaining Time First (SRTF) : The data item that is with shortest time is being selected.

(*ii*) Preemptive Longest Wait First (PLWF) : The PLWF is a version of 'Longest wait first' algorithm. The LWF is used so that to select subsequent data item, that has to be broadcast.

(*iii*) Longest Total Stretch First (LTSF) : The data item that has largest current stretch is selected for broadcast.

$$\text{Stretch time period of pending request} = \frac{\text{Time for which request is in system}}{\text{Service time}}$$

***(iv)* MAX Algorithm :** In this approach a dead line is being assigned to every request that arrives. In the broadcast scheduling the item with earliest deadline is given priority.

$$\text{Deadline} = \text{Arrival time} + [\text{Service time} \times S_{max}]$$

S_{max} → Maximum stretch value of individual request

6.4.4 Energy Efficient Scheduling

In this approach of scheduling energy saving is given top priority. The algorithms broadcast data items in batches that was requested, and it uses indexing techniques. It is notable that a mobile user can tune to a portion of broadcast of his interest rather than monitoring the entire broadcast channel.

$$\text{PRIORITY} = (\text{IF}^{\text{ASF}})\ (\text{PF})$$

where I F → Ignore factor (Number of times the data is not included)

ASF → Adaptive scaling factor

PF → Popularity factor (Number of requests for the item)

6.4.5 Hybrid Data Scheduling

The demerits of on-demand scheduling algorithms are :

- More uplink messages and there is high bandwidth demand.
- Consume more battery power on mobile clients.
- Access latency is very high.

But in the last hybrid data scheduling approach it combines, the 'push-based' and the 'on-demand' scheduling techniques such that their advantages are combined. The important issues to be considered in hybrid approach is,

(i) Access method.

(ii) Channel/Bandwidth allocation.

(iii) Assigning data item to push-based or on-demand broadcast or both the types.

Note : Some of the examples of the above approach are;

- Balancing push-pull technique
- Adaptive hybrid broadcast.

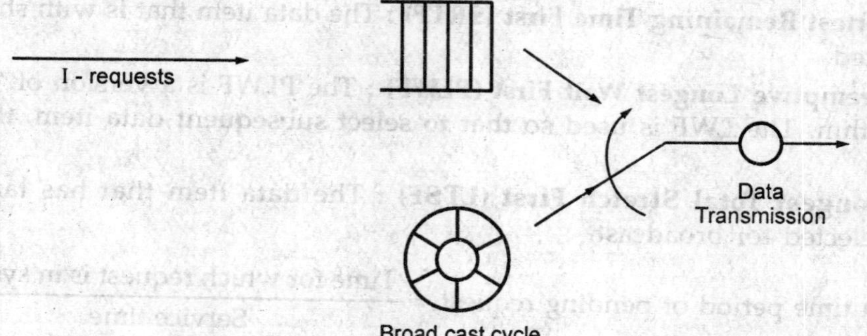

Fig. 6.5 *Hybrid broadcast-Architecture*

In the hybrid broadcast the data items are segregated either frequently requested (F-requests) or Infrequently requested (I-request). In the example shown here the requests are served using the broadcast cycle and the I-requests are served on demand basis.

The push and pull methods are integrated. For improving system scalability the various techniques used are;

1. Adjusting assignment of bandwidth to push and pull.
2. Setting a threshold value.
3. Chopping off the items pushed from the broadcast schedule. It leads to better bandwidth utility.

6.5 INDEXING TECHNIQUES OR SELECTIVE TUNING TECHNIQUES

Power Conserving Indexing

The power conserving is a main issue in battery-powered mobile system. For this the air indexing techniques are used for predicting arrival time of the data items requested. By the prediction the client is aware of the arrival time and it can ship into those mode for a while and then come back (switch) to active mode when its data item is available.

This technique saves battery consumption.

The protocol involved in the access technique has following steps. They are :

- Initial probe
- Search
- Retrieve

Note : When there is no index used, a broadcast cycle consists of data frames alone and it is called as non-index.

6.5.1 Hashing Technique

There should be a balance that has to be maintained between access time and tune-in-time. In hashing based technique a control information is carried with each frame along with the data. This control information is sent to guide and improve tune-in-time. For this it contains a hash function and a shift function. The hash function is capable of hash a key attribute to the address of the frame that is holding the desired data.

The shift function is used in case of any collision. If the tune-in-time is not so rigid, the hashing technique can be selected.

Some of the other indexing techniques are

- Index tree technique
- Signature technique
- Hybrid index technique
- Unbalanced index tree technique
- Multiattribute air indexing

We will discuss the first two techniques here.

6.5.2 Index Tree Technique

In conventional disk-based environments the index tree technique is applied to the data broadcasts on the wireless channels. Here locations of disk records are not stored. But the index tree stores the arrival times of the information frames.

For example an index tree for the broadcast cycle consists of 81 information frames. The lowest level of index tree contains square boxes that will represent collection of three information frames. Here each index node will have three pointers.

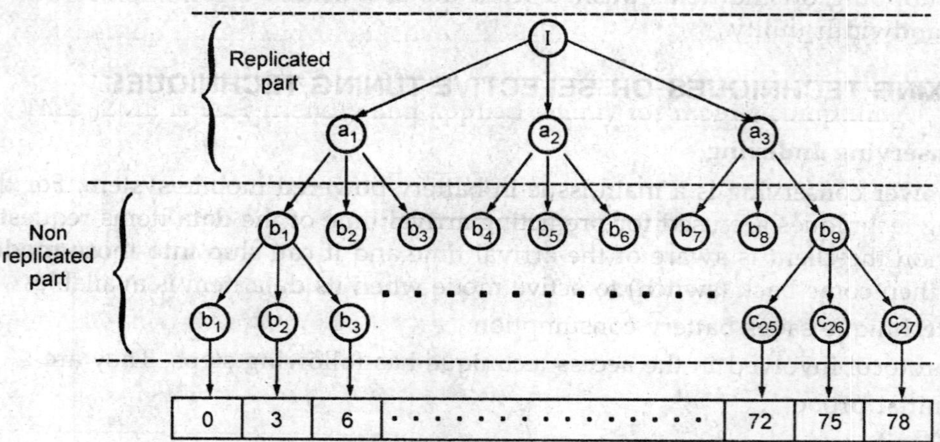

Fig. 6.6 A portion of an index tree

For reducing tune-in-time when maintaining a better access time for clients and it is possible to replicate and interleave the index tree with information frames. In case of distributed indexing this index tree is divided into two parts as replicated and nonreplicated parts. The upper levels of tree are contained in replicated part whereas the lower levels of the tree are contained in nonreplicated part. In this approach each broadcast tree contains only replicated part and nonreplicated part which indexes the proper data frame following it immediately.

To facilitate distributed indexing each frame has an offset to the beginning of root of next index tree. Also at the beginning of replicated index there is a control index for directing clients towards proper branch in the index tree.

6.5.3 Signature Technique

This technique is used for retrieving information. A signature is a bit vector that is generated by hashing the values in information frame into the strings and then they are superimposed on top of one another.

There are signature algorithms available called as simple signature. Integrated signature and multilevel signature. In first one signature will be sent before corresponding information frame.

In second, an integrated frame is formed for a group of consecutive frames known as frame group. In third type multilevel signature a combination of simple signature and integrated signatures is used, such that the upper level signatures are the integrated signatures whereas the lowest level signatures are the simple signatures.

Simple Signature ⇒ Number of signatures are equal to number of information frames in the broadcast cycle.

An example of multilevel signature structure is shown below.

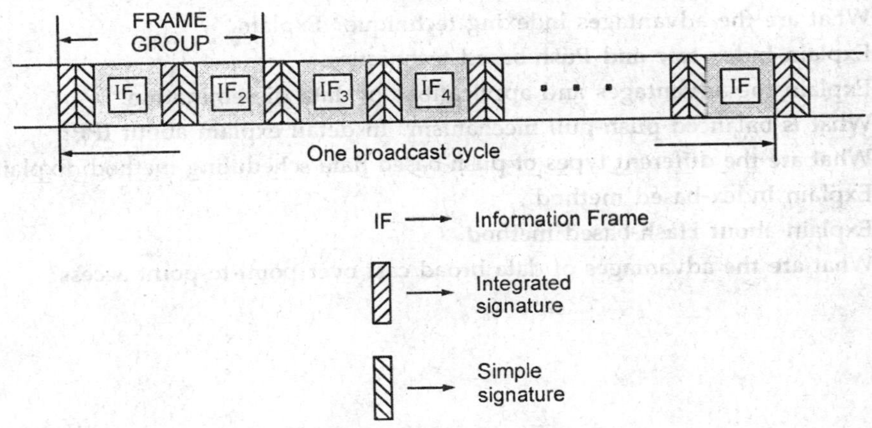

Fig. 6.7 Multilevel signature

An integrated signatures indexes the data frames between two data frames. But in case of nonclustered data frames the number of data frames is indexed by the integrated signature is kept small for maintaining filtering capabilities of the integrated signature in the system. Or otherwise if similar dataframes are grouped together then the number of frames indexed can be large in number.

REVIEW QUESTIONS

1 What is known as data dissemination?
2. Define data scheduling.
3. What is a push-based scheduling ?
4. What is a pull-based data scheduling?
5. What is known as flat broadcast?
6. What are the uses of optimal push scheduling?
7. What is the significance of heuristic algorithm?
8. Write short note on On-demand data scheduling.
9. What are the types of On-demand scheduling?
10. What are the advantages of energy-efficient scheduling?
11. Explain data dissemination in detail.
12. Explain (*i*) Pull-based and (*ii*) Push-based mechanisms.
13. Explain On-demand data scheduling in detail.

14. Explain (*i*) Energy efficient scheduling (*ii*) Push-based scheduling.
15. Write short notes on (*i*) Hybrid data scheduling
    and (*ii*) Indexing.
16. Explain indexing mechanisms in detail.
17. Explain (*i*) Hashing technique and
    (*ii*) Index tree technique.
18. What are the advantages indexing technique? Explain.
19. Explain Index tree and Push-based techniques.
20. Explain the advantages and applications of data dissemination.
21. What is balanced push-pull mechanism? In detail explain about IPP?
22. What are the different types of push-based data scheduling method. Explain each in detail.
23. Explain Index-based method.
24. Explain about Hash-based method.
25. What are the advantages of data broad cast over point-to-point access?

❑❑❑

Unit 7

Mobile Ad-hoc Networks (MANET's)

7.1 INTRODUCTION TO AD-HOC NETWORKS

In recent years wireless network nodes became popular and as the applications using Internet is high. Sometimes an user may be interested in using a laptop computer without making routing functions via global Internet. For such cases Internet protocols will not be required. Thus the mobile computer users can be allowed to set up a short lived network with wireless communication devices, for a particular moment. This network is known as ad-hoc network. It is independent of infrastructure. Thus even when there is no infrastructure available an ad-hoc network can be formed.

> The wireless computing devices are able to communicate with each other in ad-hoc networking, it is possible even there is no,
>
> - Routers or
> - Base stations or
> - Internet service providers

The ad-hoc network and mobile ad-hoc network (MANET) are discussed in this chapter.

7.1.1 Characteristics of Ad-hoc Networks

- The topology of ad-hoc networks is dynamic in nature and changes in their topology is possible. But to attain a reliable output quality frequent changes can be avoided.
- Due to wireless transmission their physical security is limited.
- The capacity of these network is lower when compared with wired networks.
- They experience higher loss rates, higher delays and also the jitter than the fixed type of networks.
- They use either exhaustible power supplies or batteries for getting energy. In network design it is very important to consider power saving.
- In a perfect 'ad-hoc network' it has all the seven layers from physical layer to application layer.
- In designing an ad-hoc network their exists high complexity with physical layer setups but in case of mobile networks it will be taken care by their base stations.
- The informations related to network destiny, link failures, nodes distributions has to be clearly defined for ad-hoc networks.

- To obtain a better network structure it is important that the MAC layer and network layer should collaborate with each other.
- The ad-hoc network is independent of any central control or infrastructure.

The ad-hoc networks has ability of providing

- Instant infrastructure in case of sudden meetings, unplanned interpersonal communications etc. Planned infrastructures are not required.
- Remote area networking : In paresely populated areas where infrastructure setup is difficult ad-hoc networks can be established.
- Effective system : The ad-hoc packet oriented network setup is less expensive and also effective. These ad-hoc networks provides a better solution for application specific cases.

A working group at IETF under ad-hoc networks focused on mobile ad-hoc networking termed as 'MANET' in the year of 2002.

A relation between MANET and mobile IP is shown in the Fig. 7.3.

7.2 OVERVIEW OF MANET'S

The "mobile ad-hoc networks" MANETs have many advantages and one of the most important advantage is its "Infrastructure independent" nature. The ad-hoc networks does not need infrastructure's that is required for other wireless networks. The term infrastructure includes need of base stations, routers etc.

The ad-hoc networks are composed of the equal nodes that can communicate with each other through wireless links. Their is no central control for their work.

The important features of ad-hoc networks and MANET's are discussed in detail in this chapter.

The term MANET describes mobile, wireless, distributed multihop networks that could operate independent of infrastructure. A MANET network is composed of mobile, autonomous, wireless nodes that could be connected at network edges to that of the fixed wired Internet. Initially MANET is developed due to military requirements where infrastructure less, line of sight operations are required.

Salient features of MANET includes

1. Network size

It refers to the geographical coverage area that could be covered by the network. The number of nodes for a given geographical area represent network density.

2. Connectivity

It refers to many issues. One such is the number of neighbouring nodes that could link to them directly. This link may be bidirectional. Connectivity also refers to link capacity between any two nodes.

3. Network topology

The user mobility can affect the network topology. Due to it the network protocols has to adapt to topology changes. Conversely when nodes are inoperative due to dead batteries their will be rapid changes in topology.

4. User traffic

The design of MANET is thick related with user traffic. It includes some conditions like,

- Does the user traffic consist of bursty, shorter packets without periodic delays ?
- Does it contain longer packets sent periodically with fixed time bounds ?
- Or is it a combination of these two situations ?

5. Operational environment

It refers to terrain whether it is a urban, rural or maritime etc. Due to any one of this LOS may not exist.

6. Energy

In MANET there is no availability of fixed base stations. A low energy network approach is tried with battery operated store and forward nodes in the network.

If some nodes are not participating in network operations shutting them for some time can be done.

In addition to there issues cost involved in MANET designed is also high that has to be planned with a proper balance with network features.

Example of MANET

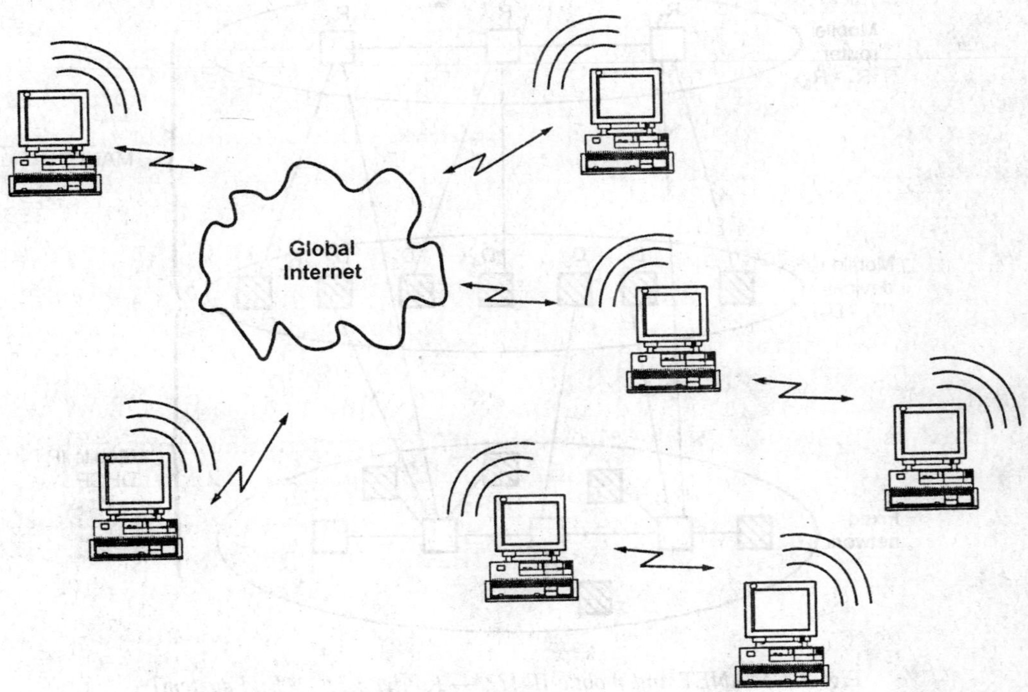

Fig. 7.1 MANET connected to Internet

An example of MANET connected to Internet is shown above. Individual nodes transmits and receives data with globalized Internet arrangement.

A simple an-hoc network composed of nodes and the complexity involved with network setup are shown in the following diagrams.

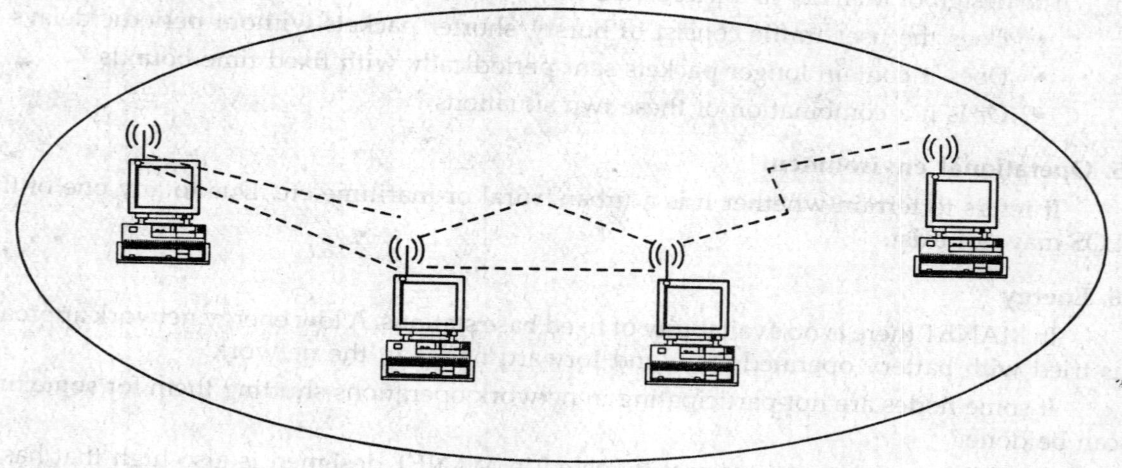

Fig. 7.2 Mobile ad-hoc network (MANET)

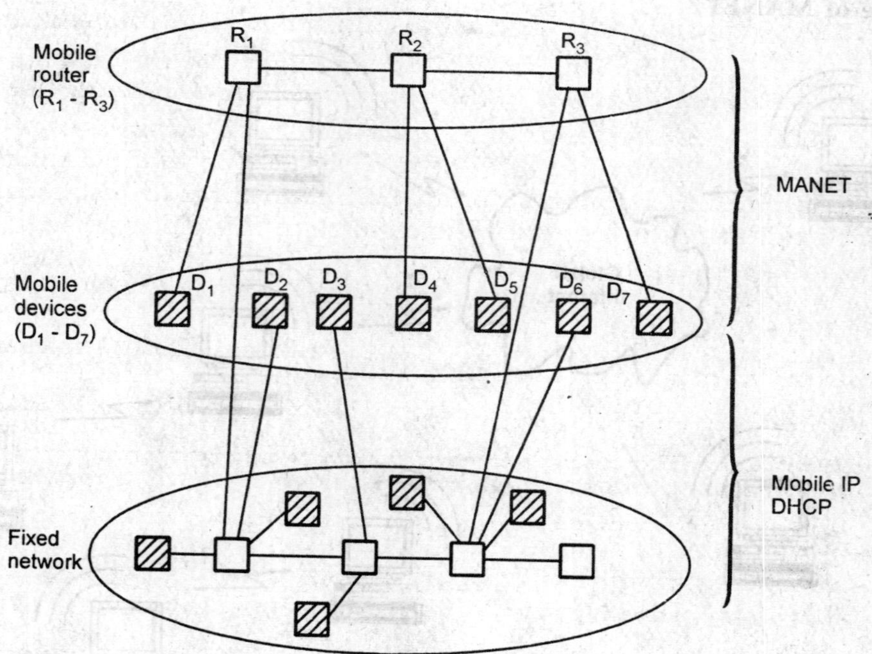

Fig. 7.3 MANET and mobile IP [?? → Router ; ?? → End system]

The mobile router (I) and mobile devices (II) forms MANET as shown here. It's relation with fixed network is established.

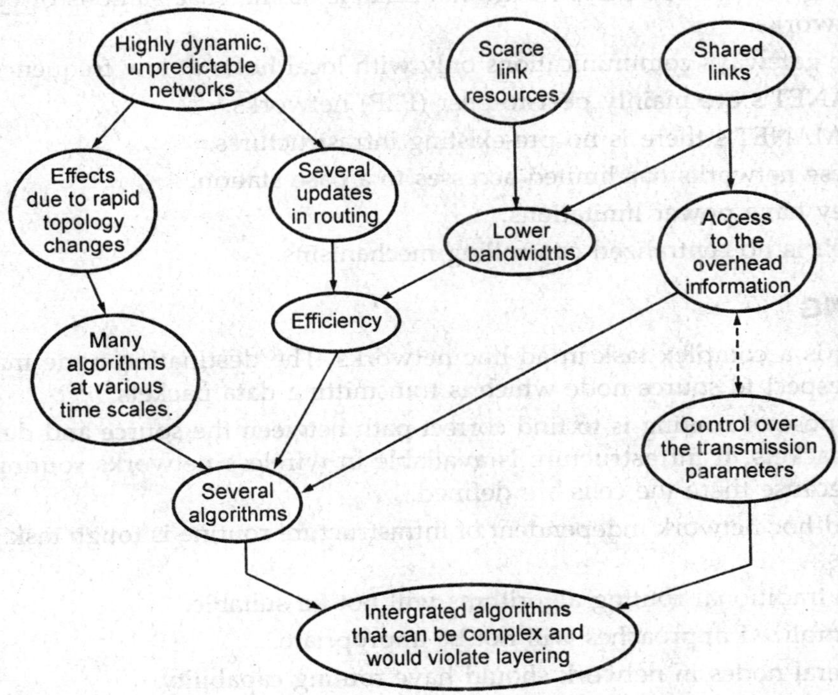

Fig. 7.4 Complexities in 'ad-hoc' network arrangement

7.3 PROPERTIES OF AN AD-HOC NETWORK

- The protocol design of ad-hoc networks are different from the fixed wired networks.
- In mobile ad-hoc network (MANET) their is no dedicated network infrastructure devices available. The MANET is an architectureless wireless network. The radio propagation range of MANET is limited.
- Because of its range limitation, for covering a short distance it has to undergo many hops.
- In few specific scenarios for communication with other networks outside some of the devices have network connections with the outside base stations (BTS) and these devices acts as gateways for ad-hoc networks.
- The gateway devices are known as weakly connected ad-hoc networks.
- MANET's have two main features of wireless computing known as
    1. Weak connectivity and
    2. Resource constraints
- MANET's have difficulties in managing bandwidth efficiency and data availability.

- Data management policies of architecture based wireless network cannot be applied directly to MANET's.
- The gateways of MANET's are not reliable as the base stations of other wireless networks.
- The gateways communications only with local hosts at low frequencies.
- MANET's are mainly peer-to-peer (P2P) networks.
- In MANET's there is no pre-existing infrastructures.
- These networks has limited accesses to a base station.
- They have power limitations.
- Their is no centralized controlling mechanisms.

7.4 ROUTING

Routing is a complex task in ad-hoc networks. The destination node may be out of range with respect to source node which is transmitting data packets.

The purpose of routing is to find correct path between the source and destination for forwarding packets. If infrastructure is available in wireless networks routing will be an easier task because there the cells are defined.

But in ad-hoc network independent of infrastructure routine is tough task. Thus in ad-hoc networks,

- The traditional routing algorithms will not be suitable.
- Centralized approaches will not be appropriate.
- Several nodes in network should have routing capability.
- They have no connection and ad-hoc network between nodes and they experience fast changing environment.
- If the load is less a method called as "flooding" can be applied in ad-hoc networking. But flooding is not an efficient method. To avoid looping as packets are forwarded, a hop counter should be used because the knowledge of maximum number of hops is very important. Still this flooding technique is not much used for packet forwarding.

7.4.1 Fundamental Steps in Routing

(*i*) Forwarding the packets to next hop. That is from an input interface to an output interface in a traditional wired network.

(*ii*) While forwarding packets sender much check for following parameters.

- (*a*) Packet reaching the destination.
- (*b*) Minimize the number of hops/path length.
- (*c*) Minimize the delay.
- (*d*) Minimize the packet loss.
- (*e*) Minimize cost involved.

7.5 MANET VS TRADITIONAL ROUTING

- In MANET's each node is a potential router whereas most of the nodes in traditional wired networks do not route the packets.
- In MANET the nodes transmit and receive their own packets and they also forward packets to other nodes.
- In MANET the topology is dynamic because of the mobile nodes but relatively it is static in case of traditional routing methods.
- The routing in MANET must consider the layer 2 and layer 3 informations whereas in traditional routing protocols they rely on layer 3 information only.
- In MANET the link layer informations includes the data about connectivity and interferences.

Main issues to be addressed by routing protocol in MANET are :

1. Routing discovery
2. Data forwarding
3. Route maintenance

7.5.1 Types of MANET Routing

The MANET's routing protocols are classified as proactive (table-driven) and reactive (on-demand) types.

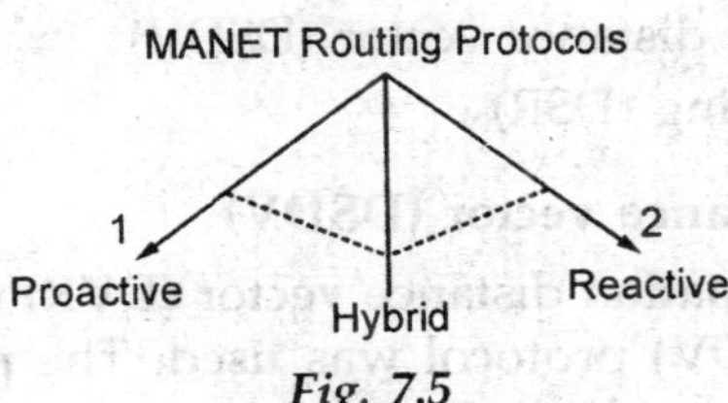

Fig. 7.5

These classification depends upon how they respond to any changes in network topology.

If a host is running a proactive protocol will react to topology change by propagating routing related informations to the neighbours. Such information transmission takes place whenever there is a change in link state is detected.

Two broader classification of routing protocols are unicast and multicast types.

1. Unicast routing protocols

(*a*) Proactive protocols : Examples of the proactive (table-driven) protocols are :

(*i*) Destination sequenced distance vector (DSDV) protocol,

(*ii*) Wireless routing protocol (WRP).

(*b*) On-demand routing protocol : In this routing protocol routes are constructed according to the demand. It tries to find or maintain routes whenever necessary. Examples of on-demand protocol is

(*i*) Dynamic source routing (DSR)$_r$

(*ii*) Signal stability based adaptive routing (SSA)

(*iii*) Ad-hoc on-demand distance vector routing (AODV)
(*iv*) Temporally ordered routing algorithm (TORA)

These protocols are reactive natured.

(*c*) Hybrid routing protocol : A combination of reactive and proactive approach is also made. It is known as hybrid routing protocol.

Example of hybrid routing protocol proposal is zone routing protocol (ZRP).

DSDV is like traditional distance vector routing technique. It is also called as "Bellman-Ford routing algorithm". The DSDV has few modified procedures to reduce routing loops.

Important operations of DSDV.

(*i*) Each router in the network collects informations from all its neighbours.
(*ii*) After gathering information node searches for a shortest path to route the packet.
(*iii*) A new routing table is generated.
(*iv*) Then the router will broadcast this table to its neighbours. Due to this function the other node (neighbours) are triggered to recompute their respective routing table.
(*v*) This process continues till the routing information becomes stable.

Importance of DSDV and DSR routing algorithms in MANET

Two important routing algorithms commonly used in MANET are,

(*a*) Destination sequence distance vector (DSDV)
(*b*) Dynamic source routing (DSR)

(*a*) Destination sequence distance vector (DSDV)

In ad-hoc networks Destination distance vector (DVR) was used at first and then On-demand distance vector (AODV) protocol was used. The performance of DVR is not so good, due to count-to-infinity problems. Because every node exchanges with its neighbour table at regular periods. Changes that takes place at a node in network slowly propagates and thus it is not a better protocol to apply.

Some features added to DVR algorithm is known as Destination sequence distance vector (DSDV) routing algorithm. Two features appended with DVR are namely,

(*i*) Sequence numbers
(*ii*) Damping

(*i*) Sequence numbers

Every routing advertisement should come with a sequence number. These sequence numbers helps to apply the advertisements in a proper order. It helps to avoid looping.

(*ii*) Damping

If the transient changes in network topology prolongs for negligible time then it may not degrade the performance of routing mechanisms. A node waits if changes are unstable and this waiting time will depend on the time taken between first and the best advertisement of routing path to a definite destination node.

(*b*) Dynamic Source Routing (DSR)

In this routing the routing task is divided into two different problems. It was analyzed in the period 1996 to 2002.

- Route discovery : It is nothing but the node searches for a correct destination for transmitting packet and currently their may be no correct route available.
- Route maintenance : If node has discovered a correct node it starts forwarding packets through it. But if the node transmits packets for a long time then in that case it has to make sure weather the route is held upright. Thus route maintenance is essential for making sure of packet delivery to the intended node.

Like token rings in fixed type of networks also this DSR can be used. The periodic routing updates are not applied in this method.

Routing mechanism in DSR

Whenever a node discovers a route it will broadcast a route request with two parameters namely,

1. Identifier
2. Destination address

If a node receives a route request it has to do the following things.

- If the node had received the request that is identified by unique identifier the node will drop its request packet.
- Once the node recognizes its destination node's address it shows that request has reached its target.

If it does not recognize the node will append its address to the list and then broadcast the new updated route request in the network.

2. Multicast protocols for MANET's

In multicasting protocols the two classification are

(*i*) Source-based protocol
(*ii*) Core-based protocol.

These classification is based on how multicast tree constructions are made. The source-based protocol attempts to maintain a per source multicast tree from every source host to the members in the corresponding multicast group. Thus there will be many multicast trees in the network.

In core-based protocol there will be one multicast tree that is rooted at core host. There are several applications served by multicasting. One such is video conferencing.

In MANET due to its host mobility, broadcasting nature of wireless environment, interference, applying multicasting is difficult than in the case of other wireless and wired networks.

Under on-demand multicast routing protocol (ODMRP) the multicast tree is formed by periodical JOIN packets of host source.

Consider the source node 'S'. It will flood the JOIN_DATA packets to all other nodes in the network. When a host node receives first JOIN_DATA packet it will rebroadcast it to form a reverse path with the previous host. Each host in the network acts as multicast receiver. It receives JOIN_DATA packet and replies in turn with a JOIN_TABLE packet to the upstream to establish reverse paths.

The process repeats until source host 'S' is reached. The method of packet forwarding is for Fig. 7.6 (*a*) is shown in Fig. 7.6 (*b*).

As the JOIN_TABLE is received a host has to build a multicast table so as to facilitate future packet forwarding.

For example the host B receives the R_1's JOIN_TABLE as shown in Fig. 7.6.

It will add R_1 as its next hop step. Assume B receives R_2's JOIN_TABLE. Now it will also add R_2 as its next hop step.

A simple final multicast table for each host is shown in Fig. 7.6 (*c*) in propagation of data packets.

7.6 MULTICAST AODV PROTOCOL

The on-demand distance vector routing protocol known as multicast AODV is an extension of unicast AODV protocol. Here the multicast tree is updated whenever a new host joins the multicast group. For making process of tree updation easier the route request packet (RREQ) is being broadcast.

In case a host receives a RREQ and if the host is not a member of multicast group, then it will rebroadcast RREQ to the neighbouring members of the network.

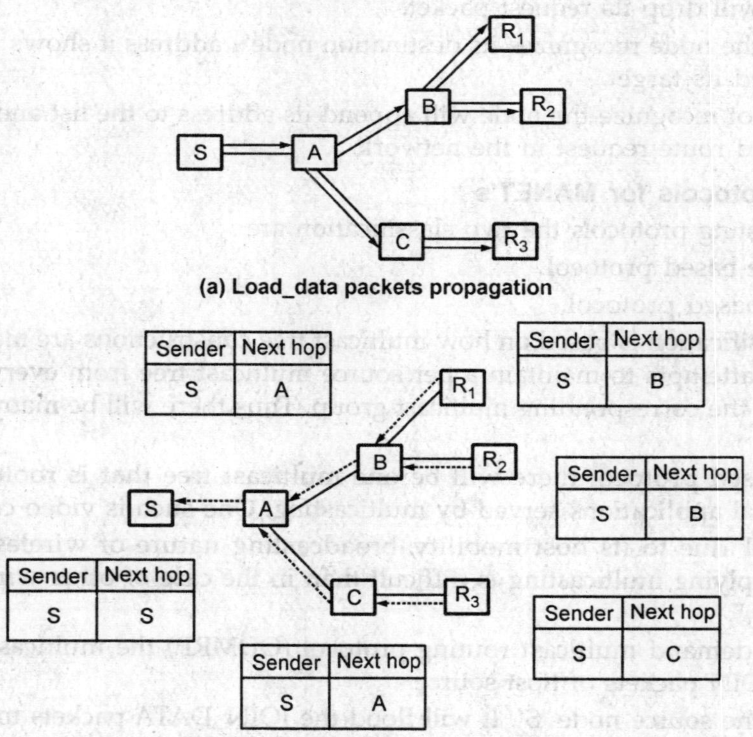

Fig. 7.6 On-demand multicast routing protocol

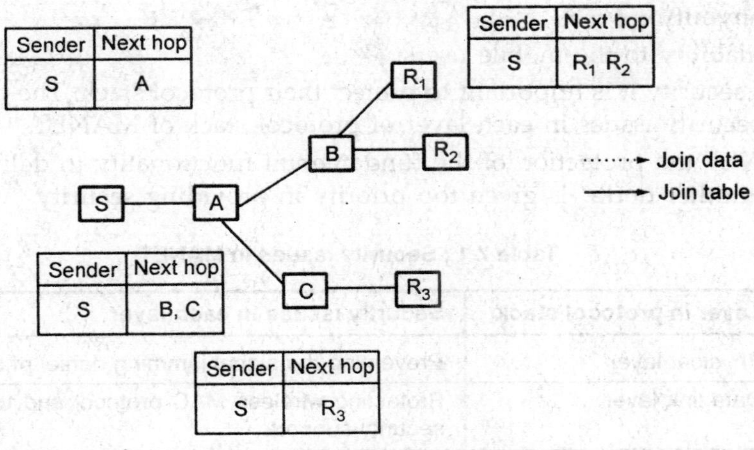

(c) Last multicast table

But if the host is a member of multicast group and if this host receives a RREQ then it will give route reply (RREP) packet data to the sending host (S). Now the multicast table will be updated. By these processes forward path will be created.

If two RREQ's are received at a time then depending upon minimum number of hop count the one with minimum hop count will be selected.

MACT

It is multicast activation (MACT) packet. The source S will unicast a MACT packet to the next hop step. On receiving a MACT packet the next hop will enable for source host (route with minimum hop count) and it leads to multicast tree.

This procedure continues till a multicast meaber is reached successfully. Distance vector algorithm design issues.

- The distance of each link in the network is a metric that has to be minimized.
  - (*a*) Distance of each link may have 'distance' 1 to reduce hop count.
  - (*b*) The algorithm attempts to reduce distance.
- The routing table at each node
  - (*a*) Specifies the next hop for each destination.
  - (*b*) Specifies the distance to the destination.
- Neighbours can also exchange routing table.

  Information for finding a route (or a better route) to reach the destination.

7.7 SECURITY IN MANET'S

In recent years the mobile ad-hoc networks (MANET's) have attained tremendous attention due to its self configuration and self maintenance features. The aim of security solutions in MANETs is to provide security services like

- Confidentiality
- Integrity

- Anonymity
- Availability to the mobile users

Thus for security it is important to protect their protocol stack. The table shown below describe the security issues in each layer of protocol stack of MANET.

"In MANET the protection of the fundamental functionality to deliver data bits from one node to another node" is given top priority in providing security.

Table 7.1 : Security issues in MANET

Sr. No.	Layer in protocol stack	Security issues in each layer
1.	Physical layer	Preventing the signal jamming deniel of service attacks.
2.	Data link layer	Protecting wireless MAC protocol and to provide link layer security support.
3.	Network layer	Protecting the ad-hoc routing and forwarding protocols.
4.	Transport layer	Securing and authenticating end-to-end communications through data encryption techniques.
5.	Application layer	Detection and prevention of viruses, worms, malicious codes etc.

The multihop connectivity *is* provided in mobile ad-hoc networks in two different steps.

Step 1 : Ensuring single hop connectivity through the link layer protocols.

Example : Wireless Medium Access Control (MAC).

Step 2 : Extending connectivity to multiple hops through the network layer routing and data forwarding protocols.

Example : Ad-hoc routing

There are two approaches for protecting MANET's namely proactive (prevents attacker in first place through cryptographic techniques) and reactive (detects security threats and react accordingly and it is posteriori natured) approaches.

The proactive approach is used for ensuring correctness of routing states whereas in the reactive approach is used for protect packet forwarding functions.

But as the number security features are increased there will be more computational complexity and it is also not economical.

Multifence security solution

In MANET multi-hop connectivity is provided through the distributed protocols in link and network layers. A better security approach is to have both proactive and reactive methods and all the three components should be encompassed. The three components are

(*i*) Prevention
(*ii*) Detection
(*iii*) Reaction

The prevention component find the attacker by increasing the difficulty of entering the system. The detection and reaction components discovers only the occasional intrusions and take reactions so as to avoid pertaining adverse effects. The prevention component is achieved by secure ad-hoc routing protocols.

Network layer security

It is concerned with protecting network layer's functionalities for delivering packets through multihop ad-hoc forwarding method between mobile nodes. The proposals can be classified into two categories,

(*i*) Secure ad-hoc routing protocols.

(*ii*) Secure packet forwarding protocols.

Message authentication primitives

The messages are being transmitted between the nodes in the network. The content of these messages has to be authenticated and for security there are three cryptographic primitives are widely used. They are,

1. Message authentication codes
2. Digital signature
3. One-way HMAC key chain.

1. Message authentication codes (HMAC)

In this technique two node share a common secret symmetric key (k). They can generate and also check a message authenticator $h_k(\cdot)$ with help of a hash function 'h'.

A 'HMAC' could be verified by an intended receiver only; the HMAC is a popular security primitive used for network layer.

2. Digital signature

It is based on asymmetric key cryptography. It includes signing / decrypting and the verifying / encrypting functions. It is not resilient against disk operating system attacks because an attacker may include false signatures and blocks verification process. If public key is known to all nodes then each node can verify digital signature such that digital signatures are more scalable to several receivers.

3. One-way HMAC key chain

There are many one-way cryptographic functions are available so that if output $\int(x)$ is given it not feasible to calculate input x value. Just by applying $\int(\cdot)$ in repeated manner on an initial input value then a chain of outputs can be found.

The computations incorporated in one-way key-chain-based authentication is less and an authenticator can verify larger number of receivers.

Notes

- Hash-chain based authentication need dock synchronization.
- Receivers should buffer a message for verifying when the key was revealed.
- A timer should be gauged carefully to monitor any second round of communication taking place due to key release.

REVIEW QUESTIONS

1. What is known as MANET?
2. What are the advantages of MANET?
3. Write short note on properties of MANET?
4. What are the routing algorithms used in MANET?
5. Write short note on security in MANET.
6. Draw the structure of MANET and mobile IP.
7. Differentiate wired and ad-hoc networks.
8. Define routing.
9. Write sort note on dynamic topology.
10. Write short note on DSDV.
11. Explain destination sequence distance vector in detail.
12. Explain dynamic source routing in detail.
13. Write short notes on (*i*) DSDV and (*ii*) DSR.
14. Explain MANET in detail
15. Explain security in MANET's in detail.
16. Explain the structure of MANET's and mobile IP with a neat sketch.
17. Explain various routing algorithms in detail.
18. Explain security in MANET's and applications of ad-hoc networks.
19. Write short notes on (*i*) DSDV and (*ii*) Advantages of routing.
20. Explain the properties and advantages of MANET in detail.
21. Why is routing in Multi-hop and ad-hoc networks complicated? What are the special challenges?
22. Explain in detail AODV routing algorithm for MANETs.
23. Distinguish between proactive and reactive routing protocols.

❑❑❑

Unit 8

Wireless Local Area Networks

8.1 NETWORKS : DEFINITION

A Network is defined as a set of nodes or devices connected by the media links. A node generally refers to a computer or any device that is capable of transmitting and/or receiving data generated by the other devices/nodes in the networks. The links used to connect the nodes in the networks is also called as 'channels'.

The wireless local area networks (WLAN) can be understood well with a few terminologies and they are discussed below.

There are three parameters considered to define an efficient network. They are :
(*i*) Performance (*ii*) Security (*iii*) Reliability

(*i*) Performance

Performance is measured in several methods like measuring 'response time' and 'transit time'. The response time is the time taken to respond to an inquiry. The transit time is the time required for message travel (journey) between any two devices.

(*ii*) Reliability

The network is said to be 'Reliable' if it generate minimum (less frequent) numbers failures between nodes in real time data transfer. The network should also be 'robust' in nature, that is even if a node fails the job in process should not be affected and it should be continued to make faithful reproduction of data reception at the receiver end.

(*iii*) Security

In any network data security is very important and data/information should be properly encrypted so that any unauthorised intruder cannot access it. Also a perfect network should protect the data/information from virus attacks by using antivirus software in designing and establishing the network.

Wireless Network

A network that is established without wires is called as wireless network.

8.2 NETWORK TAXONOMY

A network can be broadly classified into three groups.

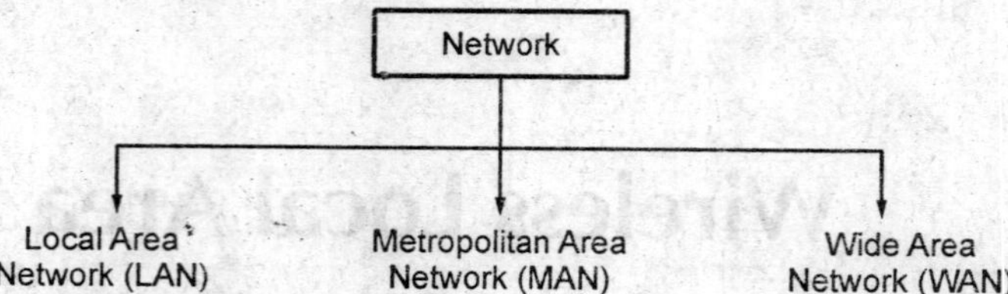

Wireless networking technology dates back to 1800's and the early messages were similar to Morse code. The wireless networking is broadly classified as below.

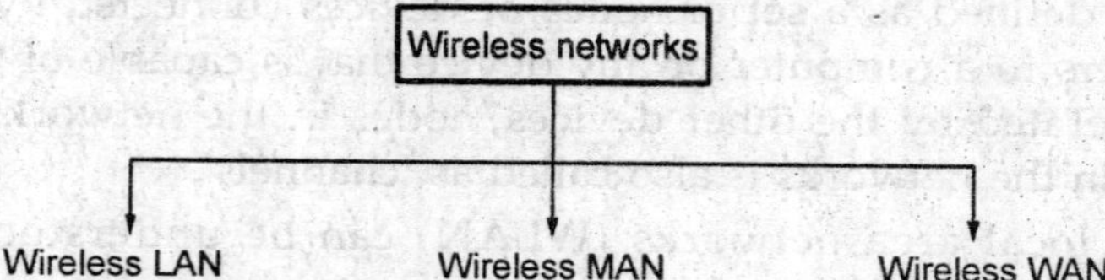

They are namely wireless local area network, metropolitan area network and wide area network. We focus on wireless LAN. It enables a simple protocol that can support network management and facilitates numerous applications. It is economical to install networks under WLAN.

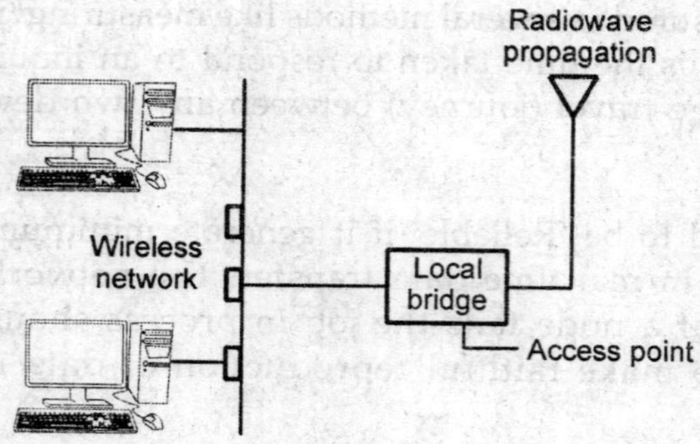

Fig. 8.1 Wireless LAN-an example

Any network is connected to another network through an access point or a local bridge. The two types of wireless LAN are given below.

The wireless local area network (WLAN) activities are mainly based on the orientation of medium access control (MAC) layers.

The IEEE 802.11 standard is a connectionless WLAN standard evolved from the computer communication technology.

Initially the first IEEE 802.11 standard with 1 to 2 Mb/sec data rate supported three techniques in physical layer namely direct sequence spread spectrum (DSSS), frequency hopping spread spectrum (FHSS) and diffused infrared (DFIR).

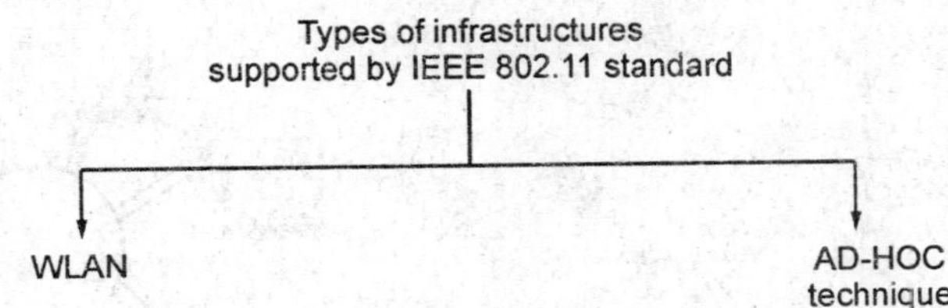

The IEEE 802.11 standard specification supports mobility and security. It provides connectionless applications with medium access control (MAC) and physical (PHY) layers. Some of the basic requirements are :

(*i*) Single MAC layer to support many physical layers.

(*ii*) Mechanisms to handle all the terminals.

(*iii*) Should support time-bound services.

8.2.1 Local Area Network (LAN)

A local area network (LAN) links several devices within a building premises, single office or an individual campus. LAN includes few computers (nodes) which can be two or many numbers in the network. It is established to a limited range of few kilometers and usually owned by a private agency.

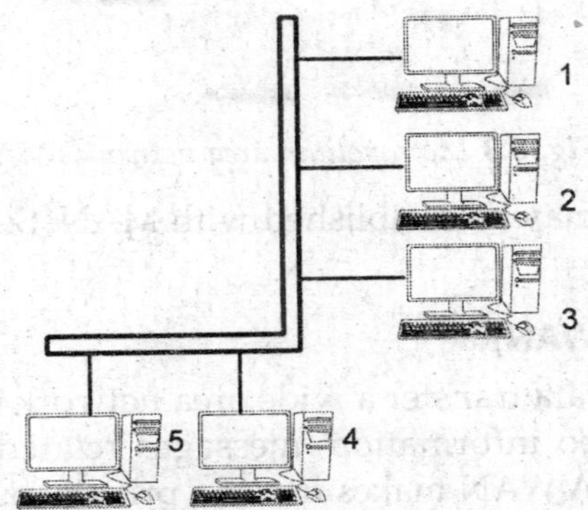

Fig. 8.2 Local area network (LAN) with five nodes in a building

The goal of LAN is to have shared communication between workstations or a set of personal computers. In the network any one computer will be given total control over all other computers and accessing data by the nodes is made possible. The data rate in LAN is generally 4 to 16 Mb/sec and the LAN topologies (physical structure) may be bus, star or ring.

8.2.2 Metropolitan Area Network (MAN)

The metropolitan area network (MAN) designed and developed to cover an entire city and the range of MAN is greater compared to LAN setup. MAN can connect several LAN's to form a larger network. It may be a single network with enhanced distance to share the resources between many LAN's within MAN. For instance a corporation can make use of MAN to develop connectivity between many LAN's in many offices in the entire city.

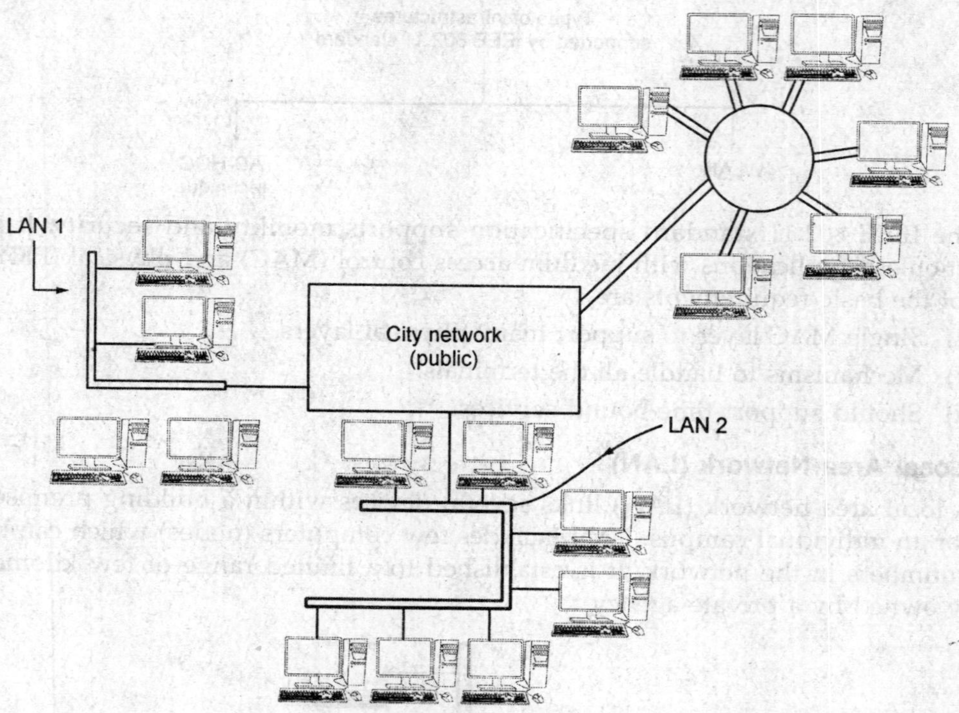

Fig. 8.3 Metropolitan area network (MAN)

A telephone company may be established with MAN. Several LAN's are interlinked to develop a MAN.

8.2.3 Wide Area Network (WAN)

For any long distance data transfer a wide area network (WAN) is used. It may include voice, data, image and video information/messages related to a particular geographical region (country/continent). A WAN makes use of a private, public or leased communication devices. It has no restrictions of range in developing a network.

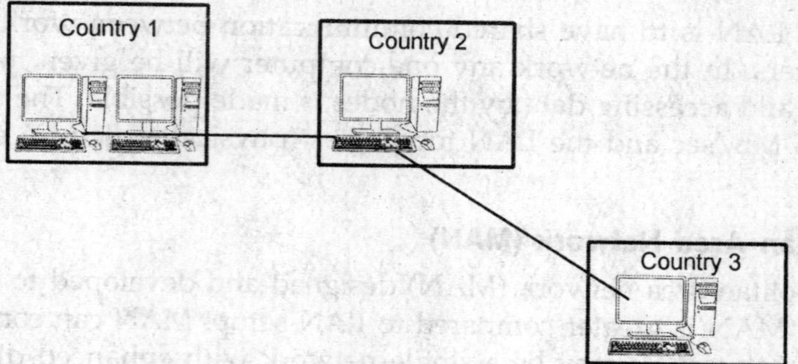

Fig. 8.4 Wide area network

Many MAN's can be connected to form a WAN.

It may even cover world wide.

Note : **Internetwork**

Whenever two or more networks (different types of networks) are interconnected by internetworking devices it forms a 'internetwork'. It is also known as internet.

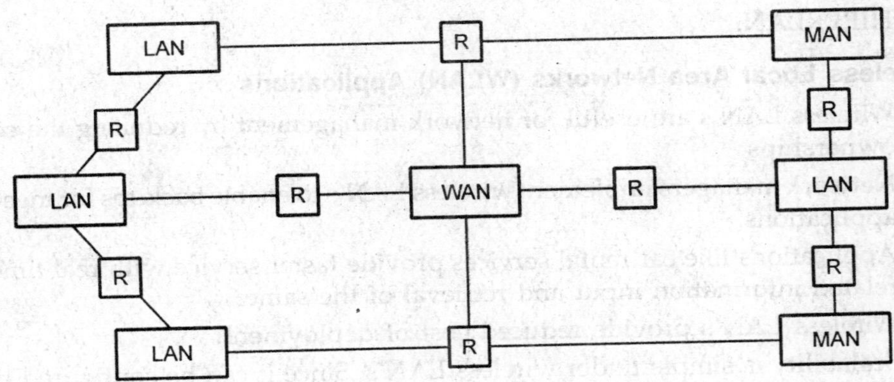

Fig. 8.5 Internetwork R → Router

The internetworking devices may include gateways, routers etc. Here routers (R) are used to interconnect different networks LAN, MAN and WAN to form an internetwork or internet.

8.3 WIRELESS LOCAL AREA NETWORK—INTRODUCTION

The wireless local area network (WLAN) is a technology developed for wideband local accesses. The coverage area is upto 100 meters WLAN enables data related LAN functioning. WLAN is generally restricted to a campus, office building or a room and not operated by very large network owners. WLAN has a goal to achieve flexible ad hoc communications.

The attractive features of WLAN are :

1. Design is simple.
2. Flexible radio coverage.
3. Robust in nature.
4. Quality of service (QoS) is good.
5. Has slow standardization and proprietary solutions grows higher.
6. Security.
7. Safety.

There are many design goals for developing WLAN as a competing technology :

It should provide ;

1. Low power.
2. Global operation (acceptance).

3. Robustness.
4. Simplicity in real time functioning.
5. Transparency.
6. Flexible with other networks.

Main standards for WLAN are :

1. IEEE 802.11.
2. HIPERLAN.

8.3.1 Wireless Local Area Networks (WLAN) Applications

- Wireless LAN's are useful for network management by reducing the cost of LAN ownerships.
- Network managers implement wireless LAN's to enable backups for meeting critical applications.
- Applications like car rental services provide faster service with real time customer related information input and retrieval of the same.
- Wireless LAN's provide reduced cost of deployment.
- Scalability is simple under wireless LAN's. Since it can be configured in a variety of topologies.
- Productivity is increased by usage of WLAN's.
- Warehouse workers use these wireless LAN's for exchange of information with the central database hence the efficiency of the entire system is greatly enhanced.

8.4 IEEE 802.11 STANDARD PROTOCOL ENTITY

The protocol entities of IEEE 802.11 standard are namely Data link layer (DLL), Physical layer (PHY) and station managements. The DLL and PHY layers are given below in detail.

The logical link control (LLC) is the main layer from which the medium access layer (MAC) receives a set of (block of) data. There are two layers in the 802.11 standard, data link layer (i.e. LLC and MAC) and the physical layer (PMD, PLCP). The important characteristics of this LLC under implementation of 802.11 standard are:

(*i*) LLC should support multiaccess and the shared-medium functions,

(*ii*) LLC also controls the data flow between any two users.

The two layers (DLL and PHY), they are divided for functional simplicity as given below in Fig. 8.6 (*b*),

- DLL → LLC, MAC; Logical link control, Medium access control.
- PHY → PMD, PLCP; Physical medium dependant, Physical layer convergence protocol.

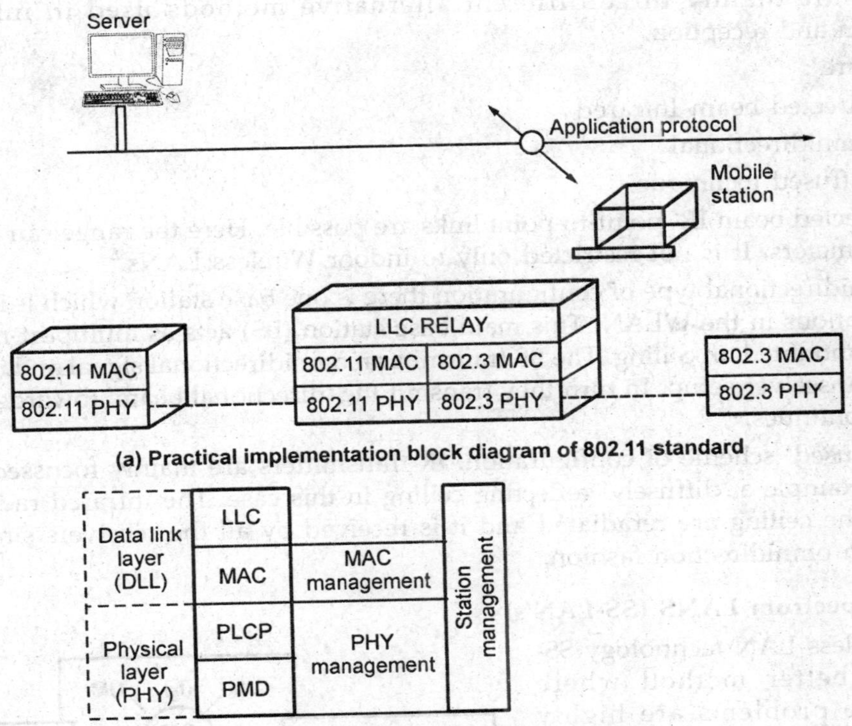

(a) Practical implementation block diagram of 802.11 standard

(b) Protocol stack entities for IEEE 802.11 standard

Fig. 8.6

The operation of these layers DLL and PHY are continuously monitored by their corresponding MAC management, PHY management and an overall station management.

Wireless LAN (WLAN) technologies-Examples

Wireless LAN technology can be classified into three groups as given below.

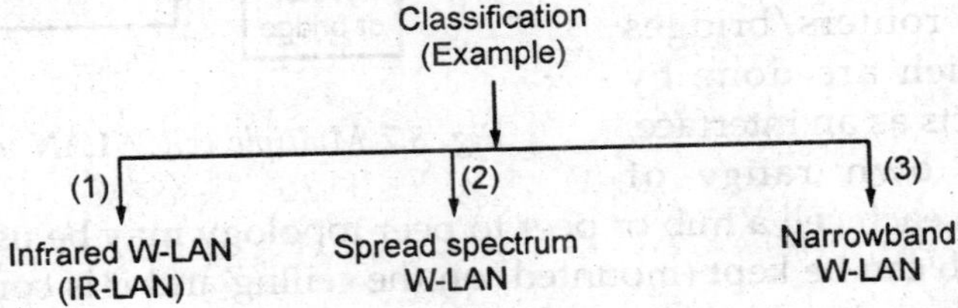

1. Infrared LAN

This method is restricted to range, as it is Line Of Sight (LOS) dependent technique. But this LAN can produce higher data rates. It is best suited for LAN configurations. It also has better security and minimum interference problems.

It is economical to implement Infrared LAN schemes. Infrared LAN has few demerits like power consumption and high radiations inside room environment.

There are mainly three different alternative methods used in infrared data transmission and reception.

They are :

(*i*) Directed beam Infrared

(*ii*) Omnidirectional

(*iii*) Diffused technique.

In 'directed beam IR' point-to-point links are possible. Here the range can be extended ever to kilometers. It is not restricted only to indoor Wireless LANs.

In omnidirectional type of configuration there is one base station which is in LOS of all the other stations in the WLAN. This main base station (BS) acts as multiport repeater and it is usually mounted on ceiling. The BS transmits an omnidirectional signal and it is received by the IR transceiver setup. In turn they transmit the 'directional beam' towards BS and the operation continues.

In 'diffused' scheme of configuration, IR transmitters are mainly focussed at a point that is for example a 'diffusely' reflecting ceiling in this case. The infrared radiations that are hitting the ceiling are reradiated and it is received by all the receivers since they are reradiated in omnidirection fashion.

2. Spread Spectrum LANS (SS-LAN's)

In wireless LAN technology SS-LAN is a better method where interference problems are highly reduced. Many cells (for example) may overlap with other with same centre frequencies but by using SS techniques interferences are reduced.

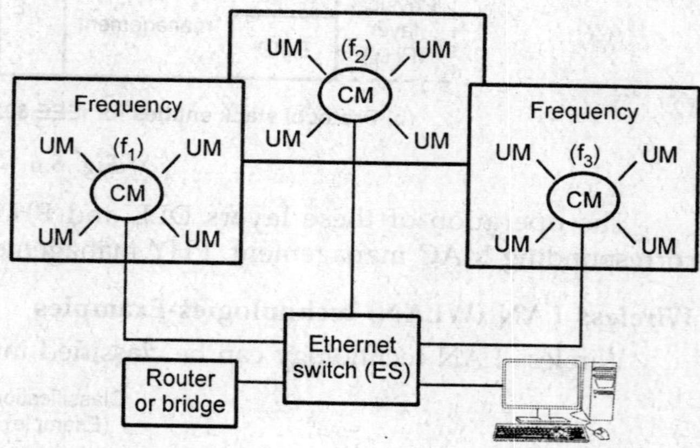

Fig. 8.7 Multiple cell WLAN using hub topology

For example, in multiple WLAN, in each cell there are control module (CM) and user modules (UM). The wireless LAN's are linked to backbone by using routers/bridges functionalities which are done by control module. It acts as an interface. Each CM has its own range of transmission. Within each cell a hub or peer to peer topology may be used. In the above hub topology, WLAN hub can be kept (mounted) on the ceiling and it is connected to that of the WLAN. It is possible to have automatic hand off of mobile stations by such WLAN hub topologies. On the other hand in a peer to peer configuration there will be no hub and a MAC algorithm can be applied for control mechanisms.

This is well suited in ad hoc type of LAN's. The SS-WLAN's are limited to data rates of 1-3 Mbps.

3. Narrow band LAN's

An example for this narrow band LAN's are narrow band microwave LAN's where a narrow band of microwave frequency is used for communication. They are two categories commonly used. They are licensed narrow band RF and unlicensed narrow band RF. A dynamic relay function in LAN is made possible by which every station acts like a repeater to drag data/message between stations if they are out of range. This is done in narrow band WLAN.

8.5 INTRODUCTION TO 802.11 STANDARD

The 802.11 IEEE standard is very popular today because of its low cost and easy deployment. The 802.11a and 802.11b standards are discussed in this chapter. The future of the standard will rely on 802.11e which gives provision for hybrid co-ordination function, that is two medium access mechanisms (MAC). They are controlled channel access and contention based channel access. The electronic hardware IEEE 802.11 based WLAN is applied in different categories as given below.

1. Residential areas.
2. Airports.
3. Apartments.
4. Classrooms etc.

While the ability or efficiency of the network is increased the quality of service (QoS) is continuously ensured.

This standard operates at either 2.4 GHz frequency for industrial. Scientific and medical band (ISM band) or the 5 GHz unlicensed national information infrastructure (UNI) band. A common radio channel can be shared and the procedures required for 802.11 standard is defined by medium access control layer (MAC). This standard supports both ad hoc and infrastructure mode.

Table 8.1 A mapping between the user priorities in 802.11 D and the access categories in 802.11E standards

Priority status	User Priority in 802.11 D	Access category	Informative designation
Lowest	1	AC [0]	Background
	2	AC [0]	Background
	0	AC[1]	Best effort
	3	AC[1]	Video
	4	AC [2]	Video
	5	AC [2]	Video
Highest	6	AC [3]	Video

3.6 IEEE 802 PROTOCOL AND OPEN SYSTEM INTERCONNECT (OSI)

A Comparative study

In IEEE 802.11 standard is mainly concerned with data link layer (DLL) and physical layer (PHY). In DLL as shown below there are logical link control (LLC) and medium access control (MAC).

In OSI model there are seven layers, and the top four layers are architecture independent. The lowest layer of IEEE 802 standard and OSI model are physical layer.

The main functions of a physical layer is

(*i*) Encoding and decoding processes.

(*ii*) Bit transmission and reception.

(*iii*) Preamble generation and removal processes for the cause of synchronization.

In IEEE 802 standard the transmission medium and the type of topology used are specified.

Above this first (physical) layer the DLL is available. It provides services to the LAN users.

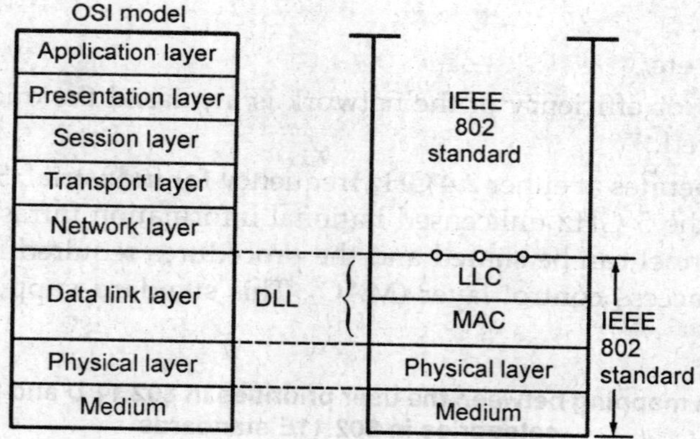

Fig. 8.8 Comparison of OSI and IEEE 802 model

Some of the main functions of DLL are,

- Fragmentation of data.
- In transmission it assembles data in the form of frame will all address and error detecting field informations.
- In reception, it does the apposite functions like dissemble frames, recognizing addresses and error detection functionalities.
- It also facilitates access to next higher layers of the model.

The two main functions of DLL is grouped or subdivided into two partitions called as medium access control (MAC) and logical link control (LLC) to interact with higher layers.

8.7 802.11 STANDARD-SECURITY ISSUES

The IEEE 802.11 standard provides both authentication and privacy mechanisms. At the transmitter end encryption process is done and at receiver end decryption is done.

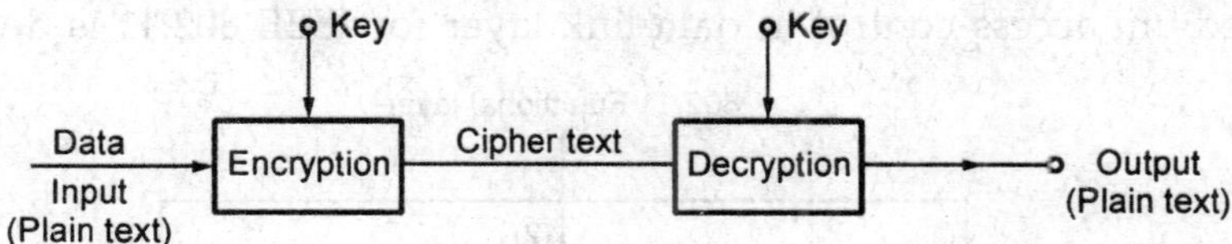

Fig. 8.9 Concept of security of data

The encrypted input signal is called as cipher text which consists of plaintext the original data as hidden information. A secret key is used at transmitter which may be private or public key. The decryption algorithm along with secret key helps to get back the plain text from cipher text.

8.7.1 Authentication

The IEEE 802.11 standard has two types of authentication schemes namely open system and shared key system.

In the open system authentication, an "authentication frame" (MAC control frame) is sent by first party to the second party. If such a frame is sent it is assumed that an open system type of authentication is an process. The second party responds by sending its authentication frame to first party and finally they exchange information without the security concerns being addressed.

In shared key authentication a common secret key is shared between two parties and it is kept confidential, so that any intruder cannot access the data.

8.7.2 Procedure of shared key authentication

Consider the two parties namely x and y.

Step 1 : 'x' transmits an authentication frame (MAC frame), shared key identification with that of the station identifier for identifying the sending station.

Step 2 : 'y' responds to this authentication frame with 128 octet text called as challenge text.

Step 3 : Then 'x' sends an authentication frame which includes the challenge text (128 octet) sent previously from y. The complete frame is finally encrypted.

Step 4 : At last 'y' receives this encrypted frame of step 3 and decrypts it using same secret key and wired equivalent privacy (WEP) used by 'x'. Once decryption procedure is completed by checking redundancy values, y then compares the incoming challenge text with the same text that was sent under second step. The 'y' transmits a 'Status code' to indicate 'success/failure' case to 'x' in the form of an authentication code.

The open system and shared key authentication schemes are very much used in IEEE 802.11 security mechanism.

8.7.3 Deauthentication

Whenever the existing authentication has to be terminated then this deauthentication will be invoked.

The medium access control in data link layer for IEEE 802.11 is dealt below.

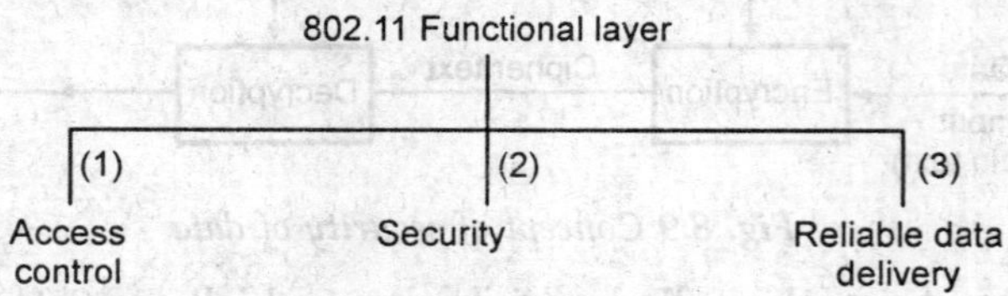

8.8 IEEE 802.11-MAC CONTROL

The architecture of IEEE 802.11 protocol consists of MAC layer with logical link control for providing many services. The MAC layer consists of three functional layers.

1. Access Control

There are two important protocols considered for access control. First, the distributed access protocol to distribute decision to transmit data and second a centralized access protocol by which 'centralized decision' is made. It is used to connect many wireless stations. The distributed access protocol enables an ad hoc network.

2. Security

The data transfer under 802.11 standard is more secure. The content of the signal is retrieved only by proper recipient and the content remains hidden for an unauthorised user.

3. Reliable data delivery

The wireless LAN that applies IEEE 802.11 MAC and physical (PHY) layers faces unreliability as the data transfer basically involves exchange of frames. But the probability of interferences, noises and other propagation effects which may result in loss of few frames is greater. The losses may be immune to error correction coding techniques. As a solution 802.11 group suggests data transfer with "two frames exchange" and "four frames exchange" methods. The transmitter and receiver should posses knowledge of frame transfer at any instant of time.

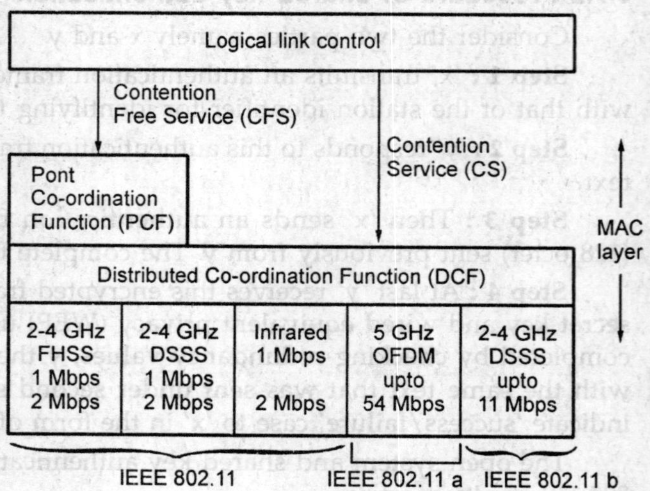

Fig. 8.10 Architecture of IEEE 802.11 protocol standard

The transmitter sends ready to send (RTS) information to the receiver before frame transfer and waits for the response from receiver side which responds by a clear to send (CTS) signal. Likewise the transmitter alerts the receivers that are within the reception range with RTS signalling. These methods also help only to a certain extent but does not guarantee the system reliability to deliver data.

In IEEE 802.11 MAC layer covers three areas namely reliable data delivery, access control and security issues. In reliable data delivery for increasing reliability two frames 'request to send' (RTS) and 'clear to send' (CTS) are sent between source and destination. Under access control the lower sublayer of MAC is known as distributed co-ordination function (DCF) which enables traffic regulation. This DCF uses carrier sense multiple algorithm (CSMA) for data transmission. For proper functioning of DCF certain delays known as interframe space (IPS) are introduced in data transmission.

The three delay (IPS) periods are shown below.

1. DIPS : It is distributed co-ordination function IPS. It is a longest IPS used for asynchronous frames waiting for access.

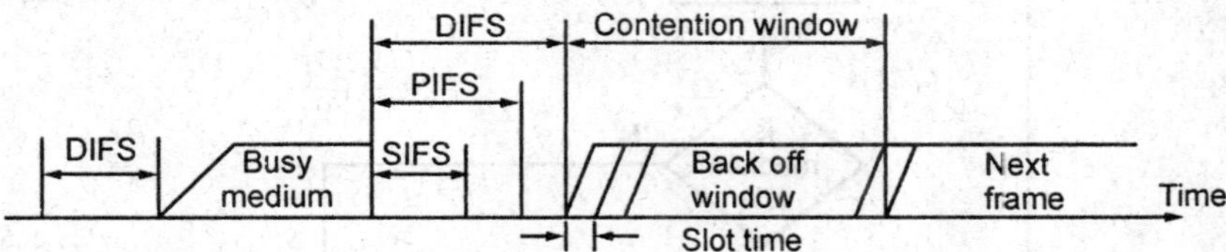

Fig. 8.11 Back access scheme in IEEE 802.11-'MAC Timing'

The station will access the medium immediately if the medium is free for a period longer than DIPS.

2. PIFS : It is point co-ordination function IPS, and it is usually a midlength IPS. PIFS is used whenever issuing polls by the centralized controller.

3. SIFS : It is short IPS, and generally used for immediate actions as responses. These three IPS values establish MAC timing under IEEE 802 model.

The 802.11 standard MAC frame structure is given below.

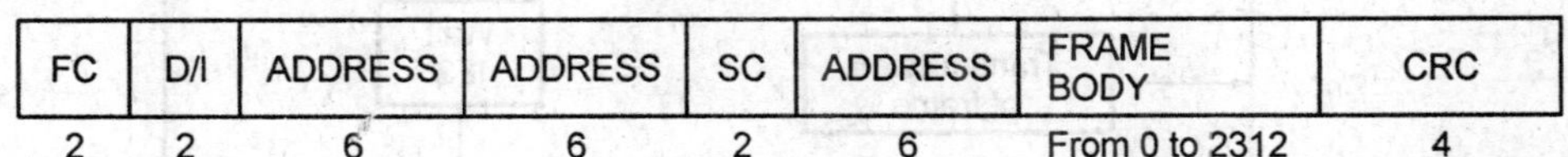

FC	D/I	ADDRESS	ADDRESS	SC	ADDRESS	FRAME BODY	CRC
2	2	6	6	2	6	From 0 to 2312	4

- **Frame Control (FC) :** It indicates type of frame and also provides control information.
- **Duration/Connection ID :** Whenever it is used as duration field, it indicates the time a channel will be allocated for a successful transmission of a MAC frame. It may also contain an association or connection identifier.

8.9 SEQUENCE CONTROL

It consists of a 4 bit fragment number subfield. It is used for fragmentation and reassembly and a 12 bit sequence number is vised to number the frames sent from transmitter.

Addresses

The address fields depends on context. The address types includes source, transmitting station and receiving station.

Frame Body

It generally contains a MAC service data units (MSDU) or a fragment of an MSDU. This MSDU is a logical link control (LLC) protocol data unit (or) the MAC control information.

Frame check sequence (CRC)

For checking the frame sequence a 32 bit cyclic redundancy check is done. The MAC logic is represented in flow chart as below in Fig. 8.12.

(*i*) When the station has a frame to send it senses that medium, and if medium is found idle it will start transmission. Station checks this idle state for a time (IPS).

(*ii*) Whenever that medium is found busy, the station will simply watch, till the medium completes the job. The busy time during IPS is measured.

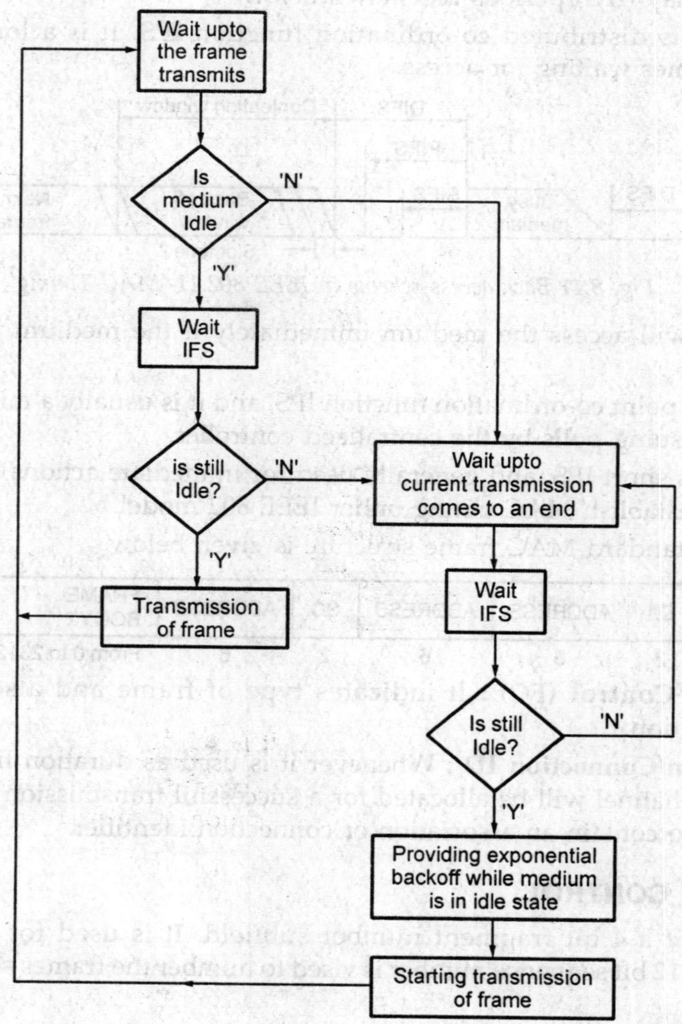

***Fig. 8.12** MAC logic of IEEE 802.11 standard*

(iii) Station will delay another delay period IPS in last step whenever the transmission gets over. During this kind of idle IPS period the station will back off for some random period sensing that medium again. For maintaining stability in this entire back off phase a binary exponential back off technique is used. This is mainly used to handle the heavy load.

Note : If there is longer back off time periods it will smooth out the heavy load condition in MAC logic of IEEE 802.11 standard.

8.10 802.11 STANDARD-ARCHITECTURE

In the year 1987 the analysis of wireless local area network (wireless LAN) began with the IEEE 802 standard. In particular the IEEE 802.11 standard was dedicated for the development of wireless LAN operation. The medium access protocol called as MAC protocol is widely related to this standard. In a way the 802.11 standard is somewhat similar to Ethernet, and it also adapts Ethernet technology to serve the wireless world.

The important components of IEEE 802.11 standard are listed as four groups. They are wireless medium, Access points, distribution system and the corresponding station. These four groups will be dealt later in this chapter.

The architecture of IEEE 802.11 standard is given below. The building block of a wireless LAN is a basic service set (BSS). It uses the MAC protocol to access the wireless medium.

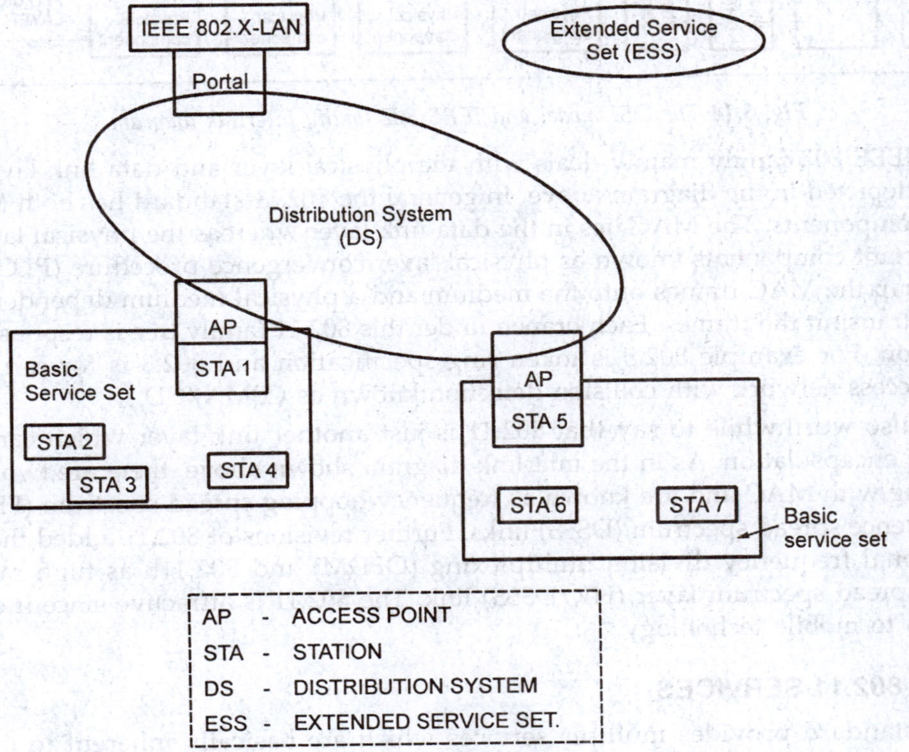

Fig. 8.13 Architecture of IEEE 802.11 standard

Each station in the entire system belongs to a particular BSS, and their association is dynamic. The two or more services are interconnected through a distribution system known as DS. The extended service set (ESS) will usually consist of two or more basic service sets. The ESS is like one logical LAN to the logical link control (LLC) level. Whenever an access to the distribution system from station is required the logic access point AP enables to establish connectivity between station and distribution system. Similarly to integrate the wired local area network and 802.11 standard a portal is used. It is nothing but a logic implemented in a device like router or bridge, which is a part of the wired LAN and it can be attached to the distribution system.

The entire family of this IEEE 802.11 standard in connection to the open system (OSI) model will ease the understanding of the underlaying concept of it.

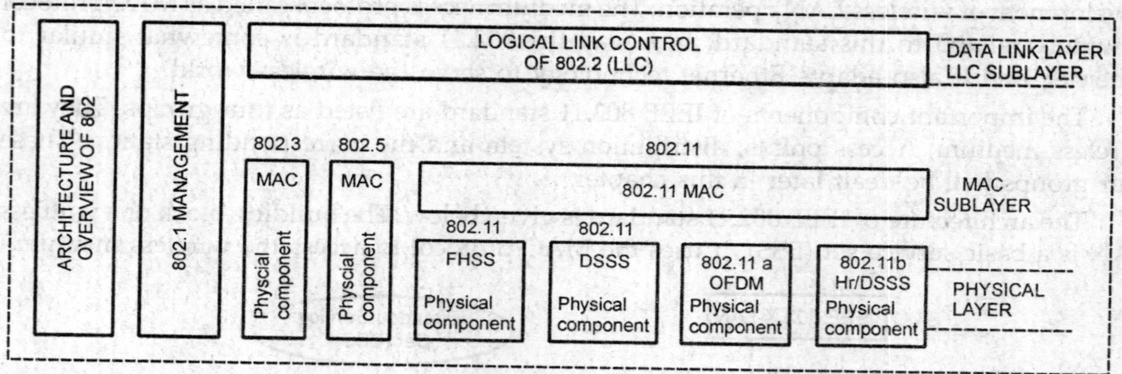

Fig. 8.14 The OSI model and IEEE 802 family interlink diagram

The IEEE 802 family mainly deals with the physical layer and data link layer of OSI model as depicted in the diagram above. In general the 802.11 standard has both MAC and physical components. The MAC lies in the data link layer whereas the physical layer holds two important components known as physical layer convergence procedure (PLCP) which helps to map the MAC frames onto the medium and a physical medium dependent (PMD) system to transmit the frames. Each branch under this 802.11 family tree is responsible for a specification. For example 802.5 is token ring specification and 802.3 is for carrier sense multiple access network with collision detection known as CSMA/CD.

It is also worthwhile to say that 802.11 is just another link layer which can use the 802.2/LLC encapsulation. As in the interlink diagram shown above, there are two physical layers along with MAC and are known as frequency hopping spread-spectrum (FHSS) and direct sequence spread spectrum (DSSS) links. Further revisions of 802.11 added the 802.11a as orthogonal frequency division multiplexing (OFDM) and 802.11b as high rate direct sequence spread spectrum layer (HR/DSSS) link. The 802.11 is attractive since it enhances its services to mobile technology.

8.11 IEEE 802.11 SERVICES

This standard provides multiple services which are basically inherent to the wired systems. A list of services and their corresponding providers are tabulated below.

Sr. Number of Service	Service	Provider of Service
1	Authentication	Station.
2	Association	Distribution system.
3	Deauthentication	Station.
4	Disassociation	Distribution system.
5	Distribution	Distribution system.
6	MSDU delivery	Station.
7	Reassociation	Distribution system.
8	Privacy	Station.

The IEEE 802.11 standard also defines three services which are Authentication, Privacy and Deauthentication.

8.11.1 Authentication

It is mainly applied to provide identity to different stations. The IEEE 802.11 needs mutually acceptable authentication before a particular station establishes its connection with the help of access point AP.

8.11.2 Privacy

It provides security to the messages. An unauthorised user can't steel the information. The data is hidden such that the core.

8.11.3 Deauthentication

When an authentication is to be revoked then this service of deauthentication is enforced.

IEEE 802.11a and 802.11b

The IEEE 802.11 infrared scheme is omnidirectional rather than a point to point scheme. The modulation used is pulse position modulation. The two schemes 802.11a and 802.l1b are the two important specifications of 802.11 standard.

Types

1. 802.11a standard :

The 802.11a standard group utilizes 5 GHz frequency. The larger frequency band is chopped into many number of channels (subchannels) using orthogonal frequency division multiplexing (OFDM) scheme.

The subchannels in OFDM are used to transmit the data, and set of all the sub channels are combined as one common channel. The data rates allowed are upto 54 Mbps.

In conventional frequency division multiplexing (FDM) scheme guard bands are inserted between consecutive bands of information to avoid overlapping.

In OFDM scheme all the subchannel frequencies overlap as shown below but still maintains transmission without interference. It is possible using the technique known as orthogonality.

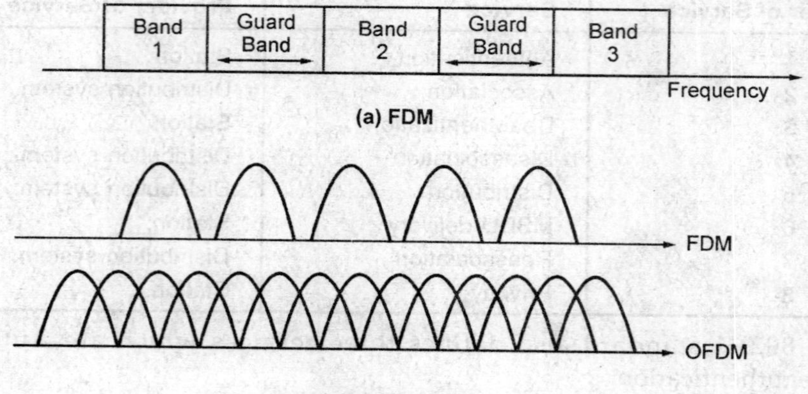

(a) FDM

(b) FDM & OFDM

Fig. 8.15

With the OFDM technique intersymbol interference may not make a big problem. But if the subcarriers are tightly packed into a particular channel it may cause inter carrier interference (ICI).

For 802.11a IEEE standard the convolutional code at different data rates forward error correction is allowed to correct any errors in reception.

The Fig. 8.15 (a) shows the basic protocol implementation block. The layers considered are MAC and PHY layers. In the functionality aspect MAC layer plays a vital role as detailed below.

1. Access mechanism.
2. Fragmentation.
3. Reassembly of the packets.

The first type of management deployed to carry out these events known as MAC sub layer management. It is also responsible for,

1. Power management.
2. Association.
3. Dissociation.
4. Reassociation processes.

The second important management is physical layer management. The physical layer under IEEE 802.11 standard is divided into three sublayers.

1. Physical layer convergence protocol (PLCP).
2. Physical medium dependent protocol (PMD).
3. Physical layer management sublayer.

The first sublayer is responsible for carrier sensing and forming packets for different PHY layers. The second sublayer PMD specifies modulation and coding techniques for signalling purposes. The third sublayer management governs the channel turning to various options for each physical layer.

2. 802.11b standard

The 802.11b standard is an extension of IEEE 802.11 DSSS scheme providing data rates of 5.5 Mbps and 11 Mbps. The 11 Mbps data rate scheme with complementary code keying (CCK) modulation method is used for 802.11b Mbps in a some what complex method.

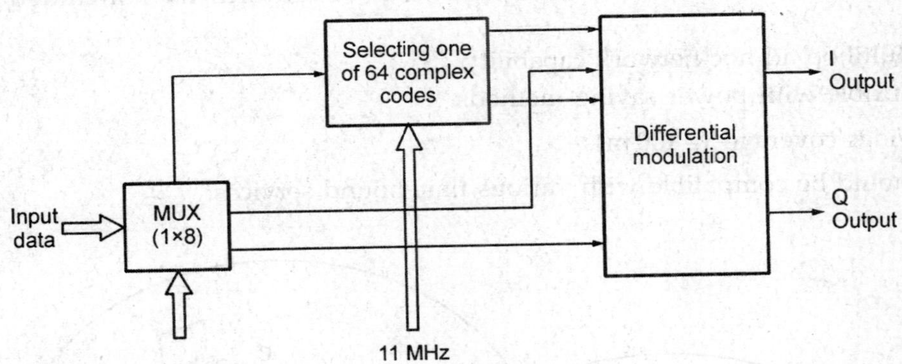

Fig. 8.16 Modulation scheme

In this scheme the input data are treated in blocks each with 8 bits at a data rate of 1.37 MHz (approx.) so that 1.37 MHz multiplied with 8 bits per symbol representation is 11 Mbps proper mapping can be done for 6 bits of each 8 bits persymbol with one of the 64 codes sequence using a 8 × 8 Walsh matrix. The output of the mapping process summed with two bits will be taken as input to a quadrature phase shift keying (QPSK) modulator unit. Walsh codes are used since they are common orthogonal codes applied in code division multiplication access (CDMA) linked applications.

8.12 HIPERLAN

The HIPERLAN is "High Performance Radio LAN" and it is a European standard. This HIPERLAN standard was initiated in 1999. The HIPERLAN-1 technology is acutally based on some functional requirements that is specified by ETSI. The frequency spectrum of 5.15 to 5.35 GHz band was first used by WLAN standard (≅ 5 GHz).

The two standards HIPERLAN-1 and HIPERLAN-2 have some functional requirements.

- Data rate - 23.5 Mbps.
- Ad hoc - Multihop networking capability.
- Provides coverage upto 100 m.
- Enhanced power saving.
- Provides time bounded services.

In HIPERLAN-1 multihop topology is followed and overlapping of two WLAN's is possible.

Actually this standard group had its origin in 1992 and the maximum work was completed in 1997. It satisfies some of the functional requirements specified by a group of European standard and for high speed wireless local networks known as ETSI. Also

CEPT released the frequency spectrum at 5 GHz to 17 GHz for the implementation of HIPERLAN-1 standards. HIPERLAN-1 was followed by HIPERLAN-2 which mainly focussed on high data rates. The HIPERLAN and HIPER ACCESS were used for remote access functions where as HIPER-LINK was used to interconnect switches in the backbone of network. Some of the functional requirements of HIPERLAN-1 included features like,

(*i*) Multihop ad hoc network capability.

(*ii*) Flexible with power saving methods.

(*iii*) Wider coverage ($\cong$100 m).

(*iv*) Should be compatible with various time-bound services.

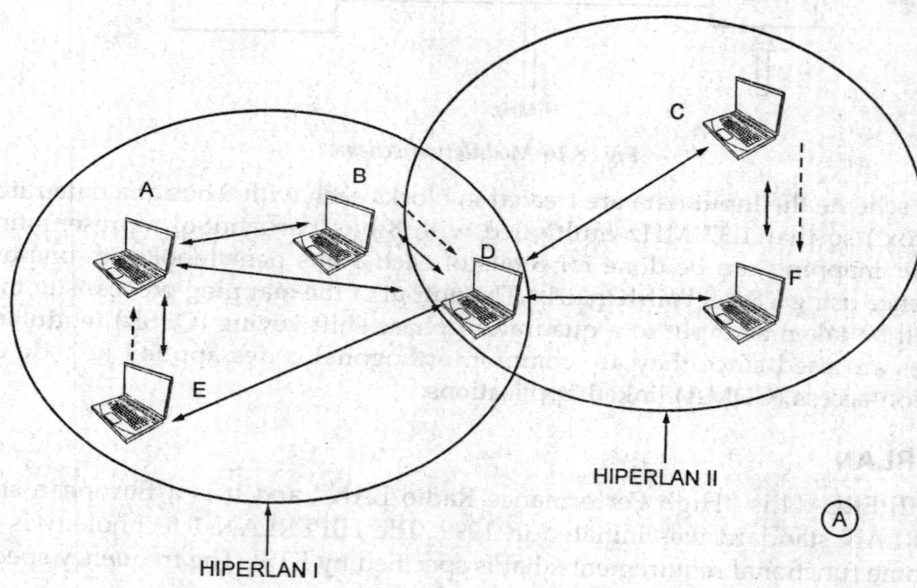

Fig. 8.17 (a) Architecture of ad hoc network in HIPERLAN-1

The ad hoc network architecture in HIPERLAN-1 is shown in Fig. 8.17 (*a*). The solid lines shows the peer to peer communications between two terminals whereas the dashed lines shows the forward link lines, inside the HIPERLAN. Three terminals A, D and F. have the forward link connections. The terminal 'D' is a member of HIPERLAN-1 and HIPERLAN-2. Since it is located at the overlapping portion of the two HIPERLAN's Multihop operation between the terminals is made possible. A forwarder node accepts the packet and if the packet has no address of its own then forwarder node retransmits the packet to some other terminal in its neighbourhood. But a Non-forwarder node accepts the packet as it is. Also a non-forwarder should select atleast one of its neighbour as a forwarder node.

The InterHIPERLAN needs a bilateral co-operation and agreement between the two HIPERLAN's is involved. In peer to peer type of communication shown by solid lines below and the dotted lines represent connections for forwarding.

The architecture of ad hoc network (B) is shown below in Fig. 8.17 (*b*) with forwarding and non-forwarding network. It is related to the previous Fig. A shown in Fig. 8.17 (*a*).

As the two HIPERLAN's (1 and 2) overlap with each other a common node falls in the intersecting area. It is also a forwarding node. In this architecture the forwarding node is denoted as 'f'.

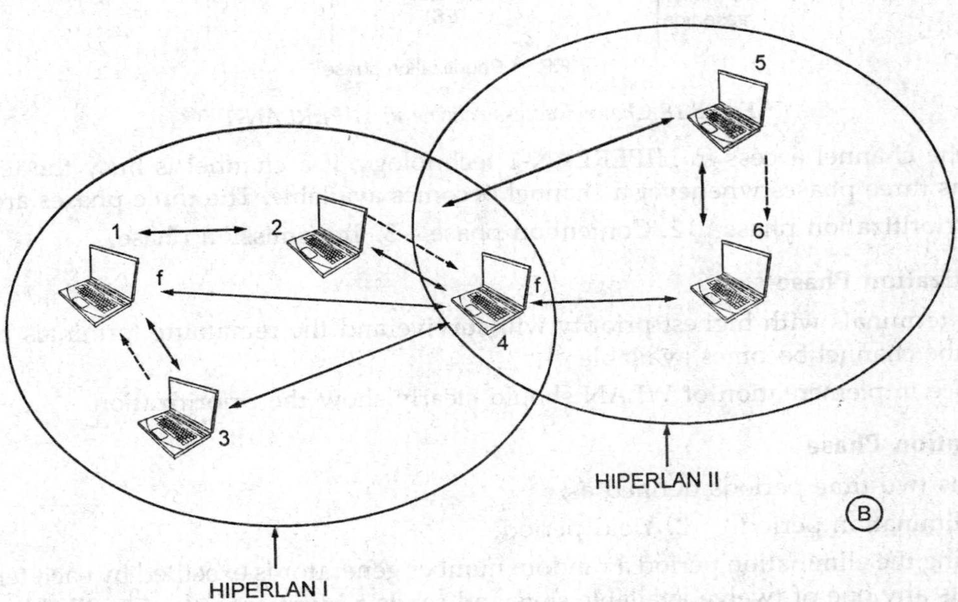

Fig. 8.17 (b) Architecture of Ad hoc network in HIPERLAN-1 related to Fig. 8.17 (a)

The physical layer (PHY) uses 200 MHz at 5.15 to 5.35 GHz which can be divided into 5 channels with a spacing of 40 MHz in European countries and divided into 6 channels with a spacing of 33 MHz spacing in U.S. The modulation used is single carrier Gaussian minimum shift keying (GMSK) scheme with a transmission power of 1 W. The data rate is upto 23 Mbps. A simple implementation of fall back data rates is possible with multisymbol quadrature amplitude modulation (QAM) embedded in OFDM scheme. In HIPERLAN-1, maximum of 47 codewords per packet is possible.

A Listen before talk protocol known as Non preemptive multiple access (NPMA) type protocol is used by HIPERLAN-1. It has similarities with 802.11 standard and also supports voice oriented transmission and asynchronous transmissions.

A "priority scheme" is defined by HIPERLAN-1 MAC scheme.

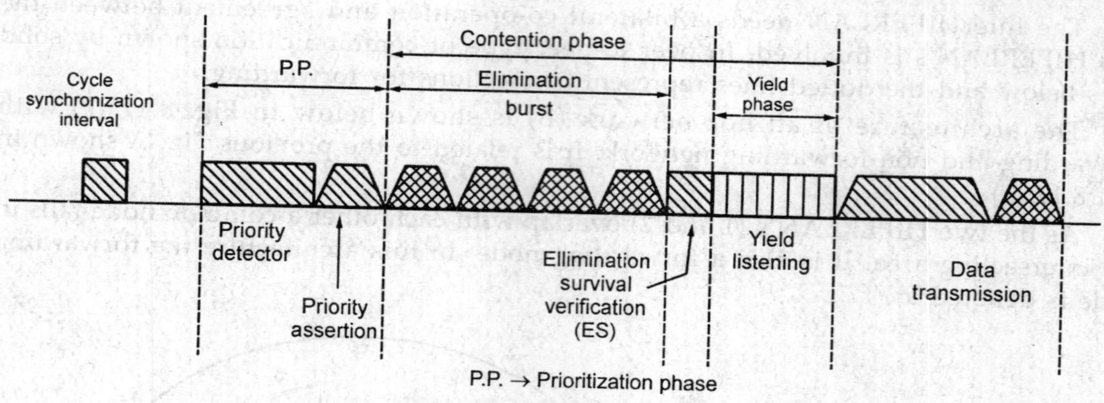

Fig. 8.18 Channel access scheme in HIPERLAN-1

In the channel access in HIPERLAN-1 technology, if a channel is busy the terminal access has three phases whenever a channel becomes available. The three phases are;

1. Prioritization phase 2. Contention phase 3. Transmission phase.

1. Prioritization Phase

The terminals with highest priority will survive and the remaining terminals have to wait till the channel becomes available.

Hence implementation of WLAN should clearly show the prioritization.

2. Contention Phase

It has two time periods defined as,

1. Elimination period 2. Yield period.

During the elimination period a random number generator is executed by each terminal and selects any one of twelve available slots and sends a burst consisting of 256 bits. Upto 256-bit durations it verifies (listens) to the channel and if the terminal does not hear any burst after the transmission it will again transmit as burst after twelfth slot in elimination survival (ES) verification zone.

If the terminal hears a burst signal in elimination survival (ES) zone period they will climate themselves. The rest of the terminals alone will enter to yield time period of the contention survival interval. The duration of yield period of each terminal is determined from an exponentially distributed random variable. It helps to reduce average waiting time required to run the counter. Later HIPERLAN-2 followed this HIPERLAN-1 WLAN standard. HIPERLAN-2 supported WLAN in many aspects. It uses two types of major topologies known as Infrastructure and Ad hoc structures. HIPERLAN-2 standard mostly co-ordinates in all sense with IEEE 802.11 standard and some examples are,

1. Working on higher layers.
2. Transmission technique.

It enables integration of WLAN into cellular systems for which 2 features are important.

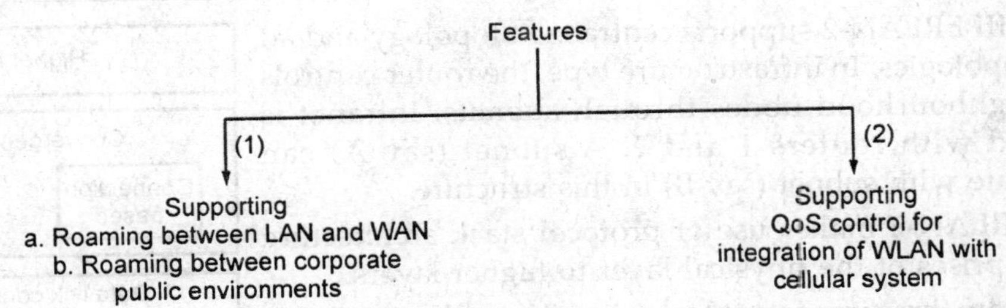

HIPERLAN-2 focuses on ATM and IP services with high data rates. It also supports connection less and connection oriented services. The demerit of HIPERLAN-1 is that it supports connectionless services.

Transmission phase

If a node have survived both the prioritization and contention phases can send data. This protocol data unit (PDU) can be either unicast or multicast. In unicast transmission the sender will expect to receive acknowledgment immediately. This acknowledgment is sent from destination node.

Two types of topologies are possible with HIPERLAN-2 standard.

The architecture of HIPERLAN-2 may follow Ad hoc or infrastructure topology.

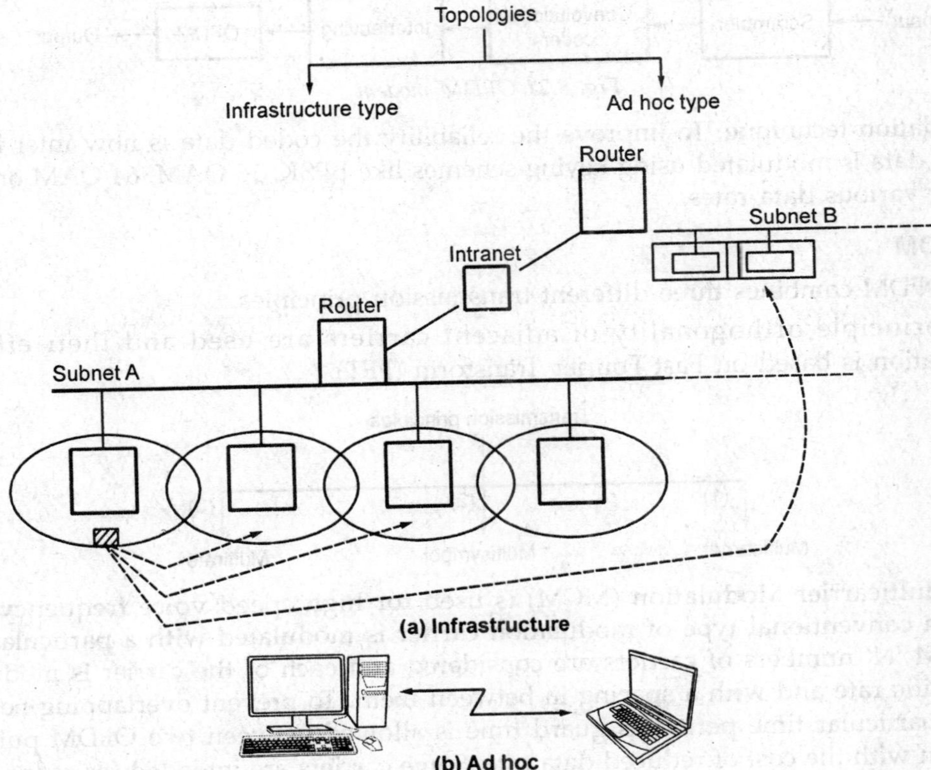

Fig. 8.19 HIPERLAN-2 topologies

The HIPERLAN-2 supports centralized topology and ad hoc type topologies. In infrastructure type, the router controls all the neighbourhood nodes through subnets. Intranet is established with routers 1 and 2. A subnet (say A) can communicate with subnet (say B) in this structure.

HIPERLAN-2 makes use of protocol stack architecture which comprises of the physical layer to higher layers.

There are three important layers known as physical layer, data link layer and convergence layer.

The data link layer provides logical link and includes the function of communication management and medium access control for handling connections. The data link control facilitates the mapping of convergence layer packets onto a single physical (PHY) layer. The PHY layer of the HIPERLAN-2 standard uses orthogonal frequency division multiplexing (OFDM) type of modulation.

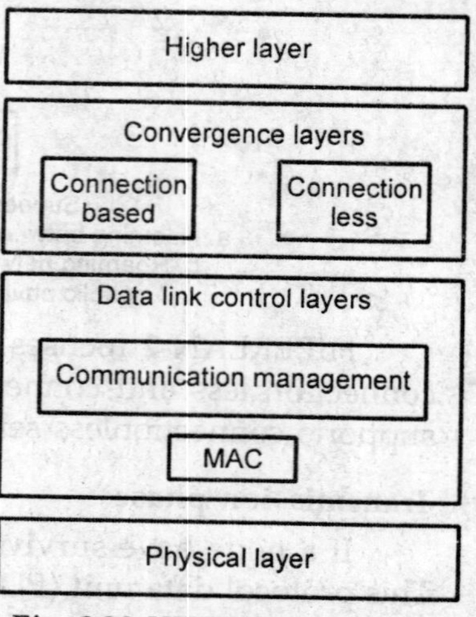

Fig. 8.20 HIPERLAN-2 protocol stack structure

The data received in HIPERLAN-2 is scrambled. This scrambled data is passed through convolutional coder which uses one of the rates 1/2 or 3/4 etc. That is used

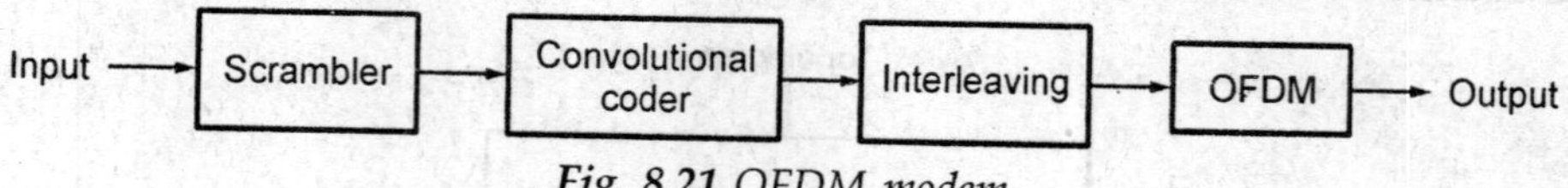

Fig. 8.21 OFDM modem

as a modulation technique. To improve the reliability the coded data is now inter leaved. Finally the data is modulated using keying schemes like BPSK, 16 QAM, 64 QAM or QPSK supporting various data rates.

8.12.1 OFDM

The OFDM combines three different transmission principles.

The principle orthogonality of adjacent carriers are used and their efficient implementation is based on Fast Fourier Transform (FFT).

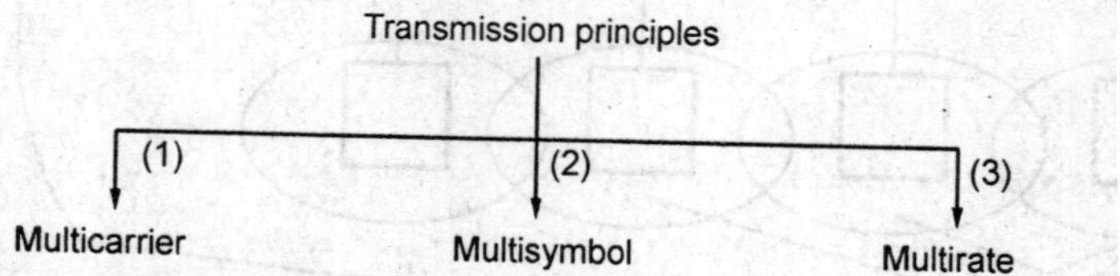

The Multicarrier Modulation (MCM) is used for high speed voice frequency band modems. In conventional type of modulation carrier is modulated with a particular rate. But in MCM 'N' numbers of carriers are considered and each of the carrier is modulated with a specific rate and with a spacing in between them. To prevent overlapping between symbols a particular time period as guard time is allowed between two OFDM pulses in transmission with the cost of reduced data rate. Some carriers are intended for redundancy and synchronization purposes.

The multisymbol modulation scheme uses multiphase modulation and multiamplitude modulation techniques which helps to avail the data rate. Quadrature Phase Shift Keying (QPSK) is a traditional keying method that can be used where four symbol system is followed encoding two bits in one of the four transmitted symbols and the signal constellation is such that four points represents amplitudes and phases of the symbols. The symbol transmission rate is double with this scheme when it is compared with Binary Phase Shift Keying (BPSK) scheme.

In multirate transmission approach under OFDM even in channel degradation conditions reliable data transmission is possible.

The signal to noise ratio (SNR) increases as the modulation efficiency increases. If the subscriber moves away from base station SNR value will reduce and the error rates can be measured.

8.13 DATA LINK CONTROL (DLC) LAYER

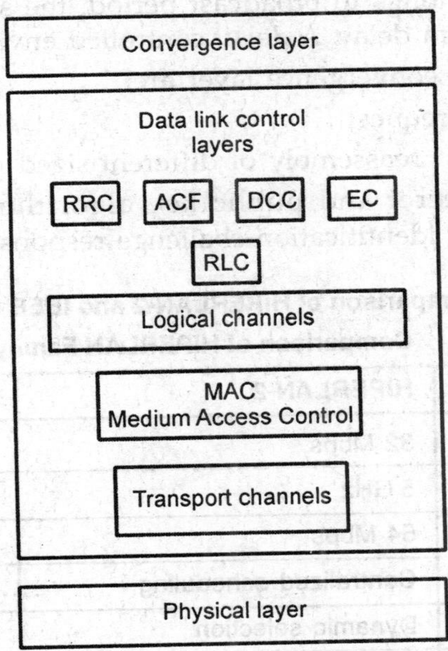

Fig. 8.22 Logical and transport channels in HIPERLAN-2

In the DLC layer the medium access control (MAC) and frame format plays vital role. Four protocols are implemented in HIPERLAN-2 standard. They are

1. Radio Link Control (RLC).
2. DLC Connection Control (DCC).
3. Association Control Function (ACF).
4. Radio Resource Control (RRC).

The Error Control (EC) mechanism is supported by DLC. The MAC protocol is dynamic in nature. It supports unicast and multicast communications. Collision free-transmission is possible. HIPERLAN-2 also supports mechanisms to calculate power establish communication such that Dynamic Frequency Selection (DPS). To improve Quality of Service (QoS) HIPERLAN-2 facilitates changing periodicity of message transmission.

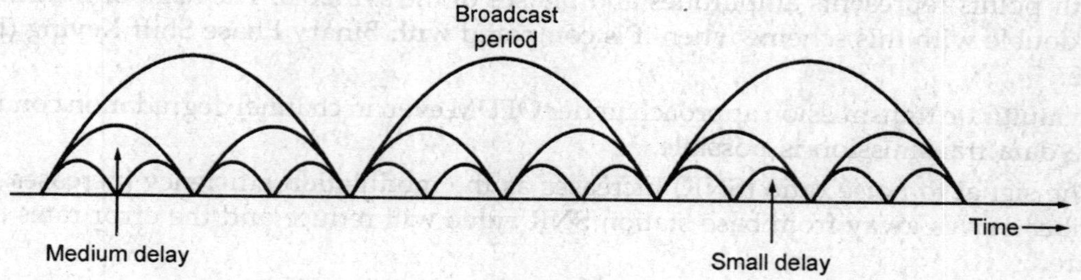

Fig. 8.23 Delay control mechanism

The longest period belongs to broadcast period, the shortest belongs to small delay. The other one is the medium delay. A delay controlled environment is possible.

The responsibilities of convergence layer are,

1. Adapting service request.
2. Fragmentation and reassembly of different sized packets.

In security issues, secret and public key algorithms can also be employed for authentication purpose. For identification challenge response mechanisms are applied.

Table 8.2 Comparison of HIPERLAN-2 and IEEE 802.11 standard

Comparison of HIPERLAN Family

Parameter	HIPERLAN-2	802.11 Standard
Maximum throughout	32 Mbps	1.2 Mbps
Frequency	5 GHz	2.4 GHz
Maximum transmission rate	54 Mbps	2 Mbps
Medium access (MA)	Centralized scheduling	Through sensing method
Frequency management	Dynamic selection	None
QoS support	ATM/802.1P/RSVP	PCF
Wired backbone	Ethernet/ATM/UMTS/IP	Ethernet
Connectivity	Connection-oriented	Connectionless
Encrypton	Possible	Possible
Link quality control	Link adaptation is possible	None

Table 8.3 HIPERLAN family for wireless networks

Sr.	Parameter	HIPERLAN type 1	HIPERLAN type 2	HIPERLAN type 3	HIPERLAN type 4
(a)	Datarate power conservation	32 Mbps	1.2 Mbps	> 20 Mbits/s	– 155 Mbits/s
(b)	Power conservation	Necessary	Necessary	Not necessary	Not necessary
(c)	Application	Wireless LAN	Access to the ATM networks	Wireless local loop.	Point-to-point wireless ATM connections uses HIPERLAN type 4
(d)	Frequency	≈ 5 to 5.5 GHz	≈ 5 to 5.5 GHz	≈ 5 to 5.5 GHz	17 to 17.3 GHz
(e)	Topology	Decentralized ad hoc or infrared	Centralized and cellular types.		
(f)	Antenna	Omnidirectional type is used.	Omnidirectional type is used.	Directional antenna is used.	Directional antenna is used.

8.14 BLUETOOTH TECHNOLOGY

The Bluetooth technology lies under Wireless Local Area Network (WLAN). The wireless LAN setup provides more benefits than wired LAN by avoiding the cost of installing LAN cabling and makes simple relocation whenever a network's structure has to be changed.

The Wireless Personal Area Network (WPAN) uses infrared rays and radio waves for communication, establishment, i.e. It is made possible for a Personal Computer (PC) to communicate with another Infrared device, IRDA (Infrared Data Association) like another Personal Digital Assistant (PDA) or a PC or a mobile phone.

One of the PAN technology standard is known as Bluetooth. It mainly uses radio instead of infrared. The data rate is of 1 Mbps for a distance of 10 meters, approximately.

It is independent of line of sight technique. Hence the wireless PAN (WPAN) works in ad-hoc mode only.

In Latin generally the term 'ad-hoc' means "for this particular purpose only". It means 'spontaneous' small area network. The new devices like Bluetooth or 802.11 IEEE standard used this "ad-hoc" technique. Hence Bluetooth deals with short range wireless technology. It provides low cost solution. Also it provides links between mobile computers, portable handheld devices, cellular phones etc. The Bluetooth ad-hoc technique is considered as a challenge and interesting topic to develop by the Bluetooth special Interest Group.

The Denmark king Herald had nickname Bluetooth. He united Denmark and Norway regions. Since this technology combines both personal communication and communication devices it was named, after the king as "Bluetooth technology."

8.14.1 Bluetooth Radio

- **Introduction**

The bluetooth technology was mainly intended to work in 2.4 GHz band frequency. The wavelength of the Bluetooth radio signal is around 12.5 cms. The antenna useful for Bluetooth signal transmission and reception can be vertical antenna and dipole antenna.

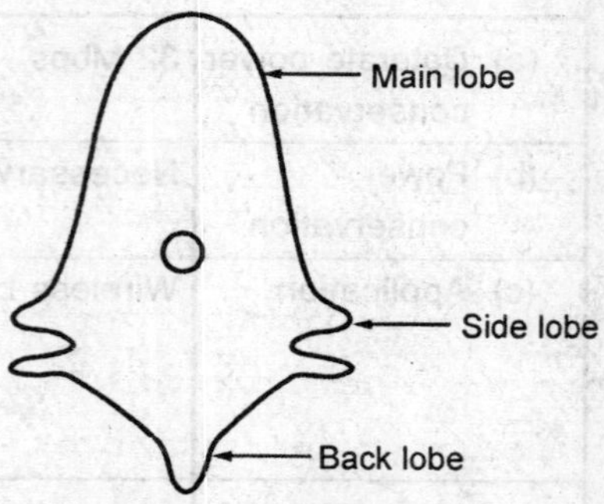

Fig. 8.24 Vertical antenna-an example

8.14.1.1 Vertical Antenna

The vertical antenna is electrically equivalent to the one half of a dipole antenna. It is important to note that erecting antenna in clearest vertical spot installing in a proper ground system beneath the antenna will probably reduce the level of interferences are losses.

8.14.1.2 Dipole Antenna

It is a straight electrical conductor measuring the half wavelength from ends and then connected at the centre to a RF (Radio Frequency) feedline. It is also called as doublet and basically it is a balanced antenna.

These two types vertical and dipole antennas are compatible with Bluetooth radio broadcasting.

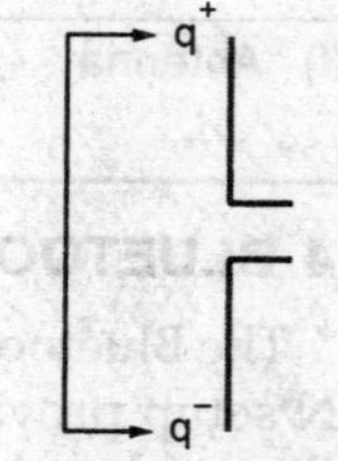

Fig. 8.25 Halfwave dipole-an example

8.14.2 Antenna Parameters

The antenna parameters are important which determine the efficiency of the entire Bluetooth system. The parameters are,

- Voltage standing wave ratio
- Bandwidth
- Efficiency
- Return loss
- Polarization

8.14.2.1 Voltage Standing Wave Ratio (VSWR)

It is a measure of mismatch between the antenna and transmitter. VSWR will be unity for a perfectly matched antenna. If the value of VSWR is less then the performance of the antenna will be good.

8.14.2.2 Bandwidth

Bluetooth technology uses 2.4 GHz ISM bandwidth of frequency for its operation. The frequency band is divided into 79 channels for frequency hopping type of spread spectrum technique with each channel 1 MHz frequency wide.

8.14.2.3 Efficiency

It is defined as the ratio of power level of transmitted signal and the received signal. The compatibility of the transmitter and receiver should hold good for better power level which in turn enables higher efficiency.

8.14.2.4 Return Loss

The return loss is used to measure the antenna performance, and it is expressed in decibel units. If the antenna can absorb 50% of the signal where the remaining portion of signal is reflected then the return loss is – 3 dB.

8.14.2.5 Polarization

Polarization is a parameter that expresses the direction of electric field in comparison with that of the earths surface. The polarization may be any one of the three types, vertical, horizontal (or) circular polarization.

8.14.3 User Scenarios

For Bluetooth piconets we can assume several user scenarios.

(*i*) Connection of peripheral devices

Many of the devices are linked to desktop computer through wires. These devices include peripherals like keyboard, mouse, joystick, headset, speakers etc. But each of them need their own specific cables, plugs etc. The connecting wires are used for data transfer and also to supply power to these devices.

(*ii*) Bridging of networks

A mobile phone can be connected to laptop or personal digital assistant (PDA) using wireless piconets.

Fig. 8.26 Bluetooth-based piconet configuration

Mobile phone can have a Bluetooth chip. Thus mobile phone can act as a bridge between a global GSM network (base station) and a local laptop as shown in Fig. 8.26.

(*iii*) Support of ad-hoc networking

Wireless networks can support any kind of interactions including discussions and meetings related to sales, preparing schedules, copying classroom lecture notes into student's PDA etc. Bluetooth chips are used to enable these facilities at less cost than using WLAN adapters in small devices.

8.15 AD-HOC NETWORK BLUETOOTH

Ad-hoc network represents connectivity establishment within a particular distance for an application. For example when two Bluetooth devices are brought into vicinity of each other, an instant connection is setup. If a network is developed by the dynamic type of connection then it is called as ad-hoc-network. The ad-hoc networks can be formed without a central administration.

For example in a place like airport it is possible to access LAN's and WAN's through the ad-hoc Bluetooth network connections, from the portable devices interconnected such as WCDMA, mobile units, PDA's (personal digital assistant) etc. Mail checking through a HIPERLAN interface to notebook computer is also possible with ad-hoc Bluetooth networks.

8.15.1 Networking Architecture

(*i*) Point-to-point connection (P2P)

It is a simple and direct network scheme which connects two devices with each other. It is also known as P2P connection. Out of the two devices one device is assumed to be a piconet master device (M) and the other device is assumed as a slave (S).

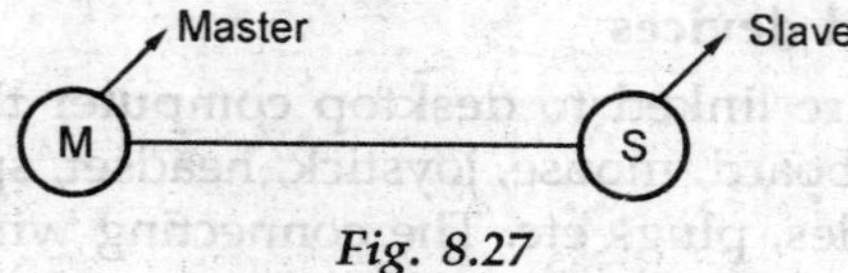

Fig. 8.27

(*ii*) Point-to-multipoint and piconet connection

In a point to multipoint connection minimum of more than two devices form a network. It is also called as piconet where a maximum of eight devices can be connected in a network.

One device acts as a master device (M) and other devices are called as slave devices (S).

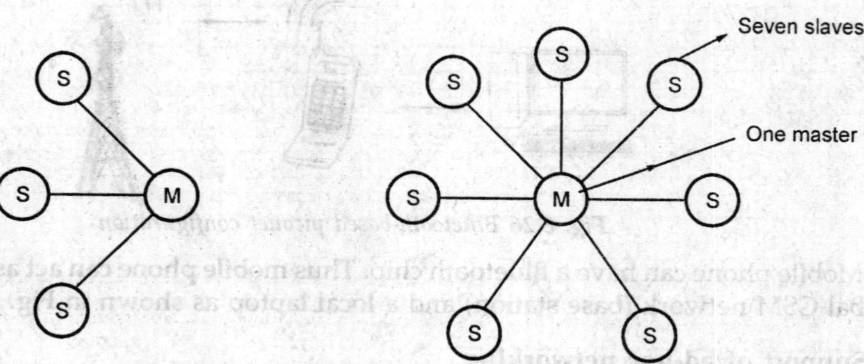

(a) One master and three slaves communication

(b) One master with seven slaves communication under piconet

Fig. 8.28

Note : A piconet for Bluetooth can contain upto 256 devices in a communication network but only eight devices can actively participate among them. No data transfer is allowed between slaves (S) of same piconet and allowed only through the master (M) device.

(*iii*) Scatternet blue architecture

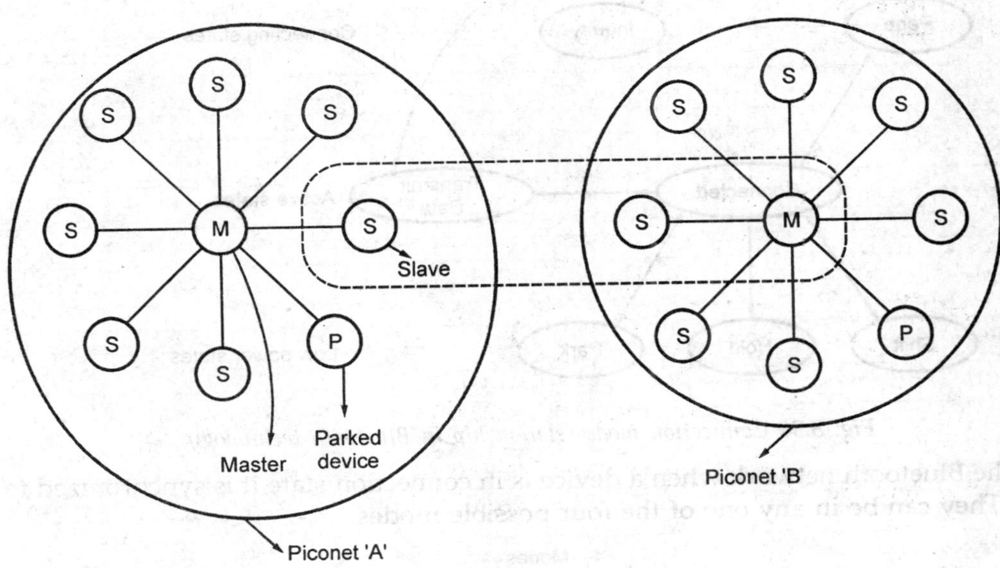

Fig. 8.29 Bluetooth architecture example of scatternet where slave of piconet A communicates with master of piconet B

Scatternets provides maximum data transfer. It enables Bluetooth devices to communicate with many piconets at a time. Scatternets are actually formed by overlapping of multiple piconets over their coverage areas. The spectrum utilization is optimized. A device in scatternet can play master/slave roles in different piconets but at the same time no single device can act as master in more than one piconet within a scatternet.

8.16 BLUETOOTH DEVICE ADDRESS

It is denoted as (BD_ADDR), and the Bluetooth transmitter-receiver is allocated a 48-bit address as BD_ADDR which follows the IEEE 802 standard. The Bluetooth adder of 48-bits is divided as three fields.

1.	Lower Address Part - LAP	-	24-bits.
2.	Upper Address Part - UAP	-	8-bits
3.	Non-significant Address Part	-	16-bits
	Total	-	48-bits long

In the three fields Lower Address Part (LAP) is assigned for company and the two Upper Address Part (UAP) and non-significant address part is for identification (ID) of the company.

8.17 BLUETOOTH CONNECTION MODE RELATIONSHIP

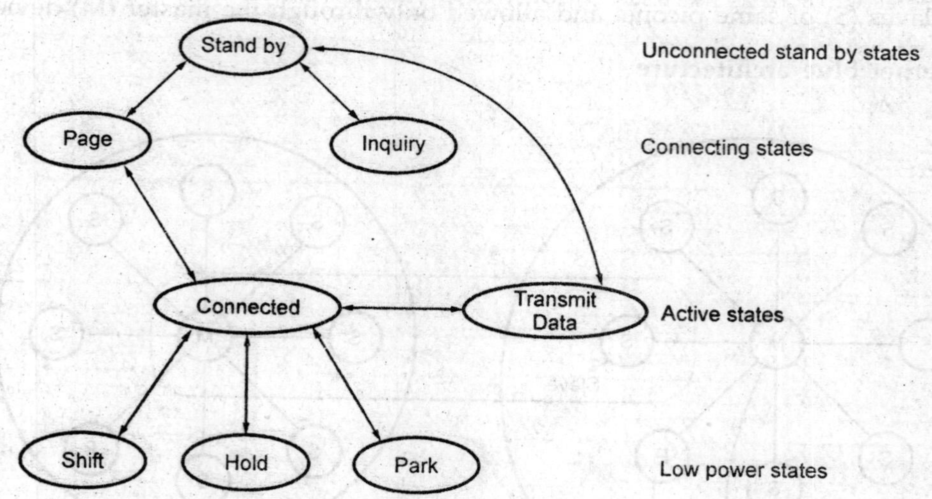

Fig. 8.30 Connection mode relationship in Bluetooth technology

In the Bluetooth network when a device is in connection state it is synchronized to the piconet. They can be in any one of the four possible modes.

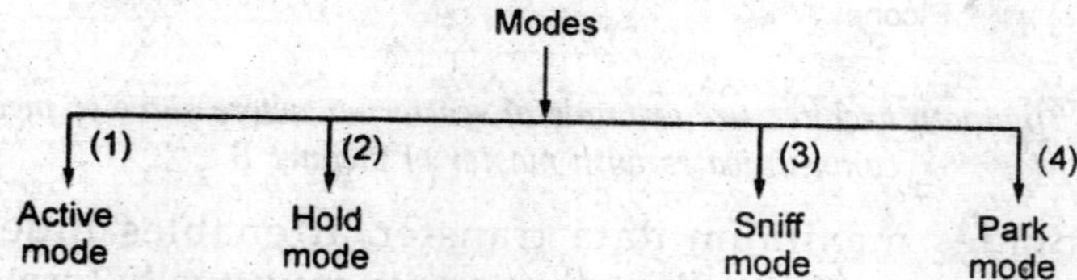

If a Bluetooth device is in active mode it transmits and receives packets, which may be of data or control packets. Each slave is assigned a bit address to differentiate it from a packed device. It is valid as long as the slave is a member of the piconet setup. The other three modes are mainly intended for saving power by reducing their own duty cycles.

When the device is in hold mode it has intermediate power efficiency which is achieved by making the particular device inactive temporarily for short time intervals. For this purpose a timer is used internally.

The sniff mode is good in prolonging or safe guarding the life of battery by minimizing unnecessary transmission of the poll packets. Whenever communication between master and slave is large sniff mode is more suitable. Devices that are in sniff mode have least power efficiency with highest duty cycle than other modes.

When a slave decides to be inactive for a particular time interval it enters into park mode that has larger duration than hold and sniff modes. Though this slave device does not participate in data traffic it maintains its synchronization with the master device in piconet.

There are four modes compatible with Bluetooth devices in a piconet arrangement.

8.17.1 Protocol Stack of Bluetooth

In Bluetooth the protocol stack enables communication with many devices. It includes voice, data and control signalling in Bluetooth. Radio modem is specified by RF layer. The link control at packet and bit levels are specified by the baseband layer. The Link Management Protocol (LMP) is capable of configuring links with other devices. It provides power modes, traffic scheduling, packet format, state of units in piconet, authentication and encryption. With L2CAP connection-oriented and connectionless data services to that of the upper layers protocol. It may include services like segmentation, reassembly protocol multiplexing and also group abstractions for the data packets. The control informations can be exchanged. The Service Discovery Protocol (SDP) enables two or more Bluetooth devices in case of supporting a particular service. The Telephone Control Protocol (TCP) is used to define the both call control.

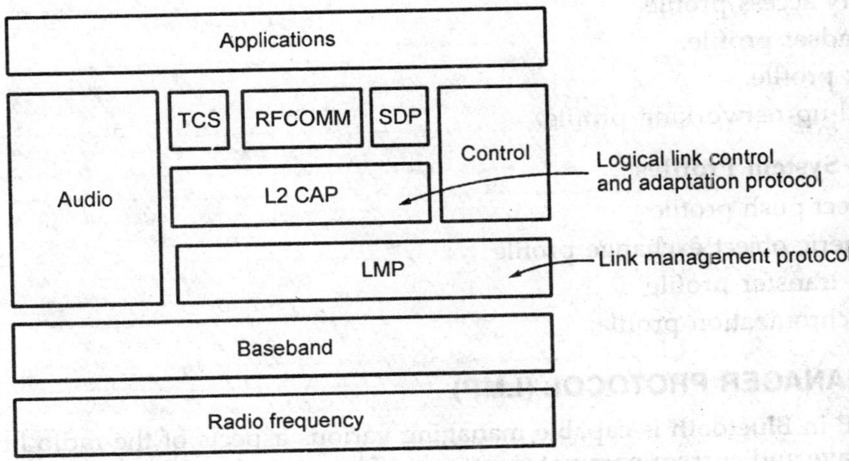

Fig. 8.31 Bluetooth protocol stack-architecture

Signalling and mobility management in connection with cordless telephone applications. Finally the RFCOMM in Bluetooth stack is a 'cable replacement' protocol that will provide RS232 control and data signals of Bluetooth baseband signal.

8.17.2 Example - Bluetooth Specification : [Version 1.1]

In Bluetooth specification Bluetooth 1.1 version is taken as an example that is used commercially.

The Bluetooth specification 1.1 version consists of two parts. They are core and profile.

In Bluetooth profile the layers are defined. The stack in it is used to provide physical and data link layers with higher level protocols that needs to communicate with this standard. The Bluetooth specific protocols are RFCOMM and TCS. The layers of the protocol stack in this version are radio layer, link management layer, logical link and adaptation layer, service discovery layer, RFCOMM layer, TCS layer and host controller interface. Also the high-layer adaptation functionalities are enabled by the non-bluetooth specific protocols (OBEX, WAP etc.) that can be implemented by the layers in this Bluetooth 1.1 version.

Under the Bluetooth 1.1 version profiles, is used to segregate the Bluetooth applications. These applications can be divided as two broad classifications application and system profiles and it is given below in detail.

In Bluetooth 1.1 version there are two main kinds of profiles supported namely application profile and system profile. They are listed below.

8.17.2.1 Nine Application Profiles

1. Service discovery application profile.
2. Generic access profile.
3. Intercom profile.
4. Serial port profile.
5. Cordless telephone profile.
6. LAN access profile.
7. Headset profile.
8. Fax profile.
9. Dial-up networking profile.

8.17.2.2 Four System Profiles

1. Object push profile
2. Generic object exchange profile
3. File transfer profile
4. Synchronization profile

8.18 LINK MANAGER PROTOCOL (LMP)

The LMP in Bluetooth is capable managing various aspects of the radio link between master and slave and current parameter setting of Bluetooth devices. The functions covered by LMP are listed below.

1. Authentication pairing and encryption of data
2. Capability negotiation
3. Synchronization
4. Power control
5. Quality of service
6. State and transmission mode change
7. Link supervision.

8.18.1 A- Physical Links

In Bluetooth there are two types of links namely :

(*i*) Synchronous connected-oriented link (SCO),

(*ii*) Asynchronous connectionless link (ACL).

(i) Synchronous connected-oriented link (SCO)

The telephone connections need circuit-switched point-to-point and symmetrical type of connections.

The master node reserves two slots (forward and reverse slots) at fixed time intervals. A master node is capable of supporting three SCO links at a time to same or different slave nodes.

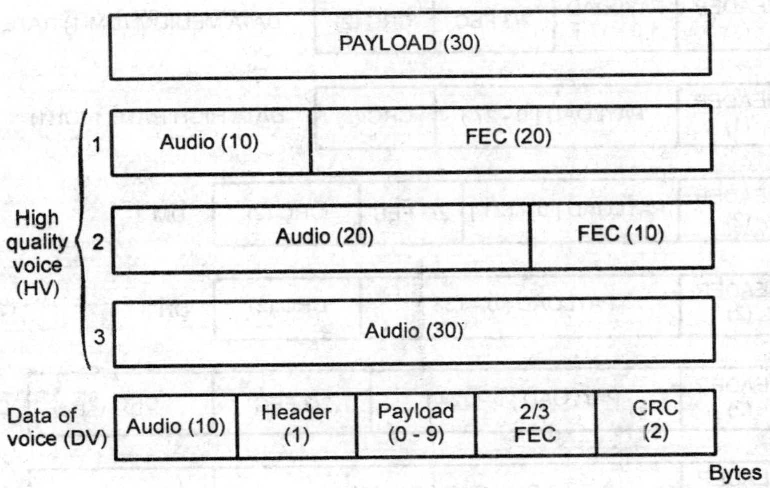

Fig. 8.32 Synchronous connection-oriented link (SCO) payload types

The forward error correction (FEC) is helpful in noisy environment, of high error rate. Bluetooth offers an automatic repeat request (ARQ) for efficient transmission.

The payload header consists an identifier for a logical channel (LC). The header is of 1 byte length for 1-slot packets and 2 bytes for multi-slot packets. The payload in physical link is protected by cyclic redundancy check (CRC).

Supporting three simultaneous links. It may be either to same slave or to different slaves. A slave node can support either three links with one master or upto two links from different master nodes. The SCO link carries voice data at 64 kb/sec and 2/3 forward error correction (FEC) or $\frac{1}{3}$ FEC can be selected. Different FEC schemes can be applied depending on channel error rate.

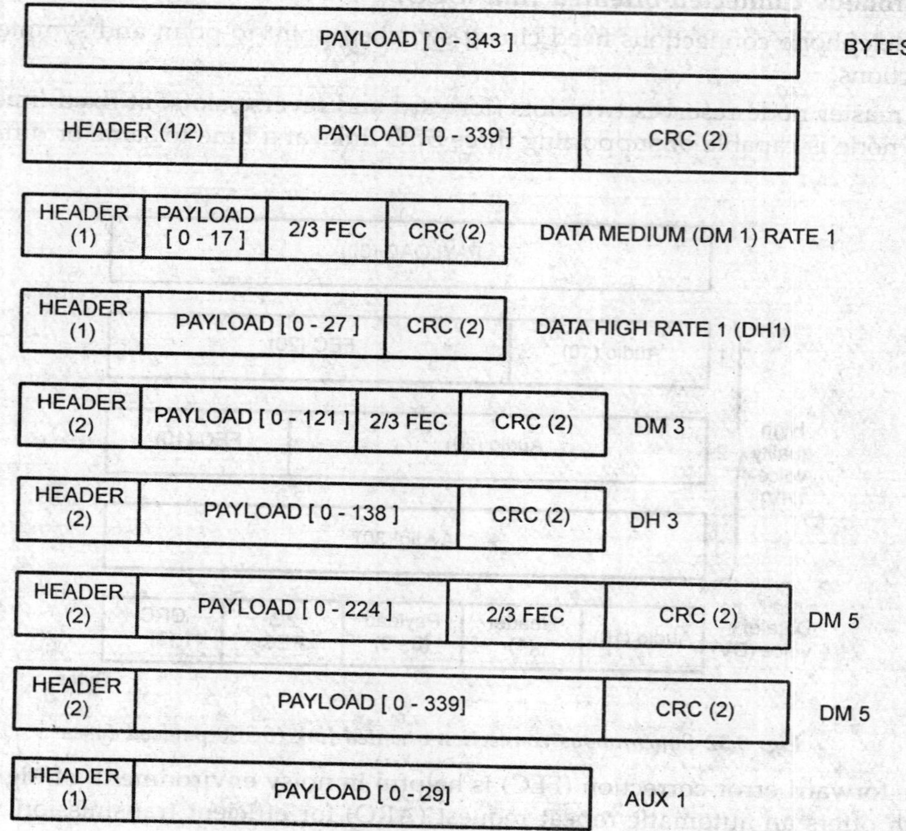

Fig. 8.33 Payload type in ACL

(ii) Asynchronous Connectionless Link (ACL)

In ACL the master node uses a polling scheme. A slave node would answer only if it was addressed in preceeding time slot. Between the master and slave only one ACL link can exist. The "ACL payload types" is shown above. For data carrying purpose in ACL. 1 or 3 or 5 slots packets could be used.

8.18.2 Logical Link Control and Adaptation Protocol (L2CAP)

The L2CAP is a data link control protocol, present on top of the baseband layer and offers logical channels between the Bluetooth devices with relevant quality of service. L2CAP is present in asynchronous connectionless link (ACL) only. Three different channels are being provided by L2CAP.

They are :

1. Connectionless
2. Connection-oriented.
3. Signalling.

These logical channels are transported between slave and master devices/nodes.

There are also three packet types belongs to logical channels. They are tabulated below.

Sr. No.	Three packet formats	Allowed payload (Bytes)
1.	Connectionless Packet Data Unit (PDU)	0 - 65533
2.	Connection-oriented PDU	0 - 65535
3.	Signalling command PDU	One or more commands

Fig. 8.34 Packet formats in L2CAP in Bluetooth

Some of the main functions provided by L2CAP are :

- Flow specification
- Multiplication
- Group management
- Segmentation and reassembly functions

Note : The larger packets has to segmented into smaller packets depending on the baseband capabilities of the system.

8.18.3 Summary of Protocols Bluetooth Architecture

The layered Bluetooth protocol stack architecture consists of core protocols, cable replace and telephony control protocols and the adopted protocols.

The five-layer stack formed by core protocols consists of below elements.

1. Radio : It specifies details of air interface that includes

(*i*) Frequency (*ii*) Use of frequency hopping

(*iii*) Modulation scheme (*iv*) Transmit power

2. Baseband : It is concerned with connection establishment inside a piconet arrangement and other tasks like,

(*i*) Packet format (*ii*) Timing

(*iii*) Power-control (*iv*) Addressing

3. Link manager protocol (LMP) : It is responsible for link setup between the bluetooth devices and link management that is ongoing.

It also includes some security issues like

(*i*) Authentication and encryption.

(*ii*) Negotiation and control of baseband packet sizes.

4. Logical link control and adaptation protocol (L2CAP) : It enables linking the baseband layer to upper-layer protocols. This L2CAP can provide

(*i*) Connectionless services and (*ii*) Connection-oriented services.

5. Services discovery protocol (SDP) : It can supervise and enable connection between two or more bluetooth devices for specific service application.

SDP includes informations like

(i) Device information (ii) Services

(iii) Service characteristics.

Note :

RFCOMM : It is a cable replacement protocol used in Bluetooth specification. RFCOMM represents a virtual serial port designed so as to replace cable technologies. With minimum changes in existing devices RFCOMM replaces serial port cables and provides data transport in Bluetooth.

TCP : Bluetooth also specifies telephony control protocol. If defines mobility management functions so that groups of TCS devices can be handled. TCS is telephony control specification bit-oriented protocol that defines call control signalling. Because of it speech and data calls between the Bluetooth devices can be established.

Adopted Protocols : The adopted protocols are defined by other standards-making org's and they are incorporated into overall Bluetooth architecture. Some of the adopted protocols are :

(i) Point-to-point protocol

(ii) Foundation protocols of TCP/IP protocol suite known as TCP/UDP/IP

(iii) Object exchange protocol (OBEX)

(iv) Wireless application environment/wireless application protocol (WAE/WAP).

8.19 SOME OF THE ADVANTAGES OF BLUETOOTH

- Eliminates the usage of cables linking computers to keyboards, mouse and printers.
- Call home from a distant place to turn any appliances on and off, set alarm etc.
- Enables MP3 players in wireless fashion, to other machines.
- To make calls from a wireless headset which is connected remotely to a cellular phone.
- It also helps in monitoring remotely the home networks, air conditioners, ovens etc.
- The control is possible with Bluetooth upto 10 meters. It is developed such that can be used by many users.
- The 'piconet setup' i.e. eight small devices can communicate in a small network helps to develop networking for a short range. Also upto ten piconets can be in a same coverage range of the Bluetooth radio.
- To provide security each link is protected and encoded and hence Bluetooth technology assures user authentication.
- The short range wireless connectivity oriented applications like cable replacement, Ad-hoc networking and data-voice accessing are possible with Bluetooth.

8.20 THREE CLASSES OF BLUETOOTH PROTOCOL

Bluetooth protocols can be divided into three different classes or groups.

Class 1

The Bluetooth specific protocols mainly for its baseband are LMP, L2CAP and SDP.

Class 2

The Bluetooth protocols that are developed based on the already existing protocols are TCP and RFCOMM.

Class 3

It mainly comprises of the existing protocols which are actually adopted by the Bluetooth Special Interest Group (SIG). It includes protocols like PPP, WAP, WAE, UDP/TCP/IP, OBEX, V-card, V-cal etc.

8.20.1 Bluetooth MAC-Mechanism

The access mechanism under Bluetooth is a voice oriented system. The MAC in Bluetooth is fast FH-CDMA/TDD method which employs polling scheme for establishing a link. That is a fast hop of even 1600 hops per second is possible. Bluetooth is mainly a CDMA system and implemented using the frequency hopping spread spectrum scheme.

8.20.2 Topology of Bluetooth

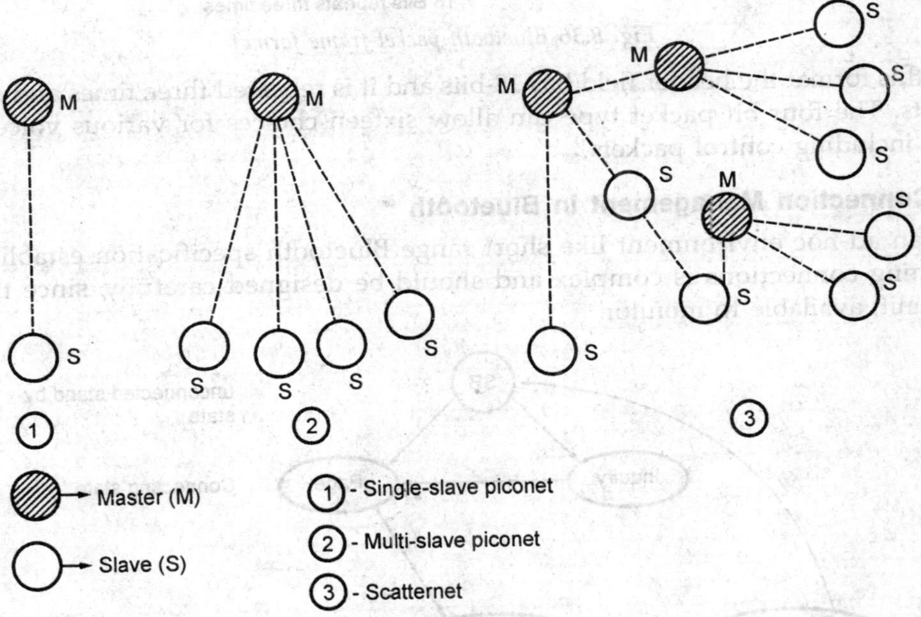

Fig. 8.35 Topologies of networked Bluetooth modules

The Bluetooth devices in a piconet consists of master and slave configuration. The piconet has structures like single-slave piconet, multi-slave piconet and scatternet. In single-slave piconet one slave is connected to a single master.

Generally Bluetooth topology adopts multiple piconet structure. It may take point-to-point (or) point to multipoint type of connection. The third type other than single-slave and multi-slave piconets is the scatternet. It has several piconets linked together within it.

8.20.3 Frame Format in Bluetooth

In the Bluetooth specification one packet per hop is enabled and a single slot packet with duration of 625 μsec is extended to three other slots of 1875 μsec duration is allowed. Different data rates (speed) of data and voice applications regarding to form a piconet is possible. In the frame format given below there are 74 bits for accessing a code field and 54 bits for the header field different payloads that can even be 5 slots are enabled in Bluetooth packet setup.

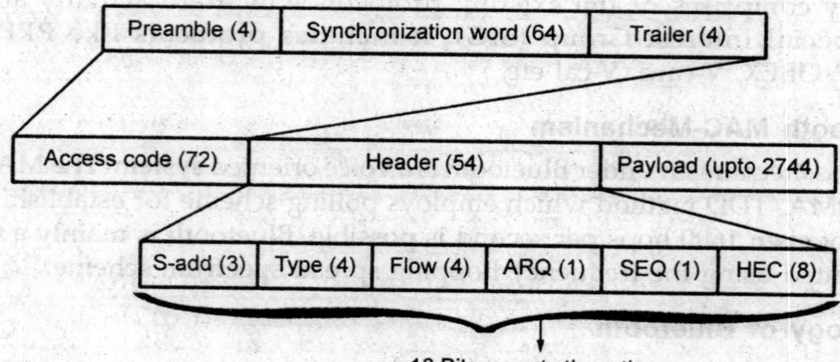

Fig. 8.36 Bluetooth packet-frame format

In this format the header field has 18-bits and it is repeated three times and considered as 54-bits. The four bit packet type can allow sixteen choices for various voice and data services including control packets.

8.20.4 Connection Management in Bluetooth

In an ad-hoc environment like short range Bluetooth specification establishing and maintaining connections is complex and should be designed carefully, since there is no central unit, available to monitor.

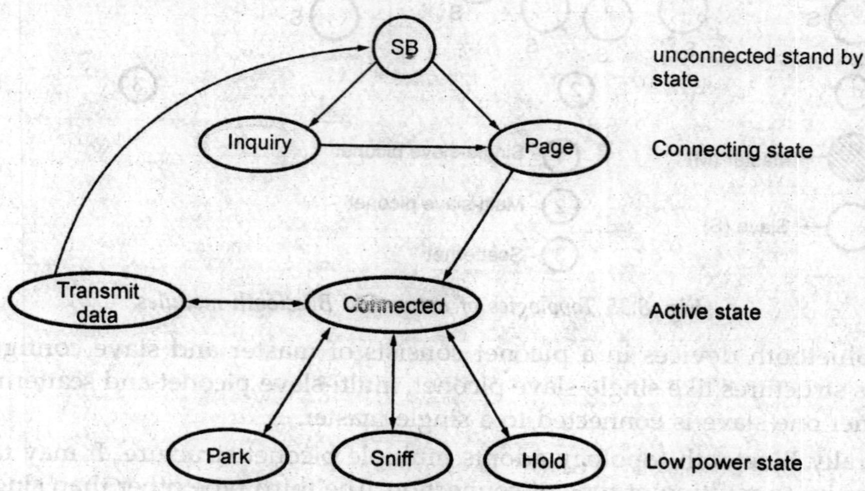

Fig. 8.37 Bluetooth "functional overview"

Bluetooth uses unique inquiry and page algorithm. In the state diagram given above in a piconet initially all the devices are in standby (SB) mode. Then one terminal becomes a 'M' terminal (master). It registers all the standby (SB) terminals and then it becomes a slave (S) terminal, during the time of inquiry. Using the FHS packets timing of all the 'S' terminals are sent to 'M' terminals. Connection starts with that of a 'PAGE' message sending the information about 'M' terminal to 'S' terminal and then a communication session follows. The hold, sniff and park are three power saving methods. In hold mode the data transfer will restart. During the sniff mode the slave (S) mode carefully listens to piconet, and in the park mode a device will give up its MAC address and it will be still synchronized with that of the piconet of the setup. A device in this park mode will not be a part of broadcasting phase.

The connection establishment thus in Bluetooth specification is more effective though it is an ad-hoc mode.

8.21 SECURITY IN BLUETOOTH

In Bluetooth there are several security mechanisms available. At first the transmitters make use of lowest power needed for receiving their data.

It uses channel hopping technique that can provide additional security measure so that snooping on data stream is difficult. Due to faster hopping rate it is tough to 'sniff' data stream off of a single channel. In otherwords due to faster hopping rate it is difficult to predict hopping sequence, though hopping technique is not a security mechanism. The security modes, security components and protocols are dealt below.

- **Bluetooth security modes**

  There are three modes of Bluetooth security. They are,

  (*i*) Non-secure mode

  (*ii*) Service-level enforced security

  (*iii*) Link-level enforced security.

- (*i*) **Non-secure mode :** If the Bluetooth device is in this mode it will not initiate any security procedure. This mode is used for public use device (e.g. walk-up printer).
- (*ii*) **Service-level enforced security :** If the device is in this mode allows access to itself and it depends on service request. A PC may be permit an user to download files whereas it may not allow to read its own files.
- (*iii*) **Link-level enforced security :** If the device is in this mode it requires authorization and authentication for any use.

Bluetooth standard defines security to both, it's devices and services. The security levels in Bluetooth are classified as

→ Trusted level

→ Untrusted level

In untrusted level the untrusted devices does not allow access to all services whereas trusted devices allows access to all the services. Also the Bluetooth services lies in one of the three security levels namely,

→ Open level
→ Authentication level.
→ Authentication and authorization level.

In first case services are open to all the devices. But in second case it requires authentication from devices. In third case both authentication and authorization are needed from devices.

8.21.1 Basic Bluetooth Security Mechanism

The structure of security components and protocols in Bluetooth are shown in below diagram.

Bluetooth uses two main keys, known as link-layer keys and encryption keys.

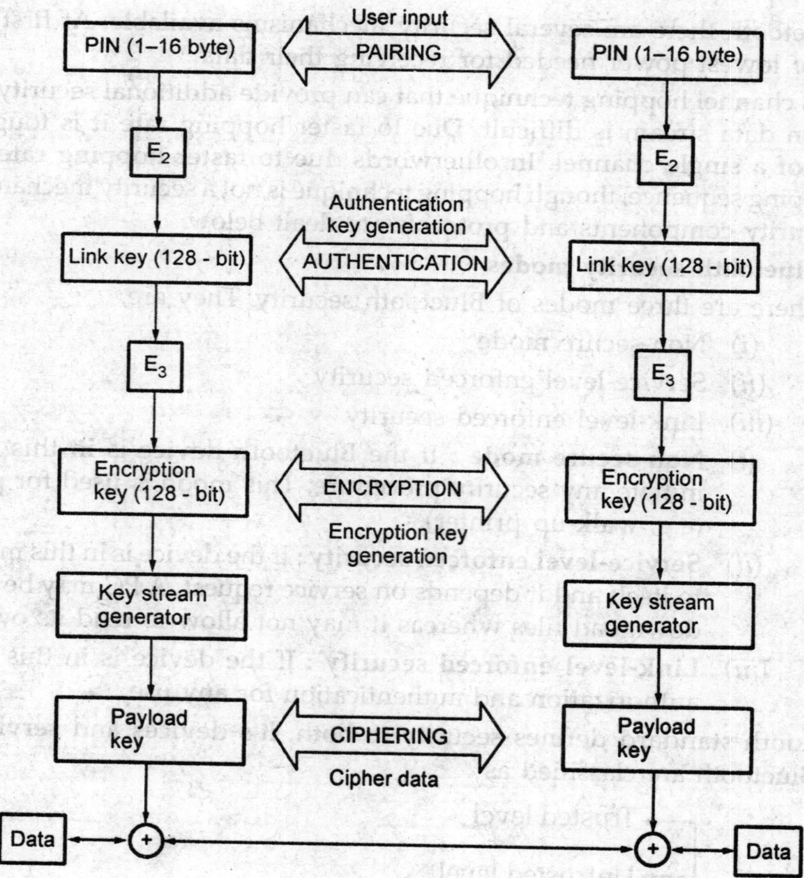

Fig. 8.38 Security components and protocols of Bluetooth

Link-layer key lifetimes are of any one of the type temporary or semipermanent.

The temporary Bluetooth keys are used only in current session. In point-to-multipoint communication temporary keys are used. The semipermanent keys can be applied after the current sessions for authenticating Bluetooth devices.

For link-layer security there are four entities available :

1. A 128-bit pseudorandom private key is used for authentication.
2. A 48-bit device address unique for every device is followed.
3. A 128-bit pseudorandom number is being generated by device.
4. An 8-bit to 128-bit private key for encryption is used.

The security algorithms uses publicly available device identify. For every transaction a random number (new) is generated by Bluetooth chip. Key management is a main task in security and it is fully assigned to higher layer software.

There are systematic steps followed in security architecture of Bluetooth.

The first step is called as pairing is done if two Bluetooth devices are meeting for first time. To develop trust user enters a secret PIN into two devices, and it is of length up to 16 byte. Depending on the parameters,

(*i*) PIN

(*ii*) Device address

(*iii*) Random number generated, many keys shall be computed that can be used as link key for authentication purpose. These link keys are stored in persistent storage. Based on the link key the authentication which is a challenge response process takes place. It is followed by random number generation and verification of device address. During authentication values are generated based on link key. The encryption key is generated during encryption stage of the security architecture of Bluetooth.

The encryption key has size of maximum of 128-bits and it can generated individually for every transmission.

Depending on the device address encryption key and current clock period a 'payload key' is then generated for cliphering purpose of user data. This payload key consists of a stream of pseudorandom bits format. The process of ciphering is just a 'XOR' operation done for user data with payload key value.

Thus in Bluetooth high level of security is possible. But there are also some demerits incorporated like fixed PIN's quality of random number generators are not specified etc.

8.22 LINK MANAGEMENT

The Link Manager Protocol (LMP) can manage different aspects of radio link between the slave and master and the setting of current parameter of devices. The LMP enhances baseband functionality but the higher layers can directly access baseband. The functions covered by LMP are given below.

1. Synchronization
2. Authentication pairing devices and encryption under security.
3. Capability negotiation.

4. Quality of service negotiation.
5. Link supervision.
6. Power control
7. State and transmission mode change.

There are four main baseband states available in Bluetooth. A simple structure of it is shown below.

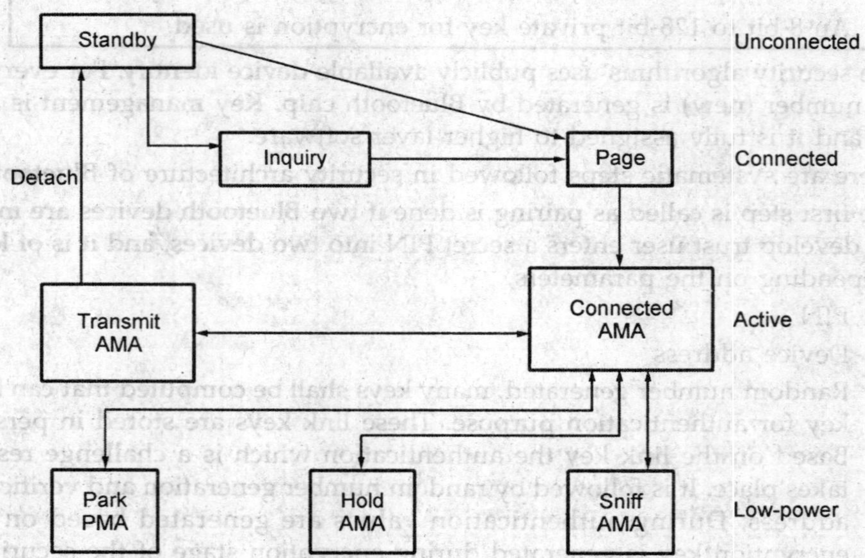

Fig. 8.39 Baseband states of a Bluetooth device

Some of the typical transitions are shown. Each device that is not taking part in piconet but not in off state is in standby by mode. The inquiry mode takes place in two ways. It is either when the device need to establish a piconet or if a device wants to watch for any change that may happen.

In the page state there are also two functions defined and they include setting up a piconet and starting the hopping sequence. The slave should co-ordinate and respond to master in piconets with synchronization. The connection state consists of both active state and there low power states. This low power state includes park, sniff and hold modes. A master should synchronize with slaves at regular time periods.

In active state slaves participates in piconet transmissions effectively. All the devices that are active should have a 3-bit address known as "Active Member Address"(AMA).

Through the delach procedure the device can again enter into standby state at the end.

Note : For power saving Bluetooth device goes into any one of three low power states namely sniff, hold or park state.

8.23 BLUETOOTH NETWORKING

The key features of Bluetooth including its operation on 79 channels in 2.4 GHz band with a carrier spacing of 1 MHz and hopping techniques the architecture of Bluetooth protocol stack enables an effective networking procedures. All the devices has networking capability acting as master or slave.

A piconet as discussed earlier is consists of slaves and a master. If more one piconets are linked it forms a scatternet. One device in a piconet acts as master (M) and other devices acts as slaves (S). An overview of formation of piconet is shown here. A master device sends its clock and device address (ID) to other devices. All other devices also has same networking capacity. They can act as master or slave. The unit that establish piconet acts as master and automatically other devices becomes slaves.

The master sends its device ID and the hopping pattern is determined by the device ID and it is globally 48-bit unique identifier whereas phase in hopping pattern is decided by master's clock. When the internal clock of other device is adjusted according to master it participates in that piconet. The devices are allocated with a 3-bit active member address (AMA).

The other parked devices has a 8-bit parked member address (PMA).

The devices in standby mode do not require an address.

The users in one piconet networking has same hopping sequence.

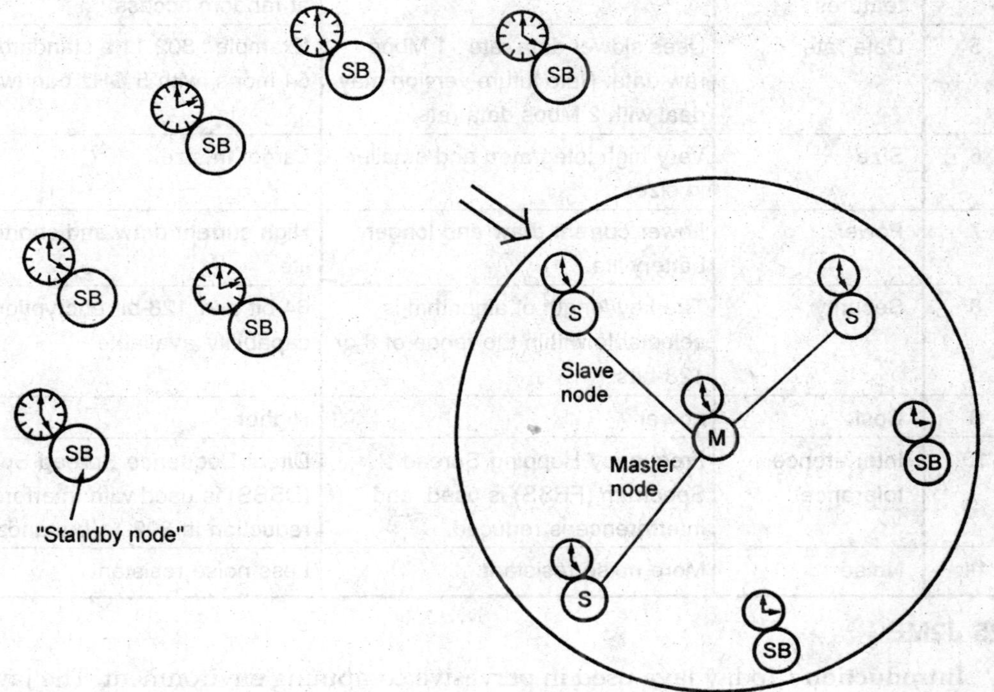

Fig. 8.39 Formation of Bluetooth Piconet in Networking

All the users shares same 1 MHz frequency channel.

If the internal clock of other devices is adjusted according to clock of master that device is connected to master as in figure, and it will take part in the piconet.

Atlast if the number of piconet formed are high the throughput of the network may gradually drop. To avoid it few piconets are combined and scatternets are formed. The piconets in a scatternet must exchange data. Many piconets can also overlap coverage simultaneously. An efficient networking is decided by formation of piconets and scatternets with real effective data transfer among them.

8.24 COMPARISON OF WIRELESS LAN AND BLUETOOTH TECHNOLOGY

Sr. No.	Parameter	Bluetooth technology	Wireless LAN (WLAN)
1	Developed for	Helps cable replacement with limited wireless network capabilities.	Office WLAN/Campus/home.
2	Distance	For 10 meter, 100 meter distances with high transmit power.	For 15-150 meters/300 meters for indoor and outdoors areas.
3	Frequency	2.4 GHz, 1600 hops/sec radio, 1 MHz channels over 79 MHz.	Example : 802.11a-5 GHz in 20 MHz channels.
4	Network features	It is Ad-hoc in nature.	No usage of piconets. It is effective at random access.
5	Data rate	Uses slower data rate : 1 Mbps raw data. Rate future version may deal with 2 Mbps data rate.	Example : 802.11 a standard : 24 to 54 mops, with 5 GHz bandwidth.
6	Size	Very high integrated and smaller in size.	Larger in size.
7	Power	Lower current draw and longer battery life.	High current draw and shorter battery life.
8	Security	The key length of algorithm is selectable within the range of 8 or 128-bits.	64-bit and 128-bit encryption capability available.
9	Cost	Lower	Higher
10	Interference tolerance	Frequency Hopping Spread Spectrum (FHSS) is used, and interference is reduced.	Direct Sequence Spread Spectrum (DSSS) is used with interference reduction in 802.11 b standard.
11	Noise	More noise resistant.	Less noise resistant.

8.25 J2ME

Introduction : Today Java used in pervasive computing environment. The Java 2 Micro Edition (J2ME) is introduced to overcome the limitations of pervasive computing devices. Java application environments can be defined on this platform.

Profile of J2ME includes language subsets for various groups of devices. J2ME is one of the popular micro edition used for many applications.

Micro Edition

Java 2 Micro Edition includes

(*i*) Virtual machines

(*ii*) Tools for deployment purposes and for device configuration.

8.25.1 Concept of J2ME

The process of selection of subsets of Java language particularly for specific device class is the basic concept of J2ME where each subset is called as a "profile".

Every profile is based on any one of the two configurations mentioned below. They are as follows :

1. Connected Device Configuration (CDC)
2. Connected Limited Device Configuration (CLDC)

1. Connected Device Configuration (CDC)

It is used for devices which have a minimum of 512 kb memory used to run Java. It can provide high bandwidth network connectivity.

2. Connected Limited Device Configuration (CLDC)

It is used for devices with 128 kb memory to run Java with limitations in network bandwidth, power supply and user interface.

The software stack architecture of J2ME is shown below.

It consists of specific and native applications, profile classes application, specific classes, J2ME configuration classes, operating system and the mobile unit/device.

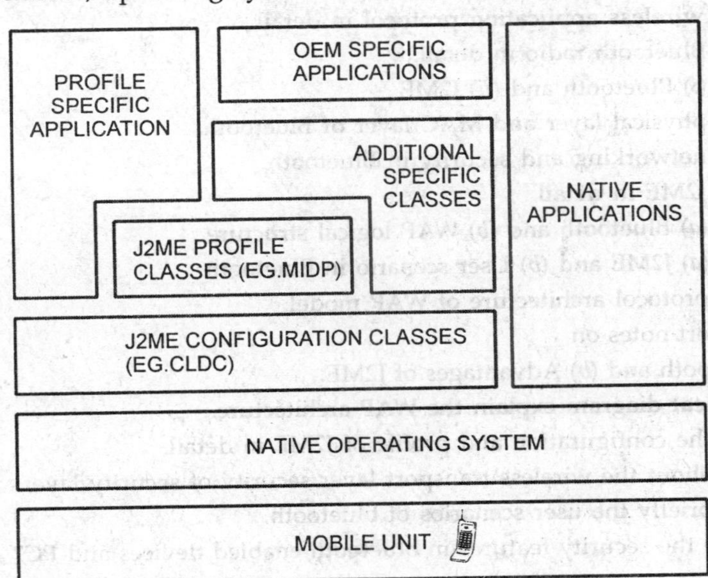

Fig. 8.31 Software stack architecture of J2ME

In the Fig. 8.30 the Mobile Information Device Profile (MIDP) is to define Java functionality, that fit the required screen size and also obeys memory constraints of Personal Digital Assistants (PDA's). In J2ME the configurations and profiles are specified by Java Community Process (JCP). The working groups develops profile currently for several applications. It includes ;

(*i*) Handheld computers.
(*ii*) Wireless mobile phones and communicators
(*iii*) Automotive systems.
(*iv*) Set-top boxes and interactive televisions
(*v*) Network-connected consumer devices that use graphic user interface (GUI)

Thus J2ME is user-friendly and applied mainly for mobile computing.

REVIEW QUESTIONS

1. What is known as WAP?
2. Draw the WAP logical structure.
3. Write short note on protocols.
4. What are the advantages of WAP?
5. What are the applications of Bluetooth?
6. Write short note on Bluetooth.
7. Write short note on WAP.
8. What is known J2ME?
9. What are the advantages of J2ME?
10. What are the applications of Bluetooth?
11. Explain wireless application protocol in detail.
12. Explain Bluetooth radio in detail. -
13. Explain (*i*) Bluetooth and (*ii*) J2ME.
14. Explain physical layer and MAC layer of Bluetooth.
15. Explain networking and security in Bluetooth.
16. Explain J2ME in detail.
17. Explain (*a*) Bluetooth and (*b*) WAP logical structure.
18. Explain (*a*) J2ME and (*b*) User scenario in Bluetooth.
19. Explain protocol architecture of WAP model.
20. Write short notes on
    (*a*) Bluetooth and (*b*) Advantages of J2ME.
21. With a neat diagram explain the WAP architecture.
22. Discuss the configuration and profile of J2ME in detail.
23. Discuss about the wireless transport layer security of security layer.
24. Discuss briefly the user scenarios of bluetooth.
25. What are the security features in bluetooth enabled devices and PC?

❑❑❑

MOBILE COMPUTING

A - Question Bank

B - Solved Problems

A - Question Bank

Q. 1. *Define a cell.*

Ans. The smallest geographical area covered by wireless communication is said to be a cell.

Q. 2. *What are the shapes related to a cell?*

Ans. In early days three shapes namely

(*a*) Circle

(*b*) Square

(*c*) Hexagon

Were suggested for a cell. But coverage of signal was very accurate with hexagonal shaped cells and in later stage it was taken as standard.

Q. 3. *Give an example for Non-co channel interference.*

Ans. Adjacent channel interference (ACI).

Q. 4. *What is an umbrella cell pattern?*

Ans. In a biggest cellular region say 'macrocell' there may be many small cells called as microcells and is known as umbrella cell pattern.

Q. 5. *What is use of an umbrella cell?*

Ans. In umbrella cell design signal strength is more and coverage of radio signal is high.

Q. 6. *What are the advantages of broadband cellular service?*

Ans. (*a*) Convenience

(*b*) Reduced cost.

Q. 7. *What is CDMA?*

Ans. It is a multiple access technique used for cellular communication and known as Code division multiple access.

Q. 8. *What is AMPS?*

Ans. The first generation (IG) cellular network was 'Advanced mobile phone system' denoted as AMPS.

Q. 9. *What is known as WAP?*

Ans. It is Wireless Application Protocol that is widely used for mobile communication technology.

Q. 10. *Define a signal.*

Ans. When a function is realizable it constitutes a signal.

Q. 11. *What is information bearing signal?*

Ans. Information is the message or original data. When a signal carries message it is said to be an information bearing signal.

Q. 12. *What is a periodic signal?*

Ans. In a signal if a particular signal pattern repeats over a time period systematically it is a periodic signal.

Q. 13. *What is a "Aperiodic" signal?*

Ans. In a signal if the same signal pattern does not repeat itself over a time period it is known as 'Aperiodic' signal.

Q. 14. *Give an example for a periodic and aperiodic signals.*

Ans. (*a*) periodic signal → $x(t + T) = x(t)$.

where $-\infty < t + \infty$

(*b*) Aperiodic signal → $x(t + T) \neq x(t)$.

Q. 15. *Differentiate analog and digital signals.*

Ans. If there is no discontinuity in a signal such a smooth signal is an analog signal. All the input signals are usually of analog in nature.

On the otherhand if there are discontinuities or break in the signal it is a digital signal. The signal strength varies in this signal. It is always better to have signals in digital format for processing.

Q. 16. *What is the importance of digital signals?*

Ans. The signal processing is better with digital signal formats (0's and 1's) where noise is minimized. Hence analog to digital converters are used to convert input analog signal to its equivalent digital signal and after processing the signal is again converted to original analog signal with digital to analog signal at the end entity for proper reception of the signal.

Q. 17. *Define wavelength.*

Ans. The wavelength of a signal represents its distance or range it takes for one cycle. It is denoted as 'λ'.

$$\text{Wavelength } \lambda = \frac{c}{f}$$

Where c → speed of light in free space which is 3×10^8 m/sec.

f → frequency in Hertz.

Q. 18. *Explain harmonics and fundamental frequency.*

Ans. Electromagnetic wave or electromagnetic signal constitutes many frequency components.

In this multiple frequencies the second and other frequencies are integer multiples of the first frequencies and known as harmonics where the first frequency is called as fundamental frequency.

Q. 19. *Define data rate.*

Ans. The data rate in communication represents the speed at which the message is transmitted.

Q. 20. *What is a bandwidth?*

Ans. Bandwidth is the range of frequencies and represented as $BW = f_2 - f_1$, where f_1 and f_2 are the first and last frequencies of the signal graph.

Q. 21. *Give an example for analog data.*

Ans. Audio signal is an example for analog data.

Q. 22. *Differentiate between signal and data.*

Ans. The term 'data' represents message or information where the signal is the representation of the data, and it is also termed as information bearing signal.

Q. 23. *Define attenuation.*

Ans. It is nothing but reduction in signal strength mainly at higher frequency ranges, and at receiving end this attenuated signal has reduced voltage levels.

Q. 24. *Tabulate two differences between analog and digital signals.*

Ans.

Analog signal	Digital signal
1. It is a continuously varying signal.	It is a regular sequence of voltage pulses.
2. Media used for signal propagation is like (*a*) Space propagation, (*b*) Copper wire media.	Media used for propagation is like (*a*) Copper wire medium.

Q. 25. *What is main advantage of digital signalling over analog signalling.*

Ans.
1. Noise interferences are less.
2. Cost is less.

Q. 26. *Give the equation for Nyquist Criterion.*

Ans.

$$C = 2B \log_2 M$$

Where $C \rightarrow$ Channel capacity.

$M \rightarrow$ Number of discrete signals.

$B \rightarrow$ Bandwidth.

Q. 27. *What is a channel capacity?*

Ans. In a communication the maximum possible data rate (speed) at which data can be transmitted is called as channel capacity.

Q. 28. *Tabulate and explain :*

(*a*) *Analog signal.*

(*b*) *Digital signal.*

(*c*) *Analog data.*

(*d*) *Digital data.*

Ans.

Type of Data	Digital Signal	Analog Signal
Analog data	Analog data can be encoded using a codec unit which produces digital bit streams.	The signal can occupy the same particular spectrum as analog data.
Digital data	Signal consists of two different levels as 0 and 1 (binary values).	Using modem units of digital data can be encoded to produce analog signals.

Q. 29. *What is 'digital data, analog signal'?*

Ans. It is related to the media that uses the signal. For example satellites and optical fibers relays (or propagates) analog type of signals.

Q. 30. *Define analog transmission.*

Ans. It refers to analog signal transmission where content may be analog data or digital data.

Q. 31. *Define digital transmission.*

Ans. It refers to digital signal transmission where the content has to be digital data combinations of 0's and 1's.

Q. 32. *Define Noise.*

Ans. Noise is an unwanted form of energy.

e.g. 1. Man made noise.

2. Industrial noise.

Q. 33. *Give the equation for signal to noise ratio.*

Ans. Signal to noise ratio (SNR) $= 10 \log_{10} \left(\frac{4\pi D}{\lambda}\right)^2$ dB

It is expressed in decibel units.

Q. 34. *Give the equation for loss (L) in microwave transmission.*

Ans. Loss $= L = 10 \log \left(\frac{4\pi D}{\lambda}\right)^2$ dB

Where D $\rightarrow$ Distance or range.

$\lambda \rightarrow$ Wavelength.

dB $\rightarrow$ Decibel units.

Q. 35. *What are the two links in satellite transmission?*

Ans. (*a*) Uplink

(*b*) Downlink

Q. 36. *What is a DTH?*

Ans. It is an application of satellite communication and called as 'direct to home'. It enhances television transmissions.

Q. 37. *Give four applications of satellites.*

Ans. (*a*) Private business networks (PBN).

(*b*) Television distributions (DTH/DBS).

(*c*) Communication applications like weather forecasting.

(*d*) Telephone transmissions with larger ranges.

Q. 38. *What are the types of transmission medium?*

Ans.

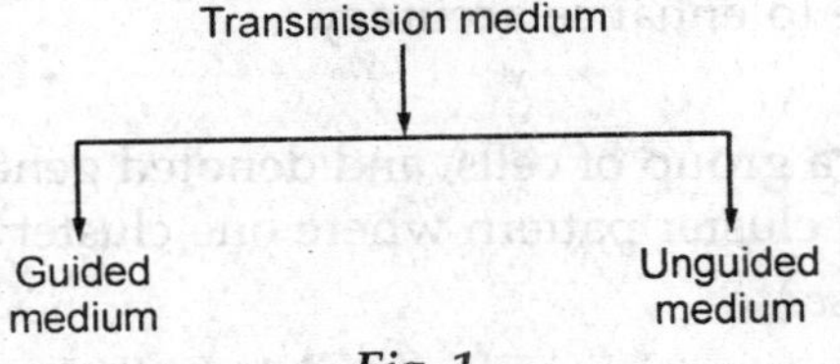

Fig. 1

Q. 39. *Differentiate guided and unguided medium.*

Ans. In guided medium the electromagnetic waves are guided by transmission medium. e.g. Copper coaxial cable.

In unguided medium the electromagnetic wave is not guided by the medium. e.g. The radiated energy is not guided in wireless communication.

Q. 40. *What is the normal operating range of frequency for cell phones?*

Ans. The operating frequency range for cell phones are 825 MHz to 845 MHz (approx).

Q. 41. *What are the frequency range of microwave transmission?*

Ans. The frequency of microwave transmissions are 2 GHz to 40 GHz.

Q. 42. *Draw the diagram of multiplexing.*

Ans.

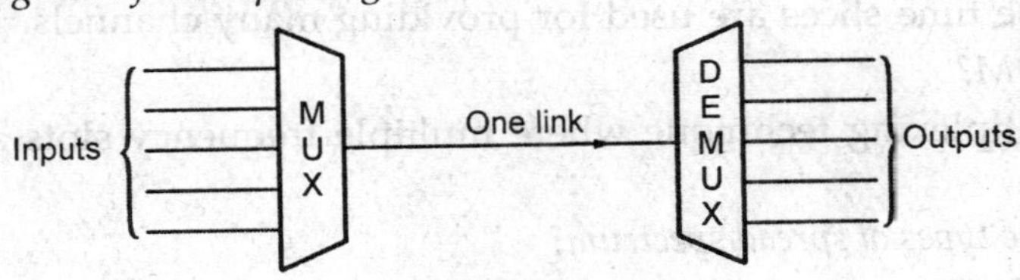

Fig. 2

Q. 43. *What is the principle used in multiplexers?*

Ans. The principle used in multiplexer is 'many to one' concept. Many inputs are combined as one link or one output from a MUX unit where a DEMUX unit at the receiver reproduces the same many units at the end entity.

Q. 44. *What are the important multiplexing schemes?*

Ans.

Multiplexing

Frequency Division Multiplexing (FDM) | Time Division Multiplexing (TDM) | Code Division Multiplexing (CDM)

Fig. 3

Q. 45. *What are the multiple access schemes?*

(*a*) FDMA

(*b*) TDMA

(*c*) CDMA

Q. 46. *Define guard band.*

Ans. It is a unused (dummy) frequency inserted with actual spectrum to reduce adjacent channel interference to enhance accuracy.

Q. 47. *Define cluster.*

Ans. It is a term used for a group of cells, and denoted generally as 'N'. If N = 7 then it is termed as seven cell cluster pattern where one cluster consists of seven cells with it.

Q. 48. *What is frequency reuse?*

Ans. The same carrier frequencies are reused in cellular communication for effective spectrum utilization.

Q. 49. *Draw the seven all (N = 7) cluster pattern.*

Ans.

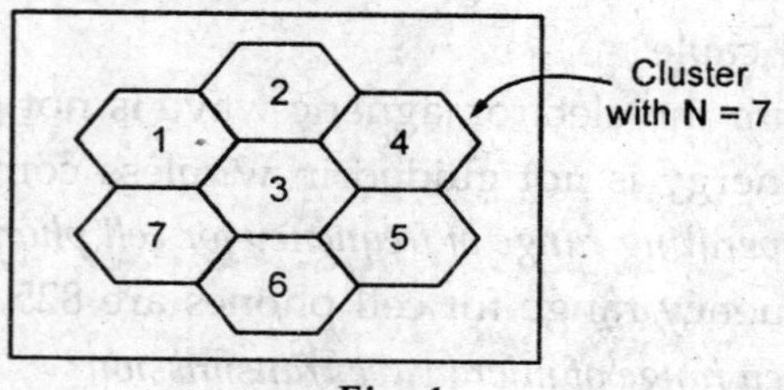

Fig. 4

Q. 50. *Define TDM.*

Ans. In TDM the time slices are used for providing many channels.

Q. 51. *What is FDM?*

Ans. It is a multiplexing technique where multiple frequency slots are providing many channels.

Q. 52. *What are the types of spread spectrum?*

Ans. (*a*) FHSS

(*b*) DSSS.

Q. 53. *What is DSSS?*

Ans. It is direct sequence spread spectrum.

Q. 54. *What is FHSS?*

Ans. It is frequency hopping spread spectrum.

Q. 55. *Differentiate DSSS and* FHSS.

Ans.

DSSS	FHSS
Each bit in transmission can be represent as multiple bits.	Signal is transmitted in random series at fixed time intervals. Synchronization between transmitter and receiver is a must.

Q. 56. *Represent FHSS concept in a graph.*

Ans.

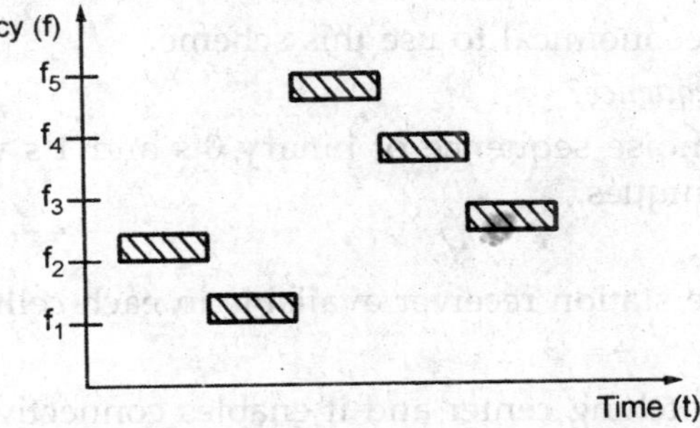

Fig. 5

Q. 57. *What is the advantage of spread spectrum?*

Ans. Security is guaranteed in communication, channels with this technique.

Q. 58. *Draw the spread spectrum diagram.*

Ans.

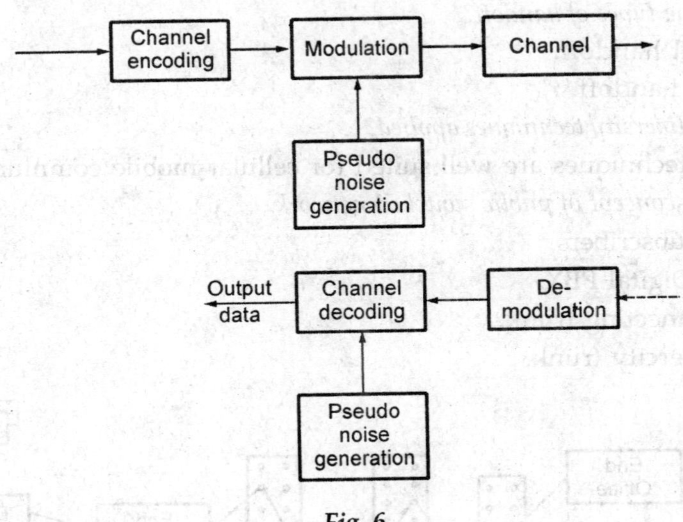

Fig. 6

Q. 59. *Define spread spectrum.*

Ans. The signal or message is modulated with a sequence of digits or spread code termed as pseudocode and this stretched signal improves higher safety (encryption) of data.

Q. 60. *Give one application of spread spectrum.*

Ans. FHSS technique can be used in defense applications.

Q. 61. *What shift keying technique is mainly used in cellular transmission?*

Ans. Gaussian minimum shift keying (GMSK) scheme.

Q. 62. *How GMSK signal is generated?*

Ans. When a MSK signal is passed through a gaussian filter GMSK is generated.

Q. 63. *What is the merit and demerit of CDMA technique?*

Ans. - It provides interference free cellular communication.
- It is not economical to use this scheme.

Q. 64. *What is a PN sequence?*

Ans. It is a pseudonoise sequence of binary 0's and 1's which can be used for spread spectrum techniques.

Q. 65. *Define BTS.*

Ans. BTS is the base station receiver available in each cellular region.

Q. 66. *What is a MSC?*

Ans. It is mobile switching center and it enables connectivity between BTS and PSTN.

Q. 67. *What is known as 'handoff?'*

Ans. Handoff is a principle used to continue the call established in mobile communication. When the subscriber is towards the cell boundary the signal strength reduces by which the BTS of that cell handover the call to the next BTS of another cell where the subscriber enters.

Q. 68. *What are the types of handoff?*

Ans. (*a*) Hard handoff.
(*b*) Soft handoff.

Q. 69. *Where are diversity techniques applied?*

Ans. Diversity techniques are well suited for cellular mobile communication.

Q. 70. *Draw basic concept of public switched network.*

Ans. S_1, S_2 → Subscribers.
DPBX → Digital PBX.
CT → Connecting trunk.
ICT → Intercity trunk.

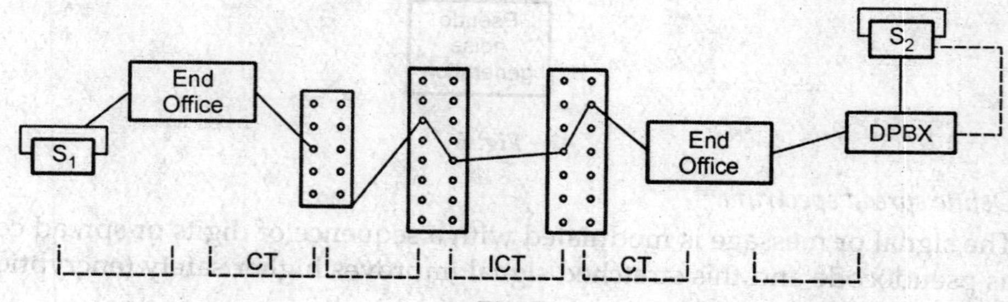

Fig. 7

Q. 71. *What are the main components of the public telecommunication network?*

Ans. (*a*) Subscribers.
(*b*) Exchange
(*c*) Subscriber lines.
(*d*) Trunks.

Q. 72. *How many wires are involved in a telephonic conversation?*

Ans. In wired telephony system a pair of wires are used for handling a subscriber call.

Q. 73. *What are the three types of switching methods?*

(*a*) Circuit switching,

(*b*) Message switching,

(c) Packet switching.

Q. 74. *Give the demerits of circuit switching in data transmission.*

Ans. (*a*) This scheme is inefficient in a terminal that hosts data connections where most of the time the line is idle.

(*b*) Constant datarate is used in this scheme and it degrades network utility because all the time the end devices have to stick on with same datarates.

Q. 75. *Give two size of packets in data transmission.*

Ans.

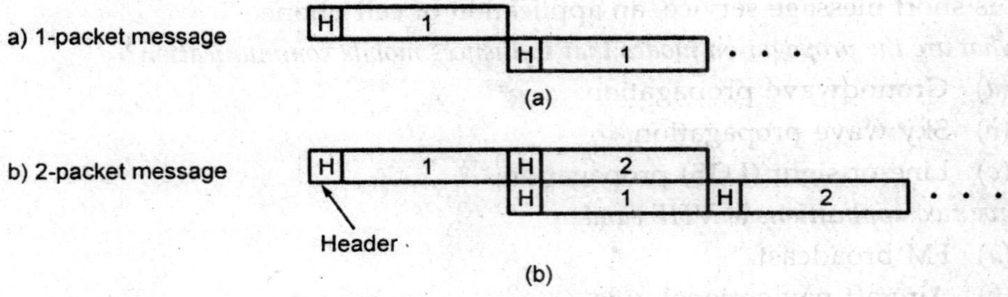

Fig. 8

Q. 76. *Draw the ATM connection setup.*

Ans.

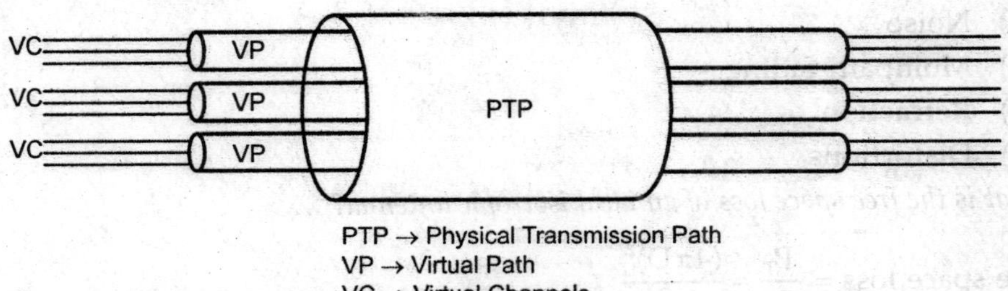

Fig. 9

Q. 77. *What is VCC?*

Ans. The logical connection in the asynchronous transfer mode is called as VCC.

Q. 78. *What is a VP?*

Ans. It is the virtual path, that describes unidirectional transport of the ATM cells, which belongs to a virtual channels.

Q. 79. *Give abbreviation of VCI and VPC.*

Ans. VCI - Virtual Channel Identifier.

VPC - Virtual Path Connection.

Q. 80. *Give ATM cell format.*

Ans.

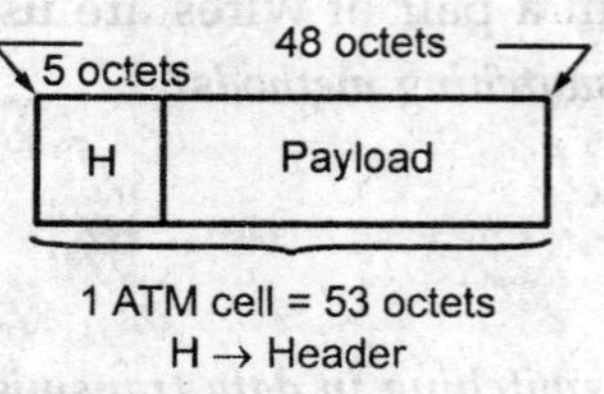

Fig. 10

Q. 81. *What are the two advantages of mobile communication over wired telephonic communication?*

Ans. (*a*) It is possible to locate the subscriber wherever he is.

(*b*) Communication gap between different parts of world is eliminated.

Q. 82. *What is SMS?*

Ans. It is short message service, an application of cell phone.

Q. 83. *What are the propagation modes that influences mobile communication?*

Ans. (*a*) Groundwave propagation

(*b*) Sky wave propagation.

(*c*) Line of sight (LOS) propagation.

Q. 84. *Give two applications of VHF band.*

Ans. (*a*) FM broadcast.

(*b*) Aircraft navigational aids.

Q. 85. *What are the demerits of LOS wireless transmissions?*

Ans. (*a*) Free space loss

(*b*) Noise

(*c*) Multipath fading

(*d*) Refraction

(*e*) Distortions

Q. 86. *What is the free space loss of an ideal isotropic antenna?*

Ans. Free space loss $= \frac{P_T}{P_R} = \frac{(4\pi D)^2}{\lambda^2}$

Where $P_T \rightarrow$ Signal power at transmitting antenna.

$P_R \rightarrow$ Signal power at receiving antenna.

$\lambda \rightarrow$ Carrier wavelength.

$D \rightarrow$ Propagation distance.

Q. 87. *What is known as intermodulation noise?*

Ans. When some transmission medium is shared by signals with different frequencies it may result in a noise called as intermodulation noise.

Q. 88. *Give the significance of E_b/N_o.*

Ans. The bit energy to output noise ratio is important in mobile communication where the bit error rate of data is a function of this above mentioned ratio. It is generally expressed in decibels.

Q. 89. *What is known as multipath?*

Ans. When signal from a cell phone emerges due to many obstacles it radiates in many directions and finally reaches its base station receiver and viceversa. Such multiple signals takes multipaths to reach the base station or the cell phone.

Q. 90. *What are the propagation mechanisms?*

Ans. (*a*) Reflection.

(*b*) Diffraction.

(*c*) Scattering.

Q. 91. *What are types of fading?*

Ans. (*a*) Fast fading.

(*b*) Slow fading.

(*c*) Flat fading.

(*d*) Selective fading.

Q. 92. *Draw the 10 packet message structure.*

Ans.

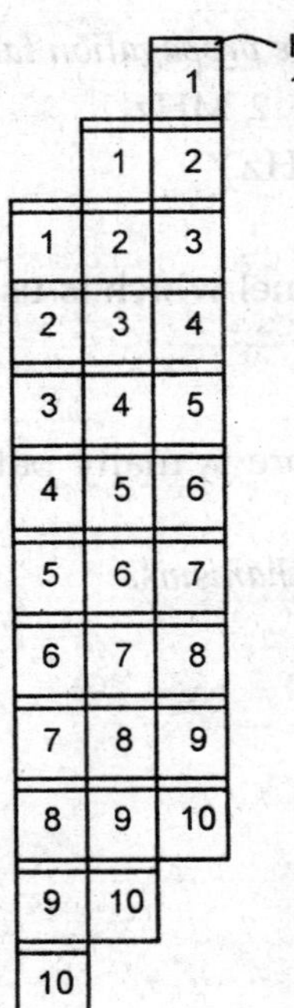

Fig. 11

Q. 93. *Give two modes of data transfer.*

Ans. (*a*) Synchronous transfer mode (STM).

(*b*) Asynchronous transfer mode (ATM).

Q. 94. *Give the similarity of ATM with, packet switching.*

Ans. Asynchronous transfer mode (ATM) is also known as 'cell relay' which resembles packet switching scheme.

Q. 95. *What is the frequency band used in cellular communication?*

Ans. UHF-ULTRA high frequency range.
(300 to 3000 MHz).

Q. 96. *What is a LOS propagation?*

Ans. LOS is line of sight propagation.

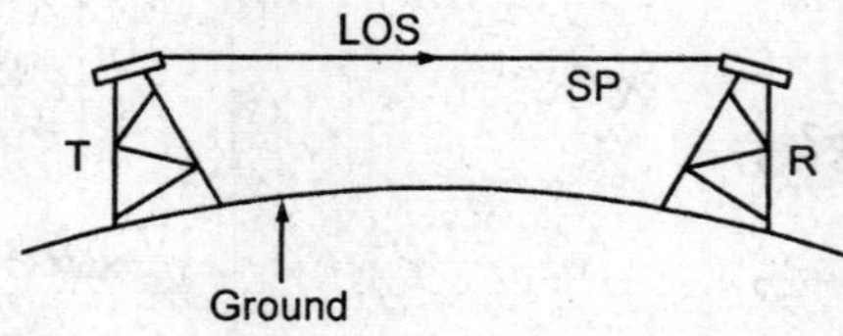

Fig. 12

T, R → Transmit and receive antennas.
SP → Signal propagation.

Q. 97. *At what frequencies groundwave and sky wave propagation takes place?*

Ans. (*a*) Groundwave propagation → below 2 MHz.
(*b*) Skywave propagation → 2 to 30 MHz.

Q. 98. *What is AWGN channel?*

Ans. It is Additive White Gaussian Noise channel which is used for analysis of multipath fading and noise in the mobile channel.

Q. 99. *When does Rayleigh fading occur?*

Ans. Rayleigh fading will take place when there is many paths between the transmitter and receiver.

Q. 100. *Give two examples for error compensation mechanisms.*

Ans. (*a*) Forward error correction.
(*b*) Adaptive equalization.

Q. 101. *Give two diversity techniques.*

Ans. (*a*) Time diversity.
(*b*) Space diversity.

Q. 102. *What are the basic shift keying methods?*

Ans. (*i*) Amplitude shift keying
(*ii*) Frequency shift keying
(*iii*) Phase shift keying

Q. 103. *How many signal levels are possible in QPSK?*

Ans. Four levels (00, 01, 10, 11) are possible with QPSK scheme.

Q. 104. *In minimum shift keying technique what is the value of* β?

Ans. In minimum shift keying (MSK) scheme under FSK scheme, the $\beta = 0.5$.

Q. 105. *What are two types of angle modulation?*

Ans. (*a*) Frequency modulation.

(*b*) Phase modulation.

Q. 106. *Define phase modulation.*

Ans. In phase modulation the phase of the carrier signal is varied in accordance with that of the modulating signal.

$$\phi(t) = N_p \, m(t)$$

Where N_p represents the phase modulation index

m(t) represents the message signal.

Q. 107. *What are the wireless LAN's standards and their corresponding frequencies used for US and Japan?*

Ans.

Wireless LAN's	Japan	US
	IEEE 802.11 f ≃ 2471 to 2497 MHz	IEEE 802.11 f ≃ 2400 to 2483 Mhz

Q. 108. *Give two user scenarios in wireless piconets.*

Ans. (*a*) Bridging of networks.

(*b*) Support of ad hoc networking.

Q. 109. *What is a Bluetooth piconet?*

Ans. Many devices using same hopping sequence of course with same phase constitutes a Bluetooth piconet.

Q. 110. *What is the aim of Bluetooth technology?*

Ans. The Bluetooth technology mainly points towards developing ad hoc piconets where 'ad hoc' is a term used for "applicable to that place" with limited coverage area.

Q. 111. *Give few advantages of Bluetooth technology.*

Ans. (*a*) Possible to represent the technology in a single chip.

(*b*) Low-cost.

(*c*) Radio based wireless network technology.

Q. 112. *What are the main services offered by Bluetooth?*

Ans. (*a*) Synchronous Connection-oriented Link (SCO).

(*b*) Asynchronous Connection less Link (ACL).

Q. 113. *Draw the format of a Bluetooth packet sent within a slot.*

Ans.

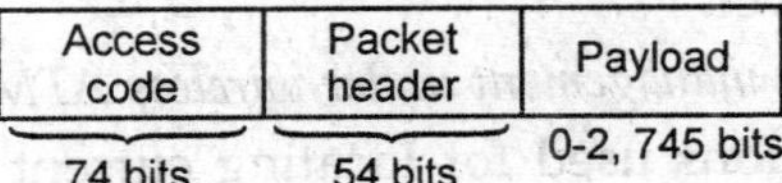

Fig. 13

Q. 114. *Draw the format of a Bluetooth packet header.*

Ans.

MAC addr	TYPE	Flow	ACK Number	SEQ Number	HEC	
3	4	1	1	1	8	bits

Fig. 13 (a)

Q. 115. *What is a scatternet?*

Ans. A group of piconets constitutes a scatternet.

Q. 116. *What is the demerit of scatternet?*

Ans. If two or more piconets use the same carrier frequency (f_c) for a particular slot, then there is a chance of collision and this may degrade the quality of information.

Q. 117. *What is WATM?*

Ans. It is wireless ATM. A special forum formed as wireless ATM working group, in the year 1996.

Q. 118. *What is a RAL and write short note about it?*

Ans. It is Random Access Layer under wireless ATM which includes wireless media access, handover issues, wireless data link control etc.

Q. 119. *Give three functions of wireless mobile terminal side.*

Ans. (*a*) Mobile Management Function (MMF).

(*b*) Identity Management Function (IMF).

(*c*) Call control and Connection Control Function (CCF).

Q. 120. *Give three requirements which are specific to RAL in wireless ATM.*

Ans. (*a*) Packet size.

(*b*) Data rate (≅ 25 Mbps).

(*c*) Transmit power (minimum 100 mW EIRP).

Q. 121. *What are the layers of RAL in wireless ATM?*

Ans. (*a*) Physical layer.

(*b*) Medium Access control layer.

(*c*) Logical link control layer.

Q. 122. *What are types of handover possible with WATM?*

Ans. (*a*) Hard handover.

(*b*) Terminal Initiated.

(*c*) Network Initiated.

(*d*) Network controlled.

(*e*) Network initiated and terminal assisted.

(*f*) Forward handover.

(g) Backward handover.

Q. 123. *What is known as location management under wireless ATM?*

Ans. There are several functions used for locating current position of mobile terminal. Also security features like authentication, privacy has to be considered. As a whole the required functions are bunched together and known as location management.

Q. 124. *What are the three part of mobile QoS?*

Ans. 1. Wired QoS.

2. Wireless QoS

3. Handover QoS.

Q. 125. *What are types of QoS supported by handover protocols?*

Ans. (*a*) Hard handover QoS.

(*b*) Soft handover QoS.

Q. 126. *What feature is highly important for mobile network?*

Ans. In mobile computing environment assigning a "topologically correct address" is very important.

Q. 127. *What are the requirements of mobile IP standard's development?*

Ans. (*a*) Transparency.

(*b*) Compatibility.

(*c*) Scalability and efficiency.

(*d*) Security.

Q. 128. *Define home and forging network under mobile IP.*

Ans. (*i*) Home network :

It is a subnet, that the mobile node belongs to with respect to the IP address. But within the home network no mobile IP is expected.

(*ii*) Foreign network :

It is different from home network and it mentions the current subnet to which the mobile node belongs to.

Q. 129. *What are the types of addresses in mobile IP?*

Ans.

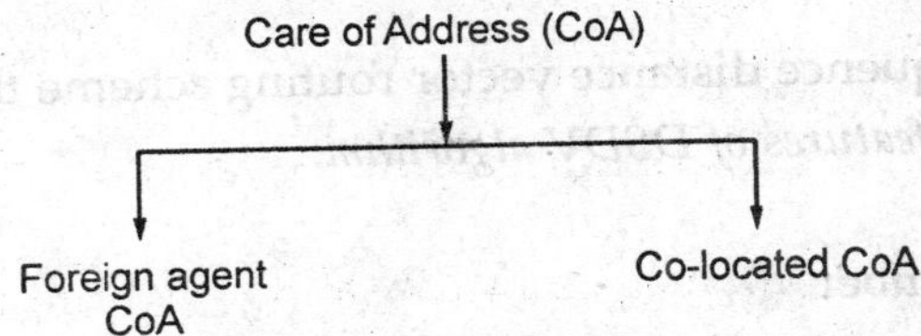

Fig. 14

Q. 130. *Draw the method of indirect registration of a mobile node in a mobile IP.*

Ans.

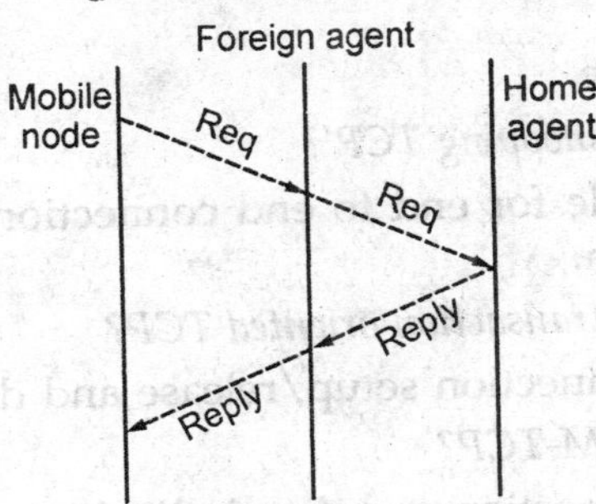

Fig. 15

Q. 131. *Draw the direct registration of a mobile node in a mobile IP.*

Ans.

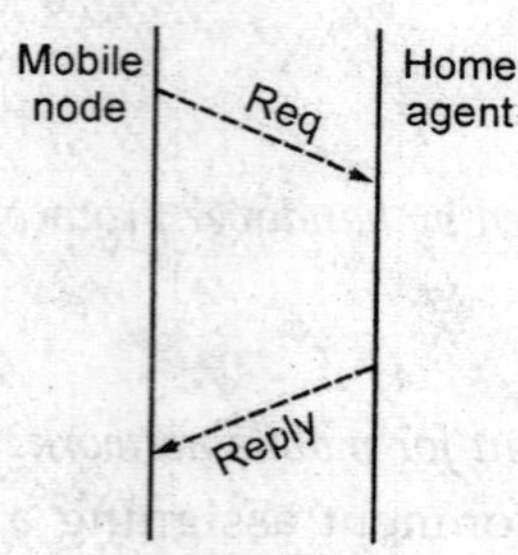

Fig. 16

Q. 132. *Give two examples of mobile IP.*

Ans. (*a*) IPV4 (IP version 4)

(*b*) IPV6 (IP version 6)

Q. 133. *Draw an example of Ad hoc network.*

Ans.

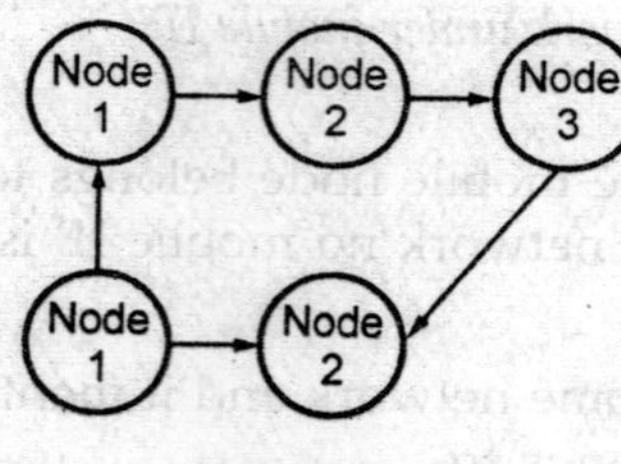

Fig. 17

Q. 134. *What is DSDV?*

Ans. It is destination sequence distance vector routing scheme that suits ad hoc networks.

Q. 135. *Give two important features of DSDV algorithm.*

Ans. It adds

(*a*) Sequence number.

(*b*) Damping (Transient changes in topology is encountered).

Q. 136. *What are the two routing schemes present in dynamic source routing?*

Ans. (*a*) Route discovery.

(*b*) Route maintenance.

Q. 137. *What is the advantage of 'snooping TCP'?*

Ans. Transparency is available for end to end connection and MAC integration is also possible in this approach.

Q. 138. *What is the mechanism of transaction oriented TCP?*

Ans. It combines both the connection setup/release and data transmission function.

Q. 139. *What is the mechanism of M-TCP?*

Ans. It mainly splits TCP connection and can choke the sender.

Q. 140. *What is the advantage of M-TCP?*

Ans. M-TCP properly maintains the end to end semantics. It can also handle long term and frequent disconnections.

Q. 141. *What is the demerit of a transaction oriented TCP?*

Ans. (*i*) It is not transparent.

(*ii*) Some changes in TCP are required.

Q. 142. *Give two examples of TCP protocols related to space communication.*

Ans. (*a*) Space communication protocol standards (SCPS).

(*b*) SCPS-transport protocol (SCPS-TP).

Q. 143. *Define HTTP.*

Ans. **The hypertext transfer protocol (HTTP) used for data transfer between the clients and servers. It is basically stateless, application level and lightweight protocol.**

Q. 144. *What is a "Ficus"?*

Ans. It is distributed file system that is not based on client/server.

Q. 145. *What is a "MIO-NFS"?*

Ans. It is system mobile integration of NFS and an extension of network file system. It applies a pessimistic approach with the tokens controlling access to files.

Q. 146. *What are modes that are supported by "MIO-NFS"?*

Ans. (*a*) Connected mode.

(*b*) Loosely connected mode.

(*c*) Disconnected mode.

Q. 147. *Give two demerits of HTTP in networking environment.*

Ans. (*a*) Caching.

(*b*) Bandwidth and delay.

Q. 148. *What is HTML?*

Ans. HTML is hypertext markup language and it is used to describe the webpage contents.

Q. 149. *What are the main solution of a wireless application protocol forum?*

Ans.

1. Scalable (compatible with customer needs).
2. Efficient (providing appropriate QoS).
3. Interoperable (Enabling various n/w softwares and terminal from different vendors to interact).
4. Reliable (provision of service deployment).
5. Secure (To increase integrity of user data).

Q. 150. *Give abbreviation of WSP and WAE.*

Ans. WSP-Wireless Session Protocol.

WAE-Wireless Application Environment.

Q. 151. *What are the classes of wireless transaction protocol?*

Ans. Please refer Fig. 18 on next page.

Three classes

Class 0 - Provides unreliable message transfer without resultant message.
Class 1 - Provides message transfer without reliable result
Class 2 - Provides message transfer with reliable result

Fig. 18

Q. 152. *What is the special of WTP?*

Ans. This protocol has the facilities of providing user acknowledgment or an automatic acknowledgment by a WTP entity.

Q. 153. *Write short note on WSP.*

Ans. It is wireless session protocol. It can function on top of datagram service WDP or transaction service WTP. The WSP can provide high security whenever required.

Q. 154. *Give three features of WSP.*

Ans. (*a*) Session management.

(*b*) Content encoding.

(*c*) Capability negotiation.

Q. 155. *What is WAE?*

Ans. The wireless application environment (WAE) is mainly used to create general purpose application environment which is based on existing techniques related to world wide web.

Q. 156. *Draw the structure of WAP.*

Ans.

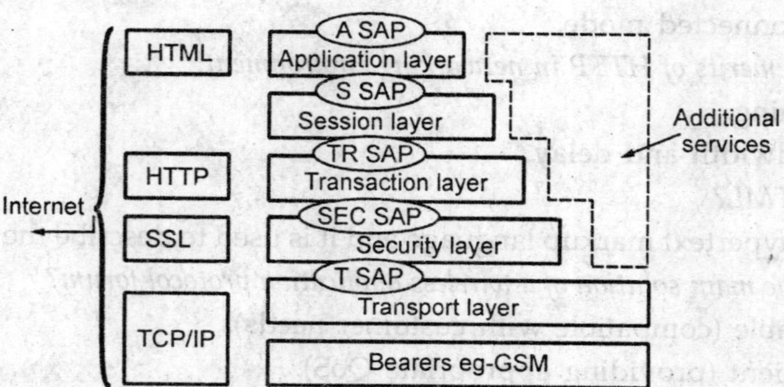

Fig. 19

Q. 157. *List two disadvantages of WLAN.*

Ans. (*a*) Quality of service (QoS).

(*b*) Safety and security.

Q. 158. *List two points related to infrared and radio transmission.*

Ans. 1. In infrared transmission technology infrared light with wavelength λ = 900 nm (approx.) is used.

2. In radio transmission it is based on GHz ranges.

3. Infrared transmission is basically simple and economic.

The radio transmission can cover larger geographical region.

Q. 159. *What are the disadvantages of infrared transmission?*

Ans. (*a*) It deals with lower bandwidth.

(*b*) Depends on line of sight (LOS) concept.

Q. 160. *What are the advantages of radio transmission?*

Ans. (*a*) It is cheap and simple in design.

(*b*) Infrared transmission are not interfered by electrical devices.

Q. 161. *Write two advantages of radio transmissions.*

Ans. (*a*) Coverage area is wider.

(*b*) It does not depend on line of sight (LOS) concept.

Q. 162. *Mention two technologies that depend on radio transmission.*

Ans. (*a*) Bluetooth technology.

(*b*) HIPERLAN.

Q. 163. *List three advantages of Infrastructure networks.*

Ans. (*a*) It provides access to other networks.

(*b*) Provides forwarding functions.

(*c*) Provides medium access control (MAC).

Q. 164. *Give two advantages of ad hoc networks.*

Ans. (*a*) It does not need a specific infrastructure to work with.

(*b*) No access point to control medium access is needed.

Q. 165. *What are the merits of IEEE 802.11 standard?*

Ans. (*a*) Provides Asynchronous service (eg. WLAN).

(*b*) Provides time bounded service (eg. WLAN).

Q. 166. *Define station under IEEE 802.11 standard.*

Ans. Station represents nodes and they are connected to access points. They have access facilities with wireless medium.

Q. 167. *Draw the format of an IEEE 802.11 PHY frame under FHSS method.*

Ans.

80	16	12	4	16	Variable	bits
Synchronization	SFD	PLW	PSF	HEC	Payload	
PLCP preamble		PLCP header				

Fig. 20

Q. 168. *What is SFD and HEC in IEEE 802.11 frame format?*

Ans. SFD - Start Frame Delimiter.

HEC - Header Error Check.

Q. 169. *What is PSF?*

Ans. It is PLCP signalling field and it is defined with 4 bits.

Q. 170. *Write two points about MAC.*

Ans. (*a*) MAC layer has to control medium access.

(*b*) In addition it provides support for

(*i*) Authentication.

(*ii*) Roaming.

(*iii*) Power conversation.

Q. 171. *What are the basic services provided by MAC layer?*

Ans. (*a*) Time bound service.

(*b*) Asynchronous data service.

Q. 172. *What is the other terminology used for MAC mechanisms?*

Ans. Distributed foundation wireless medium access control (DFWMAC).

Q. 173. *What is the significance of 1st 128 bits in PHY frame format of IEEE 802.11?*

Ans. There bits are used for

1. Synchronization.
2. Frequency offset compensation.
3. Energy detection.
4. Gain setting.

Q. 174. *What is the use of beacon in synchronization in 802.11 standard?*

Ans. The beacon frame consists of a

(*a*) Time-stamp.

(*b*) Other management information.

Q. 175. *What are types in management information?*

Ans. (*a*) Power management.

(*b*) Roaming.

Q. 176. *What are the two states for a station with respect to power saving?*

Ans. (*a*) Sleep state

(*b*) Awake state

Q. 177. *State the advantage in infrastructure based networks.*

Ans. Power management is better in infrastructure based networks.

Q. 178. *What is known as ATIM window?*

Ans. In ad hoc networks the destinations are announced with the "ad hoc traffic indication map (ATIM)" and the corresponding announcement period is called as ATIM window.

Q. 179. *What is "Roaming" in wireless networks?*

Ans. In wireless environment the station has to move as the subscriber moves from one access point to another access point. Such a moving between the access points is called as Roaming.

Q. 180. *What is the demerit of ad hoc networks?*

Ans. Power management is more complex in ad hoc networks than infrastructure-based networks.

Q. 181. *What are the steps followed in roaming between the access points?*

Ans. (*a*) Passive scanning.

(*b*) Active scanning.

(*c*) Association request.

(*d*) Association response.

Q. 182. *Write short notes on Active scanning.*

Ans. In active scanning a probe is sent on each channel and response is awaited from the channels. These are the two main functions done ultimately to decide about joining the new BSS.

Q. 183. *Give the expansion of HIPERLAN.*

Ans. It is high performance local area network.

Q. 184. *Mention the criteria related with (WPAN).*

Ans. (*a*) Market potential.

(*b*) Distinct identify.

(*c*) Economic feasibility.

(*d*) Technical feasibility.

Q. 185. *Compare HIPERLAN-1 and 2.*

Ans.

Parameter	HIPERLAN-1	HIPERLAN-2
Antenna	Omnidirectional	Omnidirectional
Application	Wireless LAN	Access to ATM fixed networks

Q. 186. *Compare HIPERLAN-3 and 4.*

Ans.

Parameter	HIPERLAN-3	HIPERLAN-4
Datarate	> 20 Mbits/sec.	155 Mbits/sec.
Range	5000 m	150 m

Q. 187. *When was HIPERLAN-1 was standardized?*

Ans. HIPERLAN-1 was standardized by ETSI in the year 1996.

Q. 188. *Compare HIPERLAN-1 and 3.*

Ans.

Parameter	HIPERLAN-1	HIPERLAN-2
Application	Wireless LAN	Wireless Localloop
Frequency	5.1 to 5.2 GHz (approx.)	5.1 to 5.3 GHz (approx.)

Q. 189. *What is the topology of HIPERLAN-4?*

Ans. Point-to-multipoint topology.

Q. 190. *Give the data rate of HIPERLAN-2.*

Ans. The data rate is 23.5 Mbits/sec.

Q. 191. *What is the topology of HIPERLAN-1 and 2?*

Ans. HIPERLAN-1 - It is decentralized. Ad hoc/Infrastructure based.
HIPERLAN-2 - It is centralized cellular based.

Q. 192. *State the applications of HIPERLAN-4.*

Ans. (*a*) Point to point and
(*b*) Wireless ATM applications

Q. 193. *What is the speciality of HIPERLAN?*

Ans. It has the ability to forward packets with many relays.

Q. 194. *Give examples that can be designed with WATM.*

Ans. Transferring
(*a*) Voice
(*b*) Video
(*c*) Classical data
(*d*) Short messages
(*e*) Multimedia etc.

Q. 195. *Give any three services related applications of* WATM.

Ans. (*a*) Industry
(*b*) Hospitals
(*c*) Office environments

Q. 196. *Draw the generic reference model of a* WATM.

Ans.

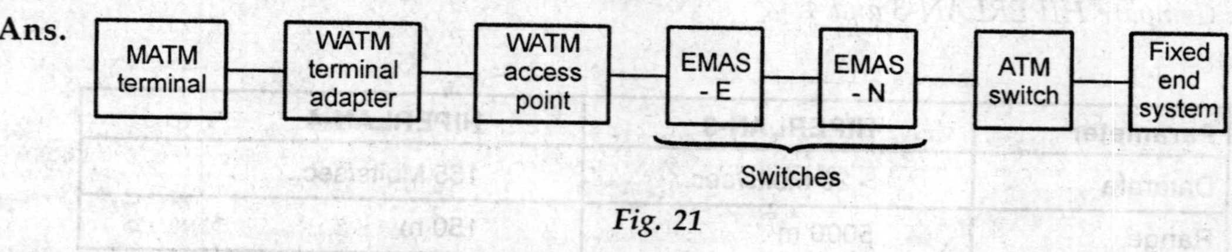

Fig. 21

Q. 197. *What are two segments of* WATM?

Ans.

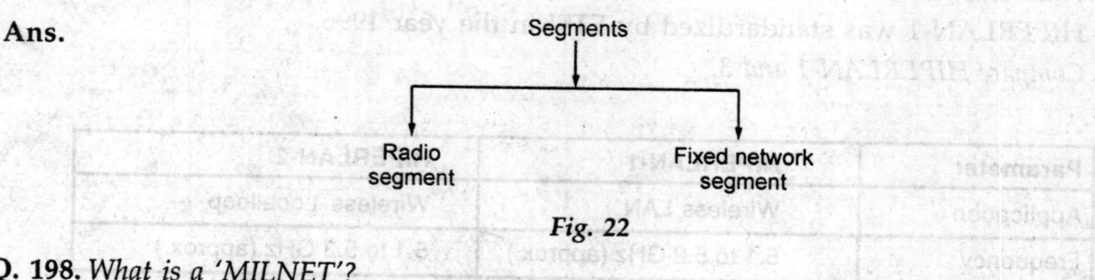

Fig. 22

Q. 198. *What is a 'MILNET'?*

Ans. In the year 1967 the advanced research projects agency (ARPA) focussed on networks which is a connection of many computers and the network was named as 'ARPANET'.

Later in 1983 the 'ARPANET' was divided into two groups. 'MILNET for military users and ARPANET for other non-military users.

Q. 199. *Write two functions of a repeater.*

Ans. (*i*) A repeater can connect all the segments of a local area network.

(*ii*) Repeater forwards each and every packet.

Q. 200. *Give the expansion of MTSA.*

Ans. MTSA is mobile terminal security agent. It focuses on security issues.

Q. 201. *List two radio access control under* WATM.

Ans. (*a*) Radio resource control function.

(*b*) ATM connection function.

Q. 202. *How may priorities are allowed for data packets ready in HIPERLAN?*

Ans. There are five different priorities possible in HIPERLAN standard. When one node completes sending packets then other nodes start transmitting.

Q. 203. *What are the three main phases in HIPERLAN?*

Ans. (*a*) Prioritization phase.

(*b*) Elimination phase.

(*c*) Yield phase.

(*d*) Transmission phase.

Q. 204. *What is DDIB?*

Ans. It is duplicate detection information base (DDIB) in HIPERLAN and it is independent of relaying, topology and routing information.

Q. 205. *Write short note on TIB.*

Ans. It reflects current (present) topology of HIPERLAN based on the information about forwarders and their source multipoint relays.

Q. 206. *Draw a simple configuration for a Bluetooth based piconet.*

Ans.

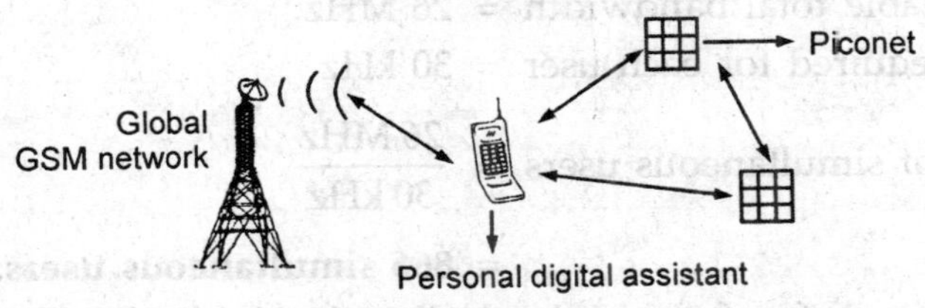

Fig. 23

Q. 207. *What are the channel borrowing techniques in network planning?*

Ans. There are two methods of channel borrowing.

(*a*) Temporary channel borrowing

(*b*) Static channel borrowing.

Q. 208. *What is ACI?*

Ans. It is adjacent channel interference. An interference takes place due to channels of different frequencies.

Q. 209. *What are the two types of interference?*

Ans. (*a*) Adjacent channel interference.

(*b*) Co-channel interference.

Q. 210. *Define co channel interference.*

Ans. In the cells of different clusters (say N_1 and N_2) same frequencies are used. The interference due to such kind of cellular frequencies is said to be "co-channel interference".

Q. 211. *Draw a diagram of two clusters from a cellular concept.*

Ans.

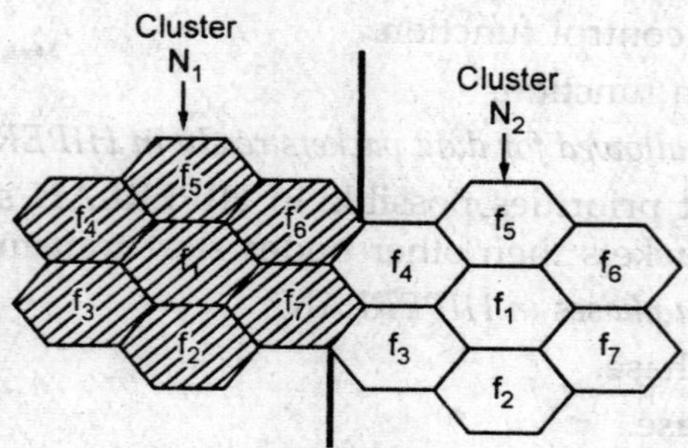

Fig. 24

Q. 212. *Give one technique to reduce ACI and CCI interferences.*

Ans. By carefully allocating channels within a cluster and also between clusters it is possible to reduce these kind of interferences.

Q. 213. *Assume the total bandwidth available is 26 MHz where each user requires 30 kHz of frequency bandwidth for the voice communication. In this case how many simultaneous are possible with single antenna availability?*

Ans. Available total bandwidth = 26 MHz.

Frequency required for each user = 30 kHz

$$\text{Number of simultaneous users} = \frac{26 \text{ MHz}}{30 \text{ kHz}}$$

= **866 simultaneous users.**

Q. 214. *In Q. 213 if there are four frequency bands allowed under dividing the total area into partitions then what will be the frequency spectrum allocation each user?*

=

Ans. Total frequency = 26 MHz

Available frequency bands = 4

$$\text{Single user frequency spectrum} = \frac{26 \text{ MHz}}{4}$$

= **6.5 MHz**

Q. 215. *In Q. 213 what will be the number of simultaneous users possible when there is four set of frequency bands available in a cluster?*

Ans. Spectrum of each user = 6.5 MHz

The number of simultaneous users per cell

$$= \frac{6.5 \text{ MHz}}{30 \text{ kHz}}$$

$$= \textbf{216 Users}$$

Q. 216. *In Q. 215 what will be the total number of the simultaneous users in a particular cluster?*

Ans. No. of simultaneous users in a cell = 216 users.

No. of cells in one cluster = 4

∴ Total number of simultaneous users per cluster

$$= 216 \times 4$$

$$= 864$$

Q. 217. *What is the advantage of cell splitting concept?*

Ans. In this technique the total number of users at a time will be increased so that traffic congestion in an area can be avoided. Also a set of lower power antennas can be used in place of single antenna for the entire region so that the cellular coverage efficiency will be definitely high.

Q. 218. *What is known as hierarchical cellular infrastructure?*

Ans. In hierarchical cellular infrastructure it is possible to have cells of different sizes.

Q. 219. *Give any two advantages hierarchical cellular infrastructure.*

Ans. (*i*) To extend increase the coverage capacity of complete cellular region.

(*ii*) To increase the cellular capacity that is the number of users in a particular cellular network.

Q. 220. *What are cell sizes defined under hierarchical cellular infrastructure?*

Ans. (*a*) Femto cells.

(*b*) Pico cells.

(*c*) Micro cells.

(*d*) Macro cells.

(*e*) Mega cells.

Q. 221. *Define 'Femto cells'.*

Ans. The femto cells are the smallest unit of the cellular hierarchy where it takes care of few meters of the coverage distance.

Q, 222. *Give two examples that are covered by femto cells.*

Ans. Femto cell are used for connection of equipments like

(*i*) Laptops.

(*ii*) Cellular telephones.

Q. 223. *Define Mega cell.*

Ans. It covers hundreds of kilometers and focused with satellite usages. These cells can cover nationwide areas.

Q. 224. *Write short note on pica cell.*

Ans. Pico cells are used for local indoor networks like LAN setup. It is possible to have upto tens of meters coverage with these cells.

Q. 225. *Define Micro cell.*

Ans. It is mainly used in urban areas. Microcells can be used for coverage upto hundreds of meters.

Q. 226. *What is known as Macro cell?*

Ans. The macro cells are used for covering metropolitan areas and they cover areas upto several kilometers.

Q. 227. *Differentiate the antenna mounting in micro and macro cell.*

Ans. In macro cells the antennas are mounted at height level than that of the root top of buildings.

In macro cells the antennas are mounted above the roof top of the buildings.

Q. 228. *What the conventional cell size that was used in early days of cellular communication?*

Ans. Macro cell was the conventional type mainly used in early days.

Q. 229. *Give two technical issues involved in planning cellular network.*

Ans. (*a*) Radio coverage and physical deployment modelling.

(*b*) Selection of frequency reuse patterns.

Q. 230. *What are the cell shapes possible with a rectangular polygon?*

Ans. (*i*) Equilateral triangle.

(*ii*) Square.

(*iii*) Regular hexagon.

Q. 231. *Draw the 60° and 120° cell sectoring shapes each with one example.*

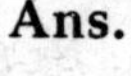

Ans.

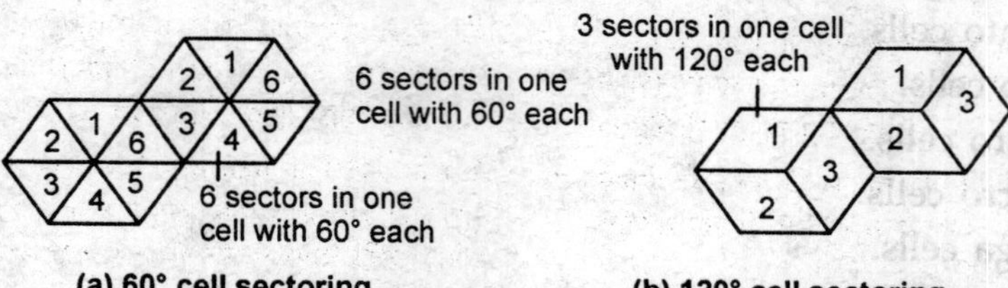

(a) 60° cell sectoring (b) 120° cell sectoring

Fig. 25

Q. 232. *Define co-channel interference.*

Ans. In a cellular coverage area when many cells use the same frequency 'f' under frequency reuse technique and those cells using same frequency is called as co-channel cells.

The interference between the different signals of these co-channel cells is known as co-channel interference.

Q. 233. *What are the types of fading?*

Ans.

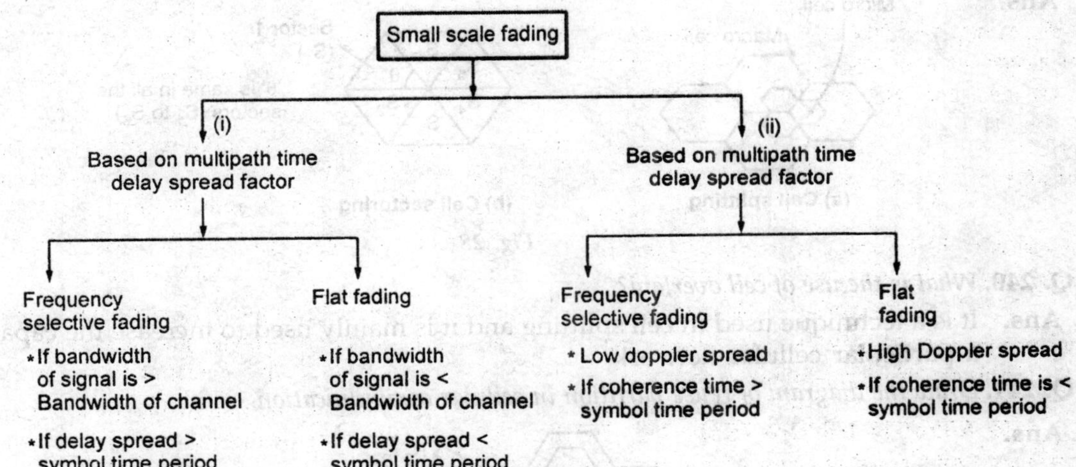

Fig. 26

Q. 234. *Draw the Hexagonal cellular pattern with two dusters.*

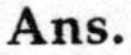

Ans.

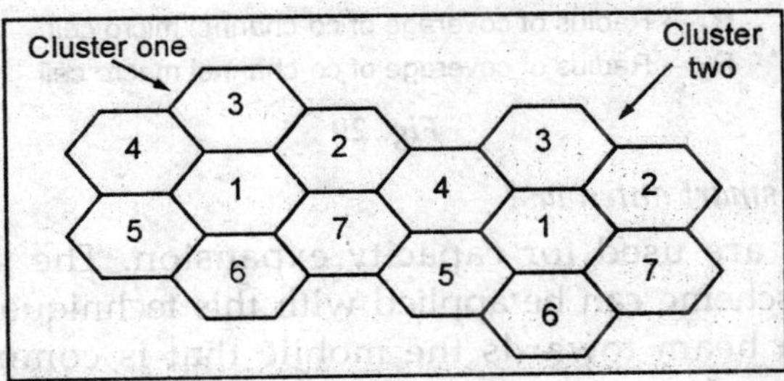

Fig. 27

Q. 235. *What is the type of modulation used with AMPS?*

Ans. In the AMPS (first telephone system used in United States) cellular communication was based on frequency modulation (FM) scheme.

Q. 236. *What was frequency spectrum allocation in AMPS?*

Ans. Mobile transmit spectrum → 824 - 849 MHz.

Mobile receive spectrum → 869 - 894 MHz.

Q. 237. *How many voice and control channels were possible in mobile transmission under AMPS?*

Ans. Voice channels → 395

Control channels → 21.

Q. 238. *What is known as cell overlaid?*

Ans. In cell splitting whenever a macro cell coexists with micro cells, it is said to be cell overlaid.

Q. 239. *Draw one example of cell sectoring and cell splitting techniques.*

Ans.

Micro cell
Macro cell

(a) Cell splitting

Sector 1 (S_1)
S_2 S_3 S_4 S_5 S_6 θ
'θ' is same in all the sectors (S_1 to S_6)

(b) Cell sectoring

Fig. 28

Q. 240. *What is the use of cell overlaid?*

Ans. It is a technique used in cell splitting and it is mainly used to increase the capacity of a particular cellular network.

Q. 241. *Draw the diagram of reuse partition in cellular communication.*

Ans.

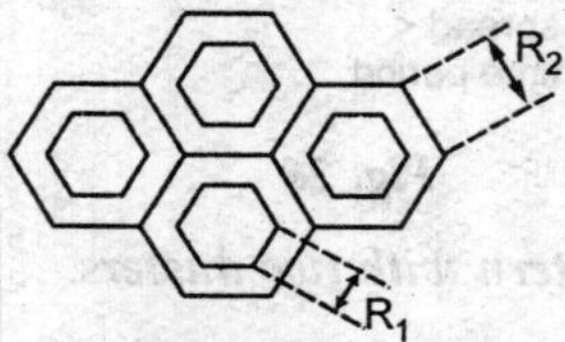

$R_1 \rightarrow$ Radius of coverage of co-channel micro cell
$R_2 \rightarrow$ Radius of coverage of co-channel macro cell

Fig. 29

Q. 242. *What is the use of smart antennas?*

Ans. Smart antennas are used for capacity expansion. The space division multiple access (SDMA) scheme can be applied with this technique by simply directing the narrow antenna beam towards the mobile that is communicating with it. The advantage of this scheme is reduced level of interference.

Q. 243. *What is FCA?*

Ans. In mobile communication FCA is fixed channel allocation scheme where the number of radio channels are preallocated.

Q. 244. *What are the channel allocation methods?*

Ans.

Channel allocation methods
1. Fixed channel allocation
2. Dynamic channel allocation
3. Hybrid channel allocation

Fig. 30

Q. 245. *What is DCA?*

Ans. It is dynamic channel allocation scheme where the radio channels are allocated on the traffic demand basis.

Q. 246. *What is HCA?*

Ans. It is hybrid channel allocation scheme where a combination of fixed channel allocation and dynamic channel allocation is applied.

Q. 247. *What are the two methods of channel borrowing?*

Ans. (*a*) Temporary channel borrowing.

(*b*) Static channel borrowing.

Q. 248. *Give two points related to non-uniform compact channel allocation (NCA) algorithm.*

Ans. In this method the algorithm defines a particular set of patterns for non-uniform distribution of radio channels. Then selection of a pattern with minimum channel blocking probability in the system is done. This is the systematic steps followed by the NCA.

Q. 249. *What is known as static channel borrowing?*

Ans. In this scheme the channels are distributed non-uniformly among the cells according the traffic availability.

Q. 250. *Compare DCA and FCA methods of channel allocation.*

Ans.

DCA	FCA
1. Good at lower traffic load.	Good at higher traffic loac.
2. Channel allocation is flexible.	Channel allocation is not flexible.

Q. 251. *Give two advantages of DCA scheme over FCA.*

Ans. In dynamic channel allocation (DCA) scheme :

(*a*) The signalling load can be moderate or high.

(*b*) The overall control mechanism can be centralized, distributed or decentralized.

The restrictions posed under FCA is not a constraint under DCA scheme.

Q. 252. *Give two advantages of FCA scheme over DCA.*

Ans. (*a*) Reusability of channels is maximum possible.

(*b*) The signalling load control mechanism is centralized.

Q. 253. *Give two demerits of FCA scheme.*

Ans. (*a*) Fluctuating grade of service (GOS).

(*b*) It is very sensitive to temporal and spatial changes which may takes place.

Q. 254. *Give two merits of dynamic channel allocation scheme.*

Ans. (*a*) Stable grade of service (GOS).

(*b*) Low probability of forced call termination.

Q. 255. *What are the three classes of algorithms under DCA?*

Ans.

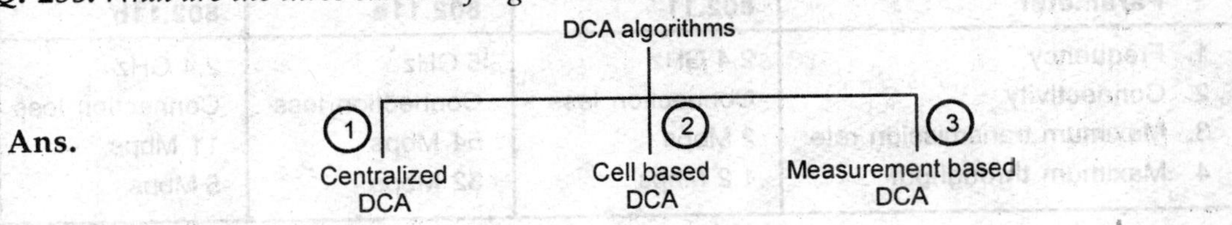

Fig. 31

Q. 256. *Give two advantages of Measurement based DCA algorithm.*

Ans. (*i*) Suboptimal channel allocation.

(*ii*) Fast real-time processing.

Q. 257. *Give two disadvantages of Measurement-based DCA algorithm.*

Ans. (*i*) Deadlock probability.

(*ii*) Instability problem.

Q. 258. *Give one merit and demerit of cell based DCA algorithm.*

Ans. Merit - It has "Near optimum channel allocation" facility.

Demerit - There is extensive communication link between base stations.

Q. 259. *Compare cell based and centralized DCA algorithms.*

Ans.

Cell Based DCA	Centralized DCA
1. It has "near optimum channel allocation".	It also has "near optimum channel allocation".
2. There is extensive communication link between base stations.	Highly centralized overhead mechanism.

Q. 260. *Compare 802.Ha and HIPERLAN-2 standards with three points.*

Ans.

Parameter	802.11a	HIPERLAN-2
Frequency	5 GHz	5 GHz
Maximum throughput	32 Mbps	32 Mbps
Transmission rate	54 Mbps	54 Mbps

Q. 261. *Compare 802.11b and HIPERLAN-2 standards.*

Ans.

Parameter	802.11 b	HIPERLAN-2
Maximum transmission rate	11 Mbps	54 GHz
Frequency	2.4 GHz	5 Mbps
Medium access	Through sensing	Centralized scheduling

Q. 262. *Compare HIPERLAN-2 and 802.11 standard.*

Ans.

Parameter	HIPERLAN-2	802.11
Maximum transmission rate	54 Mbps	2 Mbps
Frequency	5 GHz	2.4 GHz

Q. 263. *Compare 802.11, 802.11a and 802.11b standards at least with 4 points.*

Ans.

Parameter	802.11	802.11a	802.11b
1. Frequency	2.4 GHz	5 GHz	2.4 GHz
2. Connectivity	Connection less	Connection less	Connection less
3. Maximum transmission rate	2 Mbps	54 Mbps	11 Mbps
4. Maximum throughput	1.2 Mbps	32 Mbps	5 Mbps

Q. 264. *List the advantages of HIPERLAN-2 standards.*

Ans. (*a*) It is has centralized scheduling medium access facility.

(*b*) It is a connection oriented network.

(*c*) Link adaptation kind of link quality control is allowed.

(*d*) It has ATM/RSVP/802.11p QoS support.

Q. 265. *Give the frequency-bands of HIPERLAN-2 standard.*

Ans.

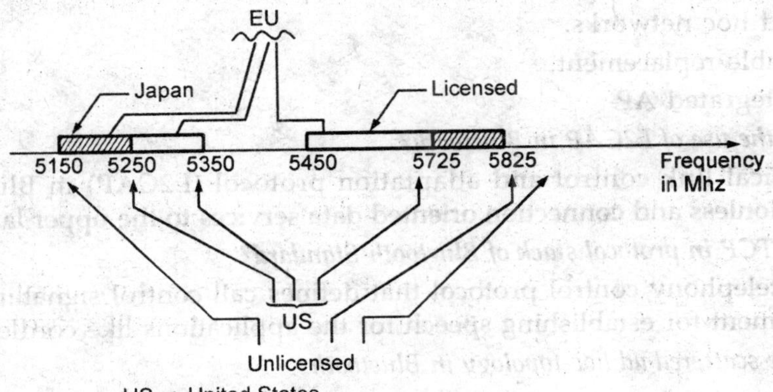

Fig. 32

Q. 266. *Comment on authentication and wired backbone parameter for HIPERLAN-2 standard.*

Ans. 1. Authentication → NAI/IEEE Add/X.509 authentication facility.

2. Wired backbone → ATM/UMTS/Ethernet/Firewire/IP/PPP.

Q. 267. *What is a "HomeRF"?*

Ans. It is a working group developed to provide wireless digital communication between consumer electronic devices and PC's in and around the home environment.

Q. 268. *What types of networks are being supported by homeRF?*

Ans. (*a*) Infrastructured network.

(*b*) Ad hoc network.

Q. 269. *Define 'SWAP'.*

Ans. In homeRF a specification is developed specially for wireless communications called as "Shared wireless access protocol" (SWAP).

Q. 270. *Write short note on SWAP.*

Ans. (*a*) SWAP specification in homeRF defines an interface that supports wireless voice communication and data networking features,

(*b*) Allows high speed data applications.

Q. 271. *Give two points related to Bluetooth standard.*

Ans. (*a*) It is a specification defined for short range wireless voice and data communications.

(*b*) It was named after the king of Denmark and Norway "Harald Blaaland" (A.D 940-981), who had nickname "Bluetooth".

Q. 272. *What is SIG?*

Ans. It is a special interest group and for example development of Bluetooth technology was expanded with a SIG of Ericsson, IBM, Nokia, Toshiba and Intel companies in the year 1998.

Q. 273. *Give some Bluetooth applications.*

Ans. (*a*) Ad hoc networks.

(*b*) Cable replacement.

(*c*) Integrated AP.

Q. 274. *What is the use of L2CAP in Bluetooth?*

Ans. The logical link control and adaptation protocol (L2CAP) in Bluetooth enables connectionless and connection oriented data services to the upper layered protocols.

Q. 275. *What is TCP in protocol stack of Bluetooth Standard?*

Ans. TCP is telephony control protocol that defines call control signalling and mobility management for establishing speech for the applications like cordless telephones.

Q. 276. *Draw the scattered ad hoc-topology in Bluetooth.*

Ans.

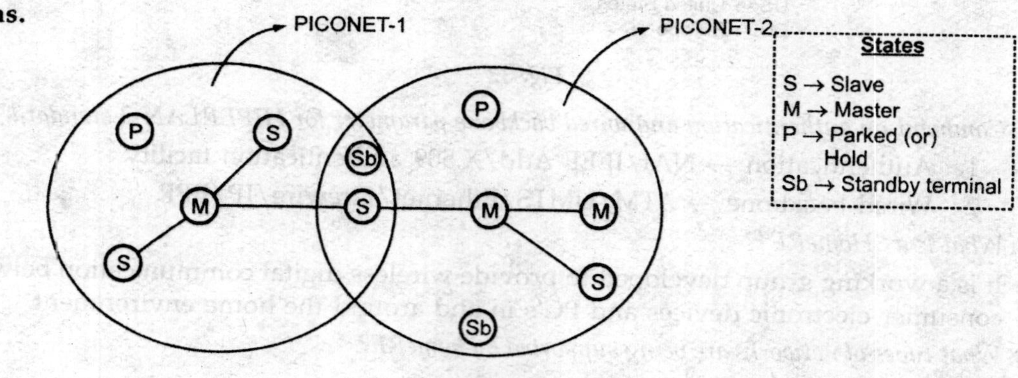

Fig. 33

Q. 277. *Draw the protocol stack for cordless phone implementation with bluetooth standard.*

Ans.

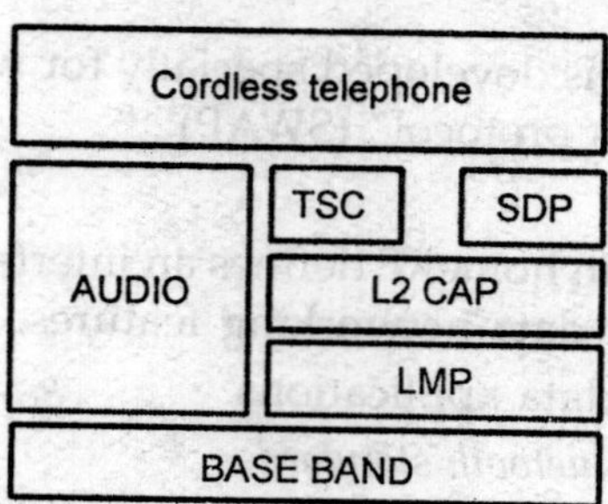

Fig. 34

Q. 278. *What are the authentication functions?*

Ans. 1. Message Encryption.
2. Message authentication code.
3. Hash (H).

Q. 279. *What are the advantages of CDMA systems?*

Ans. (*i*) Provides larger capacity.
(*ii*) Effective frequency reuse.

Q. 280. *What is known as channel borrowing technique?*

Ans. In this technique it enables the high traffic cells to borrow (receive) frequencies from the cells of low traffic. This state is maintained till a significant change in changed frequency takes place again.

Q. 281. *What is the significance of non-uniform compact channel allocation algorithm?*

Ans. It defines a set of pattern for the non-uniform distribution of channels in cellular communication. It depends on the cellular blocking probability concept.

Q. 282. *What is known as temporary channel borrowing scheme?*

Ans. In this scheme the high traffic cells return the borrowed channels to the cells which owns them after the call completion.

Q. 283. *What is known as CRC?*

Ans. The set of codes generated by a polynomial are called as cyclic codes and the corresponding block codes of this kind is known as cyclic redundancy code or simply CRC.

Q. 284. *Define a hamming distance.*

Ans. In block codes there is a distance available between any pair of codewords and this distance is always measured in terms of number of symbols or bits. It is called as hamming distance and generally it will vary from one codeword to another.

Q. 285. *What is known as hard decision?*

Ans. A received bit is sent to decode in the receiver to decide whether it is a '0' or '1' and the decoder detects or corrects any error if available at this state. This is known as hard decision.

Q. 286. *What is known as soft decision?*

Ans. In this decoding scheme, the receiver converts the received signal into several on/off levels of the output. They are the 'Q' quantized levels where upto 8 levels are possible. This is known as soft decision.

Q. 287. *Compare hard and soft decision decoding techniques with one point.*

Ans. In soft decision decoding there may be eight quantized levels of output signals. In hard decision decoding there are usually two levels of output signal.

Q. 288. *Draw the transmitted pulse shape in a bandlimited noisy channel.*

Ans.

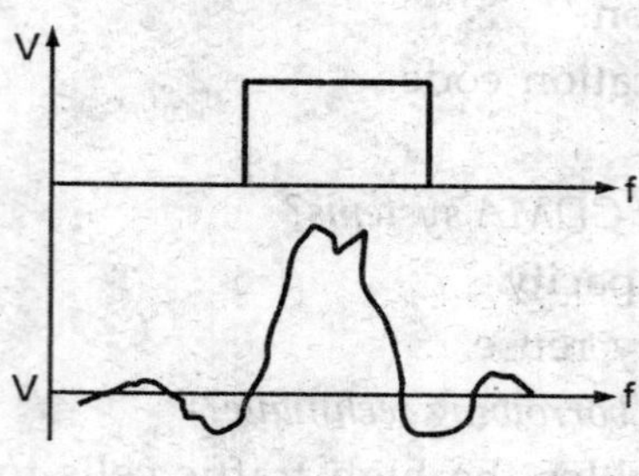

Fig. 35

Q. 289. *What is the advantage of DBPSK and NC-FSK schemes?*

Ans. These two keying schemes did not require a carrier phase reference at their receiver side. This facilitates easier implementations.

Q. 290. *Give two characteristics of a wireless medium which degraded the system performance.*

Ans. (*a*) Fading.

(*b*) Multipath propagation.

Q. 291. *Define fading.*

Ans. The large amount of fluctuations of the received power level is termed as fading.

Q. 292. *Define 'multipath-propagation'.*

Ans. In cellular mobile communication the received signals arrives through delayed multiple paths (due to obstacles in its wave travel) and this is termed as multipath propagation.

Q. 293. *What is a 'Software radio' technique?*

Ans. It is software implementation of mobile terminal and it can adapt itself dynamically with time to its radio environment location.

Q. 294. *What is the significance of software radio?*

Ans. 1. It enables software controllable user friendly transceiver architecture.

2. It provides multimode support.

Q. 295. *Give two advantages of software radio.*

Ans. (*a*) Less circuit complexity.

(*b*) Low power consumption.

(*c*) Economical.

Q. 296. *What is information contained in the transmitted bits?*

Ans. The information contained in a transmitted bit is the ratio of the energy of signal per bit to the average noise power spectral density that is (Eb/No).

Q. 297. *What, are the effects of 'fading'?*

Ans. (*a*) The error rate of the transmission system will increase.

(*b*) There will a significant fluctuation in BER value.

Q. 298. *What is known as 'delay spread' in wireless communication?*

Ans. In wireless environment there is multipath propagation problem which its leads to delayed received pulses at receiver side. The difference between first and last pulses is called as 'delay spread'.

Q. 299. *List two features of FSK.*

Ans. (*i*) FSK is less susceptible to errors.

(*ii*) It is more suitable for mobile communication.

Q. 300. *What is the complexity involved with M-ary QAM scheme of modulation?*

Ans. M-ary, QAM scheme in an amplitude dependent method and it is very critical to implement it in fading environment.

Q. 301. *What are the shift keying methods used in cellular communication?*

Ans. (*a*) MSK.

(*b*) DQPSK.

Q. 302. *What is the demerit of ASK?*

Ans. In amplitude shift keying technique the 0's and 1's are represented with presence and absence of pulses. This method cannot be used for cellular communication where fading problem is involved.

Q. 303. *Give the expansion of ISI and its eye pattern.*

Ans. ISI = Intersymbol Interference

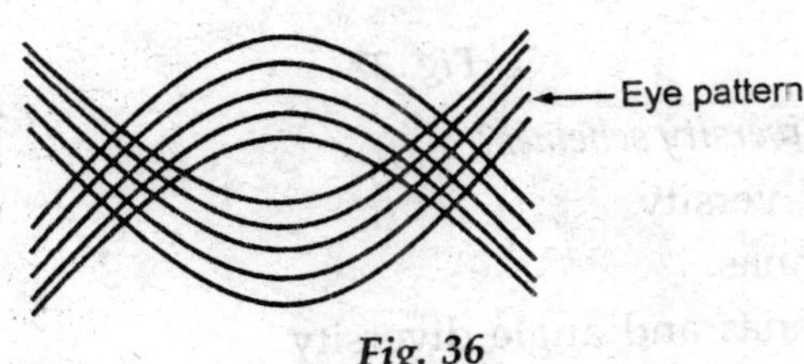

Fig. 36

Q. 304. *Write short note on frequency hopping in GSM.*

Ans. GSM standard supports slow frequency hopping transmission to introduce the frequency diversity technique. In fading situations frequency hopping equalizes the effective system performance and battery consumption among all mobile terminals.

Q. 305. *What is the level of frequency hopping in IEEE 802.11 standard?*

Ans. The frequency hopping supported by IEEE 802.11 standard is 2.5 hops per second. In fading environment a packet will be received in successive attempts or at least received in next hop to the node towards destination.

Q. 306. *Write a short note on frequency hopping in Bluetooth,*

Ans. In Bluetooth fast frequency hopping is used where upto 1600 hops per second is possible. In 'deep fade' environment a packet may get lost and if required retransmission of packet takes place.

Q. 307. *What is the use of smart antennas in CDMA?*

Ans. In systems using CDMA technique, there is a drawback of capacity limitations due to multiple access interference. But with smart antennas (array of antennas) it is possible to reduce multiple access interferences. Because smart antennas fucoses the signals in only one direction and enhances system capacity.

Q. 308. *Draw two spatial diversity schemes.*

Ans.

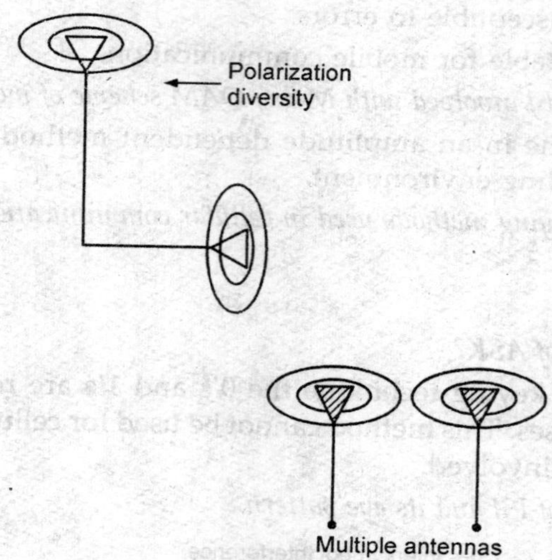

Fig. 37

Q. 309. *What are the spatial diversity schemes?*

Ans. (*a*) Polarization diversity.

(*b*) Multiple antennas.

(*c*) Sectored antennas and angle diversity.

(*d*) Adaptive angle diversity.

Q. 310. *Draw the DSSS system block diagram.*

Ans.

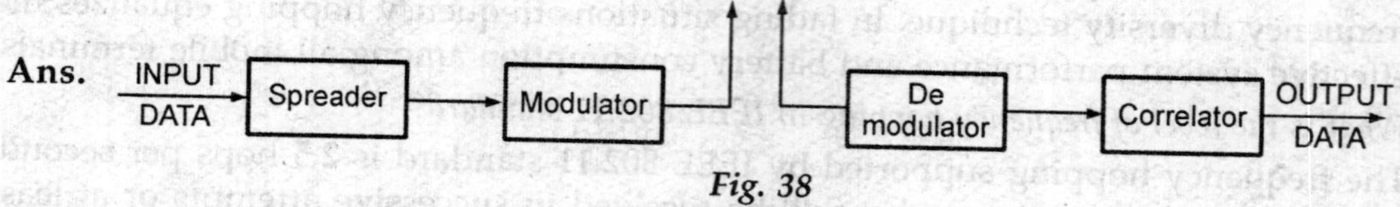

Fig. 38

Q. 311. *What is known as processing gain?*

Ans. In DSSS reception the signal is demodulated and then despreaded. The despreader correlates this signal with duplicated chip sequence and the peak of auto correlation function is mainly used to detect the transmission bit. Since autocorrelation function of a random code has high peak to sidelobe ratio and generally referred as "processing gain", of the receiver.

Q. 312. *Give an example of FHSS technique in a graph.*

Ans.

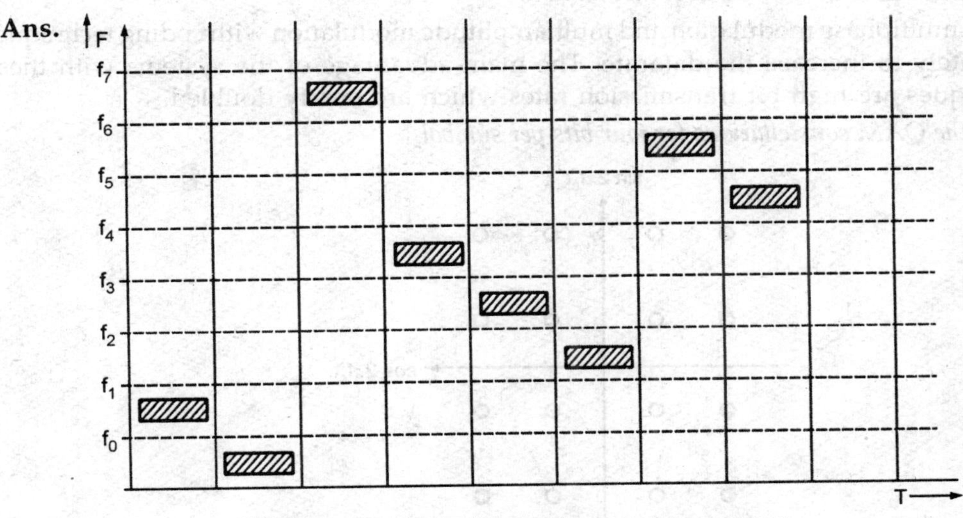

Fig. 39

Q. 313. *How many hopping channels are possible with IEEE 802.11 FHSS WLAN?*

Ans. It specifies upto 78 hopping channels where each channel is separated by 1 MHz frequency.

Q. 314. *Define 'frequency hop'.*

Ans. The frequency shift are known as frequency hops in random sequence which is known only to transmitter and an intended receiver.

Q. 315. Draw *the block diagram of frequency hopping concept (FHSS).*

Ans.

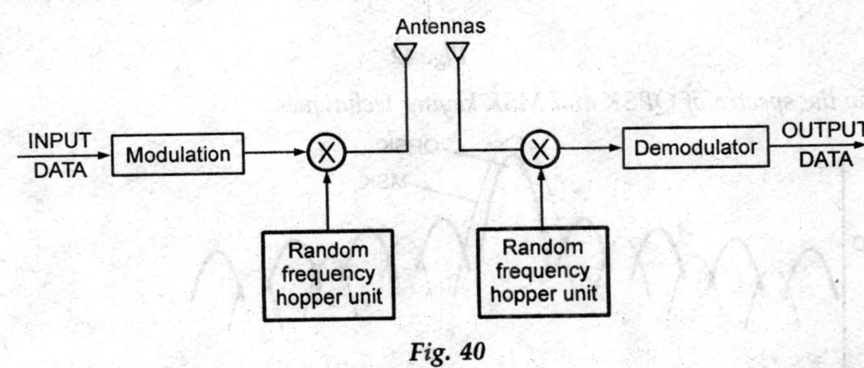

Fig. 40

Q. 316. Give two advantages of *spread spectrum technique apart from defence applications.*

Ans. (*a*) In cellular systems with CDMA spread spectrum technique provides high operational flexibility.

(*b*) The spread spectrum signals can also be over laid onto the bands related to other systems operating already, and the impact on both the systems are minimum.

Q. 317. *Write short note on multisymbol modulation.*

Ans. It uses multiphase modulation and multiamplitude modulation with coding techniques ultimately to increase the datarate. The main advantage of the systems with these techniques are high bit transmission rates which are nearly doubled.

Q. 318. *Draw the QAM constellations for four bits per symbol.*

Ans.

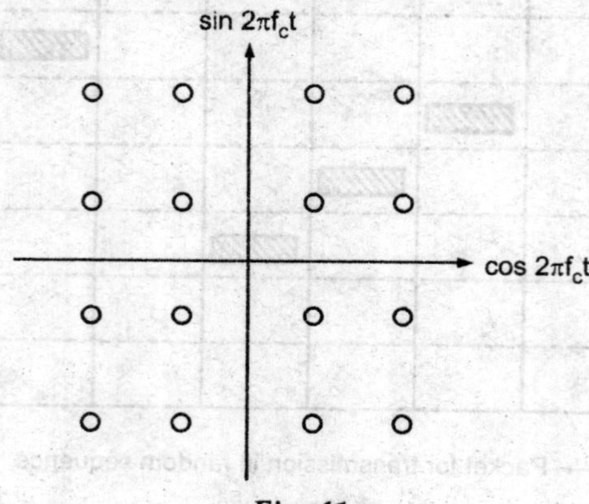

Fig. 41

Q. 319. *Draw the signal constellation of QPSK technique.*

Ans.

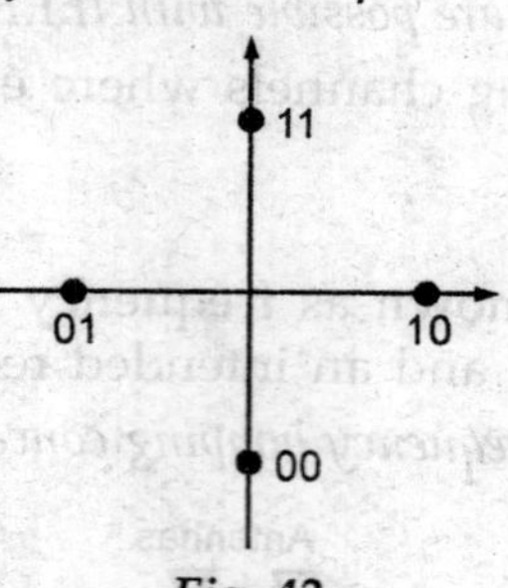

Fig. 42

Q. 320. *Draw the spectra of QPSK and MSK keying techniques.*

Ans.

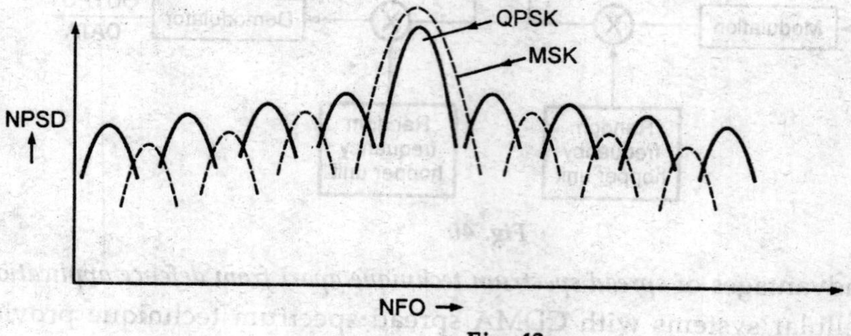

Fig. 43

NPSD → Normalized power spectral density in db.

NFO → Normalized frequency offset from the carrier signal in Hz/bit/sec.

Q. 321. *Draw the signal constellation and phase transitions of $\frac{\pi}{4}$ - QPSK.*

Ans.

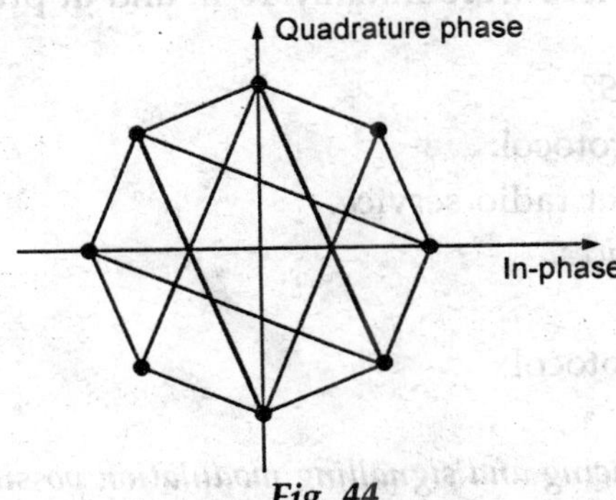

Fig. 44

Q. 322. *Give the expansion of MCHO and MDBS.*

Ans. MCHO - Mobile controlled handoff.

MDBS - Mobile database station.

Q. 323. *What is FACCH and GGSN?*

Ans. FACCH - Fast associated control channel

GGSN - Gateway GPRS support node.

Q. 324. *Define 'soft handoff'.*

Ans. The ability of mobile switching center to select between all the instantaneous received signals from various base stations is known as soft handoff. 'Call progress' is accurate in soft handoff than the hard handoff.

Q. 325. *What is DFE and DLOS?*

Ans. DFE - Decision feedback equalizer.

DLOS - Direct line of sight.

Q. 326. *Give the expansion of PPRCH and PRMA.*

Ans. PPRCH - Packet paging response channel.

PRMA - Packet reservation multiple access.

Q. 327. *Give two linear prediction methods.*

Ans. (*a*) Code exited linear prediction.

(*b*) Vector sum excitation linear prediction.

Q. 328. *What is the significance of sky wave propagation with respect to ionosphere?*

Ans. When sky waves are directed towards sky usually they are neither reflected nor refracted back to earth by the ionosphere layer. So this wave propagation is also termed as ionosphere propagation.

Q. 329. *What are the different technologies of cellular communication? Give any three example.*

Ans. (*a*) Wi-Fi technology

(*b*) GSM

(*c*) CDMA

Q. 330. *What is the range of Bluetooth technology?*

Ans. Bluetooth technology is meant for ad hoc applications in wireless networking where distance between devices were initially 10 m and at present it is extended upto 100 m range.

Q. 331. *What is FTP and GPRS?*

Ans. FTP - File transfer protocol.

GPRS - General packet radio service.

Q. 332. *Give three internet services.*

Ans. (*a*) Web browsing

(*b*) File transfer protocol

(*c*) Internet chat

Q. 333. *What is the channel spacing and signalling modulation possible with GPRS?*

Ans. Channel spacing - 200 kHz with 8/16 users per carrier.

Signalling modulation - Gaussian minimum shift keying (GMSK).

Q. 334. *List two features of PDA.*

Ans. PDA → Personal Digital Assistant.

Features :

(*i*) Used as digital clock and calender,

(*ii*) Computer games facility.

Q. 335. *What are additional functions that are possible with PDA? List any two.*

Ans. (*i*) Audio recording.

(*ii*) Media player ability.

Q. 336. *List any three operating systems that are compatible with cellular phone design.*

Ans. (*a*) Symbian

(*b*) Windows mobile

(*c*) Palm OS.

Q. 337. *Give three versions of windows mobile.*

Ans. (*a*) Windows mobile 5.0.

(*b*) Windows mobile 2003.

(*c*) Windows mobile pocket PC 2000.

Q. 338. *What is SMS and EMS?*

Ans. SMS → Short message service

EMS → Enhanced message service

Q. 339. *What are the technologies that opts for SMS facility?*

Ans. (*a*) GSM

(*b*) GPRS

(*c*) EDGE

(*d*) UMTS

Q. 340. *List two security services under GPRS.*

Ans.

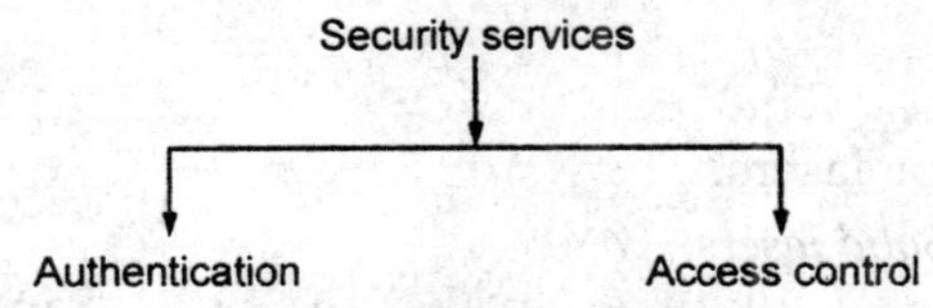

Fig. 45

Q. 341. *Write short note on QoB in GPRS.*

Ans. In GPRS the users can specify the QoS profile where the profile determines important things like reliability class, delay class and service precedence.

Q. 342. *How delay is incurred within GPRS?*

Ans. In GPRS delay is incurred due to channel access delay and transfer delays in a GPRS network.

Q. 343. *What are the network elements in GPRS?*

Ans. In GPRS architecture the network elements are termed as GPRS support nodes (GSN).

Q. 344. *What is expansion of SGSN and GR?*

Ans. (*i*) SGSN - Serving GPRS support node.

(*ii*) GR - GPRS register.

Q. 345. *What is a DECT?*

Ans. It is basically a digital cellular network termed as "digital enhanced cordless telecommunications" system and it was specified by ETS1 in the year 1999.

Q. 346. *What is the advantage of* DECT *system?*

Ans. (*a*) DECT replaced analog cordless phone system of early days.

(*b*) DECT is more flexible and powerful than other digital system. DECT's access points can be easily established with PSTN.

Q. 347. *Draw the DECT protocol architecture.*

Ans.

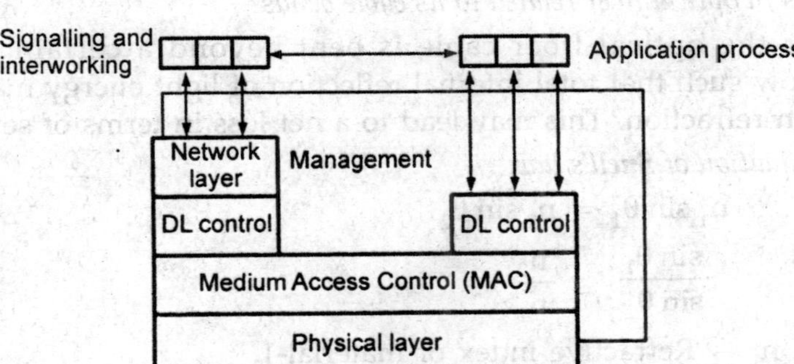

Fig. 46

Q. 348. *Give three laser types.*

Ans. (*a*) Liquid lasers

(*b*) Gas lasers

(*c*) Semiconductor lasers.

Q. 349. *Write short note on Solid lasers.*

Ans. Ruby is an example for solid laser. Each end of it is polished and the ruby is excited using a tungsten lamp that is connected to a power supply. Then the output of a laser is observed.

Q. 350. *List any two characteristics of a Laser.*

Ans. (*a*) It acts as a source that converts electrical energy to optical energy.

(*b*) Optics helps to direct the beam to a proper cone of convergence.

Q. 351. *Draw the Laser construction.*

Ans.

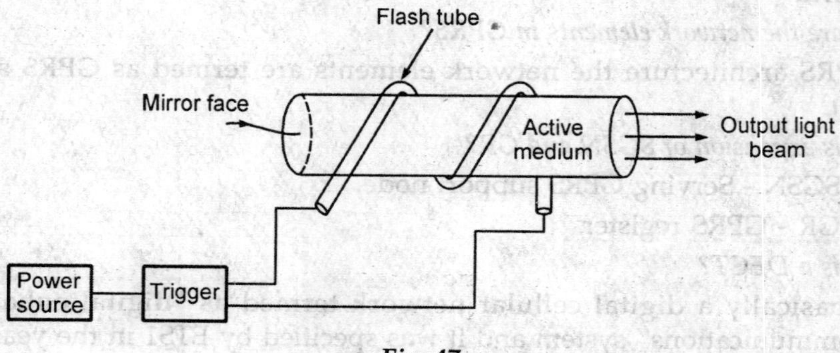

Fig. 47

Q. 352. *List any three losses of optical Fiber link.*

Ans. (*a*) Cable losses.

(*b*) Source to cable interface loss.

(*c*) Connector losses.

Q. 353. *What is loss in optical fiber related to its cable bends?*

Ans. Whenever the optical fiber cable is bent beyond a certain level the angle θ becomes low such that total internal reflection of light energy may not be achieved resulting in refraction. This may lead to a net loss in terms of several dB's.

Q. 354. *Write the equation of Snell's law.*

Ans.

$$n_1 \sin \theta_1 = n_2 \sin \theta_2$$

$$\frac{\sin \theta_1}{\sin \theta_2} = \frac{n_2}{n_1}$$

where $n_1 \rightarrow$ Refractive index of material-1.

$n_2 \rightarrow$ Refractive index of material-2.

$\theta_1 \rightarrow$ Angle of incidence in degrees.

$\theta_2 \rightarrow$ Angle of refraction in degrees.

Q. 355. *Define Refractive index.*

Ans. At the interface of two materials (m_1 and m_2) of different densities there will be a bending or refraction taking place. This amount of bending or refraction is called as "Refractive index".

Q. 356. *Write short note on Reflection.*

Ans. Reflection is nothing but the act or a means to turn back. This reflection with respect to electromagnetic waves will occur. Whenever an incident wave hits a boundary of any two media. In this case some or the total incident power of signal will not enter the second media.

Q. 357. *Define noise factor.*

Ans. $$\text{Noise factor (F)} = \frac{\text{Input signal to noise power ratio}}{\text{Output signal to noise power ratio}}$$

The noise factor (F) is unitless.

Q. 358. *What is a 'frame control' field in a IEEE 802.11 packet structure?*

Ans. The frame control field consists of 2 bytes where many sub fields are allowed, to indicate type of frame, protocol version etc.

Q. 359. *Give two field in IEEE 802.11 packet structure.*

Ans. (*a*) Duration ID field

(*b*) CRC.

Q. 360. *Define 'CRC'.*

Ans. It is the last field of IEEE 802.11 packet structure. It is provided with 4 bytes. These 32 bits (checksum) is used for protecting the frame.

Q. 361. *What is MIB?*

Ans. It is management information base (MIB) where all important parameters are stored for easy accesses whenever required by the network.

Q. 362. *What is* TSF?

Ans. It is Timing Synchronization Function and specified by IEEE 802.11 standard for synchronizing all the nodes.

Q. 363. *Give the expansion of HCSDU and HCSAP.*

Ans. 1. HCSDU - HIPERLAN CAC service data unit

2. HCSAP - HIPERLAN CAC service access point

Q. 364. *Give the expansion of EY-NPMA.*

Ans. It is elimination yield non preemptive priority multiple access, and it plays a vital role in channel access schemes.

Q. 365. *What are the three phases of EY-NPMA?*

Ans. (*i*) Prioritization

(*ii*) Contention

(*iii*) Transmission

Q. 366. *Draw the 'LBR-HBR data burst' in HIPERLAN.*

Ans.

HBR

LBR	Synchronization	$DATA_0$	$DATA_1$	...	$DATA_{m-1}$

Where LBR → Low bit rate
HBR → High bit rate

Fig. 48

where LBR → Low bit rate
HBR → High bit rate.

Q. 367. *What are the two types of burst in HIPERLAN?*

Ans. (*a*) LBR-HBR data burst.
(*b*) LBR data burst.

Q. 368. *Define LBR burst.*

Ans. It (burst) consists of low bit rate part that comprises the receiver identification. LBR burst operation is at the datarate of 1.47 Mbits per sec (approx).

Q. 369. *Give two user sceneries possible with Bluetooth.*

Ans. (*a*) Bridging of networks.
(*b*) Connecting peripheral devices.

Q. 370. *Give the format of Bluetooth packet.*

Ans.

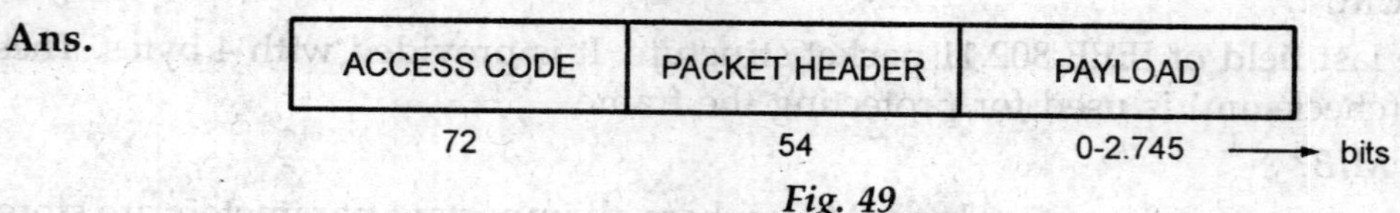

Fig. 49

Q. 371. *What are the different types of services that are compatible with Bluetooth standard?*

Ans. (*a*) Asynchronous connectionless link (ACL)
(*b*) Synchronous connection-oriented link (SCO)

Q. 372. *Give the format of Bluetooth packet header.*

Ans.

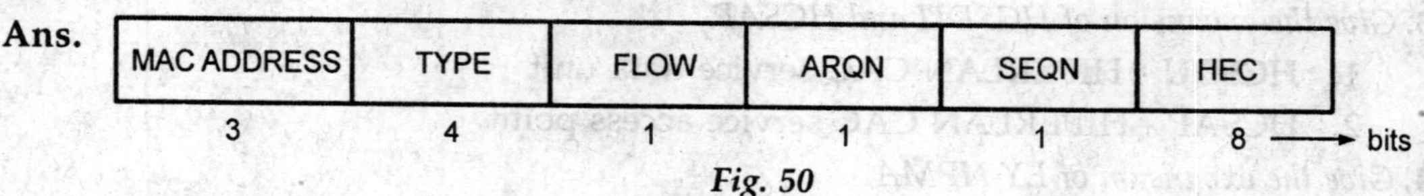

Fig. 50

Q. 373. *Write short note on link management under Ad hoc Bluetooth environment.*

Ans. The link manager (LM) manages the Bluetooth standard. It provides sending and receiving data and also it requests the names of other devices.

Q. 374. *What are the functions that are provided with link management?*

Ans. The link management is able to handle the function mentioned below.

(*a*) Authentication procedure.

(b) Link setup.
(c) Authentication parameter negotiations.
(d) Configuring links.

Q. 375. *Give two reasons for development of wireless ATM.*

Ans. (a) The ATM networks can scale from LAN's to WAN's, where ATM is extended to global environments.
(b) For integration of wireless terminals into an ATM network WATM is done.

Q. 376. *What is a BRAN?*

Ans. It is broadband radio access networks and standardized by European telecommunications standards institute (ETSI).

Q. 377. *Draw the HIPERLAN-2 reference model*

Ans.

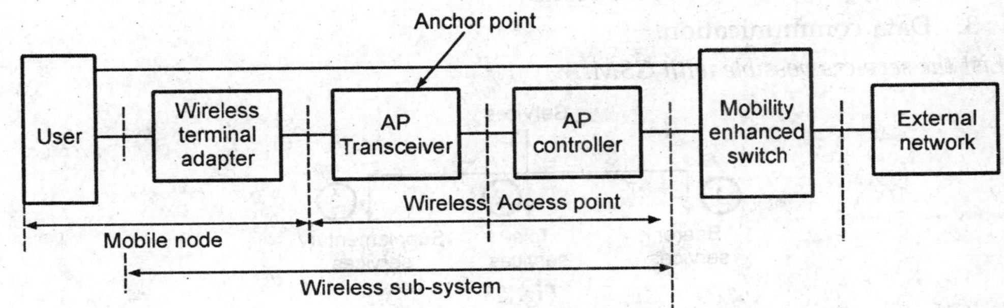

Fig. 51

Q. 378. *Mention any two types of handover possible with WATM.*

Ans. (a) Hard handover
(b) Network initiated.

Q. 379. *What is a terminal initiated handover?*

Ans. Whenever the wireless ATM (WATM) decides to initiate handover that is based on the current signal quality, it is known as terminal initiated handover.

Q. 380. *List the types of handover in WATM.*

Ans. (a) Hard handover.
(b) Terminal initiated.
(c) Network controlled.
(d) Backward handover.
(e) Forward handover.

Q. 381. *Give two important requirements of location management in wireless environment.*

Ans. (a) Security.
(b) Transparency of mobility.

Q. 382. *Give the UMTS architecture.*

Ans.

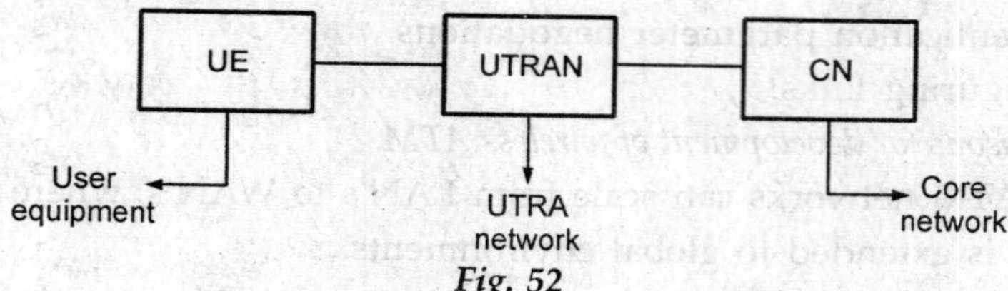

Fig. 52

Q. 383. *What is the multiple access scheme used in UTRA?*

Ans. Wideband - CDMA (W - CDMA) with DSS is used in FDD mode for UTRA network.

Q. 384. *What are the teleservices related GSM?*

Ans.
1. Message services.
2. Encrypted voice transmissions.
3. Data communication.

Q. 385. *List the services possible with GSM.*

Ans.

Fig. 53

Q. 386. *What are the subsystems under GSM?*

Ans.
(*a*) Radio subsystem (RSS)
(*b*) Operation subsystem (OSS)
(*c*) Network and switching subsystem (NSS).

Q. 387. *In wired telephony system what is the use of local subscriber loop?*

Ans. The local subscriber loop is a metallic transmission line that consists of two insulated wires as in a twisted pair.

Q. 388. *What are the parameters that the transmission characteristics depend on?*

Ans. It depends on the cable parameters like
(*a*) Conductor spacing
(*b*) Wire diameter
(*c*) Dielectric constant of the insulator.

Q. 389. *What are the distributed parameters?*

Ans. The electrical characteristics of a cable are also referred to as distributed parameters and they are generally distributed along its length.

Q. 390. *List the electrical parameters of a cable.*

Ans.
(*a*) Resistance
(*b*) Capacitance
(*c*) Inductance

Q. 391. *What are the component parts that will comprise a local loop?*

Ans. 1. Serving area interface (SAI)
2. Feeder cable (FI)
3. Drop-wire
4. Subscriber or standard network interface (SNI)
5. Distribution cable (F2).
6. Aerial
7. Distribution cable and drop-wire cross-connect point.

Q. 392. *What is a distribution cable?*

Ans. Distribution cable is a smaller version of the feeder cable which contains less wire pairs.

Q. 393. *What are the two components found on local loop?*

Ans. (*a*) Loading coils.
(*b*) Bridge taps.

Q. 394. *List three advantages of private line data circuits.*

Ans. (*a*) The transmission characteristics are more consistent.
(*b*) Line conditioning availability.
(*c*) Economical

Q. 395. *What is a* PBX?

Ans. It is private branch exchange. It is a switching machine with low capacity and the subscribers are limited (restricted) to a smaller area [like a building premises] only.

Q. 396. *What is an attenuation distortion?*

Ans. It is the frequency response of the transmission medium. Generally the voice-band frequency in a pair of cable is directly proportional to square root of the frequency.

Q. 397. *What is a C-type line conditioning?*

Ans. It actually specifies maximum limits for the attenuation distortion and also the envelope distortion.

Q. 398. *What is an envelope distortion?*

Ans. Envelope distortion is the time needed for propagation of AM envelope in a transmission medium. The corresponding distortion is called as envelope detection distortion (EDD).

Q. 399. *Give one example of correlated noise.*

Ans. Non-linear distortion is a kind of correlated noise and is mainly generated by a non-linear amplification.

Q. 400. *Define a phase jitter.*

Ans. It is one form of the incidental phase modulation, and it causes uncontrolled variations in zero crossing of the signal.

Q. 401. *Draw the phase jitter waveform.*

Ans.

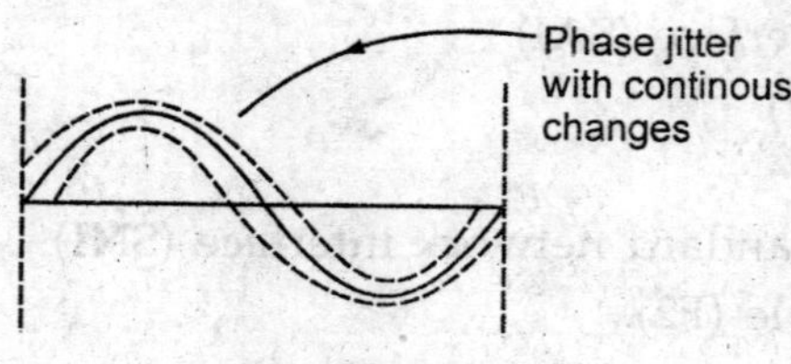

Fig. 54

Q. 402. *Draw a honey comb type of cell.*

Ans.

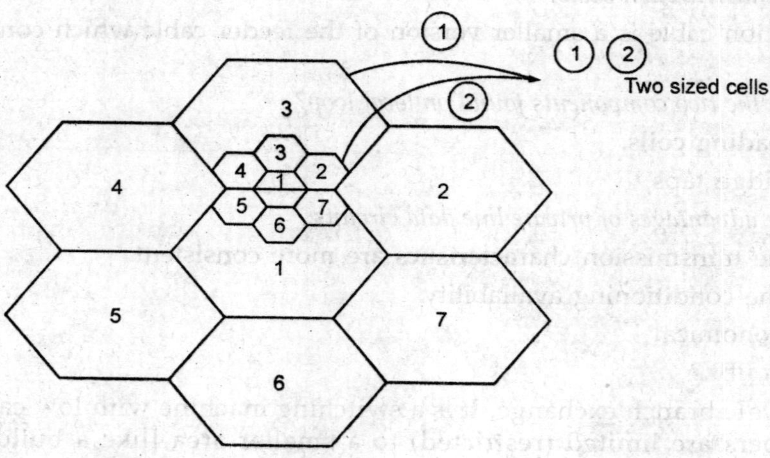

Fig. 55

Q. 403. *Draw edge and center excited cell cases.*

Ans.

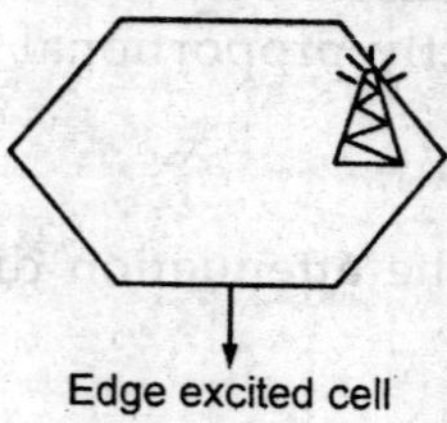

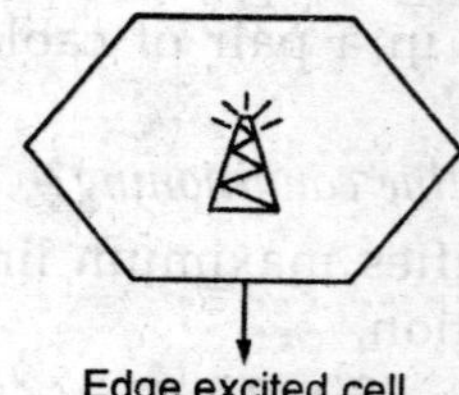

Fig. 56

Q. 404. *Draw the corner excited cell.*

Ans.

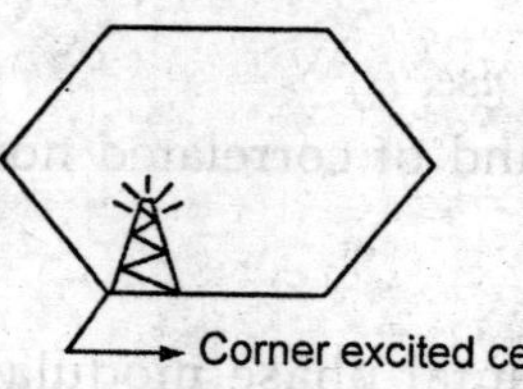

Fig. 57

Q. 405. *What is the number of cellular channels in a cluster?*

Ans.

$$f = GN$$

where f → Number of full-duplex cellular channels

G → Number of channels

N → Number cells in a cluster

Q. 406. *Write short note on 'cluster size'.*

Ans. A cluster represents a group of cells in a cellular coverage region. The cluster is denoted as 'N' which may be of sizes 4, 7 or 12 etc. The frequency reuse factor is related to cluster size by the equation.

$$\text{Frequency reuse factor} = \frac{1}{N}$$

In a hexagonal shaped cell considerations, the number cells in one cluster (N), should satisfy the relation.

$$N = i^2 + i + j^2 \text{ where}$$

i and j are two non negative integer values. For example if i = 3 and j = 2. The distance between two channel cells within a cluster N (N = 19 here) is shown below.

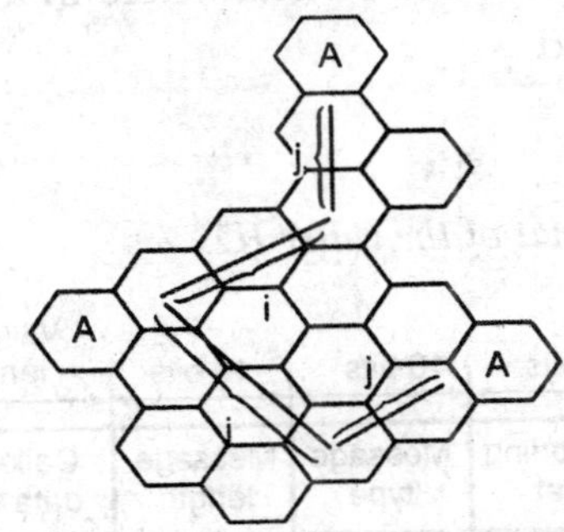

Fig. 58. A portion of cluster of N = 19 is shown here (A of A are co-channel cells)

Q. 407. *What is known as character synchronization?*

Ans. The character synchronization is done for identifying the beginning of a character and its end of which is a message.

Q. 408. *What is the other name for start-stop transmission?*

Ans. The start-stop transmission is also termed as asynchronous data transmission where the data is actually framed between start and stop bits.

Q. 409. *What is a synchronous data transfer?*

Ans. In synchronous data transfer usually a serial data is transferred as blocks or frames which represents a group of characters.

Q. 410. *What is DCE?*

Ans. Digital communications equipment (DCE) is used to denote an equipment that acts as interface between a transmission channel and data terminal equipment.

Q. 411. *Draw the cordless telephone system block diagram.*

Ans.

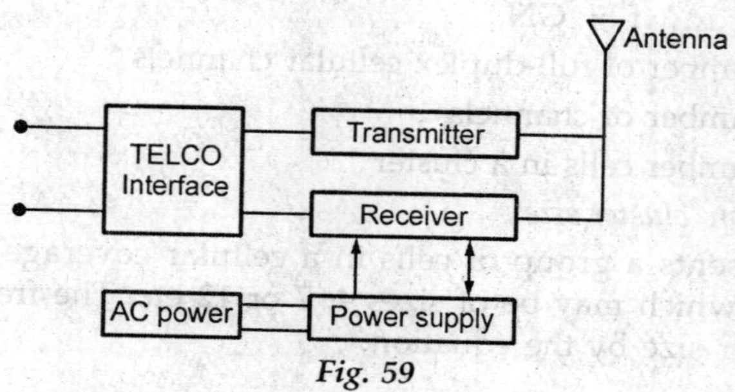

Fig. 59

Q, 412. *What is the use of caller ID?*

Ans. When telephone rings up before answering the call, with caller ID, it is possible to know the name and number of the caller party (destination).

Q. 413. *What is the frequency band utilized by cordless telephone?*

Ans. In cordless telephones 43 to 49 MHz (approx.) range of frequencies are used.

Q. 414. *How asynchronous transmission is specified in caller ID system?*

Ans. Asynchronous transmission of 16 bit characters in a frame is specified by

(*a*) Message length field

(*b*) Message field

(*c*) Caller ID data field.

Q. 415. *Draw the ringing cycle format of the caller ID.*

Ans.

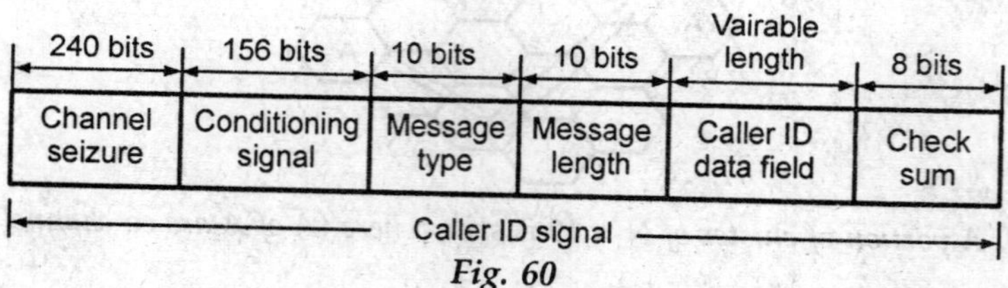

Fig. 60

Q. 416. *Draw the portable cordless phone block diagram.*

Ans.

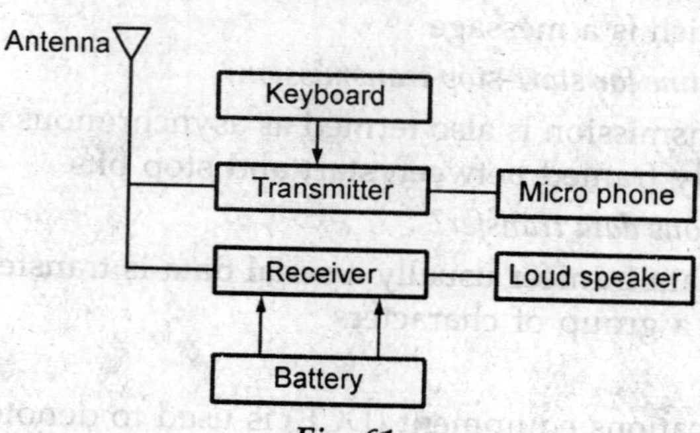

Fig. 61

Q. 417. *What is known as a paging system?*

Ans. They are simple wireless transmissions systems by which subscribers are alerted to the waiting messages.

Q. 418. *Give the electrical model of copper wire transmission line.*

Ans.

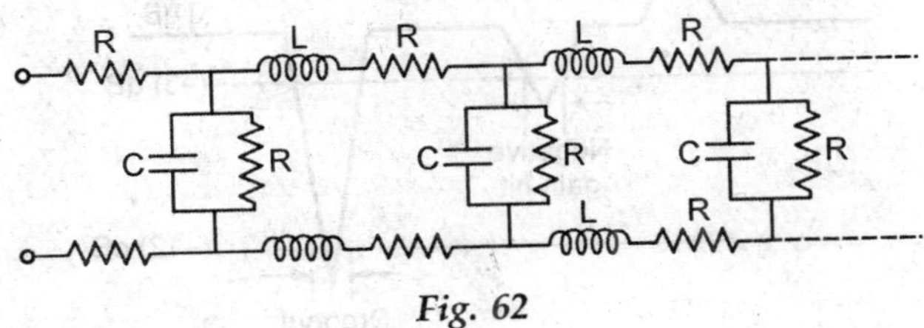

Fig. 62

Q. 419. *Write short note on bridge tap.*

Ans. It is in a random fashion at various points in cable. Bridge taps one actually unused portions of cable to serve upto subscriber location in wired telephony system.

Q. 420. *What is a total noise in a wired telephony?*

Ans. The total noise heard in a telephone receiver consists of two kind of noises.

(*a*) Noise introduced in the circuit.

(*b*) Room background noise.

Q. 421. *What is the dc loop resistance in a copper conductor in a wired telephone system?*

Ans.
$$R = \frac{0.1095}{D^2}$$

where D → Wire diameter

R → DC loop resistance

Q. 422. *What is a 'C' message weighting?*

Ans. The American telephone and telegraph company (AT&T) developed a weighting network termed as C message weighting. The noise signal components in wired telephone channels has to be considered with proper magnitude and this was done by C message weighting.

Q. 423. *What is dBm 0?*

Ans. It is dBm referred to zero (0) transmission level point.

Q. 424. *What is known as 'drop out'?*

Ans. A drop out is a decrease in the circuit gain or the signal level. It may be more than 12 dB value which can last longer than 4 msec. They occur in temporary open circuits.

Q. 425. *What is termed as gain hits?*

Ans. It is a sudden or random change in circuit gain which may result in temporary change in the signal level.

Q. 426. *What is known as phase hit?*

Ans. Phase hits are also called as 'slips'. They are random or sudden changes in the phase of the signal. Generally upto ± 20 °C peak the phase hit will not be measured.

Q. 427. *Give the gain hits and drop out in a telephonic signal.*

Ans.

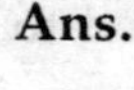

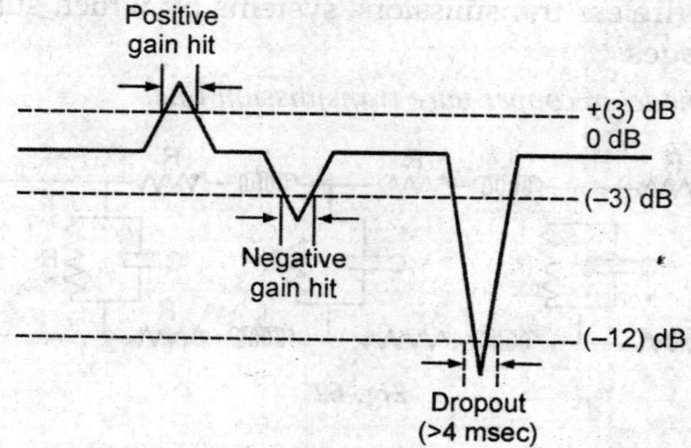

Fig. 63

Q. 428. *Draw the two wire passive cable wired circuit.*

Ans.

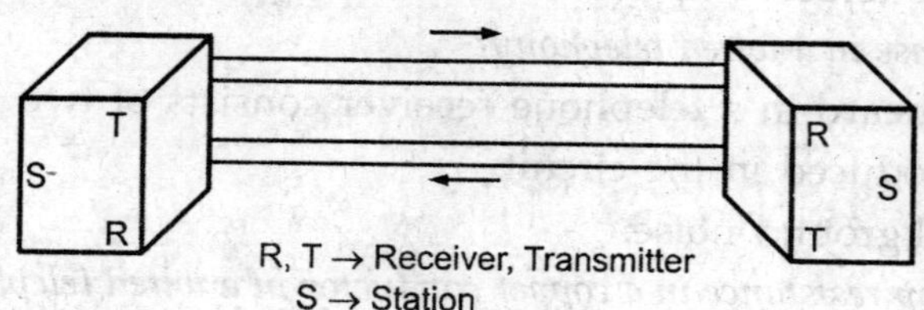

Fig. 64

Q. 429. *Draw the two wire active cable wired circuit.*

Ans.

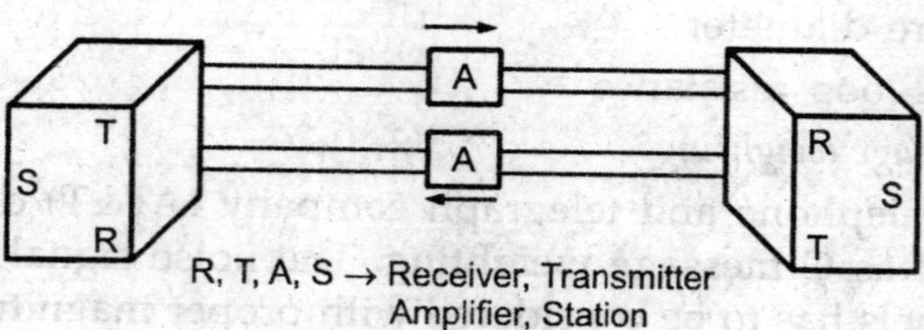

Fig. 65

Q. 430. *Draw a wireless radio carrier system.*

Ans.

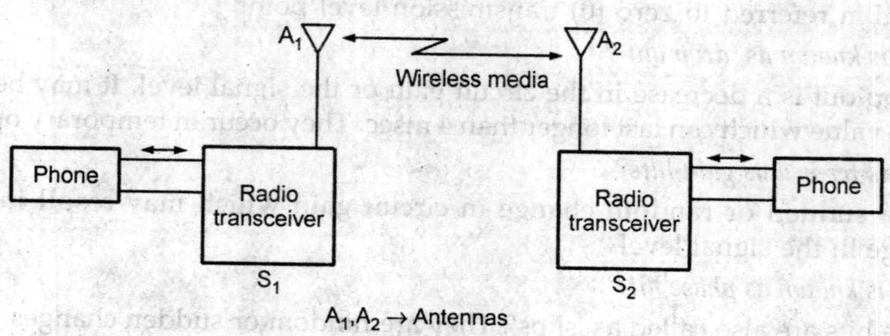

Fig. 66

Q. 431. *Define crosstalk.*

Ans. Crosstalk is an unwanted coupling that may interfere the actual signal from the original signal path into another signal path. It is mainly a kind of disturbance created in a channel by other communication channels.

Q. 432. *Give two examples for wi-fi technology.*

Ans. (*a*) IEEE 802.1la

(*b*) IEEE 802.11b

Q. 433. *What are parts of a Coaxial transmission line? (Assume it as solid flexible).*

Ans. (*a*) Sheath

(*b*) Insulation

(*c*) Branded shielding

Q. 434. *Give two examples for coaxial cable connectors.*

Ans. (*a*) BNC connector

(*b*) BNC barrel

Q. 435. *Give an equation that expresses characteristic impedance.*

Ans.

$$Z_0 = \sqrt{\frac{L}{C}}$$

where L → Inductance

C → Capacitance

Q. 436. *Define a surge impedance.*

Ans. The characteristic impedance (Z_0) is also called as surge impedance and it mainly expresses the impedance of an infinitely long line.

Q. 437. *What is the time delay that is introduced in co-axial cable?*

Ans.

$$T_d = 1.016\ \varepsilon$$

where ε → Dielectric constant of a cable

Q. 438. *What is a coupling loss?*

Ans. It occurs whenever a connection is taken from or made in a transmission line. But discontinuities leads to heat up and then dissipate power finally.

Q. 439. *What is corona?*

Ans. It is a luminous discharge that may occur between any two conductors of a transmission line whenever the potential difference is more than the breakdown voltage of a dielectric insulator. But if corona occurs transmission line get heavily damaged.

Q. 440. *Write the equation of standing wave ratio.*

Ans. Standing wave ratio = SNR = $\frac{V_{max}}{V_{min}}$

where V_{max} → Voltage maxima

V_{max} → Voltage minima

Q. 441. *Differentiate voltage and current standing waves with a graph.*

Ans.

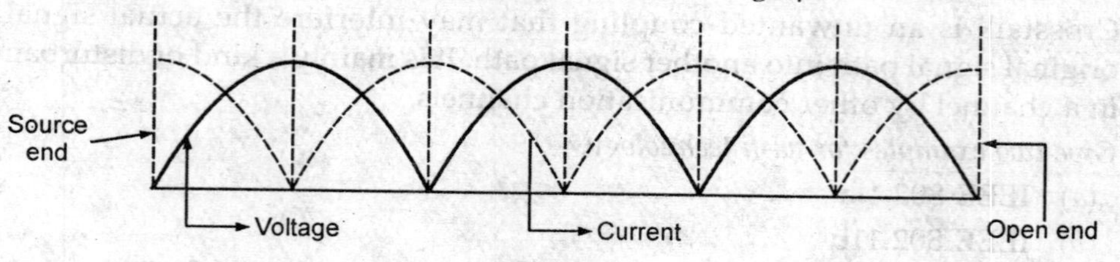

Fig. 67

Q. 442. *What is the use of quarter wavelength transformer matching?*

Ans. These transformers are used for matching transmission lines to the resistive loads (purely resistive) where their resistance is not equal to characteristic impedance (Z_0).

Q. 443. *What is a TDK?*

Ans. Time domain reflectometry (TDK) is used to locate an impairment (if any) in a metallic conductor.

Q. 444. *What is a micro strip?*

Ans. It is simply a flat shaped conductor that is separated from a ground plane by an insulating material say a dielectric.

Q. 445. *What are the three types of switching in data communication?*

Ans. (*a*) Packet switching

(*b*) Circuit switching

(*c*) Message switching

Q. 446. *What are the LAN topologies?*

Ans.

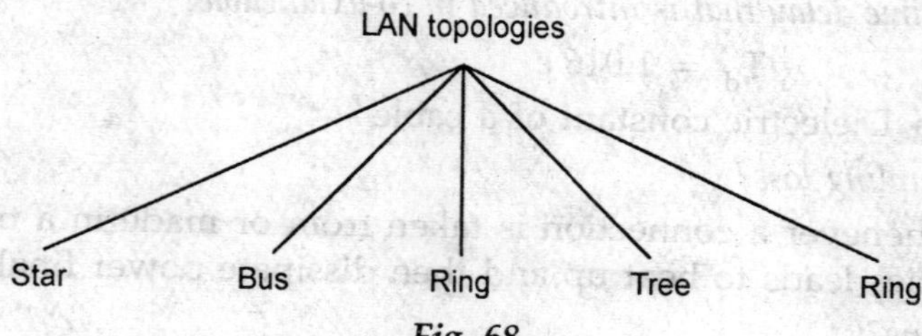

Fig. 68

Q. 447. *Compare baseband and broadband transmission format.*

Ans.

	Broadband	Baseband
1.	Analog signalling.	Digital signalling.
2.	Unidirectional	Bidirectional.
3.	Multiple traffic types are possible.	Simple.

Q. 448. *Give the ethernet standards.*

Ans. (*a*) 10 Base-5 ethernet

(*b*) 10 Base-2 ethernet.

Q. 449. *Write a note on 1000 Mbps ethernet.*

Ans. One gigabit ethernet (IGb-E) operates at 1 billion bits per sec transmission rate. It has two and four wire 1000 Base T categories.

Q. 450. *Draw an unique word correlator.*

Ans.

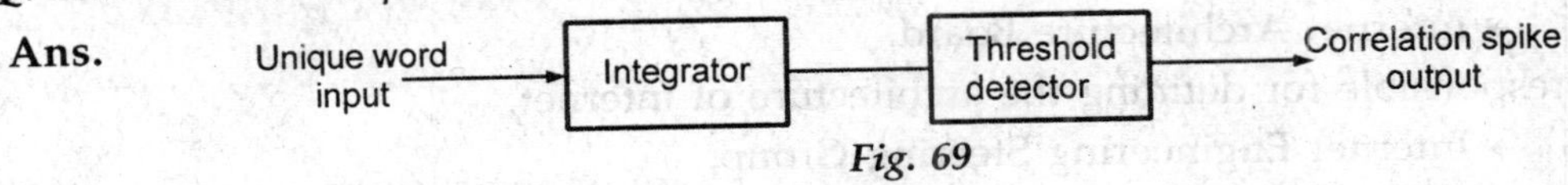

Fig. 69

Q. 451. *What is a TASI?*

Ans. The time assignment speech interpolation (TASI) is a particular form of analog channel compression technique.

Q. 452. *Draw a 60° cell sectoring shape.*

Ans.

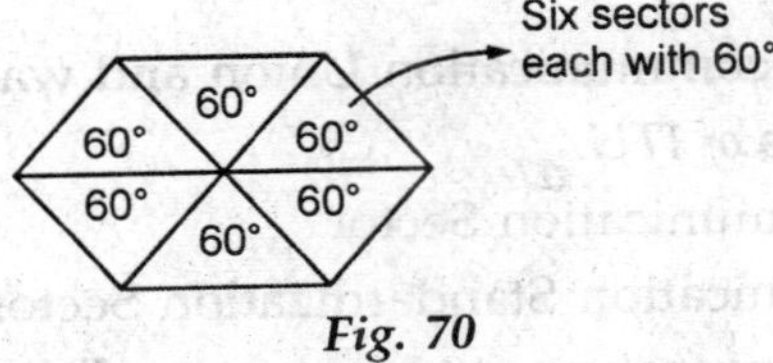

Fig. 70

Q. 453. *Express handoff in a cell with a diagram.*

Ans.

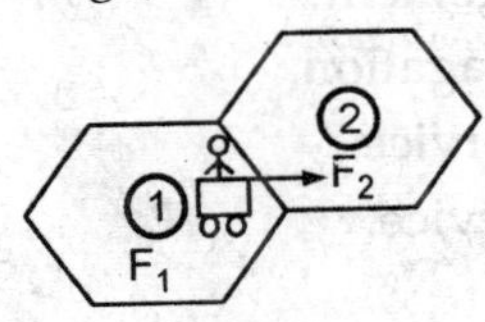

Fig. 71

A subscriber leaving cell (1) of frequency 'F_1' and enters cell (2) if new frequency 'F_2' where the base station of cell (1) hands over control to cell (2).

Q. 454. *Draw a 120° sectored cell shape.*

Ans.

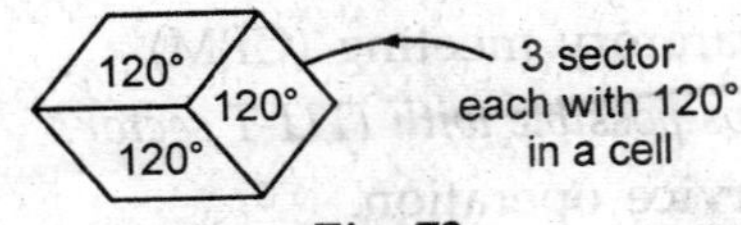

Fig. 72

Q. 455. *What are the components of a cellular telephone system?*

Ans.
1. Radio transceivers.
2. Electronic switching center.
3. Cell site controller.
4. System interconnection.
5. Common communication protocol.
6. Mobile telephone unit.

Q. 456. *What are the three types of calls in a cellular telephonic system?*

Ans. (*a*) Mobile (cell) to mobile (cell).
(*b*) Mobile to PSTN (wireline).
(*c*) PSTN (wireline) to mobile.

Q. 457. *What are IAB and IESG?*

Ans. IAB → Internet Architecture Board.

It is responsible for defining the architecture of internet.

IESG → Internet Engineering Steering Group.

It is responsible for all technical managements.

Q. 458. *Define IETF.*

Ans. It is "Internet Engineering Task Force" meant for protocol and development engineering wing of internet.

Q. 459. *Write short note on ITU.*

Ans. It is International Telecommunication Union and was created in the year 1993.

Q. 460. *Mention any two sectors of ITU.*

Ans. (*a*) ITU Radio Communication Sector.
(*b*) ITU Telecommunication Standardization Sector.

Q. 461. *What are the study groups that are organized under ITU-R?*

Ans.
1. SG-1 spectrum management.
2. SG-3 radiowave propagation.
3. SG-4 fixed satellite service.
4. SG-6 broadcasting service.
5. SG-7 science services.
6. SG-8 mobile, amateur, radio determination services etc.
7. SG-9 fixed service.
8. SC special committee on regulatory or procedural mailers.
9. CCV coordination committee.
10. Conference preparatory meeting (CPM).

Q. 462. *What are the study groups possible with ITU-T sector?*

Ans.
1. Network and service operation.
2. Tariff and accounting principle.
3. Network maintenance and telecommunications management network.
4. Protection against electromagnetic environment effects.
5. Data networks and open system communication.
6. Telemetric system characteristics.
7. Signalling requirements and protocols.
8. General network aspects.
9. Multimedia services and systems.
10. Transport system, equipment and networks.

11. End-to-end performance.
12. Software aspects for telecommunication systems.
13. Outside plant.
14. Sound and television transmission.

Q. 463. *Give any two working groups under IEEE 802 standard.*

Ans. (*a*) 802.5 Token ring working group.

(*b*) 802.6 Metropolitan area network working group.

Q. 464. *Comment on peer to peer topology for ad hoc LAN.*

Ans. In peer to peer topology there is no use of hub and this is compatible and efficient for ad hoc LAN systems. For control access a MAC algorithm can be applied.

Q. 465. *What are licensed narrowband radio frequency (RF)?*

Ans. A specific spectrum of microwave radio frequencies are suitable for voice, data and video transmissions. They are licensed within the region to reduce interferences.

Q. 466. *What is the advantage of licensed narrowband RF?*

Ans. An advantage of licensed narrowband LAN is that it reduces interferences, and guarantees faithful reception of the signal.

Q. 467. *What are the two types of narrow band RF?*

Ans. (*a*) Licensed narrow band RF.

(*b*) Unlicensed narrow band RF.

Q. 468. *What are the functions of physical layer of the OSI model?*

Ans. 1. Encoding and decoding of the signals.

2. Bit transmission and reception.
3. Synchronization.

Q. 469. *What are the two main partitions of data link layer?*

Ans. (*a*) Logical link control.

(*b*) Medium access control.

Q. 470. *What are functions of logical link layer (LLC)?*

Ans. The LLC provides proper interface between layer 2 and higher layers. It performs flow control and error control.

Q. 471. *What is the function of medium access control (MAC)?*

Ans. 1. Assembling data into the frame in transmission with relevant fields.

2. In reception disassembling the frame and performing address recognition with error detecting functions.

Q. 472. *What is LSAP?*

Ans. LSAP is service access point available in logical link control (LLC) of OSI reference model.

Q. 473. *What are the fields of a MAC?*

Ans. 1. MAC control

2. Source MAC address

3. Destination MAC address
4. CRC
5. Data

Q. 474. *What is a PCS in MAC?*

Ans. It is frame check sequence (PCS) which is also termed as cyclic redundancy check field (CRC) which is used as error detecting code.

Q. 475. *What is known as 'data'?*

Ans. Data is the original information generally represented in binary form as bits or units. The digital format of data is 0's and 1's, and processed in communication. Data may be analog data (any physical signal in nature) or digital data (0's and 1's). Today digital data transmissions are mainly used in many communication applications.

Q. 476. *List any three services provided by IEEE 802.11 standard.*

Ans.
1. Access and privacy service.
2. Association related service.
3. Distribution of messages.

Q. 477. *What is the use of frequency hopping in Bluetooth?*

Ans.
1. Frequency hopping reduces multipath effects and reduce interferences.
2. It also helps for multiple access with co-located devices of other piconets.

Q. 478. *What are the two links developed between a master and slave under physical link?*

Ans.
(*a*) Asynchronous connectionless (ACL) link
(*b*) Synchronous connectionless oriented (SCO) link.

Q. 479. *What are the fields available in Bluetooth packet format?*

Ans.
1. Access code field
2. Payload field
3. Header field

Q. 480. *What are the types of access codes in Bluetooth?*

Ans.
(*a*) Channel access code (CAC)
(*b*) Inquiry access code (IAC)
(*c*) Device access code (DAC)

Q. 481. *What are the encoding schemes possible with Bluetooth audio?*

Ans.
1. Pulse code modulation (PCM)
2. Continuously variable slope delta (CVSD).

Q. 482. *State the modes possible when the slave is in connection state in Bluetooth.*

Ans.

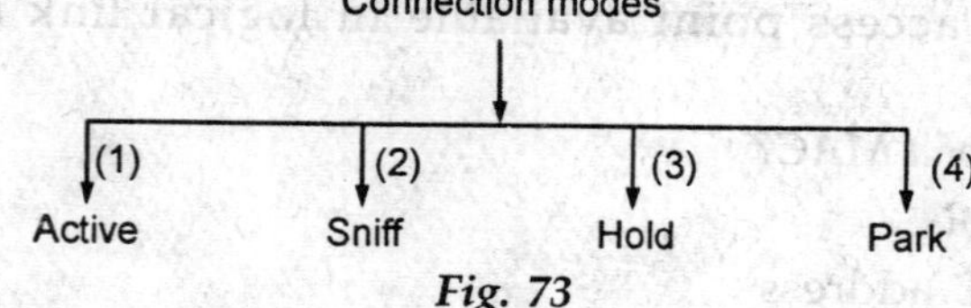

Fig. 73

Q. 483. *What are elements available under link security of Bluetooth technology?*

Ans. 1. Authentication
2. Key management
3. Encryption

Q. 484. *What is a LMP?*

Ans. It is "link manager specification" that is responsible for radio link between the master and slave in Bluetooth. This protocol also involves message exchanges in the form of LMP-PDU's.

Q. 485. *List three security services under IMP.*

Ans. (*a*) Authentication
(*b*) Change link key
(*c*) Encryption

Q. 486. *What are the synchronizing mechanisms possible under LMP?*

Ans. (*a*) Slot offset information
(*b*) Clock offset request
(*c*) Timing accuracy information request.

Q. 487. *What are the PDU's that is used to exchange messages about communicating devices in LMP?*

Ans. There are two PDU's used namely LMP version and Bluetooth radio with link controller as supported feature are related with communicating devices.

Q. 488. *What are the PDU's under LMP that are used to manage Bluetooth device states and-modes? List any five.*

Ans. 1. Slave role/switch master
2. Name request
3. Sniff mode
4. Park mode
5. Power control

Q. 489. *List any four LMP supported features.*

Ans. 1. Encryption
2. CVSD
3. Paging scheme
4. Timing accuracy

Q. 490. *What is a QoS in L2CAP?*

Ans. In logical link control and adaption protocol (L2CAP) the quality of service (QoS) defines the traffic flow specifications which expresses 'performance level' of the system.

Q. 491. *What are the parameters of flow specification under L2CAP?*

Ans. (*a*) Service type
(*b*) Token bucket size
(*c*) Token rate

(d) Latency
(e) Peak bandwidth
(f) Delay variation

Q. 492. *What are the organizations responsible for work of standards in Internet?*

Ans. (a) Internet Engineering Task Force (IETF)
(b) Internet Engineering Steering Group (IESG)
(c) Internet Architecture Board (IAB)

Q. 493. *Define header and packet.*

Ans. Header → Header precedes the user information and it is a system defined control information.

Packet → It is nothing but group of bits with source and destination address information.

Q. 494. *What is a network layer?*

Ans. It takes part in OSI model and constitutes layer 3. Functions of this layer is routing the data through the network.

Q. 495. *Differentiate syntax and semantics in data communication.*

Ans. (i) Syntax - It refers to the format or structure of the data representing the order in which the data is available.

(ii) Semantics - It represents the meaning of each section of the bits in the data.

Q. 496. *What is known as pseudonoise?*

Ans. Pseudonoise is a sequence of numbers those are random statistically. It is useful in digital transmission schemes.

Q. 497. *What is called as 'synchronous TDM'?*

Ans. It is a kind of TDM where the time slots on transmission medium shared are allotted to input-output channels on a predetermined, fixed manner.

Q. 498. *List any three Bluetooth user scenarios.*

Ans. (a) Internet bridge
(b) Cordless desktop
(c) Instant digital postcard

Q. 499. *List few functions of Bluetooth.*

Ans.
1. It can make call from a headset (wireless) to a mobile phone which is at a distant place.
2. It can trigger MP3 players on some other machines to download audio signals like music in wireless environment.
3. It mainly eliminates cables in many user applications.

Q. 500. *What is a Bluetooth?*

Ans. It is a low power short range wireless standard and it can operate in situations where several users are involved. At the maximum eight different devices can communicate in a network using this standard.

Q. 501. *Write short note on protocol architecture of Bluetooth.*

Ans. Bluetooth is said to be a layered protocol architecture and it comprises of 4 protocols namely,

1. Core protocols
2. Cable replacement protocol
3. Telephony control protocol
4. Adopted protocol

Q. 502. *What are the possible usage models defined in Bluetooth?*

Ans. The usage models in Bluetooth are a set of protocols used to implement a particular Bluetooth application. They are listed below.

1. Internet bridge
2. File transfer
3. Synchronization
4. LAN access
5. Three-in-one phone
6. Headset

Q. 503. *Differentiate piconet and scatternet in Bluetooth technology.*

Ans.
1. Piconet - It is a basic network supported by Bluetooth standard where one master and seven slaves (total eight devices) can interact.
2. Scatternet - A device in one piconet either a master or slave can interact with other device that is overlapping of one piconet on other piconet is possible and termed as a "Scatternet".

Q. 504. *List three cellular services.*

Ans.
1. Cellular Telephone Service (CTS)
2. Personal Communication Systems (PCS)
3. Personal Communications Satellite Systems (PCSS)

Q. 505. *Write short note on MTS.*

Ans. MTS refers to mobile telephone systems; and its services were introduced in 1940. It uses frequency modulation and this system was allotted with single carrier frequency as 35 to 45 MHz range.

Q. 506. *Why hexagon shaped cells are used?*

Ans. The hexagon shaped cells provided efficient transmission and coverage for cellular radio. It eliminated gaps between the cell structures.

Q. 507. *Draw a "Three cluster" cellular region.*

Ans.

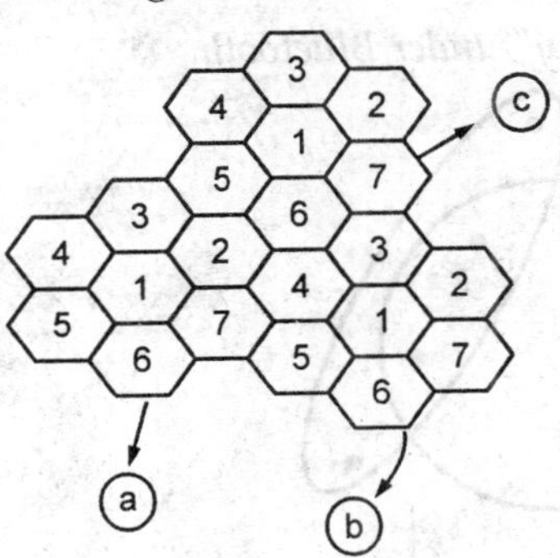

Fig. 74

Q. 508. *What is a FRF?*

Ans. FRF is frequency reuse factor. It can be expressed as

$$FRF = \frac{N}{C}$$

where

N → No. of full duplex channels, in a geographical area

C → No. of full duplex channels in a cell.

FRF is a unitless parameter.

Q. 509. *What is a co-channel cell and adjacent cell?*

Ans. The co-channel cell represents two cells of different clusters that use the same frequencies. An example is given below.

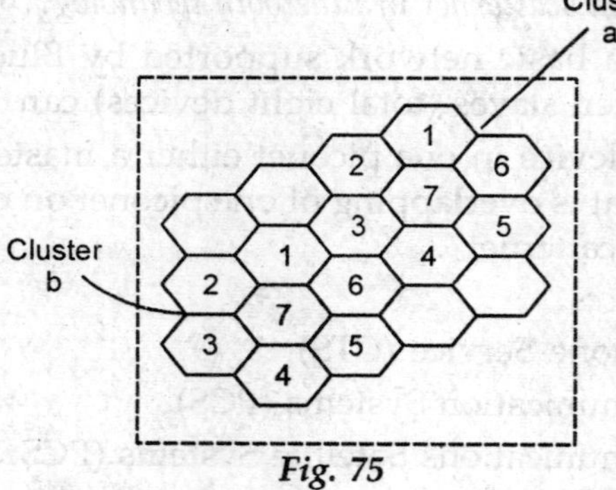

Fig. 75

The corresponding same numbers say (7, 7), (6, 6) etc. uses the same frequencies and termed as co-channel cells of different clusters a and b. An "Adjacent cell" is a neighbouring cell which is not using the same frequency, when 'frequency reuse' technique is applied.

Q. 510. *Comment on frequency hopping in Bluetooth.*

Ans. In Bluetooth frequency hopping with 1 MHz carrier frequency spacing is used. For example in a total spectrum bandwidth of 80 MHz. So different frequencies are used in this technology.

Q. 511. *Draw a "scatternet strategy" under Bluetooth.*

Ans.

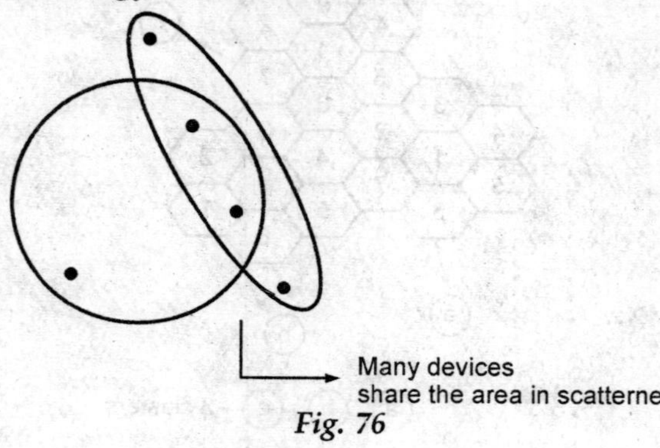

Fig. 76

Q. 512. *What is the advantage of scatternet?*

Ans. In this scatternet structure of wireless networks, several devices take part in scatternet which may overlap on each other.

Main advantage of scatternet is efficient bandwidth utilization.

Q. 513. *Draw the DSSS receiver schematic.*

Ans.

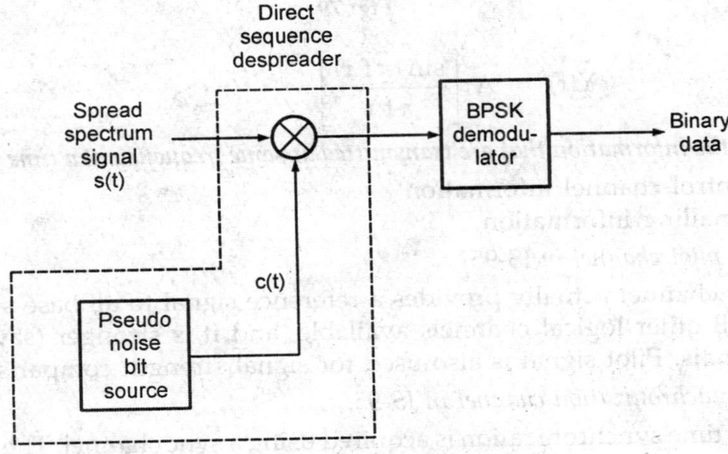

Fig. 77

Q. 514. *Draw the DSSS transmitter schematic.*

Ans.

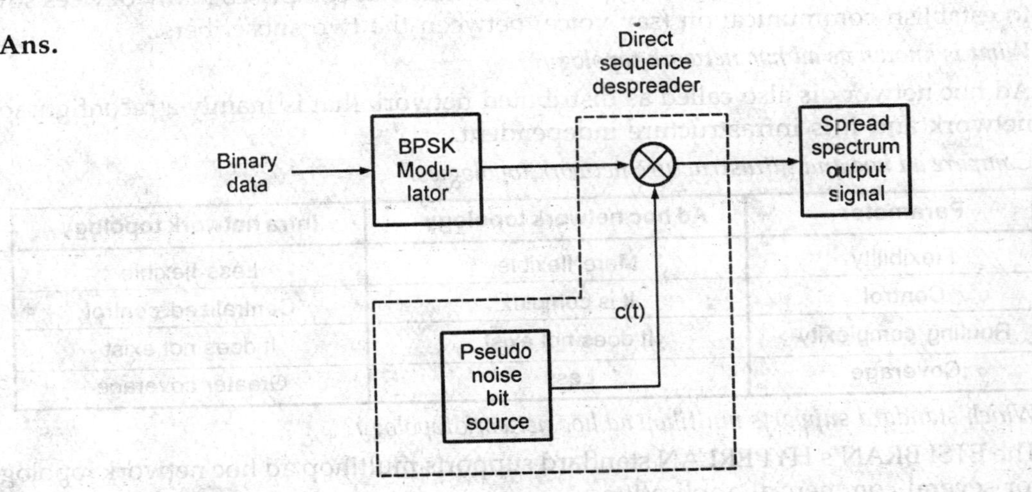

Fig. 78

Q. 515. *Write short note on CDMA.*

Ans. CDMA technique acts as both an air interface and an access scheme. It has better power control and 'handling soft handoff techniques than other methods.

Q. 516. *Draw the triangular wave y(t) with its Fourier transform y(f).*

Ans.

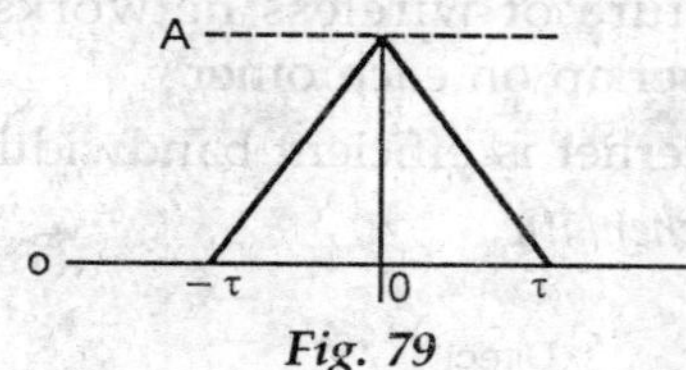

Fig. 79

$$Y(f) = A\tau\left[\frac{\sin(\pi f \tau)}{\pi f \tau}\right]$$

Q. 517. *What are the information that are transmitted at same frequency at a time in CDMA system?*

Ans. (*a*) Control channel information

(*b*) Signalling information

Q. 518. *What is a pilot channel in IS-95?*

Ans. The pilot channel actually provides a reference signal to all base stations. It is used to lock all other logical channels available, and it is stronger (say 4 to 6 dB) than other signals. Pilot signal is also used for signal strength comparisons.

Q. 519. *Define a synchronization channel in IS-95.*

Ans. An initial time synchronization is acquired using a sync channel. The sync information in IS-95 includes network and system identification.

Q. 520. *Define a telecommunication network.*

Ans. Telecommunication network is type of a medium that comprises many devices so as to establish communication (say voice) between the two subscribers.

Q. 521. *What is known as ad hoc network topology?*

Ans. Ad hoc network is also called as distributed network that is mainly a reconfigurable network and it is infrastructure independent.

Q. 522. *Compare ad hoc and infrastructure network topologies.*

Ans.

Parameter	Ad hoc network topology	Infra network topology
Flexibility	More flexible	Less flexible
Control	It is complex	Centralized control
Routing complexity	It does not exist	It does not exist
Coverage	Less	Greater coverage

Q. 523. *Which standard supports multihop ad hoc network topology?*

Ans. The ETSI BRAN's HYPERLAN standard supports multihop ad hoc network topology for several commercial applications.

Q. 524. *List four technical issues that are important for planning (deciding) a cellular network.*

Ans. (*a*) Physical deployment

(*b*) Radio coverage

(*c*) Selecting frequency reuse pattern

(*d*) Cost involved.

Q. 525. *List any three cell sizes.*

Ans. (*a*) Femto cell

(*b*) Pico cell

(*c*) Macro cell.

Q. 526. *Differentiate hexagon and circular cell shapes.*

Ans.

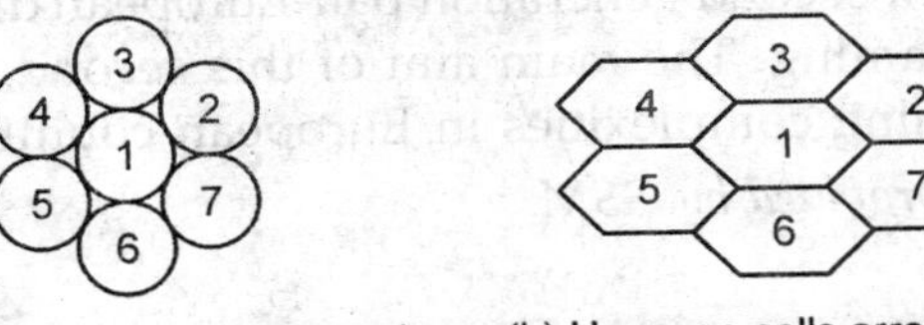

Fig. 80

Q. 527. *What is the advantage of hexagon cellular pattern over circular cellular pattern?*

Ans. In hexagon shaped cells the radio coverage is highly efficient than circular shaped cells where the coverage is poor.

Q. 528. *What are types of channel allocation?*

Ans. 1. Fixed channel allocation

2. Dynamic channel allocation

Q. 529. *What are the control types possible under fixed and dynamic channel allocation?*

Ans. Fixed channel allocation - (FCA) → Centralized control.

Dynamic channel allocation - (DC A) → Centralized/decentralized/distributed control.

Q. 530. *What are the approaches allowed to migrate from AMPs cellular scheme to IS-95 digitized cellular scheme?*

Ans.

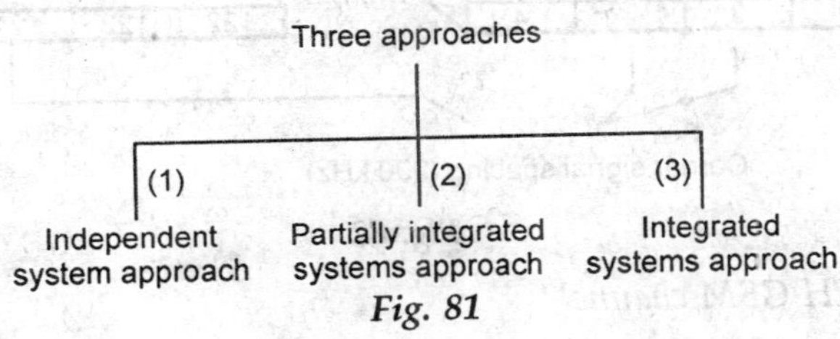

Fig. 81

Q. 531. *List two disadvantages under 'independent si/stem' approach.*

Ans. 1. Spectrum segmentation may lead to capacity loss.

2. Complexity involved in its operation.

Q. 532. *Give two advantages of the same Q. 531.*

Ans. 1. It is vendor independent.

2. Economic.

Q. 533. *List two disadvantages of partially independent system.*

Ans. 1. It requires a buffer zone.

2. Voice quality may change during handoffs.

Q. 534. *What are the advantages of an integrated system?*

Ans. 1. Efficient spectrum utilization.

2. Simplicity.

Q. 535. *Write a short note on GSM.*

Ans. Global system for mobile (GSM) is developed as an ETS1 standard in the year 1982. It was developed for second generation pan-European digital cellular with the facility of international roaming. The main aim of this second generation cellular standard was to avoid roaming complexities in European countries.

Q. 536. *List all the services provided by GSM.*

Ans. (*a*) Tele services.

(*b*) Bearer services.

(*c*) Supplementary services.

Q. 537. *What are the different managements under GSM protocol architecture?*

Ans. 1. Mobility management

2. Connection management

3. Radio resource management

4. Message transfer

5. Signal connection control

6. Link access protocol.

Q. 538. *Draw the frequency band separation structure in* GSM.

Ans.

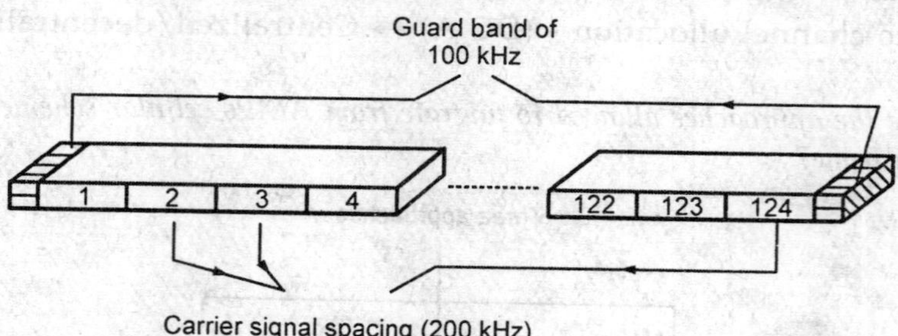

Fig. 82

Q. 539. *What is a TCH/H GSM channel?*

Ans. It is half rate traffic channel that supports traffic channels with half-rate speech coding. It can use upto 16 slots in one frame with a data rate of 11.4 kb/sec.

Q. 540. *What are the common control channels?*

Ans. The common control channels (CCCH) are used for call establishment and they are basically one way channels.

Q. 541. *What are types of CCCH?*

Ans. 1. Random access channel (RCH)

2. Paging channel (PCH)

3. Access grant channel (AGCH)

Q. 542. *What is a RCH?*

Ans. For establishing a call RCH is used by mobile station to access the base station involved.

Q. 543. *What are DCCH?*

Ans. It is duplicated control channels known as two way channels and it is useful for signalling and control operations for individual subscribers.

Q. 544. *What are the types of DCCH?*

Ans.

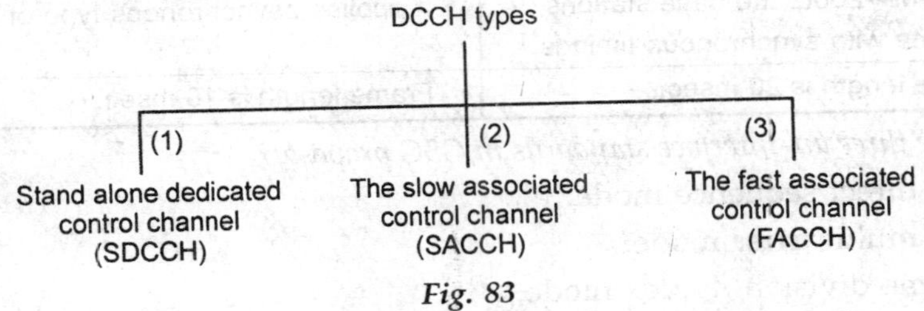

Fig. 83

Q. 545. *Write short note on IS-634 standard.*

Ans. The IS-634 is used and accepted as an interface for public wireless communication system standard. It is also named or labelled as A-interface and it is responsible for all features and services related to message communications between mobile switching center and base stations.

Q. 546. *What is the use of IS-41 standard?*

Ans. It can support many services in the core network. They are

(*a*) Authentication

(*b*) Roaming (automatic)

(*c*) Handoffs

(*d*) Message services

Q. 547. *What is the standard that resembles a SS7 signalling?*

Ans. IS-41 resembles SS7 standard in many ways. Along with that, IS-41 standard also supports mobile application part (MAP) which mainly defines message transportation between the main network elements.

Q. 548. *What are the types of logical channels in forward channel in IS-95 standard?*

Ans. There are four types of logical channels.

1. Pilot channel
2. Synchronization channel
3. Traffic channel
4. Paging channel

Q. 549. *What is the prime feature of a third generation cellular system?*

Ans. The main requirement of a 3G system is to provide several application data rates (speed), (say for example from 384 Kb/sec to 2 Mb/sec in various areas).

Q. 550. *What are the components of a global 3G system proposal?*

Ans. (*a*) Three air-interface standards.
(*b*) Support for ANSI-41 and GSM-MAP air interface modes.
(*c*) Functionality based synchronous operation is supported.
(*d*) Supports handoff operation.

Q. 551. *Compare W-CDMA and CDMA 2000 schemes.*

Ans.

CDMA 2000	W-CDMA
In CDMA-2000, the base stations operate with synchronous timings.	It applies asynchronous type of operation.
Frame length is 20 msec.	Frame length is 10 msec.

Q. 552. *What are three air-interface standards in G3G proposal?*

Ans. 1. A direct sequence mode.
2. A multicarrier mode.
3. Time division duplex mode.

Q. 553. *What are the frequency division duplex modes in G3G proposal?*

Ans. There are two frequency division duplex modes available.

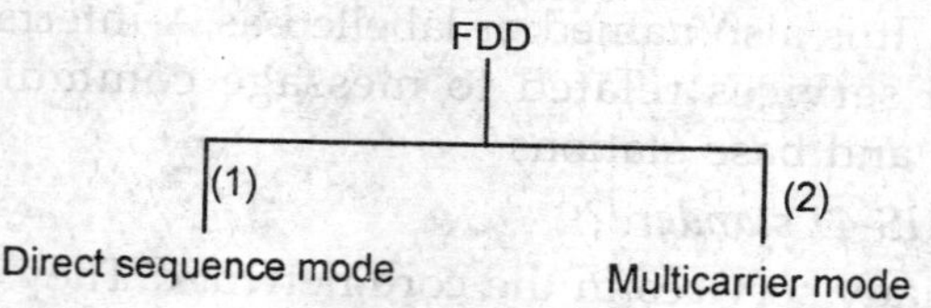

Fig. 84

Q. 554. *Write short note on W-CDMA.*

Ans. In the W-CDMA technology the base stations adopt asynchronous type of operation, and hence it requires GPS for synchronizing the base stations. W-CDMA uses orthogonal variable spreading factor (OVSF) codes.

Q. 555. *What kind of codes are used in W-CDMA with respect to uplink?*

Ans. (*a*) Gold codes (with periodicity of 38,400 chips).
(*b*) S(2) codes (with periodicity of 256 chips).

Q. 556. *What are the types of overlay mobile data networks?*

Ans.

FDD
(1)
(2)
Direct sequence mode
Multicarrier mode

Fig. 85

Q. 557. *Give an example for shared mobile data network.*

Ans. Example - CDPD network. It is a wide area mobile data technology.

Q. 558. *Draw the location management available in QPRS.*

Ans.

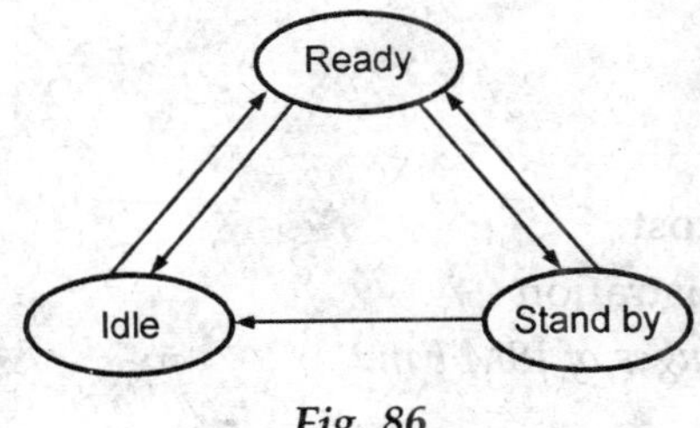

Fig. 86

Q. 559. *Give two demerits of WAP.*

Ans. 1. WAP does not support roaming between the various link level bearer services.
2. Supporting WAP on the color PDA terminals has poor quality.

Q. 560. *Give the basic WAP schematic.*

Ans.

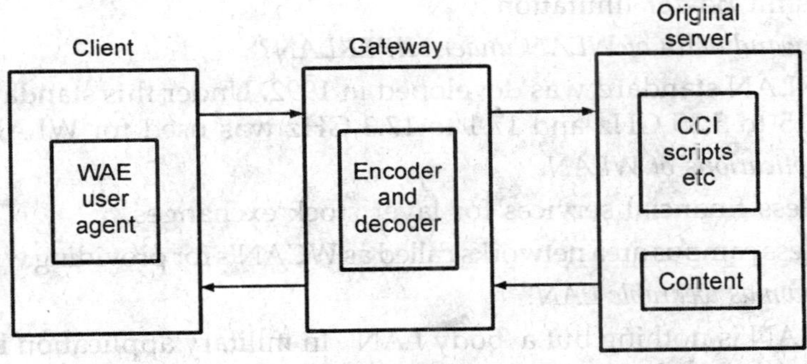

Fig. 87

Q. 561. *What are WAP and WTLS?*

Ans. WDP → Wireless Datagram Protocol
WTLS → Wireless Transport Layer Security

Q. 562. *What is WAE in WAP?*

Ans. It is wireless application environment which is an application platform that can combine the features of mobile telephony and web.

Q. 563. *What does a WAE comprise of?*

Ans. WAE consists of

1. WML
2. Micro browser
3. WML script
4. Many data formats
5. Images
6. Calenders
7. Records
8. Telephony applications etc.

Q. 564. *What are the layers available in WAP protocol architecture?*

Ans.
1. Application (WAE)
2. Session (WSP)
3. Transaction (WTP)
4. Security (WTLS)
5. Transport (WDP)
6. Other services.

Q. 565. *List few major problems that a WLAN has to meet.*

Ans.
1. Bandwidth
2. Coverage
3. Interference
4. Complexity and cost
5. Frequency administration

Q. 566. *List any two frequency ranges of ISM band.*

Ans. Frequency of operation
1. 2.4 to 2.48 GHz.
2. 5.7 to 5.8 GHz.

Q. 567. *Give two properties of ISM band.*

Ans.
1. Low power
2. Transmit power limitation.

Q. 568. *What is the bandwidth of WLAN under HIPERLAN?*

Ans. The HIPERLAN standard was developed in 1992. Under this standard the frequency band of 5.15 to 5.35 GHz and 17.1 to 17.3 GHz was used for WLAN operation.

Q. 569. *List two applications of WLAN.*

Ans.
1. Wireless financial services for layer stock exchanges.
2. Wireless campus area networks called as WCAN's for providing wireless classroom.

Q. 570. *What is known as wearable LAN?*

Ans. Wearable LAN is nothing but a 'body LAN'. In military application it can be used by soldiers where this device keeps track of body temperature, heartbeat etc. and can transmit information to next soldier if required.

Q. 571. *Give two application examples for wireless home networking.*

Ans.
1. PSTN for telephones.
2. Internet facility with systems in home.

Q. 572. *What is a HAN?*

Ans. 'HAN' is an infrastructure that can be developed to interconnect many home appliances to access internet through a central gateway.

Q. 573. What *are interfaces possible with home computing equipment?*

Ans.
1. Laptops
2. Scanners
3. Web cameras

Q. 574. *List few constraints posed by HAN.*

Ans.
1. HAN must be user friendly.
2. Always it should be flexible.
3. Should be scalable.

Q. 575. *Give two advantages of HAN.*

Ans.
1. Wired HAN's are implementable with less cost.
2. Wireless HAN's provides adhoc solutions.

Q. 576. *What is a HPNA?*

Ans. HPNA is an ethernet compatible local area network. It has a stand-alone adapter and enables connection to any device that has a ethernet card.

Q. 577. *List few basic requirements of IEEE 802.11 standard.*

Ans.
1. Multiple overlapping network should be allowed.
2. Single MAC should support several PHY layers.
3. Hidden terminal has to be handled.

Q. 578. *Compare the technologies POTS and HPNA with respect to frequency.*

Ans. POTS → Plain Old Telephone System.

HPNA → Ethernet compatible LAN.

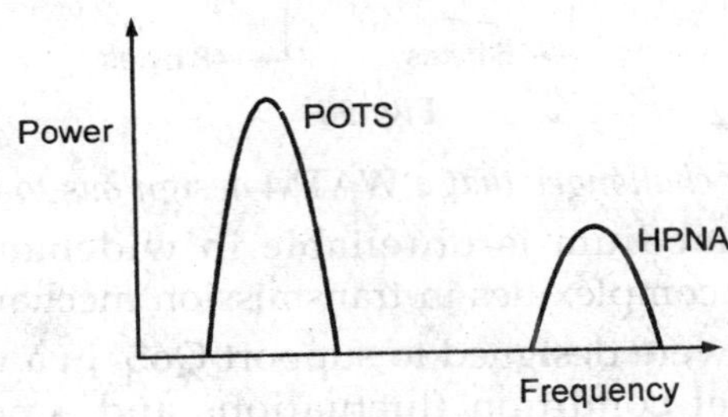

Fig. 88

POTS → 20 Hz - 3.4 kHz

HPNA → 2 MHz - 30 MHz

Q. 579. *Give one wireless and wired standard compatible with broadband home access system.*

Ans. (*a*) Wireless standard - DBS.

(*b*) Wired standard - Cable modem.

Q. 580. *What are the three main management wings under IEEE 802.11 standard?*

Ans. (*a*) MAC management

(*b*) PHY management

(*c*) Station management

Q. 581. *Represent an overlapping frequency bands for DSSS, under 802.11 standard with schematic.*

Ans.

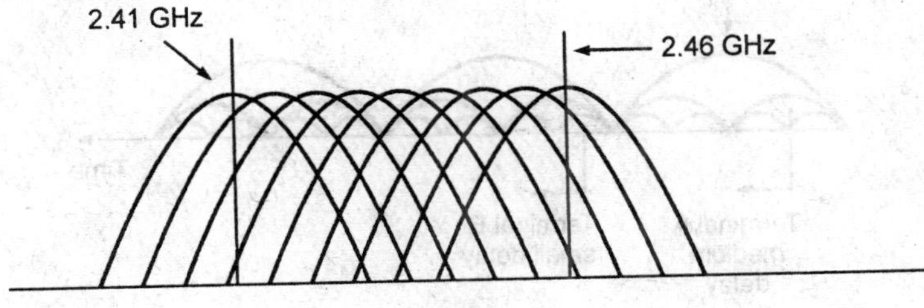

Fig. 89

Q. 582. *What are the mobility types possible with handoff in MAC management?*

Ans. 1. No transition type
2. BSS transition type
3. ESS transition type

Q. 583. *What are the two services linked with handoff mechanism in IEEE 802.11?*

Ans. 1. Reassociation service
2. Dissociation service

Q. 584. *Give the packet frame for WATM.*

Ans.

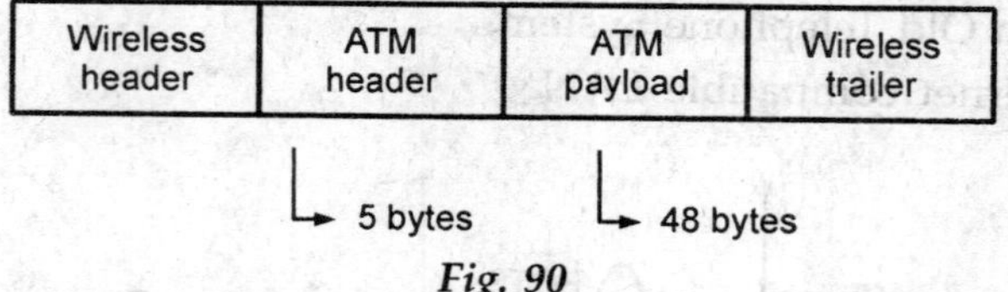

Fig. 90

Q. 585. *What are the two main challenges that a WATM design has to meet to develop the network?*

Ans. 1. The wireless medium is unreliable in wideband frequency ranges and there might be complexities in transmission mechanisms.
2. ATM switches were designed to support QoS. In a wireless environment there will be channel condition fluctuations and a negotiated QoS cannot be guaranteed, but it is the most expected feature of WATM.

Q. 586. *Give two functional requirements of HIPERLAN-1.*

Ans. (*a*) Coverage upto 100 m
(*b*) Data rates (speed) should be of 23.529 Mb/sec.

Q. 587. *What are the two features that are necessary in integration of WLAN with cellular systems?*

Ans. 1. Vertical roaming support
2. Support for QoS control

Q. 588. *What is a dynamic frequency selection (DPS)?*

Ans. The HIPERLAN-2 standard supports the basic mechanism for measuring power communicate with adjacent AP's and this is called as dynamic frequency selection.

Q. 589. *Draw the delay control mechanism in HIPERLAN-2 standard.*

Ans.

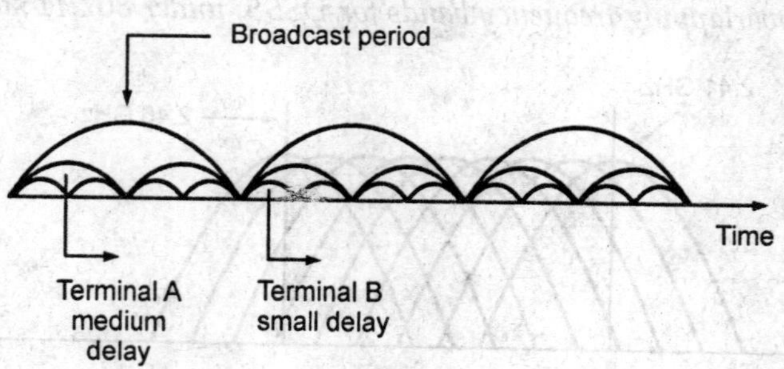

Fig. 91

Q. 590. *Mention any two standards that supports multichannel operation.*

Ans. (*a*) 802.11

(*b*) HIPERLAN-2

Q. 591. *List three functional requirement of IEEE802.15 WPAN.*

Ans. (*a*) Distance - 0 to 10 m

(*b*) Power - Low current

(*c*) Size - Small in size → 0.5 cubic inches without an antenna

Q. 592. *Give few examples for second generation cellular systems.*

Ans. (*a*) GSM

(*b*) JDC

(*c*) IS-95

Q. 593. *Compare PCS with cellular systems.*

Ans.

Feature	Cellular system	PCS
Height of antenna	> 15 meters	< 15 meters
Base station complexity	Moderate	Low
Cell size	0.5 to 30 km	5 to 500 m

Q. 594. *List five wireless local area network standards.*

Ans.
1. IEEE 802.11
2. IEEE 802.11b
3. IEEE 802.11a
4. HIPERLAN-2
5. HIPERLAN-1

Q. 595. *What is the of modulation scheme used in HIPERLAN standards?*

Ans. HIPERLAN-1 → GMSK

HIPERLAN-2 → OFDM

Q. 596. *What are the frequency bands used in IEEE 802.11b and 802.11a standards?*

Ans. IEEE 802.11b → 2.4 GHz

IEEE 802.11a → 5 GHz.

Q. 597. *Draw the CDMA type of channel allocation.*

Ans.

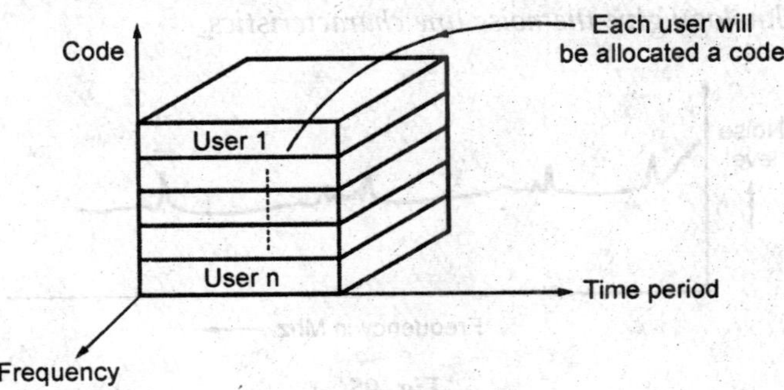

Fig. 92

Q. 598. *Draw a GMSK modulator block diagram.*

Ans. 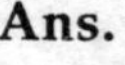

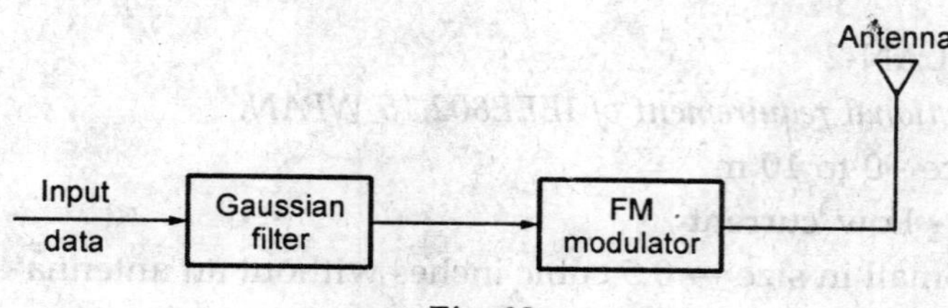

Fig. 93

Q. 599. *Represent the BPSK signal.*

Ans.

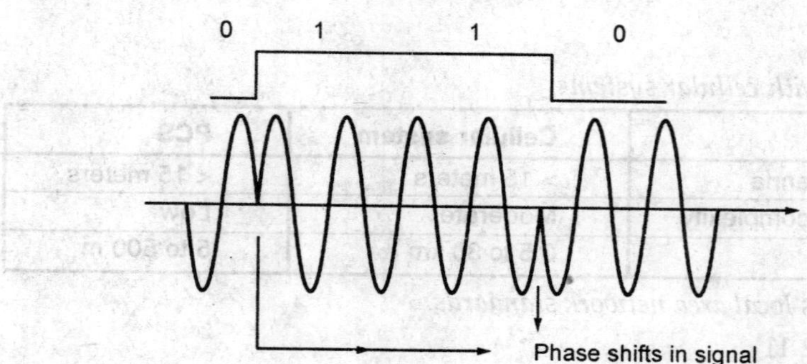

Fig. 94

Q. 600. *Mention few sensing methods under IEEE 802.11 standard.*

Ans. 1. Carrier sensing
2. Virtual carrier sensing
3. Detected data sensing.

Q. 601. *What is the need for higher data rates?*

Ans. 1. To enable interconnection of LAN and to share high speed servers.
2. To have high speed operations and multimedia applications.

Q. 602. *Give an example of LAN standard of high speed.*

Ans. Fiber distributed data interface (FDDI).

Q. 603. *In a HAN technology give the noise line characteristics.*

Ans.

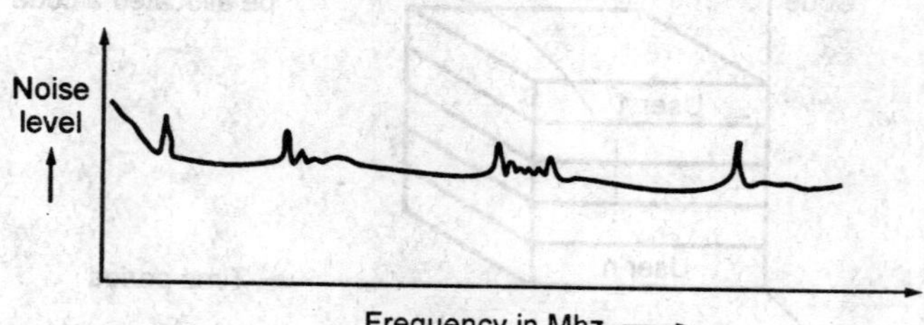

Fig. 95

Q. 604. *In a HAN technology give the power line characteristics.*

Ans.

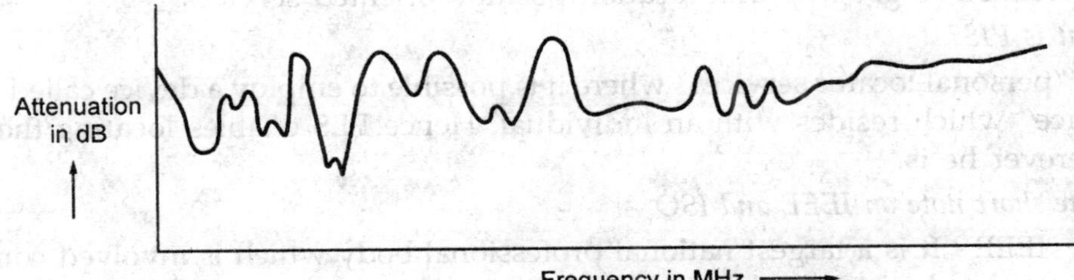

Fig. 96

Q. 605. *What are NMT and ME?*

Ans. NMT - Nordic mobile telephony

ME - Mobile equipment

Q. 606. *What are MPDU and LANE?*

Ans. MPDU → MAC PDU → Medium Access Control Protocol data units

LANE → LAN emulation → Local Area Network emulation

Q. 607. *What are HMAC and JDC?*

Ans. HMAC - Hashed message authentication code.

JDC - Japanese digital cellular.

Q. 608. *Give two CECP techniques.*

Ans.
1. Vector sum excitation linear prediction (VSELP).
2. QUAL COMM's CELP (QCELP)

Q. 609. *Define software radio.*

Ans. It is a transceiver that can define the following.
1. Modulation
2. Coding methods
3. Radio resource
4. Modulation
5. Mobility management

Q. 610. *What is the use of CRC codes?*

Ans. The CRC codes are used for error detection and correction in data transmissions.

Q. 611. *What is an AGPS?*

Ans. AGPS is an "Assisted GPS" which is a kind of technique where an entity can be appended with GPS receiver so that the satellites can be viewed by the entity like the mobile station.

Q. 612. *What is the use of geo location technology?*

Ans. Geo location technology is useful in commercial as well as military applications. It also highlights on "location aware services".

Q. 613. *What is known as location based services?*

Ans. It is related to geographical location position oriented services.

Q. 614. *What is PIS?*

Ans. It is "personal locator services" where it is possible to employ a device called "locator device" which resides with an individual. Hence PLS enables locating the person wherever he is.

Q. 615. *Write short note on IEEE and ISO.*

Ans. (*i*) IEEE - It is a largest national professional body which is involved completely in developing standards for communication, electronics, electrical engineering and computing fields.

(*ii*) ISO - It is an organization which is fully dedicated to worldwide agreement on the international standards in various fields.

Q. 616. *What is known as 'Self positioning system'?*

Ans. The mobile station can determine its own geographical position by measuring its distance from a known location like GPS receiver is called as self positioning system.

Q. 617. *Draw the geo location architecture.*

Ans.

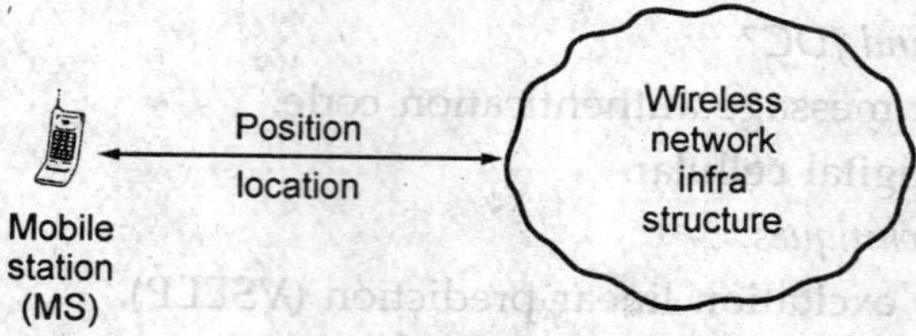

Fig. 97

Q. 618. *What is 'dead reckoning'?*

Ans. Dead reckoning is a predictive method of finding the position of the mobile.

Q. 619. *What are the two schemes to estimate the location of MS?*

Ans. (*a*) Self positioning system.

(*b*) Remote positioning system.

Q. 620. *What is known as "remote positioning system"?*

Ans. The receivers at a particular known location can find the distance of the mobile transmitter from them individually and from this data they are able to locate the position of mobile transmitter at a remote place. This is a method of locating the MS.

Q. 621. *What are the sequence of operations related to a geo location system?*

Ans. (*a*) Request location.

(*b*) Request users co-ordinates.

(*c*) Request BTS-ID etc.

(*d*) Request response.

(*e*) Response data.

(*f*) Co-ordinate operations.

Q. 622. *What is a geo location base station?*

Ans. A set of base stations (BS) are capable of obtaining the location parameters based on past information about MS and these BS's are called geo location base stations.

Q. 623. *Give two demerits of geo location system.*

Ans. (*a*) Uncertainty in locations.

(*b*) Distance error is distributed at the geo location receiver.

Q. 624. *List two advantages of geo location systems.*

Ans. (*a*) Accuracy of several services.

(*b*) Efficient coverage.

Q. 625. *Give three special features of telecommunications system.*

Ans. (*a*) Reliability

(*b*) Delay in call setup

(*c*) Accuracy

Q. 626. *Comment on Assisted GPS.*

Ans. It is also denoted as AGP's.

Features : (*a*) Superior accuracy (*b*) Indoor coverage is poor.

Q. 627. *Tabulate delay and coverage for network centric AOA.*

Ans.

GEO Location Technique

Network Centric AOA	Delay	Coverage
	Low delay : The angular information has to be transmitted mainly.	Coverage is good in outdoor areas.

Q. 628. *What are the states defined for a Bluetooth specification?*

Ans. 1. Unconnected states

2. Connecting states

3. Active states

4. Low power states

Q. 629. *What are CSMA/CA and CSMA/DA?*

Ans. 1. CSMA/CA → Carrier sense multiple access with collision avoidance.

2. CSMA/DA → Carrier sense multiple access with collision detection.

Q. 630. *What is known as BSIC, CT, and DSS?*

Ans. BSIC - Base Station Identity Code.

CT - Cordless Telephony.

DSS - Digital Signature Standard.

Q. 631. *What is the application of data communication code?*

Ans. The data communication codes are mainly used for representing characters, like letters, digits and symbols.

Q. 632. *What is a baudot code?*

Ans. It is the fixed length character code or fixed length block code where all the characters can be represented in binary form and they will have same number of symbols or bits.

Q. 633. *Write a note on ASCII code.*

Ans. It is a data communication code which was adopted by U.S from Bell system teletype code and it was termed as United states of America standard code for Information Exchange. The code's revised version was recommended by ITU. It was used for source coding the alphanumeric characters and it is a seven bit code.

Q. 634. *What is a EBCDIC code?*

Ans. The "Extended binary coded decimal interchange code (EBCDIC) is basically an 8-bit fixed length character set code. With this possibility of 2^8 codes ($2^n = 2^8$), 256 codes are possible.

Q. 635. *Define error detection.*

Ans. Error detection method is a process to monitor the data transmission link to locate the error occurrence if any in transmission.

E.g. CRC → Cyclic redundancy checking

Q. 636. *Define error correction.*

Ans. Error correction scheme provides required information about the error bit if any in data transmission and the time period when it had occurred to the intended receiver unit.

Q. 637. *Give two examples for error detection schemes.*

Ans. (*a*) Longitudinal redundancy checking

(*b*) Cyclic redundancy check.

Q. 638. *What are strategies related to error handling in data transmission?*

Ans. (*a*) Error detecting code.

(*b*) Error correcting code.

Q. 639. *What is the significance of FEC?*

Ans. Forward error correction code (FEC), is a code that is capable of correction the errors if any in data transmission in forward direction before the receiver receives the data. Hence in FEC scheme their is no need of retransmission of data.

Q. 640. *What are the different schemes involved in character synchronization?*

Ans. (*a*) Asynchronous data transmission.

(*b*) Synchronous data transmission.

Q. 641. *What is an asynchronous data transmission?*

Ans. In asynchronous data transmission scheme every data character is transmitted between a start and stop bits. Here the data can be sent without 'time' references.

Q. 642. *What is a synchronous data transmission?*

Ans. The data is sent in the form of blocks or frames with high speed. There will be no time lapses between transmitter and receiver units. Also the entire message is transmitted just as a single entity.

Q. 643. *Give the asynchronous data format of transmission.*

Ans.

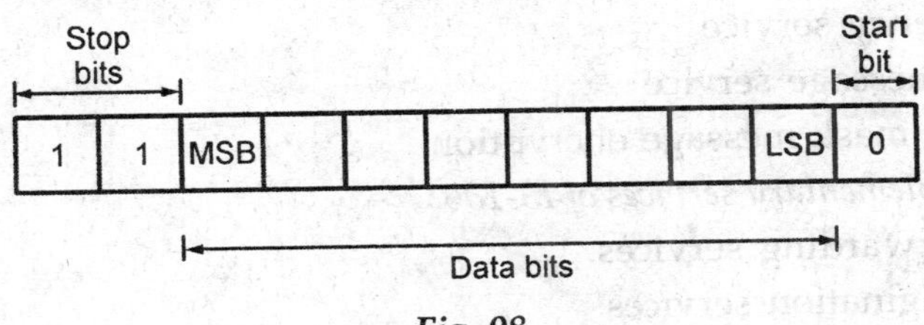

Fig. 98

Q. 644. *What is a DTE unit?*

Ans. DTE is data terminal equipment, a device available in transmitter and receiver end points.

Q. 645. *What is a DCE unit?*

Ans. It is data communication equipment and is used to represent or describe an equipment that can interface between data terminal equipment and the channel.

Q. 646. *Give examples of DCE unit.*

Ans.
1. Digital service unit
2. Channel service unit

Q. 647. *What is the other name of DCE?*

Ans. The data channels may be terminated at end of DCE's and so DCE's are also termed as data circuit terminating equipment (DCTE).

Q. 648. *What is a data modem?*

Ans. It is a DCE unit used to interface the DTE to an analog telephony circuits (POTS).

Q. 649. *What are the basic components of two point data communication circuit?*

Ans. The basic components are
1. DCE at an end point 1
2. DTE at an end point 1
3. DTE/DCE interface at 1
4. Transmission path between two points 1 and 2
5. DCE at an end point 2
6. DTE at an end point 2
7. DTE/DCE interface at 2.

Q. 650. *Represent DTE/DCE connection with a diagram.*

Ans.

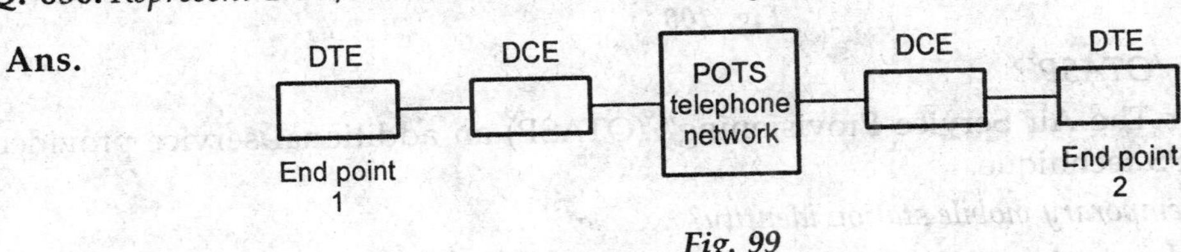

Fig. 99

Q. 651. *List any three service aspects of D-AMPS (IS 136).*

Ans.
1. Emergency service
2. Short message service
3. Rolling mask message encryption.

Q. 652. *List three supplementary services of IS-136.*

Ans.
1. Call forwarding services.
2. Call origination services.
3. Call termination services

Q. 653. *Give any three radio parameters for D-AMPS.*

Ans.
1. Modulation → $\frac{\pi}{4}$ DQPSK scheme.
2. Number of channels → 832.
3. Up/Down link frequency [mobile to BS/BS to mobile] → 824-849 MHz/869-894 MHz

Q. 654. *What are the logical channels in D-AMPS?*

Ans.
1. Traffic channels (TCH)
2. Control channels (DCCH)

Q. 655. *Give examples for privacy services.*

Ans.
1. Signalling message encryption service.
2. Voice privacy service.

Q. 656. *Give the TCH taxonomy.*

Ans.

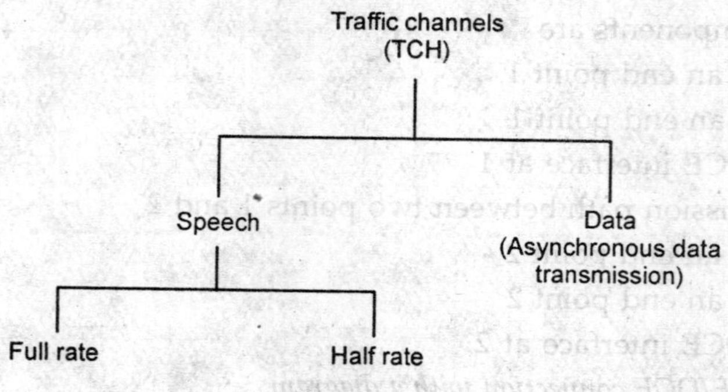

Fig. 100

Q. 657. *What is an 'OTASP'?*

Ans. It is "Over The Air Service Provisioning" (OTASP) an additional service provided by D-AMPS technique.

Q. 658. *What is a temporary mobile station identity?*

Ans. It is mainly used for maintaining user confidentiality and to reduce signalling traffic load.

Q. 659. *What is the use of pilot channel in IS-95?*

Ans. A pilot channel comprises of a DSSS signal and it is shared with all the mobile users, in a cell. Each pilot signal will send same spreading sequence (set of zeros) at various time offsets so as to differentiate the signals of the several pilots.

Q. 660. *Draw the IS-95 CDMA standard's structure. (Consider reverse traffic channel)*

Ans.

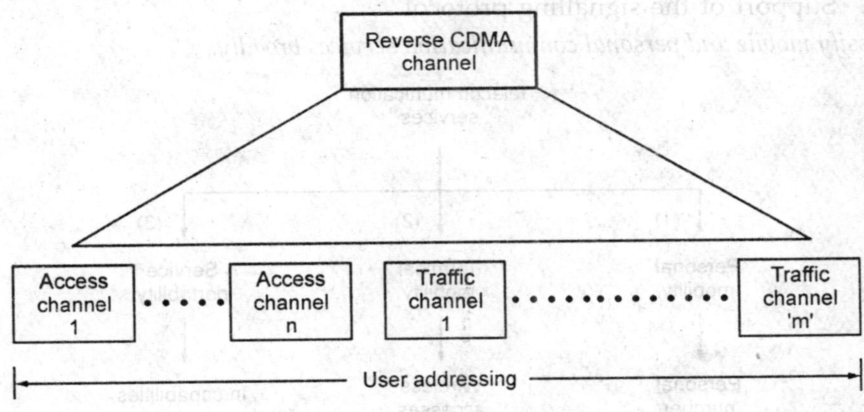

Fig. 101

Q. 661. *What a paging signal will consists of?*

Ans. (*a*) Messages related to specific mobile units.

(*b*) System parameters.

Q. 662. *Give three network layer protocol functions.*

Ans.
1. Call control
2. Interworking unit
3. Mobility management.

Q. 663. *What are the main features of personal access communication system?*

Ans.
1. A completely integrated networked approach.
2. Automatic frequency assignment.
3. Integration with other handsets is possible.
4. Error-free signal transmission.

Q. 664. *What are the general systems features in PACS?*

Ans.
1. Radio link maintenance and measurement.
2. Automatic link transfer.
3. Location registration and de-registration
4. Authentication and ciphering.
5. Call origination and delivery services.

Q. 665. *Write two functional requirements in PHS for achieving uninterrupted services.*

Ans. (*a*) Routing and delivery of the incoming calls.

(*b*) Authentication of PHS stations.

Q. 666. *What are the functions supported by cell station in PHS?*

Ans.
1. Radio access control.
2. Circuit connection control.
3. Location registration.
4. Supplementary services.
5. Support of the signalling protocol.

Q. 667. *Classify mobile and personal communication services broadly.*

Ans.

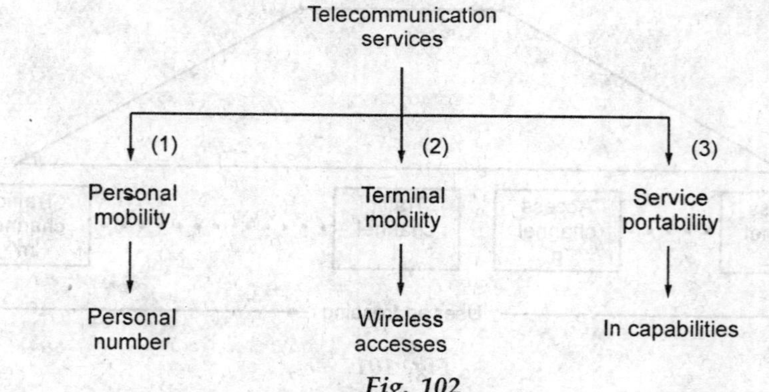

Fig. 102

Q. 668. *What is an 'IN' concept?*

Ans. It represents the intelligent network operation. 'IN' focuses on applications related to wireless and fixed networks. It decouples the functions needed to support call and connection control under new services.

Q. 669. *What is a service data function in 'IN' structure?*

Ans. The service data function (SDF) enables generic database capabilities to service control function (SCF) and also other SDF's.

Q. 670 *List any two attributes of 'IN' structure.*

Ans. (*a*) Efficient use of the information processing techniques.

(*b*) Effective usage of network resources.

Q. 671. *Write short note on soft handoff in CDMA system.*

Ans. The system has to be capable of delivering simultaneous signals to mobile phones more than one cell, so that handoff's are efficient.

Q. 672. *What are the parameters that can determine the capacity of CDMA system?*

Ans.
1. Voice activity factor.
2. Frequency reuse.
3. Processing gain.
4. Number of sectors in cell-site antenna system.

Q. 673. *What is the main advantage of CDMA cellular?*

Ans.
1. Interference is avoided.
2. Handoff is effective.

Q. 674. *Give three characteristics of CDMA 2000.*

Ans. 1. Supports radio link protocol.
2. Ability to handoffs effectively between generations.
3. It supports multicarrier and direct spread forward link.

Q. 675. *What is a DECT?*

Ans. It is digital enhanced cordless telecommunication developed by the ETSI to facilitate several digitized application.

Q. 676. *What are the applications of DECT?*

Ans. 1. Large and small business system.
2. Wireless data access systems.
3. Public cordless access systems.

Q. 677. *List two functions supported by physical layer of DECT.*

Ans. 1. Modulation and demodulation of radio carriers with data rates of bit streams.
2. Monitoring radio environment.

Q. 678. *What are the main networks that a DECT can access?*

Ans. GSM network and LAN.

Q. 679. *Give an example for interworking network operation.*

Ans. DECT/GSM interworking is made possible with GSM interworking profile (GIF).

Q. 680. *What are the special capabilities of DECT/GSM?*

Ans. 1. Service description and provision.
2. Protocol descriptions for voice oriented services.

Q. 681. *What is the significance of PACS?*

Ans. The personal access communication system is based on wireless access (WACS) communication system. It has provision to accommodate 16 pairs of channels with 10 MHz (approx.)

Q. 682. *Compare PHS and DECT systems.*

Ans.

Radio parameter	PHS	DECT
Access method	TDMA/TDD	TDMA/TDD
Spectrum allocation	1895-1918 MHz	1880-1900 MHz
Output power	80 mW	250 mW

Q. 683. *What is a CT2 system?*

Ans. It is a second generation cordless telecommunication standard used for key systems and wireless PABX, public access services etc.

Q. 684. *Tabulate two system parameters for HIPERLAN standard.*

Ans.

System parameter	HIPERLAN
Mobility limit	∠5 kmph
High bit rate modulation	OMSK
Low bit rate modulation	FSK
Error detection	CRC

Q. 685. *What is the power level and HER datarate in HIPERLAN?*

Ans. Power level - 1 W

HER - datarate - 23.52 Mbps.

Q. 686. *List few MAC protocol feature with respect to HIPERLAN.*

Ans.
1. Service access point interface.
2. Variable packet length.
3. Peer to peer structure.

Q. 687. *What are the signalling features in GSM?*

Ans.
1. Mobile call origination
2. Location updating
3. Inter MSC call handoff
4. Mobile call termination
5. Authentication
6. Ciphering.

Q. 688. *Comment on speech coder bit rate and handoff scheme in GSM.*

Ans. Speech coder bit rate - 13 kbps.

Associated control channel - Extra frame.

Q. 689. *What are the call origination services?*

Ans.
1. Priority access and channel assignment.
2. Remote feature control.
3. Voice mail retrieval.
4. Preferred language.

Q. 690. *What are the control logical channels in GSM?*

Ans.

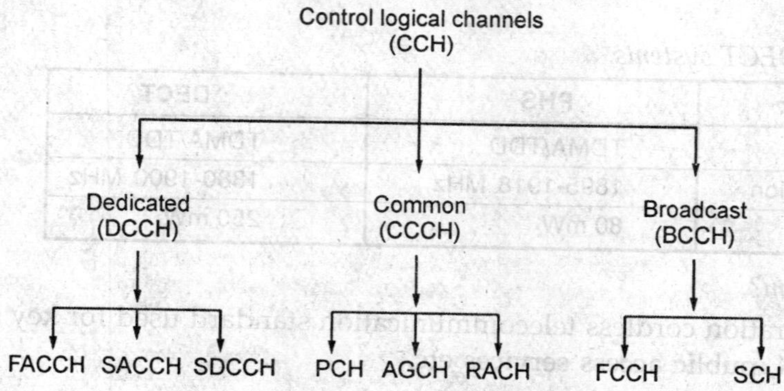

Control logical channels (CCH)

Dedicated (DCCH)
Common (CCCH)
Broadcast (BCCH)

FACCH SACCH SDCCH
PCH AGCH RACH
FCCH SCH

Fig. 103

Q. 691. *What are the call restriction services?*

Ans.
1. Selective call acceptance.
2. Subscriber PIN access.
3. Subscriber PIN intercept.
4. Password call acceptance.

Q. 692. *List any four call termination services.*

Ans. 1. Call waiting.
2. Call delivery.
3. Flexible altering.
4. Message waiting information.

Q. 693. *Draw the uplink transmission block diagram.*

Ans.

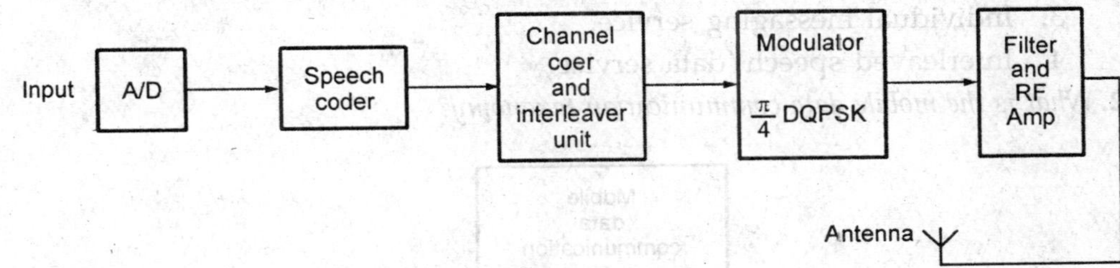

Fig. 104

Q. 694. *What is the carrier spacing and frame duration values in PDC?*

Ans. 1. Carrier spacing - 25 kHz interleaving.
2. Frame duration - 20 msec.

Q. 695. *Compare PDC D-AMPS and GSM standards.*

Ans.

Feature	PDC	D-AMPS	GSM
Bit rate of channel	42 kbps	48.6 kbps	270.8 kbps
Power level	≤ 2 W	≤ 3 W	≤ 8 W
Carrier spacing	25 kHz	30 kHz	200 kHz

Q. 696. *What are channel types under common access of PDC system?*

Ans. 1. Broadcast (BCCH)
2. Common control (CCCH)
3. User packet (UPCH)

Q. 697. *Mention two service aspects in IS-95.*

Ans. (*a*) Enhanced mobile station identities.
(*b*) Slotted paging scheme.

Q. 698. *What are the methods of channel assignment possible with packet switched data services on cellular networks?*

Ans. (*a*) Fixed assignment.
(*b*) Partial sharing.
(*c*) Full sharing.

Q. 699. *What are the significant feature of SMS implementation?*

Ans. 1. SMS is a store and forward service and it has message forwarding capabilities.
2. For transferring messages between the network entities the control and signalling channels are mainly used for data transmissions.

Q. 700. *What is a shared secret key mechanism?*

Ans. The authentication method used in IEEE 802.11 standard relays on shared secret key method where it is possible to share the keys.

Q. 701. *What are the services supported by personal access communication system?*

Ans.
1. Circuit mode data service.
2. Packet mode data service.
3. Individual messaging service.
4. Interleaved speech/data service.

Q. 702. *What is the mobile data communication taxonomy?*

Ans.

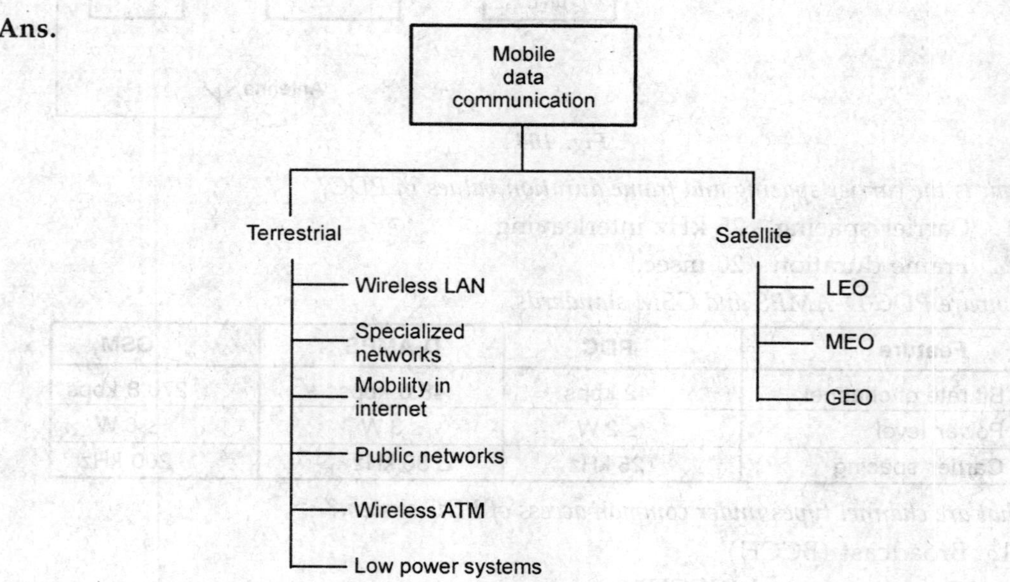

Fig. 105

Q. 703. *What are the applications possible with mobile satellite applications?*

Ans.

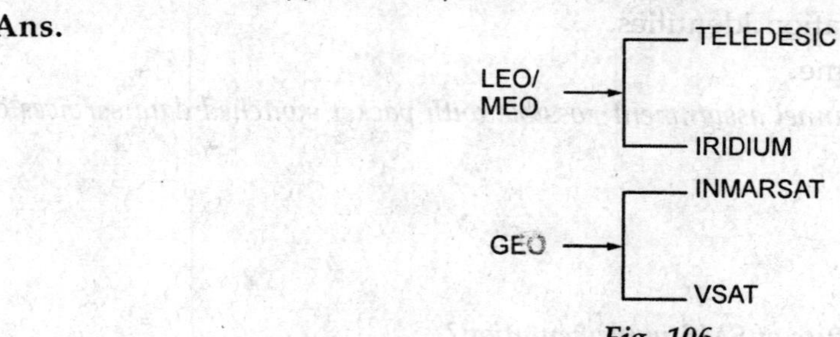

Fig. 106

Q. 704. *What are the specialized networks possible with terrestrial mobile applications?*

Ans.
1. Packet networks.
2. TETRA

Q. 705. *What are the asynchronous and synchronous bearer services possible with initial GSM?*

Ans. Asynchronous services :

1. Data circuit duplex

Synchronous services :

1. PAD access
2. Data packet duplex
3. Data circuit duplex

Q. 706. *Mention few IEEE 802.16 standards.*

Ans.

1. IEEE 802.16.1 → An air interface for frequency range 10 to 66 GHz.
2. IEEE 802.16.2 → It is co-existence of broadband wireless access system.
3. IEEE 802.16.3 → An air interface for frequency range from 2 GHz to 11 GHz.

Q. 707. *What are the three layers in IEEE 802.16 standard architecture?*

Ans.

(*a*) Physical layer

(*b*) MAC layer

(*c*) Convergence layer.

Q. 708. *What is the use of convergence layer of above question?*

Ans. It is the layer above MAC layer. It provides some functions specific to services that is being provided. For instance digital telephony and ATM are some of the bearer services.

Q. 709. *What is a physical layer?*

Ans. The fundamental features like modulation scheme, error-correction techniques, synchronization, error correcting techniques, data rates are specified by physical layer.

Q. 710. *What are the three physical layers supported by 802.11 standard?*

Ans.

1. Wireless MAN - SC2
2. Wireless MAN - OFDM
3. Wireless MAN - OFDMA

Q. 711. *List few wireless broadband applications.*

Ans.

1. Wi Fi technique.
2. Cellular mobile system.

Q. 712. *What are the Bluetooth application models?*

Ans.

1. File transfer
2. LAN access
3. Synchronization
4. Headset
5. Internet bridge.

Q. 713. *What is a RFID?*

Ans. It is radio transponder carrying an ID (Identification) and it is possible to read it through radio frequency. The transponders are also referred to as "RFID tags".

Q. 714. *What is the demerit of RFID?*

Ans. When comparing RFID with bar coding conventional method it is not economical to use these tags though they are accurate and effective.

Q. 715. *List two functional areas of RFID.*

Ans.
1. Means of interrogating or reading data in RFID tag.
2. Ways to filter a set of data if required.

Q. 716. *What are the main categories of middleware in mobile computing?*

Ans.
1. Message oriented middleware.
2. Database middleware.
3. Transaction processing middleware.
4. Distributed object and components.
5. Transcoding middleware.
6. Communication middleware.

Q. 717. *Define an ad hoc network.*

Ans. It is a small network which is designed for a particular task.

Q. 718. *What are the applications of RFID?*

Ans. Main areas of application of RFID are,
1. Manufacturing and processing mobile Computing
2. Retail stores
3. Libraries
4. Postal tracking
5. Road toll management
6. Animal tagging
7. Security etc.

Q. 719. *Write a short note on Wimax.*

Ans. Wireless MAN like IEEE 802.16 standard was developed to meet wireless access functions with telecommunication networks.

It also provides access to tall building through the exterior antennas for communicating with that of the radio base stations. The IEEE 802.16 standard protocol was established for point to multipoint broadband accesses.

Q. 720. *Draw a cellular cluster setup for K = 4.*

Ans.

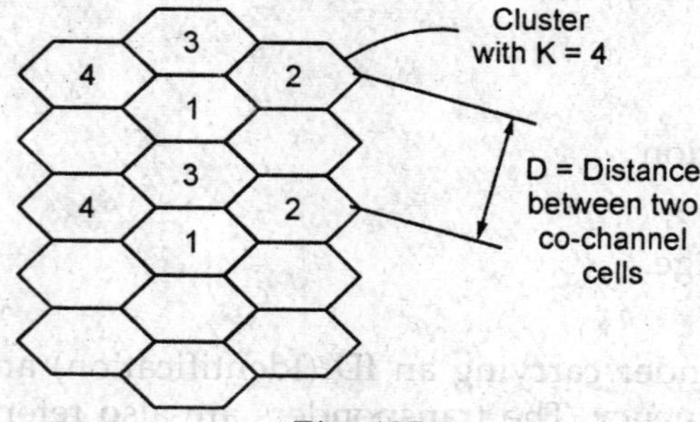

Fig. 107

Q. 721. *What are the main subsystems available in GSM architecture?*

Ans. 1. Radio subsystem.
2. Network and switching subsystem
3. Data infrastructure
4. Operation subsystem

Q. 722. *What are the two parts of BSS?*

Ans. (*a*) Base transceiver station (BTS).
(*b*) Base station controller (BSC).

Q. 723. *What are the functions of MSC in network and switching subsystem?*

Ans. 1. It is like a normal switching node for PSTN fixed telephone and for cellular subscribers of the same network.
2. It is possible to have functions like registration, location updating, authentication, call routing etc.

Q. 724. *What is the use of SS7?*

Ans. 1. In network subsystem the SS7 (signalling system number 7) is used for signalling between different functional entities.
2. SS7 is used for SMS, roaming prepaid network functicns.
3. SS7 is also used for trunck signalling.

Q. 725. *What is the function of an AuC?*

Ans. The authentication center (AuC) maintains copy of secret key that is stored in each and every subscribers SIM card. It is used to protect user's database.

Q. 726. *What is a 'SMS'?*

Ans. It is a data bearer service received as short message service in GSM. SMS also uses free capacity of signalling channel. 7 bit English characters are used and these short messages can be up to 160 characters.

Q. 727. *What are the advantages of SMS?*

Ans. 1. Stateless
2. Asynchronous
3. Non repudiable
4. Always connected
5. Self configurable

Q. 728. *What signalling is used in SMS?*

Ans. SS7 signalling is compatible with short message services worldwide.

Q. 729. *What is PSMF and RADIUS?*

Ans. PSMF - Positioning signal measurement function.
RADIUS - Remote authentication dial in user service.

Q. 730. *Give examples for value added services characteristics in mobile computing.*

Ans. 1. Standalone operation.
2. Supplementary services which adds values to the basic services.
3. Stimulates incremental demands for the core services.

Q. 731. *What is SMIL and SWAP?*

Ans. SMIL - Synchronization multimedia integration language.
SWAP - Shared wireless access protocol.

Q. 732. *What is a SIS?*

Ans. It is symbian OS Installation and this 'symbian' operating system is used for mobile communication.

Q. 733. *What are the three categories of information on demand under VAS?*

Ans.
1. Dynamic information
2. Static information
3. Real time information.

Q. 734. *Give examples for VAS.*

Ans. Some of the value added services are listed below.
1. Session based chat application.
2. Email through SMS.
3. Health care services.
4. News and stock quotes services.

Q. 735. *What are the parameters considered for defining QoS in GPRS technology?*

Ans.
1. Service precedence
2. Delay
3. Throughput
4. Reliability

Q. 736. *What are the three sublayers available when data link layer is subdivided between base station and mobile station?*

Ans.
1. Radio link control layer.
2. Logical link control layer.
3. Medium access control layer.

Q. 737. *What is known as line configuration in data communication?*

Ans. Line configuration refers to the method or way the communication devices are attached to a 'link'. This link is a physical communication pathway that can transfer data from a device to another device. The two kinds of line configurations are 'multipoint' and 'point-to-point' configurations.

Q. 738. *What are the types of signal unit under SS7?*

Ans.
1. Fill-in-signal unit
2. Message signal unit
3. Link status signal unit.

This signalling system 7 (SS7) is highly useful in cellular mobile networking.

Q. 739. *List the elements in softswitch.*

Ans. Softswitch is a combination of software and switch. The elements of it are
1. Media gateway
2. Call agent
3. Signalling gateway

4. Feature server
5. Application server
6. Media server
7. Billing, provisioning and management interfaces.

Q. 740. *What is a WIN?*

Ans. It is wireless intelligent network and is developed by telecommunications industry association (TIA).

Q. 741. *Write a short note on UPT.*

Ans. Universal personal telecommunication (UPT) is a standard in the popular International Telecommunication Union's telecommunications standardization sector intended for personal mobility functions. It will use the IN and integrated services digital network (ISDN) capabilities for supporting personal mobility applications.

Q. 742. *What is a 'nomadicity' in mobile networking?*

Ans. It represents an advantage of 'Mobile IP' that enables to change physical location of IP nodes without changing their addresses.

Q. 743. *What are the cell origination services in D-AMPS?*

Ans.
1. Priority Access and Channel Assignment (PACA).
2. Voice mail retrieval
3. Remote feature control

Q. 744. *Give some of the additional services provided by D-AMPS technology.*

Ans.
1. Enhanced Variable Rate Codec (EVRC).
2 Over The Air Service Provisioning (OTASP).
3. Smart card.

Q. 745. *What are the informations contained in synchronization channel in IS-95?*

Ans. The synchronization channel include many informations like
1. Network Identification Number (NID).
2. System Identification Number (SID).
3. PN offset of the associated pilot channel.
4. Precise time of day information.
5. Radio interface's version.

Q. 746. *What is known as 'MIN'?*

Ans. The paging channel in mobile phones are generally assigned by a hash function based on Mobile Identification Number ('MIN').

Q. 747. *How does a reverse traffic channel work in IS-95 ?*

Ans. The reverse traffic channels are mainly utilized for sending voice data from mobile phone to Base Station (BS). Here each and every channel is paired with corresponding forward traffic channel. The signalling information when a call is in progress will be again sent in "blank and burst" or "dim and burst" mode setup.

Q. 748 *Compare MEO and LEO satellite types.*

Ans.

Characteristics	MEO	LEO
Satellite lifetime	10 to 15 years	4 to 8 years
Altitude range	10,000 to 20,000 km	500 to 2000 km
Round - trip delay	40 to 80 msec	5 to 10 msec

Q. 749. *What is a GEO?*

Ans. The communication satellite (GEO) orbits in geo stationary orbit which is at 36000 km above earth's surface. The satellite revolves with same speed as that of the earth (1 Rev/day) that revolves around sun.

Q. 750. *What are examples of global mobile satellite system?*

Ans. 1. Iridium 2. Teledesic
3. Global star

Q. 751. *Give three specifications of Global star and Iridium systems.*

Ans.

Characteristic	Global star	Iridium
System type	LEO	LEO
Data speed	7.2 kbps	2.4 kbps
Launched year	1999	1998

Q. 752. *What are the values of number of planes and voice channels allowed for ICO?*

Ans. Number of planes in ICO → 2

Voice channels permissible → 4.8 kbps.

Q. 753. *Compare Global star and ICO satellite systems.*

Ans.

Parameter	Global star	ICO
Modulation	QPSK	QPSK
Output power	1000 W	2500 W
Satellite mass	450 kg	1925 kg
Foot print	5850 km	12,900 km

Q. 754. *What are the advantages of Indium satellite system?*

Ans.
1. Intersatellite links are possible.
2. Number of satellites possible is 66 and 6 numbers of satellites can be maintained as spares.
3. The terminal types can be of dual mode, mobile or handheld.

Q. 755. *What are the system type and target services under ICO satellite system?*

Ans. System type in ICO - Medium Earth Orbit (MEO).

Target services in ICO - Voice fax and low speed data.

Q. 756. *What are the number of voice channels possible with Indium, Global star and ICO?*

Ans.

Voice channel →	ICO	Iridium	Global star
	4.8 kbps	2.4/4.8 kbps	2.4/4.8/9.6 kbps

Q. 757. *List two communication parameters for Indium and Global star.*

Ans.

	Iridium	Global star
Multiple access →	TDMA/FDMA/TDD	CDMA/FDMA/FDD
Reuse pattern →	12 Cells per cluster	1 Cell per cluster

Q. 758. *Write short note on ICO.*

Ans. ICO is basically a MEO satellite system. The aim of ICO is to provide services related to handheld phones. The multiple access used here is TDMA technique.

Q. 759. *What are the four versions used by global star satellite system with maximum transmission power capability?*

Ans. Single - mode - Global star.

Dual - mode - Global star/GSM.

Dual - mode - Global star/CDMA cellular.

Triple - mode - Global star/CDMA cellular/AMPS cellular.

Q. 760. *What are the services (data and messaging) supported by personal access communication system?*

Ans. (*a*) Individual messaging service.

(*b*) Circuit mode data service.

(*c*) Packet mode data service.

(*d*) Interleaved data/speech service.

Q. 761. *What are the examples of CEO, LEO and MEO satellite systems?*

Ans.

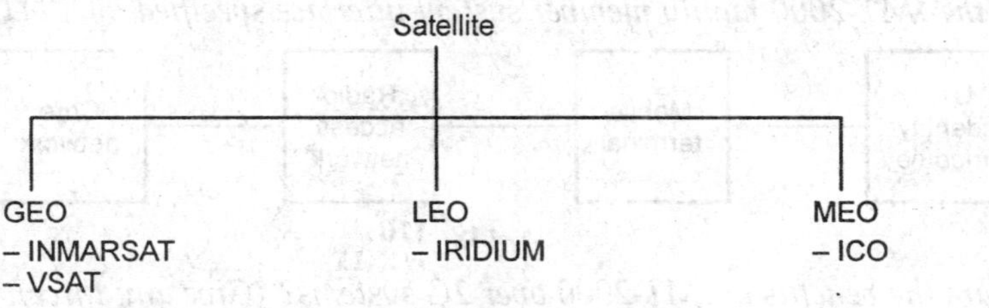

Fig. 108

Q. 762. *What are examples of low power systems?*

Ans. DECT, PACS and PHS are the main low power systems in mobile communication with respect to terrestrial services.

Q. 763. *What is a mobile multimedia?*

Ans. The Wireless ATM (WATM) primarily provides an integrated architecture for supporting end-to-end multimedia services in both wireless and wired environments. WATM is the best services that develops mobile multimedia.

Q. 764. *What are the goals of TMT-2000?*

Ans.
1. To provide mobile radio environment.
2. Flexible radio bearers for improving frequency spectrum efficiency.
3. Roaming compatibility.
4. Integration of terrestrial and satellite systems.

Q. 765. *Give a graphic representation of IMT-2000 development.*

Ans.

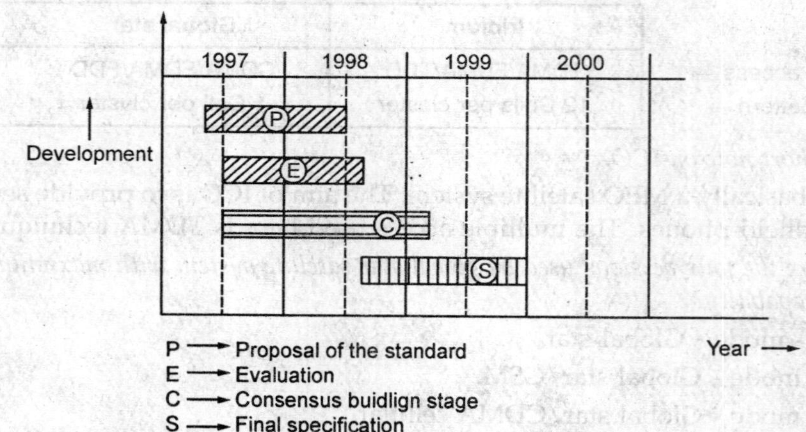

Fig. 109

Q. 766. *What are the Multiple Access (MA) and Channel Voice Codec (VC) for W-CDMA (Japan) and CDMA 2000 (U.S.A)?*

Ans.

	W-CDMA (Japan)	**CDMA-2000 (U.S.A)**
MA	WB DS-CDMA	WB DS-CDMA
VC	Variable or fixed rate	Variable rate

Q. 767. *Draw the IMT-2000 family member system interface specified by TTU.*

Ans.

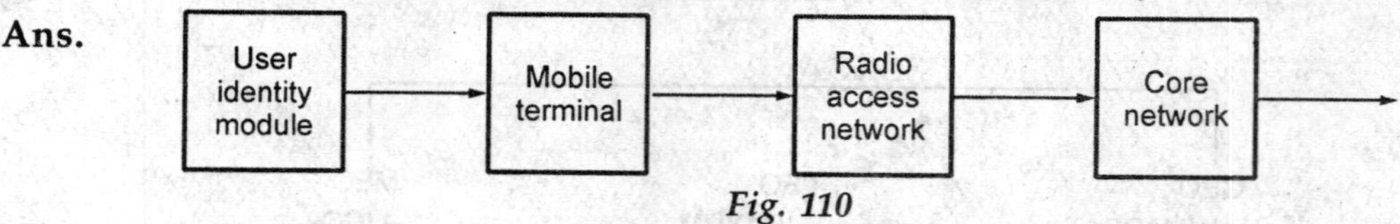

Fig. 110

Q. 768. *What are the benefits of IMT-2000 over 2G systems? (Give any three).*

Ans.
1. Circuit and packet bearer capability upto 144 kbps.
2. User authentication and ciphering.
3. Multimedia services.
4. Emergency and priority calls.

Q. 769. *Picturise the functions required for IMT-2000 standard.*

Ans.

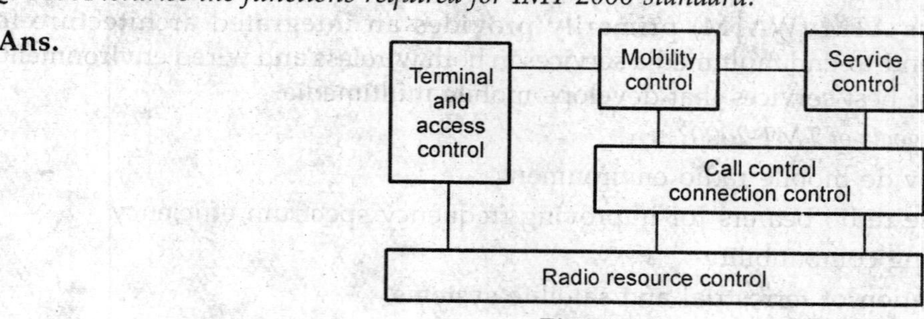

Fig. 111

Q. 770. *Give few advantages of GEO satellites.*

Ans. (*a*) They have large footprints and provides large coverage.

(*b*) Used for communication related applications.

Q. 771. *What is the demerit of GEO satellite?*

Ans. Their round trip time delay is long due to high altitudes, and it results in quality degradation.

Q. 772. *What is the goal of teledesic satellite system?*

Ans. It extends the terrestrial infrastructures to provide advanced information and communication services over earth mainly to support Internet access communication rather than mobility services.

Q. 773. *List few specifications of teledesic.*

Ans. The plan of teledesic satellite systems includes the features likes usage of 840 LEO satellites at altitude of 700 km and (roughly) it deploys 288 active low earth orbit satellites at an altitude of 1350 km.

Q. 774. *Define 'bit interval' and 'bit rate' used in digital transmissions.*

Ans. (*i*) Bit interval : It is the time period required to transmit one bit.

(*ii*) Bit rate : It is nothing but the number of bit intervals per second. It is represented as kbps, Mbps, bps etc.

Q. 775. *What is an UPT?*

Ans. The Universal Personal Telecommunication (UPT) is a kind of service focused towards personal mobility to end-users where each user/subscriber will be provided a personal number. In this call screening and call forwarding features are enriched.

Q. 776. *Give three characteristics of UPT.*

Ans.
1. User control of service profile is possible.
2. Service availability across multiple networks like ISDN, PLMN etc.
3. Network and access security.

Q. 777. *List few service features of UPT.*

Ans. (*a*) Personal charging

(*b*) Personal numbering

(*c*) Access security

(*d*) Single source billing

Q. 778. *What is UWCC and UTRA?*

Ans. UWCC - Universal Wireless Communication Consortium.

UTRA - UMTS Terrestrial Radio Access.

Q. 779. *What is a CAVE?*

Ans. The "Cellular Authentication and Voice Encryption" (CAVE) algorithm is one the main parameter that is programmed with mobile station at the time of subscription which stores the user related personal information. CAVE is used for security development.

Q. 780. *What is the handoff scheme allowed with IS-136 standard?*

Ans. The "mobile-assisted" handoff scheme is used in IS-136 standard.

Q. 781. *Represent the evolution of personal and public mobile communication technology growth as graph.*

Ans.

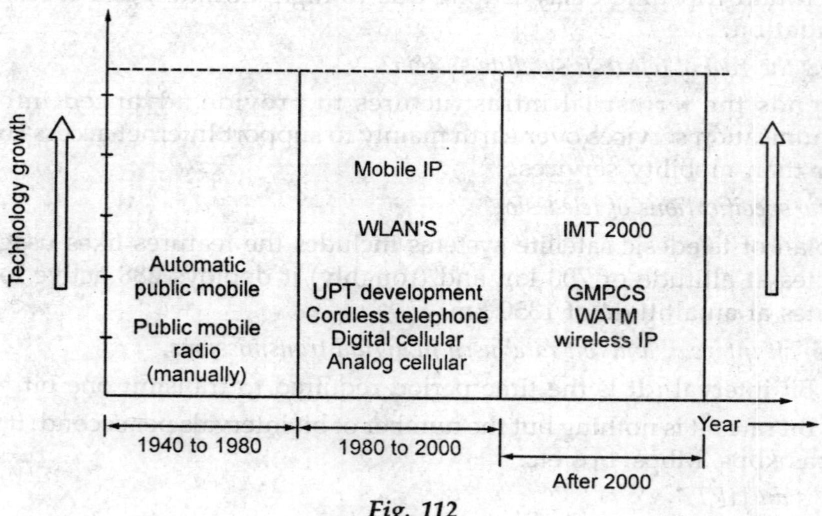

Fig. 112

Q. 782. *What are the links supported by indium system?*

Ans. The iridium system supports three types of links. The up/down link between

1. Space vehicle (SV) and gateway (GW)
2. Space vehicle (SV) and Iridium subscriber unit (ISU)
3. Space vehicle (SV) and Ka band.

Q. 783. *What is the difference between global star system and Iridium system?*

Ans. Global star depends upon the number interconnected earth stations and not the interconnected links of satellite.

Q. 784. *What are the regulatory services possible with GMPCS under global mobile satellite services?*

Ans.

1. Network interconnection.
2. Protection of interests and sovereign rights.
3. Authorization.
4. Frequency allocation.
5. Spectrum sharing.

Q. 785. *What is the main function of terminal mobility?*

Ans. The terminal mobility systems should be capable of locating and identifying a mobile terminal and should support the mobile access.

Q. 786. *What is a personal mobility?*

Ans. It depends on dynamic association between the user/subscriber and terminal where the call delivery and billing are based on personal identity.

Q. 787. *What are the logical operations possible with Universal personal telecommunication?*

Ans. There are three logical channels available in UPT termed as user recognition, user authentication, and user validation.

Q. 788. *What are the main factors that will influence the QoS in personal mobile communication?*

Ans. Authentication and privacy requirements, available frequency spectrum, speech encoding and transcoding techniques, and handoff requirements are some of the factors that will influence QoS.

Q. 789. *What are the parameters that will determine the efficiency of a mobile network?*

Ans. Speed, accuracy and dependability.

Q. 790. *What are the general parameters to be considered in mobile traffic load?*

Ans.
1. Performance (P)
2. Traffic load (L)
3. Resources (R)

Q. 791. *What are the main events involved in model mobile system?*

Ans. Call origination, call termination, call handoff location update and other features invocation are some of the events under model mobile system.

Q. 792. *What is known as round-trip speech channel delay?*

Ans. It is a delay inserted by several system components between mouth reference point (mrp)/ear reference point (erp) and the particular point of interconnection with that of the PSTN/ISDN.

Q. 793. *What arc the elements that can cause delay in a mobile network?*

Ans. The elements are speech transcoding delay, radio channel coding delay and mobile network delay.

Q. 794. *What is a satellite?*

Ans. It is a secondary body that revolves earth in an orbit as the primary body each revolves the sun.

Q. 795. *What is known as service capability?*

Ans. The service capability is the ability of the network to support and provide services at the terminal that is designated by user/subscriber.

Q. 796. *What are the main characteristics of GSM standard?*

Ans.
1. Fully digitized system using 900 MHz frequency.
2. Low data services.
3. International roaming.
4. Compatibility with ISDN.
5. Supporting SMS.

Q. 797. *List two radio aspects of GSM.*

Ans.
1. Up/down link frequencies are 890-915 MHz/935-960 MHz.
2. GSM uses TDMA and FDMA schemes.

Q. 798. *What are the main blocks of GSM?*

Ans. The main units of GSM are base station controller base transceiver station, mobile switching center, Home location register, visitor location, register, equipment identity register and authentication center.

Q. 799. *What are the physical elements of a BTS?*

Ans. BTS processor, radio transceivers, equalizers, channel coders, transcoders, encryption unit, combiners, preselectors, interleaving and deinterleaving units.

Q. 800. *What are the new supplementary services in GSM? List any three.*

Ans. Call completion to the busy subscribers, private numbering plan, and malicious call identification.

Q. 801. *What is a CAMEL?*

Ans. 'CAMEL' is 'customized applications for mobile network enhanced logic' a feature that enables GSM to support flexible customer service creations particularly for roaming subscribers.

Q. 802. *Draw the different satellite orbits.*

Ans.

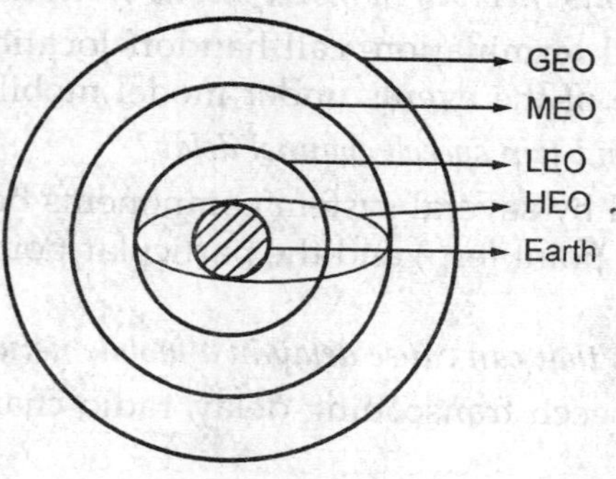

Fig. 113

Q. 803. *What are the advantages of LEO satellites?*

Ans.
1. LEO satellites provides higher global coverage.
2. High spectrum utilization.
3. The propagation delay is lower (say - 5 to 10 msec).

Q. 804. *What is known as 'ORBCOMM'?*

Ans. It refers a little LEO system, offered by ORBCOMM and it provides low bit rate, bi-directional communication services. It works with 26 LEO satellites constellation.

Q. 805. *What are the demerits of LEO system?*

Ans.
1. The network architecture is complex.
2. Satellite movement is rapid and analysis is tough.
3. Routing mechanism is difficult.
4. Long period of deployment.

Q. 806. *What are the services offered by MSAT?*

Ans.
1. Mobile Data Service (MDS).
2. Interconnected Mobile Radio Service (IMRS).
3. Mobile Radio Trunking Service (MRTS).

Q. 807. *What are the two main satellite constellations?*

Ans. The two main satellite constellations are random constellation and phased constellation.

Q. 808. *What are the merits of CEO satellites?*

Ans. GEO satellites have high data transfer and it can accommodate several transponders. Also they are more reliable than other satellite systems.

Q. 809. *What are the three control centres that are necessary for a mobile satellite system?*

Ans. The three control centres are Satellite Control Centre (SCC), Network Control Centre (NCC) and Business Management Centre (BMC).

Q. 810. *Differentiate up and down link in a mobile communication.*

Ans. Uplink : The uplink represents the signalling from mobile unit to the base station.

Downlink : It represents the signalling from base station to that of the mobile unit.

Q. 811. *What is the advanced systems taxonomy?*

Ans.
- HSCSD
- GPRS
- IMT-2000
- UMTS
- WAP

Q. 812. *Give any two functions supported by the user packet channel under personal handyphone system.*

Ans. In personal handyphone system (PHS), some of the main functions are circuit connection control, location registration, radio access control and other supplementary services.

Q. 813. *What is the significance of GPRS?*

Ans. This system mainly focuses on packet oriented data transmission. The time slots are allocated on demand basis so that channels are efficiently used. The data transfer is possible upto 150 kbits per second. GPRS is also capable of providing point to point packet transfer data services.

Q. 814. *Comment on data channels and spectrum allocation in a PHS.*

Ans. In personal handyphone system (PHS), there are four duplex data channels with each TDMA frame of 5 msec duration. The frequency spectrum is in 1895 to 1918 MHz range that can be partitioned into 77 carrier frequencies with possible separation of 300 kHz.

Q. 815. *Tabulate three characteristic features of personal communication service.*

Ans.

Characteristic	PCS system
Bandwidth	2 MHz
Channels/carrier	32
Accessing method	CDMA/TDMA

Q. 816. *Draw the personal handyphone system (PHS) taxonomy.*

Ans.

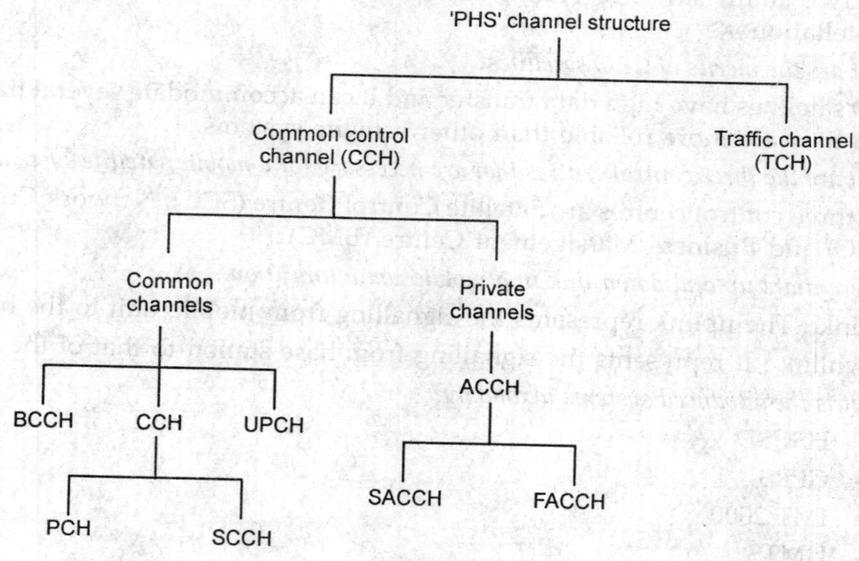

Fig. 114

Q. 817. *What type of channel assignment is used in PHS ?*

Ans. In personal handyphone system (PHS) dynamic channel assignment is used where channels are assigned according to the traffic availability.

Q. 818. *What are the channel types used in IS-95 standard?*

Ans. In IS-95 standard there are forward and reverse channels.

Q. 819. *Mention the three strategies that necessitates handoff mechanism.*

Ans. The three strategies that necessitates handoff mechanism are mobile controlled handoff, network controlled handoff and mobile assisted handoff.

Q. 820. *What are the personal communication services (PCS) technology ?*

Ans. They are cellular telephony and cordless telephony.

Q. 821. *Compare high tier and low tier cellular PCS technologies.*

Ans.

System	Low tier cellular system	High tier cellular system
Cell size	Medium	Large
Complexity	Low	High
Latency	≤ 10 msec	≤ 600 msec

Q. 822. *What are the components of SS7?*

Ans. There are three main components of SS7 namely service switching point (SSP), signal transfer point (STP) and service control point (SCP).

Q. 823. *Write short note on roaming management.*

Ans. In roaming management the functions like location tracking is important and in cellular standards as GSM a two tier system with visitor databases are used such as home location register, visitor location register.

Q. 824. *What are the three issues considered under handoff mechanism?*

Ans. The three mechanisms are handoff detection, channel assignment and radio link transfer.

Q. 825. *What are the operations that have to be considered for radio link transfer?*

Ans. First the radio link has to be transferred from old base station to new base station. Secondly, the network must be capable of bridging the link to new base station into the existing call and also dropping the link to the old base station.

Q. 826. *What are the examples for 'link transfers' in PCS?*

Ans. In PCS distinct link transfers like Intracell handoff, Inter - BSC handoff, Intercell handoff are possible.

Q. 827. *Represent mobile end station.*

Ans.

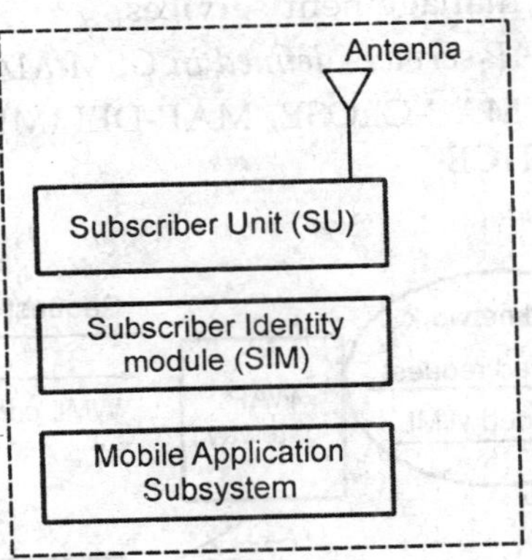

Fig. 115

Q. 828. *What is HSCSD?*

Ans. It is a circuit switched protocol used for multimedia and large file transfer applications. TDMA scheme is applied to increase HSCSD data rate.

Q. 829. *Draw the architecture of HSCSD.*

Ans.

Terminal Equipment (TE)
Mobile station
Terminal adaption functions
Radio interface
Mobile switching center
Inter working functions
PSTN/ PSDN/ ISDN/

Fig. 116

Q. 830. *What are the components of GPRS?*

Ans.
1. Home location register (HLR)
2. Visitor location register (VLR)

3. Mobile switching center (MSC)
4. Mobile station (MS)
5. Base station subsystem (BSS)
6. Terminal adaption functions (TAP)
7. Serving GPRS support node (SGSN)
8. Gateway GPRS support node (GGSN)
9. Interworking functions (IWF)
10. Terminal equipment (TE)
11. Public switched telephone network (PSTN)
12. Public switched data network (PSDN).

Q. 831. *What are the MAP services possible to complete a task in GSM?*

Ans. They are mobility, operation and maintenance, call handling, supplementary and short message service, management services.

Q. 832. *What are six common MAP services defined in GSM-MAP?*

Ans. They are MAP-OPEN, MAP-CLOSE, MAP-DELIMETER, MAP-U-ABORT, MAP-P-ABORT and MAP-NOTICE.

Q. 833. *Draw a WAP network model.*

Ans.

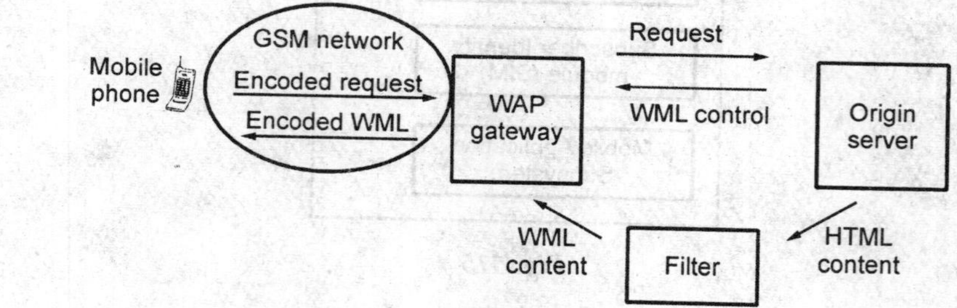

Fig. 117

Q. 834. *What are the main contents defined by WAE?*

Ans. The wireless application environment (WAE) defines content formats like images, calender informations and phone book .records. It also defines wireless telephony applications.

Q. 835. *Compare CDMA-2000 and W-CDMA technologies.*

Ans.

Specification	CDMA - 2000	W-CDMA
Chip rate	3.68 MCPS	4.096 MCPS
BS timing synchronization	Synchronous	Asynchronous

Q. 836. *What are the functions of QoS control mechanism in 3G systems?*

Ans. The 3G QoS control mechanism must (*a*) utilize the based on dynamically changing ability of QoS parameters (*b*) consider present end to end QoS to users with mapping and (*c*) Interwork with the current QoS schemes available.

Q. 837. *What is QSAFA and RD?*

Ans. QSAFA - Qausi Static Autonomous Frequency Assignment,
RD - Reject Duplicates

Q. 838. *Give the pager architecture.*

Ans.

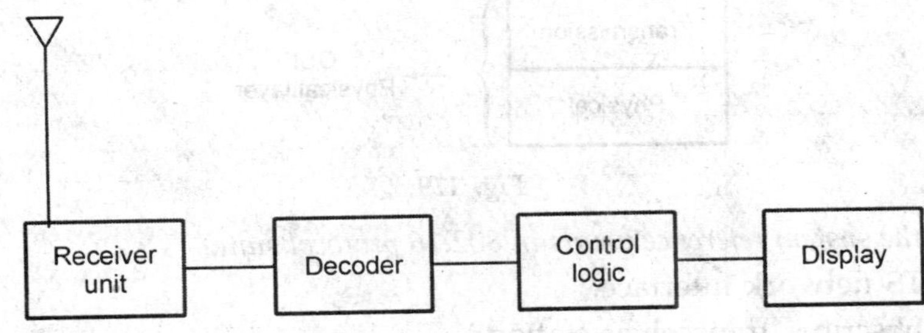

Fig. 118

Q. 839. *What is MSRN and MSISDN?*

Ans. MSRN - Mobile Station Roaming Number.
MSISDN - Mobile Station ISDN Number.

Q. 840. *Give examples for high - tier digital cellular standards.*

Ans. Global system for mobile communication (GSM), Personal digital cellular (PDC) and IS-95 CDMA based CDMA one system.

Q. 841. *Define "subrating scheme".*

Ans. "Subrating" (SRS) a process of dividing an occupied full rate channel into channels (two channels) of half the original data rates and one channel to serve the call existing where as the second channel to serve the handoff request of the instant.

Q. 842. *List any two applications possible with GSM/GPRS.*

Ans. (*a*) Telnet (*b*) Web browsing.

Q. 843. *What are the three main wireless technologies?*

Ans. The popular three wireless technologies are Bluetooth, Wi-Fi and Zig-bec technologies.

Q. 844. *Differentiate Bluetooth and Wi-Fi technologies with respect to number of devices connectivity.*

Ans. In Bluetooth technology there can be upto seven devices connected whereas in Wi-Fi it can be increased upto 32 devices that can be connected.

Q. 845. *What are the bandwidths allocated for IEEE 802.11a and IEEE 802.11b standards?*

Ans.

IEEE standard	Bandwidth
802.11a	5.6 GHz
802.11b	2.4 GHz

Q. 846. *What are the industrial applications of Wi-Fi technology?*

Ans. They are device oriented services, security services, wireless automation with controlling services, and instrumentation monitoring services etc.

Q. 847. *What are the layers of 802.16 protocol architecture ?*

Ans.

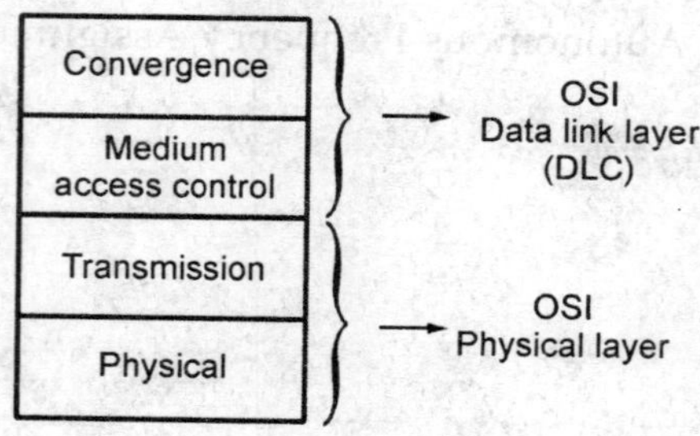

Fig. 119

Q. 848. *What are the system reference points in 802.16 protocol suite?*

Ans. SNI → STS network interface.

STS → Subscriber transceiver station.

BTS → Base transceiver station.

and BNI → BTS network interface.

Q. 849. *What are the main working groups intended for 802,16 standard development?*

Ans. The three working groups are IEEE 802.16.1, IEEE 802.16.2 and IEEE 802.16.3 specially meant for producing standards.

Q. 850. *What is the significance of a 802.16 standard?*

Ans. It is a fixed broadband wireless access standard. The IEEE 802 standard committee developed this 802.16 new working group in the year 1999 focusing on broadband wireless access applications.

Q. 851. *What is the objective of 802.16 working group?*

Ans. The aim of this group is to develop several standards that can support,

- Provide public network service.
- Metropolitan in scale.
- To provide efficient traffic with QoS.
- Broadband transmissions (72 Mbps approx).

Q. 852. *What are the physical layer modes available in IEEE 801.16.1?*

Ans. Continuous down stream (mode A) and burst down stream (mode B).

Q. 853. *What are the access method and duplexing technique under mode A and B?*

Ans.

Parameter	Mode A	Mode B
Access method	TDM	DAMA - TDMA
Duplexing technique	FDD	FDD with adaptive modulation

Q. 854. *Draw the IEEE 802.16.1 frame format.*

Ans.

MAC Header	Payload (optional)	CRC
48 or 56 bits	≥ 0 bits	32 bits

Q. 855. *What are LMDS and MMDS ?*

Ans. LMDS - Local Multipoint Distribution Service.
MMDS - Multichannel Multipoint Distribution Service.

Q. 856. *State the advantages of MMDS over LMDS.*

Ans.
1. An equipment at lower frequencies is less expensive at both subscriber and base station ends.
2. MMDS signals are less affected by rain absorption effects.
3. MMDS signal have large wavelength (λ) and can travel for long distances without power losses.

Q. 857. *What are the advantages of LMDS signals?*

Ans.
1. High data rates (in the range of Mbps).
2. It is capable of providing telephony, video and data.
3. Low cost when compared to cable systems.

Q. 858. *What is an OFDM?*

Ans. The orthogonal frequency division multiplexing (OFDM) is a multicarrier modulation that makes use of multiple carrier signals at various frequencies. Also in OFDM scheme all the subchannels are mainly dedicated to a particular data source.

Q. 859. *What is the radius of first fresnel zone?*

Ans. The radius of first fresnel zone is (r) = $\sqrt{\dfrac{\lambda S d}{(S+d)}}$

where λ → Wavelength
S → Distance from the transmitter to the measured point.
d → Distance from receiver to the measured point.

Q. 860. *Represent a first fresnel zone structure.*

Ans.

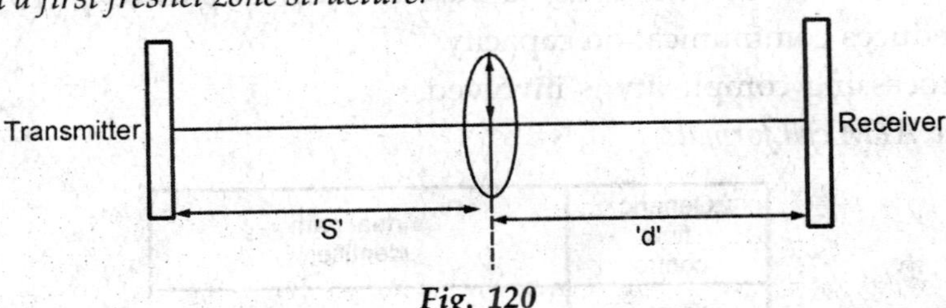

Fig. 120

Q. 861. *Compare the speech coders CELP, LPC, PCM and uncoded speech in a graph.*

Ans.

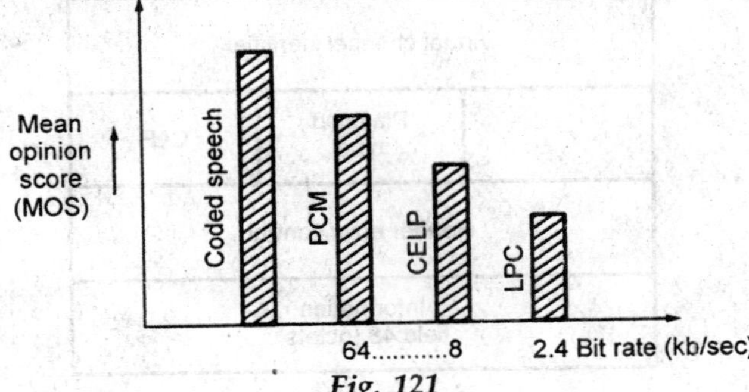

Fig. 121

Q. 862. *What is a circuit switching?*

Ans. In circuit switching there is a dedicated communication path between the stations, through nodes.

Q. 863. *What are the three phases involved in circuit switching?*

Ans. The three phases are circuit establishment, information transfer and circuit disconnect phases.

Q. 864. *What are the generic architectural components in a public telecommunications network?*

Ans. They are subscribers, subscriber lines, exchanges and trunks.

Q. 865. *What are the demerits of circuit switching network?*

Ans.
- For most of the time the terminal to host connections are idle.
- The two devices at the ends must be properly synchronized to receive the correct data.

Q. 866. *What is the operation of packet switching?*

Ans. The data/information is transmitted in block units called packets. The upper limit of packets length is 1000 bytes. Hence the entire message is broken into packets at transmitter side and re-assembled after reception.

Q. 867. *What are the advantages of packet switching?*

Ans.
1. The line efficiency is good.
2. Priorities are allowed.
3. Even when traffic load is heavy in packet switching it is possible to receive the packets with a delay but the packets will not be lost.

Q. 868. *What are the demerits of packet switching?*

Ans.
1. Each and every time delay is introduced with packet.
2. Reduces communication capacity.
3. Processing complexity is involved.

Q. 869. *Draw the ATM cell format.*

Ans.

Generic flow control	Virtual path identifier	
Virtual path identifier		
Virtual channel identifier		
	Playload type	CLP
Header error control		
Information field 48 (octets)		

Fig. 122

Q. 870. *What is the use of virtual path identifier?*

Ans. The virtual path identifier (VPI) field forms a routing field required for the network. VPI is of 8 bits at user to network interface whereas 12 bits at network to network interface.

Q. 871. *What is a payload in ATM?*

Ans. In ATM the payload field denotes the type of data/information. It is the actual data that has to be transmitted.

Q. 872. *Give an example for payload type field coding.*

Ans.

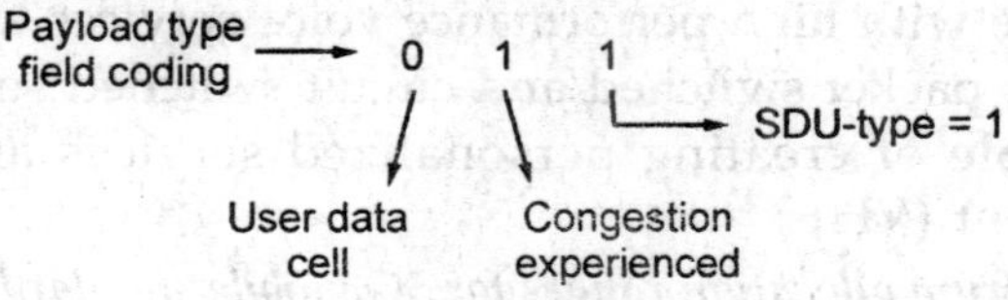

Fig. 123

Q. 873. *What is the use of* CLP?

Ans. Cell loss priority (CLP) field helps the communication network by providing guidance at the time of congestion.

Q. 874. *What are main services defined by ATM Forum?*

Ans.
1. Real time service
2. Non real time service.

Q. 875. *What is a non real time service?*

Ans. The available bit rate (ABR), unspecified bit rate (UBR) are examples of non real time service.

Q. 876. *What is the use of HEC?*

Ans. The header error control (HEC) field is a 8 bit error code and it is used to correct the single bit errors. It can also detect the double errors.

Q. 877. *Represent "ATM bit rate services".*

Ans.

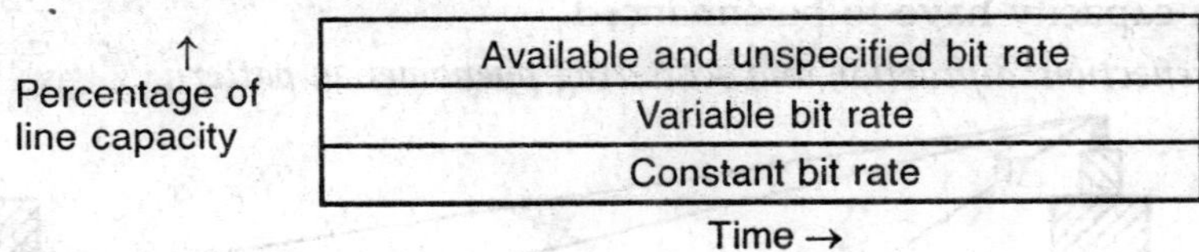

Q. 878. *List the TCP/IP layers.*

Ans.
(*a*) Physical layer
(*b*) Network access layer
(*c*) Internet layer
(*d*) Host to host on a transport layer and
(*e*) Application layer.

Q. 879. *What are bottom three layers of OSI model?*

Ans. In an OSI model there are seven layers of which the bottom three layers are network, datalink and physical layers.

Q. 880. *What is a PDU in TCP/IP?*

Ans. The protocol data unit (PDU) in TCP/IP represents the data exchanged at a protocol level and hence TCP segment is also be said to be TCP-PDU.

Q. 881. *What is the use of TELNET?*

Ans. TELNET is an application of TCP/IP. It can provide remote login facility. It has two modules known as 'User TELNET' and 'Server TELNET'.

Q. 882. *What are the important characteristics of 3G systems?*

Ans.
1. The 3G systems supports symmetric and asymmetric traffic of the network.
2. Compatible with high performance voice services and supports roaming.
3. It supports packet switched and circuit switched services.
4. It is capable of creating personalized services and enables virtual home environment (VHE).

Q. 883. *What are the spectrum allocation ranges for 3G mobile standards?*

Ans.

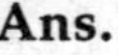

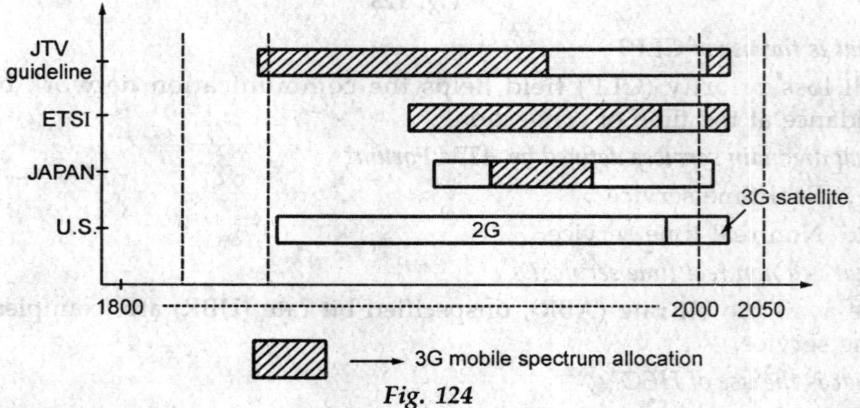

Fig. 124

Q. 884. *What is the need for increasing system capacity?*

Ans. With 3G standards intelligent antennas and multiuser detections are possible where system capacity have to be enhanced.

Q. 885. *Draw reflection, diffraction and scattering phenomenon pattern.*

Ans.

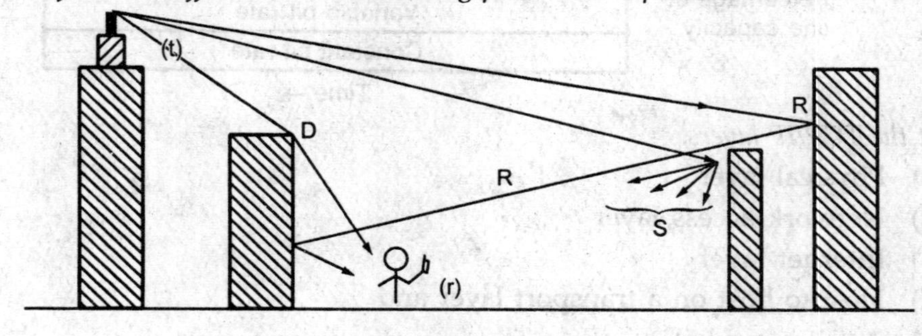

Fig. 125

Q. 886. *What are the applications of 3G standards?*

Ans.
1. Mobile commerce u-commerce field, a subset of the electronic commerce.
2. Multimedia messaging applications.
3. Broadcasting applications.
4. Geolocation based applications etc.

Q. 887. *What are the service classes?*

Ans.
- Wireless messaging
- Voice and audio
- Medium multimedia
- Switched data
- High multimedia
- Interactive high multimedia.

Q. 888. *Give the IMT-2000 specification.*

Ans.

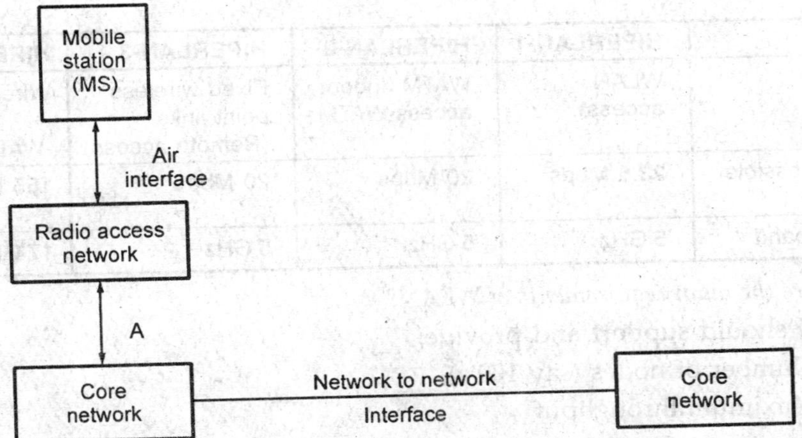

Fig. 126

Q. 889. *Draw the 8-PSK modulation scheme.*

Ans.

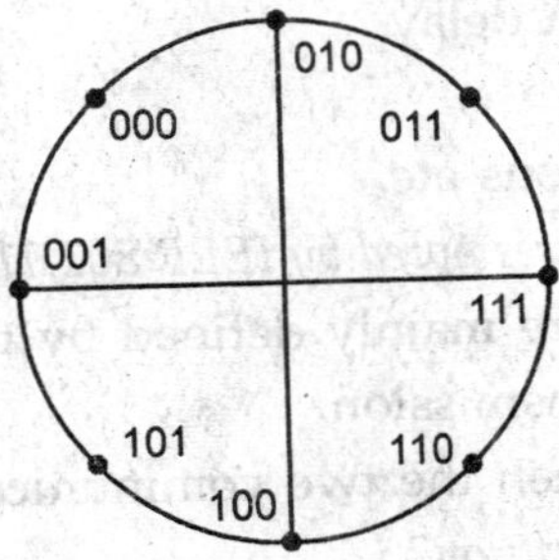

Fig. 127

Q. 890. *Write short note on EDGE.*

Ans. The 'EDGE' is Enhanced data rates for GSM evolution, and it is an air-interface that is based on TDMA technology. The goal of EDGE technology is to upgrade the networks so as to support HSCSD and GPRS advanced systems.

Q. 891. *What are the physical layer characteristics?*

Ans. They are wideband, channel coding and interleaving, downlink/uplink coherent demodulation spreading and adaptive antenna support.

Q. 892. *Compare 802.11, 802.Ha and 802.11b standards.*

Ans.

	802. 11 b	802. 11a	802.11
Application	WLAN	WLAN	WLAN
Maximum possible data rate	1 1 Mbps	54 Mbps	2 Mbps
Frequency band	5 GHz	2.4 GHz	2.4 GHz

Q. 893. *Compare HIPERLAN-1, HIPEREAN-2, HIPERLAN-3 and HIPERLAN-4 standards.*

Ans.

	HIPERLAN-1	HIPERLAN-2	HIPERLAN-3	HIPERLAN-4
Application	WLAN access)	WATM (Indoor access-WATM -	Fixed wireless point links (Remote access)	Wireless point to -WATM
Maximum possible data rate	23.5 Mbps	20 Mbps	20 Mbps	155 Mb/sec
Frequency band	5 GHz	5 GHz	5 GHz	17 GHz

Q. 894. *What are the main requirements of WLAN?*

Ans. WLAN should support and provide,

1. Number of nodes (say 100's)
2. Maximum throughput
3. Energy saving
4. Robustness and secured environment
5. Handoff - Roaming facilities
6. Reduced propagation delay
7. Dynamic topology
8. Multimedia applications etc.

Q. 895. *What are the security procedures opted by IEEE 802.11 standard?*

Ans. Two security procedures are mainly defined by this standard.

1. Encrypted frame transmission.
2. Authentication between the two communicating stations.

Q. 896. *What is a shared key authentication?*

Ans. It is a four-way handshaking mechanism used in WATM. In this method an authentication frame will be sent by the requesting station (1) and as a response the other station (2) sends an authentication frame which is a sequence of 128 bytes length. This is encrypted by the station (1) and sent to station (2) where the frames are decrypted.

Q. 897. *How power saving is achieved by IEEE 802.11 standard?*

Ans. Power saving is achieved by the principle of buffering of traffic at transmitting station that is whenever a mobile unit is in sleep mode all the traffic related to it will be buffered till the node wakes up.

Q. 898. *Write short note on IEEE 802.11g standard.*

Ans. The goals of this 802.11g group under 802.11 is to make use of OFDM scheme where data rates will be upto 54 Mb/sec. Backward compatibility should be available to support other working groups.

Q. 899. *List any three main requirements of MAC protocol in WATM.*

Ans. It should allow decreased complexity at mobile nodes with less energy consumption.

- Should support required QoS under load variations.
- Should provide low delay values under channel assignments.

Q. 900. *What are the procedures managed by radio link control protocol?*

Ans. This RLCP protocol supports and provides services to the association control function, radio resource control function and DLC connection control functions so as to enable exchange of the control information between the AP and mobile terminals.

Q. 901. *Write a short note on 'routing' in wireless Ad hoc networks.*

Ans. The routing protocols should be developed for ad hoc networks such that it has to adapt to any topology changes and the delivery of packets should not be disturbed. Routing protocols should provide assurance of packets delivery properly to the destination address irrespective of changes in network topology.

Q. 902. *What are the main metrics used by routing protocols in wired ad hoc networks?*

Ans. The routing protocols used in ad hoc networks use the metrics end to end throughput and delay metrics.

Q. 903. *What are the important performance metrics that has to be used by wireless ad hoc network routing protocol?*

Ans.

- Minimum end to end delay.
- Minimum overhead.
- Flexible and adaptive to topology changes if any.
- Reduced power consumption.
- Maximum end to end throughput.

Q. 904. *Write short note on 'Semi Ad hoc' concept.*

Ans. To increase robustness in wireless environment a dual mode of functionality can be introduced. Whenever several radio access networks are available simultaneously devices can operate either within a wireless ad hoc networks or within a cellular network with a centralized wireless control.

Q. 905. *Give an example for frequency reuse when cluster size is 3 in mobile environment.*

Ans.

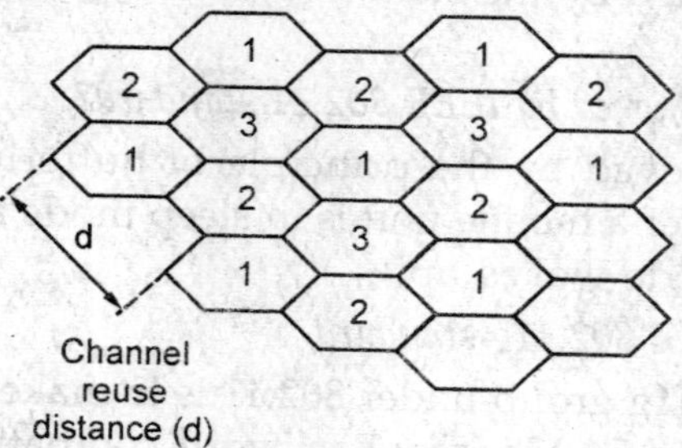

Fig. 128

Q. 906. *Give the OSI reference model.*

Ans.

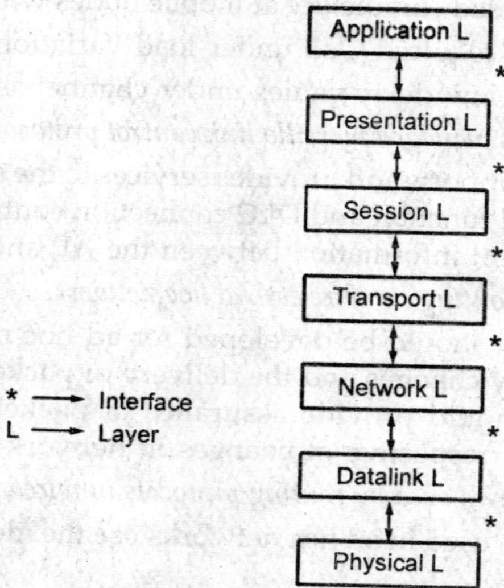

Fig. 129

Q. 907. *Give any two SAT colour codes for corresponding SAT frequencies.*

Ans.

SAT colour code SCC	Supervisory audio tone (SAT) frequency in kHz
01	6
10	6.03

Q. 908. *What are the four signals sent by signalling tones (ST)?*

Ans. They are 'Request to send', 'Alert signal', 'Disconnect signal' and 'Handoff confirmation' signal.

Q. 909. *What is the importance of smart antenna?*

Ans. The smart antennas are attractive because they are adaptive in nature, where enhanced antenna diversity is considered. Smart antennas are capable of focusing both their own transmissions and also radio transmission of the receiver in cellular environment. So the main advantage of smart antennas (array of antennas) is to reduce power.

Q. 910. *Mention any two smart antenna placement.*

Ans.

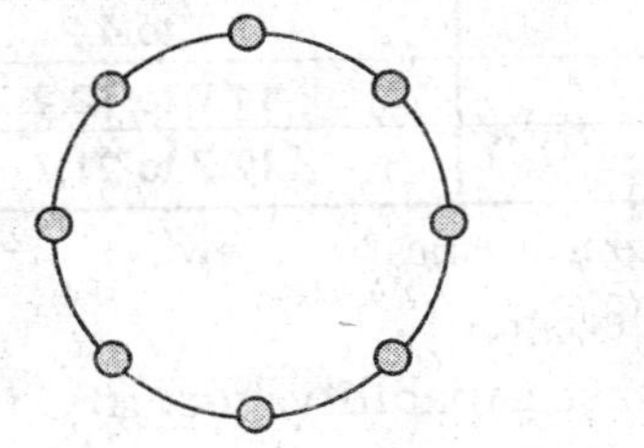

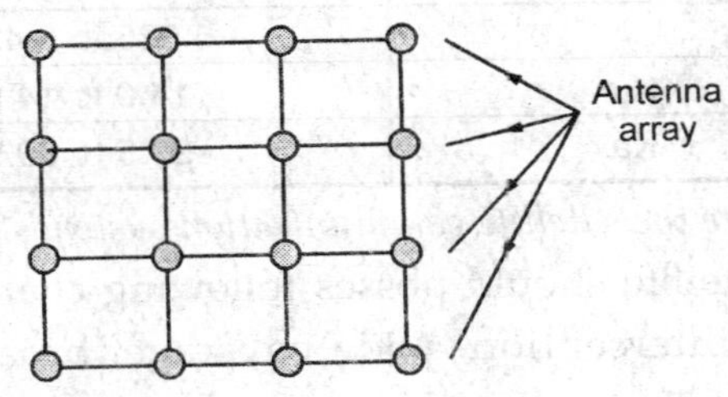

Fig. 130

Q. 911. *What is a VPN?*

Ans. Virtual private network (VPN) can connect resources and components of one network to another network. It is actually a group of several computers to a particular private network which has limited public network accesses and it is an aliter method to WEP. VPN provides good scalability and high security in wireless environment.

Q. 912. *What are the three approaches used for designing broadcasts in wireless environments?*

Ans. There are three important approaches termed as pull-based approach, push-based approach and hybrid approach for broadcast designing.

Q. 913. *What is known as hybrid approach in the previous question?*

Ans. In hybrid approach the downlink bandwidth is divided into two transmission modes known as periodic broadcast mode and on-demand mode. The combination of push and pull-based approaches constitutes this hybrid approach.

Q. 914. *Give any three design goals of 4G systems.*

Ans. The important design goals are to obtain system interoperability, overlay network enabling and to provide a common access protocol.

Q. 915. *Draw the OFDM system.*

Ans.

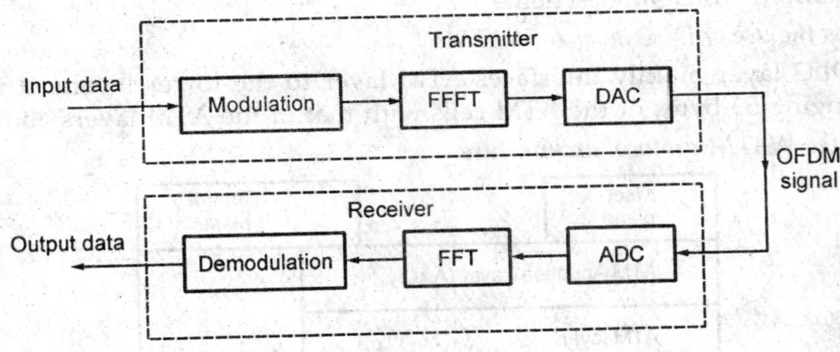

Fig. 131

Q. 916. *What are the advantages of satellites utility in developing networks?*

Ans. The main uses are mobility, broadcasting, rapid and simple deployments and provision hostile environment.

Q. 917. *What are the uplink and downlink frequencies of C, Ku and Ka bands under satellite networks?*

Ans.

Band	Uplink f (GHz)	Downlink f (GHz)
C	5.925 to 6.425	3.7 to 4.2
Ku	14.0 to 14.5	11.7 to 12.2
Ka	27.5 to 30.5	17.7 to 21.7

Q. 918. *What are the satellite communication system's characteristics?*

Ans. The satellite should posses following characteristics :

Noise interception, wide coverage, broadcast capability, security, transmission delays etc.

Q. 919. *Mention three link frequencies of global star.*

Ans.

Frequency in GHz	Type of link (up/down)
1.61 to 1.63	Mobile-satellite (up)
2.4 to 2.5	Satellite-mobile (down)
5.09 to 5.25	Gateway-satellite (up)
6.7 to 7.08	Satellite-gateway (down)

Q. 920. *What is the use of 'global star'?*

Ans. Global star is satellite based telephony system enabling the subscribers to communicate virtually from any place of the world. Global star increases the coverage area.

Q. 921. *Give a brief short note on applications of WLAN.*

Ans. The main application of WLAN are LAN extension, ad hoc networking, nomadic access and interconnection across tall buildings. The WLAN helps to develop a infrastructure independent environment for communication.

Q. 922. *What is the type of modulation and channel bandwidth used by low speed PHY in WATM?*

Ans. Channel bandwidth - 30 MHz frequency

Modulation - 16-DQPSK scheme.

Q. 923. *What is the use of DLC layer in WATM?*

Ans. The DLC layer mainly interfaces ATM layer to the lower layers. It is capable of exchanging 53 bytes of the ATM cells with that of the ATM layers above it.

Q. 924. *Draw the WATM protocol architecture.*

Ans.

Fig. 132

Q. 925. *What are the major attacks possible on wireless networks?*

Ans. The main categories of attacks are interruption of service. Interception misconfiguration, jamming, insertion attacks, attacks against passwords and encryption, client to client attacks and modifications.

Q. 926. *What are the issues that necessitates security in computer networks?*

Ans. The main issues are complexity, anonymity, sharing and multiple point of attack.

Q. 927. *What are the fields available in authentication extension contained in a registration request and reply?*

Ans. They are type, authenticator, security parameter index and length.

Q. 928. *What is known as IP Sec?*

Ans. An internet protocol security is a standard which is based on network layer '3' security protocol (SP). To authenticate the internet protocol datagrams, IP security protocol makes use of either encapsulation security payload (ESP) or authentication header (AH) protocol.

Q. 929. *Differentiate two cell shapes with diagrams.*

Ans.

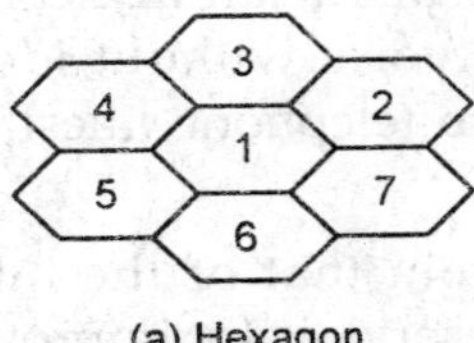

Fig. 133

Q. 930. *What are the two types of cell splitting?*

Ans. The two types of cell splitting are permanent splitting and dynamic splitting.

Q. 931. *In the figure given, find the radius of the new cell after cell splitting.*

Ans.

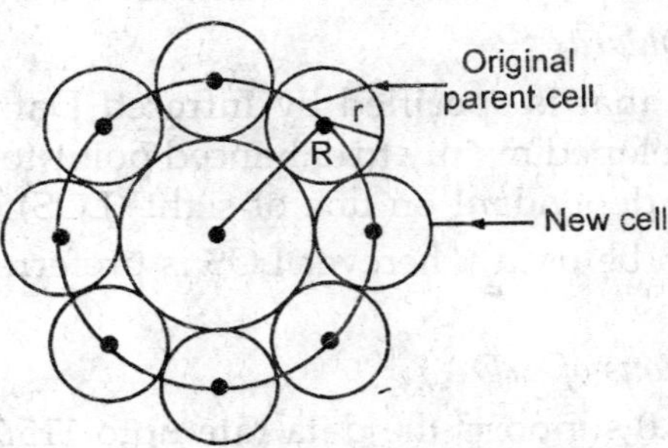

Fig. 134

$$\text{New cell radius is} = \frac{\text{Original (old) parent cell}}{2}$$

$$r = \left(\frac{R}{2}\right)$$

Q. 932. *What is known as dynamic cell splitting?*

Ans. The dynamic utilizes the allocated frequency spectrum efficiently in real time. It is a complex process to execute at high traffic hours.

Q. 933. *What is the reason behind the name "Bluetooth"?*

Ans. The name 'Bluetooth' is after the king of Denmark 'Harald Bluetooth' in 900's age. He took step for unifying a part of Norway and the Denmark as single kindom. In this remembrance the wireless standard revolutionizing communication industry was named as 'Bluetooth technology'.

Q. 934. *What is the standard indicated by Wi-Fi technology?*

Ans. The Wi-Fi represents wireless fidelity which is generally used to refer any type of the 802.11 network.

Q. 935. *Explain the characteristic of the voice channel.*

Ans. Initially cellular radio was intended to work like telephone wire lines where a pair of wires used to serve the traffic in both directions. For example, if the bandwidth is 60 kHz. Then forward path occupies 30 kHz and reverse path occupies 30 kHz. As the telephone line here also the conversation can be heard on single frequency say 'f'. That is the user receives his own voice without identifying it. This effect of crosstalk is two fold when compared to telephone lines.

Q. 936. *What is an 'AIN'?*

Ans. AIN is a kind of network evolved from that of the intelligent network (IN). It consists of an architecture that provides services for improving network performance.

Q. 937. *What is 'RFID'?*

Ans. Radio frequency identification (RFID) is a technology used to tagging of the goods and the products in commercial application area. The RFID tag acts as transmitter that sends the sensed signal when kept on a product to the RFID receiver. It is used to increase security purposes but not economical when compared to barcodes.

Q. 938. *What is an 'IrDA ' standard?*

Ans. 'IrDA' is a standard that is specified by Infrared Data Association formed in the year 1993. It was developed mainly to enhanced point-to-point or point-to-multipoint communication. It is dependant on line of sight (LOS) operation.

The infrared rays can be used wherever LOS is preferred and useful for this indoor consumer applications.

Q. 939. *What are the specifications of 'IrDA'?*

Ans. The IrDA standard 1.0 supports the data rate upto 115.2 kb/sec. for the range upto 1m and next version "IrDA 1.1" developed later supports data transfers upto 35 times faster when compared to "IrDA 1.0".

Q. 940. *What are the new specifications supported by current Bluetooth?*

Ans. The short range Bluetooth technology is improved for meeting the distance of 100 m in open air and 30 m within building infrastructures for its operation. It works with datarate of 1 Mbps.

Q. 941. *Compare four Wi-Fi standards speed.*

Ans.

Standard	Speed
802.11 a	54 Mbps
802. 11b	11 Mbps
802.11g	54 Mbps
802. 1n	100 Mbps

Q. 942. *What are MMDS, DEMS and LMDS?*

Ans. MMDS - Multichannel multipoint distribution service.

DEMS - Digital electronic messaging service.

LMDS - Local multipoint distribution service.

Q. 943. *Give the electromagnetic spectrum.*

Ans.

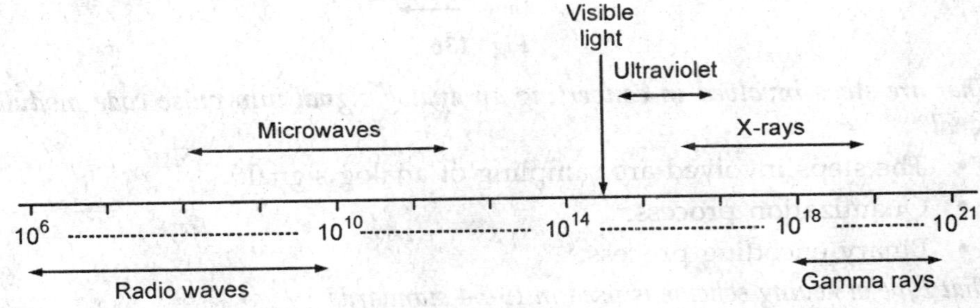

Fig. 135

Q. 944. *What is the frequency ranges of satellite and radar communication?*

Ans. Satellite → 3 to 30 GHz.

Satellites-radar → 30 to 300 GHz.

Q. 945. *Denote the super high frequency and extra high frequency.*

Ans. Super high frequency (SHF) → 3 to 30 GHz.

Extra high frequency (EHF) → 30 to 300 GHz.

Q. 946. *What is the application of satellite bands S, C and W?*

Ans. S band → Cellular application.

C band → Satellite application.

W band → For future cellular applications.

Q. 947. *Mention the microwave frequencies.*

Ans. The high frequency radio bands say ultra high frequency (UHF), super high frequency (SHF) and extremely high frequency (EHF) are denoted as microwave frequency range.

Q. 948. *What are the frequency range and application of S, C and W bands?*

Ans.

Band	Frequency range	Application
S	1.5 to 5.2 GHz	Cellular
C	3.9 to 6.2 GHz	Satellite
W	56 to 100 GHz	Future developments in cellular applications

Q. 949. *Draw a PCM signal produced by quantization.*

Ans.

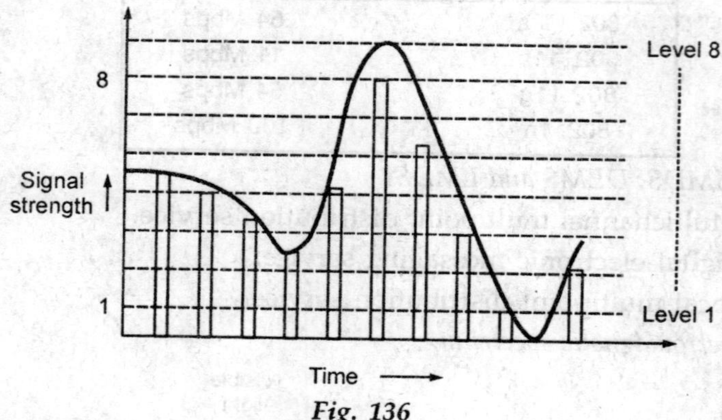

Fig. 136

Q. 950. *What are steps involved in converting an analog signal into pulse code modulated (PCM) signal?*

Ans.
- The steps involved are sampling of analog signal.
- Quantization process.
- Binary encoding process.

Q. 951. *What type of keying scheme is used in IS-54 standard?*

Ans. In IS-54 cellular standard $\pi/4$-shifted PSK scheme is used, with four combinations of bits (0's and 1's) for each phase change.

Q. 952. *What are the techniques possible with PSK variations?*

Ans. The various techniques under PSK variations are differential-PSK, $\pi/4$-shifted PSK and quadrature amplitude modulation (QAM).

Q. 953. *What are the phase changes for corresponding pair of bits used in IS-54 standard?*

Ans.

Phase change	Bits in pair
$\pi/4$	00
$5\pi/4$	01
$-\pi/4$	10
$-5\pi/4$	10

Q. 954. *What are the channel bandwidths used in early AMPS and NMT systems?*

Ans. Advanced mobile phone systems (AMPS) – 30 kHz where usable channel bandwidth is 24 kHz. (approx).

Nordic mobile telephony system (NMT) – 25 kHz where usable channel bandwidth is 9.4 kHz (approx.)

Q. 955. *Mention any two routing protocols that are used in wireless ad hoc networks.*

Ans. They are 'Destination Sequenced Distance Vector (DSDV) routing protocol' and 'Dynamic Source Routing (DSR) protocol'.

Q. 956. *What are the two main classification in routing protocol in wireless ad hoc networks?*

Ans. (*a*) Table-driven routing protocol.

(*b*) On-demand routing protocol.

Q. 957. *In above question give two examples of each type.*

Ans. Table driven routing protocol

(*i*) Destination sequenced distance vector (DSDV) routing protocol.

(*ii*) Clusterhead gateway switched routing (CGSR) protocol.

On-demand routing protocol

(*i*) Ad hoc on-demand distance vector (AODV) routing

(*ii*) Dynamic source routing (DSR)

Q. 958. *Draw the Bluetooth packet format and the packet header format.*

Ans.

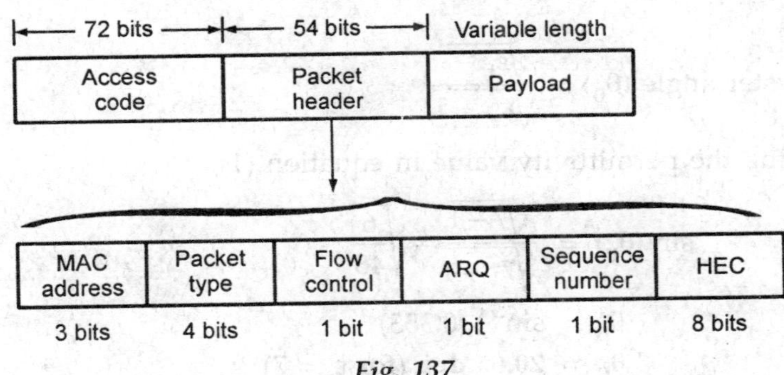

Fig. 137

Q. 959. *What are the different power levels used under Bluetooth devices?*

Ans. Bluetooth devices

Power level/class	Minimum transmit power level (mW)	Maximum transmit power level (mW)
1	1	100
2	0.25	2.5
3	N/A	1

Q. 960. *What are the two kinds of profiles in Bluetooth 1.1 version?*

Ans. The two main profile classification is nine application profiles and four system profile and as a whole thirteen profiles are supported by Bluetooth 1.1 version.

Q. 961. *What are the system profiles used in Bluetooth 1.1 version?*

Ans. The system profiles are generic object exchange, object push, file transfer and synchronization profiles.

Q. 962. *A carrier signal of 1 MHz frequency with an amplitude of IV peak value is modulated by a 3 kHz message signal with the modulation index is 0.5. Find the-upper and lower sideband frequencies and voltages.*

Ans. Carrier frequency = f_c = 1 MHz

Modulating signal frequency = f_m = 3 kHz

Lower side band frequency (f_{LSB}) = $f_c - f_m$

$$= 1 \text{ MHz} - 3 \text{ kHz}$$

$$f_{LSB} = 0.997 \text{ MHz}$$

Upper side band frequency $(f_{USB}) = f_c + f_m$

$$= 1 \text{ MHz} + 3 \text{ kHz}$$

$$f_{USB} = 1.003 \text{ MHz}$$

Voltage of the each side band is

$$E_{LSB} - E_{USB} = \frac{m F_c}{2}$$

$$= \mathbf{0.25 \text{ volts}}$$

Q. 963. *Calculate the brewster angle for a wave that impings on ground having a permittivity of $\varepsilon_r = 7$.*

Ans. The brewster angle $(\theta_B) = \dfrac{\sqrt{\varepsilon_r - 1}}{\sqrt{\varepsilon_{r^2} - 1}}$ ...(1)

Substituting the permittivity value in equation (1),

$$\sin(\theta_B) = \frac{\sqrt{7-1}}{\sqrt{7^2 - 1}} = \sqrt{\frac{6}{48}}$$

$$\theta_B = \sin^{-1}(0.353)$$

$$\theta_B = \mathbf{20.67 \text{ deg}} \text{ (for } \varepsilon_r = 7)$$

Q. 964. *Calculate the theoretical maximum possible data rate which can support a 500 kHz channel for signal to noise ratio (SNR) equal to 10 dB.*

Ans. The signal to noise ratio (SNR) = 10 dB

The channel bandwidth (B) = 500 kHz

As per Shannon's channel capacity formula, maximum possible data rate is calculated as,

$$C = B \log_2 \left(1 + \frac{S}{N}\right) \quad \text{...(1)}$$

Substituting the given values

$$C = 500 \text{ kHz} \log_2 (1 + 10) \quad \text{...(2)}$$

$$= 500000 \log_2 (1 + 10)$$

and $$\log_a^m = \frac{\log_e^m}{\log_e^a} = \frac{ln\ m}{ln\ a} \quad \text{...(3)}$$

From (3), $$\log_2^{11} = 3.459 \quad \text{...(4)}$$

Substituting equation (2) in equation (4), then

$$\text{Capacity} = C - (500 \text{ kHz})(3.459)$$

$$C = \mathbf{1729 \text{ kbps.}}$$

Q. 965. *Calculate the spectral efficiency (η_s) if the bandwidth is 684 kbps and transmission data rate is 1.152 Mbps.*

Ans. The bandwidth = BW = 684 kbps

Transmission rate = R_T = 1.152 Mbps

$$\text{Spectral efficiency} = \eta_s = \frac{R_T}{BW}$$

$$= \frac{1.152 \text{ Mbps}}{576 \text{ kbps}}$$

$$= \mathbf{1.6 \text{ bps/Hz}}$$

Q. 966. *Consider there are four cellular radio standards and select a standard which has minimum radio capacity assuming n = 4 propagation pathless.*

Ans. System 1 - B_c = 25 kHz and $\left(\frac{C}{I}\right)_{min}$ = 13 dB

System 2 - B_c = 30 kHz and $\left(\frac{C}{I}\right)_{min}$ = 17 dB

System 3 - B_c = 12.5 kHz, $\left(\frac{C}{I}\right)_{min}$ = 11 dB

System 4 - B_c = 6.25 kHz, $\left(\frac{C}{I}\right)_{min}$ = 8 dB

Assuming that each system id adopted a bandwidth of 6.25 kHz, then

$$\left(\frac{C}{I}\right)_{eq} = \left(\frac{C}{I}\right)_{min} \cdot \left(\frac{B_c}{B'_c}\right)^2 \qquad \text{...(1)}$$

Where B_c is bandwidth of particular system and B'_c is bandwidth of different system. Substituting the values in above equation (1), then

For system 1 - $\left(\frac{C}{I}\right)_{eq} = 13 + 20 \log\left(\frac{6.25}{25}\right) = 0.96$

System 2 - $\left(\frac{C}{I}\right)_{eq} = 17 + 20 \log\left(\frac{6.25}{30}\right) = 3.38$

System 3 - $\left(\frac{C}{I}\right)_{eq} = 11 + 20 \log\left(\frac{6.25}{12.5}\right) = 4.98$

System 4 - $\left(\frac{C}{I}\right)_{eq} = 8 + 20 \log\left(\frac{6.25}{6.25}\right) = 8$

Comparing all systems the largest value of $\left(\frac{C}{I}\right)_{eq}$ should be selected for minimum radio capacity. Hence the 'system 4' provides minimum radio capacity than other three systems.

Q. 967. *What will be maximum data rate that can be transmitted if the signal to noise ratio is 20 dB and channel bandwidth is 40 kHz?*

Ans. Channel bandwidth = B = 40 KHz.

Signal to noise ratio = 20 dB = 100

$$\text{Channel capacity} = C = B \log_2\left(1+\frac{S}{N}\right)$$

$$= 40 \text{ kHz } \log_2 (1 + 100)$$

$$= 40 \text{ kHz}\left(\frac{\ln 101}{\ln 2}\right)$$

Maximum data rate = C = **266.33 kbps**

Q. 968. *In a cellular mobile communication for a forward channel performance considering signal to noise ratio (SNR) of 14 dB is required as minimum requirement. Find frequency reuse factor that must be used for maximum capacity if the path loss exponent is n = 3 and n = 4. (Assuming six co-channel cells are available in first tier and key are at same distance from the mobile phone).*

Ans. Let **n = 3**

Consider a seven-cell reuse pattern in cellular cluster and N = 7.

The signal to interference ratio is $\frac{S}{I} = \frac{(D/R)^n}{i_0} = \frac{(\sqrt{3N})^n}{i_0}$

Co-channel reuse factor = Q = D/R = 4.583

For n = 3 case $\frac{S}{I} = \frac{(4.583)^3}{6}$

$= 16.04$

$\therefore \quad \frac{S}{I} = \mathbf{12.05\ dB}$

But for minimum performance the S/I should be atleast 14 dB as per, the requirement of cellular system.

Hence n = 3 is not suitable since 12.05 dB is less than standard value 14 dB.

Let **n = 4**

Consider a seven cell reuse pattern and N = 7

Co-channel reuse factor = $Q = \frac{D}{R} = 4.583$

Signal to interference ratio $= \frac{S}{I}$

$$= \frac{1}{6} \times (4.583)^4$$

$$= 73.52$$

$$\therefore \quad \frac{S}{I} = \mathbf{18.66\ dB.}$$

The signal to interference is greater than the minimum requirement standard value 14 dB and (n = 4) is a better value that can be applied, for real time performance.

Q. 969. *Consider the four cellular standards given below. Select the maximum radio capacity (assume n = 4 propagation path loss).*

Ans. In system (1), $B_c = 25\text{ kHz}, = \left(\frac{C}{I}\right)_{min} = 13\text{ dB}$

In system (2), $B_c = 30\text{ kHz}, = \left(\frac{C}{I}\right)_{min} = 17\text{ dB}$

In system (3), $B_c = 12.5\text{ kHz}, = \left(\frac{C}{I}\right)_{min} = 11\text{ dB}$

In system (4), $B_c = 6.25\text{ kHz}, = \left(\frac{C}{I}\right)_{min} = 8\text{ dB}$

where B_c is the bandwidth of particular system and B'_c is the channel bandwidth for a different system. Assuming each system with particular bandwidth 6.5 kHz (say).

In systems (1), $B_c = 6.5\text{ kHz}, \left(\frac{C}{I}\right)_{eq} = 13 + 20\log\left(\frac{6.5}{25}\right) = 1.29$

In system (2), $\left(\frac{C}{I}\right)_{eq} = 17 + 20\log\left(\frac{6.5}{30}\right) = 3.72$

System (3), $\left(\frac{C}{I}\right)_{eq} = 11 + 20\log\left(\frac{6.5}{12.5}\right) = 5.32$

System (4), $\left(\frac{C}{I}\right)_{eq} = 8 + 20\log\left(\frac{6.5}{6.5}\right) = 8$

For maximum radio capacity, the smallest value of $\left(\frac{C}{I}\right)_{eq}$ should be selected.

Hence system - 1 provides maximum capacity.

Q. 970. *Find the far field distance for an antenna with maximum dimension of 3 m and operating frequency of 800 MHz.*

Ans. The wavelength $(\lambda) = \frac{c}{f}$

$$= \frac{3 \times 10^8}{800 \times 10^4} = 0.38$$

Far field distance for an antenna is calculated as $= d_f = \frac{2D^2}{\lambda}$

$$\therefore \quad d_f = \frac{2(3)^2}{0.38}$$

$$d_f = \mathbf{47.4\ m}$$

Q. 971. *If the signal to noise ratio (S/N) of a mobile communication link is 100 dB and RF bandwidth is 65 kHz. Find the maximum possible theoretical data rate of the signal which can be transmitted.*

Ans. The signal to noise ratio $= \frac{S}{N} = 100$

Bandwidth = 65 kHz

$$\text{Channel capacity} = B \log_2 \left(1 + \frac{S}{N}\right)$$

$\therefore$ The maximum possible data is given as,

$$C = 65{,}000 \log_2 (1 + 100)$$

$$\therefore \quad C = (65{,}000)\ (6.658)$$

Maximum data rate = C = **433.33 kbps.**

Q. 972. A *dipole antenna has an efficiency of 95% and directivity is 2.14 dB Calculate the gain value in dB.*

Ans. Directivity = D = 2.14 dB

i.e. $10 \log D = 2.14$

$$D = 1.638$$

The gain value = G = (directivity) × (efficiency)

$$G = D\eta$$

$$= (1.638)\ (0.95)$$

$$G = 1.55$$

The value of gain (G) in dB is,

$$G\ (\text{dB}) = 10 \log (1.55)$$

$$G = 1.92\ \text{dB}$$

Q. 973. *Calculate the modulation index for the carrier wave of 12 V peak to peak, which is amplitude modulated by four different frequencies whose amplitudes are 4, 5, 6 and 7 volts*

Ans. The modulation index $= m = \frac{E_m}{E_c}$

where E_m is modulating signal voltage
E_c is carrier signal voltage
For four different (multiple) signal frequencies the total modulation index is calculated as,

$$m_t = \sqrt{m_1^2 + m_2^2 + m_3^2 + m_4^2}$$

where $$m_1 = \frac{E_m}{E_c} = \frac{4}{12} = 0.3$$

$$m_2 = \frac{E_m}{E_c} = \frac{5}{12} = 0.4$$

$$m_3 = \frac{E_m}{E_c} = \frac{6}{12} = 0.5$$

and $$m_4 = \frac{E_m}{E_c} = \frac{7}{12} = 0.6$$

The modulation index ($m_{total} = m_t$)

$$= \sqrt{(0.3)^2 + (0.4)^2 + (0.5)^2 + (0.6)^2}$$

$$= \sqrt{0.09 + 0.16 + 0.25 + 0.36}$$

∴ Total modulation index = m_t = **0.86**

Q. 974. *Calculate the wavelength of signal for a PCS and cellular mobile system with the ranges as 2.5 GHz and 845 MHz.*

Ans. (*i*) For personal communication systems (PCS),

The wavelength $= \lambda = \frac{c}{f}$

$$= \frac{3 \times 10^8}{2.5 \times 10^9}$$

λ = **0.12 m**

(*ii*) For cellular mobile system, wavelength (λ)

$$= \frac{c}{f} = \frac{3 \times 10^8}{845 \times 10^6}$$

λ = **0.355 m**

Q. 975. *Consider that the rms antenna current of an amplitude modulated radio transmitter is 18 Amps when unmodulated, and 20 Amps when sinusoidally modulated, find the modulation index value.*

Ans. Modulation index = m $= \sqrt{2\left[\left(\frac{I}{I_c}\right)^2 - 1\right]}$

$$= \sqrt{2\left[\left(\frac{20}{18}\right)^2 - 1\right]}$$

$$m = \mathbf{0.68}$$

Q. 976. *Find the total power P_T is amplitude modulated signal (AM), if the modulation indices are 0.3, 0.2 and 0.6 where the carrier signal power is 28 watts.*

Ans. The total power 'P_T' can be found as,

$$P_T = P_c\left[1 + \frac{m_1^2}{2} + \frac{m_2^2}{2} + \frac{m_3^2}{2} + \frac{m_4^2}{2}\right]$$

where P_c = Carrier signal power

Modulation indices $m_1 = 0.3$

$m_2 = 0.2$

$m_3 = 0.5$

and $m_4 = 0.6$

$$P_T = 28\left[1 + \frac{(0.3)^2}{2} + \frac{(0.2)^2}{2} + \frac{(0.5)^2}{2} + \frac{(0.6)^2}{2}\right]$$

$$= 28\left[1 + \frac{0.09}{2} + \frac{0.04}{2} + \frac{0.25}{2} + \frac{0.36}{2}\right]$$

$$= 28\ (1 + 0.045 + 0.02 + 0.125 + 0.18)$$

$$P_T = \mathbf{38.36\ watts}$$

Q. 977. *Calculate the signal to noise ratio in decibels for three identical links if the signal to noise ratio for any one link is 62 dB.*

Ans. The signal noise ratio at the output is

$$\left(\frac{S}{N}\right)_O = \left(\frac{S}{N}\right)_1 \text{dB} - (m)\,\text{dB, where}$$

$\left(\frac{S}{N}\right)_1 \rightarrow$ Signal to noise ratio of any one link

$m \rightarrow$ Number of links

Signal to noise ratio at the output is

$$\left(\frac{S}{N}\right)_O = [62 - 10 \log 3]$$

$$= [62 - 4.77] = \mathbf{57.23\ dB}$$

Q. 978. *An isotropic radiator is supplied with a power of 120 watts with a gain of 7 dB. Calculate the EIRP and power density at a distance of 18 km.*

Ans. The value of gain

$$(G) = 10 \log G = 7$$

$$G = 5.01$$

The effective isotropic radiated power is denoted as 'EIRP' which is expressed as,

$$EIRP = [G_t \cdot P_t],$$

which is a product of transmitter gain and power.

$$EIRP = (5.01)\ (120\ W)$$

$$= \textbf{601.2 watts}$$

$$\text{Power density} = \mathbf{P_D}$$

$$= EIRP \div 4\pi r^2$$

$$= \frac{601.2}{4\pi (18 \times 10^3)^2}$$

$$P_D = \mathbf{147.7\ nW/m^2}$$

Q. 979. *Consider if a vehicle travels through the cellular mobile system at 150 km per hour, find how often handoffs take place if the cell radius is 4 km.*

Ans. In cellular mobile system, the velocity of the vehicle with 150 kmph is considered as below

$$V = \frac{(1500\ \text{kmph})\ (1000\ \text{mpkm})}{(3600\ \text{sphr})}$$

$$V = 41.\ 6\ \text{m/sec.}$$

As the cell radius is 4 km, its diameter is 8 km.

i.e. $r = 4$ km

$d = 8$ km

$$\text{Time} = t = \frac{d}{V} = \frac{8 \times 10^3}{41.6} = \mathbf{92.3\ sec.}$$

∴ Handoff's will occur for every 92.3 sec., time intervals, when the vehicle is moving with 150 km per hour speed.

Q. 980. *For the previous question how often the handoffs will occur of the cell radius is 5 km?*

Ans. Velocity in cellular mobile environment is,

$$V = 41.6\ \text{m/sec.}$$

If cell radius $r = 5$ km then

diameter $d = 10$ km

$$\text{Time } t = \frac{d}{V}$$

$$= \frac{10 \times 10^3}{41.6}$$

$$T = \mathbf{240\ sec.}$$

Q. 981. *Find the wavelength of a radio signal in free space with a frequency of 125 MHz.*

Ans. Wavelength $= \lambda = \frac{c}{f}$

where c and f are velocity of propagation and frequency of the signal.

$$\lambda = \frac{3 \times 10^8}{125 \times 10^6}$$

$\therefore$ Wavelength = A = **2.4 m**

Q. 982. *What is known as transparency?*

Ans. The transparency responds to problems which are location dependent with respect to a file system under mobility support.

Q. 983. *Write a short note on HTTP.*

Ans. The Hypertext Transfer Protocol (HTTP) is basically a lightweight, stateless and application level protocol meant for data transfer between a server and client.

Q. 984. *What are the two main components of HTTP transaction?*

Ans.
1. HTTP transaction consisting a HTTP request given by a client.
2. HTTP response given by the server.

Q. 985. *List two advantages of MIO-NFS.*

Ans. The system mobile integration of the network file system avoids write conflicts. Also the server handles the file access.

Q. 986. *What are GIAC and DIAC?*

Ans. They are

(*i*) GIAC - General Inquiry Access Code.

(*ii*) DIAC - Dedicated Inquiry Access Code.

Q. 987. *What is IMSI?*

Ans. It is international mobile subscriber identity which is used in GSM for identifying a subscriber. It consists of mobile country code (MCC), mobile network code (MNC) and mobile subscriber identification number (MSIN).

Q. 988. *Draw the packet format in Bluetooth.*

Ans.

bits → 72	54	0-2745
ACCESS CODE	HEADER	PAYLOAD

Q. 989. *What is the basic unit of networking under Bluetooth?*

Ans. Piconet is the basic unit in Bluetooth networking. It consists of a master and slave setup where number of slaves can be from one to seven.

Q. 990. *What are the merits of infrared technology?*

Ans.
1. It is simple and economical.
2. Very less interference of electrical device during transmission.
3. Sheilding is relatively simple.

Q. 991. *Give the Nyquist bandwidth criterion.*

Ans. The channel capacity 'C' is given as,

$$C = 2 B \log 2 M \text{ where,}$$

'B' is the bandwidth and 'M' is the number of discrete voltage levels.

Q. 992. *What is BRAN?*

Ans. It is broadband radio access network. It provides network access by radio, hence it is highly flexible and easy to install. It supports asymmetrical with various kinds of traffic.

Q. 993. *Draw a comparison diagram of OSI and TCP/IP protocol structures.*

Ans.

TCP/IP layer	OSI layer
Application	Application
	Presentation
Transport from host to host	Session
	Transport
Internet	Network
Network access	Data link
Physical	Physical

Q. 994. *List any two disadvantages of WLAN.*

Ans. 1. Quality of service (QoS) is poor when compared to wired LAN.

2. Cost of WLAN is high.

Q. 995. *What is the use of bridges?*

Ans. Bridges in networking acts as an address filter and they are responsible for delivery of packets to the intended network destination. They do not alter the packets during transmission.

Q. 996. *List two functions of routers.*

Ans. 1. It provides a link between the networks.

2. Data delivery and routing on different networks are enabled.

Q. 997. *What is known as ARQ?*

Ans. Automatic repeat request (ARQ) is used in datalink and transport protocols. Error control forms an essential part of these protocols. ARQ relies on the error detecting codes.

Q. 998. *What is the principle used in RAKE receiver?*

Ans. In RAKE receiver tries to recover the original signal from multiple paths and combines them with appropriate delays.

Q. 999. *What is WSP protocol data unit?*

Ans. It is used to convey requests and response by Wireless Session Protocol (WSP). The PDU is sent to the transport layer and consists of three fields.

Q. 1000. *List any four mobile and wireless devices.*

Ans. 1. Sensor.

2. Personal digital assistant.

3. Palmtop computer.

4. Mobile phones.

❑❑❑

B - Solved Problems

Q. 1. *Assume a cellular system wherein a car travels at 200 km per hour speed. Calculate how often (approximately) handoffs would occur if the radius of the cell is 8 km?*

Ans. The speed in m/sec with which the car travels is given as,

$$V = \frac{(200 \text{ km/hr})(1000 \text{ m/1 km})}{3600 \text{ sec/hr}}$$

$$V = 55.56 \text{ m/sec}$$

The radius of the cell r = 8 km

Diameter of the cell d = 16 km

The time between the handoffs is,

$$t = \frac{d}{V}$$

$$= \frac{16 \text{ km}}{55.56 \text{ m/sec}}$$

$$= \frac{16 \times 10^3 \text{ m}}{55.56 \text{ m/sec}}$$

$$= 287.9 \text{ sec}$$

$$\therefore \quad t = \mathbf{5 \text{ min}}$$

Q. 2. *A receiver's equivalent noise figure value is 3 dB. Find its equivalent noise temperature.*

Ans. Let the noise figure in dB be NF_{dB}.

$$NF_{dB} = 10 \log NF$$

To have 3 dB noise figure in terms of noise figure ratio,

$$\log NF = \frac{NF_{dB}}{10}$$

$$\therefore \quad NF = \text{antilog}\left(\frac{NF_{dB}}{10}\right)$$

$$= \text{antilog}\left(\frac{3}{10}\right) = \text{antilog}(0.3)$$

$\therefore \quad NF = 1.995$

Noise equivalent temperature,

$$T_{equ} = 290\ (NF - 1)$$

Substituting for NF,

$$T_{equ} = 290\ (1.995 - 1)$$

$$\therefore \quad T_{equ} = \mathbf{288.63\ °K}$$

Q. 3. *An isotropic radiator is supplied with a 110 W power, and the transmitter gain is 5t dB. Calculate the effective isotropic power and the power density at a distance of 9 km.*

Ans. Transmitter power (P_1) = 110 W

Transmitter gain (G_1) = 5 dB

Expressing G_t as a ratio then G_t = 3.162

$$\left[\begin{aligned} G_t &= \log^{-1}\left(\frac{5}{10}\right) \\ &= \log^{-1}(0.5) \\ G_t &= 3.162 \end{aligned}\right.$$

(*i*) Effective isotropic radiated power

$$EIRP = G_t P_t$$

$$= (3.162)\ (110\ W)$$

$$EIRP = 347.8\ W$$

(*ii*) Power density = $P_D = \dfrac{EIRP}{4\pi r^2}$

$$= \frac{347.8\ W}{4\pi (9 \times 10^3)^2}$$

$$\therefore \quad P_D = 0.00000034\ W/m^2$$

$$P_D = 341\ nW/m^2.$$

Q. 4. *Find the processing gain if the RF transmitted bandwidth is 1.228 MHz. Assume the baseband bandwidth prior to spreading is (i) 19.2 kHz, (ii) 9.6 kHz.*

Ans. Let the processing gain be G_p.

$$G_p = \frac{B_{RF}}{B_{BS}};$$ where $B_{RF} \rightarrow$ RF bandwidth

$B_{BS} \rightarrow$ Bandwidth before spreading

(*i*)
$$G_p = \frac{1.228\ MHz}{19.2\ kHz}$$

$$G_p = \frac{1.228 \times 10^6}{19.2 \times 10^3}$$

$$\left[\begin{aligned} \because 10 \log 64 &= G_p\ dB \\ G_p\ dB &= 18.06\ dB \end{aligned}\right.$$

$$= 63.96$$

$$G_p = 64;$$

G_p in decibels is = G_p d(B) = **18.06 dB**

(*ii*)
$$G_p = \frac{B_{RF}}{B_{BS}} = \frac{1.228\ MHz}{9.6 \times 10^3}$$

$$= \frac{1.228 \times 10^6}{9.6 \times 10^3}$$

$$= 127.92$$

Gain is decibels is,

$$G_p \text{ (dB)} = \mathbf{21.07\ dB.}$$

Q. 5. *Find the minimum and maximum hopping rate for the Bluetooth ad-hoc system.*

Ans. The bluetooth system, divides the data/information into packets and transmits one packet for one hop. The length of this packet shall be in the range one to five slots, where length of one slot is 625 μ sec.

Let the minimum and maximum hopping rates be denoted as $f_{h\,(min)}$ and $f_{h\,(max)}$.

(*i*)

$$f_{h\,(min)} = \frac{1}{5\,(625\ \mu\ \text{sec})}$$

$$= \frac{1}{5 \times 625 \times 10^{-6}}$$

$$= \mathbf{320\ hertz}$$

(*ii*)

$$f_{h\,(max)} = \frac{1}{625\ \mu\ \text{sec}}$$

$$= \frac{1}{625 \times 10^{-6}}$$

$$= \mathbf{1600\ hertz}$$

Q. 6. *Calculate the block length and size of check code in Reed-Solomon code for m = 2 and t = 1.*

Ans. Given that m = 2 (Symbol length), t = 1,

In Reed-Solomon (RC codes) the block length is = $n = 2^m - 1$

Substituting for m,

$$n = 2^2 - 1$$

$$\therefore \quad n = 4 - 1 = 3 \text{ symbols}$$

$$\text{(or)} \quad n = 2^m - 1 \text{ symbols}$$

$$= m(2^m - 1) \text{ bits}$$

$$= 2(2^2 - 1) \text{ bits}$$

$$\therefore \quad n = 2(3) = 6 \text{ bits}$$

$$\text{The size of check code} = n - k$$

$$= 2t \text{ symbols (or)}$$

$$= m(2t) \text{ bits}$$

$$= 2[2(1)] \text{ bits}$$

$$\therefore \quad n - k = 2 \text{ symbols or } 2(2(1)) \text{ bits}$$

$$\text{Size of check code} = 2 \text{ symbols or 4 bits.}$$

Note : The RS codes are capable of correcting bursty errors.

Q. 7. *Consider a cellular system which consists of 34 cells with the cell radius as 1.4 km. A total frequency bandwidth is capable of supporting 343 traffic channels. Find what geographical area is km can be covered and the number of channels available per cell.*
[Assume N = 7 reuse cellular pattern].

Ans. Considering a N = 7 reuse cellular pattern with hexagon cells arranged inside. For a cell radius of 1.4 km, the full area is assumed to be an approximate square outline with hexagon cells.

The area of hexagon cells of radius r is = $1.5r^2\sqrt{3}$

$$\text{Area (A)} = 1.5(1.4)^2\sqrt{3}; \quad r = 1.4 \text{ km}$$

$$\text{Area (A)} = 1.5(1.96)\sqrt{3} = 5.09 \text{ km}^2$$

Total area covered will be (A_T) = (Area) (Number of cells)

$$= (5.09)\ (34)$$

$$A_T = 173.06 \text{ Km}^2$$

For a N = 7 frequency reuse pattern, the number of channels in one cell is equal to,

$$\frac{\text{Number of traffic channels}}{7} = \frac{343}{7} = 49 \text{ channels}$$

$\therefore$ The total capacity is (C_T) = $\begin{pmatrix}\text{Total number of} \\ \text{channels}\end{pmatrix}$ (Number of cells)

$\therefore$ C_T = (49 channels) (34 cells)

= **1666 channels.**

Q. 8. *Assume the bit error rate is 1×10^{-7} on a channel with signal to noise ratio as 13 dB. Find the bandwidth efficiency for ASK, BFSK, BPSK techniques. (Consider the graph of bit error rate for different encoding schemes) an shown in Fig. B.1 below.*

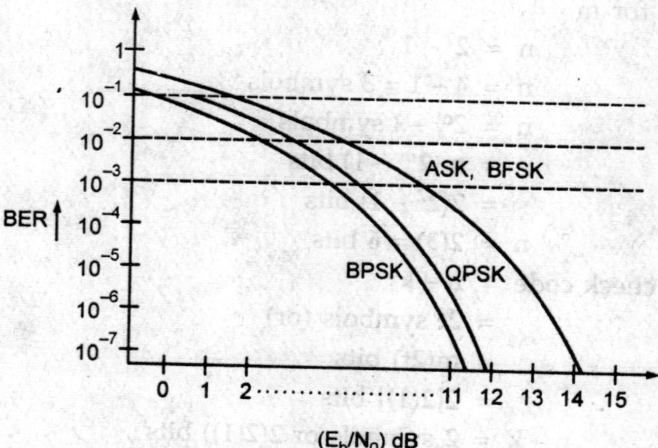

Fig. B.1

Ans. We have $\frac{E_b}{N_0} = \left[SNR - \left(\frac{R}{B_T}\right)_{dB} \right]$

Referring the graph given for BPSK technique

$$= \frac{E_b}{N_0} = 11.2 \text{ dB (approx)}$$

Substituting $\frac{E_b}{N_0}$ and SNR value in equation (1) then,

$$11.2 \text{ dB} = 13 \text{ dB} - \left(\frac{R}{B_T}\right)_{dB}$$

$$\therefore \left(\frac{R}{B_T}\right)_{dB} = 13 \text{ dB} - 11.2 \text{ dB} \qquad (1) \qquad 20 \log x = 1.8$$

$$= 1.8 \text{ dB} \qquad \log x = 0.09$$

$$\therefore \left(\frac{R}{B_T}\right) = 1.23 \qquad \therefore x = 1.23$$

For ASK, BFSK, $\frac{E_b}{N_0} = 14.2 \text{ dB (approx)}$

Substituting $\frac{E_b}{N_0}$ and SNR in equ. (1) then

$$\frac{E_b}{N_0} = SNR - \left(\frac{R}{B_T}\right)_{dB} \qquad (1) \qquad 20 \log \frac{R}{B_T} = -1.2$$

$$14.2 = 13 \text{ dB} - \left(\frac{R}{B_T}\right)_{dB} \qquad \log \frac{R}{B_T} = -0.06$$

$$\left(\frac{R}{B_T}\right)_{dB} = 13 \text{ dB} - 14.2 \text{ dB} \qquad \frac{R}{B_T} = 10^{-0.06}$$

$$= -1.2 \text{ dB} \qquad = 0.87$$

$$\therefore \frac{R}{B_T} = \mathbf{0.87}$$

Q. 9. *For a seven cell reuse pattern find the reuse if the minimum distance between centres of co-channel cells is 18 km. Radius of cell is 3 km and the distance between adjacent cells in the seven cell pattern is 6 km.*

Ans. The seven cell reuse pattern is shown below (N = 7).

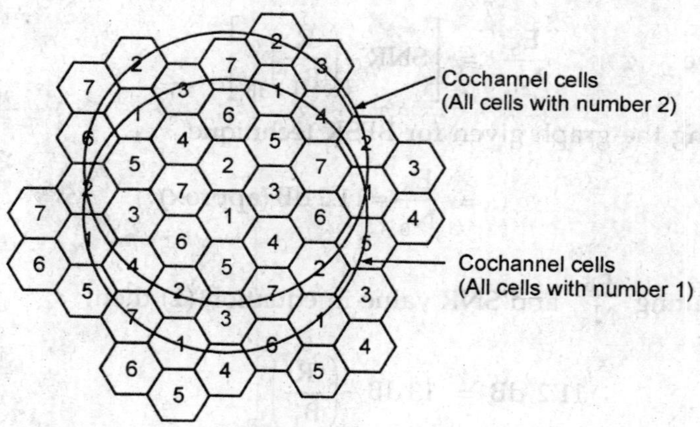

Fig. B. 2 Seven cell frequency reuse pattern (N = 7)

(1) All cells with number are connected through their centers as an example for co-channel cells using same frequency.

(2) Similarly cells with number 2 are connected through their centers.

Minimum distance between centres of co-channel is (D) = 18 km

Radius of cell (R) = 3 km

Distance between adjacent cell is = 6 km

To find reuse factor; $\frac{D}{R} = \sqrt{3N}$

Substituting the values of band R in the above equation, then,

$$\frac{D}{R} = \sqrt{3N}$$

$$\frac{D}{R\sqrt{3}} = \sqrt{N}$$

$$\frac{18}{3\sqrt{3}} = \sqrt{N}$$

$$\frac{6}{\sqrt{3}} = \sqrt{N}$$

$$3.47 = \sqrt{N}$$

$$N = (3.47)^2$$

$\therefore$ $N = 12$ cells (or) reuse factor is 12.

Thus the number of repetitive cells under reuse pattern is 12.

Q. 10. *A M-ary PSK transmitted waveform is given as* $S_i(t) = 4\cos\left(\omega_c t + \frac{i\pi}{2}\right)$ *where i = 0 to 3 and consider* $0 \le t \le T_s$. *For this data, draw the signal space diagram assuming M as 4.*

Ans. Given that $S_i(t) = 4\cos\left(\omega_c t + \frac{i\pi}{2}\right)$

$$= 4\cos\left(2\pi f_c t + \frac{i\pi}{2}\right); \text{ where } \omega_c = 2\pi f_c$$

A M-ary PSK signal can be represented as follows :

Let $\sqrt{2P_s} = 4$ [From the given $S_i(t)$]

$$2P_s = 16$$

$$\therefore \quad P_s = 8$$

In $\left(\omega_c t + \frac{i\pi}{2}\right), \frac{i\pi}{2} = \phi_i = \phi_m$ where i = 0 to 3 i = 0, 1, 2, 3

Substituting for 'i' (0, 1, 2, 3) then,

$$\phi_0 = 0$$

$$\phi_1 = \frac{\pi}{2}$$

$$\phi_2 = \pi$$

$$\phi_3 = \frac{3\pi}{2}$$

$$S(t) = \sqrt{2P_s}\cos(\omega_0 t + \phi_m)$$

$$S(t) = \sqrt{2P_s}\cos(2\pi f_0 t + \phi_m)$$

These two equations of M-ary PSK S(t) and $S_i(t)$ are compared.

We know that E_s (Symbol energy) = $P_s T_s$

and distance of each signal point with respect to origin is = $\sqrt{P_s T_s}$

$\therefore$ At $\sqrt{E_s} = \sqrt{P_s T_s}$ the signal points are placed from the origin. From this 4-ary PSK the signal space diagram will be as follows.

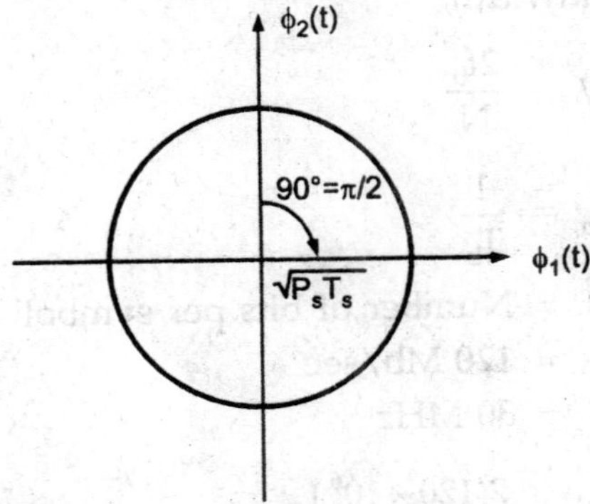

Fig. B.3 Signal space diagram for 4-ary PSK signal

Q. 11. *In mobile propagation, in a cellular system, find the correction factor and pathloss for a medium size city assuming carrier frequency as 950 MHz, height of transmitting antenna at base station is 45 m, propagation distance between antennas is 10 km and height of receiving antenna in mobile station is 5 m.*

Ans. Given :

The height of transmitting antenna = h_t = 45 m

Height of receiving antenna = h_r = 5 m

Distance = d = 10 km

f_c = 950 MHz

The correction factor for small or medium-sized city in mobile environment is,

$$\begin{aligned} A(h_r) &= (1.1 \log f_c - 0.7)h_r - (1.56 \log f_c - 0.8) \\ &= (1.1 \log 950 \times 10^6 - 0.7)5 - (1.56 \log 950 \times 10^6 - 0.8) \\ &= [1.1\,(8.98) - 0.7]5 - [1.56(8.98) - 0.8] \\ &= 45.87 - 13.2 \\ A(h_r) &= 32.67 \text{ dB} \end{aligned}$$

For medium-sized city, pathloss is given as

$$\begin{aligned} (L_{dB}) &= 69.55 + 26.16 \log f_c - 13.82 \log h_t - A(h_r) \\ &\quad + (44.9 - 6.55 \log h_t) \log d \\ &= 69.55 + 26.16 \log 950 \times 10^6 - 13.82 \log 45 - 32.67 \\ &\quad + (44.9 - 6.55 \log 45) \log 10 \\ &= 69.55 + 26.16(8.98) - 13.82(1.65) - 32.67 \\ &\quad + 44.9 - 6.55(1.65)1 \\ &= 69.55 + 234.9 - 22.8 - 32.67 + 44.9 - 10.8 \\ L_{dB} &= \mathbf{283.05\ dB} \end{aligned}$$

Q. 12. *For transmitting 120 Mb/sec data in a bandwidth of 30 MHz, which type of modulation is suitable? Discuss.*

Ans. The M-ary phase shift keying technique would be useful in transmitting 120 Mb/sec data in the bandwidth of 30 MHz.

In M-ary PSK, the bandwidth

$$BW = \frac{2f_b}{N}$$

$$\text{where } f_b = \frac{1}{T_b}$$

N = Number of bits per symbol

f_b = 120 Mb/sec

BW = 30 MHz

$$BW = \frac{2(120 \times 10^6)}{N} = 30 \times 10^6$$

$$\therefore \qquad N = \frac{2(120 \times 10^6)}{30 \times 10^6}$$

$$N = \frac{24}{3} = 8 \text{ bits}$$

In M-ary PSK technique, M will be

$$M = 2^N$$
$$= 2^8$$
$$\therefore \qquad M = 256$$

A 256-ary PSK is useful in transmitting 120 MHz signal in a bandwidth of 30 MHz.

Q. 13. *For the GSM frequency band diagram given below,*

(i) Calculate the possible number of carriers in a direction.

(ii) If the transmission rate of the system is 270.8 kB/sec, find its modulation efficiency.

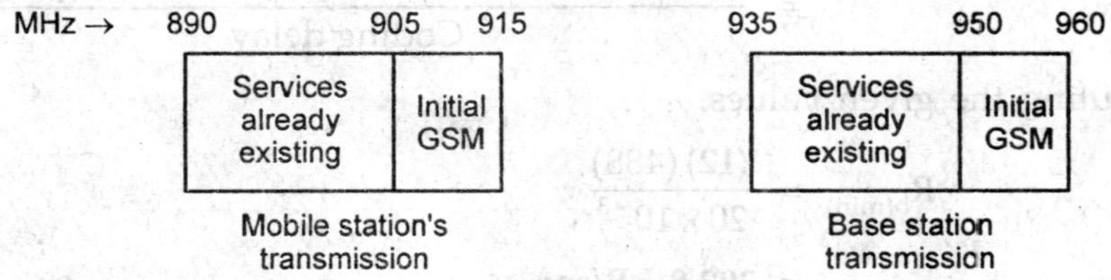

Fig. B.4

Ans. Given :

- From the diagram the carrier frequency spacing is = 200 kHz = 200 × 10^3
- Two 25 MHz frequency bands are available.
- The two bands are separated by 45 MHz frequency.

(*i*) The number of carriers possible in the system (NC)

$$= \frac{\text{Frequency of allocation of a band}}{\text{Frequency spacing/carrier signal}}$$

$$= \frac{25 \text{ MHz}}{200 \text{ kHz/Carrier signal}}$$

$$= \frac{25 \times 10^6}{200 \times 10^3}$$

$$\therefore \qquad N_c = 125 \text{ Carriers}$$

(*ii*) Modulation efficiency $= \eta = \dfrac{\text{Rate of transmission}}{\text{Frequency spacing / Carrier signal}}$

$$\eta = \frac{270.8 \times 10^3}{200 \times 10^3}$$

$$\eta = \mathbf{1.354\ bits/Hz}$$

Q. 14. *Consider in a wireless TDMA system the coding delay is 20 msec and an encoded speech into blocks of 20 msec time duration is accepted by the system. In second generation digital system, if the speech block length is 488 bits, calculate the minimum bit rate required for a 12 channels system.*

Ans. Given :

$$\text{Coding delay} = 20 \text{ msec} = 20 \times 10^{-3} \text{ sec}$$

$$\text{Number of channels} = 12$$

$$\text{Speech block length} = 488 \text{ bits}$$

The minimum bits rate $R_{b(min)}$

$$= \frac{\text{(Number of channels) (Speech of block length)}}{\text{Coding delay}}$$

Substituting the given values,

$$R_{b(min)} = \frac{(12)(488)}{20 \times 10^{-3}}$$

$$R_{b(min)} = \mathbf{292.8\ kB/sec.}$$

Q. 15. *In a data transmission, assume that there exists thermal noise and the receiver with an effective noise temperature 292 °K. Calculate the noise level at the output for a bandwidth of 12 MHz.*

Ans. The thermal noise is = N_t = KTB

where K → Boltzmann constant

T → Temperature in K

B → Bandwidth in MHz (BW)

Rewriting N_t in decibel-watts then,

$$N_t = 10 \log K + 10 \log T + 10 \log BW$$

$$= -228.6 + 10 \log T + 10 \log BW$$

Substituting for T and BW then,

$$N_t = -228.6 + 10 \log (292) + 10 \log (12 \times 10^6)$$

$$= -228.6 + 24.65 + 70.79$$

$$N_t = \mathbf{-133.16\ dBW.}$$

Q. 16. *Assume an encoding technique needs 8.2 dB for one bit error for every 10,000 bits transmitted. If the data and noise temperature are 2500 b/sec and 290 °K, find the received signal level that is needed to overcome the thermal noise problem in the system.*

Ans. Given : $\frac{E_b}{N_0} = 8.2$ dB

$$\text{Data rate (R)} = 2500 \text{ b/sec}$$

Bit error rate = one bit out of 10,000 bits = 1×10^{-4}

Temperature (T) = 290 °K and

K → Boltzmann constant

Let signal level required be S_R;

$$\left(\frac{E_b}{N_0}\right)_{dB} = S - 10 \log R + 10 \log K - 10 \log T$$

Rearranging the terms and $S = S_R$;

$$S_R = \left(\frac{E_b}{N_0}\right)_{dB} + 10 \log R - 10 \log K + 10 \log T$$

Substituting the values in the equation,

$$S_R = (8.2) + 10 \log (2500) - 10 \log (k) + 10 \log (290)$$

$$S_R = 8.2 + 33.97 - 228.6 + 24.624$$

$$S_R = -161.797 \text{ dBW}$$

$$\therefore \quad S_R = \mathbf{-161.8\ dBW}$$

Q. 17. *A carrier signal with frequency of 1.6 MHz and RMS voltage of 3 V is being modulated and the corresponding sine wave has a frequency of 600 Hz and amplitude RMS voltage of 1 V. Give the equation for the resultant signal at output.*

Ans. Let the output equation be $s(t) = [E_c + E_m \sin \omega_m t]$

where

- s(t) → the modulated output signal in volts.
- E_c and E_m → peak amplitudes of carrier and modulating signals in volts
- ω_c and ω_m → frequency of carrier and modulating signals in rad/sec

We have

RMS voltage for carrier = 3 V and

for modulating signals = 1 V

Carrier frequency (f_c) = 1.6 MHz

Modulating frequency (f_n) = 600 Hz

(*i*) Carrier voltage = $E_c = (\sqrt{2})3V = 4.24$ V

(*ii*) Modulating voltage = $E_m = (\sqrt{2})1V = 1.41$ V

(*iii*) Carrier frequency = $\omega_c = 2\pi f_c = 2\pi (1.6 \times 10^6) = 10.05 \times 10^6$ rad/sec

(*iv*) Carrier frequency = $\omega_m = 2\pi f_m = 2\pi (600) = 3.77 \times 10^3$ rad/sec

The equation $s(t) = (E_c + E_m \sin \omega_m t) \sin \omega_c t$

Substituting the above values, s(t) becomes,

$$\therefore \quad s(t) = [4.24 + 1.41 \sin (3.77 \times 10^3\ t)] \sin (10.05 \times 10^6\ t)\ \text{V}$$

Q. 18. *Find the value of modulation index of Q. 17 and give the equation including the modulation index.*

Ans. We have

$$E_c = 4.24$$
$$E_m = 1.41$$
$$\omega_c = 10.05 \times 10^6$$
$$\omega_m = 3.77 \times 10^3$$

$$\text{Modulation index} = m = \frac{E_m}{E_c} = \frac{1.41}{4.24} = 0.33$$

$$\text{Modulated signal } s(t) = (E_c + E_m \sin \omega_m t) \sin \omega_c t$$

Rearranging the equation s(t) becomes,

$$s(t) = E_c\left(1 + \frac{E_m}{E_c} \sin \omega_m t\right) \sin \omega_c t$$

$$\because \quad \frac{E_m}{E_c} = m$$

$$s(t) = E_c (1 + m \sin \omega_m t) \sin \omega_c t$$

Substituting the values the output equation is,

$$s(t) = \mathbf{4.24\ [1 + 0.33 \sin (3.77 \times 10^3\ t)] \sin (10.05 \times 10^6\ t]\ V}$$

Q. 19. *Assume a cellular phone transmitter has deviation of 11 kHz frequency. If the transmitter operates at a maximum deviation with voice frequencies 500 Hz and 3500 Hz, calculate their modulation index value.*

Ans. The frequency modulation index $= m_f = \dfrac{\delta}{f_m}$

where d → Peak deviation in Hz

f_m → Modulating frequency in Hz

(*i*) For voice frequency 500 Hz

$$m_f = \frac{\delta}{f_m}$$
$$= \frac{11\,\text{kHz}}{500\,\text{Hz}}$$
$$= \frac{11\,\text{kHz}}{0.5\,\text{kHz}}$$
$$m_f = \mathbf{22}$$

(*ii*) For voice frequency 3500 Hz

$$m_f = \frac{\delta}{f_m}$$

$$= \frac{11 \text{ kHz}}{3500 \text{ Hz}}$$

$$= \frac{11 \text{ kHz}}{3.5 \text{ kHz}}$$

$$m_f = \mathbf{3.14}$$

Q. 20. *Consider a digital communication system which makes use of sampling operation at 10 kilo samples in one second. The receiver is capable of filtering all the frequencies above 5 kHz range. Find what frequencies would appear at the receiver's output for each of the following baseband signal frequencies that is applied to the transmitter end.*

(i) 2 kHz *(ii)* 4 kHz

(iii) 6 kHz

Ans. Let the baseband signal frequencies be

$$f_{b_1} = 2 \text{ kHz}$$

$$f_{b_2} = 4 \text{ kHz}$$

$$f_{b_3} = 6 \text{ kHz}$$

The output signal s(t) will have the input frequency (f_b), sum of the output and sampling frequencies and difference of input and sampling frequencies.

(i) For $f_{b1} = 2$ kHz

$$f_s + f_{b1} = 10 + 2 = 12 \text{ kHz}$$

$$f_s - f_{b1} = 10 - 2 = 10 \text{ kHz}$$

(ii) For $f_{b2} = 4$ kHz

$$f_s + f_{b2} = 10 + 4 = 14 \text{ kHz}$$

$$f_s - f_{b2} = 10 - 4 = 6 \text{ kHz}$$

(iii) For $f_{b3} = 6$ kHz

$$f_s + f_{b3} = 10 + 6 = 16 \text{ kHz}$$

$$f_s - f_{b3} = 10 - 6 = 4 \text{ kHz}$$

Comparing the three cases mentioned above, in the first case the 2 kHz component passes through the receiver filter. In second case the input 4 kHz appears at output and 14 kHz component removed by the filter. But in third case the 16 kHz appears at output removed by the receiver filter whereas the 4 kHz component is not removed and at output 6 and 4 kHz will appear which is undesired.

Summary :

Thus the receiver filters out the components :

12 kHz ($f_s + f_{b1}$)

8 kHz ($f_s - f_{b1}$)

14 kHz ($f_s + f_{b2}$)

6 kHz ($f_s - f_{b2}$)

16 kHz ($f_s + f_{b3}$)

But the last ($f_s - f_{b3}$) component 4 kHz is not filtered and hence along with its original signal 6 kHz, it also appears. It will degrade the system hence the receiver design has to eliminate this last frequency.

Q. 21. *Give an example for finite field addition in GF(64) under RS codes for CDPD system.*

Ans. The primitive polynomial for CDPD system is

$$P_{CDPD}(x) = 1 + x + x^6; \text{ where } m = 6$$

For mapping purpose the primitive polynomial $P(\alpha)$ is equated to '0', which yields,

$$P(\alpha) = 1 + \alpha + \alpha^6 \text{ and}$$

$$\alpha^6 + \alpha + 1 = 0$$

Also the primitive polynomial rule is applied to convert α^6 to $\alpha + 1$, because the term α^6 is not available in Galois field, GF(64).

Example : Finite field addition in GF(64).

$$\alpha^5 \oplus \alpha^{27} = \alpha^5 \text{XOR} \alpha^{27};$$

$x^5 = \alpha^5 = 100000$; [since coefficient of α^5 is only 1 and others are zero; for 6 bit symbol representation the polynomial representation considered is $(x^5 + x^4 + x^3 + x^2 + x + 1)$ or $(\alpha^5 + \alpha^4 + \alpha^3 + x^2 + x + 1)$.]

$$\begin{aligned} x^{27} = a^{27} &= (x^6)^4 \cdot x^3 \\ &= ((x+1)^2)^2 \cdot x^3 \\ &= (x^2 + 2x + 1)^2 \cdot x^3 \\ &= (x^4 + 4x^2 + 1 + 4x^3 + 4x + 2x^2)\, x^3 \\ &= x^7 + 6x^5 + 4x^6 + 4x^4 + x^3 \\ &= (x^6)x + 6x^5 + 4(x+1) + 4x^4 + x^3 \\ &= (x+1)x + (6x^5) + 4(x) + 4 + (4x^4) + x^3 \\ &= 6x^5 + 4x^4 + x^3 + x^2 + 5x + 4 \end{aligned}$$

Rules used :

$$(a + b + c)^2 = a^2 + b^2 + c^2 + 2ab + 2bc + 2ac$$

$$x^6 = x + 1 \text{ or } \alpha^6 = \alpha + 1$$

$\therefore$ [using modulo 2 addition the even numbered coefficients will be zero and odd numbered coefficients will be one.]

In modulo addition odd numbered coefficients are equated to one hence.

$$x^{27} = x^3 + x^2 + 5x$$

or $\alpha^{27} = \alpha^3 + \alpha^2 + 5\alpha$

$\alpha^{27} = 001110$ (Coefficient of the polynomial for a^{27})

for finite field addition.

$$a^5 \oplus a^{27} = \left.\begin{matrix}100000\\001110\end{matrix}\right] \text{XOR}$$

$\overline{101110}$ → It corresponds to α^{55}

$\therefore \alpha^5 \oplus \alpha^{27} = \alpha^{55}$

Q. 22. *Find the power spectral density for a wide sense stationary noise process x(+) that has an autocorrelation function $R_{xx}(\tau) = C \cdot e^{-3|\tau|}$, where 'C' represents a constant.*

Ans. For a wide sense stationary process, we have power spectral density in general,

$$S_{yy}(\omega) = \int_{-\infty}^{\infty} R_{yy}(\tau)e^{-j\omega\tau}\,d\tau$$

$$S_{xx}(\omega) = \int_{-\infty}^{\infty} R_{xx}(\tau)e^{-j\omega\tau}\,d\tau$$

Substituting $R_{xx}(\tau) = C\cdot e^{-3|\tau|}$; in $S_{xx}(\omega)$ then,

$$S_{xx}(\omega) = \int_{-\infty}^{\infty} C\cdot e^{-3|\tau|}.e^{-j\omega\tau}\,d\tau$$

$$= C\int_{-\infty}^{0} e^{(3-j\omega)\tau}\,d\tau + C\int_{0}^{\infty} e^{(-3+j\omega)\tau}\,d\tau$$

$$\int e^{x} = \frac{e^{x}}{x};$$

$$S_{xx}(\omega) = C\left[\frac{e^{(3-j\omega)\tau}}{3-j\omega}\right]_{-\infty}^{0} + C\left[\frac{e^{(-3+j\omega)\tau}}{-(3+j\omega)}\right]_{0}^{\infty}$$

$$= \left[\frac{C}{3-j\omega}\right] + \left[\frac{C}{3+j\omega}\right]$$

Power spectral density

$$S_{xx}(\omega) = \frac{6C}{9+\omega^2}; C \to \text{constant}$$

Q. 23. *Consider a stationary random process whose power spectral density is*

$$S_{yy}(w) = A \qquad -C < \omega < C$$
$$= 0 \qquad \text{Otherwise}$$

find the autocorrelation value.

Ans. For a stationary random process, the autocorrelation function is expressed as,

$$R_{yy}(\tau) = \frac{1}{2\pi}\int_{-\infty}^{\infty} S_{yy}(\omega)\cdot e^{j\omega\tau}\cdot d\omega$$

$$= \frac{1}{2\pi}\int_{-C}^{C} A\cdot e^{j\omega\tau}\cdot d\omega$$

$$= \frac{A}{2\pi}\left[\frac{e^{j\omega\tau}}{j\tau}\right]_{-C}^{C}$$

$$= \frac{A}{2\pi\, jt}[2j \sin \tau \cdot C]$$

$$R_{yy}(\tau) = \frac{A}{\pi\tau} \cdot \sin C\tau$$

Q. 24. *Draw the offset QPSK and standard QPSK diagrams and show their signal states and possible transitions between the states.*

Ans. The offset and standard QPSK signal states are shown below :

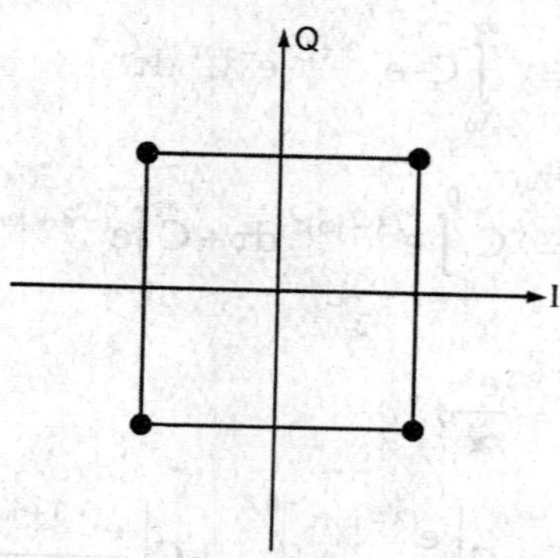

Fig. B.5

(*i*) Offset Quadrature Phase Shift Keying signal states (offset QPSK).

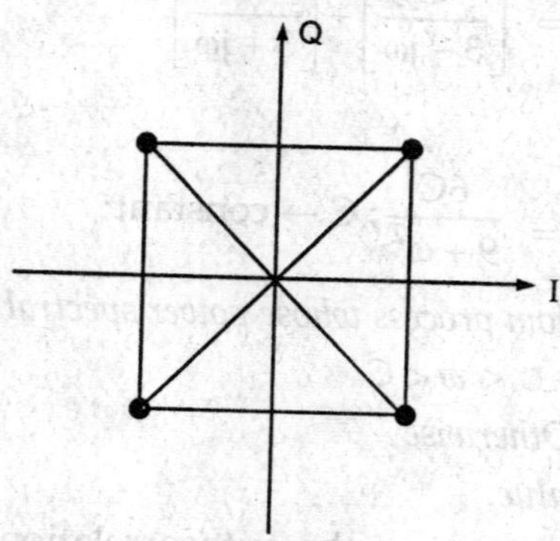

Fig. B.6

(*ii*) Standard Quadrature Phase Shift Keying signal (Standard QPSK).

Note :

• → Signal state

– → Possible transition between the signal states

- Zero crossing or signal moves through zero only in standard QPSK.
- In offset the signal will move only through Q and I and its amplitude does not goes to '0' amplitude level.

Q. 25. *If the frequency spectrum of a channel is between 4 MHz and 5 MHz and signal to noise ratio is 25 dB. Using Shannon and Nyquist criterion, calculate the channel capacity 'C' and the number of signalling levels.*

Ans. Bandwidth

$$B = 5 \text{ MHz} - 4 \text{ MHz}$$
$$= 1 \text{ MHz} = 1 \times 10^6 \text{ Hz}$$

(*i*) To find channel capacity :

Signal to noise ratio

$$(SNR)_{dB} = 25 \text{ dB};$$

1. $$SNR = \text{antilog}\left(\frac{25}{10}\right)$$

$$\therefore \quad = 316$$

From Shannon's channel capacity relation,

$$C = B \log_2 (1 + SNR)$$

Substituting the values,

$$C = 1 \text{ MHz} \log_2 (1 + 36)$$

Channel capacity C = **8.3 Mbps**

(*ii*) To find number of signalling levels (M) :

Using Nyquist's relation,

$$C = 2B \log_2 M$$

Substituting for C and B in this equation we get,

$$8.3 \times 10^6 = 2 \times 1 \times 10^6 \log_2 M$$

$$\therefore \quad \log_2 M = \frac{8.3 \times 10^6}{2 \times 10^6}$$

$$\log_2 M = 4.15$$

$$\therefore \quad M = 17.7 = 18 \text{ levels}$$

2. $$C = 10^6 (\log e^{317} \cdot \log_2^e)$$
$$= 10^6 (8.3)$$
$$C = 8.3 \text{ Mbps}$$

3. $$\log_2 M = \log_e M \times \log_2 e$$
$$= \frac{\log_e M}{\log_e 2}$$
$$= \frac{\log_2 M}{0.693}$$
$$= \frac{\log_2 M}{0.693} = 4.15$$
$$\log_2 M = 2.876$$
$$\therefore \quad M = \log_2^{-1}(2.876) = 17.7$$

Q. 26. *Calculate the maximum data rate required for transmission if the signal to noise ratio of the communication link is 20 dB and the RF bandwidth is 40 kHz.*

Ans. We have signal to noise (SNR) is = 20 dB

$$10 \log x = 20$$

$$\log x = \frac{20}{10}$$

$$\log x = 2$$

$$\therefore \quad x = 100$$

$$20 \text{ dB gain} = 100$$

$$\text{RF Bandwidth} = B_{RF} = 40 \times 10^3 \text{ Hz}$$

Maximum possible data rate

$$C = B \log_2 \left(1 + \frac{S}{N}\right)$$

$$= 40000 \log_2 (1 + 100)$$

$$C = 40000 \log_2 101$$

$$\therefore \quad C = 40000 \left[\log_e 101 \cdot \frac{1}{\log_e 2}\right] \qquad 1.\ \log_2 a = \log_e a \times \log_2 e$$

$$= 40000 \left(\frac{4.6151}{0.6931}\right) \qquad = \log_e a \cdot \frac{1}{\log_e 2}$$

$$C = \textbf{266.35 kB/sec} \qquad 2.\ \log_y x = \frac{1}{\log_x y}$$

Q. 27. *Calculate the number of radio channels available in the FDMA system with following data. A US analog mobile phone system is allocated 12.8 MHz for every simplex band. The total spectrum allocated is 12.8 MHz, the guard bandwidth is 10 kHz and the channel bandwidth is 30 kHz.*

Ans. We have total available spectrum

$$B_t = 12.8 \text{ MHz}$$

$$= 12.8 \times 10^6$$

$$\text{Channel bandwidth } B_c = 30 \text{ kHz}$$

$$= 30 \times 10^3$$

$$\text{Guard bandwidth } B_G = 10 \text{ kHz}$$

$$= 10 \times 10^3$$

Number of radio channels available in the FDMA system is devoted as 'n',

$$n = \frac{B_t - 2B_G}{B_c}$$

$$n = \frac{(12.8 \times 10^6) - 2(10 \times 10^3)}{30 \times 10^3}$$

$$n = \textbf{426 channels}$$

Q. 28. *Consider a four branch diversity scheme which is used in a mobile reception system and each branch has received unique. Rayleigh fading signal. Assume the average signal to noise ratio is 100 dB. Find the probability that the SNR value will drop below 10 dB. Also if no diversity is applied, find what will be the probability for the same case.*

Ans. (*i*) If diversity is applied and considering there are four branches.

$$\gamma = 10 \text{ dB}$$

$$G = 100 \text{ dB}$$
$$M = 4$$
$$\frac{\gamma}{\Gamma} = 0.1 \text{ dB}$$

Probability when SNR drops below 10 dB is

$$P = \left(1 - e^{\left(-\frac{\gamma}{\Gamma}\right)}\right)^M$$
$$P = (1 - e^{-0.1})^4$$
$$= (0.0952)^4$$
$$\therefore \quad P = 8.2069 \times 10^{-5}$$

(*ii*) If there is no diversity applied at receiver end then the probability is given as,

$$P = (1 - e^{-0.1})^1 \qquad \text{where } M = 1$$
$$P = (0.0952)^1$$
$$\therefore \quad P = \mathbf{0.0952}$$

If no diversity is applied, the probability that SNR will drop below 10 dB is higher than the 4 branch diversity case.

Q. 29. *Calculate the theoretical maximum data rate which could be supported in 300 kHz radio channel. Assume the signal to noise ratio as 10 dB.*

Ans. Given :

Channel bandwidth = 300 kHz

SNR = 10 dB

Maximum possible data rate is given as

$$C = B \log_2 \left(1 + \frac{S}{N}\right)$$
$$= B \log_2 (1 + 10)$$
$$= 300 \text{ kHz} \log_2 (1 + 10)$$
$$= 300 \times 10^3 \log_2 11$$
$$= 300{,}000 \log_2 11 \qquad 1. \quad \log_2 a = \log_e a \cdot \log_2 e$$
$$= 300{,}000 \log_2 11 \cdot \log_2 e \qquad 2. \quad \log_b a = \frac{1}{\log_a b}$$
$$= 300{,}000 \log_e 11 \cdot \frac{1}{(\log_e 2)}$$
$$= 300{,}000 \left(\frac{2.39789}{0.69315}\right)$$
$$= 1037.823$$
$$= \mathbf{1037.823 \text{ kB/sec}}$$

Q.30. *Calculate the Nyquist rate for the analog signal s(t) = 3 cos 50πt + 10 sin 300πt.*

Ans. The available frequencies in the analog signal s(t) are :

$f_1 \rightarrow \quad 2\pi f_1 \cdot t = 50\pi t$

$2\pi f_1 = 50\pi$

$\therefore \quad f_1 = 25 \text{ Hz}$

$f_2 \rightarrow \quad 2\pi f_2 \cdot t = 300\pi t$

$2f_2 = 300$

$\therefore \quad f_2 = 150 \text{ Hz}$

The maximum frequency in s(t) is 150 Hz.

The Nyquist rate can be given as 2 W where W is f_2 in this case. ['W' is the maximum frequency in the signal s(t)]

$\therefore$ Nyquist rate = 2W = 2 × 150

= 300 Hz

From the above it is evident that the frequency f_s has to be higher than the Nyquist rate. Thus to have a better system performance f_s should be greater than the 300 Hz.

Q. 31. *Consider a mobile located from the base station at 4 km, applying a vertical $\frac{\lambda}{4}$ antenna. Assume the carrier frequency of this system is 900 MHz and gain of the system is 2.55 dB. Calculate the length and effective aperture value.*

Ans. The wavelength

$$\lambda = \frac{c}{f}$$

$$= \frac{3 \times 10^8}{900 \times 10^6}$$

$$\lambda = 0.333 \text{ m}$$

***(i)* Length of the antenna system**

$$l = \frac{\lambda}{4}$$

$$l = \frac{0.333}{4} \text{ m}$$

$$= 0.083 \text{ m}$$

$$l = \mathbf{8.3 \text{ cm}}$$

***(ii)* Effective aperture**

$$G = \frac{4\pi A_e}{\lambda^2}$$

To convert 2.55 dB :

$$\therefore \quad A_e = \frac{G\lambda^2}{4\pi} = \frac{(G)(0.333)^2}{4 \times 3.14}$$

10 log G = 2.55 dB

$$\log G = \frac{2.55}{10} \text{ dB}$$

$$A_e = \frac{(1.798)(0.333)^2}{(4 \times 3.14)}$$

$$\log G = 0.255;\ G = 10^{0.255};\ G = 1.798$$

$$A_e = \mathbf{0.016\ m^2}$$

Q. 32. *Find the value of Nyquist rate and Nyquist interval for the signal* $x(t) = \dfrac{\sin(500\pi t)}{\pi t}$.

Ans.

$$x(t) = \frac{\sin(500\pi t)}{\pi t}$$

$$= \frac{1}{\pi t}[\sin(500\pi t)]$$

The given signal x(t) contains one frequency 500π.

$$\omega t = 500\pi t$$

$$2\pi f = 500\pi$$

$$2f = 500$$

$$f = 250 \text{ Hz}$$

Maximum frequency f_{max} or W = 250 Hz.

$$\text{Nyquist rate (NR)} = 2 \text{ W Hz}$$

$$N_R = 2(250)$$

$$N_R = \mathbf{500\ Hz}$$

$$N_1 = \frac{1}{2(250)}$$

$$= \frac{1}{500}$$

$$N_1 = \mathbf{2\ ms}$$

Q. 33. *Calculate the Nyquist rate for the given analog signal* $x(t) = 5\cos 600\pi t + 3\cos 1800\pi t$.

Ans. In x(t) there are two frequency components.

1. $\omega_1 t = 600\pi t$

$$2\pi f_1 = 600\pi$$

$$2f_1 = 600$$

$$f_1 = 300 \text{ Hz}$$

2. $\omega_2 t = 1800\pi t$

$$2\pi f_2 = 1800\pi$$

$$2f_2 = 1800$$

$$f_2 = 900 \text{ Hz}$$

In these frequency components, the f_{max} is 900.

$$f_{max} = f_2 = 900\text{Hz}$$

From Nyquist rate condition,

$$f_s = 2f_{max} = 1800 \text{ Hz}$$

$\therefore$ Sampling rate $= T_s = \frac{1}{f_s} = \frac{1}{1800}$

$$= 5.55 \times 10^{-4}$$

$$= 555.5 \times 10^{-6}$$

$$= \mathbf{555.5\ \mu sec}$$

Q. 34. *Consider a time function s(t) = 5 cos 300πt that has to be sampled at the Nyquist rate. Find the sampling rate and sampling interval.*

Ans.

$$s(t) = 5 \cos 300\pi t$$

$$= 5 \cos (2\pi t\, f_m)$$

here $2\pi f_m t = 300\pi t$

$$2\pi f_m = 300\pi$$

$$2f_m = 300$$

$$f_m = \mathbf{150\ Hz}$$

As per Nyquist criterion

$$2f_m = 2(150)$$

$$2f_m = 300 \text{ Hz}$$

is Nyquist rate $W = 2f_m = f_s = 300$ Hz

and Nyquist internal

$$T_s = \frac{1}{f_s} = \frac{1}{300} \text{ sec}$$

$\therefore$ $T_s = \mathbf{3\ sec}$

Q. 35. *Calculate the minimum sampling rate for the bandpass signal which has spectral range extending from 20 kHz to 70 kHz.*

Ans. The spectral range of the given bandpass signal is from 20 kHz to 70 kHz.

$\therefore$ The bandwidth (BW) = (70 – 20) kHz

= 50 kHz

= 2W

Minimum sampling rate (SM)

= Twice the bandwidth

= 2 (BW)

= 2 (2W)

= 2 (50 kHz)

S_N = **100 kHz**

Q. 36. *Assume that a communication channel of bandwidth 85 kHz, that is required to send binary data at a rate of 0.1 Mbps, using raised cosine pulses. Find the roll off factor a for this channel.*

Ans. Data bit rate rb = 0.1 Mbps

= 0.1 × 0^6

Time period = 10 μs.

The bandwidth present = B = 85 kHz = 85 × 10^3

$$B = \frac{r_b}{2}(1+\alpha) \Rightarrow \therefore 1 + \alpha = \frac{2B}{r_b} = \frac{2(85\text{ kHz})}{0.1\times 10^6}$$

$$\therefore \quad \alpha = \left[\left(\frac{2\times 85\times 10^3}{0.1\times 10^6}\right) - 1\right] = 0.7 \text{ where } \alpha \text{ is roll off factor.}$$

Q. 37. *Consider the direct sequence spread spectrum (DSSS) system which has a data sequence bit duration as 4.085 msec, PN chip duration is 1 μsec and E_b/N_0 is 10 for the case of average probability lesser than 10^{-5} calculate processing gain of the system.*

Ans. In PN sequence (pseudo noise) the one bit period is called as one chip duration.

T_c = I μsec = 1 × 10^{-6}

One bit duration = T_b = 4.085 μsec

T_b = 4.085 × 10^{-3}

$$\therefore \text{ Processing gain } P_G = \frac{T_b}{T_c} = \frac{4.085\times 10^{-3}}{1\times 10^{-6}}$$

P_G = **4085**

Q. 38. *For the above question, find the jamming margin value in dB for DSSS system.*

Ans. We have processing gain

P_G = 4085

E_b/N_0 = 10

Jamming margin in dB,

J_M = (Jamming margin)$_{dB}$

J_M = $(P_G)_{dB} - 10 \log_{10} (E_b/N_0)$

= $(4085)_{dB} - 10 \text{ 1og}_{10} (10)$

= $10 \log_{10} 4085 - 10 \log_{10} 10$

= 10 (3.611) – 10(1)

= **26.112 dB**

Q. 39. *Calculate the far field distance for an antenna with largest dimension 1.5 m and the corresponding frequency of 1200 MHz.*

Ans. Antenna's largest dimension is = D = 1.5 m

Operating frequency = f = 1200 MHz

$$\text{Wavelength} = \lambda = \frac{c}{f} = \frac{3\times 10^8}{1200\times 10^6} = 0.25 \text{ m}$$

Far field distance = $d_f = \frac{2D^2}{\lambda} = \frac{2(2.5)^2}{0.25}$

$\therefore \quad d_f = \mathbf{8\ m}$

Q. 40. *Consider that the magnitude of radiating portion of electric field is 0.004 V/m. Find the power flux density assuming intrinsic impedance of free space as 120π.*

Ans. Magnitude of electric field = $|E| = 0.004\ V/m$

Intrinsic impedance of free space = $\eta = 120\ \pi\Omega$

$= 376.8$

$\eta = 377\ \Omega$

Power flux density $P_d = \frac{|E|^2}{\eta}$

$= \frac{(0.004)^2}{377}$

$P_d = \frac{1.6 \times 10^{-5}}{377}$

$\therefore \quad P_d = \mathbf{4.244 \times 10^{-8}\ W/m^2}$

Q. 41. *In a cellular mobile environment, the mobile antenna height is about 3 m, average height of cell site antenna is about 49 m. Assuming communication path length as 5 km as below find the incident angle, elevation at the mobile unit's location and elevation angle at the antenna of the mobile unit.*

Ans.

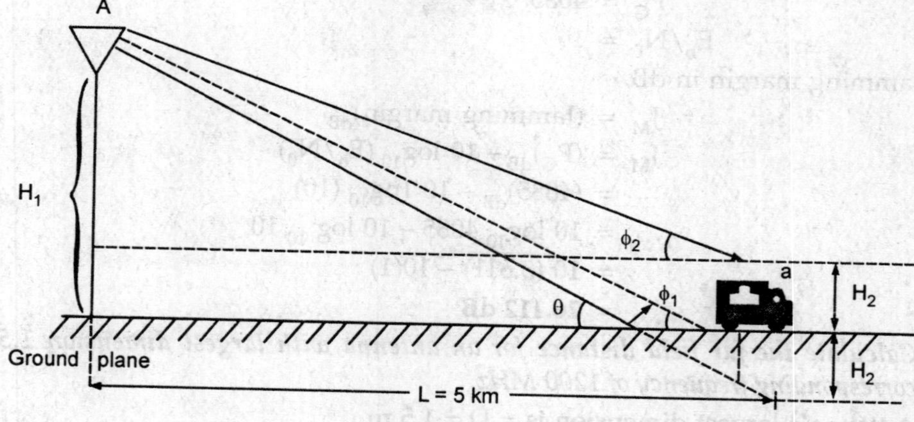

Fig. B.7

Let the elevation angle be ϕ and the incident angle be θ.

From the given data

Height of cellsite antenna (A) = H_1 = 49 m

Height of mobile antenna (a)= H_2 = 3 m

Communication path length (L) = 5 km – 5000 m

(*i*) The incident angle $\theta = \tan^{-1}\left[\frac{\text{(Summation of height of antennas)}}{L}\right]$

$$= \tan^{-1}\frac{(49+3)}{5000}$$

$$= \tan^{-1}(0.0104)$$

$$\theta = \mathbf{0.596°}$$

(*ii*) Elevation angle at the mobile unit and location is θ_1,

$$\theta_1 = \tan^{-1}\left(\frac{\text{height of cell antenna}}{L}\right)$$

$$= \tan^{-1}\left(\frac{49}{5000}\right)$$

$$= \tan^{-1}(0.0098)$$

$$\theta_1 = \mathbf{0.561°}$$

(*iii*) Elevation angle at the antenna of mobile unit is, θ_2,

$$\theta_2 = \tan^{-1}\left[\frac{\text{(height of cell site antenna – height of mobile antenna)}}{L}\right]$$

$$= \tan^{-1}\left[\frac{(49-3)\text{ m}}{5000}\right]$$

$$= \tan^{-1}(\cdot 0092)$$

$$\theta_2 = 0.53°$$

Q. 42. For the above *question, find the noise power density is dBm and energy per bit to noise power density ratio assuming the bit rate as 65 kB/sec.*

Ans. Given :

$$C = 10^{-13}\text{ W}$$

$$N = 1.2 \times 10^{-14}\text{ W}$$

$$B = 120\text{ kHz}$$

$$f_b = 65\text{ kB/sec}$$

(*i*) Noise power density

$$N_0(\text{dBm}) = 10\log\frac{N}{0.001} - 10\log B$$

$$= N(\text{dBm}) - 10\log B$$

$$= -109.21\text{ dBm} - 10\log 120\text{ kHz}$$

$$= -109.21 - 50.792$$

$$N_0 \text{ (dBm)} = -160.002 \text{ dBm}$$

(*ii*) Energy per bit to noise density ratio is,

$$\frac{E_b}{N_0} = 10 \log \frac{C}{N} + \log \frac{B}{f_b}$$

Substituting $\frac{C}{N}$ then,

$$\frac{E_b}{N_0} = 10 \log \frac{C}{N} + 10 \log \frac{120 \text{ kHz}}{65 \text{ kB/sec}}$$

$$\therefore \left(\frac{E_b}{N_0}\right) = 9.208 + 2.663$$

$$= 11.871 \text{ dB}$$

$$\frac{C}{N} = 10 \log \frac{C}{N}$$

$$= 10 \log \frac{10^{-3}}{1.2 \times 10^{-14}}$$

$$= 10 \log 8.333$$

$$= 9.208$$

Q. 43. *Calculate the transmit and receive carrier frequencies for (i) AMPS channel 4 and (ii) AMPS channel 991.*

Ans. (*i*) The transmit carrier frequency for channel 4 is determined from,

$$f_T = 0.03 (N) + 825 \qquad : \text{for } 1 \le N \le 866$$

$f_T \rightarrow$ Transmit carrier frequency (MHz)

$N \rightarrow$ Channel number = 4

$$f_T = 0.03 (4) + 825$$

$$f_T = 825.12 \text{ MHz}$$

Receive carrier frequency = $f_R = f_T + 45$ MHz

Substituting for f_T, we get $f_R = 870.12$ MHz

(*ii*) For AMPS channel 991 :

$$f_T = 0.03 (N - 1023) + 825 \qquad \text{for } 990 \le N \le 1023$$

$$f_T = -0.03 (991 - 1023) + 825$$

$$= (-0.96) + 825$$

$$f_T = 824.04 \text{ MHz}$$

Similarly $f_R = f_T + 45$ MHz

substituting for f_T we get $f_R = 824.04 + 45$

$$f_R = \mathbf{869.04 \text{ MHz}}$$

Q. 44. *What is the bandwidth efficiency if a $\pi/4$ DQ PSK supports data transmission of three various 48.6 kB/sec digitized voice signal in a bandwidth of 30 kHz?*

Ans. In $\pi/4$ DQ PSK transmission,

$$\text{Data rate of voice channel} = 48.6 \text{ kB/sec.}$$

$$\text{Bandwidth} = 30 \text{ kHz}$$

$$\text{Bandwidth efficiency} = \eta = \frac{3 \times 48.6 \text{ kB/sec}}{30 \text{ kHz}} = \frac{145.8}{30}$$

$$\eta = \mathbf{4.861 \text{ byte/sec/Hz}}$$

Q. 45. *Consider hamming codes that belongs to the family of (n, k) block error correcting codes and for minimum distance and m = 3, give the properties of the hamming code.*

Ans. The properties of hamming codes are,

(*i*) Number of data bits = $k = 2^m - m - 1$

(*ii*) Block length = $n = 2^m - 1$

(*iii*) Number of check bits = $n - k = m$

(*iv*) Minimum distance = d_{min}

(*i*) Number of data bits = $k = 2^m - m - 1$

$$= 2^3 - 3 - 1 \qquad \because m = 3$$

$$k = 4$$

(*ii*) Block length = $n = 2^3 - 1$

$$n = 7$$

(*iii*) Number of check bits = $n - k = m$

$$= 3$$

(*iv*) Minimum distance = d_{min}

$$= 3$$

Q. 46. *Consider in a climate zone z, for 0.01 % of time, rain fall exceeds 156 mm/hr with a vertically polarized wave. Calculate the attenuation 'A' for this rain rate for frequencies (i) 30 GHz and (ii) 40 GHz.*

Ans. The attenuation 'A' which has to be added to the free space for the given rain rate is,

$$\text{Attenuation} = A = aR^b$$

; R → Rain rate

a, b → coefficients for finding, attenuation due to rain fall.

Some of the values of the coefficients a and b are tabulated below for different frequencies.

Frequency GHz	a_h	a_v	b_h	b_v
20	0.075	0.069	1.099	1.065
30	0.187	0.167	1.021	1.000
40	0.350	0.310	0.939	0.929
50	0.536	0.479	0.873	0.868

(*i*) From the data given, for frequency 30 GHz the attenuation A is calculated as follows.

Applying coefficients a_v and b_v (vertical polarization) from table in the equation.

$$A = aR^b = a_v\ R^{bv}$$
$$= 0.167\ (156)^{1.000}$$
$$A = \mathbf{26.1\ dB/km}$$

(*ii*) For frequency f = 40 GHz :

$$\text{The attenuation } A = a_v\ R^{bv}$$
$$= 0.310\ (156)^{0.929}$$
$$A = \mathbf{33.79\ dB/km}$$

Q. 47. ***Calculate the time period between handoffs if the cell radius is 10 kms where the vehicle travels at a speed of 130 kmph.***

Ans. The velocity or the vehicle = $v = \frac{130 \times 1000}{32600}$ m/s

$$= 36.11\ m/s$$

$$\text{Radius of cell} = R = 10\ km$$
$$\text{Diameter} = D = 20\ km$$

Time period between handoffs is

$$t = \frac{D}{v} = \frac{20 \times 10^3\ m}{36.11\ m/s}$$
$$= \frac{20 \times 10^3}{36.11}$$
$$t = 553.86$$
$$\therefore \quad t = \mathbf{9.23\ minutes}$$

Q. 48. ***In a cellular system, there are 12 clusters available with 120 cells, and there are 10,000 subscribers. Each subscriber uses cell phone for 1 hour every day. On an average 30 minutes of the time is used during peak hours. Find the average and peak traffic for (i) Entire cellular system, (ii) For one cell considering all callers are distributed evenly over the system.***

Ans.

(*i*) Average traffic = T = NP

$$\text{Peak traffic} = P_T = 10{,}000 \times \frac{1\ hr}{24\ hr}$$
$$P_T = 416.66\ \text{Erlangs}$$
$$P_T = 10{,}000 \times \frac{30\ min}{60\ min}$$
$$P_T = \mathbf{5000\ Erlangs}$$

(ii) Average traffic in cell

$$(A_T) = \frac{416.66}{120}$$

$$A_T = 3.472 \text{ Erlangs}$$

$$\therefore \text{The peak traffic} = \frac{P_T}{\text{Number of cells}}$$

$$= \frac{P_T}{120}$$

$$= \frac{5000}{120}$$

$$P_T = \mathbf{41.66 \text{ Erlangs}}$$

Q. 49. *Assume a receiving antenna system has a gain of 42 dBi looking at sky and observed noise temperature is 18°K. The loss between LNA input and the antenna setup is 0.4 dB. Calculate the figure of merit (G/T) value if the noise temperature of LNA is of 35°K.*

Ans. The gain in dB (G) = (Antenna gain – Losses upto the reference point)

$$= (42 - 0.4)$$

$$G = 41.6 \text{ dBi}$$

Converting the feedline loss as a ratio,

$$L = \text{anti}\log\left(\frac{\text{loss in dB}}{10}\right)$$

$$= \text{anti}\log\left(\frac{0.4}{10}\right)$$

$$L = 1.096$$

$$\text{Antenna noise temperature} = t_a = \frac{(L-1)\,290 + t_{sky}}{L}$$

$$= \frac{(1.096-1)\,290 + 18}{1.096}$$

$$t_a = 42°K$$

$$\text{Figure of merit } \frac{G}{T}(\text{dB}) = G_r(\text{dBi}) - 10\log(t_a + t_{equ})$$

$$= 41.6 - 10\log(42 + 35)$$

$$= 41.6 - 18.86$$

$$\frac{G}{T}(\text{dB}) = \mathbf{22.7 \text{ dB}}$$

Q. 50. *Assume a cellular system operates with traffic of 2500 Erlangs. If each user in the system uses phone for 3 minutes of busiest hour on an average case, then find the number of users which can be accommodated under even distribution case.*

Ans. Average cellular traffic = T = n.P

where n → Number of users

P → Time period

$$T = n.P$$

$$n = \frac{T}{P}$$

$$\text{Number of users} = \frac{2500}{(3/60)}$$

$$n = \mathbf{50{,}000\ users}$$

Thus on an average 50,000 users can use phone for 3 minutes during the busiest hour.

Q. 51. *Consider maximum number of calls in one hour in one cell is 3500 and an average calling time 't' is 1.76 minutes. Calculate the offered load in the cell.*

Ans. Let offered load be A

$$A = \frac{Q_i\,t}{60}\ \text{Erlangs}$$

$$\text{Maximum calls/hr} = Q_i = 3500$$

$$\text{Average calling time} = t = 1.76\ \text{minutes}$$

$$\therefore \quad A = \frac{3500 \times 1.76}{60}$$

$$A = \mathbf{102.67\ E}$$

Q. 52. *If the number of calls per hour in a cell is 28000, what will be the offered load for Q. 51 case?*

Ans. Here

$$Q_i = 28000$$

$$t = 1.76\ \text{minutes}$$

$$\text{Offered load} = A = \frac{Q_i\,.t}{60}$$

$$A = \frac{28000 \times 1.76}{60}$$

$$A = \mathbf{821\ E}$$

Q. 53. *In a busiest hour of the day consider the number of calls per hour for each of ten cells as given below. Assume that seven percent of the car phones is used in this busiest hour and one call per phone is used during this busiest hour. Find total number of calls per hour and number of users in the system. (Q_i = 1500, 2000, 500, 3000, 1000, 1200, 1800, 2800, 2500, 900).*

Ans. Total number of calls in one hour

$$= Q_t = \sum_{i=1}^{10} Q_1$$

$$Q_i = \sum_{i=1}^{10} (1500 + 2000 + 500 + 3000 + 100$$

$$+ 1200 + 1800 + 2800 + 2500 + 900)$$

$$= 17{,}200$$

Since 70 present of car phones is used during the busy period and if considered as $\eta_c = 0.7$, then number of users in the system is given as,

Then total user traffic will be = $U_t = \dfrac{17200}{0.7}$

$= \mathbf{24571\ users}$

Q. 54. *Consider an earth station that is used for a geostationary satellite has an antenna observing a sky temperature of 28°. A receiver units connected to it has a feedline loss of 1 dB. Find the noise temperature of the system assuming receiver equivalent noise temperature as 14 °K.*

Ans. Let the feedline loss be L.

Representing 'L' as power ratio,

$$\text{Feed line loss 'L'} = \text{anti}\log\left(\frac{L\,(dB)}{10}\right)$$

$$= \text{anti}\log\left(\frac{1}{10}\right)$$

$$= 1.259$$

The antenna noise temperature

$$t_a = \frac{(L-1)\,290 + t_{sky}}{L}$$

$$= \frac{(1.259-1)\,290 + 28}{1.26}$$

$$t_a = 82°K$$

System temperature = t = Antenna noise temperature + Receiver equivalent temperature

$$= ta + t_{equ} = (82 + 14)\ K$$

$$t = 96°K$$

Q. 55. *Mention the phase changes from previous symbol to the next in DQPSK and DBPSK digital modulation techniques and draw their diagrams.*

Ans. (*i*) DQPSK technique :

Phase change from previous symbol to next	Bit
0°	00
90°	01
– 90°	10
180°	11

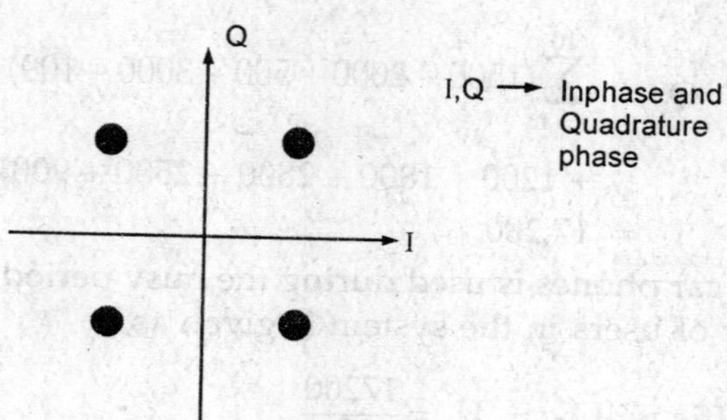

Fig. B.8 (a)

(*ii*) DBPSK technique :

Phase change from the previous symbol to next	Bit
0°	0
180°	1

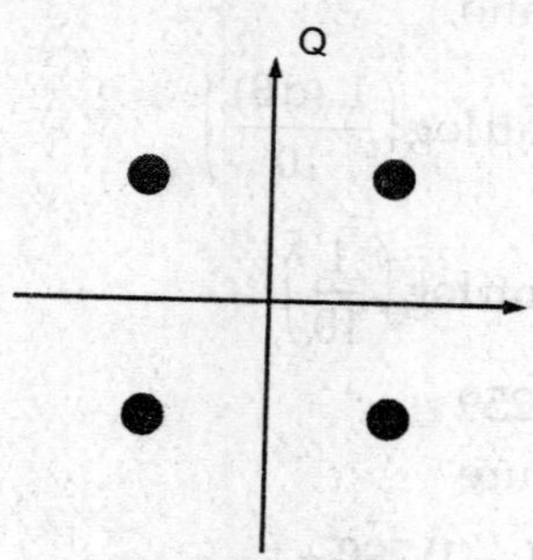

Fig. B.8 (b)

Q. 56. *Consider an original cell wherein cell splitting technique is applied and the number of new cells is 4. Find new cell area if the radius of old cell is 8 km.*

Ans. The new cell radius $(N_r) = \dfrac{\text{Old cell radius}(O_r)}{2}$

$$= \frac{8}{2} = 4 \text{ m}$$

Also new cell are $(N_a) = \dfrac{\text{Old cell are }(O_a)}{4}$

$$N_a = \frac{\pi O_r^2}{4}$$

$$N_a = \frac{\pi (8)^2}{4} \qquad \therefore N_a = \mathbf{50.24\ m^2}$$

Q. 57. *(i) find the cochannel interference reduction factor for the following cellular communication shown below with two cochannel separated by a distance D.*

(ii) Calculate the transmit power for a mobile in CDMA cellular system assuming that the mobile receives – 90 dBm signal from base station.

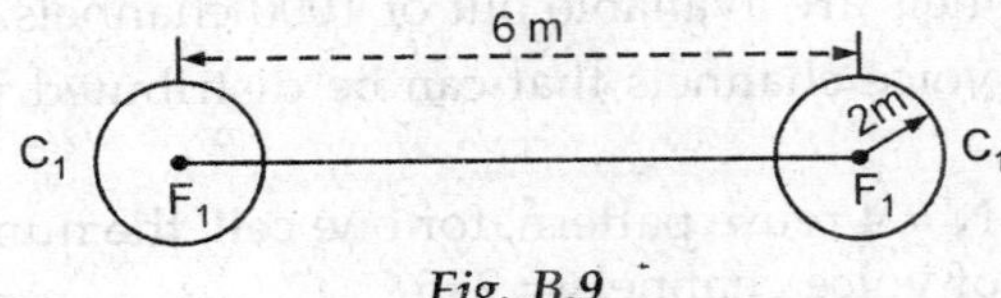

Fig. B.9

Ans. The two cochannel is denoted here as C_1 with frequency F_1.

(*i*) Distance of separation = D = 6 m

Radius of cell = R = 2 m

Cochannel interference reduction factor

$$q = \frac{D}{R} = \frac{6}{2} = 3 \text{ m}$$

(*ii*) Transmit power = P_T dBm

$$P_T = -76 \text{ dB} - P_R$$

substituting for P_R

$$P_T = \mathbf{14\ dBm}$$

Q. 58. *Consider a cellular system with four cell reuse pattern. Let the bandwidth allocated is 60 MHz to a FDD cellular telephone system using two 30 kHz simplex channels for providing full duplex control of one channel. Calculate the total number of channels available in one cell.*

Ans. If cellular system uses 4 cell reuse pattern, then each cluster has four cells.

$$N = 4$$

Total bandwidth (BW) = 60 MHz

∴ Channel bandwidth (B_c)

= Twice the number of simplex channels

= 30 kHz × 2

= 60 kHz per duplex channel

Total available channels

$$(A_c) = \frac{BW}{B_c} = \frac{60 \times 10^3 \text{ kHz}}{60 \text{ kHz}}$$

$$A_c = \mathbf{1000\ channels}$$

Q. 59. *For the above Q. 58, find the number of control channels that is available in single cell. (Assume that 1 MHz spectrum is dedicated to control channel.)*

Ans. As per reuse pattern, N = 4

The number of channels available in one cell

$$= \frac{100}{4} = 250 \text{ channels}$$

Since control channel is of 1 MHz spectrum then,

$$\text{Number of cells} = \frac{1000}{50} = 20$$

Thus 20 control channels are available out of 1000 channels.

Also the number of voice channels that can be distributed will be, 1000 – 20 = 980 voice channels.

Dividing equally for N = 4 reuse pattern, for one cell, the number of control channels = 5 and the number of voice channels = 245.

Hence total channels (control and voice) that can be assigned to one cell under N = 4 cellular system will be 250 channels.

Q. 60. *In a mobile propagation environment, find received carrier power if distance between transmitter and receiver is 79 and the constant of proportionality is 2.*

Ans. The received carrier power = $p_c = \alpha R^{-4}$

where α = Constant of proportionality

$$p_c = 2\,(79)^{-4}$$

$$p_c = 0.051 \times 10^{-6}\ \text{W}$$

$$p_c = \mathbf{51\ nW}$$

Q. 61. *Consider a modem (with QAM technique) uses sixteen different phase angles with four amplitudes. Find the number of bits that it can transmit in a symbol.*

Ans. The number states possible in a symbol is = 16 × 4 = 64 states

The number of bits per symbol is = $\log_2 64$

$$= \frac{\log_e^{64}}{\log_e^{2}}$$

$$= \frac{4.158}{0.693}$$

Number of bits = 6

Q. 62. *Find the wavelength in free space for radio waves for each of the frequencies given below.*

(a) 23 MHz *(b)* 300 MHz

(c) 450 MHz *(d)* 50 kHz.

Ans. Speed of radio wave propagation is = C = 300×10^6

$$c = f\lambda$$; f → Frequency used in MHz

λ → Wavelength in m.

$$\therefore \quad \lambda = \frac{c}{f}$$

(a) For f = 23 MHz :

$$\lambda = \frac{300 \times 10^6}{23 \times 10^6} = \mathbf{13.40\ m}$$

(*b*) For f = 300 MHz :

$$\lambda = \frac{300 \times 10^6}{300 \times 10^6} = \mathbf{1\ m}$$

(*c*) For 450 MHz :

$$\lambda = \frac{300 \times 10^6}{450 \times 10^6} = \mathbf{0.66\ m}$$

(*d*) For 50 kHz

$$\lambda = \frac{300 \times 10^6}{50 \times 10^6} = \mathbf{6000\ m}$$

Q. 63. *Consider a resistor which has a noise temperature of 400°K. Find the corresponding noise power density and draw the noise spectrum. Also if a system has noise temperature of 400°K operates at 100 MHz frequency with a bandwidth of 1 MHz, draw its noise spectrum.*

Ans. Case 1 : The noise power density = N_0 = KT

Where K → Boltzmann constant and

T → Temperature (400°K)

$$N_0 = 1.38 \times 10^{-23}\ \text{J/K} \times 400\text{K}$$
$$= 552 \times 10^{-23}\ \text{W/Hz}$$
$$= 5.52 \times 10^{-21}\ \text{W/Hz}$$

The noise power density is same for all frequencies and it is shown in the graph.

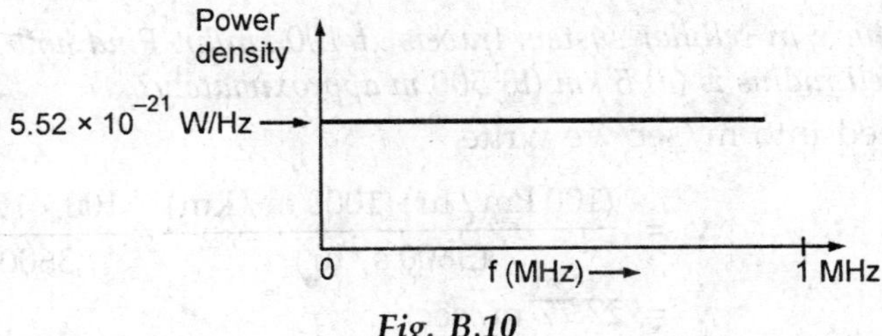

Fig. B.10

Case 2 : The noise power density is uniform over 1 MHz bandwidth. The bandwidth spectrum is shown below.

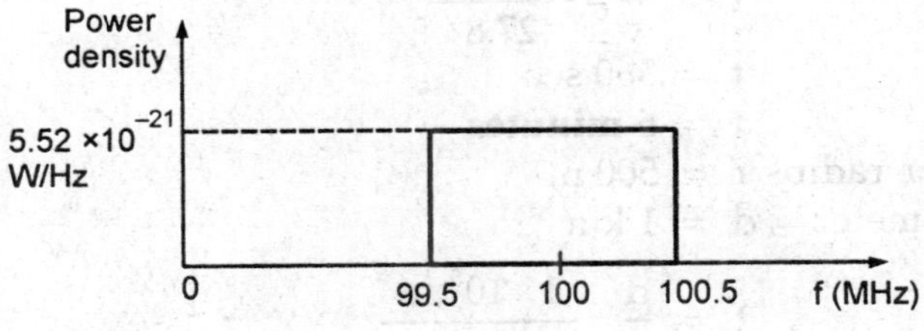

Fig. B.11

Note : Depending upon the type of filter shape of the pattern will change.

Q. 64. *Calculate the wavelengths of signals for the different cases, mentioned below.*

(i) 1.9 GHz (Personal communication systems range PCS)

(ii) 850 MHz (Cellular phone range)

(iii) 28 GHz (used in local multipoint distribution system (LMDS))

Ans. The speed of radio waves is denoted as c and it is same as the speed of light energy.

$$c = 300 \times 10^6 \text{ m/sec}$$

$$c = f\lambda \qquad ; \lambda \rightarrow \text{Wavelength}$$

$$\lambda = \frac{c}{f} \qquad f \rightarrow \text{Frequency used.}$$

(i) For PCS :

$$\lambda = \frac{c}{f} = \frac{300 \times 10^6}{1.9 \text{ GHz}} = \frac{300 \times 10^6}{1.9 \times 10^9} = \frac{3}{19} = 0.158 \text{ m} = \mathbf{158 \text{ mm}}$$

(ii) For cellular phones :

$$\lambda = \frac{c}{f} = \frac{300 \times 10^6}{850 \text{ MHz}} = \frac{300 \times 10^6}{850 \times 10^6} = \frac{30}{85} = 0.351 \text{ m}$$

$$\therefore \quad \lambda = \mathbf{351 \text{ mm}}$$

(iii) For LMDS :

$$\lambda = \frac{c}{f} = \frac{300 \times 10^6}{28 \text{ MHz}} = \frac{300 \times 10^6}{28 \times 10^9} = \frac{3}{280} = 0.011 \text{ m}$$

$$\therefore \quad \lambda = \mathbf{11 \text{ mm}}$$

Q. 65. *Assume a vehicle in cellular system travels at 100 km/hr. Find how frequency handoffs will occur if the cell radius is (a) 5 km (b) 500 m approximately?*

Ans. To have speed into m/sec we write,

$$v = \frac{(100 \text{ km/hr})(1000 \text{ m/km})}{(3600 \text{ s/hr})} = \frac{100 \times 1000}{3600}$$

$$v = 27.77 \text{ m/sec}$$

Case (*a*) : For radius r = 5 km

Cell diameter = d = 10 km

$$\therefore \quad t = \frac{d}{v} = \frac{10 \times 10^3}{27.8}$$

$$t = 360 \text{ sec}$$

$$t = \mathbf{6 \text{ minutes}}$$

Case (*b*) : For radius r = 500 m

Diameter = d = 1 km

$$\therefore \quad t = \frac{d}{v} = \frac{1 \times 10^3 \text{ m}}{27.77 \text{ m/s}}$$

$$t = 36.01 \text{ sec}$$

$$t = \mathbf{0.6 \text{ minutes}}$$

Q. 66. *A telephone voice transmission needs transmission of frequencies up to 3.6 kHz. The broadcast video using North American standard needs transmission of frequencies is upto 4.5 MHz. If certain modulation scheme requires 10 kHz for its audio transmission, find the bandwidth required to transmit video using the same scheme.*

Ans. The Hartley law states that the bandwidth is proportional to the information rate and here it is considered as baseband bandwidth.

$$B_{tv} = B_{ta} \times \left(\frac{B_v}{B_a}\right)$$ where B_{tv} → Transmission BW for video

$$B_{ta} = 10 \text{ kHz}$$ B_{ta} → Transmission BW for audio

$$B_v = 4.5 \text{ Mhz}$$ B_a → Baseband bandwidth for video

$$B_a = 3.6 \text{ KHz}$$ B_v → Baseband bandwidth for audio

Substituting for B_{ta}, B_v and B_a in the equation of B_{tv},

$$B_{tv} = 10 \text{ kHz}\left(\frac{4.5 \text{ MHz}}{3.6 \text{ kHz}}\right)$$

$$= 10 \times 10^3\left(\frac{4.5 \times 10^6}{3.6 \times 10^3}\right)$$

$$B_{tv} = \mathbf{12.5 \text{ MHz}}$$

Q. 67. *Calculate the modulation index of the AM envelope shown below. (Assume vertical : 25 mV/division, horizontal : 250 μs/division.)*

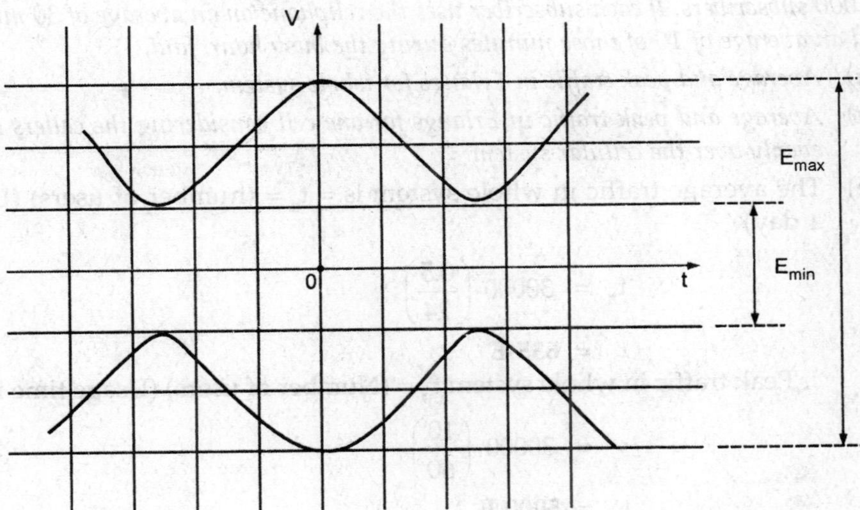

Fig. B.12

Ans. From the given data and Fig. B. 12, the minimum peak to peak voltage is Emin = (25 + 25) mV = 50 mV.

The maximum peak to peak voltage

$$= E_{max} = (25 \text{ mV} \times 6)$$

$$E_{max} = 150 \text{ mV}$$

$$\text{Modulation index (m)} = \frac{E_{max} - E_{min}}{E_{max} + E_{min}}$$

$$m = \frac{150 - 150}{150 + 50} = \frac{100}{200} = \mathbf{0.5}$$

Q. 68. *A CDMA mobileunit measures signal strength from the base station and it is – 10^5 dBm. Find what should be the mobile unit's transmitter power, as a first approximation.*

Ans. The transmitted power of mobile is = $P_t = -76 \text{ dB} - P_r$

where P_r is received power in dBm

$$P_t = -76 \text{ dB} - P_r$$

$$= -76 \text{ dB} - (-105 \text{ dBm})$$

$$= -76 \text{ dB} + 105 \text{ dBm}$$

$$= 29 \text{ dBm}$$

Converting 29 dBm to watts,

$$P_t = \mathbf{794 \text{ mW}}$$

Converting p_t in dBm to W,

$$10 \log \frac{x}{1 \times 10^{-3}} = 29$$

$$\log (x \cdot 10^3) = 2.9$$

$$(x \cdot 10^3) = \text{antilog } (2.9)$$

$$x = \frac{\text{antilog } (2.9)}{10^3}$$

$$x = 0.7943$$

$$x = 794 \text{ mW}$$

Q. 69. *A cellular mobile system uses a 12 cell reuse pattern. In this system there are 120 cells and 30,000 subscribers. If each subscriber uses the cellphone on an average of 30 minutes in a day and an average of 10 of those minutes during the busy hour, find,*

(i) Average and peak traffic in Erlangs for whole system.

(ii) Average and peak traffic in Erlangs for one cell considering the callers are distributed evenly over the cellular system.

Ans. (*i*) The average traffic in whole system is = t_a = (number of users) (Usage time in a day)

$$t_a = 30000 \cdot \left(\frac{0.5}{24}\right)$$

$$t_a = \mathbf{635 \text{ E}}$$

∴ Peak traffic in whole system t_p = (Number of users) (Usage time in busy hour)

$$= 30000 \cdot \left(\frac{10}{60}\right)$$

$$t_p = \mathbf{5000 \text{ E}}$$

(*ii*) Average traffic in one cell

$$t_A = \frac{625\text{ E}}{120}$$

$$t_A = \mathbf{5.21\ E}$$

Peak traffic in one cell

$$t_B = \frac{5000}{120} = \mathbf{41.67\ E}$$

Q. 70. *Find the maximum distance present between base station and mobile unit which can be accommodated with a guard time period of 125 μsec. The guard time has to include the round-trip propagation time.*

Ans. The radio waves travel at speed of light energy and hence the total round-trip time distance (D) will be

$$D = C.t; \qquad \text{where } C \rightarrow \text{speed of radio propagation}$$
$$t \rightarrow \text{guard time period}$$

$$= (300 \times 10^6 \text{ m/s})(125 \times 10^{-6} \text{ s})$$
$$= 300 \times 125$$
$$= 37500$$

$$\therefore \quad \text{Distance} = D = \mathbf{375\ km}$$

Q. 71. *Consider a cordless phone operating at 52 MHz frequency which has a range of 50 m. Calculate the free space pathloss.*

Ans. The free space pathloss is given by

$$L_{fs} = 32.44 + 20 \log d + 20 \log f$$

$$d = 50 \text{ m} = 0.05 \text{ km} \qquad d \rightarrow \text{path length in km}$$

$$f = 52 \text{ MHz} \qquad f \rightarrow \text{frequency in MHz}$$

$$\therefore \quad L_{fs} = 32.44 + 20 \log (0.05) + 20 \log (52)$$
$$L_{fs} = 32.44 + 20(-1.3) + 20(1.72)$$
$$= 32.44 - 26.02 + 34.32$$
$$L_{fs} = \mathbf{40.74\ dB}$$

Q. 72. *If the receiver sensitivity is 0.6 μV into 50 Ω, calculate the power in dBm.*

Ans. The voltage at receiver = 0.6 μV

$$= 0.6 \times 10^{-6} \text{ V}$$

$$\therefore \quad \text{Power (P)} = \frac{V^2}{R}$$

$$= \frac{[0.6 \times 10^{-6}]^2}{50}$$

$$P = 0.0072 \times 10^{-12} \text{ W}$$

$\therefore$ Power in dBm = P = 10 (– 11.143)

= **– 111.43 dBm**

Q. 73. *A mobile transmitter produces a power of 25 W as measured at antenna and its supply power is 47 W. Calculate its efficiency.*

Ans. Efficiency of mobile transmitter = $\eta = \frac{P_0}{P_s}$

$$\eta = \frac{25\text{ W}}{47\text{ W}} = \frac{25}{47}$$

$$\eta = 0.5319$$

$$\eta = 53.2\%$$

Q. 74. *Assume a mobile transmitter produces 26 W as it is measured at the antenna. When connected to a 13.8 V power source it draws 3.5 A of current. Calculate its efficiency 'η'.*

Ans. To find the efficiency of mobile transmitter,

We have $h = \frac{P_0}{P_s}$ where $P_0 \rightarrow$ Power produced at its output

$P_s \rightarrow$ Supply power

$$P_0 = 26\text{ W}$$

$$P_s = IR = (3.5\text{ A})(13.8\text{ V})$$

$$P_s = 48.3\text{ W}$$

$$\text{Efficiency} = \eta = \frac{P_0}{P_s} = \frac{26\text{ W}}{48.3\text{ W}} = 0.538$$

$\therefore$ η = **53.8%**

Q. 75. *Assume two handheld citizen's band (CB) transceivers are held operating at 27 MHz, 1 m above a flat terrain area. The transmitter power output is 5 W and receiver sensitivity is 0.5 μV into 500 hms. The transceiver antennas are both loaded vertical monopoles with a gain of one dBi. Consider there is no free space attenuation or interference. Find the transmitter and receiver power, path loss and path length. Also comment on limitation posed on the system. (Antenna gains increases by 2 dB).*

Ans. (*i*) The voltage at receiver is first expressed in dBm.

Voltage receiver = 0.5 μV

= 0.5×10^{-6}

and R = 50 Ω

1. $10 \log \frac{0.005 \times 10^{-12}}{1 \times 10^{-3}} = -113.01$

$$\text{Power} = P_r = \frac{[0.5 \times 10^{-6}]^2}{50}$$

$$P_r = (0.005 \times 10^{-12})\ W \quad 2.\ 10 \log \frac{5}{1 \times 10^{-3}} = 10(3.69) = 36.9$$

(*ii*) The transmitter power = P_t = 5 W
similarly expressing 5 W in dB;

$$P_t = \textbf{36.9 dBm}$$

(*iii*) The free space path loss is given as,

$$L_{fs} = 32.44 + 20 \log d + 20 \log f$$

where L_{fs} → Free space path loss in dB
d → Path length in km
f → Frequency in MHz

If the antenna gain increases the effective power by 2 dB the allowable path loss will be,

$$L_{fs} = 39.6 \text{ dBm} - (-113 \text{ dBm}) + 2 \text{ dB}$$

$$L_{fs} = 39.6 + 113 + 2 = \textbf{154.6 dB}$$

(*iv*) Substituting L_{fs} in the equation of path loss to get path length;

$$154.6 = 32.44 + 20 \log d + 20 \log f$$

$$20 \log d = 154.6 - 32.44 - 20 \log f$$

$$20 \log d = 154.6 - 32.44 - 20 \log 27$$

$$20 \log d = (154.6 - 32.44 - 28.63)$$

$$20 \log d = 93.53$$

$$\log d = 4.676$$

Path length = d = **47478 km**

From all the data it is observed that the cellular system is limited only by the distance to radio horizon and it is not limited by the transmitter power range.

Q. 76. *Find the maximum distance between transmitter and receiver if the receiver and transmitter antenna is 1 m. (Assume a flat radio horizon terrain.)*

Ans. The distance between transmitter and receiver is denoted as 'd'.

$$d = \sqrt{17h_t} + \sqrt{17h_r} \qquad h_r, h_t \rightarrow \text{Receiver and transmitter antenna heights.}$$

$$d = \sqrt{17 \times 1} + \sqrt{17 \times 1}$$

$$d = 8.246$$

$$d = \textbf{8.3 km}$$

Q. 77. *Assume a car company has a central dispatcher with an antenna setup at the top of a tower with a height of 16 m to enable communication with its vehicles. The car antennas are on the top of cars that is approximately 1.5 m above the ground level. Find the maximum communication distance available between*

(*i*) *The dispatcher and a car.*

(*ii*) *Two cars.*

Ans. (*i*) The distance = d $= \sqrt{17h_t} + \sqrt{17h_r}$

$$= \sqrt{17 \times 16} + \sqrt{17 \times 1.5}$$

$$d = 16.492 + 5.049$$

$$d = \mathbf{21.541\ km}$$

(*ii*) Distance = d $= \sqrt{17h_t} + \sqrt{17h_r}$

$$= \sqrt{17 \times 1.5} + \sqrt{17 \times 1.5}$$

$$d = 10.009$$

$$d = \mathbf{10.1\ km}$$

Q. 78. *Calculate the propagation loss for a radio signal at 850* MHz. *The transmitter antenna height is 30 m over a distance of 11 km, of using mobile propagation model and free space model and compare them.*

Ans. (*i*) Mobile propagation model (according to Hata model) is

$$L_{mp} = 68.75 + 26.16 \log f - 13.82 \log h + (44.9 - 6.55 \log h) \log d$$

where $L_{mp} \rightarrow$ Pathloss in dB

$f \rightarrow$ Frequency in MHz

$h \rightarrow$ Base station antenna height

$d \rightarrow$ Distance in km.

Substituting the given values in the equation of L_{mp}, we get,

$$L_{mp} = 68.75 + 26.16 \log (850) - 13.82 \log (30) + (44.9 - 6.55 \log 30) \log 11$$

$$L_{mp} = 68.75 + 26.16 (2.929) - 13.82 (1.477) + [44.9 - 6.55(1.477)]\ 1.041$$

$$= 68.75 + 76.62 - 20.41 + (35.23)\ 1.041$$

$$= 68.75 + 76.62 - 20.41 + 36.67$$

$$L_{mp} = \mathbf{161.63\ dB}$$

(*ii*) The free space pathloss model is denoted as L_{ts}

$$L_{fs} = 32.44 + 20 \log d + 20 \log f$$

$$= 32.44 + 20 \log (11) + 20 \log (850)$$

$$= 32.44 + 20 (1.041) + 20 (2.929)$$

$$= 32.44 + 20.82 + 58.59$$

$$L_{fs} = \mathbf{111.85\ dB}$$

Comparing case (*i*) and (*i*) it is observed that 50 dB (approx) more attenuation level is found in mobile environment than the free space environment.

Q. 79. *A truck travels at 65 km in one hour. Calculate the time period between fades if the truck uses (i) a PCS phone at 1900 MHz (ii) a cell phone at 850 MHz.*

Ans. Let us convert the truck's speed to m/sec,

$$\frac{65\text{ km}}{\text{hr}} = \frac{65\times10^3\text{ m}}{3600\text{ sec}} = \frac{650\text{ m}}{36\text{ sec}} = 18.1\text{ m/s}$$

$\therefore$ Speed of truck = 18.1 m/sec.

(*i*) For a PCS phone :

$$\text{Time} = t_{pcs} = \frac{C}{2\,fv}$$

$$= \frac{300\times10^6}{2\times(1900\times10^6)\times18.1}$$

$$t_{pcs} = \frac{300}{68780} = 0.0044 = \mathbf{4.4\ msec}$$

(*ii*) For a cell phone :

$$\text{Time} = t_{cell} = \frac{C}{2\,fv} = \frac{300\times10^6}{2\times(850\times10^6)\times18.1}$$

$$t_{cell} = \frac{300}{30770} = 0.0097 = \mathbf{9.7\ msec}$$

In the cases (*i*) and (*ii*) the fading increases very fast with both speed and frequency of transmissions respectively.

Q. 80. *Consider a metropolitan area of 1100 square km is to be covered by cells with cell radius of 2 km. Calculate the number of cells, that would be needed assuming hexagonal cell shape.*

Ans. Let area of one hexagon cell be 'a'.

Total area to be covered be 'A'.

Then the number of cells (N) required will be,

$$N = \frac{A}{a}$$

where $a = 3.464\ r^2$

Given that $A = 1100$ square km

and $r = 2$ km

Substituting for A and a total get number of cell required (N).

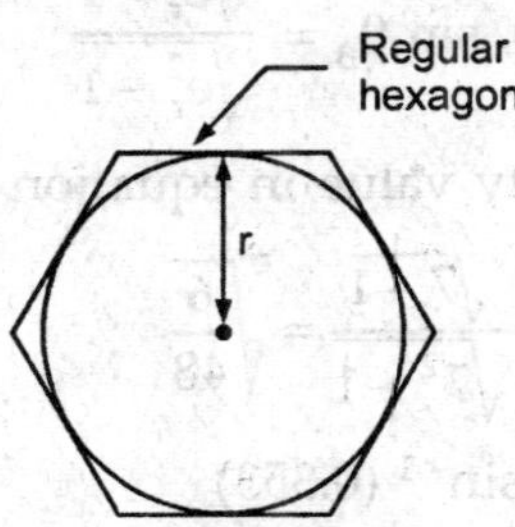

Fig. B. 13

Number of cell required

$$N = \frac{A}{a} = \frac{A}{3.464\, r^2}$$

$$N = \frac{1100}{3.464 \times (2^2)}$$

$$= \frac{1100}{13.856}$$

$\therefore$ $N = 79$ cells.

Hexagon of all sides equal is assumed and for this regular hexagon area will be a = 3.464 r² where r is radius of hexagon cell.

Q. 81. *A carrier signal of 1 MHz frequency with an amplitude of 1 V peak value is modulated by a 3 kHz message signal with the modulation index 0.5. Find the upper and lower sideband frequencies and voltages.*

Ans. Carrier frequency = f_c = 1 MHz

Modulating signal frequency = f_m = 3 kHz

Lower side band frequency $(f_{LSB}) = f_c - f_m$

$= 1 \text{ MHz} - 3 \text{ kHz}$

$\therefore$ $f_{LSB} = 0.997$ MHz

Upper side band frequency $(f_{USB}) = f_c + f_m$

$= 1 \text{ MHz} + 3 \text{ kHz}$

$f_{USB} = 1.003$ MHz

Voltage of the each side band is

$$E_{USB} - E_{USB} = \frac{m E_c}{2}$$

$$= \frac{0.5\,(1)}{2}$$

$= \mathbf{0.25}$ **volts**

Q. 82. *Calculate the brewster angle for a wave that impinges on ground having a permittivity of $\varepsilon_r = 7$.*

Ans. For the brewster angle (θ_B), $\sin \theta_B = \frac{\sqrt{e_r - 1}}{\sqrt{e_r^2 - 1}}$ ...(1)

Substituting the permittivity value in equation (1),

$$\sin(\theta_B) = \frac{\sqrt{7-1}}{\sqrt{7^2 - 1}} = \sqrt{\frac{6}{48}}$$

$\theta_B = \sin^{-1}(0.353)$

$\theta_B = \mathbf{20.67\ deg}$ (for $\varepsilon_r = 7$)

Q. 83. *Calculate the theoretical maximum possible data rate which can support a 500 kHz channel for signal to noise ratio (SNR) equal to 10 dB.*

Ans. The signal to noise ratio (SNR) = 10 dB

The channel bandwidth (B) = 500 kHz

As per Shannon's channel capacity formula, maximum possible data rate is calculated as,

$$C = B \log_2\left(1+\frac{S}{N}\right) \quad \text{...(1)}$$

Substituting the given values

$$C = 500 \text{ kHz} \log_2 (1 + 10) \quad \text{...(2)}$$

and
$$\log_a m = \frac{\log_e m}{\log_e a} = \frac{\ln m}{\ln a} \quad \text{...(3)}$$

From (3),
$$\log_2 11 = \frac{\ln 11}{\ln 2} = 3.459 \quad \text{...(4)}$$

Substituting equation (2) in equation (4), then

$$\text{Capacity} = C = (500)\,(3.459)$$

$$C = \mathbf{1729 \text{ kbps.}}$$

Q. 84. *Calculate the spectral efficiency (η_s) if the bandwidth is 684 kbps and transmission data rate is 1.152 Mbps.*

Ans. The bandwidth = BW = 684 kbps

Transmission rate = R_T = 1.152 Mbps

$$\text{Spectral efficiency} = \eta_s = \frac{R_T}{BW}$$

$$\eta_s = \frac{1.152 \text{ Mbps}}{684 \text{ kbps}}$$

$$= \mathbf{1.6 \text{ bps}}$$

Q. 85. *Consider there are four cellular radio standards and select a standard which has minimum radio capacity assuming n = 4 propagation pathloss.*

System 1 - $B'_c = 25$ *kHz and* $\left(\frac{C}{I}\right)_{min} = 13$ *dB*

System 2 - $B'_c = 30$ *kHz and* $\left(\frac{C}{I}\right)_{min} = 17$ *dB*

System 3 - $B'_c = 12.5$ *kHz,* $\left(\frac{C}{I}\right)_{min} = 11$ *dB*

System 4 - $B'_c = 6.25$ *kHz,* $\left(\frac{C}{I}\right)_{min} = 8$ *dB*

Ans. Assuming that each system id adopted a bandwidth of 6.25 kHz, then

$$\left(\frac{C}{I}\right)_{eq} = \left(\frac{C}{I}\right)_{min} \cdot \left(\frac{B_c}{B_c'}\right)^2 \qquad ...(1)$$

where B_c is bandwidth of particular system and B_c' is bandwidth of different system. Substituting the values in above equation (1), then

For System 1 - $\left(\frac{C}{I}\right)_{eq} = 13 + 20 \log\left(\frac{6.25}{25}\right) = 0.96$

System 2 - $\left(\frac{C}{I}\right)_{eq} = 17 + 20 \log\left(\frac{6.25}{30}\right) = 3.38$

System 3 - $\left(\frac{C}{I}\right)_{eq} = 11 + 20 \log\left(\frac{6.25}{25}\right) = 4.98$

System 4 - $\left(\frac{C}{I}\right)_{eq} = 8 + 20 \log\left(\frac{6.25}{6.25}\right) = 8$

Comparing all systems the largest value of $\left(\frac{C}{I}\right)_{eq}$ should be selected for minimum radio capacity. Hence the 'System 4' provides minimum radio capacity than other three systems.

Q. 86. *What will be maximum data rate that can be transmitted if the signal to noise ratio is 20 dB and channel bandwidth is 40 kHz?*

Ans. Channel bandwidth = B = 40 kHz

Signal to noise ratio = 20 dB = 100

$$\text{Channel capacity} = C = B \log_2\left(1 + \frac{S}{N}\right)$$

$$= 40 \text{ kHz} \log_2 (1 + 100)$$

$$= 40 \text{ kHz}$$

Maximum data rate = C = **266.33 kbps**

Q. 87. *In a cellular mobile communication for a forward channel performance considering signal to noise ratio (SNR) of 14 dB is required as minimum requirement. Find frequency reuse factor that must be used for maximum capacity if the path loss exponent is n = 3 and n = 4. (Assuming six co-channel cells are available in first tier and key are at same distance from the mobile phone).*

Ans. Let n = 3

Consider a seven-cell reuse pattern in cellular cluster and N = 7.

The signal to interference ratio is $\frac{S}{I} = \frac{(D/R)^n}{i_0} = \frac{(\sqrt{3N})^n}{i_0}$

Co-channel reuse factor = Q = D/R = 4.583

For n = 3 case $\frac{S}{I} = \frac{(4.583)^3}{6}$

$= 16.04$

$\therefore \quad \frac{S}{I} = \mathbf{12.05\ dB}$

But for minimum performance the S/I should be atleast 14 dB as per the requirement of cellular system.

Hence n = 3 is not suitable since 12.05 dB is less than standard value 14 dB.

Let n = 4

Consider a seven cell reuse pattern and N = 7.

Co-channel reuse factor = $Q = \frac{D}{R} = 4.583$

Signal to interference ratio = $\frac{S}{I}$

$= \frac{1}{6} \times (4.583)^4$

$= 73.52$

$\therefore \quad \frac{S}{I} = \mathbf{18.66\ dB}$

The signal to interference is greater than the minimum requirement standard value 14 dB and n = 4 is a better value that can be applied, for real time performance.

Q. 88. *Consider the four cellular standards given below. Select the maximum radio capacity (assume n = 4 propagation pathloss).*

System 1 - $B_c' = 25\ kHz$ *and* $\left(\frac{C}{I}\right)_{min} = 13\ dB$

System 2 - $B_c' = 30\ kHz$ *and* $\left(\frac{C}{I}\right)_{min} = 17\ dB$

System 3 - $B_c' = 12.5\ kHz,$ $\left(\frac{C}{I}\right)_{min} = 11\ dB$

System 4 - $B_c' = 6.25\ kHz,$ $\left(\frac{C}{I}\right)_{min} = 8\ dB$

Ans. $$\left(\frac{C}{I}\right)_{eq} = \left(\frac{C}{I}\right)_{min} \cdot \left(\frac{B_c}{B_c'}\right)^2$$

where B_c is bandwidth of particular system and B'_c is the channel bandwidth for a different system. Assuming each system with particular bandwidth 6.5 kHz (say).

$$\text{System 1 - } \left(\frac{C}{I}\right)_{eq} = 13 + 20 \log\left(\frac{6.5}{25}\right) = 1.29$$

$$\text{System 2 - } \left(\frac{C}{I}\right)_{eq} = 17 + 20 \log\left(\frac{6.5}{30}\right) = 3.72$$

$$\text{System 3 - } \left(\frac{C}{I}\right)_{eq} = 11 + 20 \log\left(\frac{6.5}{12.5}\right) = 5.32$$

$$\text{System 4 - } \left(\frac{C}{I}\right)_{eq} = 8 + 20 \log\left(\frac{6.5}{6.5}\right) = 8$$

For maximum radio capacity, the smallest value of $\left(\frac{C}{I}\right)_{eq}$ should be selected.

Hence System - (1) provides maximum capacity.

Q. 89. *Find the far field distance for an antenna with maximum dimension of 3 m and operating frequency of 800 MHz.*

Ans. The wavelength $(\lambda) = \frac{c}{f}$

$$= \frac{3 \times 10^8}{800 \times 10^6} = 0.38 \text{ m}$$

Far field distance for an antenna is calculated as = $d_f = \frac{2D^2}{\lambda}$

$$\therefore \quad d_f = \frac{2(3)^2}{0.38}$$

$$d_f = \mathbf{47.4 \text{ m}}$$

Q. 90. *If the signal to noise ratio (S/N) of a mobile communication link is 100 dB and RF bandwidth is 65 kHz. Find the maximum possible theoretical data rate of the signal which can be transmitted.*

Ans. The signal to noise ratio= $\frac{S}{N} = 100$

Bandwidth = 65 kHz

$$\text{Channel capacity} = B \log_2\left(1 + \frac{S}{N}\right)$$

The maximum possible data is given as,

$$C = 65{,}000 \text{ Iog}_2 (1 + 100)$$

$$C = (65{,}000)(6{,}658)$$

Maximum data rate = C= **433.33 kbps.**

Q. 91. *A dipole antenna has an efficiency of 95% and directivity is 2.14 dB. Calculate the gain value in dB.*

Ans.

$$\text{Directivity} = 2.14 \text{ dB}$$

i.e.

$$10 \log D = 2.14$$

$$D = 1.638$$

$$\text{The gain value} = G = (\text{directivity}) \times (\text{efficiency})$$

$$G = D\,\eta$$

$$= (1.638)\,(0.95)$$

$$G = 1.55$$

The value of gain (G) in dB is,

$$G(\text{dB}) = 10 \log (1.55)$$

$$G = \mathbf{1.92\ dB}$$

Q. 92. *Calculate the modulation index for the carrier wave of 12 V peak to peak, which is amplitude modulated by four different frequencies whose amplitudes are 4, 5, 6 and 7 volts.*

Ans. The modulation index $= m = \dfrac{E_m}{E_c}$

where E_m is modulating signal voltage

E_c is carrier signal voltage

For four different (multiple) signal frequencies the total modulation index is calculated as,

$$m_f = \sqrt{m_1^2 + m_2^2 + m_3^2 + m_4^2}$$

Where

$$m_1 = \frac{E_m}{E_c} = \frac{4}{12} = 0.3$$

$$m_2 = \frac{E_m}{E_c} = \frac{5}{12} = 0.4$$

$$m_3 = \frac{E_m}{E_c} = \frac{6}{12} = 0.5$$

$$m_4 = \frac{E_m}{E_c} = \frac{7}{12} = 0.6$$

The modulation index ($m_{total} = m_t$)

$$= \sqrt{(0.3)^2 + (0.4)^2 + (0.5)^2 + (0.6)^2}$$

$$= \sqrt{0.09 + 0.16 + 0.25 + 0.36} = \sqrt{0.86}$$

Total modulation index $= m_t = \mathbf{0.93}$

Q. 93. *Calculate the wavelength of signal for a PCS and cellular mobile system with the ranges as 2.5 GHz and 845 MHz respectively.*

Ans. (*i*) For personal communication systems (PCS), with f = 2.5 GHz

$$\text{The wavelength} = \lambda = \frac{c}{f}$$

$$= \frac{3 \times 10^8}{2.5 \times 10^9}$$

$$= \mathbf{0.12\ m}$$

(*ii*) For cellular mobile system, wavelength (λ) with f = 845 MHz

$$= \frac{c}{f} = \frac{3 \times 10^8}{845 \times 10^6}$$

$$\lambda = \mathbf{0.355\ m}$$

Q. 94. *Consider that the rms antenna current of an amplitude modulated radio transmitter is 18 Amps when unmodulated, and 20 Amps when sinusoidally modulated, find the modulation index value.*

Ans. Modulation index $= m = \sqrt{2\left[\left(\frac{I}{I_c}\right)^2 - 1\right]}$

$$= \sqrt{2\left[\left(\frac{20}{18}\right)^2 - 1\right]}$$

$$= \sqrt{2(1.23) - 1} = \sqrt{0.46}$$

$$\therefore \quad m = \mathbf{0.68}$$

Q. 95. *Find the total power P_T in amplitude modulated signal (AM), if the modulation indices are 0.3, 0.2, 0.5 and 0.6 where the carrier signal power is 28 watts.*

Ans. The total power 'P_T' can be found as,

$$P_T = P_c\left[1 + \frac{m_1^2}{2} + \frac{m_2^2}{2} + \frac{m_3^2}{2} + \frac{m_4^2}{2}\right]$$

where P_c = Carrier signal power

Modulation indices $m_1 = 0.3$

$m_2 = 0.5$

$m_3 = 0.5$

and $m_4 = 0.6$

$$P_T = 28\left[1 + \frac{(0.3)^2}{2} + \frac{(0.2)^2}{2} + \frac{(0.5)^2}{2} + \frac{(0.6)^2}{2}\right]$$

$$= 28\left[1 + \frac{0.09}{2} + \frac{0.04}{2} + \frac{0.25}{2} + \frac{0.36}{2}\right]$$

$$= 28\,(1 + 0.045 + 0.02 + 0.125 + 0.18)$$

$$P_T = \mathbf{38.36\ watts}$$

Q. 96. *Calculate the signal to noise ratio in decibels for three identical links if the signal to noise ratio for any one link is 62 dB.*

Ans. The signal noise ratio at the output is

$$\left(\frac{S}{N}\right)_O = \left(\frac{S}{N}\right)_1 \text{dB} - (m)\,\text{dB},$$

$\left(\frac{S}{N}\right)_1$ → Signal to noise ratio of any one link

m → Number of links

Signal to noise ratio at the output is

$$\left(\frac{S}{N}\right)_O = [62 - 10 \log 3]$$

$$= [62 - 4.77] = \mathbf{57.23\ dB}$$

Q. 97. *An isotropic radiator is supplied with a power of 120 watts with a gain of 7 dB. Calculate the EIRP and power density at a distance of 18 km.*

Ans. The value of gain

$$= 10 \log G = 7$$

$$\therefore \quad G = 5.01$$

The effective isotropic radiated power is denoted as 'EIRP' which is expressed as,

$$\text{EIRP} = [G_t \cdot P_t],$$

which is a product of transmitter gain and power.

$$\text{EIRP} = (5.01)\,(120)\ \text{W}$$

$$= 601.2\ \text{watts}$$

$$\text{Power density} = P_D$$

$$= \frac{\text{EIRP}}{4\pi r^2}$$

$$= \frac{601.2}{4\pi\,(18 \times 10^3)^2}$$

$$\therefore \quad P_D = \mathbf{147.7\ nW/m^2}$$

Q. 98. *Consider if a vehicle travels through the cellular mobile system at 150 km per hour, find how often handoffs take place if the cell radius is 4 km.*

Ans. In cellular mobile system, the velocity of the vehicle with 150 kmph is considered as below,

$$V = \frac{(1500\ \text{kmph})\,(1000\ \text{mpkm})}{(3600\ \text{sphr})}$$

$$V = 41.6 \text{ m/sec.}$$

As the cell radius is 4 km, its diameter is 8 km.

i.e. $r = 4$ km

$d = 8$ km

Handoffs will occur for every 192.3 sec, time intervals, when the vehicle is moving with 150 km per hour speed.

Q. 99. *In the previous question, how often the handoffs will occur if the cell radius is 5 km ?*

Ans. Velocity in cellular mobile environment is,

$$V = 41.6 \text{ m/sec.}$$

If cell radius $r = 5$ km then

Diameter $d = 10$ km

$$\text{Time } t = \frac{d}{V}$$

$$T = \mathbf{240 \text{ sec}}$$

Q. 100. *Find the wavelength of a radio signal in free space with a frequency of 125 MHz.*

Ans. $$\text{Wavelength} = \lambda = \frac{c}{f}$$

where c and f are velocity of propagation and frequency of the signal.

$$\lambda = \frac{3 \times 10^8}{125 \times 10^6}$$

$\therefore$ $$\text{Wavelength} = \lambda = \mathbf{2.4 \text{ m}}$$

❑❑❑

BIBLIOGRAPHY

Book References

1. Mobile Computing—Rajkamal—Oxford.
2. Mobile Computing—K.H. Wandra—Akshat Pub.
3. UMTS and Mobile Computing By Alexander Joseph Huber, Josef Franz Huber, Artech House 2002.
4. Mobile Computing—Technology, Applications and Service Creation by Ashoke K. Talukder and Roopa R. Yavagal—TMH.
5. Mustafa Ergen, "IEEE 802.11 Tutorial", June 2002.
6. SMS and MMS Internetworking in Mobile Networks By Arnaud Henry—Labordere, Vincent Jonack, Artech House, 2004.
7. Broadband Wireless Communications : 3G, 4G, and Wireless LAN by Jiangzhou Wang, Khuwer Academic Publishers, 2001
8. Wireless and Mobile Network Architectures, by Yi-Bing Lin and Imrich Chlamtac. John Wiley, 2001.
9. Mobile Telecommunications Networking by Michael Gallagher and Randall Snyder McGraw Hill, 1997.
10. Wireless Communications : Principle and Practice by Theodore S. Rapport, Prentice Hall, 1996.

Web Reference

1. www.ericsson.com
2. www.gsmworld.com
3. www.nokia.com
4. www.umts-forum.org
5. www..wikipedia.com
6. www.telecomspace.com
7. www.protocols.com